This Day In New York Sports

Jordan Sprechman

with

Bill Shannon

A Sports Museum Press Book
Published by Sports Publishing Inc.
Champaign, Illinois

Editor: Susan M. McKinney
Book layout: Susan M. McKinney and Jennifer L. Polson
Dustjacket design: Julie L. Denzer

ISBN: 1-57167-254-0

Printed in the United States.

All photos courtesy of Sports Museum Press, Inc.

Cover photographs, from left to right, top to bottom:
    Top row: Mets pitcher Dwight Gooden; Yankees George Selkirk, Bill Dickey, Lou Gehrig, and Joe DiMaggio; Knicks center Patrick Ewing; Jets quarterback Joe Namath; Dodgers pitcher Preacher Roe; Jets wide receiver Al Toon.
    Second row: Track star Carl Lewis; billiards champion Jean Balukas; Rangers general manager, coach and "one-time" goalie Lester Patrick; boxers Joe Louis (left) and Rocky Marciano; golf legend Bobby Jones; jockeys Bill Shoemaker (left) and Eddie Arcaro.
    Third row: Tennis great Maria Bueno; Nets forward Jayson Williams; dog show organizer Geraldine Rockefeller Dodge; Cosmos sweeper Franz Beckenbauer; Yankees outfielder Babe Ruth; Jets coach Bill Parcells; bike racing great Eddy (the Cannon) Bald; NYU's Sid Tanenbaum.
    Bottom row: Running greats Eamonn Coghlan (left) and Grete Waitz; 1933 Yale-Princeton football program cover; fencing legend James J. Murray; Columbia basketball star Buck Jenkins; bowler George Young; Islanders goalie Billy Smith.

Back cover photos:
    Giants linebacker Sam Huff; Knicks forward Nat (Sweetwater) Clifton; Yankees first baseman Don Mattingly.

SPORTS PUBLISHING INC.
http://www.SportsPublishing.Com

To Julius Sprechman, a pretty good author,
and W.O. Shannon, a really big sports fan.

————  ————

CONTENTS

A NOTE TO THE READERS AND ACKNOWLEDGMENTS

Readers will find references in this book to people, places and events that today may seem obscure, as well as mention of events that, and people who, are quite famous—or even infamous.

Right at the start, we advise you most gently, but urgently, to refer to the list of abbreviations found in Appendix I at the back of the book. Some of these abbreviations need to be explained slightly. ABL, for instance, is used to stand for two different pro basketball leagues, and AFL for four different pro football organizations, so that the focus of time is important. In the abbreviations, the time lines for some of these various groups are delineated.

Also bear in mind that when something is indicated as the "most," "best," "biggest," "longest, highest or widest," it is meant in the context that it was so at the time the event described took place, though it may no longer be the case today. "First," of course, is just that.

Records in virtually every sport have changed dramatically over the more than 150 years of history covered by this work, and there is no attempt here to be comprehensive. We have attempted merely to give the flavor of New York area sports over the period of time, places that were, people who were and events that were. Some still are (the Yankees), some lasted many years and then disappeared (the Americans), some came back several times (the Football Yankees), and ultimately failed anyway.

A word is in order here about what is meant by "New York area." We define it as that area within 75 miles of Columbus Circle in Manhattan, plus all of Long Island. We do so

because that is the charter territory of the New York Sports Museum & Hall of Fame.

This work is, therefore, part history, part nostalgia (depending upon your age, nostalgia kicks in at different times) and part contemporary reporting. We realize that sports works on different levels for different people. We hope that this book works on a lot of levels for you and provides its share of enjoyment. But our principal purpose is to provide information.

Your recollection or understanding of these events and people, to the extent you have one, may differ from the circumstances described here. We hope and expect that the reason for that difference is that we have debunked myths, corrected misperceptions and generally clarified, while adding to, the existing body of knowledge.

All the information in this book is based on the best available evidence and is derived from either contemporaneous source materials (principally newspapers, programs and media guides), encyclopedias or the authors' personal observations and notes. Any conclusions drawn or interpretations made are our responsibility.

In the course of preparing a work as extensive as this, the assistance of many people is vital. We wish first to acknowledge our debt most particularly to Barbara Paddock, without whose aid the project would perhaps never have been completed. She was able to keep tabs on all of the thousands of items by day, year, subject and sport. Otherwise, we might have been mired in electronic spaghetti for the rest of our born days.

There are, of course, numerous others to whom acknowledgment is due, including

Dennis D'Agostino, John Halligan, Dave Anderson, Lou Requena, Charlie McGill, Helen Strus, Art Campbell, Janine Angelo, Garry Garnet, Jimmy O'Neill, Edwin Prosper, Beth Reifers, Geraldine Sprechman, Bill Steinman, Lise Walsh, Marianne Winston and Mel Feldman. Of course, this work would not have been possible without the seemingly limitless facilities of the New York Public Library and the courteous staff members at the West Caldwell (N.J.) Library.

Having thanked all of those who have contributed to the collection of this material, we also need to make a final point. For a variety of reasons, we may have made mistakes compiling over 3,500 entries containing thousands of facts. For these, the authors apologize and accept full responsibility.

FOREWORD
THE DATES WE'LL NEVER KNOW . . .

By Dave Anderson

All the memorable moments in New York sports history are here, along with their dates that can be documented. But some moments can't be documented. When and where they happened, nobody knows for sure. And those moments have been just as much a part of New York sports as the documented events.

Here then is a list of those undocumented events, when:

Walter O'Malley first thought about moving the Brooklyn Dodgers to Los Angeles.

Joe Namath had his first date in his Bachelors III restaurant on Lexington Avenue.

Red Holzman, as the Knicks' new coach, first told his players to "hit the open man."

Mark Messier first decided to shave his head.

Cassius Clay, now known as Muhammad Ali, first yelled, "I am the greatest" before his fourth-round knockout of Sonny Banks at Madison Square Garden in 1962, his first bout in the New York area.

Secretariat first emptied a bag of oats at Belmont.

Arnold Palmer first hitched up his pants at the 1958 Pepsi Open at the Pine Hollow Country Club in East Norwich, Long Island, his first PGA Tour victory in the New York area.

George Steinbrenner first "fired" Billy Martin as the Yankee manager before changing his mind the next day.

Larry MacPhail first "fired" Leo Durocher as the Dodger manager before changing his mind the next day.

The America's Cup was bolted to a table at the New York Yacht Club on West 45th Street, its members assuming the trophy would never be lost.

Giants fans first chanted, "Dee-fense."

Rangers fans first chanted, "Potvin sucks."

Martina Navratilova first thought about defecting from Czechoslovakia during the 1975 U.S. Open at the West Side Tennis Club in Forest Hills.

Walt Frazier first wore the hat that inspired his "Clyde" nickname.

Jack Dempsey first sat in the window booth in his Broadway restaurant.

Willie Mays first played stickball with the neighborhood kids in the streets near Coogan's Bluff above the Polo Grounds.

Bill Bradley first learned at Princeton that he had been selected to attend Oxford University as a Rhodes Scholar.

Joe DiMaggio first wore "5" on his Yankee uniform.

Red Smith first decided to join the now-defunct *Herald Tribune* as a sports columnist.

Jimmy Cannon first decided to write a "Nobody Asked Me, But" column in the *Post*.

Jackie Robinson first jitterbugged in leading off third base at Ebbets Field.

Julius Erving was first called "Doctor" by a friend at Roosevelt High School in Hempstead.

Babe Ruth first ate a hot dog between innings after joining the Yankees for the 1920 season.

Lou Gehrig hit that memorable home run off the steps of the Columbia University library.

Pele scored his first soccer goal as a youngster in Brazil.

Felix (Doc) Blanchard first met Glenn Davis at the U.S. Military Academy at West Point.

Yogi Berra first said, "It gets late early" at Yankee Stadium during the World Series.

Willie Pep, the elusive featherweight boxing champion, won a round without throwing a punch.

Mel Ott first joined the Giants as a 16-year-old catcher and was dubbed "Master Melvin."

Frank McGuire first wore a blue double-breasted suit as the St. John's basketball coach.

Pat Riley first slicked his hair and wore a Giorgio Armani suit as the Knicks' coach.

Tom Seaver first scraped the right knee of his Mets uniform across the Shea mound's dirt.

John McEnroe first uttered an expletive during a U.S. Open match at Flushing Meadow.

Casey Stengel first decided to platoon Hank Bauer and Gene Woodling as Yankee outfielders.

Dick McGuire first threw a "no-look" pass as a kid growing up on the Far Rockaway courts.

Weeb Ewbank, taking over the Jets, first said, "I've seen sicker cows than this get well."

Reggie Jackson first mentioned "the magnitude of me."

Ned Irish, the boss of Madison Square Garden, first thought that the New York franchise in the Basketball Association of America in 1946 should be known as the Knickerbockers.

Sandy Koufax first struck out a batter in Pop Secol's Ice Cream League on the Brooklyn sandlots.

Joe Louis said that Billy Conn "can run, but he can't hide" in 1946 during their second fight.

Abe Stark first put up his "Hit Sign, Win Suit" sign at the base of the Ebbets Field scoreboard.

Joe Lapchick first played center for the Original Celtics in pro basketball's dance-hall days.

Phil Rizzuto first said, "Holy Cow."

Mel Allen first said, "How about that?"

Red Barber first said, "They're tearin' up the peapatch."

Marty Glickman first said, "Good, like Nedicks'."

Marv Albert first said, "Yessss."

Rod Laver first realized that he had a chance to complete a tennis Grand Slam in the U.S. Nationals at Forest Hills as an amateur in 1962, and again in the U.S. Open as a pro there in 1969.

A voice in the Ebbets Field grandstand first called Cardinal slugger Stan Musial "The Man."

Phil Simms first greeted first-round draft choice Lawrence Taylor as a Giants teammate in 1981.

Lew Alcindor, now known as Kareem Abdul-Jabbar, first dunked a basketball as a CYO youngster.

Bill Terry, the Giants manager-first baseman in 1934, asked, "Is Brooklyn still in the league?"

Sugar Ray Robinson first parked his flamingo-pink Cadillac convertible outside boxing promoter Mike Jacobs' office in the Brill Building at the corner of Broadway and West 49th Street.

"K" signs first appeared in the Shea Stadium stands when Dwight (Doc) Gooden was pitching for the Mets.

Indians from the Shinnecock Reservation in Southampton first began building the original Shinnecock Hills Golf Club course, the site of the second U.S. Open in 1895.

Bob Davies first dribbled behind his back at Seton Hall.

Mickey Mantle first checked into the St. Moritz hotel on West 59th Street next door to the restaurant named for him.

And now for the documented dates . . .

PREFACE

Me and my big mouth.

When, in the fall of 1996, I suggested to the real brains behind this project, Bill Shannon, that we write a book that goes day-by-day through the year, picks out the New York sports-related highlights that occurred on each day and summarizes them, I didn't know that he would think it was a good idea. Come to think of it, I'm still not sure he does.

But he and I, and a small, hardy group of other believers, have been working on a project since 1988 called the New York Sports Museum & Hall of Fame (see July 28). The Museum, which is entirely Bill's idea, is intended to, among other things, preserve the history of sports in the New York Metropolitan Area and illustrate how sports over time has woven itself into the fabric of the society's culture, as well as to use sports as a vehicle to teach educational disciplines such as history, physics, math and geography, honor the luminaries who have contributed to the history of sports, and preserve the memory of their accomplishments.

I thought it was a great concept when Bill suggested it to me. Still do. So do a lot of other people. But there is no physical museum. We have tons of stuff in storage and a bundle of ideas of how to do it right, but there is no museum, at least not yet.

On the other hand, there is an awful lot of history to learn from out there, and it seems to me to be a shame that sports—the universal cultural solvent, really—has no central venue where you can go and learn about its history.

And the history is enormously rich and varied. Look, you don't need a sports museum to figure out who won the 1953 World Series (it was the Yankees, by the way, in six over the Dodgers). Any almanac, record book or encyclopedia can tell you that. But a sports museum, done right, can be a terrific place to teach about the past:

what was going on in the world, what people wore, what music were they listening to, how they got to work, what newspapers they read—you get the idea.

For instance, baseball fans in the 1880s in New York didn't drive to Giants games at the Polo Grounds (which was at 110th Street and 5th Avenue, by the way, not 155th and 8th—but that's another story) because there were no cars, and they didn't take the subways, because they weren't opened until 1904. And they couldn't listen to the games on radio, because radio didn't exist—so what went on?

And the point isn't that they took elevated trains, or walked or rode in horse-drawn carriages, and, if they couldn't go, got the results from the evening papers (no more of those, either, in New York) because the contests were all day games (no night games then)—although all that is true. The point is that the answers to those questions give insight into the way things were then—and the way things are now.

That's why we want to build a museum. And while this book isn't exactly intended to answer those questions (though it addresses some of them), one of its goals is to give a glimpse into New York sports history.

That history, by the way, stretches back well beyond the age of television, which is only about 50 years old. It involves organizations and teams that no longer exist and sports that are no longer played—or at least don't have the status that they once did, such as bike racing (the most popular sport in the country in the first quarter of this century). It involves individuals famous in other fields, from Frederic Remington (Yale football player and painter) to Bill Bradley (Princeton basketball player and U.S. senator), and venues long since demolished (from the Newark Velodrome to Ebbets Field).

The New York region has by far the richest sports heritage of any region in the country. Every sport of any significance, from auto racing to yachting, has used New York as a significant stage at one time or another. Even today, no region can match its dozen major pro sports teams (not to mention "lesser," minor-league, college, high-school, amateur, semi-pro and club sports).

Combine this history with New York's status as the country's most important city for over 150 years, and you will find that in a very real sense, the history of New York area sports is the history of sports in the United States.

If you believe that history doesn't matter, that the people who came before have nothing to teach us, that the events of the past are meaningless, random occurrences that happened in an environment that has no relevance to today, then don't read this book—you'll only be bored.

But if you think history matters, if you think the past is prologue and a clue to the future, if you are interested in the deeds of those who came before and why they did what they did, if you think that the people in the old pictures you've seen and books you've read aren't two-dimensional figures, but were once living, breathing humans with passions, interests, biases, hopes and goals just as you are—then read this book.

Jordan Sprechman

New York
April 1998

1819
Tom Hyer, the first recognized American heavyweight boxing champion (1841-52), is born in New York.

1856
Righty Tim Keefe, who won over 300 games pitching primarily for the New York Mets of the American Association and Giants of the National League, is born in Cambridge, Massachusetts.

1900
Century A. Milstead is born in Allegheny, Pennsylvania. The Yale football star played for the Football Giants (1925, 1927-29) and Philadelphia Quakers, champions of the AFL, in 1926. The Quakers met the seventh-place Giants in a postseason game at the Polo Grounds with the Giants winning this embryonic Super Bowl, 31-0, ending the first AFL's contribution to history.

1923
"Wee Willie" Keeler, two-time National League batting champion and early star with the Highlanders, dies at age 50 in Brooklyn.

HELEN WILLS MOODY

1931
Americans' 2-0 loss to the Maple Leafs at Toronto degenerates into a third-period free-for-all that delays the game for more than a half-hour.

1933
Manhattan, in its first season under head coach Chick Meehan, plays the University of Miami in the first Palm Festival Football Game, forerunner of the Orange Bowl, but the Jaspers lose to the Hurricanes, 7-0, at Miami, Florida.

1934
Columbia becomes the last Ivy League team to win a Bowl game with a 7-0 upset over heavily-favored Stanford in the Rose Bowl at Pasadena, California. The Lions score on their "KF-79" play, with sophomore Al Barabas going around left end for a 17-yard touchdown in the second quarter.

1941
Fordham takes a 6-0 lead on Steve Filipowicz's one-yard run but Steve Hudacek's extra-point kick is blocked. Texas A&M scores twice in the third quarter and hangs on for a 13-12 win over the Rams in the Cotton Bowl at Dallas, Texas.

1942
Before 73,000 rain-soaked fans at Tulane Stadium in New Orleans, Louisiana, Fordham wins the Sugar Bowl with a 2-0 triumph over Missouri when the Rams' Alex Santelli blocks Don Greenwood's punt out of the end zone for a safety in the first quarter.

1998
Helen Wills Moody Roarke dies in Carmel, California, at age 92. Considered by many the greatest women's tennis player of all time, Helen Newington Wills (later Moody) won seven U.S. national singles titles, eight Wimbledon crowns and the French championship four times. From 1927-32, she did not lose a set, much less a match, in competition.

1871

George Lewis (Tex) Rickard, who as president of Madison Square Garden oversaw in 1925 the demolition of the second Garden in Madison Square at 26th Street and Madison Avenue and the construction of the third Garden at 49th Street and Eighth Avenue, is born in Kansas City, Missouri.

1925

Louis (Kid) Kaplan takes the vacant world featherweight title with a ninth-round KO of Danny Kramer at the Garden.

1930

Americans, who had won only once in their previous 10 meetings with the Rangers, blast their intra-building rivals, 7-1, at the Garden, and set a club record for most goals in a game. In their first 185 NHL games, the Amerks had scored six goals only three times and not since January 25, 1927, in a 6-1 win over the Ottawa Senators.

JACK SULGER

1935

Bill Bonthron of the NYAC, a former Princeton miler, wins the Sullivan Award as the nation's best amateur athlete of 1934, amassing 1,072 points in the national AAU poll.

1944

At the Garden, Boston hands the Rangers their worst home defeat ever, 13-3.

1957

Gene Fullmer wins the middleweight championship with a 15-round decision over Sugar Ray Robinson at the Garden before 18,134.

1960

Bobby Fischer wins the U.S. chess championship at age 16.

1965

St. John's tops Michigan, 75-74, in the ECAC Holiday Festival final at the Garden. The Wolverines eliminated Princeton in the semifinals on Cazzie Russell's basket (see Dec. 30).

1965

Joe Namath signs a $427,000 contract with the Jets, who drafted the Alabama quarterback in 1964 after trading quarterback Jerry Rhome to Houston for the Oilers' first-round pick in that draft.

1979

Jack Sulger, NYAC rowing coach since 1950, dies in New York at age 65.

1983

Jets lose their regular-season finale at Kansas City, 37-13, in a game postponed from October 24 by a players' strike, but still qualify for the Super Bowl Tournament. Football Giants beat the Eagles, 26-24, at Philadelphia, but finish 4-5 and miss the playoffs.

1986

Mike Bossy scores the 500th goal of his career into an empty net to seal the Islanders' 7-5 win over Boston at Nassau Coliseum.

1835

William Trotter Porter resumes publishing his weekly newspaper, *Spirit of the Times*, in New York. The first all-sports publication in America (see Dec. 10), sold to John Richards and merged in 1832, the resurrected paper becomes the leading organ of sports in America for a dozen years and opens up coverage of sports events to the public.

1920

Yankees announce the purchase of Babe Ruth from Boston for $125,000 and make a $300,000 loan secured by Fenway Park, the Red Sox' home field.

1932

Boston ices the puck 87 times in a 0-0 tie against the Americans at the Garden, outraging many NHL owners and most of the 14,000 fans. Bruins coach Art Ross and owner Charles Adams order players to ice the puck to retaliate for the Amerks' performance at Boston December 8, 1931, when they iced the puck 61 times in a 3-2 win. These fiascoes lead to the current rule penalizing icing except when shorthanded.

ARTHUR DALEY

1938

Associated Press correspondent Edward J. Neil is killed at age 38 in Zaragosa, Spain, covering the Spanish Civil War. Neil joined the *AP* as a teenager and became a respected boxing writer. The Boxing Writers Association annual award for contributions to boxing is made in his honor.

1956

Tex Sullivan, whose London Sporting Club had produced 86 consecutive weekly Monday night boxing cards at St. Nick's Arena for the DuMont Television network, announces he is ending the series January 16, claiming he cannot book fights after that date, the deadline set by NYSAC chairman Julius Helfand for all boxing managers to quit the Boxing Guild of New York, which Helfand asserts is subject to underworld influence.

1967

Mal Graham, last star of NYU's Division I basketball history, scores a school record 48 points in Violets' 100-74 win over Wagner. In his career, Graham scored 48, 47, 46, 45, and 43 (twice) points for the six highest scoring games in NYU history up to that time, and is graduated as the school's career scoring leader with 1,716 points.

1973

George Steinbrenner's syndicate buys the Yankees from CBS for $10 million.

1974

While walking to work, Pulitzer Prize-winning sports columnist Arthur Daley of *The New York Times* dies in New York at age 69 after suffering heart seizure in front of the offices of the Football Giants, for whom he once was public-address announcer.

1987

Browns eliminate the Jets, 23-20, in double overtime in an AFC playoff game at Cleveland after erasing a 20-10 deficit with 10 points in the last 1:57 of regulation.

1998

Pace basketball coach Darrell Halloran, 47, suffers a heart attack at halftime of his team's game against American International at the Pace gym in Manhattan and dies. Halloran was the winningest coach in Setters history (231-180). AIC wins, 75-74.

January 4

1878

The first annual Winter Athletic Meet of the New York Athletic Club begins at Gilmore's Gardens (which in May 1879 becomes Madison Square Garden). Although the NYAC's first meet in 1868 was held indoors, this two-day event begins the regular series of indoor games, which conclude in 1968. Outdoor meets were held every year beginning in 1868.

1898

Charles H. Byrne, founder of the Brooklyn baseball club that would become the Dodgers, dies in New York at age 54. The team, a member of the minor Inter-State League in 1883, joined the major league AA in 1884 and the NL in 1890.

1907

NYU plays its first basketball game, losing to Brooklyn Poly, 35-14. The first victory comes in the third game (a 38-16 win over Rutgers).

1936

A then-record crowd of 18,074 watches an NYU-Fordham/City College-St. John's basketball doubleheader at the Garden. NYU (52-23) and St. John's (25-22) win.

1968

United Soccer Association (USA) and the National Professional Soccer League announce a merger in New York to form the North American Soccer League, which lasts over a decade as America's first substantial nationwide soccer circuit.

1973

Raiders center Ron Ward scores five goals in New York's 9-5 WHA victory over the Ottawa Nationals at the Garden. It is the only five-goal game by a WHA player during the league's first season.

MIKE GARTNER

1987

Football Giants rout San Francisco, 49-3, at Giants Stadium in an NFC playoff game. Phil Simms completes nine passes, four for touchdowns, and Joe Morris runs for a pair of scores.

1992

Mike Gartner, in his 971st game, scores his 1,000th career point, but the Devils beat the Rangers, 6-4, at the Meadowlands.

1993

Roger Neilson, who led the Rangers to their first division championship in 48 years in 1990 and the regular season point title in 1992, is fired as head coach despite a 19-17-4 record.

1995

Jim Lee Howell, a former end and later head coach for the Football Giants, dies at the age of 80 in Lonoke, Arkansas. Howell played for the team from 1937-48 (with time out for military service) and was head coach from 1954-60, winning three division titles and the 1956 NFL championship.

1879

Jack Norworth, lyricist of "Take Me Out to the Ballgame," is born in Philadelphia, Pennsylvania.

1921

Paul V. Governali, a Columbia quarterback who in 1942 finished second in the Heisman Trophy balloting and won the Maxwell Trophy, is born in The Bronx.

1925

Lou G. Carnesecca, whose terms as St. John's head basketball coach sandwiched a three-year stint with the New York Nets, is born in New York. Carnesecca led the Redmen to the 1989 NIT title and the NCAA Final Four in 1985, and guided the Nets to the ABA final in 1972.

LOU CARNESECCA

1931

John E. McVay, Football Giants head coach (1976-78, 14-23), is born in Bellaire, Ohio.

1934

Yankees release two future Hall of Famers, pitcher Herb Pennock and infielder Joe Sewell. Pennock, 162-90 in his 11 seasons with the Bombers, finishes his career with the Boston Red Sox in 1934, while Sewell, after three years with the Yankees, goes unclaimed.

1946

While still in the U.S. Navy, catcher Walker Cooper is sold to the Giants by the St. Louis Cardinals for the staggering sum of $175,000.

1957

Sophomore Cal Ramsey scores 37 points and pulls down 30 rebounds but NYU is upset, 94-88, by Brandeis at the Garden.

1977

Defensive coordinator Walt Michaels is named Jets head coach, and Leon Hess is named acting president, succeeding the late Phil Iselin (see Dec. 28).

1979

In their home opener, the New York Stars of the new Women's Basketball League beat the Chicago Hustle, 100-99, at the Felt Forum. The WBL also includes the New Jersey Gems, who play at the Dunn Sports Center in Elizabeth, N.J. The league lasts three seasons.

1986

Bears defeat the Football Giants, 21-0, in an NFC playoff game at Chicago's frigid Soldier Field. Sean Landeta fans on a punt that Shaun Gayle runs in from five yards out in the first quarter for all the points the Bears would need.

1989

ESPN wins a four-year, $400 million contract for cable rights to some 175 major league baseball games annually beginning in 1990.

1995

After a 6-10 record in his first year, Pete Carroll is fired by the Jets, who replace him with Rich Kotite, dismissed by the Philadelphia Eagles after a 7-9 season.

January 6

1896

Garden stages the first women's six-day bike race, with Frankie Nelson winning.

1925

Paavo Nurmi, the "Flying Finn," makes his U.S. and indoor debut with a win over Joie Ray in a mile at the Garden. Ray turns in a personal best 4:14.0 but Nurmi surges in front with about 250 yards to go and is clocked at 4:13.6, a world indoor record.

1929

Garden president Tex Rickard, the promoter who introduced the million-dollar gate to boxing, dies in Miami at age 58. Rickard took control of the Garden (at Madison Square) in 1920 and was responsible for construction of Garden number three (at 49th Street and 8th Avenue) in 1925. Jack Dempsey leads the mourners when Rickard's wake is held on the floor of the Garden arena.

ALICE MARBLE

1941

Alice Marble, four-time U.S. national singles champion at Forest Hills, including three in a row from 1938-40, makes her pro debut, defeating Mary Hardwick of England, 8-6, 8-6, at the Garden in the opening of a national tour that also features Bill Tilden against Don Budge.

1948

Branch Rickey, president of the Brooklyn Dodgers, acquires the Brooklyn Football Dodgers of the AAFC from William D. Cox, who reports that he lost $350,000 operating the team during its first two seasons at Ebbets Field (see Jan. 21, 1949).

1948

Columbia's defense of its EIBL championship begins with a 55-53 win over Harvard in the second game of a doubleheader at the Boston Arena. Lions finish 11-1 in the league (23-1 overall) before a first-round loss to eventual champ Kentucky in the NCAA's at the Garden.

1966

William H. Taylor dies in Port Washington, N.Y., at age 64. In 1935, Taylor, a yachting writer for the *Herald Tribune* from 1927-42, became the first sportswriter to win a Pulitzer for his coverage of the 1934 America's Cup series won by *Rainbow* over England's *Endeavor*, 4-2.

1971

Referee Andy Hershock, 42, suffers a heart attack during an ABA game between the Nets and the Memphis Pros at Island Garden in West Hempstead, L.I. Hershock dies in the arena's medical office. Eventually the game resumes, and the Nets win, 110-101.

1976

Emile Francis, Rangers general manager since 1964, is fired and replaced the following day by former Montreal Canadiens forward John Ferguson, who also succeeds Ron Stewart as coach.

1997

Harness trainer and driver Mike Gagliardi dies at age 48 in Lakewood, N.J. Gagliardi, the winningest trainer at the Meadowlands in 1981 and 1986, spent 1993-94 in a federal witness protection program after his brother-in-law turned informant on fellow organized crime figures.

1897

M. J. Eagan wins the first National AAU handball championship at the Jersey City (N.J.) Handball Court, ousting Napoleon Levoie of the St. Roche AA, Quebec, in four sets and taking the final against William Schmidt of the Brooklyn Handball Club, 21-3, 21-9, 21-3, 21-9.

1913

John Robert Mize is born in Demorest, Georgia. The NL batting champ in 1939 with St. Louis who with the Giants tied Pittsburgh's Ralph Kiner for the NL home run title in successive seasons (51 in 1947 and 40 in 1948), Mize was traded to the Yankees in 1949 and helped them to five consecutive World Series titles.

1916

Walter (Babe) Pratt, a defenseman on the Rangers' 1940 Stanley Cup championship team, is born in Stony Mountain, Manitoba (see Nov. 27).

1923

Alvin Dark is born in Comanche, Oklahoma. Blackie Dark was the regular Giants shortstop on the 1951 pennant-winning team and 1954 world champions.

1931

Germany's Max Schmeling is stripped of his heavyweight title by the New York State Athletic Commission for refusing to sign for a June defense against top challenger Jack Sharkey.

1946

In a deal that will acquire great significance by season's end, the Football Giants obtain quarterback Frank Filchock from Washington for tackle Paul Stenn and a player to be named later (see Dec. 15).

1971

After two days of meetings in New York, the North American Soccer League elects Phil Woosnan commissioner and decides to move the league offices from Atlanta, Georgia, to New York.

1972

Richard I. (Dick) Wood and Seymour E. (Sy) Siegel, law partners in Trenton, N.J., purchase the franchise rights for New York in the newly-organized World Hockey Association. In May, the two sign a lease for their team (known as the Raiders) to play in the Garden when the league's first season opens that fall.

1988

Al Barabas, who scored the only touchdown in Columbia's 7-0 upset of Stanford in the 1934 Rose Bowl, dies in Rockville, Maryland, at age 77.

1990

Horace C. Stoneham, owner of the New York Giants from 1936-57, dies in Scottsdale, Arizona, at age 86. Stoneham moved the Giants to San Francisco after the 1957 season and sold the team in 1976.

1991

The U.S. Supreme Court refuses to hear a challenge to the NFL free agency system, effectively ending an antitrust suit by the NFL Players Association (see Oct. 15).

1992

Mets pitching great Tom Seaver, with highest percentage of the vote ever (98.8%), is elected to the Baseball Hall of Fame along with reliever Rollie Fingers. Three blank ballots and 41 write-in votes protest all-time hit leader Pete Rose's banning from the writers' ballot.

1916

Mathew (Mac) Colville, Rangers right wing on the "Bread Line" with brother Neil and Alex Shibicky, and a member of the 1940 Stanley Cup champs, is born in Edmonton, Alberta.

1944

Bill Johnson of the Yankees is selected Most Valuable Rookie of the 1943 baseball season in an unofficial poll (the official BBWAA Rookie of the Year Award does not begin until 1947).

1944

With a bitter parting shot, former Giants first baseman and manager Bill Terry quits baseball. "Baseball is too cheap for me," says Terry, who announces he is going into the cotton business. He later becomes a successful automobile dealer.

1947

Alvin Paris is convicted of attempting to fix the 1946 NFL championship game between the Football Giants and Chicago Bears (see Dec. 15).

1947

At age 79, Edward G. Barrow, Yankees general manager from 1921-45, officially retires from baseball.

1948

Don Forman's career-high 35 points lead NYU to a 77-56 win over Duke at the Garden.

1957

Dodgers' Jackie Robinson, who was traded after the 1956 season to the archrival Giants, announces his retirement in a *Look* magazine article.

1963

Former Columbia star Jack Molinas (class of 1953), who was briefly with the NBA Ft. Wayne Pistons before a lifetime suspension for betting on basketball in 1954, is convicted for his role in the 1961 college basketball point-shaving scandal.

1967

Raymond J. Kelly, sports editor of *The New York Times* from 1937-57, dies in Bronxville, N.Y., at age 68.

1972

Don Johnson wins the BPAA U.S. Open bowling championship at the Garden's Felt Forum with a 233-224 victory over George Pappas.

ED BARROW

1995

Carlos Monzon, middleweight champion from 1970-77, dies in Santa Rosa de Calchines, Argentina, at age 52. Monzon is killed in an auto crash while on a furlough from prison where he was serving an 11-year sentence for killing his estranged girlfriend, Alicia Muniz. An autopsy had revealed that Muniz was strangled before apparently falling to her death and Monzon was convicted of the killing in 1988.

1873

John J. Flanagan, later a New York City policeman and Olympic gold medalist in weight events, is born in Kilbreedy, Ireland. He won gold in the hammer throw in 1900, 1904, and 1908.

1903

Frank Farrell and Bill Devery buy the defunct Baltimore American League franchise for $18,000 and move it to New York. The team, called the Highlanders, becomes known as the Yankees by 1913.

1942

Joe Louis retains his heavyweight diadem by knocking out Buddy Baer at the Garden at 2:56 of the first round. Louis donates his net purse of $47,100.94 to the Navy Relief Fund. A crowd of 16,689 pay $189,700.

1945

Welterweight Maxie Berger of Montreal, Quebec, defeats Soloman Stewart in an eight-round bout at Brooklyn's Broadway Arena. It is Berger's 14th straight win at the Halsey Street club.

NEIL SMITH

1954

Neil Smith, the first man ever to serve simultaneously as president and general manager of the Rangers, and general manager of the 1994 Stanley Cup champions, is born in Toronto, Ontario.

1958

Oscar Robertson of the University of Cincinnati scores 56 points in the Bearcats' 118-54 rout of Seton Hall, setting an individual single-game college scoring record at the Garden. Robertson hits 22 of 32 shots and all 12 of his free throws, breaking the record set by St. John's' Harry Boykoff (see Mar. 11).

1965

One week after signing Joe Namath, the Jets sign another college quarterback, Heisman Trophy winner John Huarte of Notre Dame, to a contract worth a reported $200,000.

1972

Chick Meehan, NYU and Manhattan football coach, dies in Syracuse, N.Y., at age 78.

1979

Henry (Hinkey) Haines, quarterback of the Football Giants' first NFL championship team in 1927, dies at age 79 in Sharon Hill, Pennsylvania. Haines played for the Giants from their first season (1925) through 1928 and the Stapleton Athletic Club, Staten Island's NFL club (1929-31).

1983

Jets open their postseason with 44-17 rout of Bengals at Cincinnati as Freeman McNeil gains a club-record 202 yards on 22 carries, rushes for one touchdown and throws for another.

1990

Spud Chandler, two-time 20-game winner for the Yankees and 1943 American League MVP, dies in St. Petersburg, Florida, at age 82. In 1943, Chandler, who has the best lifetime winning percentage in club history (.717), was 20-4 with a 1.64 ERA. The right-hander was 20-8 in 1946 after being released from military service but elbow surgery in 1947 ended his career.

January 10

1911

Trotting's Grand Circuit admits to membership the half mile track at Goshen, N.Y., owned by railroad magnate E.H. Harriman. It is the only half mile track on the "major league circuit" of trotting, in part because the track is the scene of the triumphs of Hambletonian and Stamboul, two of the greatest trotting horses ever.

1917

Sid Borgia, colorful BAA and NBA referee, is born in Farmington, West Virginia.

1922

Columbia's hockey game at Princeton is postponed because the Tigers' new Hobey Baker rink isn't finished.

1928

After one season with the Giants, slugger Rogers Hornsby is traded to the Boston Braves.

1935

Nat Strong, owner of two of Brooklyn's most famous semipro baseball teams, the Bushwicks and the Bay Parkways, dies in New Rochelle, N.Y., at age 61. He was also an active promoter of black baseball, owning the Royal Giants and having interests in both the Black Yankees and Cuban Stars. Strong was also one of the owners of Dexter Park in Woodhaven, the first night ballpark in the East.

1937

Travis Jackson, longtime Giants shortstop and third baseman, is named manager of the Giants' Jersey City (International League) minor league club.

1941

Penn State beats NYU, 47-34, only the fourth loss suffered by the Violets since Alumni Gym on the University Heights campus opened in 1932 (see Dec. 17). NYU will not lose again at the Gym until 1964, winning its next 57 home games (see Mar. 3).

1944

Tommy Jones, manager of Jess Willard, the heavyweight champion from 1915-19, dies in San Diego, California, at age 69.

1946

Georgia's All-America running back Frank Sinkwich signs with the New York Yankees of the AAFC, fanning the flames of war between the infant AAFC and the established NFL.

1990

Doug Graber is hired as Rutgers head football coach. After the 1995 season, Graber is fired with a 29-36-1 record as the Scarlet Knights continue to struggle at the "big-time" level.

1994

Charles S. (Chub) Feeney, longtime Giants executive and president of the National League from 1970-86, dies in San Francisco, California, at age 72.

JESS WILLARD

1890

Maximilian Carnarius, who as Max Carey became a National League star and managed Brooklyn for the two seasons (1932-33) preceding Casey Stengel's reign, is born in Terre Haute, Indiana.

1897

A six-day military bicycle tournament sponsored by the *New York Herald* opens at the Garden. When the show closes on January 16, it has raised over $15,000 to endow rooms at New York's Hahnemann Hospital for injured or wounded National Guardsmen.

JACOB RUPPERT

1910

Rangers goalie Davey Kerr is born in Toronto, Ontario. Kerr led the Blueshirts to the Stanley Cup in 1939-40, when he won the Vezina Trophy for allowing the fewest goals in the NHL.

1911

At University Hall, Ted Kiendl scores 16 points as Columbia routs Princeton, 36-13. The Lions will win the EIBL (7-1) and Kiendl will lead the league in scoring with 100 points.

1915

Colonel Jacob Ruppert and Colonel Tillinghast L'Hommedieu Huston buy the Yankees from original owners Frank J. Farrell and William S. Devery for $460,000.

1940

Rangers defeat Chicago, 5-3, at the Garden, to tie the NHL record of 18 games in a row without a defeat. Two days later, they set a new mark, beating the Maple Leafs, 4-1, at Toronto.

1945

While still on active service with the Army Air Force, former amateur boxing champion Lieutenant Colonel Edward P.F. (Eddie) Eagen is named to the New York State Athletic Commission by Governor Thomas E. Dewey, and Eagen is later elected chairman of the commission.

1946

Bert Bell replaces Elmer Layden as NFL commissioner and the league announces its headquarters will shift from Chicago to New York. In the event, however, Bell runs the league from offices in suburban Philadelphia until his death in 1959.

1973

American League adopts the designated hitter rule on an experimental basis for the coming season.

1987

Football Giants win the NFC championship with a 17-0 victory over the Washington Redskins amid swirling 35-mph winds at Giants Stadium.

1993

Ruth Adel Torgerson, a golfer who won three Metropolitan women's amateur championships (1942, 1949, 1950), dies in Manhasset, N.Y., at age 85.

1995

After a 105-day owners' lockout that imperils the season, the NHL and Players' Association announce a labor agreement and a 48-game regular-season schedule.

January 12

1906

Representatives of two intercollegiate football rules committees meet in New York and form the organization that, in 1913, becomes the NCAA. The American Football Rules Committee, formed in 1894, is virtually run by Yale's Walter Camp, its secretary. The AFRC does not allow new tactics, while the game has become increasingly violent. In 1905, at least 18 deaths and 149 serious injuries occur. Columbia and Northwestern drop football and Harvard threatens to as well. NYU Chancellor Henry MacCracken and Army's Captain Palmer Pierce lead a new group, the Intercollegiate Athletic Association of the United States. Under pressure from President Theodore Roosevelt, the AFRC and IAAUS cooperate and, without doubt, save the sport.

1914

Stanley Saplin, creator of the first Rangers yearbook (*Inside the Blueshirt*) in 1948, sportswriter, track and field historian and athletic administrator, is born in New York.

1922

Vinnie O'Brien scores 29 of St. John's' 31 points, including all 14 in the second half, but visiting Fordham wins, 32-31.

1929

Caspar W. Whitney, creator of All-America football teams, dies. Part-owner of a small magazine, *This Week's Sport*, Whitney in 1889 conceived of the team selection as a promotion for the publication. When it folded in 1891, Whitney began selections for *Harper's Weekly* that season. Whitney consulted with Yale's Walter Camp on the first two teams and Camp picked the 1897 team when Whitney was on a world tour. Thereafter, each published separate teams.

1944

Juliette P. Atkinson, three-time U.S. national singles tennis champion (1895, 1897-98), dies in Brooklyn at age 70.

1947

The Duke and Duchess of Windsor take in an NHL game as guests of Garden management and see the Rangers beat the Toronto Maple Leafs, 3-2.

1948

Football Giants sign Columbia end Bill Swiacki, hero of the Lions' 21-20 upset over Army the preceding October (see Oct. 25).

1957

Chet Forte scores 44 points in Columbia's 93-82 win over Rutgers at New Brunswick, N.J., to set a single-game school record he will break in a little over a month (see Feb. 13).

1959

U.S. Supreme Court orders dissolution of International Boxing Club, the boxing promotion subsidiary of the Garden, on antitrust grounds. The IBC and its president, Truman Gibson, had been under investigation for several years because of allegations of corruption.

1969

Jets win Super Bowl III in one of the most famous upsets in pro football history with a 16-7 win over the Baltimore Colts at Miami's Orange Bowl. As 18-point underdogs from the upstart AFL, the Jets ride Matt Snell's four-yard first-quarter touchdown run and Jim Turner's three field goals to the win. Jets quarterback Joe Namath helps fulfill his brash "guarantee" of victory the Thursday before the game with 17-for-28 passing for 206 yards to earn game MVP honors.

1922

New Yorker Gene Tunney wins the vacant American light heavyweight title with a 12-round decision over Battling Levinsky (Barney Lebrowitz) at the Garden in a matchup of the two leading contenders for the crown.

1933

In Babe Didrickson's professional basketball debut, her Brooklyn Yankees beat the Long Island Ducklings, 19-16.

1939

Colonel Jacob Ruppert, principal owner of the Yankees for 24 years (1915-39) and bankroll who started the greatest dynasty in baseball history, dies in New York at age 71.

1942

Rangers score five goals in 3:46 of the third period during a 9-2 Garden victory over the Americans (Grant Warwick at 15:30, Alex Shibicky at 16:43, Shibicky again at 17:42, Lynn Patrick at 18:32 and Alan Kuntz at 19:16).

1942

In the fastest knockout in New York boxing annals, Joe Jakes KOs Al Foreman 11 seconds into the first round at the Broadway Club in Brooklyn.

1978

Joe McCarthy, who managed the Yankees to seven World Series titles, including four in a row, and eight pennants from 1931-46, dies in Buffalo, N.Y., at age 90.

1987

Football Giants linebacker Lawrence Taylor named MVP of the NFL by the Pro Football Writers' Association. *Sports Illustrated* reports Taylor is the first defensive player to be the league's consensus MVP.

1991

Football Giants start their journey toward a second Super Bowl with a 31-3 win over Chicago Bears in an NFC playoff game at Giants Stadium. Quarterback Jeff Hostetler, filling in for the injured Phil Simms, throws two touchdown passes and runs for another.

1995

Baseball's Executive Council announces that it plans to employ replacement players if the clubs cannot reach a contract with the Major League Baseball Players' Association, which struck the sport August 11, 1994.

1996

Bill Goodstein, a New York lawyer who during the 1980s represented, among others, Yankees Dave Righetti and Willie Randolph, and is credited by many with resurrecting Darryl Strawberry's career in the mid-1990s by persuading the Yankees to sign him, dies in New York at age 56.

JOE McCARTHY

1919

Sale of the New York Giants, one of the most valuable franchises in sports, is announced as the estate of the late John T. Brush sells the club and the Polo Grounds structure for some $2.5 million to a syndicate led by stockbroker Charles A. Stoneham. Stoneham, also the owner of a thoroughbred stable, is a member of the New York Curb Exchange (now the American Stock Exchange). His syndicate includes Francis X. McQuade, a prominent city magistrate, and Giants manager John McGraw. Stoneham becomes president of the club, succeeding Harry Hampstead, son-in-law of Brush, who had run the club since Brush's death in 1912.

1921

Benny Leonard retains his lightweight crown with a sixth-round KO of Richie Mitchell at the Garden in the first title fight of New York's second year of legalized boxing under the "Walker Law." The gate of $133,745 is the largest ever at that time for a non-heavyweight fight.

1922

Yankees file plans with the city for a new stadium in The Bronx at an estimated $750,000.

1926

In a glamour event that attracts a celebrity crowd, New York's Joe Moore wins the World Series of Speed Skating by defeating Finland's Clas Thunberg and Canada's Charles Gorman at the Garden. Moore covers three miles in 9:25.1. Thunberg, the 1924 Olympic gold medalist, leads for the first 36 of the 42 laps but fades to third as Gorman, the 1924 world outdoor champion, finishes second. Norma Shearer, Clark Gable and Jimmy Durante are among the luminaries. Four days later, the three skaters are back at the Garden for the 1 1/2-mile test and Moore wins again.

1932

Longtime National Horse Show president F.D. MacKay dies at age 60 in Brooklyn.

1940

Rangers lose to the Blackhawks, 2-1, at Chicago, ending a 10-game winning streak begun December 19 with a 5-2 victory over the Canadiens at the Garden. The loss also ends a league-record 19-game unbeaten streak (14 wins, 5 ties) that started November 23, 1939, with a 1-1 tie at Montreal. Rangers win their next five for 15 victories in 16 games and 24 victories or ties in 25 games.

1954

Joe DiMaggio, 39, marries Marilyn Monroe, 29, in San Francisco, California. The couple separate October 27 and divorce a year later (the final decree is issued October 31, 1955).

1961

Joe Foss, commissioner of the year-old AFL, sends a telegram to Pete Rozelle, commissioner of the established NFL, proposing a world championship game between the leagues' titlists. Rozelle does not respond since the NFL does not recognize the upstart league.

JOE DIMAGGIO AND MARILYN MONROE

1970

Yankees' original bullpen ace of the 1930s, and general manager of the 1969 world champion Mets, Johnny (Grandma) Murphy, dies in New York at age 61.

1892

Hobart Amory Hare Baker is born in Wissahickon, Pennsylvania. Hobey Baker, considered by many America's greatest amateur hockey player, also became a Princeton football star.

1925

Benny Leonard retires as lightweight champion due to lack of quality opposition. Leonard had held the lightweight title since 1917. He makes a comeback in 1931 as a welterweight and wins his first 19 fights but fails to beat champion Jimmy McLarnin.

1939

In the first "Pro Bowl" ever played, the Football Giants, 1938 NFL champions, defeat the Pro All-Stars, 13-10, at Wrigley Field in Los Angeles.

1971

Rick Barry scores 53 points for New York Nets in a 120-117 loss to the Pittsburgh Condors at Island Garden. It is Barry's highest-scoring ABA performance.

1971

In a startling upset, the Harlem Globetrotters lose to the New Jersey Reds, 100-99, at the Jersey City (N.J.) Armory. It is their last loss until September 1995, a span of 8,829 games, when they are beaten in Vienna, Austria.

RED SMITH

1982

Red Smith, 76, third sportswriter ever to win a Pulitzer Prize (1976), dies in New Canaan, Connecticut. Smith wrote for the *Herald Tribune* (1947-65), the *World Journal Tribune* (1966-67), *Women's Wear Daily* (1968-70), and *The New York Times* (1971-82).

1983

Scott Dierking's fourth-quarter one-yard touchdown run lifts the Jets to a 17-14 win over the Raiders at Los Angeles and into the AFC final in the Super Bowl Tournament. Lance Mehl intercepts two passes in the last 2:49 to seal the victory.

1986

Jim Crowley, last surviving member of Notre Dame's fabled "Four Horsemen" backfield and coach of Fordham football from 1933-41 (56-13-7), dies in Scranton, Pennsylvania, at age 83.

1990

Donold Lourie, a Princeton quarterback who was Walter Camp's first-team All-American in 1920 and became chairman of Quaker Oats, dies in Longwood, Florida, at age 90.

1994

In what would prove to be both quarterback Phil Simms' and linebacker Lawrence Taylor's last game, the Football Giants are hammered by the 49ers, 44-3, in a divisional playoff game at San Francisco as Ricky Watters rushes for five touchdowns.

1997

Jim Fassel is named 15th head coach of the Football Giants, 23 days after Dan Reeves is dismissed following four seasons during which the team was 31-33 and 1-1 in the playoffs.

1892

Bunker Hill pays $58.90 to win as the upset winner of the third race at Guttenburg (N.J.) race track, a three-furlong sprint for two-year-olds. Bunker Hill gets home by a head in the nine-horse field.

1932

Patrick J. Conway, founder of the Irish-American Athletic Club, dies in Freeport, N.Y., at age 72.

1945

Brooklyn's Dixie Walker is honored as the outstanding player of 1944 by the New York chapter of the BBWAA. Walker led the majors with his .357 batting average.

1945

St. John's beats Akron, 48-42, as Ray Wertis scores 15 points and Bill Kotsores 12 as the Redmen break the Zips' nine-game winning streak before 14,487 at the Garden. In the opening game of the doubleheader, NYU routs St. Francis (N.Y.), 78-33.

1947

In their first major transaction, the Knicks sell forward Ralph Kaplowitz to the Philadelphia Warriors.

1960

William D. Cox, former owner of the Philadelphia Phillies and the AAFC Brooklyn Football Dodgers, announces the formation of the International Soccer League, which will bring top teams from Europe and South America for league play starting this summer in the Polo Grounds. The ISL lasts until 1965 and paves the way for a revival of soccer interest in the United States.

1960

Knicks defeat the Cincinnati Royals, 132-106, in their final game at 69th Regiment Armory, where Knicks had played 131 home games (116 regular season and 15 in the playoffs) during their first 14 seasons.

1988

Jimmy (the Greek) Snyder, a CBS sports commentator for 12 years, is fired by the network for making racist comments to a local television reporter at a Washington, D.C. restaurant.

1993

Freddie (Red) Cochran, dies in Lyons, N.J., at age 77. Cochran was world welterweight champion from 1941-46.

1996

Rudolf W. Wanderone, better known as notorious pool hustler "Minnesota Fats," dies in Nashville, Tenn., probably at age 84.

1997

Jim Kensil, 66, former NFL executive and Jets president, dies in Massapequa, N.Y.

DIXIE WALKER

1837

William B. Curtis, one of the founders of the New York Athletic Club, is born in Salisbury, Vermont.

1916

Professional Golfers Association (PGA) is formed at the Taplow Club in New York by a group led by department store mogul Rodman Wanamaker.

1922

Benny Kauff, former Federal League batting champ (known as the "Ty Cobb of the Feds"), is denied an injunction in his effort to force the Giants and Commissioner Landis to lift his suspension from Organized Baseball. Kauff had been suspended after being arrested in 1921 on charges in connection with the sale of stolen automobiles. Even though Kauff was acquitted, Judge Edward Whitaker of the New York Supreme Court is unable to grant relief because "there was no longer a valid contract between the parties." The decision effectively ends Kauff's major league career.

1932

Brooklyn's Andy Varipapa bowls a six-game exhibition in Queens Village with a total pinfall of 1,652, an average of 275.33 pins per game. Varipapa (who bowled a sanctioned 300 in 1931) opens with a 300 and follows with 268, 279, 247, 299 and 259.

1941

Fritzie Zivic retains his welterweight title with a 12th-round KO of Henry Armstrong at the Garden, retaining the crown he won from Armstrong in October 1940. The crowd of 23,190 is the largest in Garden history for boxing and the largest indoor crowd for a fight on record.

1944

Churchill Downs president Colonel Matt J. Winn, considered the nation's foremost promoter of thoroughbred racing, is elected president of the Empire City Racing Association, succeeding the late George H. Bull. But the track is sold and becomes Yonkers Raceway in 1950.

1951

A major college basketball betting scandal breaks with the arrests of Henry Poppe and John Byrnes, co-captains of Manhattan's 1949-50 team, for taking bribes to dump games.

1967

Barney Ross, the welterweight champion who became a World War II military hero and later became addicted to painkilling drugs because of war wounds, dies in Chicago, Illinois, at age 57.

1985

Cosmos, the league's most important franchise, reveal the financial crisis that triggers the collapse of the North American Soccer League.

RAY TELLIER

1989

Ray Tellier is hired as Columbia's head football coach, succeeding Larry McElreavy, who resigned under pressure November 29, 1988. Tellier inherits a program that has won only two of its previous 54 games, but in 1996 Tellier is chosen National Coach of the Year in Division 1-AA after leading the Lions to an 8-2 record, their best in 51 years.

January 18

1895
Reigning champion Tommy Ryan TKOs Jack (The Non-Pareil) Dempsey in the third round of a welterweight bout at the Coney Island Athletic Club.

1924
Harry Greb defeats Johnny Wilson in a 15-round middleweight rematch at the Garden to retain the crown he took from Wilson in August.

1951
Selecting first overall in the NFL draft, the Football Giants pick SMU back Kyle Rote.

1954
Empire City, which has been running its thoroughbred racing meetings at other tracks for many years, withdraws from New York's racing calendar, allowing the remaining tracks (Aqueduct, Belmont, Jamaica and Saratoga) to split up its dates. A full reorganization of New York racing comes the following year with the formation of the New York Racing Association.

1955
Boston's Bob Cousy scores 20 points to lead the East to a 100-91 victory over the West in the fifth NBA All-Star Game before 15,564 at the Garden. Jim Pollard of the Minneapolis Lakers scores 17 for the West and the Knicks' Harry Gallatin has a game-high 14 rebounds.

1958
Knicks beat Syracuse, 123-120, setting a team record for the most points at the 69th Regiment Armory, surpassing the mark (122) set Jan. 26, 1957, against the Minneapolis Lakers. But the record lasts only a week (see Jan. 25).

1961
Mark Douglas Messier is born in Edmonton, Alberta. Acquired by the Rangers in October 1991 and promptly named captain, Mark Messier in 1991-92 led the Rangers to their first regular-season championship in 50 years and two seasons later to their first Stanley Cup since 1940.

1964
Neil Farber's 22 points lead four Lions in double figures as Columbia scores a major upset by defeating Princeton and Bill Bradley, 69-66, at University Hall. The Tigers finish the regular season 19-7, and lose only one other Ivy League game (at Harvard).

1985
Mets participate in a six-player, four-team deal by sending pitcher Tim Leary to Milwaukee Brewers and obtaining pitcher Frank Wills from the Kansas City Royals.

1995
Ron Luciano, flamboyant former American League umpire and author of several books, commits suicide at age 57 in Endicott, N.Y.

1880

William Muldoon wins the Greco-Roman wrestling championship at the Garden by defeating France's Thiebaud Bauer, two out of three falls. Muldoon later serves as a trainer for heavyweight champ John L. Sullivan and subsequently as chairman of the New York State Athletic Commission.

1911

Rudolf Walter Wanderone is probably born in New York. There is some dispute, which Minnesota Fats never cleared up, as to the precise year, but most authorities accept 1911.

1911

Harvey (Busher) Jackson, an Americans wing (1939-41) whose best years came on Toronto's "Kid Line" with Joe Primeau and Charlie Conacher, is born in Toronto, Ontario.

1931

NYU makes its first basketball appearance at the Garden, losing to Manhattan, 16-14, in a charity tripleheader to benefit Mayor Walker's Emergency Relief Fund that attracts some 15,600 and generates $22,854.20 in receipts. In the opener, Lou Bender scores eight points to lead Columbia to a 26-18 victory over Fordham. After Manhattan's win (its ninth straight for the season), St. John's extends its winning streak to 22 by defeating City College, 17-9.

1939

Neil Amdur, future sports editor of *The New York Times*, is born in Wilkes-Barre, Pennsylvania.

1950

Jonathan Trumpbour Matlack is born in West Chester, Pennsylvania. The third leg of the mighty Mets rotation of the early 1970s (with Tom Seaver and Jerry Koosman), Jon Matlack in 1973 blanked the Reds, 5-0, in the second game of the NLCS, allowed two unearned runs in the World Series opener, a 2-1 loss to the A's, and allowed one run in eight innings in a 6-1 fourth-game win. His remarkable streak ended in the third inning of the final game (see Oct. 21).

1952

Ted Collins sells the Yanks franchise back to the NFL after two seasons in Yankee Stadium, ending his eight-year dream of having a second NFL team in New York. Five days later, the league sells the franchise to the Dallas Texans, who fold after the 1952 season and are replaced by the new Baltimore Colts.

1973

In one of the biggest upsets in NHL history, the expansion Islanders, 4-37-4 and losers of 12 straight, beat the defending Stanley Cup champion Boston Bruins, 9-7, at Boston Garden.

1979

Alphonse (Tuffy) Leemans, a Football Giants running back whose "Day" at the Polo Grounds was spoiled by news of the Japanese attack on Pearl Harbor on December 7, 1941, dies in Hillsboro Beach, Florida, at age 66.

1986

Ivan Lendl routs Boris Becker, 6-2, 7-6, 6-2, at the Garden to win the Nabisco Grand Prix Masters, the men's championship. Lendl, the world's top-ranked player, wins for the 35th time in 36 matches to take the $100,000 first prize, and $800,000 for finishing first on the circuit. Lendl raises his earnings to $1,963,074 for the 1985 season, which concludes with this event.

January 20

1898

H.M. Spencer wins the championship .22 caliber-rifle competition at the Sportsmen's Exhibition at the Garden. He totals 2,421 (of 2,500) points in the week-long event. R.J. Young is second with 2,413. Spencer also wins the continuous competition with 149 (out of 150) points.

1909

William Dole Eckert is born in Freeport, Illinois. When, as a retired Air Force general, Eckert is named baseball commissioner in 1965, one wag says, "My God, they've named the Unknown Soldier." Eckert shortly becomes the Unknown Commissioner when he is forced out of office (and his contract bought out) in 1968.

1938

Larry MacPhail is elected executive vice president of the Dodgers with authority over all baseball operations. Shortly, MacPhail will bring Brooklyn legends organist Gladys Goodding, manager Leo Durocher, broadcaster Red Barber and shortstop Pee Wee Reese to Ebbets Field.

1977

In a swap of centerfielders, the Yankees trade Elliott Maddox to Baltimore for Paul Blair. That year, Blair singles to start the winning three-run rally in the ninth inning of the deciding fifth ALCS game in Kansas City (see Oct. 9) and drives in the winning run in the 12th inning of the World Series opener against Los Angeles at Yankee Stadium.

NED IRISH

1982

Rangers beat the Islanders, 3-2, at the Garden, for the visitors' last loss until February 21, 4-3 at Pittsburgh. In between, the Isles win 15 straight to set an NHL record (see Feb. 20).

1986

George Furey dies in Nyack, N.Y., at age 71. In 1936, Furey returned the opening kickoff of the second half for a touchdown at the Polo Grounds that gave Columbia another 7-0 win over Stanford in a rematch of the 1934 Rose Bowl.

1990

Barney Kremenko, longtime sportswriter with the New York *Journal-American,* who is credited with giving Willie Mays the nickname "The Say Hey Kid," dies in Mineola, N.Y., at age 80. Kremenko covered the Giants and later the Mets. After his paper closed in 1967, he became a publicist for the Nets and Islanders.

1991

Matt Bahr's fifth field goal, a 42-yarder as time expires, gives the Football Giants a 15-13 win over the two-time defending champion 49ers at San Francisco and the NFC championship.

1995

Rangers open the strike-delayed 1994-95 season with a 2-1 loss to the Buffalo Sabres at the Garden in their first season opener as defending Stanley Cup champions since November 2, 1940, when they won, 4-1, at Toronto. An emotional banner-raising ceremony celebrates the 1993-94 division, conference, league and Cup championships.

January 21

1888

Amateur Athletic Union, which governs amateur, non-collegiate sports for most of the next century, is formed in New York. The NYAC presses its organization after withdrawing from the N4A. Embroiled in several disputes with the leaders of the N4A, the NYAC simply leads the formation of a rival, successful organization.

1921

Kennesaw Mountain Landis takes office as baseball's first commissioner, beginning a 23-year reign filled with controversy but one that restores stability and respectability to the sport.

1921

Bantamweight Packey O'Gatty is awarded a decision over Roy Moore by referee Ed Pollack at the Pioneer Sporting Club on East 24th Street. The next day an N.Y. State Athletic Commission deputy commissioner rules the fight "no contest" since O'Gatty won on a foul in the first minute of the third round. O'Gatty sues and State Supreme Court Justice John MacCrate rules Pollack's decision absolute (April 11). O'Gatty, unable to collect his purse, seeks relief, and the legislature passes a special bill to pay him. Governor Nathan Miller signs the "O'Gatty Law" March 18, 1922. O'Gatty is then paid $1,252.50, becoming the only prize fighter ever paid by the state.

1922

John McGraw, skipper since 1902, signs to manage the Giants for five more years.

1923

Sabath (Sam) Mele, later an NYU star, longtime major league outfielder, and manager, is born in Astoria, Queens.

1948

Carl M. Voyles is named head coach of the Football Dodgers, succeeding Cliff Battles.

1949

AAFC Yankees and Dodgers merge into a team based in Yankee Stadium with New York's Red Strader head coach and Brooklyn's Carl Voyles an assistant. The same day, the NFL shifts the Boston Yanks to New York as the Bulldogs share the Polo Grounds with the Football Giants, providing an NFL game every weekend against the AAFC's key team.

1954

Making its first appearance at the Garden, the NBA All-Star Game goes into overtime for the first time, and the East wins, 98-93, after an 84-84 tie after regulation. The paid crowd of 16,487 is an All-Star record not surpassed until 1965 in St. Louis (16,713). Harry Gallatin of the Knicks hauls in 18 rebounds and Bob Cousy of Boston scores 20 for the winners.

1982

Ned Irish, 76, the sportswriter who introduced regular college basketball doubleheaders to Madison Square Garden in 1934, made intersectional collegiate games a staple of the sport, served as Garden president and founded the Knickerbockers in 1946, dies in Venice, Florida.

1985

General manager Craig Patrick, Herb Brooks' assistant on the 1980 gold medal U.S. Olympic hockey team, fires Brooks as Rangers coach and takes the helm. The Rangers, 15-22-8 at the time, go 11-22-2 the rest of the way, finishing 26-44-10, their most losses ever in a single season.

1990

Nat (Feets) Broudy, colorful courtside clock operator for Knicks and college basketball games at the Garden for three decades, dies at age 76 in New York.

1922

Original Celtics win twice at the Garden, beating Wilkes-Barre in the afternoon, 38-18, for their third straight EPBL win, with Chris Leonard scoring 13 points. At night, Nat Holman scores 12 as they top Powers Brothers of Passaic, N.J., 33-21. Although there are three Powers brothers on the team, Benny Borgmann leads the losers with 13 and shortly joins the Celtics.

1929

Club president Jake Ruppert announces the Yankees will have numbered uniforms for the coming season, making them the first baseball team permanently to adopt uniform numbers.

1943

Yankees acquire Nick Etten from the Philadelphia Phillies for four players and $10,000. Etten leads the American League in home runs in 1944 and RBI in 1945.

1948

Mexican baseball commissioner Alejandro Aguilar Reyes announces that the Mexican League and U.S. Organized Baseball have made peace. During the two-year baseball border war, Mexican League teams, seeking major league parity and bankrolled by the Pasqual brothers, had signed many U.S. players. On October 28, 1947, the Mexican League reported it had lost 2.5 million pesos and promised no more player raids, appointing Reyes commissioner at that time to negotiate with the U.S. major leagues. Five-year suspensions for jumping to Mexico for big leaguers such as Max Lanier, Sal Maglie and Mickey Owen are all finally lifted by 1950.

1949

Henry W. Slocum, U.S. national singles tennis champion in 1888 and 1889 and USNLTA president from 1891-93, dies at age 86 in New York.

1951

Yankees shortstop Phil Rizzuto, the American League MVP in 1950, is presented with the first S. Rae Hickok Belt as the professional athlete of the year in Rochester, N.Y.

1957

Islanders right wing Michael Bossy is born in Montreal, Quebec. Bossy scored 573 goals in his 10 years with the Islanders, including a rookie-record 53 in 1977-78 and 69 the next year. He tallied the Cup-winning goals in 1982 and 1983.

1987

Devils beat Calgary, 7-5, at the Meadowlands before 334 fans who brave a blizzard. Only 13 New Jersey players show up despite a one-hour, 46-minute delay in the start.

1991

Johnny Balquist, Columbia baseball coach for 26 years, dies in Teaneck, N.J., at age 82.

1994

In the NHL All-Star Game at the Garden, the East beats the West, 9-8, before 18,200, and Rangers goalie Mike Richter takes MVP honors despite allowing two goals in his only period of work as he makes 19 saves, including Canucks' Pavel Bure's penalty shot (see June 7).

MIKE BOSSY

1911

A.W. de la Poer, national dueling champion, demonstrates the first electronic sword for fencing competition during a meet at the New York Athletic Club. The sword rings a bell that is hung around each competing fencer's waist when a touch is scored, eliminating un-sportsmanlike squabbling and bad judgment by officials. In the actual competition, Columbia's left-hander A.V. Clough wins the FLA President's Trophy in the novice foil competition.

1923

Horace Ashenfelter, later a prominent mile and two-mile champion, is born in Collegeville, Pennsylvania.

1944

Red Wings rout the Rangers, 15-0, at Detroit, starting a Blueshirts 21-game winless streak (0-17-4) that extends to the end of the season. The margin of defeat is the Rangers' biggest ever.

1950

In the first meeting since the "merger" of the warring pro football leagues, the combine known, briefly, as the National American Football League assigns the Football Giants to what becomes the National Conference and the Bulldogs (soon to be called the Yanks) to the American Conference.

EMILE GRIFFITH

1951

Knicks play the longest game in their history (four overtimes) but lose to the Royals, 102-92, at Rochester.

1954

Isaac B. Grainger of New York is elected president of the U.S. Golf Association.

1967

Emile Griffith decisions Joey Archer in a 15-round bout at the Garden to retain his world middleweight championship.

1968

NBA All-Star Game returns to the Garden for the first time since 1955 and the East wins, 144-124, as Boston's John Havlicek scores 26 points and Philadelphia's Hal Greer adds 21 (including a record 19 in the third quarter). The game was planned as a feature of the new (fourth) Garden, but construction delays back up the opening of that building to February and causes the game to the played in the third Garden instead, where a capacity crowd of 18,422 watches.

1983

Dolphins defeat the Jets, 14-0, in the AFC championship game in the soaked and muddy Orange Bowl in Miami, Florida. Jets quarterback Richard Todd throws five interceptions, one of which is returned 35 yards in the fourth quarter by A.J. Duhe for Miami's second touchdown.

1989

George Washington Case, Rutgers baseball coach in the 1950s and 1960s and a six-time American League stolen base king, dies in Trenton, N.J., at age 73.

1842

Yankee Sullivan (James Ambrose) KOs Tom Secor at 1:07 of the first round of a heavyweight fight in Staten Island. Sullivan later claims the American heavyweight title.

1903

Morris Ward sets two amateur speed skating records at Verona, N.J., with a 9.6-second clocking in the 100 yards and a 19 seconds flat in the 220.

1911

Charlie Barr, pilot of three successful America's Cup defenses for the New York Yacht Club, dies in Southampton, England, at age 46.

1930

In his U.S. boxing debut, Italian Primo Carnera, later heavyweight champion, KOs Big Boy Peterson at 1:10 of the first round before 20,000 at the Garden.

1938

James J. Mutrie, Mets manager from 1883-84 and field boss of the Giants championship teams of 1888 and 1889, dies in New York at age 86. Mutrie is generally credited with giving the team its nickname by calling his players, "My Giants."

1953

Ed Conlin hauls down a school-record 32 rebounds and scores 16 points as Fordham defeats Army, 63-54, at West Point.

1953

Mike Jacobs, longtime boxing promoter, dies in Miami Beach, Florida, at age 72. Jacobs, a New York ticket broker, dominated boxing from 1937-46 through his 20th Century Sporting Club and its control of heavyweight champion Joe Louis' contract. Jacobs sold his interests to Madison Square Garden and its International Boxing Club in 1949 for $110,000.

1980

A group led by Nelson Doubleday and Fred Wilpon that includes City Investing Co. purchases the Mets for $21.1 million, the most yet paid for a baseball franchise, from the family of original owner Joan Whitney Payson. Mrs. Payson's daughter, Lorinda deRoulet, and grandchildren had been running the team since her death in 1975.

1981

In the 50th game of the season, Mike Bossy scores twice to give him 50 goals, the second player in NHL history to reach that milestone that quickly (after Montreal's Maurice Richard in 1944), as the Islanders beat Quebec, 7-4, at Nassau Coliseum.

1992

Dr. Anthony Pisani, team physician for the Dodgers and later the Football Giants, dies in Boynton Beach, Florida, at 80. Dr. Pisani resigned his position with the Giants under a cloud of suspicion during a gambling investigation.

1997

Mike Milbury steps down as Islanders coach, bowing to the wish of new owner John Spano (see Nov. 26). Milbury led the Isles to a 22-50-10 record in 1995-96 and the club is 14-23-9 when Rick Bowness takes over. Milbury remains general manager. The Isles are 15-18-3 under Bowness and eliminated from playoff contention in the season's last week.

1925

John B. Day, 77, founder of the original Metropolitan Baseball Club (the Mets of the AA) and the NL New York (now San Francisco) Giants, dies in New York.

1926

Richard (Dick) McGuire, a Dartmouth and St. John's star who led the NBA in assists once with the Knicks, for whom he was later coach and chief scout, is born in Huntington, N.Y.

1936

Don Maynard, a Giants reject who starred for 13 years with the Titans/Jets, and who at his retirement held the NFL record for most pass receiving yardage, is born in Crosbyton, Texas.

1939

In his first title defense since the smashing first-round victory over Germany's Max Schmeling the previous summer (see June 22), heavyweight champ Joe Louis knocks out John Henry Lewis, the reigning light heavyweight champion, in the first round at the Garden.

DON MAYNARD

1942

Rangers rout the Detroit Red Wings, 11-2, at the Garden, matching their all-time high goal total for a game.

1945

Colonel Larry MacPhail, Dan Topping and Del Webb purchase the Yankees from the estate of the late Jacob Ruppert for $2.8 million (for 96.88% of stock), with MacPhail replacing Ed Barrow as president and general manager.

1958

Knicks beat Minneapolis, 128-116, in an NBC game at the 69th Regiment Armory and, in the process, set a team record for most points at the Armory, and both teams combine to break an Armory record of 243 points set the week before.

1965

Less than one month after signing his first contract with the Jets, Joe Namath undergoes surgery on his right knee at Lenox Hill Hospital to repair cartilage and ligament damage.

1967

Defenseman Harry Howell is honored on the first "night" ever held by the Rangers for an individual player. Four days earlier, Howell became the first Blueshirt ever to play 1,000 games for the team. The Rangers beat Boston, 2-1, to climax the evening.

1968

At the Millrose Games at the Garden, Bob Seagren sets the world indoor pole vault record (17' 4 $\frac{1}{4}$").

1987

With 39-20 victory over Denver, the Football Giants win Super Bowl XXI at Pasadena, California. Game MVP Phil Simms completes 22 of 25 passes for 268 yards and three touchdowns as the Giants erase a 10-9 halftime deficit by scoring the first 24 points of the second half.

January 26

1893

At Stamford, Connecticut, Joseph H. Donohue sets world professional skating records for 30, 40, 50, 60, 70, 80, 90 and 100 miles (7:11:38$^1/_5$).

1893

Abner Doubleday, who helped start the Civil War (as a Union general stationed at Fort Sumter, S.C.), but had nothing to do with starting baseball (as his own voluminous diaries attest) dies in Mendham, N.J., at age 73.

1897

Edward Reynolds of Chicago wins the mile in 2:56.2 at the National Amateur Skating Association championships at Silver Lake, Staten Island. The next day, Reynolds wins the quarter-mile (37.4 seconds) and Edward A. Thomas of Newburgh, N.Y., takes the five-mile in 18:29.4. The championships, originally scheduled for Cove Pond, near Stamford, Connecticut, on Jan. 22, are moved when the Cove Pond ice proves to be inferior.

1933

William S. Gummere, organizer of Princeton's team for the first intercollegiate football game in 1869, dies in Newark, N.J., at age 82. Gummere, later Chief Justice of New Jersey, was the Princeton captain in the game played against Rutgers (see Nov. 6).

1935

Jay Gould, II, grandson of the railroad magnate and financier, and a longtime world champion court tennis player (1914-22), dies in Margaretville, N.Y., at age 46.

1940

A major pro basketball merger takes place as the ABL champions two of the three prior seasons, the Jersey Reds (1938) and the New York Jewels (1940) combine into a single New York-based team.

1940

Mineola's Nassau County Fairgrounds is granted a Grand Circuit trotting week for July 22-28. A discussion of night racing at the Mineola half-mile, favored by Cornelius N. Bliss, is held but no action is taken. E. Roland Harriman, president of the Grand Circuit stewards, makes the announcement after a meeting at the Prince George Hotel on East 28th Street.

1944

Mark James Roth, former Yankees road secretary, dies at age 62 in Floral Park, N.Y. While a sportswriter for the New York *Globe*, he is credited with creating the name "Yankees."

1960

Alvin (Pete) Rozelle is elected commissioner of the NFL on the 23rd ballot of a week-long owners' meeting in Miami, Florida, finally breaking a deadlock between San Francisco lawyer Marshall Leahy and NFL treasurer Austin H. Gunsel. Leahy loses support by refusing to move the league office to New York, which Rozelle, general manager of the Los Angeles Rams, agrees to do. Rozelle serves until 1989, presiding over the greatest growth in NFL history and the merger with the rival AFL.

1980

Lynn Patrick, son of Lester, brother of Muzz, and father of Craig, dies in St. Louis, Missouri, at age 67. Patrick was a winger on the Rangers' 1940 Stanley Cup champions and coached New York to the Cup final in 1950.

1981

Constance Applebee, who introduced field hockey to U.S. in 1901 and coached the sport in this country for 50 years, dies in Hampshire, England, at age 107.

1897

Harley Davidson sets world pro speed skating records for the 100 yards (9.0 seconds) and the 300 yards (23.4 seconds) the next day, both aided by a pushing wind, at Red Bank, N.J.

1914

Will Henry Grimsley, later a famed sports columnist for The *Associated Press* for nearly three decades, is born in Monterey, Tennessee.

1921

Yankees transfer five players, including Frank (Lefty) O'Doul, to Pacific Coast League clubs. O'Doul, an undistinguished pitcher in three seasons for the Bombers, eventually converts to the outfield and wins National League batting titles for Philadelphia (1929) and Brooklyn (1932).

1940

In a college basketball doubleheader before 3,000 at the Cross-County Center in White Plains, N.Y., Yale beats Tulsa, 42-33, after Geneva tops Brooklyn College, 40-39.

1947

Middleweight contender Rocky Graziano admits he received a $100,000 offer to throw a fight with Ruben Shank.

LEE MACPHAIL

1972

Yankees general manager Lee MacPhail announces that an agreement has been reached for the Bombers to play two seasons in Shea Stadium (1974-75) while Yankee Stadium undergoes renovation.

1979

Rangers hand the Islanders their first home loss of the season after a 15-0-8 start, strafing the Isles, 7-2, at Nassau Coliseum. Ten days earlier, the Rangers ended Isles goalie Glenn Resch's 15-0-8 personal streak to start the season, 5-3, at the Garden.

1981

Bill Brendel, 58, colorful TV sports publicist for ABC and CBS, dies in New York.

1986

Roone Arledge, head of ABC Television Sports since 1968, gives up responsibilities for daily operations of the sports division, becoming group vice president of ABC News. He is succeeded by Dennis Swanson.

1987

Allison Danzig, the nation's premier authority on tennis and other racquet sports during his long career with *The New York Times*, dies at age 88 in Ridgewood, N.J.

1991

Football Giants win Super Bowl XXV at Tampa, Florida, with a 20-19 victory over the Buffalo Bills. Rallying from a 12-3 second-quarter deficit, New York takes the lead for good on Matt Bahr's 21-yard field goal in the fourth quarter. Buffalo kicker Scott Norwood barely misses a 47-yarder for the win as time expires.

1808

Messenger, whose progeny become the blood stock of U.S. harness racing, is buried with full military honors in Oyster Bay, L.I., on the grounds of what is now Piping Rock Golf Club.

1875

Guy V. Henry is born in Red Cloud, Nebraska Indian Territory. Henry became commander of United States Cavalry at Fort Riley, Kansas, the leader of U.S. Olympic equestrian teams and a major presence at the National Horse Show in the Garden.

1890

New York Supreme Court refuses to enjoin John M. Ward from playing for and managing the Players League Brooklyn club being formed by the Brotherhood of Professional Baseball Players.

1914

First indoor invitational games of the Millrose AA are held at the Garden.

1934

William DeKova White is born in Lakewood, Florida. After one season (1956) with the Giants and a successful career as a first baseman, mostly with St. Louis, Bill White joined the Yankees broadcasting crew in 1971 and in 1989 was elected National League president, becoming the first black to head a major professional sports league.

1950

In a hotly-disputed finish at the Garden, Don Gehrmann is awarded the win in the Wanamaker Mile at the Millrose Games over Fred Wilt in a near dead heat. Both are timed at 4:09.3.

1957

James Murray, 85, NYAC Fencing Master who in 50 years as Columbia fencing coach tutored numerous Olympic greats as well as Mayor John Purroy Mitchell, dies in New York.

1958

Dodgers catcher Roy Campanella suffers a broken neck in an accident caused when his car skids on a rain-slicked Dosoris Lane in Glen Cove, Long Island, at 3:34 a.m. Campanella is permanently paralyzed from the neck down.

1974

Muhammad Ali decisions Joe Frazier in a successful 12-round defense of his NABF American heavyweight title at the Garden. In his next fight, Ali knocks out George Foreman, Frazier's conqueror in 1973, in Kinshasa, Zaire, to regain the world championship.

BILL WHITE

1986

Denis Potvin's 271st career goal breaks Bobby Orr's record for most goals by a defenseman as the Islanders beat Toronto, 9-2, at Nassau Coliseum.

1991

Red Grange, the fabled "Galloping Ghost" of football, who played two seasons for the Football Yankees in 1926 and 1927, dies in Lake Wales, Florida, at age 87. Grange was an All-American at Illinois and played most of his pro career with the NFL Chicago Bears.

1914

William Peter Turnesa (a.k.a. "Willie the Wedge"), the leading amateur golfer in a family that also produced six professional golfers, is born in Elmsford, N.Y.

1918

William Joseph (Bill) Rigney, last field manager of the New York Giants, is born in Alameda, California. Rigney, who succeeded Leo Durocher, managed the Giants in 1956 and 1957 in the Polo Grounds before their move to San Francisco.

1928

Visiting Rangers rout the Americans, 7-0, at the Garden, to set "road" game margin of victory record matched many times but not broken until 1984 (11-2 at New Jersey, October 25).

1929

James R. Price, former sports editor of the New York *Press*, commits suicide in Boston. After the *Press* was merged into the morning *Sun* in 1916, Price took over the grounds of the old Newark Federal League ballpark in Harrison, N.J., and rented it out for various sports. Later, he was an Eastern representative of the American League (then based in Chicago) with an office in New York.

WILLIE TURNESA

1946

A Brooklyn Dodgers farm club, the Montreal Royals of the International League, signs pitcher John R. Wright of New Orleans. Wright is the Royals' second black player, Jackie Robinson having signed November 23, 1945.

1949

At the Millrose Games in the Garden, Bill Dwyer joins the list of 60-yard indoor sprinters with a 6.1-second time for the event. Don Gehrmann wins the Wanamaker Mile and Belgium's Gaston Reill the Toussaint Two-Mile.

1960

Continental League, continuing to make moves toward becoming a third baseball major league, admits Buffalo, N.Y., as its eighth club in an owners' meeting in New York.

1964

Nick Werkman sets a Seton Hall record with 52 points in the Pirates' 111-80 victory over Scranton at Walsh Auditorium in South Orange, N.J. Werkman, as a junior the previous season, had led the nation in scoring (29.5) by the narrowest margin ever over NYU's Barry Kramer (29.3) but fails to repeat despite increasing his point-per-game average to 33.2 in 1963-64.

1985

Bryan Trottier, in his 726th career game, scores his 1,000th point as the Islanders tie Minnesota, 4-4, at Nassau Coliseum.

1986

Terrance Bailey ties the Wagner record with 49 points in a triple-overtime 105-103 win over Brooklyn College at Sutter Gym (see Dec. 3). Bailey, the national Division I scoring leader, has 854 points in 29 games, averaging 29.4 points per game.

January 30

1907

Edmund Enoch (Ned) Price, a former American heavyweight champion who later became a New York attorney, dies en route from his Brooklyn home to a Manhattan hospital at age 65.

1923

Yankees acquire left-hander Herb Pennock, "The Squire of Kennott Square," from the still-cash-poor Boston Red Sox (see Jan. 3) for infielder Norm McMillan, outfielder Camp Skinner, and $50,000. Pennock would win 162 games in 11 years with the Bombers, including 19 in 1923 (plus two more in the World Series).

1943

David Allen (Davey) Johnson, who managed the Mets to the 1986 World Series title and the 1988 National League East Division title, and who made the last out of the 1969 World Series (against the Mets) as a member of the Baltimore Orioles, is born in Orlando, Florida.

1948

Former Yankees pitching star Herb Pennock, general manager of the Philadelphia Phillies, dies of a cerebral hemmorhage in New York at age 53.

1949

Rangers defeat Montreal Canadiens, 9-0, at the Garden, to equal the largest victory margin in team history (eventually surpassed—see Nov. 21).

1959

Graham-Paige Corp., a closed-end investment company derived from two old auto manufacturers, buys a 40% interest (and, thus, working control) of the publicly-held Madison Square Garden Corp. for nearly $4 million from James D. Norris. About a year later, Graham-Paige, headed by Adm. John J. Bergen, nearly doubles its stake in the Garden and merges itself into the Garden Corp., which is listed on the New York Stock Exchange.

1960

John Thomas of Boston University sets a world indoor high jump record at Wanamaker Millrose Games at the Garden for the second straight year, raising his mark to 7' $1\frac{1}{2}$".

1964

John Thomas breaks his own Millrose Games high jump record by clearing 7' $2\frac{1}{4}$".

1973

In the first NHL All-Star Game ever played in New York, the East beats the West, 5-4, at the Garden, on a goal by Vancouver's Bobby Schmautz at 13:59 of the third period. The crowd of 16,986 generates the largest receipts ever in 26 All-Star Games ($120,767).

1996

Boxing manager and promoter Dan Duva dies in New York at age 44.

1845

Robert Vavasour Ferguson, who earns the nickname "Death to Flying Things" for his fielding exploits in the error-prone early years of professional baseball, is born in Brooklyn. He led the Brooklyn Atlantics to their stunning upset of the Cincinnati Reds in 1870 (see June 14), and later both played for and managed several New York and Brooklyn clubs.

1919

Jack Roosevelt Robinson is born in Cairo, Georgia. Jackie Robinson became the first black man to play major league baseball in the 20th century when he joined Brooklyn in 1947.

1923

Five world indoor records are set in the Millrose AA Games at the Garden. Loren Murchison (Newark AC) breaks the oldest mark, knocking a fifth of a second off Lon Myers' 1882 60-yard dash record. Richmond Landon (NYAC) and LeRoy Brown (Dartmouth) in the high jump (6'5 $1/_4$"), Jimmy Connolly (Georgetown University) in the $2/_3$ mile, Joie Ray (Illinois Athletic Club) in the 1 $1/_2$ mile and the Valcour Girls Club in the quarter-mile relay also set new standards.

1945

A basketball scandal hits Brooklyn College as five players admit they accepted a $1,000 bribe to throw a game with Akron scheduled that night in Boston. A Kings County grand jury indicts Harvey Stemmer, Henry Rosen and a third man identified only as "a John Doe known as Danny" on charges of conspiracy and intent to defraud. The five (Robert Leder, Stanley Simon, Lawrence Pearlstein, Jerome Greene and Bernard Barrett) are unindicted coconspirators and are expelled by the school February 2. Stemmer and Rosen are convicted May 9. It is later discovered that Pearlstein is not even enrolled. He just went out for basketball and made the team.

1945

Lieutenant Al Blozis, a star with the Football Giants before entering the service, is killed by German machine gun fire during an assault on the Vosges Mountains in France at age 26.

1948

Gil Dodds sets a world indoor mile record at the Wanamaker Millrose Games at the Garden with a clocking of 4:05.3.

1959

With all other events finished at the Garden, 17-year-old Boston University freshman John Thomas keeps 15,000 fans at the Millrose AA Games in their seats. The fans are rewarded with the world's first indoor seven-foot high jump.

1988

Al Laney dies at 92 in Spring Valley, N.Y. One of America's leading writers on golf and tennis, Laney was with the *Herald Tribune* for 40 years, based in Paris from 1925-39 and New York from 1939-65. He was the first regular sportswriter to cover the Wimbledon championships and other major European tennis events for an American newspaper.

1992

Mel Hein, former All-Pro center for the Football Giants from 1931-45 whose number "7" was retired by the club in 1963, dies in San Clemente, California, at age 82.

MEL HEIN

February 1

1896

Yale and Johns Hopkins play the first intercollegiate hockey match, a 2-2 tie in Baltimore, Maryland. After a loss in its next game, Yale wins twice to finish its first season at 2-1-1.

1908

Famed Yale quarterback Albie Booth (1929-31) is born in New Haven, Connecticut.

1926

Joe Stecher retains his world heavyweight wrestling title by pinning "The Mad Russian" Ivan Poddubny in 1:38:47 before 10,000 at the 71st Regiment Armory, 34th Street and Park Avenue.

1947

Joe Fulks' 31 points lead the Philadelphia Warriors to a 71-63 victory over the Knicks at the 69th Regiment Armory. In the 29 regular-season BAA games played in New York during the league's first season, Fulks' output is the highest single-game scoring total by any player.

WEEB EWBANK

1954

Giants trade Bobby Thomson and catcher Sam Calderone to Milwaukee for lefties Johnny Antonelli and Don Liddle, catcher Ebba St. Claire and $50,000. Antonelli helps the Giants to the pennant with a 21-7 record and a league-leading six shutouts. In March, Thomson breaks his ankle sliding in spring training and is replaced by infielder Henry Aaron in the Braves outfield.

1973

Jets announce Charlie Winner will succeed father-in-law Weeb Ewbank as head coach following the 1973 season when Ewbank will retire as coach, although he will remain as general manager.

1977

Bob (Nasty) Nash, 84, an original Football Giant (1925) and the team's first captain, dies in Winsted, Connecticut. A tackle, Nash was the first player in NFL history known to have been traded, having been peddled by Akron to Buffalo in 1920 on the day of the game for $300 and 5% of the game's gate receipts.

1981

Frederick W. Leuhring dies at age 99 in Swarthmore, Pennsylvania. Leuhring, Princeton's first full-time basketball coach, led the Tigers from 1912-20, compiling a record of 100-43 (.699).

1984

Steve Burtt scores 40 points to lead Iona to a 93-73 victory over Holy Cross at the Mulcahy Center in New Rochelle, N.Y.

1989

C. Everett Bacon, Walter Camp's All-America quarterback while a senior at Wesleyan in 1912, dies in Southampton, N.Y., at age 98.

1997

Fordham and Football Giants star Ed Danowski dies in East Patchogue, N.Y., at age 85. A hero of the "Sneakers Game" (see Dec. 9), he coached Fordham for eight seasons before the Rams dropped "big-time" football in 1954.

1855

Jacob F. Schaefer, Sr., probably the greatest billiards player in America in the late 19th century, is born in Milwaukee, Wisconsin.

1876

National League of Professional Baseball Clubs is formed in a meeting by representatives of clubs from eight cities in the Broadway Central Hotel in New York. Morgan G. Bulkeley is elected first president but the Chicago contingent of Al Spalding and Bill Hulbert is the driving force. William Cammeyer's Mutuals club represents New York despite playing their games at Cammeyer's Union Grounds in the City of Brooklyn. Several Brooklyn clubs, including the celebrated Eckfords and Atlantics, decline to join the new league, which has been wrought out of the wreckage of the National Association, an oft-chaotic player-run organization. The league is controlled by club owners who bring stability to the sport and create a model for all professional leagues since.

1886

A cockfighting main that draws adherents of the blood sport from the entire area is held at Union Hill, N.J. Newark wins decisively over archrival Paterson, 9-2, in a seven-hour event. The highlight is the ninth fight, in which Newark's four-pound, two-ounce white pyle kills Paterson's gray after a 12-minute battle hailed by the *Herald* as "one of the greatest ever fought."

1927

Alan B. Helffrich, a former Penn State star running for the NYAC, wins the 600 at the Millrose Games at the Garden for the fifth straight year in 1:13.8, the slowest of his five wins.

1936

Former Syracuse University captain Lou Robbins scores two goals and has 11 assists to lead Westchester to a 22-19 win over Washington Heights in a Greater New York Indoor Lacrosse League game at the Cross-County Center in White Plains, N.Y.

1949

Charley Ewart, a former Yale quarterback and general manager of the Philadelphia Eagles, becomes coach of the NFL New York Bulldogs after Maurice (Clipper) Smith, who coached the team in Boston, resigns to accept the head coaching post at Lafayette (see Jan. 21).

1956

Charles West's 39 points set a Wagner record and lead the Seahawks to their second upset victory in three years over St. John's, a 92-90 win at the Redmen's DeGray Gym in Brooklyn.

1962

John Uelses is the first indoor 16′ pole vaulter in the Millrose Games at the Garden.

1967

American Basketball Association is formed with an announcement at the Hotel Carlyle. It lasts nine seasons as a challenger to the NBA. Ten franchises begin play that fall—New York (New Jersey), Indianapolis, Minneapolis-St. Paul, Pittsburgh, New Orleans, Dallas, Houston, Kansas City (shifted to Denver April 2), Oakland and Anaheim. (Louisville is added March 5.) Former pro great George Mikan is named commissioner. The ABA introduces the red, white, and blue ball and promotes the three-point shot, which now permeates all levels of basketball.

1991

Robert Tisch buys a 50% interest in the Football Giants from Mrs. Helen Mara Nugent (widow of Jack Mara, one of founder Tim Mara's two sons) and her two children, Tim Mara and Maura Mara Concannon. Tisch has an equal share with Wellington Mara, Jack Mara's brother.

February 3

1890

Leland S. (Larry) MacPhail, who brought night baseball to the major leagues as the general manager of Cincinnati, ran the Dodgers and later owned part of the Yankees, is born in Cass City, Michigan.

1909

John Heron sets a Yale single-game hockey record with eight goals in an 11-4 victory over Columbia at New Haven.

1938

Boxing champion Emile Griffith is born in St. Thomas, V.I. Griffith held the welterweight title three times from 1961-65 and the middleweight title twice, in 1966 and 1967.

1939

Melio Bettina KOs Tiger Jack Fox in the ninth round at the Garden to be recognized as light heavyweight champion by New York State, but loses the crown to Billy Conn in July.

LARRY MACPHAIL

1939

Charles C. (Cash and Carry) Pyle, famed sports promoter of the 1920s, dies in Los Angeles, California, at age 56. Pyle, who as Red Grange's agent used the Illinois All-American's name to start the first AFL in 1926 (including the New York Yankees, for whom Grange starred), created the professional tennis tour the same year when he signed flamboyant French champion Suzanne Lenglen (to play veteran Mary K. Browne) as well as men including Vinny Richards. He also invented odd events such as the New York-to-California "Bunion Derby."

1940

Francis Asbury Tarkenton is born in Richmond, Virginia. Fran Tarkenton quarterbacked the Football Giants for five seasons (1967-71) between stints with the Minnesota Vikings.

1959

A record NBA crowd of 18,496 attends a Garden doubleheader to watch the St. Louis Hawks defeat Boston, 104-97, and the Knicks edge the Syracuse Nationals, 115-114.

1961

Manhattan College relay team (Dan Corry, Kye Courtney, Larry St. Clair and Arthur Evans) sets a two-mile indoor record in the Millrose Games at the Garden (7:32.8).

1971

Rangers bow, 4-2, to Chicago at the Garden, their first home loss of the season, ending a club-record 24-game home unbeaten streak (matched in 1995-96). The Blueshirts end the year 30-2-7 at home.

1968

Homer H. Hazel, Rutgers football star and an All-America running back in 1924, dies at age 73 in Marshall, Michigan.

1977

Reverend Gil Dodds, onetime world record holder for the indoor mile, dies at age 58 in St. Charles, Illinois.

1912
Golf great John Byron Nelson, Jr., is born in Fort Worth, Texas.

1915
Hobey Baker's three goals pace the St. Nicholas Hockey Club to a 5-1 win over the Irish-American AC at the St. Nick's Rink.

1926
Millrose AA track and field meet makes its first appearance in Garden No. 3.

1937
Harry Wolverton, 63, Highlanders manager in 1912 (50-102), dies in Oakland, California.

1943
Frank Calder, president of the NHL since its founding in 1917, dies in Montreal, Quebec, at age 65. Calder took over the Americans when they ran into financial difficulties in 1936 and appointed Red Dutton to run the club. Dutton became Calder's successor as league president.

1959
Lawrence Taylor, the Football Giants linebacker considered by many the greatest ever at his position, is born in Williamsburg, Virginia.

1961
Knicks play the St. Louis Hawks during a heavy snowstorm and the game draws 1,300 fans, the smallest Garden crowd in team history. St. Louis wins, 128-111.

1963
Mayor Robert Wagner signs a bill formally naming the new municipal stadium in Flushing Meadow after New York attorney William A. Shea. Shea Stadium becomes the home of the New York Mets in 1964. Shea led the effort to get a new NL team in New York after the Giants and Dodgers had left following the 1957 season.

1989
In his return to the Montreal Forum after coming out of retirement with the Rangers, Guy Lafleur thrills the crowd with two goals and an assist as the Rangers build a 5-2 lead after two periods. The excitement continues as the Canadiens rally to win, 7-5.

1997
Jets announce the hiring of Bill Belichick as head coach for the 1997 season with his former boss, Bill Parcells, to serve as a "consultant" until free of his contractual obligations to the New England Patriots. The Jets had sought to clear Parcells to coach for them with an offer to the Pats of $1 million and a package of draft choices. But New England insisted on getting the Jets' first-round pick in 1997, the No. 1 overall choice in the upcoming draft. The Jets refused to part with that pick.

1998
Bob Mulcahy, president of the NJSEA since 1979, becomes athletic director at Rutgers, succeeding Fred Gruninger.

BILL SHEA

February 5

1894
Harold J. Parker, twice CCNY head football coach (1924-33 and 1947-48), is born in New York.

1915
Patrick Powers, former International League president, announces that he has secured the Kansas City franchise in the Federal League, the outlaw "third major league," and is moving it to Newark (see Feb. 25).

1915
In a contentious annual meeting at the Waldorf-Astoria, the USNLTA votes, 129-119, to award the national singles and interscholastic tennis championships to New York's West Side Tennis Club starting this year. Since 1881, singles had been held at the Casino in Newport, R.I. Former champion Henry Slocum leads the Newport faction while Karl N. Behr and WSTC president Julian Myrick lead the New York contingent. Behr's spirited speech is considered decisive.

1923
Welterweight Andy Thomas (whose real name is Anthony Perino) collapses before the 12th round of his bout with Jimmy Clinton at Brooklyn's Broadway Arena. He dies the next morning, becoming the second ring fatality in less than a year at the Arena (see Apr. 24).

1930
Karl Schafer of Vienna wins the world figure skating championship before 13,000 at the Garden. U.S. champ Roger Turner is second. Norway's Sonja Henie wins her fourth straight ladies singles crown with Miss Cecil Smith of Canada second and Boston's Maribel Y. Vinson third.

1938
Columbia's Ben Johnson sets a world record in the 60-yard dash final in 6.0 seconds at the Millrose Games at the Garden. AAU officials, believing no one could run that fast and the timing is incorrect, instead credit Johnson with his 6.1 time in his semifinal heat. Barney Ewell in 1942 (and seven others) tie Johnson's meet record before it is broken by Sam Perry in 1965.

1949
Tony Lavelli sets an EIBL record with 40 points as Yale routs Princeton, 74-48, at Payne Whitney Gymnasium in New Haven, Connecticut.

1955
Ernest A. Blood, coach of the fabled Passaic High School "Wonder Teams" that won 159 consecutive basketball games from 1919-25, dies in New Smyrna Beach, Florida, at age 82.

1967
Francis P. Meehan dies at age 70 in Newark, N.J. "Stretch" Meehan at 6'7" was probably the first good big man in basketball. After leaving Seton Hall in 1919 he turned pro and toured with several teams. He was a box office attraction because of his height, which was extraordinary for the time. He later became a lawyer in Newark.

1972
Nets play their final game at Island Garden in West Hempstead, L.I., home since 1969, losing to the Virginia Squires, 126-117. The Nets played their first 26 home games of that season there before moving to the partly-completed Nassau Coliseum (see Feb. 11).

1987
Mike Burke, president of the Yankees from 1966-73 and later head of Madison Square Garden, dies in Galway, Ireland, at age 70.

1888

James Alberts tries to set running endurance records but is unable to eclipse overall marks set six years earlier by Charles Rowell (see Feb. 27). He does set world records for four days on February 9 (450 miles, 220 yards) and five days February 10 (544 miles).

1895

George Herman (Babe) Ruth, probably the best and certainly the most famous player in baseball history, and likely the most famous athlete in sports history, is born in Baltimore, Maryland.

1915

Dauntless, the famous racing yacht built at Mystic, Connecticut in 1866, once owned by James Gordon Bennett, sinks at Essex, Conn., while being used as a houseboat by Colonel C.L.F. Robinson.

1925

Led by center Howie Bollerman, Hackensack High School ends Passaic's 159-game winning streak, 39-35, handing Passaic its first loss since March 15, 1919, when it was beaten by Union Hill in the New Jersey High School championship final at New Brunswick.

1925

Ground is broken for Madison Square Garden No. 3, a $5.5 million building designed by theater architect Thomas W. Lamb. The "new" Garden is finished in 249 days.

1935

Yale's 33-29 overtime victory at New Haven snaps 11-0 NYU's 27-game winning streak, longest in Violets history. NYU finishes the season 20-1.

1944

Will B. Johnstone, sports cartoonist for the *Evening Telegram* and *World-Telegram*, dies in West Palm Beach, Florida.

1950

Longtime Yankees coach Art Fletcher dies in Los Angeles at age 65.

1957

Despite 36 points by the Lions' Chet Forte, Yale defeats Columbia, 103-87, at University Hall en route to the Ivy League championship.

1991

Mouse Davis is named first head coach of the New York-New Jersey Knights of the World League of American Football. The Knights open the season only 45 days later and Davis steers them to a 5-5 mark.

1993

Arthur Ashe, tennis' first U.S. Open men's singles champion in 1968, dies in New York at age 49 after contracting AIDS in a blood transfusion.

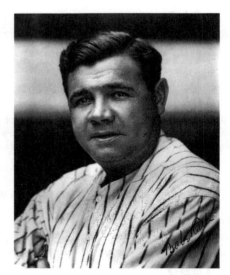

BABE RUTH

1996

Published reports state that after 14 years, World Team Tennis will not have a New Jersey team.

February 7

1921

In the last of the 20 fights between the two champions, Jack Britton decisions Kid Lewis in a 15-round welterweight title defense at the Garden. They first met March 26, 1915, with a 10-round bout at the 135th Street Sporting Club.

1923

Joie Ray of the Illinois Athletic Club sets a record for the Newark AC meet with a 4:17.4 clocking in the mile, his fastest of the indoor season.

1923

Fordham breaks a seven-game losing streak with a 37-26 win over Holy Cross at the Hunt's Point Palace.

1925

Paavo Nurmi sets a world indoor two-mile record (9:09) during the Wilco AC meet at Brooklyn's 13th Regiment Armory. The Flying Finn's 14th world indoor record, 0.4 seconds faster than Joie Ray's 1923 mark, is the night's highlight for the 7,000 who jam into the Armory.

CAL RAMSEY

1931

NYU beats St. John's, 27-23, to end at 24 the longest winning streak in St. John's basketball history.

1938

George Herbert Daley, sports editor of the *Herald Tribune*, dies at age 68 in New York. Daley's passing leads to Stanley Woodward's first hiring as sports editor.

1942

Cornelius Warmerdam, who 15 times had cleared the height outdoors, becomes the first man ever to clear 15 feet indoors in the pole vault at the Millrose AA Games at the Garden. Warmerdam, on earlier vaults, breaks Sueo Ohe's meet record of 14'3", set in 1937, and the world record of 14'7 $^1/_8$" set by Earle Meadows at the Garden in 1941.

1949

Joe DiMaggio signs his largest contract yet ($90,000 for one year) with the Yankees. He misses the first half of the season after surgery on bone spurs in his heel but returns to hit .346 with 14 homers and 67 RBI over the last 76 games to carry the Yankees to the pennant.

1959

Cal Ramsey's 40 points lead NYU to a 94-57 drubbing of Hunter at Alumni Gym.

1979

Warren Giles, National League president from 1951-69, dies in Cincinnati, Ohio, at age 82.

1996

Seton Hall coach George Blaney gets ejected for the first time in 20 years of coaching, star guard Danny Hurley suffers a mild concussion in the first half and Rutgers beats the Pirates, 70-61, at the Meadowlands before 7,423. It was the Scarlet Knights' first win over Seton Hall since 1983, ending a seven-game losing streak to the Pirates.

February 8

1896

In its first annual meeting at Delmonico's (see Dec. 22), the USGA awards the second U.S. Open and Amateur championships to the Shinnecock Golf Club Links in Southampton, N.Y., to be held July 18, and the women's championship to Morristown, N.J.

1905

Yale Athletic Association reports the largest profit in its history ($31,222) for the fiscal year ended September 10, 1904. Yale received $30,340 for its 1903 football game at Harvard, $28,743 for its home game with Princeton and $9,329 for its game with Columbia.

1928

Lloyd Hahn of the Boston AA wins his eighth straight indoor race and sets a track record (2:15.2) in the 1000 yards at Newark's 113th Regiment Armory in the Newark AC Games. Prudential AA's Catherine Donovan sets the record in the new women's half-mile (2:38).

1943

Harry Boykoff scores a Garden-record 45 points in leading St. John's to a 76-46 win over St. Joseph's (Pa.). After DePaul's George Mikan surpasses that with 53 in an NIT semifinal in 1945, Boykoff sets a new mark (54) in 1947 after his return from military service (see Mar. 11).

1955

Harry Gallatin, in his 500th straight game for the Knicks, receives a night in his honor at the Garden between games of an NBA doubleheader. The Knicks beat Minneapolis, 98-95, after Syracuse thumps Boston, 115-88.

1959

William J. (Wild Bill) Donovan dies at age 76 in Washington, D.C. A Columbia football quarterback in 1904 and '05, later a life trustee at the university and instrumental in persuading the school administration to accept the bid to the 1934 Rose Bowl, Donovan during World War II organized the Office of Strategic Services (OSS), which became the CIA after the war.

1968

In the final college basketball doubleheader at Garden No. 3, a pair of local rivals having off years collide with NYU defeating Manhattan, 76-73, after defending NIT champion Southern Illinois is beaten by Duke, 78-54.

1979

Islanders' Mike Bossy has a goal and an assist in the NHL All-Stars' 4-2 win over the Soviet Union at the Garden in the opener of the three-game "Challenge Cup Series." The Soviets rally for a 5-4 win in the second game and in the finale embarrass the NHL, 6-0.

1991

Sportswriter Herb Goren, 74, who became "The Old Scout" columnist at *The Sun* at age 19, and later served as publicist for the Rangers and ABC Sports, dies in Manhasset, N.Y.

1993

Slew Hester, 80, an independent oil producer who, as United States Tennis Association president, was the force behind the building of the National Tennis Center in Flushing Meadow, dies in Jackson, Mississippi.

1998

In the first NBA All-Star Game at the Garden in 30 years, the East beats the West, 135-114, before 18,323. Chicago's Michael Jordan leads all scorers with 23 for the winners and is voted game MVP. Jayson Williams, one of seven first-time All-Stars, represents the Nets, but no Knicks were selected for the East squad.

1859

John Joseph Killion is born in the Greenpoint section of the City of Brooklyn. As Jake Kilrain, he became bare-knuckles era world heavyweight champ and lost his crown to John L. Sullivan in the last heavyweight title bout fought under London Prize Ring Rules in 1889.

1897

St. Nicholas Hockey Club defeats the Cambridge Hockey Club of Boston, reportedly "the best squad in the East," 2-1, at the St. Nicholas Rink, 69 West 66th Street, Cambridge's first loss of the season.

1917

Fordham football running back Dominic Principe is born in Brockton, Massachusetts.

1940

Arturo Godoy of Chile loses a 15-round heavyweight title fight decision at the Garden to Joe Louis. In a June rematch, Louis KOs Godoy in the eighth round. In a span of 22 title defenses from 1938 to 1946, Godoy is the only opponent to survive 15 rounds against Louis.

FREDDIE SPENCER

1944

Judges' and referee's scorecards are announced for the first time as announcer George Kobb reveals the breakdowns on Tippy Larkin's unanimous Garden win over Lulu Constantino.

1944

Charles J. Harvey dies in Brooklyn at age 79 while walking to the subway to attend an evening of boxing at the Garden. "Handlebar Charlie" Harvey was a ring announcer at the second Madison Square Garden in the early days of the century, became the first secretary of the New York Boxing Board under the Frawley Law in 1911, and, in 1920, a manager of fighters. Among the fighters he managed were Tom Heeney and Steve Hamas, a pair of heavyweight contenders.

1945

Jimmy Herbert of the Grand Street Boys, a former NYU runner, wins the Millrose 600 for the fifth time, tying Alan Helffrich's record (1923-27) for most wins in the event. Herbert is clocked in 1:15, well off his best time of 1:12.4 in 1942. He also won in 1937, '38, '40, and '42.

1968

In the final track meet at the third Garden—the Madison Square Garden Invitation—Jim Ryun of Kansas wins in 3:57.5, "The Last Garden Mile." Garden president Ned Irish makes a special presentation to him as the last winning miler in the old building.

1983

Walt Michaels "retires" under pressure as Jets coach with a 39-47-1 record in six seasons.

1984

Leon Hess buys Helen Dillon's 25% interest in the Jets, making him the 100% owner.

1992

Freddie Spencer, who rode on four winning teams in six-day bike races at the Garden, dies in Rahway, N.J., at age 89. Spencer was a two-time U.S. sprint champion and set several world records at both the Newark and New York Velodromes.

1930

Holy Cross' Bernie McCafferty wins the 500 yards in 59.0 seconds at the Newark (N.J) Armory in the fourth annual Seton Hall Games, missing Joe Tierney's world record by one second.

1933

Primo Carnera knocks out Ernie Schaaf, 24, of Elizabeth, N.J., in the 13th round of their heavyweight bout at the Garden. Not everybody is convinced the fight is on the square. The *Evening Journal* runs a headline over Bill Farnsworth's article the next day that reads, "FAKE! FAKE! FAKE!" It is the first time in 98 fights that Schaaf has been knocked out, and on February 13, he dies.

1936

Eddie Babe Risko decisions Tony Fisher in 15 rounds at Laurel Gardens in Newark, N.J., to retain his American middleweight championship.

1951

Don Gehrmann wins the Baxter Mile at the NYAC Games at the Garden and takes permanent possession of the Baxter Cup. Gehrmann, a Wisconsin student, beats Fred Wilt, an FBI agent, by a yard in 4:08.2.

1956

Joe Lapchick resigns after almost nine years as Knicks coach (326-247, .569). Vince Boryla replaces him. Lapchick guided the Knicks to the NBA final three times (1951-53).

1962

Cassius Clay of Louisville, Kentucky (later Muhammad Ali), makes his Garden debut with a fourth-round knock-out of Sonny Banks.

1968

Knicks play their final game at the third Garden, defeating the Philadelphia 76ers, 115-97, before a capacity crowd of 18,499.

1976

Former North Carolina State head coach Lou Holtz signs a five-year contract to coach the Jets. In the event, Holtz lasts 13 games (3-10).

1989

Glenna Collett Vare, one of the most famous women amateur golfers from the 1920s to the 1940s, dies in Gulfstream, Florida, at age 86.

1997

After a meeting lasting almost six hours in the offices of the NFL's law firm, commissioner Paul Tagliabue announces that Bill Parcells will coach the Jets in 1997 and that New England will receive four Jets draft choices in return—Nos. 3 and 4 in 1997, No. 2 in 1998 and No. 1 in 1999. Jets owner Leon Hess also donates $300,000 to a Boston-area youth football organization as a gesture to Patriots owner Bob Kraft (see Feb. 4).

1998

Linda Miles has 18 points and 11 rebounds as Rutgers beats No. 2-ranked Connecticut, 74-70, in the women's basketball upset of the year. The defeat at Piscataway, N.J., ends the Lady Huskies' 53-game winning streak over Big East opponents that dates from Jan. 2, 1996.

1905

Yale wallops Princeton, 9-3, before a record overflow crowd of 3,000 in hockey at the St. Nicholas Rink. Karl Behr nets four goals for the Elis.

1942

St. Nicholas Hockey Club defeats Harvard, 6-4, at the Playland Casino in Rye, N.Y., as Fred Moseley, a former Cantab, scores three goals and assists on two others.

1945

Hype Igoe, 59, a sportswriter and cartoonist, dies in New York. He was with the *World, Journal* and *Journal-American* from 1927-45. His column was called "Pardon My Glove."

1948

Carl Braun scores 32 points in the Knicks' 86-63 win over Providence at the 69th Regiment Armory, the best up to then by any Knick player at home, surpassing Bud Palmer's 30 in a loss to Philadelphia on November 22, 1947, at the Armory.

CARL BRAUN

1950

Bob Zawoluk scores 38 points to lead St. John's to a 72-63 win over Niagara.

1962

Chuck McKinley tops Whitney Reed in a 63-game match (4-6, 6-3, 4-6, 9-7, 10-8) in the final of the U.S. National Indoor Tennis Championship at the 7th Regiment Armory.

1966

Kansas freshman Jim Ryun makes his first Garden appearance and wins the mile in 4:01.6 in the inaugural U.S. Track & Field Federation Invitational Meet. As a schoolboy, Ryun had run 3:55.3 outdoors, making him the first U.S. high school runner in history to run a sub-4:00.

1968

Final Rangers game is played at Garden No. 3, a 3-3 tie with Detroit, in the afternoon, and that night Bob Hope and Bing Crosby formally open Garden No. 4 with a USO benefit.

1972

Nets move to Nassau Coliseum and Rick Barry scores 45 points in a 129-121 win over the Condors. Pittsburgh's Mike Lewis scores the first basket and Billy Paultz gets the Nets' first hoop. A crowd of 7,892 fills all the available seats as the Nets not only christen their new home but also wear new uniforms designed by Mrs. Deon Boe, wife of club owner Roy L.M. Boe.

1981

Major Indoor Soccer League All-Star Game is held at the Garden, with the Western Division's five-goal fourth quarter producing an 8-5 win over the Eastern Division before 13,170. Adrian Brooks of the Denver Avalanche scores two goals during the rally and is picked the game's MVP. Steve Zungul of the New York Arrows scores twice for the East, which held a 4-3 lead after three.

1995

Jimmy Powers, sports editor of the *Daily News* and a television voice of boxing in the 1950s, dies at Bal Harbour, Florida, at age 92.

February 12

1908

Great Around-the-World auto race, sponsored by *The New York Times* and *Le Matin,* begins in New York at 11 a.m. Six cars take off for Paris via Alaska and Siberia with the first leg north to Albany, N.Y. On July 30, the German and American cars arrive in Paris with the U.S. team declared the winner because the Germans shipped their vehicle to Seattle by rail. A huge welcome is held in New York when George Schuster and his team return.

1909

Ch. Warren Remedy wins the Westminister Kennel Club best-in-show for the third straight year.

1913

Hannes Kolehmainen of Finland, running for the Irish-American AC, sets a world indoor record in the three-mile run (14:18.2) at Brooklyn's 13th Regiment Armory. That night, Kolehmainen wins the five-mile run in the NYAC Games at the Garden in 24:29.0.

1923

Willie Ritola deals Joie Ray his first loss of the indoor season by winning a 1 $^3/_4$-mile run in 7:59.8 in the 71st Regiment AA meet at the Regiment's Armory.

1942

NYU's Les MacMitchell wins the Metropolitan Intercollegiate Mile at the Bronx Coliseum in 4:08, sixth-fastest ever by collegian.

1949

New York Renaissance, one of the most legendary of black basketball teams, replaces the Detroit Vagabond Kings as a member of the NBL. Playing out of Dayton, Ohio, and coached by Pop Gates, the Rens pick up Detroit's standing and schedule. Founded in 1925 by Bobby Douglas, the Harlem-based Rens were one of the best and most popular of the touring teams for over two decades. Eventually, the team was sold to the Harlem Globetrotters of Chicago.

1959

Charles D. Daly, 78, the only man ever to play in a Harvard football win over Yale and Army football win over Navy, dies. An All-America quarterback at Army (1902), he coached eight seasons there (1913-16, 1919-22), with a 58-13-3 mark and three unbeaten teams (1914, 1916, 1922).

1962

Alastair B. Martin, later president of the USLTA (1969-71), wins the Tuxedo Gold Racquet court tennis championship with a 5-6, 6-4, 6-4, 6-5 win over defending champ James C. Bostwick at Tuxedo Park, N.Y.

1979

Forward Bob McAdoo is traded by the Knicks to Boston for three 1979 first-round draft choices and a player to be named. Tom Barker (on February 14) is that player and the draft choices turn out to be Bill Cartwright (No. 3), Larry Demic (No. 9) and Sly Williams (No. 21).

1995

Nat Holman dies in The Bronx at age 98. Considered one of basketball's greatest players while starring with the Original Celtics in the 1920s, Holman coached CCNY to the NCAA and NIT titles in 1950, the only time a team has won both tournaments in the same season.

1997

Delaney Kiphuth, longtime Yale athletic director and son of the famed Olympic swimming coach Bob Kiphuth, dies in Hamden, Connecticut, at age 78.

February 13

1896

Trotter Patchen Wilkes sells for $10,025 during the W.B. Fasig auction at the Garden to Mike Bowerman of Lexington, Kentucky. It is the highest price paid for a trotting horse in New York since 1893, when E.H. Harriman paid $41,000 for Stamboul (see Jan. 10).

1899

In the first round of the national amateur racquets championships at the Racquet & Tennis Club, snow halts the program. Quincy A. Shaw (who wins the tournament March 18) defeats W.B. Dinsmore, Jr., in the opening match, and J.S. Hoyt defeats T.E. Meredith, but the third match is postponed when snow begins falling through the skylights and the floor gets slippery.

1914

Baking magnate Robert B. Ward announces he has been granted the Federal League franchise first awarded to Toronto, Ontario, and that the team will play at a rebuilt Washington Park at 4th Avenue and Third Street in Brooklyn. The FL expands from six clubs to eight in a move to major-league status, with Cleveland shifting to Baltimore and Buffalo, N.Y., joining along with Brooklyn.

1948

Dick Button, 18, of Englewood, N.J., wins the world figure skating title at Davos Platz, Switzerland, completing a clean sweep of 1948's major honors. Button, the U.S. and North American champion, won the European championship at Prague, Czechoslovakia, on January 14 and the gold medal (191.77 points) in the Winter Olympics on February 5 in St. Moritz, Switzerland.

1957

Chet Forte scores 45 points, setting a Columbia school record that will last 34 years as the Lions rout Pennsylvania, 93-75, at University Hall (see Feb. 15).

1964

Tom O'Hara sets a world indoor mile record (3:56.6), winning the Baxter Mile in the NYAC Games at the Garden. (He will break his record less than a month later in Chicago.)

1968

To its oldest tenant, the Westminister Kennel Club, falls the honor of conducting the final event in the venerable third Madison Square Garden, which is ending a 43-year history that saw the birth of sporting institutions including the Rangers (1926), Knicks (1946) and the NIT (1938).

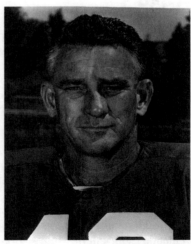

1990

Bryan Trottier tallies his 500th career goal but the Islanders bow to Calgary, 4-2, at Nassau Coliseum.

1996

Charley Conerly, 74, Football Giants quarterback (1948-62), dies in Memphis, Tennessee. He helped the Giants to the 1956 NFL championship and division titles in 1958, '59, '61 and '62.

CHARLEY CONERLY

1998

In the Wanamaker Mile at the Chase Millrose Games at the Garden, Kenya's Laban Rotich wins (3:55.69) but the story is Marcus O'Sullivan, whose 3:58.84 (for third) is his 100th sub-4:00 mile. He is the third miler (after John Walker and Steve Scott) to reach that milestone.

February 14

1896

Yale defeats Johns Hopkins, 2-1, on a return trip to Baltimore to gain its first intercollegiate hockey victory.

1903

Joseph W. Daniels sets six world swimming records in the Columbia University pool for distances of 225 yards (eight turns), 275 yards (10), 325 (12), 375 (14), 425 (16) and 475 yards (18), covering the final distance in 6 minutes, 39.8 seconds.

1907

At the Garden, Ch. Warren Remedy, a Fox Terrier (smooth), takes the first best-in-show ever awarded by Westminister Kennel Club.

1908

Ch. Warren Remedy does it again.

1920

On closing night for the four-day run of the Westminister Kennel Club, 624 dogs and their handlers at the Grand Central Palace finish the seventh and last WKC show held anywhere but the Garden. It is the fourth time the show has been held at the Lexington Ave. site (1912-14) (see Apr. 26).

1953

A Grand Street Boys quartet (Herb McKinley, Mal Whitfield, George Rhoden and Andy Stanfield) sets a world indoor record in the 1,060-yard sprint medley relay during the AAU Nationals at the Garden.

1967

Everett B. Morris, a founder of the NIT, longtime basketball and yachting writer for the *Herald Tribune* and a beachmaster at the D-Day landings in Normandy during World War II, dies at age 67 in Port Washington, N.Y.

1968

Knicks play their first game in the "new" Garden (No. 4) and beat the San Diego Rockets, 114-102. In the first game of an NBA doubleheader that night, Boston downs Detroit, 118-96, with the Pistons' Dave DeBusschere, shortly to be a Knicks hero, scoring the first basket ever in the new building. Walt Frazier gets the first Knicks points.

1969

New York Chapter, Knights of Columbus track meet observes its 50th anniversary and makes its first appearance at Garden No. 4. The meet originated at the 22d Regiment Armory, then a mecca for track meets, in 1920, and moved to the second Garden in 1925.

1975

Julius Erving scores 63 points, but the Conquistadors beat the Nets, 176-166, in San Diego, in four overtimes. The clubs set an ABA record for combined points in a game.

1979

George Young, former Baltimore Colts assistant coach, is named general manager of the Football Giants. His appointment, suggested by NFL commissioner Pete Rozelle, is designed to end the on-field consequences of friction between co-owners Wellington Mara and nephew Tim.

1899

Lon Myers, the world's dominant runner in the 1880s, dies in New York at age 40. Myers, who ran for the Manhattan AC in its heyday, was the first U.S. runner to defeat the British best on their soil and set world and U.S. records at virtually every distance from 100 yards to a mile.

1913

Abel Kiviat, captain of the Irish-American track team, sets a world indoor record for the mile on a 10-lap track of 4:18.2. It gives him four world indoor records (the 600 yards, 800 meters, 1000 yards and mile). In 1912, he broke the 1,500-meter record three times in 13 days.

1916

Hobey Baker scores three goals in leading the St. Nicholas Hockey Club to a 9-2 victory over the New York Hockey Club, getting the last on a rush nearly the full length of the St. Nick's rink.

1916

Yankees buy third baseman Frank (Home Run) Baker from the Philadelphia Athletics for $37,500. Baker, who refused to report to the A's in 1915, was a regular for four years, did not play in the majors in 1920, and rejoined the Yanks in 1921.

BUCK FREEMAN

1953

Robert Grant, III, of New York wins his 10th U.S. Amateur racquets championship by defeating David Milford of Great Britain at the Racquet & Tennis Club.

1959

John Patrick McEnroe, Jr., winner of four U.S. Open and three Wimbledon titles, and the world's best doubles player in his prime, is born in Wiesbaden, West Germany.

1961

Maribel Vinson Owen, age 49, dies in an air crash near Brussels, Belgium. The crash takes the lives of 18 members of the U.S. figure skating team, including five reigning champions (two of them Mrs. Owen's daughters) and causes the world championships, scheduled for Prague, Czechoslovakia, to be cancelled.

1963

Jim Beatty runs New York's first sub-4:00 mile, a 3:58.6 clocking to win the Baxter Mile in the NYAC Games at the Garden.

1964

Bill Bradley sets a Princeton single-game mark with 51 points in the Tigers' 87-56 win over Harvard at Dillon Gym.

1974

Buck Freeman, a former St. John's star and college basketball coach who helped elevate the school to major status, dies in West Columbia, South Carolina, at age 71.

1991

Sophomore Buck Jenkins scores a school-record 47 points in Columbia's 92-77 victory at Harvard, surpassing the 45 scored by Chet Forte in 1957 (see Feb. 13).

1858

Track great Lon Myers is born in Richmond, Virginia.

1915

Middleweight Al McCoy no-decisions an opponent fighting under the *nom de guerre* of "The New Al McCoy" in a 10-round bout at the Broadway Club in Brooklyn.

1924

Frank Benjamin Saul, Jr., is born in Oradell, N.J. Pep Saul was one of Seton Hall's basketball stars right after World War II, scoring 1,011 points during his career (1946-49).

1931

Richard Blair Modzelewski is born in West Natrona, Pennsylvania. Dick Modzelewski, better known as Little Mo, was a defensive tackle on the Football Giants from 1956-63.

1954

Philadelphia's Neil Johnston sets a Garden single-game pro record by scoring 50 points in the Warriors' 95-77 win over the Syracuse Nationals in the opener of an NBA doubleheader.

1959

Tim Mara, 71, one-time legal bookmaker and founder of the Football Giants, dies in New York.

1968

New York Athletic Club's 100th anniversary indoor track meet is held at the 4th Garden, the first track meet in the new building and the last for the NYAC, which decides to abandon the event because of demonstrations over accusations of racism, which the club vigorously denies. The end of the NYAC Games starts a chain reaction which causes the Knights of Columbus, the IC4A, and, eventually, the AAU to leave the Garden, with only the Millrose AA remaining.

1970

Joe Frazier KOs Jimmy Ellis in the fifth round at the Garden to unify the world heavyweight title.

1972

Edgar P. Feeley, Giants treasurer from 1944-57, dies in New York at age 79.

1972

Mac Kinsbrunner, member of the fabled St. John's "Wonder Five" of the 1930s, dies in Kiamesha Lake, N.Y., at age 62.

1986

Rangers Pierre Larouche and Mike Ridley are awarded penalty shots and both are stopped by Detroit goalie Corrado Micalef, but New York wins anyway, 3-1, at the Garden.

TIM MARA

1995

Joe Griffin sets an LIU record with 46 points but the Blackbirds lose at Marist, 128-98.

February 17

1902

Raymond W. Pond is born in Torrington, Connecticut. Ducky Pond coached Yale football during the era of Larry Kelley and Clint Frank, who won the Heisman Trophy in 1936 and 1937, respectively.

1923

Thomas Irving Brown's speedy ice yacht *Say When* wins both the Commodore's event and the point race in the first ice boating competition of the season on the North Shrewsbury River near Red Bank, N.J.

1931

Roger Lee Craig is born in Durham, North Carolina. Widely credited with popularizing the "split-finger" fastball as a pitching coach in the 1980s, righthander Roger Craig, a member of the 1955 world champion Brooklyn Dodgers, led the National League in losses in 1962 (24) and 1963 (22) pitching for the infant Mets.

1950

Charles (Mile-A-Minute) Murphy, a bicyclist who set a world speed record in 1899 that stood for over 40 years (see June 30), dies in New York at age 79.

1953

State Supreme Court Justice Bernard Botein overrules the New York State Athletic Commission, which awarded a victory to welterweight Billy Graham after a fight at the Garden December 19, 1952. Commission chairman Robert K. Christenberry ruled that "an error in judgment" by judge Joe Agnello had given the decision to middleweight Joey Giardello. Botein restores Giardello's victory.

1977

Thoroughbred racing trainer Nick Combest dies in an auto accident in Hewlett, N.Y., at age 52. After a brief career as a jockey, Combest started his successful training career in 1954.

1983

Georgia's Heisman Trophy winner, halfback Herschel Walker, signs a three-year, $3.9 million contract plus a $1.5 million signing bonus, with the New York-New Jersey Generals of the USFL. Walker, a junior, then announces he wants to stay at Georgia, but reverses himself again and reports to the Generals February 26, eight days before the team opens its first season in the spring-summer football league (see Mar. 6).

1983

Chancellor John Brademas announces that, 11 years after quitting the "big-time" version of the sport, NYU will resume varsity basketball starting with the 1983-84 season at the Division III level. Mike Muzio, who has been coaching a junior varsity team, will be the first coach and home games will be played at the Coles Center on Mercer Street.

1989

Vernon (Lefty) Gomez, star southpaw who was 189-101 from 1930-42 with the Yankees, dies in Larkspur, California, at age 78. A colorful character who played to his "screwball southpaw" image and was known by nicknames "Goofy" and "El Goofo," Gomez was a four-time 20-game winner, 6-0 in the World Series, started five All-Star Games and twice led the American League in ERA.

1997

Nets make a nine-man trade with the Dallas Mavericks, sending center Shawn Bradley, guards Robert Pack and Khalid Reeves and forward Ed O'Bannon to the Mavs for guards Chris Gatling, Jimmy Jackson and Sam Cassell, forward George McCloud and center Eric Montross.

1897

William Barnard of Brooklyn's Montauk Club beats Ferdinand Poggenburk (Liederkranz Club of Manhattan), 200-171, to win the inter-city billiards trophy at Maurice Daly's Academy.

1901

Paul Berlenbach is born in New York. "The Astoria Assassin" won the AAU light heavyweight amateur wrestling championship in 1920 and then turned to professional boxing, winning the light heavyweight crown in 1925.

1931

Bill Tilden makes his pro tennis debut, defeating Czech Karel Kozeluh, 6-4, 6-2, 6-4, before 13,800 at the Garden, who pay $36,000 to watch the seven-time U.S. national champion.

1951

Three CCNY basketball players (Ed Warner, Ed Roman and Alvin Roth) are arrested for point shaving. Also arrested at the start of a scandal that is of national scope are Edward Gard of LIU's 1949-50 team, charged with encouraging others to accept bribes; Harvey (Connie) Schaff, an NYU player charged with accepting money to sound out players about the scheme; and Salvatore T. Sollazzo, a 45-year-old jewelry maker, ex-convict and alleged mastermind. Roberto Sabatini, Sallazzo's bookmaker, is held as a material witness (see Jan. 17 and Feb. 19).

COLIN CAMPBELL

1951

America's best miler, Don Gehrmann of Wisconsin, misses the National AAU championships at the Garden, having been grounded by a snowstorm in Milwaukee. The New York Pioneer Club wins the team championship.

1953

Jack Molinas sets a Columbia record with 41 points as the Lions clout Princeton, 81-58, at University Hall.

1955

Richie Guerin scores 40 points but Iona loses to John Carroll, 77-70, at the Cross-County Center in White Plains, N.Y.

1967

A basketball game between Niagara and St. Francis at the 69th Regiment Armory is postponed after Niagara's Manny Leaks shatters a backboard with a slam dunk in warm-ups and no spare is available. St. Francis posts a surprising 81-72 win when the game is played the next afternoon (Sunday) at Brooklyn's Bishop Ford High School gymnasium.

1968

Rangers play their first game at Garden No. 4 and defeat the Philadelphia Flyers, 3-1.

1998

With the Rangers in fourth place in the Atlantic Division (17-24-16), general manager Neil Smith fires Colin Campbell, who was 118-108-43 in just over three seasons as head coach. The next day, Smith names former Edmonton and Buffalo coach John Muckler to succeed Campbell.

1897

Charles H. Kilpatrick, world amateur half-mile champion, leaves Princeton to become a professional, engaging in a series of races against E.C. Bredin, the English champion, in the British Isles.

1916

Eddie Arcaro, the only jockey ever to steer two horses to thoroughbred racing's Triple Crown (Whirlaway in 1941 and Citation in 1948), is born in Cincinnati, Ohio.

1929

Americans' six-game unbeaten streak (4-0-2) ends with a 1-0 loss to the Montreal Maroons at the Garden. The loss is the Americans' last until March 14 at Toronto as another six-game unbeaten streak (3-0-3) follows.

1937

Freddie Steele gains a 15-round decision over Eddie Babe Risko at the Garden in the first defense of his world (National Boxing Association) middleweight championship.

1951

Three LIU players (Adolph Bigos, LeRoy Smith, Sherman White) are arrested in the burgeoning college basketball point-shaving scandal. White is the nation's leading scorer and 1949-50 *The Sporting News* Player of the Year. Other schools involved to varying degrees are Manhattan, NYU, Bradley and Kentucky. Salvatore Sollazzo is indicted on Federal income tax evasion charges February 28 and on 13 counts of bribery March 8 (see Jan. 17 and Feb. 18).

1957

Richie Guerin scores 35 points against Boston, the most points ever scored by a Knick at the Garden up to that time, and the Knicks edge the Celtics, 112-110.

1957

Yankees trade for lefthander Bobby Shantz in a 10-player deal, sending pitchers Walter Coleman, Tom Morgan and Mickey McDermott, second baseman Milt Graff, shortstop Billy Hunter and outfielder Irv Noren to the Kansas City A's for Shantz, fellow pitchers Art Ditmar and Jack McMahan and first baseman Wayne Belardi.

1968

George Hackenschmidt, a celebrated professional wrestling champion at the turn of the century, dies at age 90 in London, England.

1976

Frank Sullivan, a well-known sportswriter for *The New York Times*, among other papers, dies at age 83 in Saratoga Springs, N.Y.

1977

At Nassau Coliseum, the Rangers right wing Rod Gilbert notches his 1,000th career point with a goal in his 1,027th career game, but the Islanders beat the Blueshirts, 5-2.

1983

Charles G. Bluhdorn, the Austrian-born founder and chief executive of Gulf + Western Industries, dies of cardiac arrest while on a private-flight jet from Santo Domingo, Dominican Republic, to New York. Bluhdorn, 56, is the owner, through G + W, of Madison Square Garden, and his death sets in motion the chain of events that will result in the Garden's sale (twice) over a decade later.

1902

St. Francis Xavier College of Manhattan scores two second-half goals to forge a 3-3 tie with City College in hockey at the St. Nicholas Rink.

1920

Joe Stecher defeats Jim Londos in a heavyweight wrestling match before 10,000 at the 71st Regiment Armory. The one-fall victory takes 2:13, not an uncommon time in that era when a single mistake could cost a wrestler the match and the sport was more athletic competition than showmanship. Stecher returns to the Armory later in the year and loses his championship to Ed (Strangler) Lewis (see Dec. 13).

1923

Charley White of Chicago is ordered to pay a $2,500 forfeit to Rocky Kansas for failing to make weight for their lightweight fight at the Garden February 9 when he weighs in at 135 $^3/_4$ pounds.

1939

A record crowd of over 6,000 packs St. Nicholas Arena to witness a lightweight bout between a pair of New Yorkers. Al (Bummy) Davis wins a split decision over Mickey Farber in the eight-round feature to run his record to 32-0.

1942

Philip Anthony Esposito is born in Sault Sainte Marie, Ontario. Phil Esposito, a record-high scoring center with Boston, was dealt from the Bruins to the Rangers on November 7, 1975, in the most celebrated trade in hockey history up to that time and stayed with the Rangers organization as a player (until 1981), broadcaster (1986) and general manager and occasional coach (1989), when he was dismissed after three years of constant trades and on-ice mediocrity.

1951

In the wake of the college point-shaving scandal that implicated several of its players, LIU drops basketball (despite a 20-4 record) and all other intercollegiate sports. Basketball will not be revived at LIU until 1957 when "Operation Rebound" begins.

1960

St. John's makes its 26th and final appearance at the 69th Regiment Armory, defeating St. Francis, 86-61. The Redmen first played in the Lexington Avenue drillshed January 19, 1921 (winning over Cathedral, 28-17), and used the Armory for a few home games in the 1940s and 1950s.

1982

John Tonelli scores with 47 seconds left in the game off former Islanders goalie Chico Resch (playing his first game at Nassau Coliseum since his trade) to give the Isles a 3-2 victory over the Colorado Rockies and an NHL-record 15th straight win.

1988

Jim Woods, television and radio broadcaster for both the Yankees (1953-55) and Giants (1956-57), dies in Oviedo, Florida, at age 71. While with the Yankees, Woods worked with both Mel Allen and Red Barber and when he moved to the Giants teamed with Russ Hodges.

JOHN TONELLI

1892

Marshall Cassidy, inventor of the modern thoroughbred racing starting gate, is born in Washington, D.C.

1917

Ollie Kinney scores 38 points, a Yale record that will stand for 29 years, in the Elis' 75-20 rout of the Springfield YMCA.

1942

John Borican, running for the Asbury Park (N.J.) AA, wins the Matt Halpin Half Mile at the NYAC Games in the Garden in 1:51.4 and equals the American indoor record for distance set by Lloyd Hahn of the Boston AA in 1928.

1948

Harrison Dillard of Baldwin-Wallace matches the world record in the 60-yard high hurdles (7.2 seconds) and Billy Mathis of Illinois ties it in the 60-yard dash (6.1 seconds) in the National AAU championships at the Garden. The NYAC wins the team title and Brooklyn's Boys High wins the interscholastic championship.

1960

Philadelphia's Wilt Chamberlain scores 58 points, a pro record for the Garden, in the Warriors' 129-122 victory over the Knicks. Chamberlain's performance erases the mark set six years earlier by Neil Johnston (see Feb. 16).

1972

Tom Seaver signs a long-term contract with the Mets for $172,500, making him baseball's highest-paid pitcher. But the contract leads to a rupture between the Mets and Seaver when the club will not renegotiate after the advent of free agency, leading to Seaver's trade in 1977 (see June 15).

1980

Frank Cashen is named Mets general manager. Cashen remains GM until 1991 and helps build a perennial contender that wins the 1986 World Series.

1981

Don Maloney scores three times, two shorthanded, in 2:30 of the second period at the Garden, a club record for individual fastest three goals in a game, and the Rangers beat Washington, 6-4.

1987

Kansas defeats St. John's, 62-60, to end the Redmen's 14-game winning streak on the Madison Square Garden court that began December 1, 1985, with a win over Louisville.

1987

Eric Riggins ties Bob Lloyd's 22-year-old Rutgers record of 51 points in a game in the Scarlet Knights' overtime 102-99 loss to Penn State at the Rutgers Athletic Center. Oddly, Lloyd is on hand, for a ceremony retiring his uniform number.

FRANK CASHEN

February 22

1938

Young Corbett III (Ralph Giordano) decisions Freddie Apostoli in a non-title bout in San Francisco, setting the stage for a Nov. 18 rematch, when, at the Garden, Apostoli knocks out the former welterweight champ (for 96 days in 1933) in the eighth round of a middleweight title bout.

1949

George Mikan hits for 48 points, most ever scored against the Knicks on their own court up to that time, leading the Minneapolis Lakers to a 101-74 rout of New York at the Garden.

1950

Carl Braun sets a 69th Regiment Armory pro scoring record of 38 points in the Knicks' 89-81 victory over the Washington Capitals.

1950

Julius Erving, who led the New York Nets to two ABA titles in his three seasons with the team (1973-76), is born in Roosevelt, N.Y.

1950

LaVern Roach, a middleweight making a comeback after a loss to Marcel Cerdan, is knocked out at 1:57 of the 10th round by George Small at St. Nick's Arena on his 24th birthday. He dies the next day at St. Luke's Hospital of a cerebral hemorrhage.

1960

Manhattan captain Bob Mealy scores a school-record 51 points in the Jaspers' 109-67 pasting of CCNY at the Beavers' Wingate Gym.

1964

Facing a second straight year of missing the playoffs, the Rangers trade captain and all-time leading scorer Andy Bathgate and center Don McKenney to Toronto for wingers Bill Collins, Bob Nevin and Dick Duff, and defensemen Arnie Brown and Red Seiling. While these players help the Rangers long-term, the Maple Leafs receive immediate dividends as Bathgate scores the Stanley Cup-winning goal in the seventh game of the final against Detroit.

1975

Women's college basketball comes to the Garden as Immaculata defeats Queens College, 65-61, with Mary Schraff getting 12 points and nine rebounds. In the second game, Fairfield's men defeat Massachusetts, 78-67, but most of the crowd of 11,969 leaves by halftime.

1992

Matt Cusack dies in Yonkers, N.Y., at age 82. Cusack was the ring announcer for the Golden Gloves tournament from 1941-90 and announced track meets at the Garden.

1997

In a very suspicious coincidence, a "fan" named Daniel Artest has his name drawn for a halftime shot worth two airline tickets during the Seton Hall-West Virginia basketball game at the Meadowlands. Artest happens to be the younger brother of Ron Artest, a 6'7" high school All-America basketball star being recruited by Seton Hall. Fortunately for all concerned, he misses not only his original shot but a second try at a closer distance. Seton Hall officials insist the drawing was "random" and Artest's seat just happened to be picked from among the 7,771 fans on hand. On April 9, Ron Artest commits to St. John's. West Virginia wins the game.

1883

William V. (Big Bill) Dwyer, owner of the NFL Dodgers and the NHL Americans, is born in Manhattan. "The King of the Bootleggers," Dwyer in 1925 bought the NHL Hamilton Tigers for $75,000 and moved the club to New York. After his release from federal prison in 1928 for violations of the Volstead Act (which was passed after the 18th Amendment to the Constitution, enacting Prohibition, became law), he became an NHL Governor.

1912

R. Kenneth Fairman, a Princeton basketball player and coach who succeeded Asa Bushnell as the school's athletic director in 1938 when Bushnell took over as commissioner of what later became the ECAC, is born in Spring Valley, N.Y.

1923

Gene Tunney regains the American light heavyweight championship from Harry Greb with a 15-round decision at the Garden. Badly beaten by Greb the previous May for what proves to be his only professional loss, Tunney revitalizes his career with this win.

1933

Olympic track star and later Yale coach Lee Calhoun is born in Laurel, Mississippi.

1934

Casey Stengel is hired as Dodgers manager, replacing Max Carey.

1935

Glenn Cunningham sets the 1500-meter record (3:50.5) in National AAU championships at the Garden and the NYAC wins the team title with 36 points.

1945

Mal Graham, an NYU basketball player who set virtually all of the school's scoring records when the Violets still played a major-college schedule, is born in White Plains, N.Y.

1960

Demolition of Ebbets Field begins (see Oct. 30).

1963

NYU defeats St. Francis of Brooklyn, 72-62, in the Violets' last appearance at the 69th Regiment Armory, which serves as the Terriers' home court.

1963

Jim Beatty wins the mile in 3:59.0 at the AAU Nationals at the Garden, his second mile under four minutes in eight days and just the second ever in New York (see Feb. 15).

1983

Mark Pavelich's five goals tie a Rangers record in an 11-3 Garden win over Hartford.

1989

Knicks acquire forward Kiki Vandeweghe, whose father played for the club from 1949-56, in a deal that sends their first-round draft choice that spring to the Portland Trail Blazers.

1996

Ernie Grunfeld is named president and general manager of the Knicks.

1896

National League finds John Montgomery Ward a free agent since he was not tendered a contract by New York for 1895 and was kept improperly on its reserve list. As it happens, the point is moot since Ward, a New York attorney, continues to work in his law practice in 1896.

1923

Former great heavyweight Joe Jeannette is licensed as a boxing referee and judge, the first black licensed by the New York State Boxing Commission.

1923

Princeton's Ralph Hills sets a world indoor record (48'9") in the 16-pound shot put at the NYAC Games at the 2d Regiment Armory. Columbia's Walter Koppisch wins the Buermeyer 500-yard run in 59.6 seconds.

1940

Allan Tomlich of Detroit, reigning king of the hurdlers, sets a world indoor record in the 70-yard high hurdles at the AAU Nationals at the Garden, hitting the tape in 8.4 seconds to beat L.G. O'Connor and Joe Batiste. Tomlich, like hundreds of other athletes of the late 1930s, is denied a chance at Olympic glory by World War II, which cancels the 1940 and 1944 Games.

1951

William F. Carey, Garden president from 1929-33, dies in Indio, California, at age 72. Carey, a skilled engineer, helped build the Panama Canal and later constructed the mammoth Madison Square Garden Bowl in Long Island City, the site of many famous boxing events in the 1930s.

1951

Manhattan wins the team title at the IC4A Championships in the Garden but the big news is the special Zamperini Mile. Again, Don Gehrmann and Fred Wilt finish in a virtual dead heat at 4:08.6. Again, Gehrmann gets the win, on a 3-1 vote of the finish judges (see Jan. 28).

1968

Wall Street broker Peter Elser is awarded a New York NASL franchise. A partner in the Generals (with R.K.O. General) in the 1967 National Professional Soccer League season, Elser brings in 10 partners for 1968 on March 30, but the Generals fold after the season, leaving New York without an NASL team until 1971, when the Cosmos begin play.

1968

Right wing Rod Gilbert pours an NHL-record 16 shots on Montreal's goal and scores four times as the Rangers strafe the Canadiens, 6-1, at the Montreal Forum.

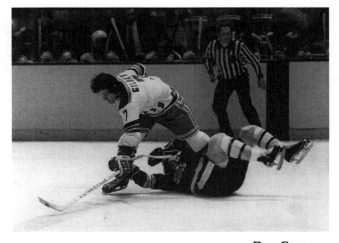

ROD GILBERT

1978

Nets' Kevin Porter sets an NBA record with 29 assists in a 126-112 victory over the Houston Rockets before 3,873 fans at the Rutgers Athletic Center in Piscataway, N.J., erasing the record shared by Bob Cousy and Guy Rodgers. Super John Williamson is a major beneficiary, scoring 39 points. Porter leads the NBA that year with 801 assists, a Nets club record.

February 25

1915

Pat Powers announces he will build a ballpark for the Federal League Newark club in Harrison, N.J., right across the Passaic River from downtown Newark. But the next day, Kansas City officials get an injunction to prevent their team from being moved. FL president Jim Gilmore hastily arranges for Powers to acquire league champion Indianapolis, which shifts to Newark instead (see Feb. 5).

1928

Sabin W. Carr in the pole vault (14'1") and Lancelot Ross in the 300 yards (32 seconds) give Yale two winners in the indoor AAU Nationals at the Garden. NYU's Phil Edwards wins the 600 in 1:14.2 but every other event (except the 60-yard dash) is won by senior club athletes, with the Illinois AC taking three firsts and winning the team title.

1934

John McGraw, 60, dies in New Rochelle, N.Y. He managed the Giants from 1902-32 and won 2,840 of 4,879 games (.589), 10 National League pennants and three World Series (1905, '21, '22).

1940

Rangers beat the Canadiens, 6-2, at the Garden, in the first televised NHL game, which is shown by NBC experimentally to a few hundred sets in the New York area.

1952

Johnny Lattner, the Notre Dame halfback who would win the 1953 Heisman Trophy, scores the winning basket, his only points of the game, with nine seconds left in overtime for a 75-74 win over No. 6-ranked NYU at the Garden. Lattner plays less than a half-minute in the game.

1954

Despite the recommendation of a special trial committee of the City Board of Higher Education that CCNY coach Nat Holman (suspended November 18, 1952) be absolved in the 1951 basketball dumping scandal, the board fires him. State Education Commissioner Lewis Wilson on August 27 orders him reinstated with 21 months back pay. He eventually returns as head coach.

1966

James B. Norris, 59, dies in Chicago. Norris at one time owned a controlling interest in Madison Square Garden, Chicago Stadium (in partnership with Arthur Wirtz), and Detroit's Olympia, and held a note against Boston Bruins owner Weston Adams, causing sportswriters to dub the NHL the "Norris House League." Norris was also president of the International Boxing Club, successor to Mike Jacobs' 20th Century Sporting Club as the dominant force in major championship fights. Forced to divest his New York holdings and break up the IBC as the result of antitrust rulings by the U.S. Supreme Court, he sold the Garden to the Graham-Paige Corporation in 1960.

1983

Carl Lewis becomes the second man in the history of the national championships to win the 60-yard dash (6.04) and long jump (27'4 $^3/_4$"), in a meet at the USA/Mobil Indoor Track & Field Championships at the Garden. Stephanie Hightower sets a world indoor record in the 60-yard hurdles (7.36), beating Kim Turner and Candy Young. Young and Hightower shared the indoor record (7.37) after a dead heat in the previous year's Millrose Games.

1998

The long-awaited sale of the Islanders by John Pickett to Steven Gluckstern and Howard Milstein is completed for $195 million, after Spectacor Management Group (SMG), operator of Nassau Coliseum, under threat of litigation, drops its demand that the seller sign a letter vouching for SMG's good performance in operating the arena.

1897

Pennsylvania beats Columbia, 5-0, at the St. Nicholas Rink in New York's first intercollegiate hockey game.

1923

R. Earl Fink defeats Jay Gould, 15-10, 15-10, to win the national squash title at the courts of Brooklyn's Crescent AC.

1926

Middleweight Tiger Flowers dethrones Harry Greb with a 15-round Garden decision.

1935

After 15 seasons, seven pennants, four world titles and 659 homers, baseball's most famous team and its most famous player part ways as the Yankees release Babe Ruth.

BABE RUTH (L.) WITH BOSTON BRAVES MANAGER BILL McKECHNIE

1937

Bernard William St. Jean Thompson, sports editor of *The New York Times* since December 1915, dies at age 63 in New York and is succeeded by 39-year-old Raymond J. Kelly.

1938

Glenn Cunningham sets a world indoor 1500-meter record (3:48.4) in the AAU Nationals at the Garden. Allan Tomlich of Detroit's Wayne University sets a world indoor record in the 65-meter high hurdles in his semifinal heat (8.5) but Forrest Towns wins the final in 8.7 seconds. NYU's Jimmy Herbert wins the 600 meters (1:21) while Ben Johnson in the 60 meters (6.6), Frank Ryan in the 16-pound shot (52'8 $^1/_4$"), and Dick Ganslen in the pole vault (13'6") win firsts for Columbia. The NYAC wins the team title with 23 points while Columbia (18) is second, and the New York Curb Exchange AA and NYU (17) tie for third.

1949

Tony Lavelli breaks his own record with 52 points as host Yale routs Williams, 100-64.

1949

Robert Grant, III, wins the U.S. amateur racquets championship for the seventh time since 1937 with a victory at the Racquet & Tennis Club on Park Avenue.

1951

NYU routs Notre Dame, 87-72, at the Garden, its largest margin of victory in the first 22 annual meetings of the showcase series. The Violets win, 102-78, in 1966, when the series renews after a brief break, but it ends for good in 1971 with the Irish ahead, 23-9 (see Dec. 29).

1966

Famed sports cartoonist Burris Jenkins, Jr., whose work appeared primarily in the New York *Journal-American*, dies in Hollywood, Florida, at age 69. Jenkins' father, a fiery Midwest Protestant minister, was portrayed by Burt Lancaster in the film *Elmer Gantry*.

1969

Danny Lynch's 21-year career as head coach at St. Francis ends as the Terriers are beaten, 91-82, by Fairleigh Dickinson in Rutherford, N.J. Lynch finishes with a 282-237 career record.

1882

Charles Rowell, England's most famous go-as-you-please pedestrian, wins a 142-hour, $9,000 pro walking race at the Garden and sets records along the way with 150 miles, 392 yards in one day, 258 miles, 220 yards for two days, and 353 miles, 220 yards for three days.

1902

Swimming great Ethelda Bliebtrey is born in, aptly, Waterford, N.Y.

1902

Golf great Eugene Sarazen is born in Harrison, N.Y. Sarazen won the U.S. Open in 1922 and 1932, as well as three PGAs and the 1935 Masters. In his 1932 Open win at the Fresh Meadows Country Club in Flushing, he shot a final-round 66, a record until 1960.

1912

Yankees (Highlanders) announce they'll wear pinstriped uniforms.

1951

Floyd Lane of CCNY admits to taking $3,000 in bribes in the widening point-shaving basketball scandal. His arrest is the 11th in the investigation so far. CCNY cancels its final two games of the season. The day before, Nathan Miller, a former LIU player, was arrested for throwing two games in December 1948.

1958

Sunnyside Gardens in Queens, closed for over 15 months, reopens when Manny Heicklen promotes a card featuring a six-rounder (Al (Rocky) Milone taking a unanimous verdict over Gene Hamilton) with tickets priced at $1.00 and $2.00.

1964

Tom O'Hara of Chicago's Loyola University runs his second sub-four-minute mile in the Garden with a 3:58.5 clocking in the Frank A. Brennan Columbian Mile at the New York Chapter, Knights of Columbus Games.

1977

Rutgers plays its final game after 46 years at "the Barn," as it is affectionately known, closing out with an 87-81 victory over Villanova as James Bailey scores 25 points. The 2800-seat Rutgers Gym on College Ave. in New Brunswick, N.J., which opened in 1931, is replaced by the Rutgers Athletic Center in nearby Piscataway. Rutgers won 314 of the 480 games played in the College Avenue gym.

1983

Ireland's Eamonn Coghlan leads the field as three of the five fastest indoor miles ever run are turned in at the Vitalis/U.S. Olympic Invitational at the Meadowlands Arena. Coghlan is clocked in 3:49.78 (the fastest indoor mile ever up to then), countryman Ray Flynn in 3:51.20 and Steve Scott of the U.S. in 3:52.28.

1994

Former heavyweight champion Jersey Joe Walcott dies at age 80 in Camden, N.J.

1998

Braheen Cotton scores 22 points as Hunter wins its 24th straight, a 76-55 thumping of York to capture the final of the CUNY conference tournament in Queens. The win also gives the Hawks a berth in the NCAA Division III tournament. On the same day, Suzette Henry overcomes a sprained ankle to score 23 points as Hunter's women's team beats the College of Staten Island, 63-52, in their championship game, snapping CSI's 29-game winning streak.

February 28

1903

Harvard beats defending champion Yale, 5-1, at the St. Nick's Rink to win the intercollegiate hockey title. The Elis play without injured captain Charley Hitchcock.

1923

Willie Ritola beats Joie Ray by a yard in a special three-mile run in the 22d Regiment Armory at the first New York Chapter, Knights of Columbus Games. Ritola sets a world record of 14:17.6, breaking the record set outdoors by Alfred Shrubb of England in 1903.

1940

NBC's W2XBS shows a Garden doubleheader as college basketball is televised for the first time. Pittsburgh tops Fordham, 57-37, before NYU beats Georgetown, 50-27.

1943

J. Gregory Rice of the NYAC sets a world indoor record for the three-mile run, being timed in 13:45.7 at the AAU Nationals at the Garden.

1947

Gus Lesnevich knocks out Billy Fox in the 10th round at the Garden to defend the light heavyweight championship he has held since 1941. Owing to World War II, the defense is only the third since Lesnevich gained world recognition with a 15-round win over Tami Mauriello.

1953

In a spectacular night at the Knights of Columbus Games at the Garden, Mal Whitfield sets world indoor records for 600 yards (1:09.5) and 500 meters (1:04.4) and also wins the 880-yard run.

1962

City College ends its season with a 96-83 victory over Bridgeport to finish 9-9 as Tor Nilson scores a school-record 48 points, surpassing the mark of 38 set by Mervyn Schorr in 1954.

1964

Gus Lesnevich, former light heavyweight champion and longtime fight referee in New York and New Jersey, dies in Cliffside Park, N.J., at age 49.

1970

St. Peter's and Manhattan leave defense in the locker rooms at the Cardinal Spellman High School Gym in The Bronx, with the Peacocks winning, 137-112, an average for both teams of over 6.2 points per minute. Almost lost in the shower of statistics are Tom Schwester's 53 points, a St. Peter's record. The game is one of three Jaspers home games played that season at Spellman.

1983

With the final episode of the long-running television show M*A*S*H, due to air tonight, Manhattan decides to postpone its first-round MAAC playoff game to the next night. The Jaspers' opponent was willing to play as scheduled—Army.

1987

In the first round of the MAAC tournament at the Meadowlands, Kevin Houston's 53 points, a Cadets single-game standard (eclipsing Mark Binstein's 51 in 1955), lift Army to a 98-94 overtime win over Fordham. Army is eliminated in the next round by Fairfield.

1892

Thomas Conneff, a popular running champion of the Manhattan Athletic Club, decides not to turn professional and announces he will represent the club in the English and Irish athletic championships this summer.

1916

A police detective stops a boxing exhibition at Grupp's AC between Young Atkinson and an actress named Hildreth Whitehouse in the second round. Owner Billy Grupp protests that the boxing board had given its approval since both are members of the club, but the detective says, "If they did approve it, they shouldn't have."

1924

Helen Wainwright wins the AAU senior diving championship in the pool at the People's Palace in Jersey City, N.J. Miss Wainwright wins the 10-foot springboard title with 129.34 points to WSANY teammate Aileen Riggins' 129.10, the closest finish in the event up to that time (.24 points).

1936

Columbia routs Cornell, 59-26, at University Hall, for its eighth straight EIBL win and assures itself of no worse than a tie for the league championship as sophomore Cliff Wolff scores 17 points and Bill Nash adds 16. The Lions finish 12-0 in league play and Nash leads the league in scoring (11.5 points per game).

1936

Gustav Kilian and Heinz Vopel of Germany win the 60th six-day bike race at the Garden. It is the pair's sixth straight victory in U.S. events since October. Kilian and Vopel have a one-lap edge after 2,572 miles in the 144-hour grind over Belgians Alfred Verhaege and Omar DeBruycker.

BRIAN LEETCH

1960

Onetime leading welterwight contender Isaac Logart KOs Peter Schmitt in the first round at St. Nicholas Arena. Although he never won the title, Logart fought five successive welterweight champions: Virgil Akins, Don Jordan, Luis Rodriguez, Emile Griffith and Nino Benvenuti.

1988

Nets name Willis Reed as head coach. Reed is 33-77 before becoming vice president and general manager in August 1989.

1988

Defenseman Brian Leetch, fresh from his tour of duty on the U.S. Olympic team, makes his NHL debut and gets an assist as the Rangers beat St. Louis, 5-2, at the Garden.

1996

Neil O'Donnell, who quarterbacked the Pittsburgh Steelers to the Super Bowl a month earlier, signs a five-year, $25 million contract with the Jets, a deal that includes a $7 million signing bonus.

1880

Behind the performances of George Frazier, skip on rink No. 1, and William Kellock, skip on rink No. 2, Yonkers defeats Empire City, 54-42, in a curling match at the Madison Avenue Skating Rink.

1904

Harry Fisher scores 11 points to lead Columbia to a 23-12 win over Pennsylvania at Philadelphia's 1st Regiment Armory to clinch the EIBL championship. Marcus Hurley has four points for the Lions. Later that year, Hurley would win the Olympic gold medal at St. Louis and the world amateur championship as a cyclist.

1907

Yale rallies from an 11-7 halftime deficit to defeat Pennsylvania, 20-17, at New Haven and clinches a tie for the EIBL title. When Penn beats Columbia, 20-16, a week later, the Elis win the crown outright with a 9-1 league record under first-year coach William Lush, first professional coach of Yale basketball.

1948

NYU, ranked No. 1 and the nation's only unbeaten team at 19-0, is upset by Notre Dame, 64-59, in their annual meeting at the Garden. The Violets' Dolph Schayes is held to nine points and Kevin O'Shea scores 18 for the Irish in a wild game that has 17 lead changes.

1949

Allen Stack of Yale sets four U.S. backstroke records at New Haven, clocking 5:02.8 in the 100 meters, 5:05 in the 400 yards, 5:49.9 in the 500 yards and 6:25.1 in the 500 meters.

1953

Seton Hall's 27-game winning streak is stopped as the nation's No. 1 team is upset at Dayton, 71-65. The Flyers (14-13 on the season) are led by Jim Paxson, Sr., with 23 points, while the Pirates' Walter Dukes is held to 19.

1959

Albie Booth, Yale's famed "Little Boy Blue," dies in New York at age 51. Booth was the Elis quarterback from 1929-31 and later became a leading Eastern college football official.

1969

Mickey Mantle announces his retirement in Fort Lauderdale, Florida, ending his 18-year career with the Yankees. "I can't hit anymore," Mantle tells sportswriters at spring training. Mantle hit just .237 the year before with 18 homers in 144 games, but his career total of 536 is third all-time. A three-time MVP, Mantle was the most powerful switch-hitter ever.

1983

Army eliminates Manhattan, 74-69, in a MAAC playoff game at Draddy Gym postponed from the night before (see Feb. 28).

1991

In a major shakeup of sports management at Madison Square Garden, Al Bianchi is fired as Knicks general manager, Dave Checketts is named president of the NBA team, and John C. (Jack) Diller is appointed president of the Rangers.

1996

Sportswriter Patrick J. McDonough dies at age 89 in Hoboken, N.J.. Pat McDonough joined the New York *Evening Telegram* July 1, 1925, and his fascination with sports statistics soon earned his the nickname "Figur' Filbert." He later served as official statistician for the Brooklyn Football Dodgers and the New York Titans and Jets, and edited the *National Bowling Weekly* after his newspaper folded in 1967.

March 2

1889

With over 800 competitors at the Garden and before an overflow crowd, the N4A stages its last indoor track championships, the largest event of its type yet held. Manhattan AC's A.F. Copeland sets a world record in the 250-yard hurdles (32.2). U.S. champion Tom Conneff (Manhattan AC) defeats British champion A.B. George (Spartan Harriers) by 20 yards in the three-mile.

1904

Indoor polo is introduced for the first time at the Durland Riding Academy on West 66th Street. In the three periods of 10 minutes each, the team captained by H.A. Brachley defeats the team captained by J.C. Wilmerding, five goals to four.

1929

America's best freestyle women swimmer yet, Martha Norelius, completes her *tour de force* in the AAU Nationals at Chicago's Lake Shore AC. Norelius wins the 500-yard freestyle in a world indoor record 6:26 and anchors a winning relay. Earlier, she had won the 100 and the 220 (also with a world indoor record time 2:34.8). Her WSANY easily wins the team championship (see June 12 and July 5).

1935

With a rare bench technical helping the momentum, Pennsylvania (9-2 in the league) beats Columbia (8-2), 34-22, before an overflow 10,275 at the Palestra to temporarily move past the Lions into first place in the EIBL. Penn scores the game's first five points and official Dave Tobey's unusual call helps the Quakers pad their lead early in the second half. Veteran observers could not recall a similar foul called in the EIBL (see Mar. 13).

1949

At the Pioneer Club Games run at the 369th Regiment Armory, the NYAC's Henry Laskau sets a world indoor mile walk record (6:22.7), lowering the mark he had set February 12 at the NYAC Games (6:24.6). NYU's Jim Gilhooley wins the Borican Memorial 600 in 1:11.7, the fastest flat-floor time ever.

1962

Yale wins the Ivy League basketball championship with an 81-66 win over Dartmouth at Payne Whitney Gym in New Haven, Connecticut.

1968

Frank Erickson, "King of the Bookmakers," dies in New York at age 72. Erickson was a primary figure in the Kefauver investigations of big-city corruption in the 1950s.

1974

Princeton thrashes Columbia, 70-43, in the final game of the 74-year history of University Hall as the Lions' home court. Columbia opens its new Levien Gymnasium in December.

LEON HESS

1981

Leon Hess acquires Townsend Martin's 25% interest in the Jets, increasing his stake to 75%. The only other co-owner, Mrs. Helen Dillon, retains 25%.

March 3

1891

Leonard W. Jerome, 82, dies in Brighton, England. The socially prominent Wall Street financier was once part-owner of the *The New York Times*, and one of the most famous names in thoroughbred racing during the post-Civil War era. He led the syndicate that founded Jerome Park in The Bronx (1866) and Brooklyn's Sheepshead Bay Course (1880). Jerome went to England for his final days to be near his three daughters, all married to Englishmen. One, Jenny, was Lord Randolph Churchill's wife, making Jerome Winston Churchill's maternal grandfather.

1914

St. Nicholas outscores the Wanderers, 9-7, at the St. Nick's Rink to clinch a tie for the Amateur Hockey League championships. (St. Nick's would win the title on March 11 with a 4-3 win over the Hockey Club of New York.)

1942

Rangers and Americans tie, 4-4, in their final meeting. The Rangers finish with a 56-24-14 all-time edge over the co-occupants of the Garden, who drop out of the league (they thought temporarily, for the duration of World War II) after a season-ending 8-3 loss at Boston March 17.

1947

Bowling great Johnny Petraglia, one of the top money-winners in the history of the PBA Tour and two-time president of the PBA, is born in Brooklyn.

1951

St. John's' Bob Zawoluk scores a school-record 65 points as the Redmen overwhelm St. Peter's, 105-61, at DeGray Gymnasium in Brooklyn. It's the first time in its 43-season history that a St. John's team has scored over 100 points in a game.

1951

Fred Wilt finally defeats Don Gehrmann and ends Gehrmann's 39-race winning streak, taking the Columbian Mile in the Knights of Columbus Games at the Garden in 4:08.4 for the first win over his archrival, to whom he had lost several disputed decisions (see Jan. 28).

1964

Rider beats NYU, 66-63, at the Violets' Alumni Gym on University Heights, halting their 23-year, 57-game home court winning streak (see Jan. 10). It is only the fifth loss in 123 games in Alumni Gym since its 1932 opening (see Dec. 17). Happy Hairston and Barry Kramer score 19 each for NYU but it isn't enough to stop the Broncs from winning in The Bronx.

1965

Sophomore George Barbezat, averaging only 7.4 ppg, scores 26 as LIU wins the Tri-State League title with a 78-69 playoff win over Wagner at Hofstra in Herb Sutter's last game as Seahawks coach after 27 years (352-251). LIU qualifies for the NCAA college division tournament, its first postseason berth since basketball was restored in 1957.

1992

Allan Roth dies at age 74 in Los Angeles, California. Roth, a Montreal, Quebec, native, became statistician for the Brooklyn Dodgers in 1950 and is credited with revolutionizing the use of baseball statistics.

1997

Demolition begins on Palmer Stadium, home of Princeton football and other events since 1914. The Tigers, 283-161-17 at Palmer, will play their football games on the road this season before opening a new $45 million stadium on the same site against Cornell September 19, 1998.

1893

Arthur C. Vance is born in Des Moines, Iowa. Dazzy Vance, briefly a Yankee, led the NL in strikeouts seven straight seasons (1922-28) with the Dodgers, and won a league-leading 28 and 22 games for Brooklyn in 1924-25.

1904

The Wanderers, a new club formed by the former NYAC and St. Nicholas players, win the Amateur Hockey League title with a 3-1 victory over the Crescent AC at the St. Nicholas Rink.

1918

Margaret Evelyn Osborne is born in Joseph, Oregon. Perhaps the best-ever women's doubles player, Margaret Osborne (later duPont) captured 10 straight U.S. national doubles titles (1941-50), the last nine with Louise Brough. She also won three U.S. national singles titles (1948-50).

1925

John Montgomery Ward dies at age 65 in Augusta, Georgia. Ward, who hurled the second perfect game in major league history, later played shortstop for the Giants before helping to organize the Players League in 1890. He then managed the Giants before retiring to become a prominent New York attorney.

1950

An Italian team of Severino Rigoni and Fernando Terruzzi wins in a revival of the International Six-Day Bike Race (last staged at the Garden in 1939) (see Mar. 5). Rigoni and Terruzzi log 2,081.8 miles at the 22d Regiment Armory.

1960

J. Watson Webb, a polo star for the team that brought the Westchester Cup back to the U.S. from England in 1909, dies at age 75 in New York.

1968

Pro boxing comes to the fourth Garden in a big way as a pair of title fights top the card. Nino Benvenuti recaptures the world middleweight title from Emile Griffith and Joe Frazier stops Buster Mathis for the New York version of the heavyweight crown vacated by Muhammad Ali. The crowd of 18,096 pays an indoor record of $658,503 to help cover the $505,000 in purses guaranteed to the headliners. The first fight, and thus the first in the new Garden, is a middle-weight scrap in which Dennis Heffernan knocks out Tony Smith in the third round.

JOE FRAZIER (L. WITH MURRAY GOODMAN)

1978

Knicks get only one offensive rebound but beat Boston anyway, 99-91, at the Garden.

1991

John Cunniff is fired as Devils coach and is replaced by Tom McVie, who begins his second stint in New Jersey.

1991

Joe Dey dies at age 83. Known as "Mr. Golf," Dey was USGA executive director from 1934-68 and headed the Tournament Players Division of the PGA from 1969-74.

1904

E.A. Taylor sets an indoor mile record in speed ice skating (2:49.6) at the Clermont Avenue Rink in Brooklyn. Phil Kearney is second at 2:50.4

1913

Robert Joseph Kelleher, president of the USLTA in 1968 at the dawn of the open era of tennis, is born in New York.

1921

Walter Higgins of Columbia wins the Baxter Mile in the NYAC Games at the 22d Regiment Armory. Higgins is timed in 4:21 while beating J.J. Connelly of Georgetown by inches at the finish with Sid Leslie (unattached) third.

1929

Casey Tibbs, colorful world champion rodeo star, is born in Fort Pierre, South Dakota.

1938

Columbia wins the IC4A indoor track and field championship at the Garden with 27 points. Ben Johnson and Herb Weast finish 1-2 in the 60-yard dash and Dick Ganslen finishes second in the pole vault for the Lions.

CASEY TIBBS

1949

In a revival of the six-day bike races that were a staple of the Garden's prewar sports menu, a Swiss team wins the grind at the 22d Regiment Armory. Hugo Koblet and Walter Diggelman log 2,384 miles even, with Italy's Alvaro Georgetti and Greece's Henri Surbati finishing second on points. A crowd of 11,000 is on hand for the finale.

1954

Paddy DeMarco wins the lightweight championship by decisioning James Carter in 15 rounds at the Garden, but only 5,730 pay, the second-smallest Garden crowd for a title fight since the building opened in 1925.

1965

Willis Reed scores 46 points, the second most ever in a single game by a Knicks rookie, but the Los Angeles Lakers win, 105-103, at the Garden.

1968

Jim McMillian scores 37 points as Columbia wins its first Ivy League basketball title since 1951 with a 92-74 pounding of Princeton in a league playoff game at St. John's Alumni Hall. Both teams had 12-2 league records in the regular season. Columbia would lose in the Eastern Regional final of the NCAA tournament, ending its season with a 23-5 record, ranked sixth in the nation.

1983

Butch Graves' 39 points lead Yale to a 103-98 victory over Harvard at Payne Whitney Gym. A junior, Graves will have five more 30-point or more games as a senior and finishes his four-year career as Yale's top career scorer (2,090 points).

1885
Famed sportswriter Ring W. Lardner is born in Niles, Michigan.

1904
Andy Aitkenhead, who as a rookie goalie led the Rangers to the 1933 Stanley Cup, is born in Glasgow, Scotland.

1917
LIU All-America basketball player Irving Torgoff is born in Brooklyn.

1935
Miler Ron Delany is born in Arlow County, Wicklow, Ireland. Delany won all 17 of his mile races at the Garden, including the Millrose Games' Wanamaker Mile four times (1956-59).

1938
Brooklyn sends outfielder Eddie Morgan and $45,000 to Philadelphia for first baseman Dolph Camilli. Morgan never plays for the Phils but Camilli has 100 or more RBI four times in his first five years in Brooklyn and leads the National League in homers (34) for the 1941 pennant-winners.

1973
Jimmy McDermott coaches his last game for Iona, a 77-66 loss at Siena. McDermott finishes his 26-year career as the Gaels' basketball coach with a 319-253 record.

1976
"Slapsie" Maxie Rosenbloom, middleweight contender before embarking on an acting career, dies in South Pasadena, California, at age 71.

1984
Eleanor Twitchell Gehrig, widow of Lou, dies in New York at age 79.

1984
In a game neither team appears to want, the Devils beat the Penguins, 6-5, at Pittsburgh. By winning, New Jersey gives itself the upper hand in the race to avoid finishing with the NHL's worst record. Though they close 1-11-1, the Devils wind up ahead of Pittsburgh which, by finishing last, drafts first, and selects Mario Lemieux. New Jersey gets Kirk Muller.

JULIA JONES PUGLIESE

1993
Julia Jones Pugliese, a fencer at NYU and longtime fencing coach at Hunter College, dies in New York at age 84.

1997
Rutgers fires basketball coach Bob Wenzel after the team's fifth straight losing season. Wenzel posts a 128-135 record in nine seasons as the Scarlet Knights' head coach. Rider's Kevin Bannon takes the job April 3 after the school interviews several candidates (at least two, Drexel's Bill Herrion and Texas' Tom Penders, turn it down).

1997
Ed Furgol, winner of the U.S. Open golf title in 1954 at the Baltusrol Golf Club in Springfield, N.J., dies at age 77 in Miami Shores, Florida.

1885

First six-day roller-skating race at the Garden is won by Willie Donovan of Elmira, N.Y., who logs 1,090 miles in the 142 hours for a $500 first prize and a medal, but two competitors die within slightly more than a month. Joseph Cohen of Brooklyn, who did not finish in the money, dies March 16 and Donovan dies in April (see Apr. 10).

1938

Steve McKeever dies at age 84 at his home, 31 Maple Street, Brooklyn. More than 1,500 friends, baseball executives, and fans attend his funeral three days later. McKeever, one of two brothers who owned the construction company that built Ebbets Field, was Dodgers president from 1933-37. When the ballpark cost more than owner Charles Ebbets could pay, he satisfied the debt in stock. This fragmentation in 1913 continued the dispersal of stock that was not substantially consolidated until Walter O'Malley bought out Branch Rickey's interest in 1950.

1953

Cornell wins the final event, the mile relay, beating Columbia by eight yards and ties the Lions for first in the sixth annual Indoor Heptagonal Track and Field Championships at Ithaca, N.Y. Each team finishes with 33 points.

1959

Rudy LaRusso's last-second shot lifts Dartmouth to a 69-68 win over Princeton in a playoff for the Ivy League title at Yale's Payne Whitney Gym. The loss ends the season for the Tigers' "Iron Man" quintet of Carl Belz, Herman Belz, Jim Brangan, Joe Burns and Art Klein, who started every game as a unit and scored all but 26 of Princeton's 982 league points.

RAY ARCEL

1977

Charles Bluhdorn's New York-based conglomerate Gulf + Western, owner of 39% of the Garden, announces a tender for all 2.9 million remaining shares at $10 each. Madison Square Garden, listed on the New York Stock Exchange since 1925, goes off the Big Board after this tender offer. Rumors of the tender prompted shares to jump $5, to $9.75, the Friday before this Monday announcement.

1994

Ray Arcel, 94, one of boxing's most famous trainers and cornermen, dies in New York.

1995

Jack Rohan retires as Columbia basketball coach after 18 seasons in two hitches (1961-74, 1990-95). He had three 20-win seasons (all in a row) and led the 1968 Ivy League champions (23-5) but was 217-248 overall.

1997

I.T.T. announces the sale of 38.5% of its ownership interest in Madison Square Garden to its partner, Cablevision Systems, for a reported $500 million. Cablevision, which now owns 88.5%, has the right to buy the remainder for $150 million over the next 24 months. On March 31, NBC acquires a 25% stake in the Garden valued at about $325 million by converting some of the cable television holdings it shares with Cablevision.

1860

Teams from New York and Boston start a two-match telegraphic chess competition played out before live audiences in each city. In New York, the team assembles at the University Building and sends its moves to the telegraph office on Wall Street. The match drags on until March 16, when each team concedes one of the two matches, halving the competition at 1-1.

1894

Thoroughbred racing executive James McGowan, 70, dies at his home, 21 Prospect Place, Brooklyn. "Uncle Jim" McGowan was one of the creators of the auction pool system of betting.

1910

Lou Bender, an All-America basketball player at Columbia and the EIBL's leading scorer in 1930-31, is born in New York.

1921

Commissioner Kennesaw Mountain Landis summons Giants outfielder Benny Kauff from spring training in San Antonio, Texas. On April 7, he places Kauff on the disqualified list due to alleged complicity in the sale of stolen cars, prompting Kauff to sue Landis and the Giants (see Jan. 17).

PETE DAWKINS

1938

Pete Dawkins, Army's Heisman Trophy winner in 1958, is born in Royal Oak, Michigan.

1959

One of the more prestigious U.S. curling events winds up as an intramural affair for the Winchester (Massachusetts) Country Club. Winchester's No. 1 team defeats its No. 3 team, 11-7, to win the St. Andrew's mixed bonspiel at Hastings-on-Hudson, N.Y.

1960

NYU defeats Connecticut, 78-59, in the finale of an opening-round tripleheader in the NCAA tournament at the Garden. The Violets earn a trip to the "Final Four" by winning twice at the Eastern Regional at Charlotte, N.C., the next weekend (see Mar. 18).

1967

Dr. Edward S. Elliott, Columbia's first full-time Director of Athletics in 1931, dies in London, England, at age 89.

1971

"The Fight of the Century" at the Garden. For the first time, undefeated heavyweight champions meet. Joe Frazier (26-0) scores a unanimous 15-round decision over Muhammad Ali (31-0) to become the undisputed champ. The Garden's 17th heavyweight title bout, the fifth since Garden No. 4 opened, draws 20,455 fans and a $1,352,951 gross, both world indoor records.

1986

Willie Glass scores 19 points and Walter Berry adds 16 as St. John's wins the Big East tournament at the Garden, squeezing past Syracuse, 70-69.

1996

Knicks fire Don Nelson (34-25) as head coach. Jeff Van Gundy succeeds him.

March 9

1897

AAU meeting at the Astor House Hotel creates the first national amateur basketball committee. Dr. Luther H. Gulick is named chairman with C.C. Hughes and J.W. Kelly, Jr., as members. The committee arranges a national championship tournament before year's end.

1921

Bill Roper is rehired as Princeton's football coach. Roper was 10-2-2 in his first two seasons and remains until 1930, compiling a 53-23-10 record for 12 seasons, a tenure not exceeded by any Tigers coach 75 years later.

1928

Rodman Wanamaker dies at age 65 in Atlantic City, N.J. Wanamaker was scion of the department store family and one of the prime supporters of the store's Millrose AA who helped build its indoor meet into one of the world's premier track and field events.

1935

France's Alf Letourner and Italy's Franco Georgetti, the "Red Devil" team, take the 58th six-day bike race at the Garden by three laps with 2,359 miles and nine laps. It is Letourner's 16th career win in the U.S., counting wins in Boston and Chicago.

1938

NYU rallies from a huge 20-14 halftime deficit to beat LIU, 39-37, in the second game of the opening night of the first NIT. The Violets trail by five with four minutes left but score eight of the game's last nine points with Dan Dowd scoring four and sophomore guard Bobby Lewis three in the late run.

1940

Americans surprise the league-leading Bruins, 4-2, at Boston in a nasty game in which Boston's Dit Clapper had his nose broken and Amerks' coach Red Dutton is ejected for constantly hectoring referee Bill Stewart.

1948

Rangers' Billy Taylor is suspended for life for gambling on NHL games. League president Clarence Campbell, in Lansing, Michigan, imposes the penalty after hearing testimony by John Tamer, a rearrested Michigan parolee, that Taylor had bet $500 on the Chicago Blackhawks in their game against the Boston Bruins Feb. 18.

1955

Bud Haabestad scores 28 points to lead Princeton to an 86-69 win over Columbia in the final playoff to break a three-way tie for the Ivy League title. Columbia had eliminated Penn, 73-71, two nights earlier, also at the Rutgers Gym in New Brunswick, N.J.

1965

Frank Graham, longtime sports columnist with *The Sun* and *Journal-American*, dies in New York at age 70.

1985

Bill Martin's 18 points lead Georgetown to a 92-80 win over St. John's in the Big East final at the Garden despite Chris Mullin's 25 for the Redmen (see Mar. 30).

1996

Pete Carril's 29-season tenure as Princeton's head coach begins its final chapter as the Tigers beat Penn, 63-56, in overtime, at Lehigh's Stabler Arena in Bethlehem, Pennsylvania, in an Ivy League title playoff. The Tigers dominate in overtime to give Carril his 12th league title. After the game, Carril tells his players he is retiring when the NCAA tournament ends. In the postseason, Princeton upsets the defending NCAA champs, UCLA, 43-41, in the first round before losing in the next round.

March 10

1858

Baseball's first national organization, the National Association of Base Ball Players, is formed in a meeting at 298 Bowery, headquarters of the Gothams Base Ball Club. Dissatisfied with organizational efforts of the Knickerbockers, 22 clubs call the convention to form a governing body. William H. Van Cott of the Gothams is elected president, L.B. Jones (Excelsiors) first vice president, Thomas S. Dakin (Putnams) second vice president, J. Ross Postley (Metropolitans) recording secretary, Theodore P. Jackson (Putnams) corresponding secretary and E.H. Brown (Metropolitans) treasurer. A year later, another convention is called by the four oldest clubs (Knickerbockers, Gothams, Empires and Eagles) and is attended by 50 clubs.

1897

In what is believed to be the first basketball game ever played by a New York city college, Pratt Institute loses to the champion Adelphi Club, 30-3, at the Pratt gymnasium.

1905

Harry Fisher scores an astonishing 26 points (on 13 field goals) to lead Columbia to a 56-16 rout of Penn at University Hall as the Lions finish 19-1. Fisher's total is a Columbia single-game record until Bill Hasslinger scores 28 at Navy in 1941.

1906

Harold L. Markson is born in Kingston, N.Y. Harry Markson was a sportswriter for the *Bronx Home News*, a press agent for fight promoter Mike Jacobs and president of Madison Square Garden boxing from 1960-75.

1938

Led by Madeleine Dalton, the Salle D'Armes Vince wins the women's national foil championship at the Fencers Club, defeating Salle Santelli-Greco, 5-2. Miss Dalton is 3-0 in the finals and Maria Cerra 2-0. Geisha Fernandez is 0-2 in the final round.

1941

John Borican, running for the Shore AC, sets a meet record in the 1,000-yard run (2:16.2) at the New Jersey State AAU Indoor Championships at the Elizabeth (N.J.) Armory, but Seton Hall takes the team title. The Pirates earn 32 $\frac{1}{3}$ points.

1946

Sonny Hertzberg scores 12 points as the Gothams edge the Paterson Crescents, 49-47, at St. Nick's Arena in the final game of the ABL season. On March 17, the Baltimore Bullets, the eventual league champion, beat the Gothams, 70-59, in the semifinal playoffs (see Mar. 31).

1948

In the final game of the season, Buddy Hatchett sets a Rutgers record with 40 points in the Chanticleers' home 94-53 victory over Delaware.

1953

NYU Chancellor Henry T. Heald announces the school is dropping football, canceling the eight games scheduled for that fall and ending 80 years of Violets football.

1997

Larry Keating, Seton Hall athletic director for 12 years, resigns in the morning, apparently after refusing to fire head basketball coach George Blaney. In the afternoon, Blaney is dismissed by school president Msgr. Robert Sheeran after a 10-18 season and a 38-48 record for his three years (see Mar. 19 and Apr. 16).

1887

Meeting at the Hoffman House, the USNLTA endorses an American tennis ball for official usage for the first time. Wright & Ditson's ball replaces the Ayre English ball that had heretofore been official. Delegates also approve shifting the national doubles final to the Orange Lawn Tennis Club in Mountain Station, N.J., from Newport, Rhode Island.

1914

Harold Rosenthal, *Herald Tribune* sportswriter (1931-66), is born in New York.

1915

Hobey Baker's hat trick leads St. Nick's to a 5-2 victory over the Boston AA at the St. Nicholas Rink to clinch the Amateur Hockey League championship for the second straight year.

1921

Edwin Binney of Yale cuts one-fifth of a second off the league record for the 50-yard freestyle (24.2) as the Elis defeat CCNY, 48-3, in an Intercollegiate Swimming League match at New Haven, Connecticut. Yale also wins the water polo match, 20-11.

SUNNY JIM FITZSIMMONS

1927

Vince Boryla, a Knicks forward who averaged 11.2 ppg over five seasons (1959-54) and who later coached them (80-85, .485) for parts of three (1956-58), is born in East Chicago, Illinois.

1947

Harry Boykoff of St. John's sets a Garden single-game individual scoring record for basketball with 54 points in the Redmen's 71-52 victory over St. Francis of Brooklyn.

1948

James M. McMillian, Haggerty Award winner as the best college basketball player in the metropolitan area three straight years (1967-70) while leading Columbia, and who later played two seasons (1976-78) with the Knicks, is born in Raeford, North Carolina.

1958

In a major upset, Manhattan eliminates West Virginia, 89-84, in a first-round NCAA tournament game at the Garden behind Jack Powers, who scores 29 points.

1966

Sunny Jim Fitzsimmons, one of thoroughbred racing's most celebrated trainers, dies in Miami, Florida, at age 81. He trained two Triple Crown horses (Gallant Fox in 1930 and Omaha in 1935) and produced 2,275 winners worth over $13 million in purses.

1995

G. Herbert McCracken, the Lafayette College football coach who is credited with creating the huddle, dies in Boynton Beach, Florida, at age 95.

1995

Alf Goullet, who was a part of eight six-day bike race championship tandems in the Garden during the heyday of the sport, dies in Toms River, N.J., at age 103.

1904

John Flanagan adds over a foot to his world record in the 56-pound weight throw with a toss of 29'6 $\frac{1}{2}$" and Yale defeats Penn in a thrilling mile relay in the Irish-American AC Games at the Garden.

1921

Formed to govern USNLTA clubs within 35 miles of New York City Hall, the Metropolitan Tennis Association is organized by 35 clubs at the Hotel McAlpin. Charles S. Landers of the West Side Tennis Club is elected as the group's first president.

1932

Newark Women's AC finishes second in the team standings at the women's indoor AAU Nationals in Newark, N.J., despite first-place finishes by Cathrine Capp in the 220-yard dash and Nellie Sharka in the 50-yard hurdles. The Meadowbrook Club Women's Team of Philadelphia wins the title with 21 points to the Newark WAC's 14.

1938

Jimmy Herbert, pushed by Glenn Cunningham, sets a world indoor record (1:11.1) in the Casey 600 at the Knights of Columbus Games at the Garden. Howie Borck (Manhattan College) is second (1:11.2) and Cunningham third in 1:11.3 (which equals the previous indoor 600-yard record). Earlier, Cunningham thrills the 18,000 fans with a quick 4:07.4 mile victory.

1946

Paul Mooney, Columbia's basketball coach since 1933 (except for three years of World War II military service), resigns to enter private business (Junior varsity coach Gordon Ridings is named his successor March 17.) Mooney was 101-81 in 10 seasons with an EIBL title in 1936. Mooney was a standout four-sport athlete at NYU.

1954

Christina Gehrig, mother of Lou, dies in New York at age 72.

1973

Frankie Frisch, 74, dies in Wilmington, Delaware, after injuries sustained in a car accident. "The Fordham Flash" was a star with the Giants, playing manager of the 1934 world champion St. Louis Cardinals and broadcaster famed for the phrase, "Oh, those bases on balls."

CHRIS MULLIN

1982

St. John's starts its NCAA title drive with a 66-56 win over Penn at Nassau Coliseum in Uniondale, N.Y. The same night, Northeastern surprises St. Joseph's (Pa.), 63-62. Two nights later, the Redmen drop a 69-68 thriller to Alabama.

1983

St. John's wins the championship with an 85-77 win over Boston College in the final of the first Big East basketball tournament played at the Garden. Freshmen Chris Mullin scores 23 for the Redmen and is voted tournament MVP.

1886

Jake Schaefer, Sr., wins the 14-inch balkline billiards championship and a $1,000 purse with a 1,145-point victory in a five-day match at Manhattan's Cosmopolitan Hall. Schaeffer has 3,000 points to 1,855 for French and European champion Maurice Vignaux. Schaefer also pockets $2,500 in side wagers.

1914

Leon Hess is born in Asbury Park, N.J. Originally the junior member of the consortium that bought the Titans (see Mar. 28), Leon Hess became over time sole owner of the Jets.

1919

Carlos Martin, sportswriter for the *Hudson Dispatch* in Union City, N.J., and public-address announcer for both the Rangers and U.S. Open tennis, is born in West New York, N.J.

CARL MARTIN

1920

NYU wins the national amateur basketball championship by defeating Rutgers, 49-24, before a capacity crowd of 4,000 at the Auditorium in Atlanta, Georgia, in the final of the AAU tournament. The Violets and Chanticleers each won three games to reach the final.

1935

Captain Bob Freeman sinks a 52-foot shot with less than five seconds left to lift Penn to a 35-34 victory over Columbia in the playoff game for the EIBL title at the Rutgers gym in New Brunswick, N.J. Columbia leads, 34-27, with fewer than five minutes to play before Freeman starts a Quakers rally with a basket.

1963

Having called the round in which he would KO his opponent in nine straight fights since 1961, Cassius Clay, 21, has his streak snapped by veteran Doug Jones at the Garden. Clay called for Jones to go in four. Instead, the 10-rounder goes the distance and Clay wins a hotly-disputed decision to raise his record to 18-0. *Ring Magazine* later rates it the "Fight of the Year."

1968

In the final ABA game at the Teaneck (N.J.) Armory, the New Jersey Americans beat the Denver Nuggets, 96-87. The team draws only 79,872 in 39 home games (26-13) and that summer moves to Long Island to become the New York Nets (see July 15).

1971

In the first major bowling event televised (ABC) from the Felt Forum at the Garden, Earl Anthony defeats Roy Buckley, 226-181, to win the $85,000 Cougar Open. The first three days of the tournament were rolled in the Garden's Bowling Center.

1971

Fordham notches a first-round NCAA tournament win over Furman, 105-74, at St. John's Alumni Hall, but loses in the next round to Villanova, 85-75, at Raleigh, North Carolina.

March 14

1925

Walter Camp, father of American football, dies in New York at age 65 while attending a football rules committee meeting. Camp is responsible for the fundamental structure of the game, having introduced the line of scrimmage, the concept of downs and 11-a-side squads.

1944

In tennis' first major match between an amateur and a professional, the amateur, Coast Guard cadet Jack Kramer, beats the pro champ, Don Budge, 6-3, 6-2, in Budge's last match for the duration of World War II. At the time, amateur players were prohibited from playing pros, who in turn were barred from all major tournaments such as Forest Hills and Wimbledon. This match is permitted as a benefit for wartime charities.

1946

In the opening game of the NIT, Rhode Island State's Ernie Calverley hits the most famous single shot in Garden college basketball history. As time expires, Calverley sinks a 55-footer to force a tie with Bowling Green. Rhode Island State wins in overtime, 82-79, and advances all the way to the championship game before losing to Kentucky.

1953

Charles T. McManus, superintendent of Yankee Stadium for the first 30 years of its existence, dies at age 62 in The Bronx.

1953

Seton Hall (31-2) wins its first NIT title with a 58-46 Garden win over St. John's before an NIT record crowd of 18,496. Walter Dukes scores 21 points and has 20 rebounds, finishing as the tournament's high scorer (70 points) and MVP.

1962

New York Tapers play their final home game at the Long Island Arena in Commack and lose to the Hawaii Chiefs, 110-95. This vagabond club started the American Basketball League season in Washington, D.C., and relocates to Philadelphia for 1962-63, but the league folds on New Year's Eve 1962.

1962

Andy Bathgate's third-period penalty-shot goal gives the Rangers a 3-2 Garden win over Detroit, despite Gordie Howe's 500th career tally. Referee Eddie Powers makes the call when Wings goalie Hank Bassen throws his stick at the Rangers' Dean Prentice and awards the penalty shot to Bathgate, who last touched the puck on the offensive team when the whistle blew. The win virtually clinches the Rangers' first playoff berth in four years.

1968

Elnardo Webster scores 51 points (the second highest ever in an NIT Garden game) to lead St. Peter's to a wild 102-93 double overtime win over Marshall.

1972

Norman Armitage dies at age 65 in New York. Armitage, one of America's greatest fencers, won 10 U.S. sabre championships in 16 years. A Columbia graduate, he won his first national title in 1930 and took three titles while an NYU law student (1934-36).

1979

With former Queens College All-America Althea Gwyn of the New York Stars scoring 19 points and hauling down 16 rebounds, the East beats the West, 112-99, in the WBL All-Star game before 2,731 at Madison Square Garden's Felt Forum. Debra Waddy-Rossow of the Chicago Hustle scores 26 for the West.

1886

Jack (the Non Pareil) Dempsey of New York defeats Boston's George LaBlanche in the 13th round of a middle-weight title fight held under clandestine circumstances on a Sunday morning on the shores of Long Island Sound near Larchmont, N.Y. The bout was hastily shifted from Mamaroneck, N.Y., the day before to avoid interference by the local authorities. Dempsey wins a $2,500 purse and a little extra from wagers by the Bostonian's backers.

1897

Irving Brokaw wins the St. Nicholas club figure skating championship at the St. Nick's Rink by one point over Erskine Hewitt.

1933

East Rutherford (N.J.) High School girls basketball team wins its 104th straight game since 1926. But coach Marian Hackbarth's team is forced to give up the sport when it cannot schedule enough opponents for the following season.

1939

St. John's forward Bill Lloyd sets an NIT scoring record with 31 points in leading the Redmen to a 71-47 first-round win over Roanoke. Lloyd's 31 is also a Garden collegiate record, eclipsing the 25 scored by Illinois center Pick Dehner in a regular-season win over Manhattan earlier in the season. St. John's gets bounced by Loyola of Chicago, 51-46, in the semis.

1941

Columbia scores the college fencing upset of the season, 15 $^1/_2$-11 $^1/_2$, over Navy at University Hall, handing the Midshipmen (6-0) their first dual-meet loss since 1936. Herb Spiselman, Armand Mascia and Eaton Bayer each win twice to lead a 6-3 foil win that keys the upset. Kermit Lanser also wins twice in sabre for the Lions.

1942

With a surprising 6-3 victory over eventual Stanley Cup champion Toronto, the last-place Americans, New York's first NHL team (1925), play their last home game ever at the Garden.

1962

Bill van Breda Kolff becomes Princeton's head basketball coach, succeeding Joey L. (Jake) McCandless, who resigned March 6. Paul Lynner is hired March 19 to fill the vacancy created by van Breda Kolff's resignation at Hofstra.

1973

Raiders play their final home game (against the Los Angeles Sharks) of the WHA's inaugural season, a financial disaster. They average only 5,868 announced attendance for their 39 Garden games. During the off-season, the team is sold (see Nov. 19).

BILL VAN BREDA KOLFF

1987

Red Dutton, 88, dies in Calgary, Alberta. Americans defenseman, coach and club president, and later NHL president (1943-46), Dutton, a longtime Rangers antagonist, supposedly cursed the Blueshirts after they forced his club out of the Garden in 1942. "The Rangers will never win the Stanley Cup again in my lifetime," he may have said. And they never did.

March 16

1894

With the Coney Island Jockey Club (Sheepshead Bay Racetrack) joining, the Jockey Club has jurisdiction over thoroughbred racing at all major New York area tracks. Already members are the Brooklyn Jockey Club (Gravesend), the New York Jockey Club (Morris Park) and the Monmouth Park (N.J.) Association. Within a week, however, unfavorable government action knocks out the New Jersey track (see Mar. 21).

1927

Junius Kellogg is born in Haverstraw, N.Y. A Manhattan College basketball star, Kellogg made the revelations that triggered the 1951 point-shaving scandals (see Jan. 17).

1938

Temple, led by Don Shields and Ed Boyle, routs Colorado, 60-36, at the Garden, to win the first NIT, America's oldest postseason college basketball tournament.

1941

Behind two goals from George Roberts, Bob Bordley, and Ralph Wyer, the St. Nicholas Hockey Club beats Clinton (N.Y.), 10-3, to win the national AAU hockey title at the New Haven Arena.

SONNY WERBLIN

1946

Metropolitan Intercollegiate "indoor" track and field championships are held outdoors on the eight-lap board track at Columbia's Baker Field. Among the record-breakers is NYU's Irv Kintisch (ETO shotput champ in 1945 when in the military), who heaves the shot 51' 8 $\frac{5}{8}$".

1946

Pancho Segura of Ecuador becomes the first Latin American player to win a major USLTA championship by beating Don McNeill, 1-6, 6-3, 6-4, 7-5, in the final of the U.S. Indoors before 2,000 at the 7th Regiment Armory.

1949

In the first BAA doubleheader ever at the Garden, the Chicago Stags beat Boston, 107-82, and the Rochester Royals down the Knicks, 94-89. Doubleheaders become a staple of the Garden's NBA programs for the next 20 years.

1962

Brian Mullen is born in New York. A left wing, Mullen scored 100 goals in four years (1987-91) with the Rangers, and played one year for the Islanders. His brother Joe, also a native New Yorker, was the first U.S.-born player to score 1,000 NHL points.

1969

Nets' Bob Lloyd misses his third free throw attempt of the game, ending his ABA record streak of 49 straight (his first miss since February 8) in a 123-109 loss to the Floridians at the Long Island Arena in Commack. Kentucky's Luvie Dampier breaks Lloyd's mark in 1970-71 with 57 straight.

1978

Jim Roach, *The New York Times* sports editor (1958-73), dies in New York at 70.

1871

Meeting at Collier's Cafe, 13th Street and Broadway, 10 clubs organize baseball's first professional league—the National Association of Professional Base-Ball Players. For a $10 membership fee, nine sign up to start the season: the Mutuals, the Athletics (Philadelphia), Bostons (Boston)—the three charter members who play all five National Association seasons—White Stockings (Chicago), Forest City (Rockford, Illinois), Haymakers (Troy, N.Y.), Olympics (Washington, D.C.), Kekiongas (Fort Wayne, Indiana), and Forest City (Cleveland, Ohio). James N. Kerns of Troy is elected president. The season opens May 4 in Fort Wayne but the Kekiongas withdraw after 28 games and the Eckfords of Brooklyn, the skeptical 10th team, pay the $10 to replace them.

1910

David A. Werblin is born in Brooklyn. Sonny Werblin led the consortium that bought the Titans in 1963 (and changed the name to Jets and colors to green and white). His involvement in the Meadowlands project gave it the credibility to raise the money to build the complex. He later served as president of Madison Square Garden, was an officer of Monmouth Park race track and owned his own thoroughbred stable.

1925

Billed as "The Race of the Ages," Willie Ritola of the Finnish-American AC wins the 5,000-meter run as the heavy favorite, Paavo Nurmi, staggers off the boards with four laps to go. Nurmi is ill with an upset stomach he later blames on a beef pot pie he ate at 5 p.m. The race is the highlight of the first Knights of Columbus track meet held at Garden No. 2. It is also the last as this Garden closes that summer (see Nov. 28).

1932

Princeton (18-4) ends Columbia's bid for a third straight EIBL championship with a 38-35 playoff victory at the Palestra in Philadelphia. John Seibert with 14 points and Ken Fairman with 13 lead the Tigers, while Owen McDowell has 13 for Columbia. It is Tigers coach Al Wittmer's last game after nine seasons (115-86).

1936

Welterweight Lou Ambers KOs Tony Scarpati, 22, in the seventh round at Brooklyn's Broadway Arena. Scarpati, winner of his previous 19 bouts, dies three days later of a cerebral hemorrhage without regaining consciousness, New York's second ring death in three years.

1937

For the fifth straight year, Glenn Cunningham wins the Columbian Mile in the New York Chapter, Knights of Columbus Games before 13,000 at the Garden. He is clocked in 4:08.7.

1940

On the final night of the regular season, Pat Egan replaces Wilf Field on defense for the Americans and scores a hat trick in a 5-2 win over Toronto at the Garden.

1951

Ray Rudzinski pours in 26 points to lead St. Francis (19-11) to a 93-79 win over Seattle in the title game of the third National Catholic Basketball Championship at Albany, N.Y. Vernon Stokes has 22 and Roy Reardon 21 for the Terriers, who go 4-0 in the tournament. St. Francis had lost to Siena in the semifinals the year before.

1989

Katha Quinn, sports information director at St. John's, dies in New York at age 34.

1997

Helped by the Devils' Bobby Holik, who bats the puck into his own net to break a 1-1 tie, the Florida Panthers defeat New Jersey, 4-1, at the Meadowlands, snapping New Jersey's 15-game home unbeaten streak.

1848

Nathaniel G. Herreshoff is born in Bristol, Rhode Island. Captain Herreshoff designed five yachts that defended the America's Cup six times (Columbia twice, 1899-1901).

1897

The first AAU national gymnastics championship held since 1894 is staged at the Knickerbocker Athletic Club on Madison Avenue at 54th Street. E.J. Linderman of the Camden (N.J.) Turn Verein wins the all-around title with 165.60 of a possible 195 points.

1900

Oliva Chapdelaine is born in St. Francis, Quebec. As Jack Delaney, he held the world light heavyweight championship from 1926-27 and engaged in several legendary battles with Paul Berlenbach.

1905

Bowling great Lou Campi is born in Verona, Italy.

1938

Robert Frank Nevin is born in South Porcupine, Ontario. Bob Nevin had five 20-goal seasons in his seven years (1964-71) in New York and his six-plus seasons as Rangers captain from February 5, 1965, until his trade to Minnesota May 25, 1971 (for winger Bobby Rousseau), is the second-longest tenure in club history behind Bill Cook (1926-37).

1950

City College sets the stage for its unprecedented sweep of postseason basketball tournaments with a 69-61 victory over Bradley in the NIT final at the Garden.

1960

In a national semifinal NCAA basketball game at San Francisco, NYU loses, 76-54, to eventual national champion Ohio State.

1961

Army makes its first postseason basketball appearance ever, losing an opening-round NIT game to Temple, 79-66, on a Saturday afternoon at the Garden, but George Hunter's Cadets finish 17-7, most wins for West Point since 1923, when Harry Fisher's team was 17-0.

1968

Wilbur Wood, sports editor of *The Sun* from 1934 to its closing on January 4, 1950, dies at age 76 in Hollywood, Florida. Wood helped organize the Boxing Writers Association of America and served as its first president in 1926.

1974

Charles Hoerter, *Daily News* sports editor (1957-67), dies in Palm Beach, Florida, at 67.

CAROL BLAZEJOWSKI

1983

Franco Georgetti, winner of eight six-day bike races (with five different partners) at the Garden during the 1920s and '30s, dies in Bovisio Mombello, Italy, at age 80.

1882

John L. Dwyer, one of the leading pugilists of the 1870s, dies in Brooklyn at age 34. Dwyer held wins over Steve Taylor and Jimmy Elliott before retiring to become Chief Clerk of the Kings County Court in Brooklyn.

1894

National AAU boxing championships open with preliminary rounds at the Garden. Two nights later, the tournament resumes with the quarterfinals and so many bouts are fought the finals don't begin until after 11 p.m. Those hardy fans who remain see some excellent fights, including the victory of Jimmy Madden of the Pastime AC over George Ross of the Lexington AC in the 105-pound final.

1915

Norwegian Molla Bjurstedt defeats Marie Wagner, 6-4, 6-4, at the 7th Regiment Armory to win her first U.S. national indoor singles tennis title. Between them, Wagner (6) and Bjurstedt, later Mrs. Franklin I. Mallory, (5), combine to win 11 indoor nationals. That fall, Miss Bjurstedt wins the first of her record eight U.S. national singles titles.

1938

Americans and Maple Leafs combine to score eight goals in 4:52 in the Leafs' 8-5 win at Toronto. The Leafs score five and the Amerks three during the third-period spree.

1938

Former Fordham star Joe McCluskey breaks his own world indoor steeplechase record (9:43.3) in the Metropolitan AAU championships at the Jersey City Armory.

1944

Utah is eliminated by Kentucky, 46-38, in the NIT quarterfinals at the Garden. But Garden fans haven't seen the last of the Utes, who go west to capture the NCAA Regionals and return east to win the season's second championship at the Garden (see Mar. 28). Oddly, Kentucky duplicates Utah's feat five years later, being knocked out in the NIT quarters but winning the NCAA championship in Seattle.

1946

Ruth Kreppdin's game-high 14 points lead NYU's women's basketball team to a 30-24 win over Brooklyn College, who get 13 from Diana Marcus at Evangeline Gym.

1966

Top-seeded Brigham Young tops NYU, 97-84, to win the NIT at the Garden. It is the Violets' eighth (and last) NIT appearance and second second-place finish (1948 was the other).

1972

Eddie Giacomin becomes the first goalie in the club's 46-season history to record two assists in a game as the Rangers beat Toronto, 5-3, at the Garden.

1978

Carol Blazejowski, the nation's scoring leader, pours in 50 points as her Montclair (N.J.) State Squaws rout Queens College, 75-50, before 1,750 at the Rutgers Athletic Center to win the AIAW Eastern Regional final and a trip to Los Angeles for the women's Final Four. Blazejowski's 50 points raise her career total to 3,118 for 99 games.

1997

Seton Hall introduces former Duke assistant Tommy Amaker as its new head basketball coach. A top assistant without any head coaching experience, Amaker at 31 is the youngest head coach in the Big East.

1896

Yale and Pennsylvania play what is thought to be the first intercollegiate five-a-side basketball game, with the Bulldogs winning, 32-10, at New Haven. Earlier, Yale had played several games against YMCA and amateur Athletic Club teams.

1901

Yale defeats Brown, 5-1, at the St. Nicholas Rink, to win the Intercollegiate League hockey championship.

1928

Bespectacled Donald Noble sinks his only basket with two minutes left as Penn beats Princeton, 24-22, at the Palestra in Philadelphia to win the EIBL championship playoff. Princeton had won, 29-12, at Penn on the final night of the season to create a tie.

1939

LIU (24-0) wins the NIT with a 44-32 victory over the Loyola of Chicago Ramblers (21-1) at the Garden in a rare clash between unbeaten teams in postseason tournament play.

1947

John M. Chapman, a leading executive during the heyday of bike racing in the United States, dies in Santa Monica, California, at age 69.

1948

Brooklyn's Prospect Park YMCA (Division Street branch) wins the national "Y" tournament with a 58-45 win over Hoboken at the Manual Training High School. Prospect Park, as the "Y" champion, earns a berth at the Olympic trials in the Garden the following week but loses in the first round to tournament winner Phillips 66 Oilers (Bartlesville, Oklahoma), national AAU champs.

1951

Illinois beats Columbia (22-0), 79-71, in a first-round NCAA game at the Garden, sending the Lions to their first loss. The same night, St. John's beats Connecticut, 63-52, to advance to the second round.

1965

In Joe Lapchick's final game as a coach, St. John's edges Villanova, 55-51, to win the NIT for a record fifth time before 18,499 at the Garden. In 19 seasons at St. John's over two terms, Lapchick compiled a 335-129 mark.

1965

In his final college game, Bill Bradley pours in 58 points, a Final Four record, as Princeton clouts Wichita State, 118-82, in the national third-place game of the NCAA Final Four at Portland, Oregon.

1981

Irwin Jaffee, 74, national champion speed skater in the 1920s and '30s, dies in San Diego.

1997

Carlo Fassi dies in Lausanne, Switzerland, at age 67, during the World Figure Skating Championships. A native-born Italian who rebuilt the U.S. figure skating program in the 1960s following the plane crash that killed 18 team members (see Feb. 15), Fassi coached Olympic champions Peggy Fleming and Dorothy Hamill.

1997

Tony Zale, middleweight champion from 1941-47 and in 1948, dies in Portage, Indiana, at age 83. Zale won the first and last of his three now-legendary brawls with Rocky Graziano in 1946 at Yankee Stadium and in 1948 at Ruppert Stadium in Newark, N.J.

1889

John Bain Sutherland, a famous college football coach at Lafayette and Pittsburgh who later led the Brooklyn Football Dodgers, is born in Coupar-Angus, Scotland.

1894

Chief Justice Mercer Beasley of the New Jersey Supreme Court announces that the court finds invalid acts by the state senate licensing race tracks, permitting bookmaking and limiting fines for gambling. Although part of a larger issue over political control of the Senate, the ruling effectively shuts down the state's tracks. Affected are Monmouth Park and the well-known Elizabeth Jockey Club, as well as smaller tracks at Linden, Guttenberg, Gloucester and Clifton.

1917

Joie Ray, a Chicago taxi driver running for the Illinois AC and America's most famous miler, clocks 4:19 at the Garden to beat Yale's John Overton by 15 yards. A special feature of the John Wanamaker Commerical Institute Games (forerunner of the Millrose AA), "The Greatest Mile Race Ever Run Indoors" also features Sid Leslie and the Millrose's Mike Devaney, but neither one finishes.

JOCK SUTHERLAND

1929

Butch Keeling's goal at 29:50 of overtime gives the Rangers a 1-0 Garden win over the Americans in an opening-round Stanley Cup playoff game and the series. The opener of the two-game, total goals series was a 0-0 tie, making Keeling's goal the only one in 149:50 of play.

1939

Mel Hill's goal at 59:25 of overtime gives Boston a 2-1 win over the Rangers at the Garden in the first game of their Stanley Cup semifinal. Two nights later, Hill scores at 8:24 of overtime to lift the Bruins to a 3-2 win at Boston (see Apr. 2).

1945

DePaul's George Mikan explodes for a Garden-record 53 points to lead the Blue Demons to a 97-53 semifinal victory over Rhode Island State in the NIT (see Mar. 11). Mikan scores 120 points in three games as DePaul rolls to the NIT title.

1970

Marquette wins the NIT, beating St. John's, 65-53, in the final at the Garden. The Warriors had been extended an NCAA bid but declined. As a result, the NCAA passes a rule that henceforth, any team extended a bid to the NCAA tournament may decline, but cannot accept an invitation to any other postseason tournament.

1983

Drawn largely to see Heisman Trophy winner Herschel Walker, 53,370 turn out to watch the New Jersey Generals home opener in the USFL, a spring-summer pro football league. But visiting Tampa Bay wins, 32-9, at Giants Stadium.

1991

Josh Barney, one-time president of the NHSA dies in Sarasota, Florida, at age 79.

March 22

1897

Arena AC opens at Broadway and 42nd Street and Dan Creedon of Australia delivers a KO of Charley Strong of Newark, N.J., in the fourth round of their scheduled 20-round feature bout.

1928

Major General George W. Wingate, founder of New York's PSAL, dies at age 85 in Brooklyn.

1941

LIU halts Seton Hall's 43-game winning streak with a 49-26 NIT semifinal victory over the Pirates at the Garden. Two days later, the Blackbirds win the NIT for the second time in three years with a 56-42 win over Ohio University.

1952

With Bob Zawoluk setting an NCAA tournament record with 32 points, St. John's stuns Kentucky, 64-57, at Raleigh, North Carolina, ending the Wildcats' 23-game winning streak and sending the Redmen to the semifinals in Seattle, Washington (see Mar. 26).

1967

Muhammad Ali makes the eighth successful defense of his WBC heavyweight championship by knocking out Zora Folley at 1:48 of the seventh round at the Garden. But it will be Ali's last championship bout for nearly four years as he is stripped of his title for his refusal to be drafted into the U.S. Army during the Vietnam War. Ali claims a religious exemption from the draft (see June 20).

1968

New Jersey Americans forfeit their special ABA playoff game with the Kentucky Colonels for fourth place in the Eastern Division. Forced from their home court at the Teaneck (N.J.) Armory by a circus, the Amerks, who earned home court by winning seven of 11 regular-season games with the Colonels, choose to play at the Long Island Arena in Commack. The Arena's floor is declared unplayable due to condensation by league commissioner George Mikan. The decision sends the Colonels into the playoffs and the Americans home for the summer.

1971

Newly-formed New York Cosmos of the North American Soccer League sign their first player, outside left Jorge Siega, 23, from the German-Hungarians of the New York's German American Soccer League.

1972

Yankees trade infielder Danny Cater to the Red Sox for Boston reliever Sparky Lyle.

1975

Asa S. Bushnell, Princeton athletic director and first commissioner of the ECAC, dies in Princeton, N.J., at age 75.

1990

Tate George's 17-footer off a length-of-the-court pass by Scott Burrell as time expires lifts Connecticut to a stunning 71-70 win over ACC champion Clemson in the NCAA East Regional semifinal at the Brendan Byrne Arena in East Rutherford, N.J.

1997

Marsha Harris scores 26 points, including a last-second basket, to give the NYU women's basketball team the NCAA Division III national championship with a 72-70 victory over Wisconsin-Eau Claire at the NYU gym. The Violets rally from a 15-point deficit early in the second half and finish with a 29-1 record.

1889

Pat Cahill of the Scottish-American AC stops W.H. Stuckly of the National Turn Verein of Newark, N.J., to successfully defend his middleweight boxing title in the AAU championships at the Metropolitan Opera House. Fencing and wrestling finals are also held with Luis Francke winning the sabre crown over B.F. O'Connor, and two Philadelphians stage the best wrestling final with William Law (Valencia Boat Club) downing D.W. Windsor (Schuylkill Navy) at 4:51 of their 158-pound match.

1914

Montreal's Wanderers lose to the Quebec Bulldogs, 8-6, at the St. Nick's Rink but win the two-game, total-goals tournament, 15-12, and the $5,000 prize. The Vancouver Millionaires were eliminated during the opening round-robin series. These outstanding Canadian teams were invited to St. Nick's to show New York the pro league game.

1932

Gregory Mangin of Newark, N.J., defeats Francis X. Shields, 10-8, 2-6, 6-4, 6-3, to win the USLTA men's national indoor singles championship at the 7th Regiment Armory. Mangin makes the indoor final five straight years, a record, and wins four (losing only in 1934). In the international match that accompanies the event, the U.S. beats France, 3-2, with Shields winning the clinching singles over Christian Boussus, 6-1, 6-4, 10-8. Jean Borotra wins his two singles to account for the French points.

1948

Kentucky defeats Baylor, 58-42, in the NCAA basketball final at the Garden.

1952

In the season's last game, Bill Mosienko scores three goals in 21 seconds (6:09, 6:20 and 6:30 of the third period), an NHL record for fastest three goals by an individual or team, as Chicago rallies from a 6-2 deficit for a 7-6 win over the Rangers at the Garden.

1960

Franklin P. Adams, who wrote for the *World* and penned the "saddest words that were ever heard—Tinker to Evers to Chance," dies in New York at age 78.

1975

Princeton becomes the first Ivy League team to win the NIT with an 80-69 Garden win over Providence as Mickey Steuerer scores 26 points and Todd Van Bloomesteyn 23.

1979

With a 14-7 win over the Philadelphia Fever at Nassau Coliseum, the New York Arrows take the opener of the best-of-three MISL championship series. Two nights later, the Arrows complete the sweep and win the league's first title, 9-5, at Philadelphia.

ADAM GRAVES

1994

Adam Graves sets a Rangers record for goals in a season with 51 when he scores twice in the first period against his former team in a 5-3 win at Edmonton. Graves' first ties Vic Hadfield's 1971-72 record of 50 and his second comes 2:54 later.

March 24

1859

English boxing champion James Massey heads the list of participants in a "sparring exhibition" at Hoym's Theater in the Bowery (then part of the theater district). Massey spars with Johnny Mackey while American heavyweight champ John Morrissey leads the preliminary bill of 11 brief matches, the best of which pits Barney Aaron against Johnny Sweetman.

1896

St. Nicholas Hockey Rink opens to the public for the first time. Manager Charles M. Pope shows off the 200-foot-by-90-foot rink as well as the main floor and balcony seating.

1897

New York Athletic Club beats the St. Nick's, 3-1, at the St. Nicholas Rink to win the first Amateur Hockey League championship of America and a trophy donated by Frank L. Slazenger. The NYAC team is largely composed of former members of the Hockey Club of New York, a group of expatriate Canadians, seven of whom joined the NYAC shortly before the league season began.

1915

For the second straight year, the Montreal Wanderers win the invitational hockey tournament at the St. Nicholas Rink. The Wanderers beat the Quebec Bulldogs, 15-12, to take the two-game, total-goals series, 27-18.

1929

John Ross Roach blanks Toronto, 1-0, at the Garden, in the first game of the Rangers' semifinal against the Maple Leafs, his third straight shutout, tying an NHL playoff record.

1944

St. John's becomes the only team ever to win the NIT in successive years with a surprising 47-39 win over DePaul. Tournament MVP Bill Kotsores scores 10 points and Ray Wertis 12 for the Redmen, who effectively shackle DePaul's heralded big man, George Mikan.

1945

Down by 10 points with two minutes left in regulation time, NYU stuns Ohio State, 70-65, in overtime in the semifinals of the NCAA tournament at the Garden. Dolph Schayes hits two key rebound baskets and Don Forman adds a critical set shot to the miracle rally. But three nights later, Oklahoma A&M wins the NCAA title with a 49-45 win over the Violets.

1962

Emile Griffith regains his welterweight crown with a knockout of champ Benny Paret at 2:09 of the 12th round at the Garden. The badly-battered Paret dies of his injuries on April 3.

1980

Pierre Etchebaster, court tennis world champion (1928-54) who coached the sport at the Racquet & Tennis Club from 1927-66, dies at age 86 in Saint Jean de Luiz, France.

1990

Patrick Ewing scores a career-high 51 points, but the Celtics beat the Knicks, 115-110, at the Garden.

1886

Famous thoroughbred owner Francis Morris dies at age 76 in Oakland Manor, Maryland. Morris imported the fabled Eclipse from England and bred such great horses as Ruthless (the first Belmont Stakes winner), Relentless, Regardless, and Remorseless.

1897

George Dixon, the world featherweight champion, defeats Frank Erne of Buffalo, N.Y., at the Broadway Athletic Club on the decision of referee Dick Roche. Erne had a 20-round decision over Dixon and the pair previously fought a 10-round draw, so Dixon agreed to the match, even though Erne was over the weight, to redeem his reputation.

1913

Harry Harris, long-time *Associated Press* photographer, is born in New York.

1916

Heavyweight champ Jess Willard decisions Frank Moran at the Garden in his first New York appearance since winning the crown from Jack Johnson in Havana, Cuba, the year before.

ALTHEA GIBSON

1928

In the fourth game of a "world championship" series, the Original Celtics win the basketball crown and continue their dominance of the sport with a 27-26 victory over Fort Wayne (Indiana) at Brooklyn's Arcadia Hall. Holding a 16-4 lead at the half, the Celtics withstand a late rally to win the best-of-five series, three games to one. Davey Banks leads the winners with 11 points while Nat Holman adds six and Dutch Dehnert five. The first three games of the series were played in Fort Wayne, with the Celtics winning March 21 (30-21), losing March 22 (28-21) and winning again March 23 (35-18).

1931

Canadian-born brothers Russell and Lloyd Blinco score two goals each as the Crescent Athletic Club of Brooklyn wins the National AAU hockey championship at the Garden with a 4-2 victory over the Atlantic City (N.J.) Sea Gulls.

1950

In the U.S. Amateur indoor tennis championships at the 7th Regiment Armory, Don McNeill wins the men's title, 11-9, 4-6, 6-2, 6-2 over Fred Kovaleski, but the women's final makes history when Althea Gibson becomes the first black player ever to make a national singles final, though she loses to Nancy Chafee (later married to baseball slugger Ralph Kiner), 6-0, 6-2.

1968

Tom Okker of the Netherlands faces Jim McManus of the U.S. on one court and Zeljko Franulovic of Yugoslavia meets Allen Fox of the U.S. on another as the inaugural USLTA International for the Garden Challenge Trophy gets underway at the Garden. Despite some brilliant highlights, the 48-player, six-day event is not a financial success.

1976

Fred Schmertz, meet director of the Millrose Games for the last 41 years of his life, dies in Baton Rouge, Louisiana, at age 87. He is succeeded by his son Howard.

March 26

1898

Ernest Roeber retains his world Greco-Roman wrestling championship at the Garden on a foul when Ishmael Yousouf, "The Terrible Turk," is (not surprisingly) disqualified. Roeber retains the title until 1900 when he loses to Beck Olsen of Denmark, wins it back from Olsen in 1901 and retires in 1902 (see Apr. 30 and Dec. 14).

1909

In a controversial finish, "Philadelphia Jack" O'Brien is saved by the bell after being knocked down three times by Stanley Ketchel, "the Michigan Assassin," at the National Sporting Club on East 24th Street. O'Brien is down for the count in the final round of the 10-rounder when the bell sounds, ending the fight in a draw. Many observers think the bell is rather premature.

1914

In probably the fastest knockout ever in amateur boxing, William Smith, Jr., of the Bronx Church House decks William J. Jackson of the Grace Club with his first punch in the first round of their 135-pound opening bout in the Metropolitan AAU championships at the NYAC.

1915

Meeting in Baltimore, Federal League owners approve the shift of the Indianapolis club to Newark and the transfer of league batting champ Benny Kauff from Indianapolis to Brooklyn.

1946

Led by Bob Kurland's 23 points, Oklahoma A&M wins the NCAA championship with a 43-40 victory over North Carolina at the Garden. The game is the first NCAA final televised, being shown locally by the CBS Network's New York outlet, WABC-TV (Ch. 7).

1949

Regis defeats St. Francis in the final game of the National Catholic Basketball Tournament, 51-47, at Denver, Colorado, despite 24 points by the Terriers' Tom Gallagher. Gallagher finishes his season with 496 points, thought to be the most ever by a player from a New York City college in a single season up to then.

1952

After reaching the NCAA final with a 61-59 win over Illinois the night before, St. John's is beaten for the championship by Kansas, 80-63, at Seattle, Washington, as Jayhawks center Clyde Lovellette wipes out Bob Zawoluk's single-game tournament scoring record with a 33-point performance. Zawoluk leads the Redmen with 20.

1968

Eleanora Randolph Sears, Boston socialite and America's the most famous woman athlete at the turn of the century, dies in Palm Beach, Florida, at 87. Eleo Sears was also a standout horsewoman who won ribbons at the National Horse Show, the first women's national squash champion in 1928 and a member of four national tennis championship women's doubles teams (1911, 1915-17). She also teamed with Willis F. Davis in 1916 to win the national mixed doubles tennis title.

1989

For the third time in four years, Duke wins the East Regional in the NCAA tournament, defeating Georgetown, 85-77, at the Brendan Byrne Arena in East Rutherford, N.J..

1997

Governor John G. Rowland announces that Connecticut will accept a buyout from the NHL Hartford Whalers, allowing the state's only professional major sports team to leave. The Whalers will pay $20.5 million to end their lease. (On May 6, the Whalers announce they are moving to Raleigh, North Carolina, to become the Carolina Hurricanes.)

1879

Miller James Huggins is born in Cincinnati, Ohio. Huggins managed the Yankees for 12 seasons, taking them to their first six pennants and three world titles.

1897

Columbia scores first, but Yale takes a 3-1 lead and coasts to a 7-2 hockey win over the Lions at the St. Nick's Rink. The game helps restore athletic relations between the two old rivals, who had not played for several years, and is a prelude to the famous 1899 Columbia football win over the Elis.

1921

Frank L. Kramer wins the "Mayor Gillen 5-Mile Open Pro Stakes" on opening day at the Newark (N.J.) Velodrome. Mayor Charles P. Gillen fires the opening gun and Kramer comes home first 11:04 later with Peter Moeskops second, Reggie McNamara third, Alf Goullet fourth and John Bedell fifth.

1938

Lorne Carr's goal 40 seconds into the fourth overtime lifts the Americans to a 3-2 victory over the Rangers in the longest NHL game ever played at the Garden. The win gives the Amerks, who had trailed, 2-0, going into the third period, the best-of-three Stanley Cup opening-round series, two games to one.

1939

Hal Sharkey, sports editor of the *Newark Evening News* (1933-39) whose energetic booking of dates during California vacations made the modern PGA tour possible, dies in Montclair, N.J., at age 43.

1949

Bobby Jahn of Brooklyn and Mary Lynch of Newburgh, N.Y., sweep the titles in the Eastern States Indoor Speed Skating Championships at the Brooklyn Ice Palace. Jahn wins the men's 880-yard race (1:29), the $^3/_4$-mile (2:21.1) and the mile (3:19) while Miss Lynch takes the women's 440 (0:50) and 880 (1:44.7).

1956

William H. Cane dies at Miami Beach, Florida, at age 81. Born in Jersey City, N.J., in 1874, Cane bought out his father's contracting business and built, among other projects, Boyle's 30 Acres (see July 2). Retiring in 1925, Cane turned his attention to harness racing, built Good Time Park in Goshen, N.Y., took over the Hambletonian and moved it there in 1930 and, in 1950, led the syndicate that converted the old Empire City Racetrack into Yonkers Raceway.

1956

New York State Supreme Court Justice Morris Eder upholds the revocation of the London Sporting Club's promoter's license at St. Nicholas Arena. The New York State Athletic Commission revoked the license February 28 while fining promoter Tex Sullivan and matchmaker Willie Gilzenberg $5,000 each for unapproved practices. Teddy Brenner's New York Boxing Club, Inc. had been granted promotional rights at St. Nick's and DuMont Network Vice President Ted Cott announces a two-year contract with Brenner for Monday night fights.

1976

Rutgers rides into the NCAA basketball tournament semifinal at the Spectrum in Philadelphia with a 31-0 record but loses to Michigan, 86-70. Two days later, the Scarlet Knights also lose to UCLA, 106-92, in the third-place consolation game.

March 28

1896

In the first hockey game played at the St. Nicholas Rink, the new St. Nick's team routs the Cornell varsity, 8-0, in a game of two 20-minute halves. Malcolm Chace scores the first goal as the St. Nick's take a 2-0 halftime lead and Bill Larned, who later won seven U.S. national singles tennis championships, has a three-goal hat trick in the second half.

1935

Bill Thieben, Hofstra basketball's career scoring leader, is born in Brooklyn. The Dutchmen were 56-20 from 1953-56 as Thieben scored 1,837 points, 22-4 in his senior season when he averaged 26.7 points per game. His best year was 1954-55 (29.2).

1940

Kevin Michael Loughery, who later coached the Nets to their two ABA championships in 1974 and 1976, is born in Brooklyn.

1944

Utah, eliminated in the NIT (see Mar. 19), wins the NCAA basketball tournament with a 42-40 overtime victory over Dartmouth at the Garden.

1950

City College completes its unique sweep of college basketball's major postseason tournaments with a 71-68 defeat of Bradley in the NCAA final at the Garden. No other team has ever matched this feat. It is also the last NCAA final at the Garden.

1963

AFL officials announce that the bankrupt New York franchise has been sold to a syndicate of five men headed by Sonny Werblin, president of MCA, the entertainment organization. On April 15, the new owners announce that former Baltimore Colts head coach Weeb Ewbank has been hired as general manager and head coach and that the team, known as the Titans, will now be called the Jets.

1981

Knicks beat the Nets, 90-88, in the final NBA game at the Rutgers Athletic Center, before 8,515, who raise season attendance to 302,001. (Nets drew 382,611 to the RAC in their first New Jersey season in 1977-78.) The team loses 14 of its last 18, including another to the Knicks the next night at the Garden.

1989

William D. Cox, who founded the International Soccer League and was principal owner of two New York pro football teams (as well as the Philadelphia Phillies before being forced to sell for betting on his own team), dies in Mount Kisco, N.Y., at age 79.

1989

A New Zealand syndicate's suit against the use of a catamaran in an America's Cup defense is upheld by New York Supreme Court Judge Carmen B. Ciparic but the San Diego Yacht Club gets a stay pending an appeal. (The New York Court of Appeals reverses Ciparic's ruling September 19. New York courts have jurisdiction in America's Cup litigation because New York is the site of the original "Deed of Gift" of the Cup.)

1995

In his first game at the Garden since ending his 1 $\frac{1}{2}$-year retirement, Chicago's Michael Jordan scores 55 points, a pro record for the 4th Garden, and sets up Bill Wennington's basket in the closing seconds as the Bulls beat the Knicks, 113-111.

1898

Charles McVeigh is born in Kenora, Ontario. Charley (Rabbit) McVeigh was a winger for the Americans for seven seasons (1928-35), accumulating 66 goals and 77 assists in 311 games. He tied for the club lead in assists in 1930-31.

1928

Rangers wrap up their first playoff series victory with a loss, 4-2 to Pittsburgh at the Garden. The Blueshirts take this first-round, two-game, total-goals series, 6-4, on the strength of an opening-game 4-0 win over the Pirates at the Garden March 27.

1929

In the first meeting in the Stanley Cup final between two American-based teams and the first Cup final game ever played at the Garden, Bill Carson's goal with 1:58 left in the third period gives Boston a 2-1 win over the Rangers and a two-game sweep of their best-of-three final. Carson is set up by Harry Oliver, who scored Boston's first goal.

1938

Til Huston dies on Butler Island, Georgia, at age 71. Colonel Tillinghast L'Hommedieu Huston and Jake Ruppert bought the Yankees in 1915 and were co-owners until Ruppert bought out Huston's interest in 1922.

1945

Knicks guard and captain Walt Frazier is born in Atlanta, Georgia. A four-time first-team All-Star and a seven-time selection on the All-Defensive team, Frazier retired as the Knicks' all-time leading scorer, with a 19.3 ppg average over 10 seasons (1967-77). He later became a lyrical Knicks broadcaster.

WALT FRAZIER

1951

Jerry Travers dies at 63 in East Hartford, Connecticut. Travers, one of America's finest golfers before World War I, won the Metropolitan Amateur title five times (1906-07, 1911-13) and the U.S. Open in 1915. He was a four-time U.S. Amateur champion and his legendary battles with Walter Travis helped popularize the sport.

1951

Hardy Astrom is born in Skelleftea, Sweden. Astrom went 2-2 in his only four games as Rangers goalie, but one of them, a 6-3 victory in Montreal February 25, 1978, snapped the Canadiens' 28-game unbeaten streak, then longest in NHL history.

1959

Findlay S. Douglas dies at age 83 in New York. Douglas won the U.S. Amateur in 1898 and the Metropolian Amateur in 1901 and 1903. He later served as president of the Metropolitan Golf Association (1921-25) and the USGA (1929-30).

1982

Amado Credidio, Jr., is killed at age 24 after being thrown from his mount, Spartan Monk, in the ninth race at Aqueduct Racetrack. The Panamanian-born jockey is the 113th rider killed in on-track accidents in the U.S. since 1940.

March 30

1883

Famed NYU track and field coach Emil von Elling is born in New York.

1889

John B. Day's Manhattan Exhibition Company offers to contribute $10,000 to charity if the city council will leave the Polo Grounds undisturbed until October. Day writes to Mayor Hugh Grant, but Grant and the Council reject the request and order a street cut into the property at 110th Street and 5th Avenue.

1892

Floyd Bostwick Odlum is born in Union City, Michigan. Odlum, a lawyer with the New York law firm of Simpson, Thacher & Bartlett from 1917-20 and president of Atlas Corporation, an investment company, in 1933 organized a group that took over Madison Square Garden and returned it to profitability during the Great Depression. He replaced Colonel John S. Hammond with Colonel John Reed Kilpatrick as Garden president.

1919

Ossie Schectman, LIU guard and original Knick (1946), is born in Kew Gardens, N.Y.

1921

Newark, which lost two International League teams in the previous six years, gains one when the Akron, Ohio, franchise moves there, where it will remain until the end of the 1949 season.

1943

Wyoming defeats Georgetown, 46-34, in the final of the first of seven NCAA basketball championships to be held at the Garden.

1944

Utah, the NCAA champ, beats St. John's, the NIT winner, 44-36, in a benefit game at the Garden that generates over $48,000 for the Red Cross War Relief Fund.

1975

Marie Wagner, winner of six U.S. national indoor singles tennis titles at the 7th Regiment Armory (1908-09, 1911, 1913-14, 1917), dies in Freeport, N.Y., at age 88.

1979

Conditional NHL franchises are awarded to four WHA teams subject to a merger agreement ending the competition between the two leagues. On June 22, the four (Edmonton Oilers, Quebec Nordiques, Hartford Whalers, Winnipeg Jets) are admitted to the NHL and allowed to protect a limited number of players. The WHA ceases to function and all remaining WHA players return to their original NHL teams (if any) or go into a common draft pool.

1985

In their fourth meeting of the season, Georgetown tops St. John's, 77-59, in the semifinals of the NCAA basketball tournament at Lexington, Kentucky. The Redmen had eliminated Arkansas, Kentucky and North Carolina State in their three prior tournament games. Two days later, Villanova (a semifinal loser to St. John's in the Big East tournament) upsets the defending champion Hoyas, 66-64, to win the NCAA title.

March 31

1879

Completing a home-and-home sweep, the Brooklyn Gun Club defeats the Social Gun & Rifle Club of Philadelphia, 107-103, in a clay pigeon shoot at Riverton, N.J. The 10-man teams take 15 shots per man with James Bryer and William Wynne each hitting 14 of 15 for Brooklyn.

1881

John L. Sullivan, the first heavyweight champ to appear regularly in New York, makes his first New York appearance with a two-round win over Steve Taylor at Harry Hill's Hotel. Sullivan, who became the champion in 1882, earns $750 this night.

1911

Featherweight champ Abe Attell pounds Frankie Burns in a 10-round bout at the National Sporting Club, decking Burns for nine-counts in each of the last two rounds. Attell, featherweight king from 1906-12, finishes the fight despite an injured left shoulder that makes him, in effect, a one-armed boxer. This bout is the only fight from January 31 to September 20 for Attell, who averaged 15 matches a year over the previous three years.

1929

John Salvo of Passaic, N.J., along with hundreds of other competitors, starts out from New York in C.C. Pyle's cross-country run (known as the "Bunion Derby"). Salvo will set a record for the event by finishing in Los Angeles on June 16 after running 3,610 miles in 525 hours, 57 minutes, 20 seconds.

1946

Tony Kappen's 21 points lift the Gothams to a 66-60 exhibition win over Paterson in the team's final game at the St. Nicholas Arena. For the 1946-47 season, the Gothams shift to Brooklyn and remain in the ABL for three more seasons before succumbing to the Knicks' dominance of the pro basketball market in the city.

1962

Hunter's Larry Yellin pitches eight innings of no-hit ball but gives up two singles in the ninth as Bridgeport, aided by a Hunter error, scores twice for a 2-0 win at Hunter. Yellin fans 12 and walks none but is outpitched by Bridgeport's Mike McLanglin, who throws a no-hitter and fans 14, although he issues six walks.

1962

New York Tapers are eliminated in the ABL semifinals, bowing to the eventual league champion Cleveland Pipers, 107-84, in Kansas City. This one-game playoff sets up a Pipers-Kansas City final won by Cleveland, three games to two. The Tapers reached the semis with a 125-116 overtime win over Hawaii at Pittsburgh March 29 and a 115-108 upset of the Chicago Majors at Cleveland March 30. In the loss to Cleveland, New York's top scorer, Dan Swartz, is ejected with 8:53 left in the third quarter when he slugs the Pipers' Jim Darrow with a right hook, scoring a one-punch KO. In the basketball portion of the evening, Dick Barnett leads Cleveland with 25 points while Cy Blye has 26 and Roger Kaiser 16 for the Tapers.

1965

For only the third time since 1923, a team wins the IFA title without winning any individual weapon. Columbia scores 71 three-weapon wins to NYU's 68 and Penn's 65 in the two-day competition at Columbia. Penn wins "The Little Iron Man," the oldest continuous college sports trophy in the nation (1894), by capturing the foil team title. NYU's Howie Goodman wins the individual sabre crown.

1980

Track great Jesse Owens, 66, winner of four gold medals at the Berlin Olympics (1936) and the 60-yard dash at the Millrose Games at the Garden in 1935, dies in Tucson, Arizona.

April 1

1898

Joseph Alexander, the first player ever signed by the Football Giants (1925), their player-coach in 1926 and center on the 1927 NFL champs, is born in Silver Creek, N.Y.

1907

Maureen Orcutt is born in New York. Orcutt won the Metropolitan Amateur golf title 10 times over a period of 42 years (1926-68) and the Eastern Amateur seven times. She was also a sportswriter for the *World, Evening Journal* and *Times* from 1937-72.

1921

Sidney Walker is born in Augusta, Georgia. As Beau Jack, he was twice lightweight champion (1941-42, 1943-44), and fought more Garden main events (22) than any other boxer.

1952

Caterpillar Diesels of Peoria, Illinois, the AAU champions, win the Olympic Trials tournament final by beating NCAA champion Kansas, 62-60, on Howie Williams' layup in the final seconds at the Garden, giving the Peoria Cats the lion's share of berths on the U.S. Olympic team that wins the gold medal at the Helsinki Games that summer.

MAUREEN ORCUTT

1966

Commissioner Spike Eckert draws a "Mets" slip out of a hat and Tom Seaver, to become the greatest pitcher in club history, is awarded to the team for $50,000. Only the Mets, Philadelphia and Cleveland entered the drawing after Eckert ruled that Seaver's signing by Atlanta was illegal, as it occurred after the start of the college season.

1972

A baseball strike that leads to improved funding for the players' pension fund begins as spring training ends. Settled April 13, the walkout costs 86 games (six for the Mets and seven for the Yankees). Play resumes April 15, but the labor-owner warfare that will dog the sport for more than two decades has just begun.

1977

New York Nets play their final NBA game at Nassau Coliseum, losing to the Indiana Pacers, 89-88, before 8,782. The Nets move to New Jersey during the off-season.

1989

For the third straight year, Columbia wins the NCAA fencing title, with 88 points in the three-day tournament at Evanston, Illinois. Defender John Normile leads the Lions by winning the individual epee competition again. The championship is the ninth outright for Columbia, who twice (1954, '71) tied NYU for first.

1992

NHL Players Association calls the first general in-season strike in NHL history. The season resumes April 12.

1996

Tony Delk scores 24 points and Ron Mercer 20 as Kentucky wins its sixth NCAA title (first since 1978), beating Syracuse, 76-67, at the Continental Air Arena before 19,229 in East Rutherford, N.J. John Wallace leads the Orangemen with a game-high 29 points and 10 rebounds.

1921

In the first brother-versus-brother national championship tennis final ever, Frank Anderson defeats his elder, Fred, 6-2, 6-1, 6-3, for the U.S. indoor title at the 7th Regiment Armory.

1939

For the third time in the series, Mel Hill scores in overtime to beat the Rangers. Earning the nickname "Sudden Death," Hill scores at 8:00 of the third overtime at the Boston Garden to give the Bruins, the eventual Cup champions, a 2-1 win and the series, the first best-of-seven series in Stanley Cup history, four games to three. New York forced a seventh game by winning three in a row after dropping the first three. It is Lester Patrick's last game as Rangers coach.

1954

Pudge Heffelfinger, a three-time Yale All-America guard (1889-91) and the first openly pro football player, dies in Blessing, Texas, at age 86. Heffelfinger was considered by his contemporaries the greatest guard in football history.

1956

In the 98th consecutive and last Monday night fight program presented by Tex Sullivan's London Sporting Club at St. Nicholas Arena, Brooklyn middleweight Hardy (Bazooka) Smallwood wins a unanimous 10-round decision over Mexico's Gaspar Ortega (see Jan. 3 and Mar. 27).

1969

Willis Reed sets a team playoff record with 43 points as the Knicks, third in the Eastern Division in the regular season, finish a four-game sweep in the first round of the NBA playoffs with a 115-108 Garden win over the division champion Baltimore Bullets.

1970

Willis Reed has 36 points and 36 rebounds as the Knicks blast the Bullets, 101-80, at the Garden, to take a three-games-to-two first-round NBA playoff series lead.

1972

On the last day of the regular season, Vic Hadfield scores two goals, the second in the third period, as the Rangers bow to the Montreal Canadiens, 6-5, at the Garden. The left wing ends the campaign with 50 goals (the first Ranger to reach that milestone), 56 assists and 106 points, all figures that would prove to be career highs by far.

1993

Pierre Turgeon's 50th goal of the season, at 3:41 of overtime, lifts the Islanders to a 3-2 victory over the Rangers at the Garden, boosting the Isles' playoff qualification chances and severely crippling those of the Blueshirts.

1994

Rangers, with four second-period goals, erase a 2-0 deficit and beat the Devils, 4-2, at the Meadowlands to extend their lead in the race for the NHL's best overall record to four points over New Jersey. It is the visitors' sixth win in six meetings on the season with the Devils.

WILLIS REED

1896

Hockey Club of New York defeats the St. Nicholas Hockey Club, 4-2, at the St. Nick's Rink. The HCNY, New York's first organized hockey team, was formed by Canadians living in New York who largely contented themselves with intramural matches on natural surfaces until the opening of the St. Nicholas Rink (see Mar. 24) created the momentum for the first hockey league to be formed in the United States.

1896

The national court tennis championship at the Racquet & Tennis Club is won by L.M. Stockton of Boston, who defeats E.A. Thomson of New York, 6-4, 6-2, 6-2.

1938

In the third and deciding game of their Stanley Cup semifinal series, Chicago beats the Americans, 3-2, at the Garden. It is the closest the Amerks will ever come to the Stanley Cup final. The Blackhawks go on to win the championship.

1948

City College, led by foil champion Robert Axelrod, wins the NCAA fencing championship at Annapolis, Maryland.

1957

Knicks trade veteran forwards Nat (Sweetwater) Clifton and Harry Gallatin, and guard Dick Atha, to Detroit for forwards Mel Hutchins and Charlie Tyra.

1962

Benny (Kid) Paret, the welterweight champion who lost his title to Emile Griffith March 24 at the Garden, dies of his injuries at age 25.

1969

Max Hirsch dies in New Hyde Park, N.Y., at age 88. A thoroughbred trainer for 60 years (1908-68), Hirsch trained 1,933 winners, including 1946 Triple Crown champion Assault.

FRED CAPOSSELA

1988

On the last night of the season with the Rangers and Devils tied for the last playoff spot, the Rangers score three third-period goals to beat Quebec, 3-0, at the Garden. Needing a win to qualify for their first-ever berth, the Devils, in a game starting an hour later in Chicago, wait until overtime when John MacLean's goal at 2:21 of the five-minute session puts the Devils in, 4-3. New Jersey 7-0-1's spurt catches the Rangers, whose 8-3-2 close is not enough.

1989

Seton Hall comes within a single basket of the NCAA basketball title but loses, 80-79, to Michigan in overtime at Seattle. John Morton scores a game-high 35 for the Pirates and the loss leaves P.J. Carlesimo's club with a 31-7 record.

1991

Famed thorougbred racing announcer Fred Capossela ("It is now post time") dies in Upland, California, at age 88.

1900

Edgar William Garbisch, a three-time All-American football player at Army and captain of the 1924 Cadets team, is born in Indiana.

1905

Tony Manero, 1936 U.S. Open golf champion at Baltusrol when he shot a then-record 282, is born in New York.

1921

Ed (Strangler) Lewis defends his world heavyweight wrestling title by pinning John Pesek in 1:34:32 at the 71st Regiment Armory.

1924

Gilbert Raymond Hodges, slugging first baseman for the Brooklyn Dodgers, an original Met in 1962, and manager of the 1969 Miracle Mets, is born in Princeton, Indiana.

1941

Lou Nova knocks out former heavyweight champion Max Baer in the eighth round of the first boxing match televised from the Garden. It is the second time Nova has KO'd Baer and it is also the final fight of the ex-champ's career.

1948

Werner Roth is born in Bosnia, Yugoslavia. A Pratt graduate, Roth was a Cosmos defender from 1972-79 and captain of the 1977 and 1978 NASL champions. At his retirement, he had played 123 games, a club record.

1975

With a 3-2 victory at Atlanta, the Rangers assure themselves of a Stanley Cup playoff berth for the ninth straight year and put the three-year-old Islanders in for the first time ever.

1977

In their first game ever at Giants Stadium, the Cosmos trounce Victory of Haiti, 9-0, as Giorgio Chinaglia scores four goals, Pele two and Tony Field, Terry Garbett and Jomo Sono one each. In the opener of the "Cosmos' Tournament of Champions" doubleheader, Tampa Bay beats Toronto's Metro-Croatia, 1-0, in a shootout (1-0), before only 7,212.

1987

Denis Potvin becomes the first defenseman in NHL history to notch 1,000 career points as the Islanders tie Buffalo, 6-6, at Nassau Coliseum.

WERNER ROTH

1995

Dale Hopp, an end for the Columbia football team from 1951-53, dies in Greenwich, Connecticut, at age 62.

1891

Alfred J. Goullet, greatest six-day bike racer of his time (1910s and 1920s), is born in Emu, Australia.

1898

Henry Dehnert is born in New York. Dutch Dehnert was a star center with the Original Celtics in the 1920s when the team dominated professional basketball.

1913

With 21 delegates and 30 observers from virtually every major soccer organization and club meeting at the Astor House, the U.S. Football Association is formed. This ends the rivalry of the mainly-pro American Football Association (AFA) and the American Amateur Football Association (AAFA), and leads to full international recognition of U.S. soccer. At a meeting June 21 at the Broadway Central Hotel, Dr. G.R. Manning, former AFA head, is elected president of the organization that in 1945 puts "soccer" in the title to become the USSFA.

1941

Edward Baker Talcott, Giants principal owner with partner C.C. Van Cott (1893-94) and president before the team's 1895 sale to Andrew Freedman, dies in Point Pleasant Beach, N.J., at 83.

PIERRE TURGEON

1947

In their first playoff game at the Garden, the Knicks beat Cleveland, 86-74, evening their first-round best-of-three series at a game apiece. In the deciding game, April 9 at the 69th Regiment Armory, the Knicks win again, 93-71, to take the series.

1970

Trailing Montreal by two points in the East Division for the final Stanley Cup playoff berth entering the last day of the season, the Rangers fire a club-record 65 shots at the Red Wings goal and defeat Detroit, 9-5. That night, the Canadiens, needing at least a tie or five goals in a loss, bow at Chicago, 10-2, allowing New York to qualify. The spectacle of the Rangers pulling their goalie with a 9-3 lead in an effort to score more goals coupled with the Canadiens pulling their goalie facing a 5-2 deficit leads the NHL to abolish its rules specifying total goals scored as a criterion to determine playoff qualification if teams finish with identical records.

1991

P.J. Boatwright, who succeeded Joseph C. Dey as executive director of the United States Golf Association in 1969, dies in Morristown, N.J., at age 63.

1995

Islanders acquire former Devils and present Canadiens captain Kirk Muller, defenseman Mathieu Schneider and center Craig Darby from Montreal for center Pierre Turgeon and defenseman Vladimir Malakhov. Muller's refusal to sign a new contract, owing to his unwillingness to participate in the Isles' rebuilding scheme, creates tension in the organization that contributes to Don Maloney's dismissal as general manager (see Dec. 2).

1878

What is thought to be the first gloved boxing bout under Marquis of Queensberry Rules in New York sees W.H. McClellan win over Mike Donovan on a foul in round 16. Donovan, later longtime NYAC boxing coach, wins the rematch May 18 (and a $500 purse) when McClellan cannot answer for the eighth round. Donovan's son, Arthur, becomes a famous boxing referee and his grandson, Arthur Jr., an All-Pro tackle with the NFL champion Baltimore Colts.

1910

James McDermott is born in New York. Jimmy McDermott was the basketball coach at Iona for 26 seasons (1947-73), compiling a record of 319-253 (.558).

1940

New York's West Side YMCA team wins the AAU national wrestling championship, thanks to Henry Wittenberg's victory in the 174-pound class, at Ames, Iowa. West Side has nine points overall (with Wittenberg as its only individual champ), the Baltimore YMCA has eight and host Iowa State College finishes with six.

1943

Carl Ford Lockhart is born in Dallas, Texas. Spider Lockhart was a free safety for the Football Giants from 1965-75.

1950

Chuck Rayner posts the only playoff shutout of his Rangers career as the Blueshirts beat the Canadiens, 3-0, at Montreal, to take their Stanley Cup semifinal series, four games to one.

1955

Francis X. McQuade, 78, former city magistrate and Giants treasurer, dies in New York.

1967

In their first playoff game in five years, the Rangers blow a 4-1 third-period lead and lose to the Canadiens, 6-4, at Montreal.

1972

Chick Wergeles, fight manager of, among others, Beau Jack, dies at 81 in New York.

1982

A spring blizzard buries New York and causes the postponement of the Yankees' opening game against Texas. Snow drifts covering Yankee Stadium prevent games until Easter Sunday, April 11, when the Yankees finally open by dropping a doubleheader to the Chicago White Sox.

1988

In their first Stanley Cup playoff game, the Devils lose, 4-3, to the Islanders at Nassau Coliseum on Pat LaFontaine's goal at 6:11 of overtime.

BEAU JACK

1991

In the home opener for the WLAF New York-New Jersey Knights, 36,546 show up on this Saturday night at Giants Stadium, but quarterback Mike Perez throws three scoring passes to lead the Frankfurt (Germany) Galaxy to a 27-17 victory.

1917

A fire at Belmont Park causes over $1,000,000 in damage but news coverage is minimal because the United States entered World War I the day before.

1923

Vinnie Richards defeats Frank Hunter, 6-1, 6-3, 7-5, to win the national indoor tennis title at the 7th Regiment Armory with a record 5,000 fans on hand.

1928

In the second period of the scoreless second Stanley Cup final game, Montreal Maroons forward Nels Stewart's shot hits Rangers goalie Lorne Chabot in the eye, knocking him out of the game. Maroons coach Eddie Gerard refuses permission to use a pro goalie in attendance at the Montreal Forum, so 44-year-old Rangers coach Lester Patrick dons the pads. The inspired Rangers win in overtime, 2-1, on Frank Boucher's goal, evening the series. The NHL then adopts the "house goalie" rule requiring the presence of a substitute netminder in case either starter is injured. Meanwhile, the Rangers, playing all final games at the Forum, the circus having forced them from the Garden, use former Americans goalie Joe Miller for the next three games (see Apr. 14).

HIRSCH JACOBS

1932

With Garden ice unavailable because of the circus, the Rangers elect to play the second game of the Stanley Cup final against Toronto at the Boston Garden. The setting doesn't help as the Maple Leafs paste New York, 6-2, to take a 2-0 series lead.

1944

Inglis M. Uppercu, once the major Cadillac-LaSalle auto dealer in New York, dies in Manhattan at age 66. Uppercu was an auto race driver in the Vanderbilt Cup events on Long Island and a promoter of bicycle racing during the sport's heyday.

1951

Led by MVP Sol Walker and center Ray Felix, Carlton Branch becomes Brooklyn's second national YMCA champion in three years, winning the tournament hosted by Boston's Huntington Avenue "Y," beating Buffalo (N.Y.) Downtown, 88-62, in the title game.

1966

Joe Foss resigns as AFL commissioner. The next day, Oakland Raiders general manager and head coach Al Davis is named to succeed him, indicating that the upstart league prefers conflict to accommodation with the NFL (see June 8).

1977

For the second time this year, apprentice jockey Steve Cauthen rides six winners in a nine-race card at Aqueduct. Cauthen also rode six winners January 7. The trick had last been turned by Angel Cordero, Jr. (March 12, 1975). Cauthen leads the nation with 487 winners for the year.

1983

Nets coach Larry Brown is forced to resign with six games remaining in the season. Brown had accepted the head coaching job at Kansas and agreed to finish the season, but Nets officials rejected the offer.

1899

Veteran walker Peter Hegelman wins the 24-hour professional walking race at the Grand Central Palace (120 miles) with John A. Glick second (113) and James M. Dean third (107).

1904

Hirsch Jacobs, trainer of 3,596 thoroughbred winners during his career and the nation's leading trainer (measured by winners) 11 times in 14 years from 1933-46, is born in New York.

1922

Jay Gould defends his U.S. court tennis championship with a 6-2, 6-1, 6-0 victory over Hewitt Morgan at the Racquet and Tennis Club in New York. Gould, a grandson of the famed railroad magnate, holds the title from 1906-25 and is world champion from 1914-22.

1946

James Augustus Hunter is born in Hertford, North Carolina. Righty Catfish Hunter, the 1974 Cy Young Award winner, joined the Yankees as the first celebrated baseball free agent Dec. 31, 1974 (though his signing preceded the general player emancipation—see Dec. 23) and won a league-leading 23 games for the Bombers in 1975.

1964

Jack Fugazy, a promoter of boxing title fights at both the Polo Grounds and Ebbets Field who retired in 1931 and came out of retirement by 1950, and who once planned to build a huge boxing arena in Manhattan, dies in New York at age 79.

1971

For the first time, gambling in New York on horse and harness races at locations other than the racetracks is legal, as the first Off-Track Betting shops open, accepting wagers on racing from Roosevelt Raceway.

1979

In the season finale, Mike Bossy scores his 69th goal, the second-highest total yet in NHL history, as the Islanders beat the Rangers, 5-2, at the Garden. With Montreal losing to Detroit, the Isles win their first regular-season league championship by one point.

1980

Steve Vickers chips in a short backhand 33 seconds into overtime for the fastest Stanley Cup playoff goal ever by a Ranger as the Blueshirts beat Atlanta, 2-1, in the opener of their opening-round playoff series. Vickers also scores the tying goal in the third period. It is the Rangers' first Garden win over the Flames since March 30, 1977 (0-7-2).

1982

Mikko Leinonen sets an NHL record with six assists in a playoff game as the Rangers beat Philadelphia, 7-3, at the Garden to even their first-round series at 1-1.

1985

J. Fred Coots, composer of the "Rangers Fight Song" (as well as "Santa Claus is Coming to Town"), dies in New York at age 87.

1997

Tampa Bay's Jason Wiemer scores on a deflection at 11:43 of the second period to end Devils goalie Martin Brodeur's attempt at a fourth straight shutout. New Jersey scores once in the third to gain a 2-2 road tie, but Brodeur's shutout streak ends at 2:13:52.

1898

Paul Robeson, an All-America end at Rutgers in 1917-18 and later a controversial actor and political activist, is born in Princeton, N.J.

1912

Joseph Frederick Cullman, III, is born. A Yale graduate, Joe Cullman was chairman of the U.S. Open tennis championships at Forest Hills in 1969 and 1970.

LEO DUROCHER

1913

In the first regular-season game at Ebbets Field, Philadelphia scores off Nap Rucker in the first inning and wins, 1-0, as Tom Seaton throws a six-hitter. The Dodgers had beaten the Yankees, 3-2, in an exhibition game April 5 when writers discover the new park had no press box.

1932

In the finale of what came to be known as the "Tennis Series," Toronto beats the Rangers, 6-4, at Maple Leaf Gardens to complete a sweep of the Stanley Cup final series, 3-0, winning the three games 6-4, 6-2, 6-4.

1943

Charles S. Mercein, Yale and Football Giants fullback, is born in Milwaukee, Wisconsin.

1947

Dodgers manager Leo Durocher is suspended for one season by baseball commissioner A.B. (Happy) Chandler for "an accumulation of unpleasant incidents detrimental to baseball." Durocher's most recent offenses relate to his alleged consorting with known gamblers during Brooklyn's spring training in Havana, Cuba.

1956

In the first card presented by Teddy Brenner's New York Boxing Club Inc. at the St. Nick's Arena, unbeaten middleweight Rory Calhoun of White Plains, N.Y., scores a unanimous 10-round decision over Jackie LaBua of East Meadow, N.Y. The crowd of 1,800, the largest at St. Nick's in three years, generates a gross gate of $3,652.

1971

Will Harridge, secretary to American League president Ban Johnson from 1911-27 and president of the league from 1931-59, dies in Evanston, Illinois, at age 89.

1993

Pittsburgh's Mario Lemieux scores five goals as the Penguins embarrass the Rangers, 10-4, at the Garden, to post their NHL-record 16th straight win. The Devils finally end the streak at 17 at the Meadowlands April 14, holding on for a 6-6 tie.

1993

Abie Bain dies in Ormond Beach, Florida, at age 86. Bain fought over 100 pro bouts as a middleweight and light heavyweight from 1924-34 and was later an actor in "Requiem for a Heavyweight" and technical advisor for many films about boxing.

1994

Associated Press sportswriter Jim Donaghy dies in New York at age 37.

April 10

1859
America's first championship billiards match for which admission is charged and the public admitted is staged at Fireman's Hall in New York. Dudley Kavanagh defeats Michael Foley of Detroit for a side bet of $750.

1880
Frank Hart wins the sixth international walking match at the Garden, hoofing a record 565 miles in 142 hours to become the second holder of the O'Leary Championship belt. Hart also collects $7,175 as the winner's share of the $28,683 gate money, the $9,000 in entry fees, and a $1,000 bonus for setting a world record. The next seven finishers divide $21,508.

1885
Willie Donovan, winner of the first six-day roller-skating race at the Garden, dies at 8:00 a.m. at the Putnam House hotel in New York (see Mar. 7).

1896
New Britain (Connecticut) YMCA, the New England champions, scores a 5-2 victory over the Brooklyn Central YMCA basketball team in Brooklyn.

1916
Jim Barnes wins the first championship of the recently-organized Professional Golfers Association at the Siwanoy course in Bronxville, N.Y. (see Jan. 17).

1951
Mark Roth is born in Brooklyn. One of the first hard-throwing bowlers who now dominate the pro ranks, Roth in 1984 became the second PBA bowler to earn more than $1,000,000 in prize money.

1953
Despite a game-high 19 points by Carl Braun, the Minneapolis Lakers beat the Knicks, 91-84, at the 69th Regiment Armory to win the NBA final in five games. It is the third straight loss in the final for the Knicks, and they will not reach that round again for 17 years.

1972
Nets (44-40 during the regular season) complete their upset of the 68-16 Colonels by beating Kentucky, 101-96, before 11,533 at Nassau Coliseum to take their first-round ABA playoff series, four games to two.

1984
Ken Morrow's goal at 8:56 of overtime gives the Islanders a 3-2 win over the Rangers in the fifth and decisive game of their first-round playoff series at Nassau Coliseum. The Rangers force overtime with 39 seconds remaining in the third period when Don Maloney swats a high rebound past Islander goalie Billy Smith.

1988
Brent Sutter scores a shorthanded overtime goal, second in NHL playoff history, at 15:07 of the extra session, as the Islanders beat the Devils, 5-4, at the Meadowlands, to tie their first-round Stanley Cup playoff series, two games each.

1992
After 10 days, the first league-wide NHL players' strike ends with players getting a slight improvement in free agency rights and a substantial boost in the rookie salary minimum (up to $100,000 from $25,000). Games resume April 12 and the season ends April 16 with the Rangers (105) the only team to finish with more than 100 points.

1920

Andrew Levane is born in Brooklyn. A guard on the St. John's NIT champions of 1943, Fuzzy Levane was the Knicks' fourth coach.

1936

Dr. Harry March, long associated with the Football Giants, announces the formation of a new AFL after two days of meetings at the Hotel Biltmore. Franchises are granted to New York; Boston; Providence; Syracuse; Cleveland; Pittsburgh; and Philadelphia. By the time play begins in September, Providence and Philadelphia have dropped out.

1940

Defenseman Muzz Patrick's goal at 11:43 of the second overtime gives the Rangers a 2-1 win over Toronto at Maple Leaf Gardens and a three-games-to-two lead in the Stanley Cup final series.

1948

Dr. Jock Sutherland, famous coach of Lafayette (1919-23), the University of Pittsburgh (1924-38) and the Pittsburgh Steelers (1939-40), who coached the NFL Brooklyn Football Dodgers for two seasons (1941-42), dies in Pittsburgh, Pennsylvania, at age 59.

1950

World pocket billiards champion Andrew Ponzi dies in Philadelphia, Pennsylvania, at age 47.

1970

In a turbulent game marked by goalie Eddie Giacomin's first-period baiting of Bruins center Derek Sanderson before a faceoff that results in a melee when the puck drops, the Rangers beat Boston, 4-3, at the Garden, to narrow their Stanley Cup first-round playoff series deficit to 2-1 and end the Blueshirts' 10-game playoff losing streak, then an NHL record.

1975

J.P. Parise scores 11 seconds into overtime to give the upstart Islanders a 4-3 win over the established Rangers at the Garden in the third and decisive game of their first-round playoff series. The Rangers had rallied for three third-period goals to erase a 3-0 Islander lead. The win signals the ascendancy of the Islanders, in only their third year in the league, as the dominant local hockey team. The Rangers would miss the playoffs the next two seasons.

1979

In their third NBA season, the Nets play their first playoff game, losing, 122-114, at Philadelphia. The 76ers win two nights later at the Rutgers Athletic Center, 111-101, to take the series, two games to none.

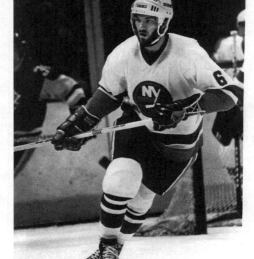

KEN MORROW

1980

Ken Morrow's goal at 6:55 of overtime gives the Islanders a 4-3 win over the Kings at Los Angeles and a two-games-to-one lead in their first-round best-of-five playoff series. Morrow's goal caps a comeback from a 3-1 deficit and is the first of six overtime wins (against one loss) the Isles will have in winning their first Stanley Cup.

1900

Joseph Bohomiel Lapchick, who played for the Original Celtics when they dominated pro basketball in the 1920s, and coached St. John's for 19 years from 1937-65 in two stints interrupted by a nine-year term as Knicks coach (1947-56), is born in Yonkers, N.Y.

1939

Lucien Fontaine, who drove 3,458 winners in 6,615 races and amassed over $21 million in career purse earnings, is born in Pointe aux Trembles, Quebec.

1960

Tomas Jonsson, a smooth defenseman on the Islanders' last two Stanley Cup champions (1982-83) who scored 333 points in 532 games with the Isles, is born in Falun, Sweden.

1968

Adam Graves, holder of the Rangers' single-season record for goals and inseparable from Mark Messier's left side during their six years together in New York, is born in Toronto, Ontario.

LUCIEN FONTAINE

1974

For the fifth time in six years, the Knicks knock the Bullets out of the playoffs, beating Capital (as the team is now called), 91-81, at the Garden, to take the series, four games to three.

1981

Heavyweight champ Joe Louis dies in Las Vegas, Nevada, at age 66. Louis held the world title for the longest uninterrupted stretch in heavyweight history (1937-49) before retiring.

1986

Within 38 seconds of the third period, the Rangers score three times (Jim Wiemer at 12:29, Bob Brooke at 12:43 and Ron Greschner at 13:07) to snap a 2-2 tie and beat Philadelphia, 5-2, for a 2-1 lead in a best-of-five first-round Stanley Cup playoff series.

1986

After rallying from a two-games-to-none deficit against the Caps a year before to win their first-round best-of-five series (see Apr. 16), the Islanders find themselves in the same predicament. But this time, there is no rebound as Washington closes out the Isles, 3-1, at Nassau Coliseum. It is the first time the Islanders have not won a game in a playoff series, and is the last game of coach Al Arbour's first term.

1988

Karol Kristin Fageros Short dies in South Miami, Florida, at age 53. Karol Fageros was a modestly talented tennis player in the 1950s who parlayed good looks and gold lame underwear into a sizeable reputation on the international circuit.

1989

Sugar Ray Robinson, five-time middleweight champ and considered by many the best fighter, "pound-for-pound," in boxing history, dies in Culver City, California, at age 68.

1995

Dorothy Wise, U.S. Open women's billiards champion from 1967-71, dies at age 80.

1903

Norman Himes, who played his entire nine-season career with the NHL Americans (1926-35), is born in Galt, Ontario. Himes led the Amerks in scoring four times.

1931

Auto racing great Daniel Sexton Gurney is born in Port Jefferson, N.Y. Gurney, ranked as high as sixth in the world in 1964, won the Manufacturers' 500 in New York in 1963 and the Bridgehampton (L.I.) segment of the Can-Am series in 1966.

1933

Bill Cook's power-play goal at 7:33 of overtime gives the Rangers a 1-0 win at Toronto and their second Stanley Cup. The Rangers take the best-of-five series, three games to one.

1940

Bryan Hextall scores at 2:07 of overtime to give the Rangers a 3-2 win over Toronto at Maple Leaf Gardens and the Stanley Cup. New York, which had erased a 2-0 third-period deficit, wins the series, four games to two.

1962

After losing April 11 in St. Louis and being greeted by Mayor Wagner the next day, the Mets play their first home opener ever on Friday the 13th at the Polo Grounds. Ray Daviault, the Mets' third pitcher, walks Dick Groat to open the eighth, wild pitches him to second and, after Groat goes to third on an infield out, wild pitches him home to give Pittsburgh 4-3 victory. A crowd of 12,447 pays to watch history on a dark, wet, chilly afternoon. Following seven more losses (nine in a row to start the season), the Mets finally win (9-1) at Pittsburgh April 23.

1982

In the fifth and deciding game of their first-round playoff series against the Penguins at Nassau Coliseum, the two-time-defending Stanley Cup champion Islanders, having blown a 2-0 series lead, trail Pittsburgh, 3-1. But Mike McEwen scores with 5:27 left in the third and John Tonelli ties it with 2:21 remaining. It seems inevitable that the Islanders will then win in overtime, and they do, Tonelli providing the coup de grace at 6:19.

DAN GURNEY

1994

Phil Fox, 80, a referee in the BAA (1946-49) and NBA (1949-51), dies in Brooklyn.

1996

MetroStars play their first Major League Soccer (MLS) match ever, losing, 2-1, at Los Angeles. The home opener is April 20 against the New England Revolution, a 1-0 loss caused when Nicola Caricola kicks the ball into his own net, startling MetroStars goalie Tony Meola and the Giants Stadium crowd of 46,826.

1996

In the season's denouement, the defending Stanley Cup champion Devils lose their finale, 5-2, to Ottawa at the Continental Air Arena and are eliminated from playoff contention despite a 37-33-12 record. New Jersey is the first Cup defender to miss the playoffs since 1969-70 (Montreal—see Apr. 5). Devils coach Jacques Lemaire was a center on that Canadiens team.

1890

Heavyweight contender James J. Corbett knocks out Dominic McCaffrey at 0:20 of the fourth round at the Brooklyn Casino in his first New York bout. "Gentleman Jim" had appeared at the New York Athletic Club, sparring three rounds with the club's boxing instructor, Mike Donovan, March 20.

1897

Thirty-two clubs gather to organize the Metropolitan Golf Association, which will have jurisdiction within 55 miles of New York. The meeting at Delmonico's Hotel elects H.B. Hollins as the organization's first president.

1900

Marvin Allen Stevens is born in Stockton, Kansas. Dr. Mal Stevens, a star on the undefeated Yale football team of 1923 (8-0), was the Bulldogs' head coach from 1928-32 (21-11-8), NYU coach from 1934-41 (33-34-2) and AAFC Brooklyn Football Dodgers coach in 1946 before being fired with a 2-4-1 record.

1911

Fire destroys the main grandstand at the Polo Grounds, leaving the Giants temporarily homeless. The Highlanders offer the use of Hilltop Park at 168th Street and Broadway until the Polo Grounds can be rebuilt. The offer eventually leads to the team soon to be known as the Yankees moving to the rebuilt Polo Grounds as a tenant in 1913.

JAMES J. CORBETT

1927

Don Mueller, .296 lifetime hitter who played 10 years for the Giants (1948-57), is born in St. Louis. Called "Mandrake the Magician" for his ability to hit 'em where they weren't, he led the National League in hits in 1954 (212) but lost the batting race to teammate Willie Mays (.345 to .342).

1928

Frank Boucher scores twice and the Rangers hold on to beat the Maroons, 2-1, at the Montreal Forum to take the Stanley Cup final series and their first Cup, three games to two.

1947

Martin F. Domres is born in Ithaca, N.Y. Domres set 15 school, 12 Ivy League and three ECAC records as Columbia quarterback (1966-68), and played one year (1977) for the Jets.

1967

Red Sox rookie Billy Rohr outpitches veteran Whitey Ford (and nearly hurls a no-hitter, allowing only an Elston Howard single with two out in the ninth) as Boston beats the Yankees, 3-0, in the Bombers' home opener. Organist Eddie Layton makes his Stadium debut.

1988

Devils complete their first-ever Stanley Cup playoff series with a 6-5 win over the Islanders at the Meadowlands to win the first-round matchup, four games to two.

1993

Rangers finish their home season with a second consecutive shutout loss, 2-0 to Washington, for their seventh straight home loss, tying a club record.

April 15

1883

Making their first appearance as a local team, the National League baseball club that will soon be known as the Giants defeat the AA Mets, 8-3, in an exhibition game at the Polo Grounds in 1:50. John Montgomery Ward outpitches the Mets' Tim Keefe as 5,584 curious fans look on.

1900

The first significant auto race in the U.S. is held at Springfield, L.I., and A.L. Riker wins it in his electric battery-powered car. Riker covers the 50-mile course in two hours, three minutes.

1915

Giants lefty Rube Marquard pitches a 2-0 no-hitter against Brooklyn at the Polo Grounds, but by the end of the season is traded to the Dodgers.

1937

Earl Robertson shuts the Rangers out for the second straight game as the Red Wings win the Stanley Cup for the second straight year, topping New York, 3-0, at Detroit, to take the final, three games to two.

1938

Bill Dwyer loses control of the Americans when his option to repurchase the team from the NHL expires. The league took over the club when Dwyer's financial difficulties, related to tax disputes with the IRS (which Dwyer ultimately loses), prevented him from operating it.

1951

Arthur Poe dies at 72. Poe, youngest of five brothers to play for Princeton over 19 years, was an end who as a junior in 1898 ran for a 95-yard touchdown to help beat Yale, 6-0, and as a senior in 1899 bedeviled the Bulldogs again with a 35-yard field goal for an 11-10 Tigers win.

1968

In the major leagues' longest 1-0 game to date, the Astros beat the Mets at the Astrodome in 24 innings with Les Rohr taking the loss and Wade Blasingame getting the win, both in relief.

1971

Bob Nevin scores 9:07 into overtime as the Rangers beat Toronto, 2-1, at Maple Leaf Gardens to take their first-round Stanley Cup playoff series, four games to two. It is the Blueshirts' first playoff series victory since the 1950 semifinals (0-9).

1976

Remodeled Yankee Stadium opens and 54,010 watch the Yankees wipe out a 4-0 deficit and beat the Twins, 11-4. Minnesota's Dan Ford belts the first Stadium homer.

1986

Bill McCarthy dies in Palm Beach, Florida, at age 91. McCarthy was NYU's baseball coach from 1922-61, compiling a 476-258-12 record with his teams winning the Metropolitan Conference championship nine times.

1998

Forced out of Yankee Stadium due to the falling of an expansion joint there two days earlier that causes temporary closure of the ballpark, the Yankees beat the Anaheim Angels, 6-3, at Shea Stadium. That evening, the Mets beat the Cubs, 2-1, also at Shea. The Bombers return to The Bronx Friday, April 24, after flipping weekend series with the Detroit Tigers.

1906

William John Peden is born in Victoria, British Columbia. Torchy Peden won three six-day bike races at the Garden in the 1930s, with three different partners.

1915

Baltimore's Terrapins defeat the Newark Peps, 6-2, in the Federal League opener at Harrison, N.J. (see Feb. 25). A crowd of 26,500 packs the new park and sees Newark Mayor Thomas L. Raymond and other dignitaries dedicate the building, home of New Jersey's first (and only) major league baseball team. Peps business manager Billy Murray introduces women ushers in the grandstand, a baseball first (see Oct. 3).

1938

Righthander Gene Bowe throws a three-hitter and strikes out 18 as host Fordham slugs Lehigh, 10-0. The Rams, 3-0 on the season, score five runs in the first inning.

1968

Paul J. Schissler, head coach of the Brooklyn Football Dodgers in 1935-36 (8-14-2) and in 1951 the founder of the "Pro Bowl" as a charity promotion for the *Los Angeles Times*, where he worked as director of special events, dies in Hastings, Nebraska, at age 74.

1974

Ron Harris scores 4:07 into overtime off a faceoff win by Pete Stemkowski to lift the Rangers to a 3-2 win over the Canadiens at Montreal and a 3-2 lead in their first-round playoff series. Bruce MacGregor scores twice for the Blueshirts, including the tying goal in the last minute of regulation with the goalie pulled.

1979

Joe King, a sportswriter who covered the Giants and Football Giants for the *World-Telegram* from the 1930s into the '60s, and who in 1967 helped organize the New York Professional Football Writers' Association, dies in Ridgewood, N.J., at age 70.

1980

Frank Crowley, a Manhattan College track and field star who was the NCAA two-mile champion in 1934, dies in Clarkston, Michigan, at age 70.

1983

Gus Mauch dies in St. Petersburg, Florida, at age 81. Mauch was a trainer of Manhattan College football, the Football Yankees, Football Giants, Yankees and Mets (including world championship teams with both baseball clubs).

GUS MAUCH

1985

Establishing another new standard of resilience, the Islanders beat the Washington Capitals, 2-1, at the Cap Centre, in the fifth game of their first-round Stanley Cup playoff series, to become the first NHL team to win a best-of-five series after losing the first two games.

1997

Susan Carolyn Dilley Regan, wife of former Athletic Director Richie Regan, is appointed Seton Hall AD for at least the next calendar year (see Mar. 10).

# April 17

1820

Alexander Joy Cartwright, a surveyor who established many of the modern rules of baseball, including 90 feet between bases, three outs to an inning and forcing runners at bases (rather than "soaking" runners between them), is born in New York. If any one person can be given credit for "inventing" baseball as we know it today, it is Cartwright.

1859

Walter Camp, the undisputed father of American football, is born in New Haven, Connecticut.

1890

Set up after the league champion Brooklyn club jumped to the National League, the new rival Brooklyn AA team opens its season with a 3-2 home loss at Ridgewood Park, often used by established teams to play Sunday games in an effort to avoid City of Brooklyn and New York "Blue Laws" that prevent games on the Christian Sabbath.

1913

Having accepted the Giants' offer to become tenants, the Yankees play their first game at the Polo Grounds but lose, 9-3, to Washington. The Yankees will remain in the Polo Grounds until the end of the 1922 season.

1915

Floyd MacFarland, 39, a former champion rider and manager of the Newark (N.J.) Velodrome, is killed when the concession manager, David Lantenberg, stabs him in the head with a screwdriver during an argument over posters the latter is mounting at the track. Lantenberg, charged with manslaughter, is acquitted in a Newark court June 23.

1938

Led by former NYU star guard Hagan Anderson, who has 10 points, the Jersey Reds win the ABL championship by edging the New York Jewels, 30-28, before 2,800 at Brooklyn's Arcadia Hall to take the final series, four games to two.

1951

Rookie Jackie Jensen's homer highlights the Yankees' 5-0 win over Boston as 44,860, the largest opening-day crowd since 1946, looks on at Yankee Stadium. Centerfielder Joe DiMaggio starts his final season in pinstripes, rightfielder Mickey Mantle plays the first of his 2,401 games as a Yankee and Bob Sheppard mans the public address mike for the first time, starting a career that will span more than four decades. Pfc. Edward Charles Ford throws out the first pitch.

1953

Batting righty, Mickey Mantle slams a two-run homer off the Senators' Chuck Stobbs that clears the leftfield bleachers at Washington's Griffith Stadium. Yankees publicist Red Patterson announces the ball traveled a measured distance of 565 feet.

1964

Bill Mazeroski's ninth-inning single off Ed Bauta drives in the tie-breaking run as the Pittsburgh Pirates beat the Mets, 4-3, in the opening game at Shea Stadium. The crowd of 50,312 includes 48,736 paying customers and an assortment of local dignitaries.

1995

Steve Lewis and Brian Fitzsimmons get three hits each as St. John's beats Iona, 15-6, at Redmen Field to give baseball coach Joe Russo his 600th career victory in 904 decisions. The win makes the Redmen 6-10 for the season.

April 18

1902

Jesse W. Sweetser is born in Cobb, Kentucky. Yale alumnus Sweetser won the intercollegiate golf championship in 1920, took two Metropolitan Amateurs (1922, '25), the U.S. Amateur in 1922 and in 1926 became the first American to win the British Amateur, then a major championship.

1923

Yankee Stadium, "The House That Ruth Built," opens and an announced crowd of 74,217 watches the Yankees beat the Red Sox, 4-1, on the strength of, fittingly, Babe Ruth's three-run homer in the third off Boston starter Howard Ehmke.

1923

Although he fans a school-record 17, Lou Gehrig's pitching gets mixed reviews as he allows eight hits, walks four, hits a batter, throws a wild pitch and commits an error as Columbia loses, 5-1, to Williams at South Field.

1925

Charles Ebbets, the president and principal owner of the Brooklyn Dodgers since 1897, dies in New York at 65.

1947

Former lightweight champion Benny Leonard, 51, dies in the ring at St. Nicholas Arena while refereeing a bout between Mario Roman of Mexico City and Harlem's Bobby Williams. Leonard collapses during the first round and is pronounced dead as a result of a cerebral hemorrhage by ring physician Dr. Vincent Nardiello at 10:55 p.m. Leonard had worked six preliminary fights on a hot night. Another referee is brought in for the night's main event, a 10-rounder matching lightweights Eddie Giosa and Julio Jiminez.

1951

Max Zaslofsky scores 23 points as the Knicks beat the Rochester Royals, 80-73, at the 69th Regiment Armory to tie the NBA final series three games each. Like their brethren, the Rangers, in 1939, the Knicks, in their first best-of-seven series, lose the first three games and then win the next three. And just like their brethren (see Apr. 2), they lose the seventh game (see Apr. 21) and never duplicate the feat of rallying to tie a playoff series after trailing 3-0.

1970

Denny Doyle's first-inning leadoff single is the only hit allowed by Nolan Ryan as the Mets beat Philadelphia, 7-0, at Shea Stadium.

1974

For the third straight year, the Rangers oust the defending Stanley Cup champs in the first round of the playoffs. As in 1972, Montreal is victimized, losing the sixth game of the series at the Garden, 5-2, after leading, 2-0, in the second period.

1984

After six straight losses (three series), the Nets, in their eighth NBA season, win a playoff game, beating the defending champion 76ers, 116-101, at Philadelphia, in the series opener.

1987

Pat LaFontaine ends the longest game in Islanders history with a goal at 8:47 of the fourth overtime at Washington's Capital Centre in Landover, Maryland. LaFontaine gives the Islanders a 3-2 win over the Capitals and a 4-3 series victory in the opening-round Stanley Cup series, which New York had trailed, 3-1.

1995

Brian Leetch sets a club record for assists in a game by a defenseman and ties his own club record for points in a game by a backliner as he gets assists on all five New York goals, but the Rangers lose, 6-5, at Pittsburgh.

April 19

1890
Brooklyn makes its National League debut and gets buried, 15-9, by Boston at Eastern Park, as pitcher Adonis Terry gets shelled (see Apr. 28).

1897
After journeying to Elizabeth, N.J., for an exhibition game, the Giants probably can't help wondering why. They win, 40-1, as George Van Haltren pounds out seven hits.

1908
Gordon Phelps is born in Odenton, Maryland. Babe Phelps was a catcher for the Brooklyn Dodgers from 1935-41.

1931
Alexander Webster is born in Kearny, N.J. Red Webster was a star running back for the Football Giants from 1955-64 and head coach from 1969-73 (29-40-1).

1944
Tommy Hitchcock, "the Babe Ruth of polo," dies in a military plane crash at age 44. Hitchcock gained the maximum rating of 10 goals every year but one from 1922-40 (in 1935 he was rated at nine goals) and helped popularize the sport, which was centered on Long Island.

1946
Jackie Robinson makes his professional baseball debut, playing for the Montreal Royals (a Brooklyn Dodgers farm club) at Jersey City. Robinson has four hits (including a homer) and scores four runs to lead the Royals to a 14-1 win over the Giants. The paid crowd is announced as 51,872 (about double the capacity of Roosevelt Stadium).

1956
In their first National League game at Jersey City's Roosevelt Stadium, the Dodgers beat the Phillies, 5-4, in 10 innings.

1960
Wilfred (Shorty) Green dies in Sudbury, Ontario, at age 63. Green, like his brother Red, was an original American in 1925-26, scoring eight goals in 32 games.

1971
Bullets dethrone the Knicks, taking the seventh game of their NBA semifinal playoff series, 93-91, at the Garden. Baltimore center Wes Unseld tips Bill Bradley's last-second shot.

1971
Russ Hodges, 59, play-by-play announcer for the Yankees (1946-48) and Giants (1949-57), whose uncharacteristically emotional "The Giants win the pennant!" call in reporting the Bobby Thomson home run (see Oct. 3) became a part of baseball lore, dies in Mill Valley, California.

1984
Bernard King sets a club playoff record with 46 points, including 23 in a row in the first quarter, but the Knicks lose at Detroit, 113-105, to square their first-round playoff series 1-1. In the next game (Apr. 22), King matches his point total in a 120-113 Knicks win over the Pistons at the Garden.

1878

Cyrille Dion is the winner of the Grand National Tournament of 15-ball billiards at the Union Square Billiard Rooms. Sweden's Gottlieb Wahlstrom is second in the international field that includes such champions as George Slosson, Joseph Dion, William Sexton, Clark Wilson, A.P. Rudolph and George Frey.

1908

Henry Chadwick dies in Brooklyn at age 83. A longtime sportswriter, Chadwick, known as "Father Baseball," invented the baseball boxscore and was a relentless partisan of the sport and its foremost historian.

1928

Dominic (Dom) Alagia is born in Union City, N.J. He announced St. Peter's college basketball games (1960-78) and also worked at minor-league baseball, NFL football and Meadowlands Arena college basketball games, in addition to Army football and other New York-area events.

DOM ALAGIA

1930

Alex Smith, long-time golf professional at the Westchester Country Club, dies at age 58 in Baltimore, Maryland. Smith won the 1906 U.S. Open in Lake Forest, Illinois, while serving as the pro at the Nassau Country Club and the 1910 Open at Philadelphia while the pro at Wykagyl in New Rochelle, N.Y. He was also considered one of golf's great coaches, tutoring such stars as Jerry Travers, Marion Hollins and Glenna Collett.

1950

Rangers center Don Raleigh does it again. His overtime goal (his second in as many games) at 1:38 gives the Rangers a 2-1 victory over the Red Wings at Detroit and a 3-2 series lead in the Stanley Cup final.

1967

Tom Seaver pitches a 6-1 win for the Mets over the Chicago Cubs at Shea Stadium for his first major league victory. Seaver finishes the year 16-13 and becomes the first National League Rookie of the Year ever selected from a last-place team.

1970

Posting the biggest margin of victory in the team's playoff history, the Knicks wallop Milwaukee, 132-96, at the Garden, to take their semifinal matchup, 4-1. For the fifth straight game, Willis Reed is the Knicks' leading scorer, with 32 points. As the rout progresses, Garden fans serenade former Power Memorial High School superstar and Bucks rookie center Lew Alcindor (later Kareem Abdul-Jabbar) with chants of "Goodbye, Lewie," as the Knicks reach the NBA final for the first time since 1953.

1974

Yale's Don Gallagher throws a no-hitter at archrival Harvard in a 2-1 win at Yale Field.

1983

In the first playoff meeting between New York-area NBA teams, the Knicks take the opener of their best-of-three series with the Nets, 118-107, at the Meadowlands.

1895

Rocco Tozzo, who as Rocky Kansas was lightweight boxing champion from 1925-26, is born in Buffalo, N.Y.

1906

Elmer Kenneth Strong is born in West Haven, Conn. Ken Strong, the nation's leading scorer as a star back for NYU in 1928, played his entire pro football career in the New York area, starting with the NFL Stapletons of Staten Island (1929-32), followed by the Giants (1933-35), the AFL Yankees (1936-37) and Jersey City Giants (1938) before rejoining the Football Giants in 1939. During World War II and after (1943-47) he was primarily the Giants' placekicker. The team retired his uniform No. 50.

1936

James Young, Army's head football coach from 1983-90 (51-39-1), is born.

1937

Charles D. White dies in Cortlandt, N.Y., at age 77. A baseball historian, statistician, and salesman for Spalding's Sporting Goods Co., White created the statistics and records publication known as the "Little Red Book of Baseball" and, after he left Spalding in 1932, "Charlie White's Little Red Book." In 1938, publication was taken over by the Elias Baseball Bureau, which continued it through 1971.

1951

Arnie Risen scores a game-high 24 points and leads both teams with 13 rebounds to pace the Rochester Royals to a 79-75 victory over the Knicks in the seventh game of the NBA final at Rochester's Edgerton Park Sports Arena.

1951

Stephen James Vickers is born in Toronto, Ontario. Steve Vickers, who spent his entire 10-year career with the Rangers, was NHL Rookie of the Year in 1972-73 and was voted Second Team NHL All-Star two years later when he posted a career-high 41 goals and 89 points.

KEN STRONG

1958

Frank J. (Buck) O'Neill, Columbia head football coach from 1920-22 (11-14) after coaching at Colgate and Syracuse, dies in Hamilton, N.Y., at age 82.

1980

One of the first relief specialists, Joe Page, the flame-throwing Yankee lefty instrumental to the Bombers' championships in 1947 and 1949, dies in Latrobe, Pa., at age 62.

1993

Hal Schumacher, the "Prince" to Carl Hubbell's "King" in the Giants' starting rotation in the 1930s, dies in Dolgeville, N.Y., at age 82. Schumacher was 158-120 in a 13-year Giants career from 1931-46 (interrupted by war) and 2-2 in three World Series.

1995

In the last NBA regular season game ever at the Boston Garden, the Knicks beat the Celtics, 99-92.

April 22

1905
Because their home opener was rained out the day before and they didn't issue rain checks, the Highlanders admit over 25,000 fans to Hilltop Park free on Saturday to watch their 5-3 win over Washington. Rain checks shortly become a part of the standard baseball ticket.

1921
Harvey Biemiller pitches a no-hitter for the Jersey City's International League club, beating Buffalo, 1-0, at Jersey City. He walks four and fans five.

1965
Johnny Dundee, 71, "the Scotch Wop" who was featherweight champ (1923-24) and fought the last boxing match ever at Garden No. 2 (see May 5), dies in East Orange, N.J.

1967
In the home opener of the first (and only) National Professional Soccer League season, the Generals edge Chicago, 2-1, at Yankee Stadium. The Generals finish third in the league's Eastern Division (11-13-8) but are the surviving New York team when the two warring soccer leagues merge, and play in the North American Soccer League in 1968 before folding.

1970
By striking out the last 10 Padres (a record), Tom Seaver ties the major-league mark of 19 strikeouts in a game and pitches the Mets to a 2-1 win over San Diego at Shea Stadium.

1973
Wiping out a 76-60 deficit in the last 10 minutes, the Knicks outscore the Celtics 33-17 in the fourth quarter at the Garden and go on to beat Boston, 117-110, in double overtime in the fourth game of their NBA semifinal to take a 3-1 series lead.

1979
Vic Obeck, NYU athletic director from 1957-67, general manager of the Westchester Bulls of the minor-league Atlantic Conference Football League and a television analyst for high school football games on WPIX, dies at age 61 in New York.

1983
For the third straight year, the Islanders knock the Rangers out of the playoffs, finishing off their quarterfinal matchup with a 5-2 Garden win to take the series, 4-2.

1984
Ruby Goldstein, the "Jewel of the Ghetto," a former welterweight contender and later a famous boxing referee, dies in Miami Beach, Florida, at age 76.

1988
Patrik Sundstrom sets an NHL playoff record with eight points (three goals, five assists) as the Devils stomp Washington, 10-4, at the Meadowlands Arena to take a 2-1 lead in their Stanley Cup quarterfinal series. Sundstrom's center, Mark Johnson, scores four times.

1990
Bob Davies, a star guard at Seton Hall from 1939-42 who played 10 years for Rochester, helping the Royals win the 1950-51 NBA title, dies in Hilton Head, South Carolina, at age 70.

1903

Known as the Highlanders, the team that would become the Yankees wins its first American League game, 7-2, over the Senators at Washington.

1946

Ed Head of the Dodgers no-hits the Boston Braves, 5-0, at Ebbets Field. Head is making his first start after a year's military service and is 3-2 in 13 games this season, his last in the majors.

1948

Billiards great Alfred DeOro dies in North Pelham, N.Y., at age 86.

1950

Pete Babando scores at 8:31 of the second overtime, giving the Red Wings a 4-3 win over the Rangers at Detroit and the seventh and deciding game of the Stanley Cup final. Because Madison Square Garden is occupied by the circus, New York, which led the series 3-2 after consecutive overtime wins in Games 4 and 5, is forced to play all seven final games on the road, five in Detroit and Games 2 and 3 in Toronto, where Maple Leafs fans obligingly root for the "home" Blueshirts.

DRAZEN PETROVIC

1952

Giants relief-pitching knuckleballer Hoyt Wilhelm gets his first big-league win (over the Boston Braves at the Polo Grounds) and helps his own cause with a home run in his first at bat. The homer turns out to be more remarkable. In his next 1,069 games, Wilhelm earns 142 more victories but never hits another homer.

1952

Leonard Wayne Merrick is born in Sarnia, Ontario. A three-time 20-goal scorer before his 1978 trade to the Islanders, Wayne Merrick became a steady contributor to the Isles' four straight Stanley Cups (1980-83), amassing 197 points in 411 games.

1982

For the third time in the series, and the eighth time in 10 games over four playoff meetings since 1975, the Islanders beat the Rangers at the Garden, winning the sixth game of their quarterfinal Stanley Cup playoff, 5-3, to take the series, four games to two.

1992

Drazen Petrovic sets a Nets NBA playoff record with 40 points, but the Cavaliers beat New Jersey, 120-113, at Cleveland, in the first game of their first-round series. It is the Nets' first playoff game since 1986.

1995

Famed sports announcer Howard Cosell dies in New York at age 77.

1997

Wayne Gretzky scores the fastest hat trick in Rangers playoff history, tallying three times in a 6:23 span of the second period as the Rangers beat Florida, 3-2, at the Garden to take a 3-1 first-round series lead.

April 24

1917

Yankees lefty George Mogridge no-hits the Red Sox, 2-1, at Fenway Park in Boston.

1921

Lucio Rossini is born in The Bronx. Lou Rossini was head basketball coach at Columbia, NYU and St. Francis. His 1950-51 Lions went 22-0 before losing their first-round NCAA game, and his 1959-60 Violets reached the NCAA Final Four.

1922

Lightweight Frankie Pitcher knocks out fellow Brooklynite Lew Brody in the ninth round of their scheduled 10-rounder at the Broadway Arena. Brody dies of a cerebral hemorrhage at Bushwick Hospital the next morning (see Feb. 5).

1940

Fight manager Joe B. Jacobs dies in New York at age 42. Adder to the lexicon of the phrases "We wuz robbed" (see June 21) and "I shoulda stood in bed" after going to a baseball game on a cold day with boxing promoter Mike Jacobs (no relation), Jacobs also helped Max Schmeling win the heavyweight title in 1930 when he ordered his charge to stay down on the canvas after being "fouled" by Jack Sharkey.

1954

Bill Shoemaker rides Correlation to victory in the Wood Memorial at Jamaica, covering the mile-and-an-eighth in 1:50. High Gun, two months later the winner of the Belmont Stakes, is third, three lengths off the pace. It is the first New York victory for Shoemaker in a major stakes. He would go on to win nearly two dozen others.

1965

Casey Stengel gets his 3,000th managerial victory (including minor league wins) as the Mets beat the Giants, 7-6, in San Francisco. On July 25, Stengel fractures his hip in a fall, ending his career. Coach Wes Westrum is named interim manager on July 26. Stengel finishes with 3,026 wins, announcing his retirement on August 30.

1970

In the first NBA final game played at the Garden, the Knicks take the opener from the Los Angeles Lakers, 124-112, behind Willis Reed's game-high 37 points. All nine previous final games in New York had been held at the 69th Regiment Armory.

1974

It's the end of an era for the Knicks as the Celtics win their semifinal series, four games to one, with a 105-94 win at Boston, in Willis Reed's, Jerry Lucas' and Dave DeBusschere's last games. Phil Jackson leads all Knicks with 27 points and nine rebounds.

1975

Brigadier General John T. Cole dies in Denville, N.J., at age 78. Gen. Cole served as a director of the NHSA and as non-riding captain of the U.S. Army equestrian team.

1994

Rangers roar past the Islanders, 5-2, at Nassau Coliseum to sweep their first-round Stanley Cup playoff series. In the four games, the Rangers outscore the Isles, 22-3.

1997

It's the last night of play at Julian's on East 14th Street as New York's oldest billiards parlor closes forever. Opened in 1929 (when New York had 3,800 pool rooms), Julian's by 1983 is the only operating billiards hall south of 125th Street in Manhattan. Several scenes in the movie "The Hustler" with Jackie Gleason and Paul Newman were shot in this second-floor establishment.

1907

John W. Kennedy is born in Brooklyn. Don Kennedy was the St. Peter's basketball coach for 22 seasons (1950-72), posting a 323-195 record as St. Peter's received seven postseason bids, including three straight NIT invitations (1967-69).

1918

Martin Joseph Egan is born in Blackie, Alberta. Defenseman Pat (Box-car) Egan led the NHL in penalty minutes with 124 as a member of the Brooklyn Americans, the franchise's last team in 1941-42. He also played two seasons for the Rangers (1949-51).

1928

Polar aviator Floyd Bennett dies at age 37 in Quebec City, Quebec.

1931

Garry Hermann, from 1903-20 chairman of the National Commission, the governing body of baseball before the creation of the commissioner's office in 1921, and president of the Cincinnati Reds from 1903-27, dies in Cincinnati, Ohio, at age 71.

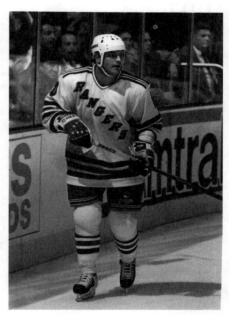

ESA TIKKANEN

1952

George Mikan's game-high 22 points and 19 rebounds lift the Lakers to an 82-65 win in the seventh game of the NBA final over the Knicks at Minneapolis and the NBA championship. Max Zaslofsky has 21 for the Knicks.

1958

Erudite Herman Hickman, a guard for the Brooklyn Football Dodgers from 1932-34 and Yale head coach from 1948-51 (16-17-2), dies in Washington, D.C., at age 46.

1991

Laz Barrera, a thoroughbred trainer whose Affirmed won horse racing's Triple Crown in 1978, dies in Downey, California, at age 66.

1991

Knicks absorb the worst playoff loss in team history, losing, 126-85, at Chicago in the first game of their open-ing-round best-of-five series.

1992

Bridge champion Billy Seaman dies at age 74 in Miami Beach, Florida.

1993

Devils end the Penguins' NHL-record 14-game Stanley Cup playoff winning streak with a 4-1 first-round victory at the Meadowlands. But the win merely cuts Pittsburgh's series lead to 3-1, and the defending Cup champions fin-ish the job a day later, 5-3, at Pittsburgh.

1997

Esa Tikkanen's second overtime goal of the series, scored at 12:02, gives the Rangers a 3-2 win over the Pan-thers at Florida and a four-games-to-one opening round series victory. Tikkanen's goal at 16:29 of overtime had given the Blueshirts a 4-3 win in Game 3 on April 22.

1881

With 1,113 entries, the Westminster Kennel Club opens its four-day run at the American Institute Fair Building. It is the first of seven times the event is not staged at Madison Square Garden. The WKC will return to this site in 1882 and in 1890 (when the second Garden is being built but not yet completed) (see Feb. 14).

1897

Theodore A. Havemeyer, 62, among the founders and the first president of the USGA, dies in New York. Havemeyer was even more widely known as the "Sugar King" because of his leadership position in the American Sugar Refining Company, heavily attacked then as a monopoly.

1908

Cecil Graham Dillon is born in Toledo, Ohio. Cecil Dillon led the NHL in playoff goals (eight) and points (10) in 1932-33 as the Rangers won the Stanley Cup. A right wing, he shared first-team All-Star honors with Toronto's Gordie Drillon (!) in 1937-38, the only time since selecting began in 1930-31 that two players have ever shared first-team honors.

1917

Salvatore Anthony Maglie is born in Niagara Falls, N.Y. Sal Maglie, known as the Barber because of the close shaves he gave opposing batters, pitched for the Giants, Dodgers and Yankees, most memorably as a Giants hurler on the 1951 pennant-winners.

1921

Daniel Chauncey, a Wall Street broker who was president of the Metropolitan Golf Association from 1905-06 and the USGA from 1907-08, dies in New York at age 71.

1927

Harry Gallatin is born in Roxana, Illinois. "Harry the Horse," a steady scorer (12.7 ppg in 610 games over nine seasons, 1948-57, as a Knick) and rebounder (leading the team six times), still holds the club record for consecutive games played at 610. He later briefly coached the team, for 63 games over two seasons in 1965.

1961

Mickey Mantle's two-run 10th-inning homer gives the Yankees a 13-11 win over the Tigers in Detroit. Mantle's homer is his second of the game and seventh of the season. Roger Maris hits his first of the year in the fifth inning of the Bombers' 11th game.

1975

In only the second such reversal in NHL history, the three-year-old Islanders, in only their second playoff series, complete a stunning comeback from a three-games-to-none deficit and beat the Penguins, 1-0, at Pittsburgh, in the seventh game of their quarterfinal playoff, taking the series, four games to three. Eddie Westfall scores the game-winner with just over five minutes left in the third period and Chico Resch stops all 30 shots. Only the Toronto Maple Leafs (in the 1942 Cup final against Detroit) had ever before pulled off such a feat (see May 11).

1982

Gene Michael becomes Yankees manager for the second time, replacing Bob Lemon, who is fired for the second time, this time with the Bombers at 6-8.

1984

In one of the great upsets in NBA playoff history, the Nets, after winning the first two games of their opening-round series at Philadelphia and losing the next two at the Meadowlands, rally in the closing minutes to beat the defending NBA champion 76ers, 101-98, at Philadelphia, to take their first-round series, three games to two. It is the Nets' first (and to date, only) NBA playoff series victory.

1874

P.T. Barnum opens his Hippodrome at 26th Street and Madison Avenue. Barnum, America's most famous showman, has leased a railroad station abandoned by the New York Central & Hudson River Railroad, spent $35,000 and six months refurbishing it and planned a successful run of circus attractions to play in it. But within three years, popular bandmaster Patrick Gilmore takes over the lease and renames the place Gilmore's Gardens. In 1879, this building becomes the first Madison Square Garden (see May 31).

1896

Rogers Hornsby, a Giant for one season (1927) a Mets coach for another (1962), and the holder of the highest lifetime average for a righthanded hitter (.358), is born in Winters, Texas.

1903

Jamaica Race Course is opened by the Metropolitan Jockey Club. Blackstock, a four-year-old bay colt ridden by Grover Cleveland Fuller, wins the featured Excelsior Handicap and its $10,000 purse. The new track attracts 18,000 improvers of the breed for its opening, including such notables as Diamond Jim Brady, Lillian Russell and "Bet-a-Million" Gates, founder of Texaco.

1915

Perry Schwartz, an end for the Brooklyn Football Dodgers from 1938-42 and the AAFC Yankees in 1946, is born in Chicago.

1934

Joe Vila, a sportswriter for the *Journal* and *Herald* and sports editor of *The Sun*, dies in New York at age 67.

1950

Yonkers Raceway opens as a major harness racing track under the guidance of Bill Cane, who converted the Empire City one-mile track to a half-mile at the renovated 1899 grandstand (see Sept. 4). On this opening night, 27,178 turn out and wager $688,009.

1959

John G. Jackson, a golfer for Columbia in 1901 and USGA president from 1936-37, dies in New York at age 79. Jackson, a prominent New York attorney, was also president of the state's Bar Association and a life trustee at his alma mater.

1974

Walter L. Pate, a tennis official and administrator, and the non-playing captain of three U.S. Davis Cup championship teams (1937, 1938, 1946), dies at age 95.

1978

John Doeg, who ended Bill Tilden's bid for a record eighth U.S. national singles tennis title in the 1930 semifinals at Forest Hills, and went on to take the crown, dies in Redding, California, at age 69.

1984

For the fourth straight playoff game, Bernard King scores over 40 points, tallying 44 this time in leading the Knicks to a 127-123 overtime win over the Pistons at Detroit and a three-games-to-two series victory in their first-round matchup.

1994

After 125:43 of scoreless hockey, Dave Hannan's goal gives the Sabres a 1-0 victory at Buffalo, tying their first-round playoff series with New Jersey at 3-3. The loss is the longest game in Devils history but they win the series, 2-1, in the seventh game two nights later.

1883

Playing its first game against organized opposition, Charlie Byrne's Brooklyn entry in the minor Inter-State League beats Manhattan College, 14-8, in Brooklyn. The winners will join the AA in 1884 and eventually grow up to become the Dodgers.

1886

Monterey, a bay gelding, wins the first race at the formal opening of Fleetwood Park in what is now The Bronx by the Driving Club of New York. Fleetwood Park will serve as New York's premier trotting track until 1897.

1890

On opening day at home for the new Players League major league baseball organization, Brooklyn clubs win two (both over Philadephia) and lose one. The National League team wins, 10-0, before 2,870 at Washington Park, the PL team wins, 3-1, before 4,750 at Eastern Park and the AA team loses, 5-1, at Rochester. Before the season ends (see Aug. 25), the AA entry gives up the ghost and at season's end, the PL folds.

IKE GELLIS

1977

Islanders beat the Canadiens in the third game of their Stanley Cup semifinal series, 5-3, at Nassau Coliseum, ending Montreal's 11-game playoff winning streak to cut their series deficit to 2-1. The prior Montreal loss had been May 4, 1976, a 5-2 Isles win at the Coliseum in the fourth game of the semifinals. Montreal goes on to take the series, four games to two.

1981

Mickey Walker dies in Freehold, N.J., at age 79. World middleweight champion from 1926-31, "The Toy Bulldog" also operated a bar-restaurant on 49th Street and Eighth Avenue, directly south of Garden No. 3.

1985

With the Yankees off to a 6-10 start, Yogi Berra is fired as manager and replaced by Billy Martin, who starts his fourth term. Martin leads the Yankees to a 91-54 record and a second-place finish, but is fired again, this time on October 17, and replaced by Lou Piniella.

1988

Ike Gellis, sports editor of the *New York Post* from 1948-78, dies in Nyack, N.Y., at age 80.

1992

Nets beat Cleveland, 109-104, at the Meadowlands, to narrow Cleveland's first-round playoff series lead to two games to one for their first playoff win since May 5, 1984, after 10 straight losses. The Cavs wrap up the series two nights later, 98-89, at New Jersey.

1993

After scoring an insurance goal to help seal an Islanders win over Washington, 5-3, and thus the sixth game of their first-round playoff series, and the series itself, 4-2, Pierre Turgeon is checked hard into the boards well after the play ends by Capitals center Dale Hunter. Hunter gets suspended for 21 games at the beginning of the following season and Turgeon suffers a separated shoulder. Though he returns in time for the semifinal series against Montreal, his effectiveness is limited, and the Isles bow out in five games.

1993

Jim Valvano dies in Durham, North Carolina, at age 47. The energetic Valvano, who scored 1,122 points in his playing career at Rutgers, was head coach at Iona for five seasons (1975-80), guiding the Gaels to a 94-47 record. In 1983, he led underdog North Carolina State to the NCAA basketball championship.

1906

For the first time ever, Sunday sports events are conducted in New York City without legal interference as the Highlanders and Brooklyn play baseball benefits for the victims of the recent San Francisco earthquake and fire. At Hilltop Park, the Highlanders beat the Philadelphia A's, 11-3, but the big news is the crowd of just under 20,000 pays $5,552.25 for the S.F. fund. One fan, John Hostein, is so pleased with the idea of Sunday games that he donates $50 to the fund. In Brooklyn, Elmer Stricklett's five-hitter gives the home team a 1-0 win before 10,000 at Washington Park. But it will still be 13 years before Sunday sports become legal.

1909

A late snowfall postpones the Highlanders' home opener against Boston at Hilltop Park, the first April "snowout" in New York baseball history.

1922

Ross Youngs has a 5-for-5 day, hitting for the cycle with an extra double as the Giants' 20 hits bury the Braves, 15-4, at Boston. Youngs' homer is a two-run inside-the-park drive to left in the fourth inning. He also scores five runs.

1925

Edward J. McKeever, president of the Dodgers for only eight days (beginning three days after predecessor Charles Ebbets' death), dies of pneumonia in Brooklyn.

1931

St. John's athletic director Ray E. Lynch announces that the school has decided to discontinue varsity baseball and football after completing the upcoming seasons. Lynch already has six football games scheduled for the now-abandoned 1932 season. An official statement says the board of trustees has decided the value to the school is not enough "as to justify the present outlay of funds."

1970

Lakers guard Jerry West beats the buzzer with a shot from behind the midcourt line to force overtime in the third game of the NBA final at the Forum in Los Angeles, but the Knicks win anyway, 111-108, to take a two-games-to-one series lead.

1970

Andre Agassi, the flamboyant but erratic baseliner, is born in Las Vegas, Nevada. Agassi entered the 1994 U.S. Open unseeded, but beat five seeds on his way to taking the title. He rose to No. 1 within six months.

1971

After Chicago's Stan Mikita hits both posts while shooting at an empty net in the second overtime, Pete Stemkowski scores at 1:29 of the third overtime to lift the Rangers to a 3-2 win over the Blackhawks at the Garden and even their Stanley Cup semifinal series, 3-3. It is Stemkowski's second overtime goal of the series. The Blackhawks win the series finale, 4-2, at Chicago Stadium May 2.

1973

With Walt Frazier leading them with 25 points and 10 rebounds, the Knicks beat the Celtics, 94-78, at Boston, to take their semifinal NBA playoff series, four games to three, and advance to the final for the third time in four years. For the Celtics, it is the first time they have ever lost the seventh game of an NBA playoff series.

1982

Elmer Ripley, a pro basketball player for 20 years (including a stint with the Original Celtics) and college coach for 26 years with seven schools, including Wagner (1922-25), Yale (1929-35), Columbia (1943-45) and Army (1951-53), dies in Staten Island at age 90.

1877

Hartford plays a 12-inning tie with Boston in the National League opener at Brooklyn's Union Grounds. With the New York Mutuals expelled from the National League (see Dec. 7), Hartford plays its home games in Brooklyn and is unofficially known as "Brooklyn-Hartford."

1891

Australian Frank Slavin, the champion of England, appears at the Garden in a sparring exhibition facing noted heavyweights Charley Mitchell and Jim Daley.

1898

Philadelphia beats Brooklyn, 6-4, before 15,000 fans at the opening game of the new Washington Park at 4th Avenue and 3rd Street in Brooklyn.

1898

World Greco-Roman wrestling champion Ernest Roeber's rematch against Ishmael Yousouf, "The Terrible Turk," ends in a riot at the Metropolitan Opera House (see Mar. 26). When the two wrestlers get into a shoving match, their managers, Billy Brady (Roeber's) and Martin Julian (Yousouf's), jump into the ring and begin a private brawl related to their management of heavyweight boxing champs Jim Corbett (Julian) and Bob Fitzsimmons (Brady). When Fitzsimmons joins the festivities and several fans decide to participate, referee Herman Wolff, a wrestler of some note himself, calls the bout "no contest" and flees the ring. Opera House officials decide rentals for wrestling contests in the future are not beneficial to its image.

1903

In their first home game, the Highlanders defeat Washington, 6-2, at Hilltop Park, 168th Street and Broadway.

1940

Brooklyn's Tex Carleton no-hits the Reds, 3-0, at Cincinnati.

1944

Phil Weintraub comes within one RBI of the big league record for a single game, driving in 11 as the Giants clout the Dodgers, 26-8, in the opener of a doubleheader at the Polo Grounds before 58,068 (52,057 paid). Weintraub's four hits include two doubles, a triple and a homer. The 18-run margin is the Giants' largest in this century but Brooklyn wins the nightcap, 5-4.

1946

Cleveland's Bob Feller no-hits the Yankees, 1-0, at the Stadium. It is the first no-hitter against the Yankees since 1919 and the first ever pitched against them at Yankee Stadium.

1946

George T. Hepbron, the first basketball official in the New York area and the first outstanding referee in basketball history, dies in East Orange, N.J., at age 82. Hepbron, the referee at a national AAU tournament in Bay Ridge in 1897, was the editor of the *Official Basketball Guide* from 1896-1915, wrote the first "How to Play" book in 1904 and was secretary of the Joint Rules Committee from 1915-33.

1946

Donald Arthur Schollander is born in Charlotte, North Carolina. The first Olympian to win four swimming gold medals at a single Olympics (Tokyo 1964), Don Schollander enrolled at Yale in February 1965 and set numerous college and national pool records.

1878

"Honest John" Morrissey, 47, a boxer who claimed the American heavyweight title after beating John C. Heenan in 1858, dies in Saratoga, N.Y. After refusing a rematch with Heenan, Morrissey retired to run gambling houses in New York and Saratoga and later was elected to serve two terms in the U.S. Congress. In 1877, he was elected to the New York State Senate but fell ill and never took his seat before his death.

1883

In the first National League game ever played in New York, the Giants defeat Boston, 7-5, at the Polo Grounds, 110th Street and Fifth Avenue. Former President Ulysses S. Grant is among the more than 15,000 in attendance to help inaugurate 75 seasons of NL history. Mickey Welch pitches a seven-hitter and the Beaneaters commit eight errors. The Giants score three runs in the first inning and pound out 16 hits.

1898

Famous basketball referee (1918-45) David Tobey is born in New York. Tobey also coached the Savage Institute and Cooper Union.

1906

Philadelphia's Johnny Lush pitches a no-hitter against Brooklyn at Washington Park in a 1-0 Phillies victory. Lush will also pitch a six-inning no-hitter at Washington Park after being traded to St. Louis, winning 2-0 on August 6, 1908.

1920

In the longest game by innings in major league history, Brooklyn and Boston play a 26-inning 1-1 tie at Braves Field. Starting pitchers Leon Cadore of the Dodgers and Joe Oeschager of the Braves both go the distance.

STEVE CAUTHEN

1926

Davey Brown's first-half goal starts a local all-star team to a 3-0 win over the touring Hakoah All-Stars of Vienna, Austria, before 46,000 at the Polo Grounds, the largest crowd at a U.S. soccer match for 51 years. The New York team is composed of players from Indiana Flooring and the New York Giants, two American Soccer League teams.

1946

Bill Johnston dies at age 51 in San Francisco, California. Twice a U.S. national men's singles tennis titlist (the first in 1915, the initial championship played at Forest Hills), "Little Bill," 5'8 $^1/_2$" and dwarfed in comparison to his great rival, "Big Bill" Tilden, also lost six national singles finals, five to Tilden, four of those in a row (1922-25).

1960

Steve Cauthen, the child prodigy jockey who rode Affirmed to the Triple Crown in 1978, is born in Covington, Kentucky. He then moved to England, where three times he was riding champion.

1992

Rangers beat the Devils, 8-5, at the Garden, to take their first-round Stanley Cup playoff series, 4-3.

May 2

1885

In their first game as defending AA champs, the Mets score four in the first inning and beat Brooklyn, 8-2, at Washington Park.

1885

Mickey Welch loses his no-hitter with one out in the eighth but finishes with a two-hitter as the Giants beat Boston, 2-1, before 5,500 on opening day at the Polo Grounds in 97 minutes.

1929

Thomas Aloysius Dorgan dies in Great Neck, N.Y., at age 52. Tad Dorgan was a famous sports cartoonist for the *Journal* and *American*, and inventor of the phrase "hot dog" to describe the steaming sausages sold by Harry M. Stevens at the Polo Grounds.

1936

Leroy Herrmann of the Maple Leafs pitches a 10-inning International League no-hitter, winning, 1-0, over Newark at Toronto, Ontario.

1939

Lou Gehrig benches himself in Detroit, snapping his streak of 2,130 consecutive games played. Babe Dahlgren takes over at first and the Yankees pound the Tigers, 22-2, as Dahlgren doubles and homers (with one on) and Charlie Keller drives in six runs.

1975

Mrs. H. Norman Engelsen dies in New York at age 67. As Ethel McGary, she was a member of the WSANY and an Olympic swimmer in 1924 and 1928.

1976

Dan Bankhead, the first black pitcher in the National League (with Brooklyn in 1947), dies in Houston, Texas, at age 55.

1977

Daniel J. Ferris, sportswriter for the New York *Evening Mail* from 1919-26 and secretary-treasurer of the AAU from 1927-57, dies in Amityville, N.Y., at age 87.

1980

John Chapman, winner of 3,915 harness races with over $21 million in winnings, dies in Westbury, N.Y., at age 51.

1987

After rallying from a three-games-to-one deficit to beat Washington in the first round of the Stanley Cup playoffs (see Apr. 18), the Islanders have rallied from an identical deficit to force a seventh game against Philadelphia in the quarterfinal round. But, as they did in 1975 (see May 11), the Flyers spoil the Isles' comeback dreams, beating New York, 5-1.

1991

Vitas K. Gerulaitis, Sr., dies at age 76 in Woodhaven, N.Y. Father of his namesake, the nationally-ranked player, Gerulaitis was tennis teacher and coach, and the first head professional at the National Tennis Center in Flushing Meadow (1979-85).

1851

Yacht *America* is launched from William H. Brown's shipyard on the East River at 12th Street. The boat measures 93$\frac{1}{2}$ feet at the water line and costs $30,000 (see Aug. 22).

1870

Under new rules of the National Association designed to improve competition, the trotting season begins at the Union Course.

1886

Mary Outerbridge, one of the pioneers of tennis in the 1870s and a member of the family for whom the Outerbridge Crossing connecting Staten Island to New Jersey is named, dies in Staten Island.

1920

Brooklyn loses, 2-1, in 19 innings to the Braves in Boston to end an incredible three-game, three-day stretch in which the Robins play 58 innings to get two defeats and a tie. On May 1, Brooklyn and Boston play a record-breaking 26-inning 1-1 tie. Then the Robins go home on Sunday only to drop a 4-3 decision to Philadelphia in 13 innings at Ebbets Field before returning to Boston for Monday's 19-inning loss.

1920

Walker Smith, Jr., later known as boxing great Sugar Ray Robinson, is born in Detroit, Michigan.

1934

Harry M. Stevens, who transformed a baseball souvenir program printing niche into the nation's dominant ballpark concession business, dies in New York at age 78.

1936

Edward Grey Cooke is born in Norfolk, Virginia. Ed Cooke, a defensive end, was an original Titan from 1960-62 and played with the Jets in 1963.

1940

A pair of ribbons in the evening's first event, the triple-bar jump, enables the Army Cavalry team to finish first in total ribbons in the 10th annual Newark (N.J.) Horse Show at the 102d Cavalry Armory.

HARRY M. STEVENS

1950

Somewhat befuddled by the new balk rule, Yankees righthander Vic Raschi gets called for four balks by home plate umpire Bill Summers. Raschi commits an error, gives up 10 hits and balks in the game's first run but wins anyway, 4-3, over the Chicago White Sox at Yankee Stadium.

1981

Maud Rosenbaum Blumenthal dies in New York at age 79. As Baroness Giacomo Giorgio Levi, she was a nationally-ranked tennis player before her marriage to Mr. Blumenthal in 1935. She was the top-ranked player in the East in 1933.

1903

Elmer Layden, one of Notre Dame's "Four Horsemen" and commissioner of the NFL from 1941-46, when his contract was not renewed, is born in Davenport, Iowa.

1905

On opening day at the new Belmont Park, the featured 14th running of the Metropolitan Handicap ($10,000 added) winds up in a dead heat with Sysonby (Willie Shaw up) and Race King (Leslie Smith up) dividing top money.

1912

John Abbott Lardner, son of famed sportswriter Ring Lardner and a sports columnist himself, is born in Chicago, Illinois. John Lardner was a sports columnist for *Newsweek* from 1939-57.

1919

In the first legal Sunday baseball games ever played in New York, the Phillies beat the Giants, 4-3, at the Polo Grounds, and the Dodgers defeat the Boston Braves, 6-2, at Ebbets Field.

1947

Alfred Beard is born in Hardinburg, Kentucky. Butch Beard, a Knicks reserve guard for parts of four seasons (1975-76 to 1978-79), was later a color commentator on Knicks broadcasts and coach of the Nets for two seasons (1994-96).

1951

Pete Castiglione's leadoff single is the only hit allowed by Sal Maglie in the Giants' 5-1 victory over the Pittsburgh Pirates at the Polo Grounds.

1970

With the Knicks trailing, 25-15, in the first quarter of the fifth game of the NBA final, Willis Reed collapses on the court with a pulled leg muscle. Down 53-40 at the half and without their best player for the rest of the game, the Knicks, in one of the most famous comebacks in league history, beat the Lakers, 107-100 at the Garden, to take a 3-2 series lead.

1972

Completing their comeback from a 2-0 series deficit, the Nets beat the Squires, 94-88, at the Norfolk (Va.) Scope, before 10,410, to take the ABA Eastern Division final in seven games and advance to their first ABA final (see May 20).

1972

Defenseman Brad Park tallies two first-period power play goals and adds two assists as the Rangers, playing their first home Stanley Cup final game since 1940, beat the Bruins, 5-2, at the Garden, narrowing the Boston series lead to 2-1.

1990

Patrick Ewing scores 44 points, pulls down 13 rebounds and ties a club playoff record with seven steals, as the Knicks, accumulating a team playoff-record 43 assists, pound Boston, 135-108, to tie their first-round best-of-five playoff series at two games each.

BUTCH BEARD

1849

Fabled trotter Hambletonian is born on Jonas Seeley's farm near Sugar Loaf in Orange County, N.Y. Seeley's employee, William Rysdyk, later purchased both the foal and his mother for $125, raising and training the great horse on his own small farm nearby.

1877

In the first collegiate dual meet in New York, Columbia's track team takes all but two of the 12 events from Princeton at the Mott Haven Grounds. George Parmley in the hammer throw (79' 1") and Alonzo C. Hunt in the broad jump (18') are winners for the Tigers while W.J.G. Bearns leads the Lions by winning the mile in 5:21.25 with Princeton's William Phrainer second. The event is Columbia's 10th annual Athletic Field Day, but the first time another college has been invited to compete in the events.

1925

In the last boxing card at the "old" Garden (No. 2) at Madison Square, Sid Terris wins the featured 12-round main event with a decision over former featherweight champ Johnny Dundee, "the Scotch Wop."

1971

New York Cosmos open their first home season as a member of the NASL with a 1-0 win over the Washington Darts at Yankee Stadium.

BILL COOK

1981

Islanders beat the Rangers, 5-2, at the Garden, to sweep their Stanley Cup semifinal playoff series. In the four games, the Isles outscore the Rangers, 22-8.

1984

Nets beat Milwaukee, 106-99, at the Meadowlands Arena to even their quarterfinal playoff series at two games each. It is the Nets' first home NBA playoff win (after six losses). But the Bucks take the next two games and the series, 4-2.

1986

Bill Cook dies in Kingston, Ontario, at age 89. An original Ranger as a right wing and the team's first captain, a position he held for his entire 11-season NHL career (making him the captain with the longest tenure in club history), Cook led the NHL in goals and scoring in 1926-27, his rookie year, and 1932-33. Later a Rangers coach (1951-53), Cook, with his brother Bun on the left and Frank Boucher at center, formed the first great line in Rangers history, one that stayed intact from the club's inception until Bun's sale to Boston in 1936. Cook's 223 goals remained a club record until broken by Andy Bathgate in 1962.

1997

Arena Football League competition returns to the Garden, but the CityHawks lose their regular-season home opener to the Orlando Predators, 50-42, before only 7,422 (see May 9).

1903

Famed restaurateur Bernard (Toots) Shor is born in Philadelphia, Pennsylvania.

1907

Wilbur C. Ewbank is born in Richmond, Indiana. Weeb Ewbank coached the Jets to their 1969 Super Bowl victory over his former team, the Baltimore Colts.

1915

Luther Cook's 11th-inning RBI single gives the Yankees a 4-3 win over the Red Sox at the Polo Grounds, but Boston pitcher Babe Ruth surprises Yankees starter Jack Warhop and the 5,000 fans by leading off the third inning with a home run. It is Ruth's first major-league homer.

1925

Shortstop Everett Scott doesn't play in the Yankees' 6-2, 10-inning loss to the Philadelphia A's at the Stadium, ending his streak of consecutive games played at 1,307. Scott's streak, which began June 20, 1916, when he was with the Boston Red Sox, is then the longest in baseball history. Less than a month later, Scott's teammate, Lou Gehrig, will begin a streak of his own that will establish a record lasting more than half a century.

1929

David Anderson, sportswriter for the *Brooklyn Eagle, Journal-American,* and *The New York Times,* is born in Troy, N.Y. In 1981, Dave Anderson won a Pulitzer Prize for distinguished commentary.

1978

Ethelda Bliebtrey, freestyle swimming star and a member of the Women's Swimming Association of New York, dies in West Palm Beach, Florida, at age 76.

DAVE ANDERSON

1988

Displeased with the officiating during a 6-1 semifinal playoff loss to the Bruins at the Meadowlands to fall behind in the series, two games to one, Devils coach Jim Schoenfeld accosts referee Don Koharski in the corridor after the game and apparently shoves him while certainly saying, referring to Koharski's weight, "Have another doughnut, you fat (bleeping) pig." Schoenfeld's actions prompt his suspension for the fourth game, but an injunction allows him to coach, provoking officials assigned to the game to boycott it, forcing the NHL to use amateur officials in the game on May 8, won by the Devils, 3-1, after a 66-minute delay. Schoenfeld serves his suspension in the fifth game in Boston (May 10), won by the Bruins, 7-1.

1990

Completing a stunning turnaround after losing the first two games by an aggregate of 40 points, the Knicks beat the Celtics, 121-114, at the Boston Garden, snapping a 26-game losing streak there and becoming the third team in NBA history to win a best-of-five series after dropping the first two games.

1994

In their second playoff meeting, the Knicks again oust the Nets, beating New Jersey, 102-92, at the Meadowlands, to wrap up the first-round series, three games to one.

1866

Outgoing Commodore Edwin A. Stevens is feted by his fellow New York Yacht Club members at the elegant Delmonico's. A silver punch bowl by Tiffany is presented to Stevens by incoming Commodore H.W. McVickar.

1914

Kenneth A. Norton, for 22 years coach of Manhattan College basketball, is born in Queens. Norton was 312-205 (.603) from 1946-68 as Jaspers coach.

1922

Giants hurler Jess Barnes no-hits the Phillies, 6-0, at the Polo Grounds.

1946

Jimmy Johnston, "the Boy Bandit" and Madison Square Garden boxing promoter in the 1930s before Mike Jacobs, dies in New York at age 70.

1960

General John Reed Kilpatrick dies in New York at age 70. An All-America end at Yale in 1909-10, Kilpatrick served war-interrupted terms as president of both Madison Square Garden and the Rangers from the mid-1930s-1960. His father Frank was a founder of the New York Athletic Club.

1960

Leo O'Mealia, *Daily News* sports cartoonist from 1929-60, dies in Brooklyn at age 76. He drew the classic "Who's A Bum!" cartoon that graced the entire front page of the paper the day after the Dodgers won their only World Series in 1955.

1970

At Shea Stadium, Wes Parker of the Dodgers becomes the first player ever to hit for the cycle against the Mets, helping Los Angeles to a 7-4 10-inning win.

1972

Despite a 31-point effort by Walt Frazier, the Knicks lose, 114-100, at Los Angeles, and the Lakers win the NBA final, 4-1, to take their first league title since moving from Minneapolis in 1959.

1974

New York Sets play their first match in World Team Tennis at Nassau Coliseum. With 4,990 on hand, they lose to the Hawaii Leis, 29-25.

1983

Mike Bossy sets an NHL record with his fourth game-winning goal of the series as the Islanders beat Boston, 8-4, at Nassau Coliseum, and take the semifinal, 4-2. Bossy notches four goals in the game and nine for the series. It is also his second hat trick, as he had three goals in the Isles' 8-3 fourth-game win at the Coliseum May 3.

1987

Bob Cooke, 75, *Herald Tribune* sports editor (1948-59), dies in Riverhead, N.Y. Cooke's tenure was sandwiched by the two terms of Stanley Woodward, who was fired by publisher Helen Reid Rogers in 1948 and reinstated in 1959 when John Hay Whitney bought the paper.

1995

Jack Hand, noted sportswriter for *The Associated Press* who wrote the wire service's leads on many World Series, dies in New Milford, Pennsylvania, at age 82.

1877

At 10 a.m., Superintendent Charles Lincoln throws open the doors for the first Westminster Kennel Club dog show. A day crowd of 4,000 pours into Gilmore's Gardens (renamed Madison Square Garden in 1879) and another 6,000 turn out in the evening when General A.S. Webb, the WKC president and Henry Burgh, the featured speaker, do the formal opening. An English setter, Leicester, owned by L.H. Smith of Strathroy, Canada, is one of the first breed winners selected from 1,177 entries by the panel of four judges, including two from Great Britain.

1909

Albert Raines sets a world marathon record of 2:46:04.6 in the Northwestern AC event on a day when three marathons are run in and around New York City. Raines runs the first 385 yards and the last two miles at the Bronx Oval while most of the rest of the 24 miles are run through the hills of Westchester. In a pro event at the Polo Grounds, over 15,000 watch France's Henri St. Ives win, while at Brooklyn's Saratoga Park, George Obermeyer of the National AC wins the Acorn AA Marathon. Raines breaks a world record set February 12 by James Clark of the Xavier AA of 2:46:52.6 in Brooklyn, who ran from the 13th Regiment Armory to Sea Gate and back.

1913

Ferdinand Zivic is born in Pittsburgh, Pennsylvania. Fritzie Zivic was welterweight champion from 1940-41.

1915

Hannes Kolehmainen wins the *Evening Mail* "modified marathon" from 184th Street and the Grand Concourse in The Bronx to City Hall by covering the 13 miles, 200 yards in 1:14:09.6.

1929

Left-hander Carl Hubbell becomes the last New York Giants pitcher to hurl a no-hitter with an 11-0 triumph over Pittsburgh at the Polo Grounds.

1937

Henry W. Dreyer, who introduced trap shooting to Brooklyn in 1888 and founded the Bergen Beach Gun Club, dies at age 79 in Brooklyn.

1942

Famed jockey Angel Cordero, Jr., is born in Santurce, Puerto Rico.

1961

Eddie Donovan is named the Knicks' sixth head coach, replacing Carl Braun.

1968

Craig Wood dies in Palm Beach, Florida, at age 67. Wood won 34 PGA tour events, as well as the 1941 Masters and U.S. Open, the 1942 Metropolitan PGA and the 1940 Metropolitan Open, at which his 72-hole 264 set a PGA record.

1970

Led by Walt Frazier's 36 points and 19 assists, and inspired by injured center Willis Reed's appearance on the court just before tip-off and two baskets to start the game, the Knicks beat the Lakers in the seventh game of the NBA final, 113-99, at the Garden, to take the first league title in their 24-year history.

1979

Don Murdoch and Ron Greschner score second-period goals to offset Mike Bossy's first-period tally as the Rangers complete their upset of the regular-season champions by beating the Islanders, 2-1, at the Garden, and taking their Stanley Cup semifinal series, 4-2.

May 9

1888

First baseman Roger Connor becomes the first Giant and only the second National League hitter to belt three homers in a game as he drives in six runs to lead an 18-4 rout at Indianapolis. Pitcher Tim Keefe also takes advantage of the 267-foot rightfield corner with a homer as the Giants hit seven in the game. Connor homers in the second, third, and seventh innings, each of the last two with a man on.

1912

Leland Shaffer, quarterback and running back for the Football Giants from 1935-43 and in 1945, is born in Minneola, Kansas.

1937

Matched up against the last pitcher to beat him, the Cubs' Bill Lee, Giants lefty Carl Hubbell wins his 20th straight decision, a 4-1 victory over Chicago before 36,529 at the Polo Grounds. Lee had defeated Hubbell, 1-0, at Chicago on July 19, 1936, before the New York screwballer started his streak (which would end in his next start).

1941

Howard Komives is born in Toledo, Ohio. Butch Komives, the Knicks' second-round choice (13th overall) in the 1964 NBA draft, was the team's point guard before the ascension of Walt Frazier (see Dec. 19).

1942

Graham McNamee, legendary sports announcer who in 1922 broadcast the first World Series game ever heard on radio, dies in New York at age 53.

1959

Before the largest crowd in baseball history (93,103), the Yankees beat the Dodgers, 6-2, at the Los Angeles Coliseum in an exhibition game to raise money for former Dodgers catcher, the paralyzed Roy Campanella.

1963

Joe Cirella, who played with the Devils for seven seasons, including their first in New Jersey (1982-83), before spending three with the Rangers, is born in Hamilton, Ontario.

1973

Milton Gross, longtime sports columnist for the *New York Post* whose daughter Jane became a sportswriter for *The New York Times*, dies in New York at age 61.

HOWARD KOMIVES

1988

New York Knights open their Arena Football season at the Garden with 13,667 on hand for their 54-48 loss to the Detroit Drive.

May 10

1841

James Gordon Bennett, Jr., is born in New York. Son of the founder of the *New York Herald*, the youngest member of the New York Yacht Club in 1857, winner of the first trans-Atlantic race in 1866, creator of the first intercollegiate track event at Saratoga, N.Y., and a well-known playboy who spent a good deal of his time in Europe, Bennett imported polo to the United States in 1876 and helped build a field, the Polo Grounds, on which to stage matches. To satisfy his desire to read his own newspaper while in France, he also founded the *Paris Herald*, lineal ancestor of the *International Herald Tribune*.

1842

In another match race pitting the best horse of the North against the best of the South, Fashion beats the South's Boston in straight heats, 2-0, at Union Course (see May 27).

1878

Princeton's baseball team is shut out by Harvard for the first time, 8-0, and the Cantabs complete the sweep of the two-game series at Princeton the next day, 3-1.

1911

Gordon F. (Skim) Brown, a Yale guard who is one of only three players in college football history to be voted All-America four times (1897-1900) (the others being the Bulldogs' Frank Hinkey and Penn's T. Truxton Hare), dies in Glen Head, N.Y., of diabetes at age 30.

1916

Albert George DeMarco is born in North Bay, Ontario. Center Ab DeMarco led the Rangers in goals, assists and points two years in a row (1944-45, 1945-46). His son, Albert Thomas (also called Ab), a defenseman, also played for the Blueshirts, in the early 1970s.

1930

George Allen Summerall is born in Lake City, Florida. Placekicker Pat Summerall converted 136 of 138 PATs in four years with the Giants (1958-61) and became the No. 1 play-by-play pro football announcer for both the CBS and FOX television networks.

1945

Randy Rasmussen is born in St. Paul, Nebraska. An offensive guard for the Jets from 1967-81, he played in 207 games, a club record for total games until surpassed by Pat Leahy.

1946

Yachting historian Billy Stephens dies in Bayside, N.Y., at age 91.

1971

At Governor William T. Cahill's and State Treasurer Joseph McGrane's urging, the New Jersey's legislature passes legislation enabling the creation of the New Jersey Sports & Exposition Authority. The NJSEA is to issue bonds, build, and operate a sports complex in northern New Jersey.

1973

Winning their second NBA championship, the Knicks beat the Lakers, 102-93, at Los Angeles to close out the final series in five games. Earl Monroe leads the Knicks with 23 points while Gail Goodrich has 28 for the Lakers.

1974

Larry Kenon gets 23 points, Billy Paultz 21 and Julius Erving 20 as the New York Nets defeat the Utah Stars, 111-100, at Nassau Coliseum before 15,934 to take their first ABA championship, four games to one.

# May 11

1878

Only eight of 34 starters finish in the championship walking competition at Manhattan's American Institute Fair Building on Third Avenue at 63rd Street. In the 36-hour professional event, Charles A. Harrison of Haverhill, Massachusetts, does 160 miles in 34:26:14 to win the $200 top prize. Among the amateurs, J.B. Gillie of the Scottish-American AC wins a gold watch for doing 108 miles in 23:04 while M.J. Ennis of the Harlem AC gets a gold medal for his 103 miles in 23:31:06. The amateur event is 24 hours, and Gillie sets pedestrian race-walking records by walking 50 miles in 9:29:22, 75 miles in 15:15 and 100 miles in 21:42.

1883

In their first home opener as AA members, the Mets lose to the Philadelphia Athletics, 11-4. On the same afternoon, Brooklyn has better luck in its first Inter-State League game at Washington Park (5th Avenue and 3rd Street) with a 13-6 win over Trenton before 6,000.

1900

Jim Jeffries successfully defends his heavyweight title with a knockout of Jim Corbett in the 23d round at the Seaside AC in Coney Island.

1914

Only 88 days after announcing the team was coming to Brooklyn, the Tip Tops open their first Federal League home season with a 2-0 loss to Pittsburgh before over 18,000 at rebuilt Washington Park. Pittsburgh's Howie Camnitz fires a five-hitter and outpitches the Brookfeds' Tom Seaton.

1921

Jack Lang is born in the Ridgewood section of Brooklyn. Lang joined the *Long Island Daily Press* in 1941, and after a stint in the Army, was a baseball writer there from 1945 until the paper folded March 25, 1977. He then joined the *Daily News*, where he worked until 1987.

1957

Chris Leonard, a basketball star with the New York Whirlwinds (1918-21) and Original Celtics (1921-27), dies in Manhasset, N.Y., at age 67.

1970

Tom Seaver's 16-game winning streak (including 6-0 this season) ends as Expos left-hander Dan McGinn shuts down the Mets, 3-0, before 15,016 at Shea Stadium.

1972

For the second time in its history, the Garden is witness to the awarding of the Stanley Cup, and for the second time, Boston skates off with the chalice. The Bruins beat the Rangers, 3-0, in the sixth game of the final. Bobby Orr scores the winning goal.

1975

For the second straight series, the Islanders erase a 3-0 deficit, beating the defending Stanley Cup champion Flyers, 2-1, at Nassau Coliseum, on Gerry Hart's third-period goal to even their series. Two days later, facing playoff elimination for the ninth time, the Isles finally succumb, bowing out, 4-1, at Philadelphia.

1994

George Gregory, Jr., 88, the first black basketball All-American (Columbia, 1930-31), dies in New York.

1997

Adam Graves scores at 14:08 of overtime to give the Rangers a 2-1 win over the Devils at the Meadowlands and a 4-1 victory in their quarterfinal playoff series.

1871

Scoring at least three runs in every inning except the ninth, the Mutuals crush the Resolutes of Elizabeth, N.J., 39-0, at Union Grounds. Joe Start has five hits while the Resolutes manage only four as a team. The score is still the largest professional game shutout.

1897

Louis P. Bayard of Princeton wins the first championship of the Inter-collegiate Golf Association with a 45-46-91 round at the new Ardsley Casino course in what was then Irvington, N.Y. Two days later, Yale wins the first team title.

1925

Lawrence Peter Berra is born in St. Louis, Missouri. The best catcher in team history, Yogi Berra was American League MVP three times during his 18-year Yankees career (1946-63).

1928

W.J. Hurley, 72, national sculling champion (1880-83), dies in Port Washington, N.Y.

1929

Edward Payson Weston, one of the noted pedestrians during the walking craze of the post-Civil War era, dies at his home in Brooklyn at age 90. He first came to public notice in 1868 when he walked from Portland, Maine to Chicago. Weston won the Astley World Championship belt in London in 1879 by walking 550 miles in a six-day competition (141 hours, 44 minutes) at Agricultural Hall. In 1909, he walked from New York to San Francisco in 104 days. In 1913, he strolled 1,546 miles in 51 days at the invitation of the Minneapolis Athletic Club to officiate at the cornerstone laying of the club's head-quarters building.

JIM JEFFRIES

1952

Middleweight Georgie Small of Brooklyn knocks out Jimmy Herring of Ozone Park, N.Y., at 2:46 of the ninth round at the opening of Eastern Parkway Arena in Brooklyn. Promoter Emil Lence opens the arena after signing an agreement with the DuMont Network to produce Monday night fights. Ted Husing calls the action, which is shown locally on WABD, Channel 5.

1956

Brooklyn's Carl Erskine gets his second career no-hitter, stopping the Giants, 3-0, at Ebbets Field.

1985

In a nationally-televised drawing, the Knicks, eligible for the NBA lottery by virtue of having missed the playoffs, win the right to select first overall. Elated Knicks general manager Dave DeBusschere pounds the table when commissioner David Stern reveals that the Knicks have won the first pick, knowing they will take Georgetown's dominant center, Patrick Ewing.

1995

Randy McKay's overtime goal at 8:51 of overtime gives the Devils a 1-0 win over Boston at the Meadowlands in the fourth game of their first-round series and a 3-1 series lead. New Jersey goalie Martin Brodeur gets the shut-out, his third in four games.

1863

Jim Dunne is awarded a decision over Jimmy Elliott on a foul in the 12th round of their bout at Bull's Ferry in Weehawken, N.J., under London Prize Ring rules. Elliott is subsequently arrested and imprisoned for two years as a result of his conduct during the bout but later wins the American heavyweight championship (see June 26 and July 4).

1911

Fred Merkle drives in six runs as the Giants score 13 times in the first inning and go on to beat the St. Louis Cardinals, 19-5, at Hilltop Park, where the National League club is playing because of a fire at the Polo Grounds the month before. Merkle hits a three-run homer and a bases-loaded double in the 13-run frame.

1914

Joseph Louis Barrow is born in Lafayette, Louisiana. Joe Louis was world heavyweight boxing champion from 1937-49.

1922

Gladys Medalie Heldman, co-founder of *World Tennis* magazine (1953), who persuaded Joe Cullman of Phillip Morris in 1970 to underwrite a women's professional tennis tour that came to be known as the Virginia Slims circuit, is born in New York.

1928

James Shoulders is born. Jim Shoulders made frequent appearances at the Garden with the rodeo. Five times he was all-around rodeo cowboy champion (1949, 1956-59).

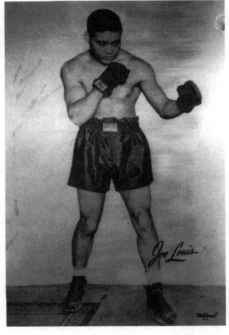

JOE LOUIS

1954

Frank G. Menke, editor of *The Encyclopedia of Sports*, dies at age 68 in Cincinnati, Ohio, while on a cross-country trip. Menke was a sportswriter for the International News Service from 1911-32, served as publicist for the Kentucky Derby (1938-45) and produced his first *All-Sports Record Book* in 1930, eventually leaving his INS job to produce sports books.

1961

Lefthander Roy Lown wins a record payoff of $15,000 by beating Don Robinette, 196-191, in the third game of the PBA Invitation at the Paramus (N.J.) Bowling Center. Lown beats Pat Patterson in the semifinals and then takes two of three games from Robinette before 500 fans and a national television audience.

1976

By defeating the Denver Nuggets, 112-108, at Nassau Coliseum, the New York Nets win the ABA title for the second time in three years, 4-2. That summer, the league vanishes in a merger with the NBA, making this game the last one in ABA history (see June 17). Nets forward Rich Jones scores the last ABA points.

1978

Joie Ray, national AAU champion in the mile in 1915 and 1917-23, and onetime co-holder of the indoor mile world record (4:12.0 in 1925), dies in Benton Harbor, Michigan, at age 84.

1666

First organized horse racing in North America is held at Salisbury Plain (later Hempstead Plain), Long Island, in what is now Garden City in Nassau County. It is instituted by the British colonial government led by Governor Richard Nicolls.

1883

England's Charley Mitchell decks heavyweight champ John L. Sullivan in the first round of their fight at the Garden, but Sullivan then punishes Mitchell ferociously until Police Capt. Alexander Williams halts the carnage after the third round.

1887

On opening day at Gravesend, Dry Monopole, a four-year-old bay colt, produces a major surprise, winning the Brooklyn Handicap and setting an American record for 1 1/4 miles (2:07).

1899

Earle Combs, centerfielder and leadoff hitter for the "Murderers' Row" Yankees of the late 1920s, is born in Pebworth, Kentucky. Combs set a Yankees single-season hit record with 231 in 1927 that was not surpassed until Don Mattingly had 238 in 1986.

1918

James Gordon Bennett, Jr., dies in Paris, France, at age 77 (see May 10). An all-around sportsman, Bennett, in addition to owning the *New York Herald*, sponsored auto, balloon and airplane races and was a major early patron of U.S. Olympic teams.

1929

Lorne John Worsley is born in Montreal, Quebec. Gump Worsley, an outstanding goalie for generally bad teams from 1952-63, played more games (583) and absorbed more losses (271) than any other goalie in Rangers history. (When once asked which team gave him the most trouble, he replied, "The Rangers.")

1988

Devils' first visit to the playoffs finally ends, as the Bruins beat them, 6-2, at Boston, in the seventh game of their Stanley Cup semifinal series.

1993

David Volek scores 5:16 into overtime as the Islanders, after blowing a 3-1 third-period lead, pull off one of the most stunning upsets in Stanley Cup playoff history, beating the two-time defending Stanley Cup champion Penguins, 4-3, in the seventh game of their quarterfinal at Pittsburgh to take the series, four games to three.

DAVID VOLEK

1996

Dwight Gooden no-hits the Seattle Mariners, 2-0, at Yankee Stadium, walking six and fanning five. Gooden, suspended from baseball and released from the Mets in 1994 in the aftermath of his violations of baseball's drug policies, was a Met from 1984 until his suspension. Centerfielder Gerald Williams' first-inning over-the-right-shoulder catch of Alex Rodriguez's drive, the defensive gem of the night, saves a run and the no-hitter.

1862

Union Grounds, at Lee and Rutledge Streets in Brooklyn, opens as baseball's first enclosed ballpark. Two teams picked from among the Putnams, Eckfords and Constellations play an exhibition for over 2,000 people who come mainly to see the converted ice skating rink and its new grandstand. The three teams are resident for the season during which a 10-cent admission is charged, although the opening day exhibition is free. Over the next 25 years, the Union Grounds will be the site of many famous games and the home for New York's National Association and National League clubs.

1918

The first airmail flight between New York and Washington, D.C. takes off from the infield at Belmont Park.

1926

Madison Square Garden is granted an expansion hockey franchise by the NHL. The team would soon be called Tex's Rangers, owing to Tex Rickard's stewardship of the Garden, and the nickname sticks.

1926

Righthander George Earnshaw spoils the opening game at the Newark Bears' new home with a six-hitter. The Baltimore Orioles win, 7-2, in the first International League game at David's Stadium (named for Bears owner Charles L. David). The club had been playing at Newark's Schools Stadium and Sprague Field in nearby Bloomfield, N.J. (see Nov. 12).

JOE DiMAGGIO

1941

Many of the 9,040 at Yankee Stadium boo as the Yankees drop the opener of a three-game series to Chicago, 13-1, the Bombers' only run coming on Joe DiMaggio's first-inning single off Edgar Smith. DiMaggio gets at least one hit in every game for over two months, building his record 56-game hitting streak starting with this game (see July 17).

1961

Tommy Gorman, one of the founders of the NHL, a key player in bringing hockey to New York, the first coach of the Americans, and business manager or general manager of seven Stanley Cup champions, dies in Ottawa, Ontario, at age 74.

1970

Tom Seaver throws the Mets' third one-hitter in the first 33 games of the season, beating the Phillies, 4-0, at Philadelphia. It gives the Mets back-to-back one-hitters as Gary Gentry threw one at Chicago May 13 (the 14th was a travel day) and is the second of Seaver's career. He will ultimately throw five one-hitters for the Mets.

1984

Jersey City officials announce a housing development is to be built on the site of Roosevelt Stadium. The stadium was a major sports venue for some four decades.

1991

Bill Parcells resigns as head coach of the Football Giants, citing health concerns. Parcells posted a 77-49-1 record in eight seasons and led the club to Super Bowl wins in 1987 and 1991.

1881

Leading heavyweight contender John L. Sullivan reinforces his claim to challenge champ Jake Kilrain with an eight-round victory over John Flood on a barge anchored in the Hudson off Yonkers, N.Y.

1885

J.A. Snowden of Boston wins the second six-day roller skating race at the Garden with a record 1,166 miles in 142 hours slightly over two months after two contestants died in the wake of the inaugural competition (see Mar. 7). Bill Boyst, Jr., of Port Jervis, N.Y., is second (1,025 miles).

1912

Enraged by the taunts of fans, Detroit's Ty Cobb charges into the stands at Hilltop Park during the fourth inning of the Tigers' 8-4 win. Umpire Silk O'Laughlin ejects Cobb after order is restored, and the next day he is suspended by American League president Ban Johnson.

1914

Two Brooklyn clubs meet at Pawtucket, R.I., in the first national championship of the U.S. (Soccer) Football Association. The Brooklyn Football Club wins the National Challenge Cup over the Brooklyn Celtic FC, 2-1.

1924

Candy Cummings, a righthander believed to have invented the curveball during his stint with the Excelsior Club of Brooklyn in 1866-67, dies in Toledo, Ohio, at age 75.

1926

Dog racing is introduced to New York with the start of two days of competition at the Polo Grounds. On the first day of the International Dog Carnival, 16 races are run as Lion, a 16-pound fawn-shade whippet, wins the Grand National Handicap with Peter finishing second.

1954

Patrick Joseph McDonald, last of the famed "Irish Whales," dies in New York at 76. Babe McDonald was the Olympic gold medalist in the shotput in 1912 and in the 56-pound weight in 1920.

1955

Hardy (Bazooka) Smallwood of Brooklyn gains a split decision over Bob Provizzi of Freeland, Pennsylvania, in the 10-round middleweight feature at Eastern Parkway Arena. After three years and 156 consecutive shows, the arena closes when ABC does not renew its contract. Eastern Parkway operated for two years on a contract with the DuMont Network (see May 12) before DuMont switched to Manhattan's St. Nick's Arena and ABC picked up Eastern Parkway.

1975

Al Helfer, baseball play-by-play announcer for the Mutual Game of the Day, the Brooklyn Dodgers and the Giants, dies in Sacramento, California, at age 63.

1982

Islanders beat the Canucks, 3-1, in Vancouver, to win their third straight Stanley Cup, sweeping both the semifinal (against Quebec) and final rounds in four games.

1989

New York's leading thoroughbred trainer five times in the 1960s, Buddy Jacobson dies in Buffalo, N.Y., at 58. Jacobson in 1978 murdered restauranteur John Tupper, the third angle of a love triangle involving model Melanie Cain, then 23. Sentenced in 1980 to 25 years in prison, he escaped from the Brooklyn House of Detention but was captured six weeks later in California.

1887

Awaiting passage by the legislature of the so-called Ives Pool bill, which will legalize auction pool betting at New York tracks, the Brooklyn Jockey Club shuts down racing at Gravesend after its six-race program. The club plans to resume May 25 if the bill has passed by then. (The bill is passed and becomes effective May 26, when racing resumes there.)

1912

Clarence Parker is born in Portsmouth, Virginia. A Football Dodgers half-back (1937-41) and AAFC Yankees quarterback (1946), Ace Parker earned the NFL MVP award in 1940.

1939

In the first televised sports event in America, Princeton edges Columbia in 10 innings, 2-1, at Baker Field. Dan Carmichael throws a six-hitter for the winners and the Lions' Hector Dowd also goes the distance as the Tigers complete an EIBL doubleheader sweep. The second game is telecast by the National Broadcasting Company's experimental station, W2XBS, with Bill Stern calling the play-by-play and Burke Crotty as the director.

STEVE OWEN

1953

In a classic game of managerial manipulation, 41 players appear in the Yankees' 6-5, 10-inning win over the St. Louis Browns at Yankee Stadium. New York uses 23 men as Irv Noren's two-run double ties the game in the ninth and Billy Martin's two-run single wins it. The second game of the scheduled doubleheader is called in the middle of the fourth because of darkness.

1954

Stephen (Tex) Sullivan presents his first "Monday Night Fights" boxing show at Manhattan's St. Nick's Arena on the DuMont Network. Hocine Khalfi of Algeria gains a split decision in a non-title fight over world featherweight champ Sandy Saddler in the main event shown live on DuMont's 30-station network. The program is the first on a two-year deal between DuMont and Sullivan's London Sporting Club (see Jan. 3).

1964

Steve Owen, who played for the Giants' 1927 NFL champions and coached their 1933 and 1938 title teams, dies in Oneida, N.Y., at age 66.

1980

In the first Stanley Cup final game ever played at Nassau Coliseum, the Islanders rout Philadelphia, 6-2, to take a two-games-to-one lead in the best-of-seven series.

1983

Islanders beat Edmonton, 4-2, at Nassau Coliseum, to take the Stanley Cup final in four straight for the second consecutive year, and win their fourth straight Cup.

1992

Joseph F. Healy, 81, NYU track and field coach from 1957-78, dies in Westwood, N.J.

1878

A.J. Burton wins the quarter-mile (0:54.2) and the half-mile (2:08.25) at the Mott Haven Grounds as Columbia wins the IC4A title for the second of three straight years. Penn's Horace Lee wins the 100-yard dash in 10.25, only a quarter-second off his own world record set in 1877.

1878

Westchester Polo Association members open new grounds for the sport in the Fordham area, now The Bronx, but within two years move further downtown into Manhattan (see May 22).

1919

Ralph Kaplowitz, a star guard at NYU and an original Knick in 1946-47 who started in the team's first game (see Nov. 1), is born in Astoria, N.Y.

1946

Reginald Martinez Jackson is born Wyncote, Pennsylvania. Reggie Jackson helped the Yankees to four division championships, three pennants and two World Series titles during five often turbulent seasons in New York (1977-81). Dubbed "Mr. October" sarcastically by teammate Thurman Munson after starting the 1977 Series, his first with the Yanks, poorly, Jackson, by the end, had hit five homers, including three straight in the final game, proving the nickname prophetic.

REGGIE JACKSON

1947

Hal Chase dies at age 64 in Colusa, California. A former Highlanders first baseman and manager, Chase was a famously good fielder and an infamous gambler on baseball.

1962

Billy Golembiewski (with a 752 final series) and Mrs. Shirley Garms (587 in the three-game final) successfully defend their titles at the fourth Ruppert-Brunswick Tournament of Champions bowled at the Garden.

1974

Daniel Reid Topping dies in Miami, Florida, at age 61. As a wealthy young man, Topping embarked on a career of buying sports franchises, starting with the Brooklyn Football Dodgers of the NFL in 1934. He later owned the New York Football Yankees of the AAFC from 1946-49 and was part of the triumvirate (with Del Webb and Larry MacPhail) who bought the Yankees and Yankee Stadium from the Jacob Ruppert estate in 1945 (see Jan. 25).

1996

Chet "the Jet" Forte, 60, dies in San Diego, California. College basketball player of the year in 1956-57, Forte averaged 24.8 ppg over three years with Columbia and was the first director of ABC's "Monday Night Football." Forte ruined his career temporarily through compulsive gambling, though at his death he was hosting a radio sports talk show in San Diego.

1997

In his first playoff as a Ranger, Wayne Gretzky becomes the first Blueshirt ever to record two hat tricks in a single playoff year, tallying three times as New York holds off the Flyers, 5-4, in Philadelphia to even their Stanley Cup semifinal series at 1-1.

1887

In the opening of the local season, the Staten Island Cricket Club defeats St. George, 74-54, in an one-innings match at the St. George Grounds in Hoboken, N.J.

1904

John Murray Murdoch is born in Lucknow, Ontario. An original Ranger in 1926 and the first player the club ever signed, Murray Murdoch, a left wing, played every game (508 plus 66 in the playoffs) of the Rangers' first 11 seasons, setting an NHL durability record. He later coached Yale hockey for over 20 years.

1914

Clem Stralka, football coach at the U.S. Merchant Marine Academy (Kings Point) from 1951-57, is born in Glen Lyon, Pennsylvania. Stralka also started the wrestling program at Kings Point and coached it to 19 winning seasons in a row.

1928

Adolph Schayes is born in New York. Dolph Schayes was a great forward for NYU in the mid-1940s before going on to a Hall of Fame career with the Syracuse Nationals of the NBA.

1928

Gilbert James McDougald is born in San Francisco, California. Gil McDougald was a versatile infielder for the Yankees from 1951-60 and Fordham baseball coach from 1970-76, compiling a 100-79-4 record in seven seasons.

1962

Ray Camp, outdoors columnist for *The New York Times* who wrote the "Wood, Field & Stream" column, dies in Madison, Connecticut, at age 54.

1984

Islanders' drive for five straight Stanley Cups dies in Edmonton. The Oilers, signaling the eclipse of the era of New York's dominance of the NHL and the dawn of their own, beat the Isles, 5-2, to take the final, 4-1, and snap the Islanders' string of 19 consecutive playoff series won, a record in any major professional sport. Isles rookie Pat LaFontaine scores twice in the first 35 seconds of the third period to set a league playoff record for fastest two goals at the start of a period to shave the Oilers lead to 4-2, but Edmonton hangs on.

1991

Greg Rice, distance runner and winner of the 1940 Sullivan Award as the nation's top amateur athlete, dies in Hackensack, N.J., at age 75.

DOLPH SCHAYES

1994

Stephane Matteau whacks in a loose puck in front of Devils goalie Martin Brodeur 6:13 into the second overtime for an unassisted goal that gives the Rangers a 3-2 victory over New Jersey at the Meadowlands and a two-games-to-one lead in their best-of-seven semifinal series.

1842

Another great intersectional horse race is staged at Union Course with the North's Fashion easily outrunning Boston, the best of the South, as 20,000 people pour into the course. Fashion breaks all records by covering four miles in 7:32 (see May 27).

1906

Walter Fleischer is born in New York. As Walter Fletcher, he covered dog shows from 1927 into the 1990s for *The New York Times*.

1939

In the first event televised from Madison Square Garden, NBC's experimental station W2XBS shows a half-hour of a six-day bike race, eventually won by the Peden brothers.

1939

Joe Carr, president of the NFL from 1921-39, dies in Columbus, Ohio, at age 58. Carr was also president of the American Basketball League from 1925-28.

1946

Craig Patrick is born in Detroit, Michigan. Grandson of Lester, son of Lynn and nephew of Muzz, Patrick, Rangers general manager from 1980-86, never achieved his apparent destiny to bring, as his ancestors in one capacity or another did, the Stanley Cup to New York. Instead, Patrick built the Stanley Cup champion Pittsburgh Penguins, who won two in a row (1991-92).

CLAIR BEE

1948

For the second time in his career, Joe DiMaggio hits for the cycle as he homers twice and drives in six runs to help the Yankees romp, 13-2, over the White Sox at Chicago.

1967

Dan Parker, sports columnist and sports editor of the *Daily Mirror* from 1926-63 and the *Journal-American* from 1964-65, dies in Waterbury, Connecticut, at age 73.

1968

Belmont Park reopens after a $30.7 million renovation with 42,080 on hand. In the day's feature, Mrs. Frances Genter's In Reality wins the 68th Carter Handicap by 1 1/2 lengths.

1972

At Nassau Coliseum, Roger Brown scores 32 points as Indiana beats the Nets, 108-105, to take the ABA final, 4-2, disappointing most of the 10,434 fans.

1982

Dave DeBusschere is named director of operations for the Knicks, replacing general manager Eddie Donovan, and Hubie Brown is hired as head coach, succeeding Red Holzman, who retires with a 613-484 regular-season record (.559) and two NBA titles (1970, 1973).

1983

Clair Bee, LIU coach during the halcyon days of Blackbirds basketball, dies in Cleveland, Ohio, at age 87. In 18 seasons (1933-51), Bee's teams were 370-80 and won the NIT in 1939 and 1941, when it was the premier postseason college basketball tournament.

1879

Gilmore's Gardens, a major entertainment venue at 26th Street and Madison Avenue in Manhattan, is to be known as "Madison Square Garden" under an agreement between W.K. Vanderbilt, president of the New York Central & Hudson River Railroad, owners of the building, and the new lessees: J. & L.F. Kuntz & Company and Messrs. M.K. Botsford and O.H. Dodsworth. The building, originally built in 1832 as a railroad terminal for the New York & Harlem, became an entertainment venue in 1871 when the first Grand Central Depot opened on East 42d Street and the railroads moved uptown.

1881

A meeting of 31 clubs from around the country is held in New York and forms the United States National Lawn Tennis Association. Known today as the U.S. Tennis Association, it is the oldest amateur sports governing organization in the world as well as the oldest national tennis association. General Robert Shaw Oliver of Albany, N.Y., is elected as the first president.

1930

For the only time in his career, Babe Ruth hits three homers in a game (driving in six runs), but the Yankees lose, 15-7, in the first game of a doubleheader at Philadelphia. The A's complete the sweep with a 4-1 win.

1942

John T. Doyle, president of the American Sports Publishing Company from 1915-42, dies in New York at age 71.

1952

Dodgers score 15 runs in the first inning and beat Cincinnati, 19-1, before 11,850 at Ebbets Field. Sending 21 men to the plate, Brooklyn gets 10 hits, seven walks and two hit batsmen off four pitchers as every Dodger gets at least one RBI.

1960

Princeton's Cookie Krongard scores what is believed to be the first goal ever recorded by a lacrosse goalie. His tally snaps a scoreless tie and his 15 saves lift the Tigers to a 6-5 home win over Cornell that clinches a third straight Ivy League title.

1968

David A. (Sonny) Werblin, who had served as president and guiding hand of the Jets since their reorganization in 1963, is bought out by his four partners.

1979

For the third time since they last won the Stanley Cup in 1940, the Rangers are beaten in the final, losing the fifth game of the series to the Canadiens, 4-1, at the Montreal Forum.

1981

Islanders whip Minnesota, 5-1, at Nassau Coliseum, in the fifth game of the final, to win their second straight Cup. New York completes the playoffs with a 15-3 record, losing only two quarterfinal games to Edmonton and one to the North Stars.

1981

St. John's wins the opening-round game in the NCAA Northeast Regional baseball playoffs, beating Yale, 1-0, in 12 innings at New Haven, Connecticut. Southpaw Frank Viola runs his record to 10-0, outlasting Bulldogs righty Ron Darling but needs relief help from Eric Stampfl, who gets the save. Maine wins the regional title three days later by eliminating the Redman, who are making their eighth straight tournament appearance.

1880

Before an audience of about 1,000 curious onlookers, the Westchester Polo Association dedicates the Polo Grounds, soon to become New York's most important outdoor sports venue. Although there are no stands to accommodate fans on this opening Saturday afternoon, the Association decides to rectify that shortcoming by fall when a successor group, the Manhattan Polo Association, takes over the 400,000-square foot site. James Gordon Bennett, Jr., publisher of the *New York Herald*, had introduced polo to America in 1876 and strongly presses for its development (although his popular newspaper supports virtually all sports). The tract, bounded by 110th and 112th Streets between Fifth and Sixth Avenues in Manhattan, will shortly have not only polo fields but baseball diamonds and a track for bicycle and running events. At 4:30 p.m. on this day, the WPA splits into opposing teams for practice games. The "Blues," captained by August Belmont, II, capture a silver tankard by winning the best-of-five demonstration series, 3-2, over the "Reds," captained by Chauncey Oelrichs.

1930

In the Yankees' doubleheader sweep of the Athletics at Philadelphia's Shibe Park, Lou Gehrig has his third career three-homer game in the 20-13 nightcap victory. Babe Ruth also homers in that game after hitting a pair in the 10-1 opener win. Ruth has now hit six homers in four games (see May 21) and is ahead of his 1927 record pace.

1932

Sportswriter Bozeman Bulger dies in Lynbrook, N.Y., at age 54.

1944

Keene Fitzpatrick, 79, Princeton track and field coach (1911-32), dies in Princeton, N.J.

1976

Heavyweight boxer Oscar Bonavena dies in Reno, Nevada, at age 33.

1990

Rocky Graziano, the crowd-pleasing middleweight champ from 1947-48, when he took the title in the second of his three bouts with Tony Zale, dies in New York at age 68.

1992

Don Murphy, an NBA referee for 17 seasons, dies in Cincinnati, Ohio, at age 61.

1994

After being eliminated in the playoffs three straight years by Chicago, the Knicks beat the Michael Jordan-less Bulls, 87-77, at the Garden, to take the seventh game of their quarterfinal matchup, ending the Bulls' three-year reign as league champions.

1995

Defenseman Brian Leetch scores all three Rangers goals but Philadelphia wins, 4-3, at the Spectrum on Kevin Haller's goal 25 seconds into overtime, to take their second straight overtime game and a 2-0 Stanley Cup quarterfinal series lead.

1998

Mets acquire catcher Mike Piazza, former Los Angeles All-Star, from the Florida Marlins for three prospects (outfielder Preston Wilson and minor-league pitchers Ed Yarnall and Geoff Goetz). Piazza's acquisition creates a potential logjam behind the plate when incumbent Todd Hundley, the majors' all-time record holder for home runs in a season by a catcher (41 in 1996), returns from the disabled list. In the event, when Hundley returns July 11, he plays leftfield.

May 23

1877

In a cockfighting main held well after the traditional Easter Monday end of the season, breeders settle the question of whether Manhattan or Brooklyn and Long Island breed the best fighting birds. New York wins the first four matches at Newtown, Queens, before Brooklyn-Long Island wins twice. Then a four-pound black red closes out the best-of-nine and New York wins the main, 5-2, and collects the heavy betting money.

1928

Irwin Dambrot is born in New York. In 1949-50, Dambrot was an All-American and (with Joe Galiber) co-captain of the CCNY basketball team that won both the NIT and NCAA titles.

1936

Harness driving great Carmine Abbatiello is born in Staten Island.

1938

George Foster Sanford dies in New York at age 67. Sanford, a center at Yale from 1891-92, was Columbia's first pro coach who led the football team from 1899 (when the school reinstated the sport after a seven-season hiatus) to 1901, posting a 23-11-1 record. He also coached Rutgers from 1913-23, logging a 56-32-5 mark.

1944

John David Newcombe, popular winner of the U.S. national singles tennis titles in 1967 (as an amateur) and in 1973 (as a pro) at Forest Hills, is born in Sydney, Australia.

1945

Luis Tiant, Sr., is shelled in a four-run fourth inning as the Homestead Grays of Pittsburgh, Pennsylvania, defeat the New York Cubans, 8-2, in a Negro National League game before 12,000 at the Polo Grounds.

1946

Pitchers Max Lanier and Fred Martin and infielder Lou Klein jump their Cardinals contracts while St. Louis is in New York finishing a two-game series with the Giants to sign with the Mexican League. The signings climax the Pasqual brothers' campaign, begun in 1945, to challenge for major league status by luring big-league players to Mexico. Six Giants (including pitcher Sal Maglie, infielder Nap Reyes and outfielder Danny Gardella) have already jumped and the Dodgers have lost catcher Mickey Owen and outfielder Luis Olmo, who hit .313 in 1945.

1958

Billy Brown resigns as matchmaker for the International Boxing Club and is succeeded by Jack Barrett. Brown (whose real name is Dominick Mordini) was an assistant to Al Weill for two years, and became IBC matchmaker in 1952 when Weill resigned to manage heavyweight champion Rocky Marciano. The 57-year-old Brown steps down after being caught in the vortex of investigations swirling around the IBC.

1963

Joe Pepitone homers twice in the eighth inning during the Yankees' 13-7 victory over the Kansas City A's at the Stadium.

1990

Ted Tinling, longtime clothes designer for women's tennis players, dies at age 79 in Cambridge, England.

1998

In his first start since throwing a 4-0 perfect game against the Minnesota Twins at Yankee Stadium May 17, Yankee southpaw David Wells allows six hits as the Yankees pound the Red Sox, 12-3, at Boston. Chuck Knoblauch belts a second-inning grand slam to help Wells to his sixth straight win.

1888

Edward H. Coy is born in Andover, Massachusetts. Ted Coy was captain of the 10-0 Yale football team of 1909 that is generally acknowledged as that season's national champs.

1901

Lionel Conacher, a defenseman who like his Hall of Fame brother Charlie spent a portion of his career with the New York Americans (1926-27 to 1929-30), is born in Toronto, Ontario. Conacher was traded in 1930 to the Montreal Maroons for future Amerks coach and president, and eventual NHL president, Red Dutton.

1936

Second baseman Tony Lazzeri belts two grand slams, the first major leaguer ever to do so, and drives in an AL-record 11 runs as the Yankees, scoring the most runs in a game in their history and posting their largest margin of victory, cruise to a 25-2 win over the Philadelphia A's at Shibe Park. The day before, the Yanks swept a doubleheader from the A's, 12-6 and 15-1, giving them 52 runs in two days. On the same day, the Giants beat the Phillies, 13-5, and Brooklyn spanks Boston, 11-2.

1946

Joe McCarthy resigns as Yankees manager during his 16th season. Since taking over the club in 1931, McCarthy had managed the Yankees to pennants in 1932, 1936-39, and 1941-43, winning the World Series each of those years except 1942.

1946

Steve Phillips introduces the mobile starting gate at Roosevelt Raceway, revolutionizing harness racing.

1966

Jim Barnes, winner in 1916 of the first PGA championship, held at the Siwanoy Country Club in Bronxville, N.Y., and the second in 1919, held at the Engineers Country Club in Roslyn, N.Y., dies in East Orange, N.J., at age 78.

1980

Bob Nystrom's goal at 7:11 of overtime gives the Islanders a 5-4 win over Philadelphia at Nassau Coliseum and the first of their four successive Stanley Cups. The Islanders win the final series, four games to two, despite blowing a 4-2 third period lead.

BOB NYSTROM

1989

Phil Esposito is fired after three seasons as Rangers general manager. During his tenure, the Blueshirts go 107-107-26 during the regular season, missing the playoffs once, and lose eight of 10 Stanley Cup playoff games, all coached by Esposito.

1990

Augie Donatelli, a National League umpire from 1950-73, dies in St. Petersburg, Florida, at age 75. Donatelli in 1964 was the driving force behind the organization of the umpires' union, a move that apparently cost him his designation as a crew chief.

May 25

1845
William A. Muldoon is born in Belfast, N.Y. "The Great Muldoon" was a famed wrestler, amateur boxer and trainer who in 1921 was appointed chairman of the New York State Athletic Commission.

1866
A crowd of several thousand shows up at Brooklyn's Capitoline Grounds to watch the host Excelsior club edge the fabled Knickerbockers, 56-42, in the early highlight of the local baseball season. The game lasts only 2:35 despite the 98 runs.

1871
Capt. A.H. Bogardus of Elkhart, Indiana, defeats J.A. Payne of New York, 87-86, in pigeon-shooting at Fleetwood Park in Morrisania (The Bronx). A crowd of 300 well-to-do admirers of sharpshooting assemble for the match under the rules of the Rhode Island Sportsmen's Club.

1907
Jerome Travers wins the Metropolitan Amateur golf title for the second straight year, beating Findlay Douglas, 8 and 7, at the Nassau Country Club in Glen Cove, N.Y.

1922
Alexa Stirling, three-time national amateur champion from Atlanta playing out of the North Hempstead Country Club, wins the Metropolitan women's title at the Morris County CC in Convent, N.J. Miss Sirling, three-time U.S. titlist (1916, 1919-20), defeats Mrs. Pauline Mackay Jackson, herself the U.S. national champion in 1905 and 1914, 5 and 3, in the 36-hole final.

1922
Brooklyn's Jimmy Johnstone hits for the cycle and scores three times as the Dodgers beat the Phillies, 8-7, in the first game of a doubleheader at Philadelphia.

1929
Maureen Orcutt of White Beeches (N.J.) takes her fourth straight Metropolitan Women's Golf Championship with a 4 and 3 win over Helen Hicks of Hewlett, L.I., at the Greenwich CC.

1960
International Soccer League, the largest effort yet to establish the sport in the U.S., opens its 30-date season as 10,444 watch Kilmarnock of Scotland defeat Bayern-Munchen (West Germany), 3-1, at the Polo Grounds. Using 11 full teams imported from Europe and South America plus a locally-organized team called the New York Americans coached by Albert Stubbins of England, the ISL is a modest success in its first season and operates for six years.

1987
Bob Giegengack, track and field coach at Fordham from 1938-41 and in 1946, and at Yale from 1946-75, dies in New Haven, Connecticut, at age 80.

1994
Mark Messier scores three times in the third period, lifting the Rangers past New Jersey, 4-2, in the sixth game of their Stanley Cup semifinal and evening the series at 3-3. Messier, who the day before had "guaranteed" victory, starts the Rangers' comeback by assisting on Alexei Kovalev's goal late in the second period to cut the Devils lead to 2-1.

1876

Jack Root, the first recognized light heavyweight champion when he defeated Kid McCoy in 1903, is born in Czechoslovakia.

1887

After being banned for 10 years, legalized betting returns to New York racetracks. Using the auction pool system, bookmakers openly ply their trade on the third day of the Brooklyn Jockey Club spring meeting at the Gravesend Track. Saxony is the first winner, romping home in the seven-furlong first race.

1922

Playing in Washington without Babe Ruth, the Yankees lose to the Senators, 3-1, as Ruth sits out a one-game suspension. He had thrown dirt at umpire George Hildebrand during a 6-4 victory over the Senators the day before at the Polo Grounds and then chased a heckler in the stands after being ejected.

1952

Tom McMillen is born in Elmira, N.Y. A Rhodes Scholar and 6'11" center who was later elected to Congress, McMillen played 56 games for the Knicks in 1976-77 alongside fellow Rhodes Scholar Bill Bradley, a Princeton graduate, as well as Jim McMillian, late of Columbia, giving the Knicks perhaps the smartest team in NBA history. Alas, it wasn't a good one, finishing 40-42 and missing the playoffs.

1956

Norman P. (Red) Strader, coach of the AAFC Yankees in 1948 and 1949 (13-9) and the NFL Yanks in 1950 (7-5) after the AAFC folded, dies in Berkeley, California, at age 53.

1969

Franchise founder Arthur Brown sells the New York Nets to Roy L.M. Boe.

1992

Princeton becomes only the fourth school in the 16-year history of the tournament to win the NCAA lacrosse championship. Midfielder Andy Moe's goal nine seconds into the second overtime gives the Tigers a 10-9 victory over Syracuse, shocking the 13,650 fans at the University of Pennsylvania's Franklin Field. Only Syracuse, Johns Hopkins, and Maryland had won the title since the tournament began in 1977. Princeton had been ranked No. 1 four times in final national polls before 1977 (1937, 1942, 1951, 1957).

1995

Rangers' Stanley Cup defense ends ignominiously as the Philadelphia Flyers whip the lifeless Blueshirts, 4-1, at the Garden, to sweep their second-round playoff series in four games.

JIM McMILLIAN

1996

Francis X. Briante dies at age 91 in White Plains, N.Y. Frank (Five-Yard) Briante was a star running back at NYU, teaming with Ken Strong on the Violets' best teams in 1926 and 1927 before joining the NFL Staten Island Stapletons and Newark Tornadoes. He later served 10 years as president of the White Plains (N.Y.) Board of Education.

May 27

1823

Feelings run high as two of America's best horses, Henry of Navarre, representing the South, and American Eclipse, for the North, meet in a best two-of-three-heats match race for a $20,000 purse plus sizeable side bets all around at the Union Course on what is now the Woodhaven-Ozone Park border. Henry wins the first race but jockey Samuel Purdy boots Eclipse home in both the second and third of the four-mile heats to win the purse.

1871

The largest crowd of the local baseball season so far (3,500) turns out at Union Grounds in Brooklyn to see the Olympics of Washington, D.C., beat the Boston Red Stockings, 6-5, in an NA game. The crowd validates the decision to charge 50 cents a ticket for games in New York between pro clubs instead of the customary 25 cents.

1928

Andrew Payne, age 17, of Claremont, Okla., wins C.C. Pyle's "Bunion Derby" cross-country run, arriving in New York after running 3,422 miles from Los Angeles in 573 hours, 4 minutes, 34 seconds. He started March 9.

1932

Bill Morley, Columbia's first football All-American in 1899 and Lions coach from 1902-05 (26-11-3), dies in Pasadena, Calif., at age 55.

1944

Alfred B. Maclay, president of the American Horse Association from 1926-36 and breeder, exhibitor and judge of show horses, dies at age 72 in New York.

1949

Believe it or not, Bob Ripley, a sports cartoonist for the *New York Globe* from 1913-23 before achieving fame as a nationally-syndicated cartoonist, dies in New York at age 55.

1959

A husband-and-wife team sweeps the honors in the first Ruppert-Brunswick Tournament of Champions bowling event at the Garden. Don Carter eliminates Ray Bluth and finishes with 8.64 Peterson points to take the men's title and Mrs. Laverne Carter rolls a 179 and a 195 in her final two games to win the women's event.

1964

Ted Collins, Kate Smith's manager and owner of the NFL New York Bulldogs (1949), who morphed into the New York Yanks (1950-51), who became (after Collins sold them) the Dallas Texans in 1952 and the Baltimore Colts in 1953, dies in Lake Placid, N.Y., at age 64.

1982

A group led by Dr. John McMullen completes the purchase of the Colorado Rockies and announces receipt of NHL approval to move the club to the Meadowlands Arena in East Rutherford, N.J. On June 30, the nickname "Devils" is chosen from among fans' suggestions and Billy MacMillan is named general manager and coach.

1994

Stephane Matteau scores at 4:24 of the second overtime to give the Rangers a 2-1 win over the Devils in the seventh game of their semifinal at the Garden and a berth in the final against Vancouver. New York's Brian Leetch's second period goal stands up until Valeri Zelepukin tallies with 7.7 seconds left in regulation.

1997

Princeton wins the NCAA lacrosse title for the fourth time since 1992 with a 19-7 victory over unseeded Maryland before 25,317 at College Park, Md., as Jesse Hubbard scores four goals. The Tigers (15-0) stretch their winning streak to 28 games and become the first repeat champions since 1990.

1874

Fordham downs visiting NYU, 26-10, in a baseball game that marks the beginning of the storied athletic competition between the schools.

1876

Charles F. Herreshoff, an earlier designer and racer of motorized power boats, is born in Nice, France.

1888

Jim Thorpe, voted America's greatest athlete of the first half of the 20th century, is born in Prague, Oklahoma Territory.

1946

In the first night game in Yankee Stadium history, Washington beats the Yankees, 2-1.

1951

Rookie Willie Mays, hitless in his first 12 at-bats, gets his first big-league hit when he slams a first-inning homer onto the leftfield roof off Boston's Warren Spahn at the Polo Grounds. The Braves win, 4-1, disappointing most of the crowd of 23,101 this night. Mays is held in check (0-for-8) in the balance of the three-game series with Boston before breaking out against Pittsburgh.

1962

Tony Fortunato earns a 10-round decision over Stefan Redl in a welterweight bout that is the feature fight on the final night at St. Nicholas Arena. The 66-year-old arena is soon converted to a television studio by the ABC television network.

LOU LITTLE

1967

Cerro of Uruguay, playing as the New York Skyliners, open the United Soccer Association season with a 1-1 tie against Toronto (Hibernians of Edinburgh, Scotland) before 21,871 at Yankee Stadium.

1968

Oswald Tower dies in West Caldwell, N.J., at age 84. Tower was the editor of the *Official Basketball Guide* from 1914-50, a referee for 35 years and Rules Committee interpreter from 1915 until his retirement in 1959.

1979

Lou Little, head football coach of Columbia from 1930-56 and winner of the 1934 Rose Bowl against Stanford, dies in Delray Beach, Florida, at age 85.

1990

Abe Shorin, one of the brothers who presided over the growth of the Topps Gum Co. into the dominant outfit in the baseball trading card business, dies in Miami Beach, Fla., at age 91.

1994

Julius Boros, twice U.S. Open golf champion (1952, 1963) and winner of the PGA championship and Westchester Classic in 1968, dies in Fort Lauderdale, Florida, at age 74.

1875

Baseball's first no-hitter is pitched by Joseph Mann of Princeton against Yale as the Tigers win, 3-0, at New Haven.

1875

David Lewis Fultz is born in Staunton, Virginia. Fultz in 1903 got the first extra-base hit in the Highlanders history. He organized and was president of the Baseball Players' Fraternity (1912-17), and was president of the International League (1919-20). He also was NYU football coach in 1904 (3-6).

1906

Arthur Chapman is born in Winnipeg, Manitoba. In his first two full seasons with the Americans, Art Chapman led the NHL in assists (34 in 1934-35, 28 in 1935-36).

1913

Anthony Florian Zaleski is born in Gary, Indiana. As Tony Zale, he was world middleweight champion from 1941-47 and again in 1948.

1932

Richie Guerin, an Iona star and 6'4" sharpshooter who averaged 19.9 ppg for the Gaels during his three seasons there (1951-54), and who later averaged 20.1 ppg in 518 games over eight seasons (1956-64) with the Knicks, is born in New York. Guerin three times led the Knicks in scoring, with a high of 29.5 ppg in 1961-62, then a club record.

1933

Daniel O'Leary, the Irish immigrant who became a fabled 19th-century pedestrian competitor, dies at age 90 in Los Angeles, Calif. O'Leary, who defeated Edward Payson Weston (see May 12) in a six-day race in 1875 and twice won the Astley World Championship belt, walked over 300,000 miles in his lifetime, including 125,000 in competition (see July 8).

1938

Francis T. Vincent, Jr., is born in Waterbury, Connecticut. Fay Vincent, whose father was a Yale football player and longtime Eastern college football game official, was the eighth commissioner of baseball, from 1989 to September 7, 1992.

1963

Queens housewife Mrs. Barbara Weiner nearly steals the women's title at the fifth Tournament of Champions bowled at the Garden, but leaves a seven-pin in the 10th frame of the final. Judy Audsley, the 18-year-old pro, then buries a strike to win the final, 569-561, over the 24-year-old amateur. Dick Weber has a much easier time, beating Don Carter, 751-574, in the men's final.

1975

Hubert Glendon, Columbia varsity crew coach from 1934-47, dies in Hyannis, Massachusetts, at age 72. His brother, Richard J., and father, Richard A., also coached the Light Blue crew.

1988

Joe Bostic, the first black boxing ring announcer at Madison Square Garden, dies at age 79 in Southampton, N.Y.

1990

Davey Johnson, Mets manager since 1984, is fired with the team 20-22, in fourth place and 5 1/2 games out. Third-base coach Bud Harrelson takes over, and the Mets lose, 2-1, at Cincinnati that night.

1883

Five baseball games are played at the Polo Grounds, 110th Street and 5th Avenue, in a single day. A canvas fence is used to divide the grounds in half. On the 6th Avenue side, the Mets play two A.A. games, beating Cincinnati, 1-0, in the morning, and Columbus, 12-5, in the afternoon. On the 5th Avenue side, the Giants split a doubleheader with Detroit (losing 5-2 and then winning 8-4) while Yale defeats Princeton, 5-4, in between.

1885

Harvard's aggressive lacrosse team, fresh from a win over NYU the day before, wins the Oelrichs Cup tournament at the Prospect Park Parade Grounds in Brooklyn. The Crimson defeat the Williamsburg Lacrosse Club, 6-1, in the morning, and the Druids of Baltimore, Maryland, 5-0, in the afternoon after the Druids beat Princeton. NYU was eliminated by Princeton earlier in the day.

1896

Georgetown's Bernie Wefers sets a world record in the 220-yard run (20.2 seconds), breaking his own mark set in the International meet the previous fall (see Sept. 21). Yale wins the team title (44 $\frac{1}{2}$ points) with Penn second (22 $\frac{1}{2}$) in the IC4A meet at Manhattan Field.

1900

George H. Collett sets a world cycling record at Berkeley Oval by covering 24 miles, 1,472 yards in one hour. He also sets an amateur competition record by winning the one-mile handicap in 2:00.4 and the half-mile dash.

1900

Led by the Vesper Boat Club, Philadelphia rowers win four events to the New York clubs' three in the annual regatta on New Jersey's Passaic River. In the eight-oar shell race over 1 $\frac{1}{2}$ miles, Vesper beats the NYAC by a length.

1912

Columbia's R.L. Beatty sets a 16-pound shotput record (47' $\frac{1}{8}$") on the opening day of the IC4A championships at Philadelphia's Franklin Field.

1913

Racing resumes at Belmont Park after a two-year shutdown due to anti-betting laws passed by the New York legislature. During the shutdown, two famous Brooklyn tracks (Sheepshead Bay and Gravesend) close forever.

1922

Babe Ruth is among the 15,000 fans at the first opening night of the New York Velodrome, 225th Street and Broadway. Georges Columbatto of Italy (paced by James Hunter of Newark, N.J.) wins the 25-mile international motor paced feature in 39:46.2.

1938

Before 81,141, largest crowd in the history of Yankee Stadium, the Yankees sweep a Decoration Day doubleheader from the Red Sox, 10-0 and 5-4.

1962

Los Angeles beats the Mets, 13-6 and 6-5, to sweep a Memorial Day doubleheader at the Polo Grounds before 54,360, the largest National League doubleheader paid crowd in New York since 1937.

1973

Ownership syndicate headed by Ralf Brent announces that the WHA New York Raiders will henceforth be known as the Golden Blades. Club trades center Ron Ward and goalie Pete Donnelly to the Vancouver Blazers for center Andre Lacroix and left wing Don Harriman.

1879

Madison Square Garden officially opens under its new (and permanent) name as Harvey B. Dodsworth conducts a 60-piece orchestra in a concert that features numerous solo performers including noted tenor Signor Liberati.

1902

Arthur Duffey of Boston sets a world record in the 100-yard dash (9.6 seconds) at Berkeley Oval, but the record is subsequently expunged due to charges that Duffey was a professional.

1906

New York Governor Frank W. Higgins orders New York County sheriff John Hayes to enforce the state's law against prizefighting, which he believes is being widely flouted by City athletic clubs despite 110 arrests by City police since January. Hayes and his deputies convince the Long Acre AC on West 29th Street to cancel its regular Thursday night show on this date but other clubs (including the Century AC, which promotes its fights at the Garden) promise to challenge the action in court.

1909

Arthur Edmund Coulter is born in Winnipeg, Manitoba. The second captain in club history (1937-42), Rangers defenseman Art Coulter helped New York to the 1940 Stanley Cup and was elected in 1974 to the Hockey Hall of Fame.

1942

Harold Hairston is born in Winston-Salem, North Carolina. Happy Hairston scored 1,346 points (21.0 ppg) and pulled down 793 rebounds for NYU from 1961-64.

JACK DEMPSEY

1946

Charles Chicarelli's four-game 877 is good for the $1,500 first prize in the annual Landgraf Individual Classic at Manhattan's Bowlmor Recreation on University Place. Eddie Niederhaus is second ($800) with 874 and Semo Stavich third ($600) with 866.

1983

Jack Dempsey, world heavyweight champion from 1919-26, dies in New York at age 87.

1984

Doug Carpenter is named the Devils' third head coach. He stays until January 26, 1988, with a lifetime 100-166-24 mark (.386) and a 21-24-5 record on the season. Jim Schoenfeld takes over and spearheads New Jersey's drive to its first-ever playoff berth.

1991

Pat Riley is hired as head coach of the Knicks. In four years, Riley would lead the Knicks to four 50-win seasons and the NBA final in 1994.

1995

Tim Mara, Jr., who created through his control of a 50% interest in the Football Giants the impasse that resulted in George Young's hiring as general manager in 1979 (see Feb. 14), dies in Jupiter, Florida, at age 59.

June 1

1871

Opening their National Association season, the Mutuals beat the Forest City club of Rockford, Illinois, 7-3, before 2,000 at Union Grounds in Brooklyn.

1900

New Jersey Golf Association is founded by a group of 10 clubs and elects L.H. Graham as its first president.

1925

Lou Gehrig begins his 2,130 consecutive-games-played streak when he appears as a Yankees pinch-hitter.

1939

As part of its continuing experiment with sports on television, NBC's pilot station in New York shows the Lou Nova-Max Baer heavyweight fight from Yankee Stadium with Sam Taub at the microphone. Nova knocks out Baer in the 11th round.

1946

Trained by Max Hirsch and ridden by Warren Mehrtens, P.J. Kleberg Jr.'s King Ranch star, Assault, wins the Belmont Stakes to complete the seventh Triple Crown in thoroughbred racing history.

1955

Dodgers set a club record for home runs in a game with six and Duke Snider becomes the last Brooklyn player to hit three homers in a game in an 11-8 win over the Milwaukee Braves at Ebbets Field. Snider homers in the first, fourth and sixth innings while Pee Wee Reese, Jackie Robinson and Roy Campanella each hit one.

1960

Lester Patrick, the first Rangers coach (1926-39) and general manager of their first three Stanley Cup championship teams (1927-28, 1932-33, 1939-40), dies at age 76 in Victoria, British Columbia.

1961

In the third annual Ruppert-Brunswick Tournament of Champions at the Garden, Billy Golembiewski of Detroit and Mrs. Shirley Garms of Chicago both win in the final frame. For the second straight year, Golembiewski beats Don Carter in the men's final (606-582) and Garms defeats Phyllis Notaro, 575-569, before 4,300 fans.

1994

Al Arbour retires for the second time as Islanders coach. Arbour, who coached the 1980-81-82-83 Stanley Cup champions, was in his two terms (1973-86, 1988-94) behind the Isles' bench 739-537-223 (.567). In the playoffs, his Islander clubs won 119 of 198 games (.601) and 29 of 40 series, including a record 19 in a row encompassing the four consecutive Cups and three series in 1984 before the Edmonton Oilers finally ended the streak in the final.

1994

Taunting the fans, and particularly courtside spectator and film director Spike Lee, Indiana's Reggie Miller scores 25 fourth-quarter points at the Garden to lead the Pacers to their third straight win, 93-86, over the Knicks and a three-games-to-two lead in their semifinal series.

1995

Daniel Capozzi, a soccer star at Harrison (N.J.) High School and later with the Newark Portuguese and Irish-American Soccer Clubs, dies in North Bend, Oregon, at age 69.

June 2

1900

Perry Belmont's bay colt, Ethelbert, establishes himself as one of the nation's premier thoroughbreds by easily defeating W.C. Whitney's Jean Beraud in a $5,000 match race at Gravesend track in Brooklyn. Each horse carries 126 pounds and Ethelbert runs the 1 1/4 miles in 2:08.2.

1910

Ehrhardt Henry Heller is born in Kitchener, Ontario. Defenseman Ott Heller upon retiring in 1946 after 15 years had played more games (647) than anyone else in Rangers history.

1915

Colonel William E. Van Wyck, 75, a New York Athletic Club founder and its first president, dies in New York.

1923

In the first championship fight at the Polo Grounds, Eugene Criqui wins the world featherweight championship with a sixth-round knockout of Johnny Kilbane. The 30,000 fans pay over $105,000 gross. Criqui loses the title 54 days later on a 15-round decision to Johnny Dundee July 26 (also at the Polo Grounds) and never regains it.

1938

Eugene Richard Michael is born in Kent, Ohio. Gene Michael was a Yankees shortstop, coach, two-time manager, general manager and "super scout."

1941

Lou Gehrig, "The Pride of the Yankees," dies in New York at 37 of amyotrophic lateral sclerosis, now commonly called Lou Gehrig's Disease. A two-time American League MVP and 1934 Triple Crown winner, Gehrig hit 493 homers in a 15-year career, all with the Yankees, over which he batted .340. He played in 2,130 consecutive games, a major league record until Cal Ripken broke the mark in 1995, and on nine pennant winners and eight World Series champions.

R. NORRIS WILLIAMS, II

1961

Senior catcher Dick Wohlamacher drives in five runs to lift St. John's to a 10-4 victory over Villanova at Syracuse, N.Y., in the first round of the NCAA baseball tournament. Wohlamacher has a two-run double and then hits a three-run homer in the Redmen's five-run eighth inning that breaks a 4-4 tie. Larry Bearnarth is the winning pitcher for St. John's, which is eliminated from the tournament in the next round.

1968

The unsinkable Dick Williams dies in Bryn Mawr, Pennsylvania, at age 77. R. Norris Williams, II, survived the 1912 sinking of the *Titanic* by holding onto the side of a half-submerged lifeboat. He rejected a ship doctor's advice to amputate his legs and in 1914 (at Newport, R.I.) and 1916 (at Forest Hills) won the U.S. national singles tennis titles.

1978

Philadelphia Flyers coach Fred Shero is named Rangers general manager and coach, succeeding John Ferguson in the former job and and Jean-Guy Talbot in the latter.

1851

Knickerbockers, using their new standard uniform of blue trousers and white shirts with straw hats, defeat the Washingtons, 22-20, on the grounds in Harlem. (On June 17, the same two teams play with the same score but take 10 innings, baseball's first recorded extra-inning game.) The Knicks are baseball's first uniformed team.

1929

Harry H. Frazee, the cash-strapped owner of the Boston Red Sox in 1920 who sold Babe Ruth to the Yankees (in part to finance production of *No, No, Nanette*, a 1925 Broadway hit), dies in New York at age 48.

1932

Lou Gehrig becomes the first American League player, and first major leaguer in the 20th century, to hit four homers in a game as the Yankees pound the A's, 20-13, at Shibe Park in Philadelphia. In the same game, New York's Tony Lazzeri hits for the cycle with a grand slam in the ninth inning. Both events are obscured in the following day's papers, because . . .

1932

John McGraw resigns as Giants manager after 31 seasons. He is replaced by first baseman Bill Terry.

1932

Fischl Lebowitz is born in Arad, Rumania. As Fred Lebow, he was president of the New York Road Runners Club and founded the New York City Marathon in 1970.

FRED LEBOW

1933

William A. Muldoon dies at age 88 on his estate, Olympia, in Purchase, N.Y. "The Great" Muldoon was world Greco-Roman wrestling champion while a member of the New York City Police Department (although he resigned from the force in 1881 to pursue his athletic career) and served as chairman of the New York State Athletic Commission from 1921-28. He was a member of the commission at his death.

1945

Hale Irwin, U.S. Open golf champion at the Winged Foot GC in Mamaroneck, N.Y., in 1974, is born in Joplin, Missouri.

1975

Nets trade forward Larry Kenon to the San Antonio Spurs for center Swen Nater.

1980

Fred Leib dies in Houston, Texas, at age 92. Leib was a baseball writer for New York papers (1911-35), starting with the *New York Press* for five years, and then *The Sporting News* (1935-80), as well as the author of many books on baseball.

1988

Davey Moore, World Boxing Association junior middleweight champion from 1982-83, dies in Holmdel, N.J., at age 28 (see June 16).

 # June 4

1883

Meeting at Delmonico's, leaders of New York society organize the National Horse Show Association of America, with a capital stock of $100,000 (100 shares of $1,000 each). Cornelius Fellowes is elected the first president with seven vice presidents also chosen from among the new group's shareholders, who hope to rent Madison Square Garden for their annual shows (see Oct. 22).

1900

Fred William Kugler, Jr., founder of the Somerville (N.J.) bike race in 1940, is born in Somerville, N.J.

1916

Dana Oliver Mozley, a sportswriter for the *Daily News* from 1945-80, president of the Golf Writers' Association of America and founder of the Ike golf championship in 1953, an amateur competition that grew to over 700 competitors, is born in Lowell, Mass.

1921

Robert F. Wanzer is born in New York. Bobby Wanzer was a guard for Seton Hall from 1938-40 and 1945-46 and a 10-year pro for the Rochester Royals.

1938

John J. Flanagan, three-time Olympic gold medalist in the hammer throw (1900, 1904, 1908), seven-time AAU national champion in that event, five-time AAU champ in the 56-pound weight throw and a New York City policeman from 1896-1911, dies in Kilbreedy, Ireland, at 65.

1962

Famed thoroughbred racing announcer Clem McCarthy dies in New York at age 79.

1963

Rangers trade their franchise's leader in career wins for a goaltender (204), Gump Worsley, along with wingers Dave Balon, Leon Rochefort and Len Ronson to Montreal for Canadiens netminder Jacques Plante, a six-time Vezina Trophy winner as the NHL's stingiest goalie, center Phil Goyette and left wing Don Marshall.

1968

Rangers general manager Emile Francis steps down as Rangers coach and names Boom Boom Geoffrion his successor, the first of three times Francis relinquishes coaching duties. Francis twice fires his own replacement and returns behind the bench. Garden management replaces Francis before he can perform a second encore.

1974

Los Angeles Strings beat the visiting New York Sets, 25-23, to halt the Sets' 14-match season-opening winning streak. Despite the great start, the Sets finish second in the World Team Tennis Eastern Division and lose to Boston, 25-24, in the first round of the playoffs.

1976

Tom Seaver fires a shutout but Dave Kingman steals the headlines with three homers (all on the first pitch) and a club-record eight RBI as the Mets rip the Dodgers, 11-0, at Los Angeles.

1981

Herb Brooks, coach of the 1980 "Miracle On Ice" U.S. Olympic gold medal hockey team, is named Rangers coach by general manager Craig Patrick, assistant coach of that gold medal team, who steps aside as Rangers coach.

1871

Scoring their first major victory in the National Association, the New York Mutuals surprise the White Stockings, 8-5, at Brooklyn's Union Grounds, for Chicago's first loss after a 7-0 start. Despite the 50-cent admission price, some 7,000 show up.

1918

Lieutenant Leon Cadore, on leave from his military duties, throws a four-hitter for Brooklyn and beats St. Louis, 2-0, at Ebbets Field. While on furlough, Cadore appears in two games for the Dodgers during the season.

1937

Samuel D. Riddle's War Admiral, Charles Kurtsinger up, becomes the fourth horse to complete the Triple Crown with his Belmont Stakes victory.

1943

Count Fleet, owned by Mrs. John Hertz and ridden by Johnny Longdon, wins thoroughbred racing's sixth Triple Crown with a victory in the Belmont Stakes.

PATRICK EWING

1949

Baseball commissioner Happy Chandler issues official pardons to 18 players who jumped to the Mexican League in 1946. The players were originally banned from Organized Baseball for five years (see May 23).

1953

Bill Tilden, 60, dies in Los Angeles, California. Perhaps the greatest tennis player of all time, Big Bill won seven U.S. national singles titles, equaling the most ever (1920-25, 1929).

1963

Right wing Andy Hebenton, for eight years a Rangers "Iron Man" as he appeared in a then-NHL record 560 games in a row, is drafted by Boston. Hebenton, naturally, plays all 70 games in 1963-64 for the Bruins before retiring with 189 goals and 202 assists in 630 games.

1978

Three days after naming a new coach, the Rangers announce the signings of right wing Anders Hedberg and center Ulf Nilsson, Swedish natives who played four years with the WHA Winnipeg Jets. Hedberg and Nilsson help revive the Rangers, Hedberg tying for the team lead in scoring in 1978-79 (78 points) and Nilsson notching 66 in 59 games before breaking his ankle.

1992

Former Rangers coach Herb Brooks takes over as Devils coach, replacing Tom McVie, who was 42-36-15 in his second term behind the New Jersey bench and lost in the seventh game of the first round of the Stanley Cup playoffs in both 1991 and 1992.

1994

Patrick Ewing gets 24 points and 22 rebounds to lead the Knicks to a 94-90 Garden win over Indiana in the seventh game of their semifinal series. The Knicks take the last two after dropping three straight to win the series, and advance to the NBA final for the first time since 1973.

June 6

1906

Mrs. C.F. Fox of Philadelphia defeats Miss Georgianna Bishop of New York, the defending national champion, 4 and 2, and Philadelphia wins, 9-6, to capture the Griscom Cup from New York and Boston in amateur golf at the Nassau Country Club in Glen Cove, L.I.

1934

Left fielder Myril Hoag becomes the first Yankee to get six hits in a game when he strokes six singles among the Yankees' 25 hits in a 15-3 win over Boston in the opener of a doubleheader at Fenway Park. But the Red Sox take the nightcap, 7-4, to knock the Bombers a half-game behind first-place Detroit.

1936

A relatively obscure pro, New York-born Tony Manero, turns in a blistering final-round 67 for a record-low 282 to win the U.S. Open golf championship at the Baltusrol GC in Springfield, N.J. Henry Cooper is in the clubhouse with an apparently safe 284 (itself an Open record) when Manero's round on the upper course earns him the $1,000 first-place money. Ben Hogan plays his first Open but fails to make the 36-hole cut.

1939

Edward Giacomin, who in 11 seasons with the Rangers won more games (266) and recorded more shutouts (49) than any other goalie in club history, and whose waiving on Oct. 31, 1975, provoked a storm of protest (see Nov. 2), is born in Sudbury, Ontario.

1939

Setting a major league record, the Giants hit five homers in the fourth inning against the Cincinnati Reds at the Polo Grounds. Harry Danning's sixth of the season raises the Giants lead to 7-0 before Frank Demaree's three-run shot makes it 10-0. Then Burgess Whitehead (with one on), pitcher Manny Salvo (inside the park) and Jo-Jo Moore connect in succession to make it 14-0 before the inning ends. The Giants eventually win, 17-3, with Moore getting another homer and Mel Ott (his ninth) one to give the Giants a club record seven in the game.

1946

Basketball Association of America (BAA) is formed in New York by a group of arena owners, primarily in the Northeast, seeking to fill dates in their buildings with pro basketball. Eleven cities are represented the first year, including Boston and New York, the only ones that survive without relocating for 50 seasons. Others are Detroit, Cleveland, Pittsburgh, Chicago, Toronto, St. Louis, Providence, Washington, D.C. and Philadelphia. Maurice Podoloff, president of the American Hockey League, is chosen as commissioner.

1969

Quarterback Joe Namath of the Super Bowl champion Jets announces his retirement rather than sell his interest in Bachelors III, a Manhattan bar with alleged gambling connections. But on July 18, Namath announces the sale of his interest and the end of his retirement.

1977

New York Apples (nee Sets) lose to the Phoenix Racquets, 27-24, in a World Team Tennis match at the Garden that draws 13,675, the largest crowd in regular-season league history.

1990

Yankees reach perhaps the lowest point in their history, when Bucky Dent is fired. The team is 18-31 and in the process of being swept in four games at Boston. Stump Merrill takes over and the Bombers finish last for the third time ever. But before he is suspended for a second time, owner George Steinbrenner on Aug. 21 hires Gene Michael as general manager to stabilize the franchise.

1922

Leo Charles Reise, Jr., a Rangers defenseman (1952-54) whose father Leo, Sr. played for the Americans (1926-30) and Rangers (1930), is born in Stoney Creek, Ontario.

1930

For the first time since 1919, thoroughbred racing has a Triple Crown winner as William Woodward's Belair Stud saddles Gallant Fox, who takes the Belmont Stakes. Trained by Sunny Jim Fitzsimmons and ridden by Earle Sande, Gallant Fox had earlier won the Kentucky Derby and Preakness, now recognized as the first two legs of thoroughbred racing's Triple Crown.

1941

Warren Wright's Whirlaway, Eddie Arcaro up, carries the Calumet Farms colors home to win the Belmont Stakes and complete thoroughbred racing's fifth Triple Crown.

1944

Cazzie Russell is born in Chicago. The Knicks' first choice (and first overall) in the 1966 NBA draft, Russell, a popular, shifty forward and a member of the 1969-70 NBA champions, averaged 13.3 ppg in 344 games over five seasons (1966-71) with the Knicks before being traded for Jerry Lucas.

1947

Thurman Munson, appointed in 1976 the first Yankees captain since Lou Gehrig and American League MVP that year, is born in Akron, Ohio.

1972

One day before the NHL amateur draft, the expansion Islanders and Atlanta Flames choose players unprotected by their fellow clubs. The Isles get, among others, winger Eddie Westfall, their first captain, from the Stanley Cup champion Boston Bruins, and goalie Billy Smith, who would backstop them to their four straight Cups, from the Los Angeles Kings.

1993

Verlon Biggs, a Jets defensive lineman from 1965-70, dies in Moss Point, Mississippi, at 50.

SERGEI ZUBOV

1993

Drazen Petrovic, a shooting guard who was the Nets' leading scorer in 1991-92 (20.6 ppg), is killed in an automobile accident near Ingoestadt, Germany, at age 28.

1994

Rangers beat the Canucks, 4-2, at Vancouver, to take a 3-1 series lead in the Stanley Cup final. After the Canucks take a 2-0 first period lead, Brian Leetch halves the deficit in the second and Mike Richter, on a play that recalls the NHL All-Star Game at the Garden (see Jan. 22), stops Pavel Bure on a penalty shot. Sergei Zubov's power-play goal late in the second ties it, and Alexei Kovalev's power-play goal late in the third wins it.

1912

J. Walter Kennedy, public relations director for the BAA and later the NBA, and ultimately NBA commissioner from 1963-75, is born in Stamford, Connecticut.

1927

Tony Lazzeri produces the first regular-season three-homer game in Yankees history to help salvage a 12-11, 11-inning win over Chicago at the Stadium. Lazzeri drives in five runs on his homers, the last two with his third, which caps a five-run rally that ties the score in the ninth.

1927

In the first major New York outdoor sports event played at night, Hakoah of Vienna and a local all-star team play a scoreless exhibition soccer match before over 20,000 at the Polo Grounds. More than one million candlepower of light is generated by 18 portable flood lamps.

1935

For the second time in five years, William Woodward's Belair Stud captures the Triple Crown as Omaha wins the Belmont Stakes.

1953

PETE ROZELLE

In the first full international soccer match between England and the U.S. in America, England wins, 6-3, before 7,271 at Yankee Stadium. Outside right Tom Finney scores twice and sets up three others for the visitors in a match postponed from Sunday to Monday by wet grounds. England thus gains a small measure of revenge for a 1-0 loss to the U.S. in the 1950 World Cup in Brazil, the first soccer meeting between the countries and still considered in that sport's circles perhaps the greatest upset in soccer history.

1966

The 15-team NFL and nine-team AFL announce they have agreed to a merger. Each league expects to add one expansion team each and operate as a 26-club unit under incumbent NFL commissioner Pete Rozelle.

1972

Islanders, choosing first, take winger Billy Harris with their first-round pick in the NHL amateur draft. Lorne Henning is chosen in the second round and Bobby Nystrom in the third.

1978

Knicks trade forward Phil Jackson and a draft pick to the Nets for two draft picks.

1983

Stan Albeck is named Nets head coach, succeeding interim coach Bob Blair, who had finished the 1982-83 season after Larry Brown's abrupt departure (see Apr. 7).

1991

Mary Bacon Anderson, 43, commits suicide in Fort Worth, Texas. In the early 1970s, Mary Bacon was a pioneer woman jockey who won 286 races, many in New York, and once posed nude for *Playboy* magazine.

1992

Thoroughbred owner and yachtswoman Josephine Hartford Bryce, 88, dies in New York.

1863
Dudley Kavanaugh becomes the first recognized pool champion of the U.S. with a victory over seven other players in a week-long tournament in Manhattan. The games are played under the then-prevailing English 4-ball rules.

1899
James J. Jeffries becomes the world heavyweight champion with an 11th-round knockout of Bob Fitzsimmons at the Coney Island Athletic Club.

1901
Al Selbach is credited with a six-hit game (four singles, two doubles) even though the Giants win a forfeit at Cincinnati. With the Giants leading, 25-13, and two out in the ninth, part of the 17,984 on hand surges onto the field, causing the Reds to forfeit by an official 9-0 score. But all individual records count, including the Giants' 31 hits.

1946
Mel Ott becomes the first major league manager ejected from both ends of a doubleheader as the Giants drop two to the Pirates, 2-1 and 5-1, in Pittsburgh. In the nightcap, plate umpire George Magerkurth clears the Giants bench after Ott is ejected in the fifth inning, sending 10 men to the clubhouse, leaving only first-game catcher Walker Cooper to summon reinforcements to be used as pinch-hitters and subs when needed.

1959
Davey Moore, World Boxing Association middleweight champion from 1982-83 (not to be confused with 1959-63 world featherweight champion Davey Moore), is born in The Bronx.

1960
Titans owner Harry Wismer completes negotiation of the AFL's first television contract. The five-year deal with ABC calls for a first-year rights fee of $1,785,000.

1966
Rangers claim Bernie (Boom Boom) Geoffrion on waivers from the Canadiens. Geoffrion, a 14-year veteran (all with Montreal) and former 50-goal scorer, tallies 17 goals and 42 points in his first year in New York and, after playing part-time the following season, succeeds Emile Francis as Rangers coach June 4, 1968. But ulcers and the team's underperformance cost Geoffrion the job Jan. 17, 1969.

1973
In one of the most decisive races ever, Secretariat sets a track record (2:24) for $1\frac{1}{2}$ miles and completes his Triple Crown sweep. Ridden by Ron Turcotte, the Meadow Stables colt wins the Belmont Stakes by 31 lengths over Twice a Prince and earns $90,120 while becoming the ninth Triple Crown winner and first since 1948.

1978
Herman Barron, golf pro at the Fenway Country Club in Westchester County for 43 years, dies in Pompano Beach, Florida, at age 68.

1986
Milton Richman, who in 1944 joined United Press (which merged with the International News Service to form UPI) and was sports editor from 1972-85, dies in New York at age 64.

1991
Yale football coach Howard Hobson dies in Portland, Oregon, at age 87.

June 10

1857

John Cox Stevens, 71, dies in New York. Stevens was the co-founder and first commodore of the New York Yacht Club (see July 30), led the syndicate that in 1851 built the yacht *America* that won the Hundred Guineas Race, which became the America's Cup, and owned Elysian Fields, which opened in 1831. Elysian Fields was the site of what for years was thought to be the first baseball game ever played (see June 19).

1871

On opening day of the American Jockey Club spring meeting at Jerome Park, Harry Bassett beats 10 other starters to the wire in 2:56 to win the fifth renewal of the $1,500-added Belmont Stakes. Stockwood is second and August Belmont's favored By the Sea is third in the one-mile, five-furlong test before 10,000.

1890

Alexander A. Jordan of the NYAC wins the decathlon championship with 41 points at the Staten Island AC grounds. Malcolm W. Ford, who won the event four times since its inception in 1885, is not allowed to compete due to an eligibility dispute with the AAU. Michael O'Sullivan of the Pastime AC is second with 30 points.

1904

H. Chandler Egan defeats D.E. Sawyer, 8 and 6, to win the U.S. Amateur golf championship at the Baltusrol GC in Springfield, N.J.

1944

The first recorded triple dead heat for a win in an American stakes race occurs in the 46th running of the Carter Handicap at Aqueduct. After seven furlongs on a sloppy track in 1:23 2/5, Joe W. Brown's Brownie, Belair Stud's Bossnet and William Ziegler Jr.'s Wait a Bit all hit the wire at precisely the same split-second.

1962

Gene Littler wins the first Thunderbird Classic golf tournament at the Upper Montclair CC. It is also the only Thunderbird played at the club as the tournament moves to the Westchester CC for a three-year run starting in 1963.

1973

General manager Bill Torrey hires Al Arbour as Islanders head coach, succeeding Earl Ingarfield, who replaced Phil Goyette after 50 games (6-40-4) of the team's 12-60-6 first NHL season.

1975

Pele, the world's most famous soccer player, signs to play with the Cosmos of the NASL through the 1977 season.

1978

For the second straight year, racing has a Triple Crown winner as Affirmed survives a heart-stopping duel with archrival Alydar to win the Belmont Stakes. Steve Cauthen boots home Harborview Farms' Affirmed by a head over the Calumet Farms colt in 2:26 4/5 to earn $110,580 and become the 11th Triple Crown winner.

1994

In a home debut that draws 12,583 to the Meadowlands Arena, the Rockin' Rollers beat the Philadelphia Bulldogs, 11-5, in a Roller Hockey International match.

1995

Lindsey Nelson, Mets broadcaster from 1962-78, dies in Atlanta, Georgia. Nelson, Bob Murphy and Ralph Kiner formed the Mets radio and television broadcast team that remained intact for the club's first 17 seasons.

1887

Danny Richardson becomes the first Giant ever to get six hits in a game despite making the first out in an 11-run first that leads to a 26-2 walloping of the Washington Nationals at the Polo Grounds. Richardson gets singles in his next six at-bats to the delight of the 6,564 fans who watch the 1:40 affair.

1912

Daniel Reid Topping, future owner of the Brooklyn Football Dodgers, AAFC Yankees, and New York Yankees, is born in Greenwich, Connecticut.

1913

Vincent Thomas Lombardi is born in Brooklyn. Vince Lombardi was a guard at Fordham in 1935 and 1936 and an assistant coach with the Football Giants before becoming a legend as head coach of the Green Bay Packers from 1959-68.

1919

J.K.L. Ross' Sir Barton, ridden by Johnny Loftus, completes the first Triple Crown in U.S. thoroughbred racing history with a victory in the Belmont Stakes.

1929

Hard-hitting outfielder Frank Thomas, who led the original Mets of 1962 with 34 homers, is born in Pittsburgh, Pennsylvania. Thomas spent 16 seasons (1951-66) in the majors.

AL ARBOUR

1977

Karen G. Taylor's Seattle Slew becomes the 10th Triple Crown winner in thoroughbred racing history as he captures the Belmont Stakes.

1979

Jesse Abramson, longtime sportswriter for the *Herald Tribune*, dies in Mount Vernon, N.Y., at age 75.

1979

Loren Murchison, a sprint champion who won the gold medal in the 400 meters at the Olympic Games of 1920 and 1924, dies at age 80 in Point Pleasant, N.J.

1986

Harry Kessler, a boxing referee who worked over 5,000 fights, including 15 world championship bouts, dies in St. Louis, Missouri, at age 85. A millionaire metallurgical chemist, Kessler was the first non-New Yorker licensed to referee fights in New York.

1991

Moe Spahn, a basketball All-America for CCNY in 1932 and captain of the 1932-33 squad that finished 13-1, dies in New York at age 79.

1994

Tabasco Cat overhauls Go For Gin in the stretch to win the Belmont Stakes and Pat Day's mount becomes the ninth horse to win the Preakness and Belmont after losing in the Kentucky Derby, the first leg of thoroughbred racing's Triple Crown. Go For Gin won the Derby with Tabasco Cat a lagging sixth before winning the next two legs.

June 12

1839

Abner Doubleday does *not* invent baseball.

1885

Dave Orr of the AA Mets hits for the cycle with six hits, including a two-run homer and a triple in a 17-8 romp over the St. Louis Browns at the Polo Grounds.

1920

Man O'War wins the Belmont Stakes by 20 lengths over Donnacona, the only other horse in the field. His time (2:14 $^1/_5$) is an American record for 1 $^3/_8$ miles.

1929

It is revealed that Martha Norelius competed in the AAU nationals (see Mar. 2) while under a suspension for giving unauthorized exhibitions. She denies the charges but the AAU continues her suspension (and also that of WSANY teammate Helen Meany, the Olympic gold medalist in the low-board dive, on the same grounds).

1936

Ground is broken for the auto racing track to be known as Roosevelt Raceway at Salisbury Plain (now Westbury), L.I. Track president George Preston Marshall leads the dignitaries in starting construction of the four-miles-per-lap track and four grandstands with a capacity of 60,000 within sight of Charles Lindbergh's takeoff point on his trans-Atlantic flight in 1927. Major George H. Robertson, winner of the 1908 Vanderbilt Cup race, had convinced backers to revive big-time auto racing on Long Island by building the new track (see Oct. 12).

1943

Marvin Aufstrig is born in Brooklyn. As Marv Albert, he was the voice of the Knicks and Rangers for many years and became the nation's most famous sportscaster, working NBA and NFL games and boxing matches. In 1997, he pleaded guilty to assault in highly publicized Virginia case.

1948

Warren Wright's Calumet Farms wins its second Triple Crown, the eighth in thoroughbred racing history, as Eddie Arcaro brings Citation home first in the Belmont Stakes.

1981

A 50-day baseball strike that causes direct losses estimated at $164 million starts. It wipes out 712 games and causes the creation of a split season with a new (third) tier of playoff games. (The Yankees, first in the AL East will be declared first-half champions and automatically qualify.)

1988

Seve Ballesteros birdies the first playoff hole to break a four-way tie and win the $126,000 first-place money in the Manufacturers Hanover Westchester Classic at the Westchester CC. Ballesteros was tied (at 276) with David Frost, Greg Norman and third-round leader Ken Green after regulation play.

1991

America's outdoor amateur championships (conducted by The Athletics Congress rather than the AAU) return to New York for the first time since 1966 but criticism of the facilities at Randalls Island mute the occasion. Bonnie Edmondson wins the women's hammer throw on the first day of the four-day event but the absence of a wind gauge means no records can be set.

1994

Lee Janzen fires a five-under final round 66 (for a 72-hole 268) to win the Buick Classic by three strokes over Ernie Els at the Westchester CC and take the $216,000 first-place money.

1905

On his way to a 31-win season, Giants righthander Christy Mathewson hurls his second career no-hitter, beating the Cubs, 1-0, at Chicago.

1912

Christy Mathewson wins his 300th career game on a six-hitter as the Giants beat Chicago, 3-2, at the Polo Grounds.

1915

Splitting a doubleheader with Richmond, the Newark Indians play their last International League home games. Newark wins the nightcap, 12-5, after losing the opener, 4-3. Under heavy pressure from the competing Federal League club in Newark, the Indians shift to Harrisburg, Pennsylvania, at the end of a road trip July 1. In 1916, the IL returns to Newark following the FL's collapse (see Oct. 3).

1935

"The Cinderella Man," Jim Braddock, wins the heavyweight title with a 15-round decision over Max Baer before 35,000 at the Madison Square Garden Bowl in Long Island City. Less than two years earlier, Braddock had been on home relief (as welfare was then called).

1936

Don Lash of Indiana University sets a world record (8:58.3) on the two-mile run, breaking Paavo Nurmi's 1931 mark and easily beating Norman Bright (9:24.9) of the Olympic Club to the wire in the Princeton Invitational at Palmer Stadium. Penn's Gene Venzke scores an upset, beating world record-holder Glenn Cunningham by a stride in the mile but the time is a slow 4:13.4.

JIM BRADDOCK

1948

It's "Babe Ruth Day II" at Yankee Stadium. Ruth's uniform No. 3 is retired, the Bambino briefly addresses the 49,461 fans and then the Yankees beat Cleveland, 5-3. Just over two months later, Ruth dies of cancer (see Aug. 16).

1961

Ben Jones, 78, a thoroughbred trainer from 1914-61 and five-time top money-winner who trained Triple Crown winners Whirlaway (1941) and Citation (1948), dies in Lexington, Kentucky.

1985

Stan Albeck resigns as Nets coach, after guiding the team to play-off berths in each of his two seasons, to become head coach of Chicago. Dave Wohl is eventually named to succeed him.

1991

After a long battle against his two-year suspension for alleged steroid use, Butch Reynolds runs seventh in his heat in the 400-meter sprint at the TAC championships at Downing Stadium on Randalls Island. Dan O'Brien emerges as a star and Olympic hopeful with a record 8,844 points in the decathlon.

1995

In the only series game won by the home team, the Devils beat Philadelphia, 4-2, at the Meadowlands, to take their Stanley Cup semifinal, four games to two, and advance to the final.

1870

In the biggest upset in 25 years of baseball history, the Cincinnati Reds—the sport's first all-professional club—suffer their first defeat since the opening of the 1869 season, their first full pro season. Some 9,000 fans pay 50 cents each to watch the Brooklyn Atlantics halt the Reds' streak, 8-7, in 11 innings at Brooklyn's Capitoline Grounds. With the score 5-5 after nine, the Reds score twice in the top of the 11th, but the Atlantics get three in their half. Joe Start's RBI triple makes it 7-6, Bob Ferguson's single ties it and Ferguson scores the winning run on an error. Although some dispute exists as to the exact number, most observers report that the Reds had won an incredible 81 straight (with one tie) before this loss (including the first 24 in 1870).

1890

Filly Sallie McClelland, a 15-1 shot, wins the Great Eclipse Stakes at Morris Park in The Bronx, upsetting John A. Morris' two-year-old colt Russell by a head in the mud. Sallie McClelland wins a $24,385 first-prize purse against the strongest stable in the East in horse racing's upset of the year.

1934

Californian Max Baer wins the heavyweight championship with an upset 11th-round victory over Primo Carnera before 52,266 (48,964 paid) at the Madison Square Garden Bowl in Long Island City. Referee Art Donovan stops the fight after Carnera is decked twice in each of the 10th and 11th rounds.

1948

Albert B. Nixon dies at age 59 in the French Hospital in New York. Nixon was a basketball, football and track athlete and NYU's baseball captain in 1913 before serving as graduate manager of athletics (athletic director) at NYU from 1922 to his death. At his death, he was also president of the Intercollegiate Fencing Association and the Metropolitan Intercollegiate Basketball Association, the governing body of the NIT.

1959

With rain forcing the final round to Sunday for the first time, Bill Casper, Jr., holds on to the lead he took in the second round to win the U.S. Open golf championship at the Winged Foot GC in Mamaroneck, N.Y. Casper shoots a 74 for the final 18 but finishes at 282, one stroke ahead of Bob Rosburg, to earn the $12,000 top payoff.

1965

Jim Maloney of the Reds hurls 10 hitless innings against the Mets at Cincinnati. In the 11th, however, Johnny Lewis homers and the Mets win, 1-0, with two hits.

1988

John J. Farrell dies in Boynton Beach, Florida, at age 87. A native of White Plains, N.Y., Johnny Farrell won the Metropolitan Open in 1927 and beat Bobby Jones in a playoff to take the U.S. Open golf title in 1928 at Olympia Fields, Illinois.

1991

On the third of the four days of the TAC championships at Downing Stadium, Leroy Burrell steals the show with a victory over Carl Lewis and a world record time (9.90 seconds) in the 100-meter dash.

1994

Rangers defeat the Vancouver Canucks, 3-2, at the Garden in the seventh game of the Stanley Cup final to take the series, 4-3, and capture their first Cup since 1940. Brian Leetch, later voted playoff MVP, and Adam Graves give the Rangers a 2-0 lead after the first period. Mark Messier is credited with the goal that gives New York a 3-1 lead in the second during a goalmouth scramble, although teammate Brian Noonan appears to score it.

1865

Philadelphia's Athletics, who the next year will become the first non-New York, non-Brooklyn club to claim the U.S. baseball championship, rout the Resolutes of Elizabeth, N.J., 39-14, before 6,000 at Union Grounds.

1925

Gertrude Ederle swims from the Battery to Sandy Hook, N.J., 21 miles, in 7 hours, 11 minutes, 30 seconds. On August 6, 1926, Miss Ederle will set a speed record swimming the English Channel, the first woman to do so, going over 31 miles from Cape Gris-Nez, France, to Dover, England, in 14 hours, 31 minutes.

1938

General manager Larry MacPhail turns on the lights at Ebbets Field but Cincinnati's Johnny Vander Meer turns them out on Dodgers hitters. Vander Meer becomes the only major league pitcher to throw two successive no-hitters, winning, 6-0, in the first night game ever at Ebbets Field and the first big-league no-hitter under the lights. Leo Durocher flies to center for the final out after the southpaw loads the bases with walks. In his previous start on June 11, Vander Meer no-hit the Boston Braves, 3-0, at Cincinnati.

1965

Jack Mara, 57, dies after 31 years as president of the Football Giants. Brother Wellington succeeds him, and Tim Mara, Jack's son, takes Wellington's job as vice president and treasurer.

1977

Ending a very public squabble between the franchise and The Franchise, the Mets trade an unhappy Tom Seaver, their ace for 10 years, to Cincinnati for pitcher Pat Zachry, outfielder Steve Henderson, second baseman Doug Flynn and minor league outfielder Dan Norman.

ARTHUR KNAPP

1980

Forty-year-old Jack Nicklaus becomes the fourth golfer to win the U.S. Open four times and he does it in high style with a record-setting eight-under 272 at Baltusrol's lower course. (Willie Anderson, Bobby Jones and Ben Hogan had also won the Open four times.) "The Golden Bear" opens with a first-round 63 (matched by Tom Weiskopf) and either leads or is tied for the lead all the way. Japan's Isao Aoki, second at 274, posts the second-lowest 72-hole total ever at the Open up to then. Only three others break par.

1986

Ray Floyd's 279 wins the U.S. Open golf title and the $115,000 top money as the Open returns to the Shinnecock Hills GC in Southampton, N.Y., for the first time since 1896.

1992

Arthur Knapp, longtime champion sailor with the Larchmont (N.Y.) Yacht Club, dies at age 85 in Greenwich, Connecticut.

1995

Pat Riley, the loser in a power struggle over player personnel decision-making authority, resigns by fax as Knicks coach after four years (223-105, .680) while on vacation in Europe.

June 16

1871

Edward Payson Weston, America's most celebrated pedestrian, completes his walk of 400 miles in five days at the Empire Skating Rink with 18 minutes to spare. Weston starts his final day at 4:43 a.m. in his 325th mile. He finishes at 11:47 p.m., doing the final mile in 11:07 and the last lap in 1:13. He began at 12:03 a.m. on June 12.

1883

Giants stage baseball's first "Ladies Day" and win, 5-2, at the Polo Grounds as Tip O'Neill outpitches Cleveland's Hugh (One-Arm) Daly, who has only a right arm.

1890

A throng of over 12,000 attends the opening of the second Madison Square Garden at 26th Street and Madison Avenue. The audience, including all the leaders of New York society, is treated to a concert by Viennese composer Eduard Strauss and two ballets created and staged by Alfred Thompson.

1934

Kansan Glenn Cunningham becomes the first American in 11 years to hold the world record in the mile as he is clocked in 4:06.6 around the cinders at Palmer Stadium in Princeton, N.J. Princeton's Bill Bonthron is second but still has his career-best time and Penn's Gene Venzke is third. Ben Eastman, a Stanford graduate student, also thrills the 25,000 fans with the first half-mile in less than 1:50 ever run as he is timed in 1:49.8.

1974

Despite a final-round 73 that includes six bogeys, Hale Irwin makes par on the final two holes to win the U.S. Open golf title on the west course at the Winged Foot GC in Mamaroneck, N.Y. Forrest Fezler, who bogeys the par-5 18th, finishes at 289 to Irwin's seven-over-par 287. Irwin wins $35,000 and Fezler $18,000.

1983

Luis Resto of Puerto Rico brutally pounds Bill Ray Collins of Nashville, Tennessee, in a 10-round middleweight bout at the Garden on the undercard of a Roberto Duran-Davey Moore fight (in which the 32-year-old Duran, thought to be washed up, stuns the boxing world by taking Moore's junior middleweight title) and wins a unanimous decision. It is later learned that much of the padding was removed from Resto's gloves. Collins suffers brain and vision damage, never fights again and dies in a 1984 Tennessee auto crash. In 1985, Resto and his manager, Panama Lewis, are indicted and convicted of a variety of charges. Resto is sentenced to three years in prison and Lewis six.

1993

Emil Lence dies at age 76 in Delray Beach, Florida. Lence and his father John bought a roller skating rink in Brooklyn 1944 and in 1947, encouraged by Jack Dempsey, turned it into a boxing club. He was boxing promoter at the club, Eastern Parkway Arena, until 1957. He also promoted Floyd Patterson's first heavyweight title defense (see July 29).

1996

Mel Allen, 83, who split radio broadcasting duties from 1939-42 between the Yankees and the Giants before becoming the voice of the Yankees (1946-64), dies in Greenwich, Connecticut.

1997

Righthander Dave Mlicki throws a nine-hit shutout as the Mets win their first regular-season interleague game against the Yankees, 6-0, at Yankee Stadium. An almost-evenly-divided crowd of 56,188 watches as John Olerud drives in three runs with a first-inning double and a two-run single in the seventh. The Yankees win the next two days.

1866

William B. Curtis, John C. Babcock and Harry E. Buermeyer, three Civil War veterans, hold the first preliminary meeting at Babcock's home that leads to the formation of the New York Athletic Club.

1885

Irked by the bragging of rookie pitcher John Smith (who calls himself "Phenomenal"), Brooklyn commits 20 errors to help St. Louis to an 18-5 rout at Washington Park. All St. Louis runs are unearned, disgusting the 1,600 fans and owner Charles Byrne (who gives his players an angry postgame lecture). Smith goes the distance, allowing 12 hits.

1916

Righthander George Smith pitches a three-hitter, striking out 16, as Columbia closes its season with a 6-0 victory over Wesleyan at Middletown, Connecticut. In his last five starts, Smith is 5-0 with 79 strikeouts, allows 12 hits and gives up only one run. The Lions finish 18-1-1, being adjudged the best team in the East despite a loss to Cornell and a 15-inning tie with Penn.

1925

Detroit pounds the Yankees, 19-1, at the Stadium, setting a record (matched 52 years later by expansion Toronto, 19-3) for the most runs ever allowed by the Yankees in a home game.

1938

A revived version of the New York Whirlwinds, a famed name in pro basketball in the 1920s, is admitted to the ABL, along with two other teams (Wilkes-Barre, Pennsylvania and Troy, N.Y.).

1963

Jack (Doc) Kearns, heavyweight champion Jack Dempsey's manager, dies in Miami Beach, Florida, at age 79.

1976

A "merger" of the NBA and ABA is announced at Hyannis, Massachusetts, with four ABA clubs joining the NBA for an entry fee of $3.2 million each. The four new NBA teams are the New York Nets, Indiana Pacers, Denver Nuggets, and San Antonio Spurs, expanding the NBA to 22 clubs and ending the ABA's nine-season existence. The stiff fee contributes to financial troubles that cause the ABA champion Nets to sell their star and the league's marquee player, Julius Erving, to the Philadelphia 76ers before the Nets begin their first NBA season.

1976

Floyd Odlum, who made Madison Square Garden profitable during the Great Depression by reorganizing its management, dies in Indio, California, at age 84. Odlum later reorganized Paramount Pictures and owned a controlling interest in RKO Pictures.

DAVE MLICKI

1978

Ron Guidry fans 18 Angels, an American League record for strikeouts by a lefty in a nine-inning game, and the Yankees shut out California, 4-0, at Yankee Stadium.

June 18

1892

Montana, running last in an 11-horse field at the half-mile, surges home to win the Suburban Handicap at Sheepshead Bay by $3/_4$-length. Jockey Ed (Snapper) Garrison specializes in finishes of this type, putting the phrase "Garrison Finish" into the lexicon of two generations of sports fans. Montana is clocked in 2:07.4 for the 1 $1/_4$-mile race.

1915

Amateur Jerome Travers of the Upper Montclair (N.J.) Country Club wins the U.S. Open at the Baltusrol GC in Springfield, N.J., playing the last six holes in one under par to edge Tom McNamara by a stroke. Travers shoots a final-round 76 for 297 to McNamara's 75.

1938

Frustrated in his attempts to become a manager, Babe Ruth signs on as a coach with the Brooklyn Dodgers.

1941

Ahead on points after 12 rounds of his heavyweight title fight at the Polo Grounds against Joe Louis, Billy Conn decides to go for the knockout of the champ and gets knocked out himself in the 13th. It is the closest Louis comes to losing his title in 12 years as champion.

1967

Jack Nicklaus wins his second U.S. Open with a record-setting 275 for 72 holes on the lower course at the Baltusrol GC. Nicklaus' final-round 65 gives him a four-stroke win over Arnold Palmer, the only other golfer to break par. The crowd of 20,528 raises the four-day total to 88,414, an Open record.

1979

Tommy Lockhart dies in New York at 87. One of the foremost promoters of hockey in the New York area, Lockhart organized the Eastern Amateur Hockey League in 1933, the Amateur Hockey Association of United States in 1937 and served as business manager of the Rangers from 1946-52.

1984

Fuzzy Zoeller wins the U.S. Open golf title in a playoff with Australia's Greg Norman after the pair tied for the lead at 4-under 276 for 72 holes at the Winged Foot Golf Club. Zoeller's extra-day 67, lowest 18-hole Open playoff score ever, bests Norman by eight strokes for the Open's largest margin of victory in an 18-hole playoff.

1986

Terry Simpson is named Islanders head coach, succeeding Al Arbour.

1994

Ray Houghton's goal in the 12th minute stands up as Ireland scores a stunning 1-0 upset of Italy before 74,826 at Giants Stadium in an opening-round World Cup game. The game is the first of seven in the tournament to be played at Giants Stadium.

1995

Corey Pavin shoots a final-round two-under 68 to pass both Greg Norman and Tom Lehman and take the centennial U.S. Open with a four-day even-par 280 at the Shinnecock Hills GC in Southampton, N.Y. For Pavin, the victory is his first in one of golf's major tournaments.

1846

At Elysian Fields in Hoboken, N.J., an all-star New York Nine clobbers the Knickerbockers, 23-1, in what for many years was thought to be the first baseball game ever played un-der rules instituted by Knickerbockers club member Alexander Cartwright.

1867

Jerome Park, in what is now The Bronx, is the site for the inaugural run-ning of the Belmont Stakes, a one-mile, five-furlong test for three-year-olds. The first Belmont is won by Francis Morris' bay filly, Ruthless, in 3:05, who earns $1,800 for Mr. Morris. Only four horses are entered with DeCourcey finishing second and Rivoli third.

1930

James W. Garrett is born in Rutherford, N.J. Jim Garrett was football coach at Columbia for a single disastrous, controversial season (0-10 in 1985).

1936

Temporarily derailing the youngster's march to the heavyweight title, former champion Max Schmeling of Germany gives Joe Louis a fistic lesson, finally KOing "the Brown Bomber" in the 12th round of their non-title bout at Yankee Stadium.

JIM GARRETT

1945

Sid Mercer, longtime sportswriter with the Hearst newspapers in New York (*Evening Journal* and *Journal-Ameri-can*), dies at age 64 in Manhattan. The New York chapter of the BBWAA annually presents the Sid Mercer "Player of the Year" Award in his memory.

1946

In the first prizefight that offers a $100 (ringside) ticket, Joe Louis knocks out Billy Conn at Yankee Stadium in the eighth round in a rematch of their famous bout before World War II (see June 18).

1946

Monmouth Park, the most famous track in the state, is reopened for thoroughbred racing at Oceanport, N.J. Originally opened July 4, 1870, Monmouth endured lengthy closures over its 76-year history but this revival will be permanent, with the NJSEA taking over the plant in 1985.

1954

After an errant tee shot, Ed Furgol salvages a par 5 on the final hole by hitting his second shot from off the fair-way onto the 18th fairway of the adjacent upper course, and then to the green, and wins the U.S. Open at Baltusrol Golf Club's lower course with a four-over 284. Gene Littler misses an eight-foot putt on 18 to tie and finishes one shot back. This is the first Open to be nationally televised and Furgol, despite a withered left arm caused by a childhood elbow injury, takes home the $6,000 first-place money. Ropes are used for the first time to keep the gallery off the fairway as the tournament draws a record 39,600.

1985

Stepping aside as Rangers coach for the second time in his tenure as general manager, Craig Patrick names former Philadelphia Flyers assistant coach Ted Sator as head coach.

1903

Golfing great Glenna Collett is born in New Haven, Connecticut.

1911

Russell Patrick Hodges is born in Covington, Kentucky. Russ Hodges was a baseball play-by-play announcer for the Yankees (1946-48) and the Giants (1949-57) and followed the Giants when they moved to San Francisco. His "The Giants win the pennant! The Giants win the pennant!" call when Bobby Thomson hit the "Shot Heard 'Round the World" (see Oct. 3) is perhaps the most famous broadcasting moment in sports history.

1919

Bill Devery dies in Far Rockaway, N.Y., at age 65. "Big Bill," a New York City policeman who was twice indicted while a precinct captain but nevertheless became chief of police in 1898 when the city was consolidated, was a silent partner of Frank Farrell and Thomas F. Foley in American League Park at 168th Street and Broadway, and Farrell's silent partner in the New York Highlanders from 1903 until 1915, when they sold the Yankees.

1925

Doris Jane Hart, two-time winner of the U.S. national singles title at Forest Hills (1954-55), is born in St. Louis, Missouri.

1959

John Ogrodnick, a sharpshooting left wing who led the Rangers in goals (43) in 1990-91, is born in Ottawa, Ontario.

1963

Mets score a big psychological victory by defeating the Yankees at Yankee Stadium, 6-2, in the first Mayor's Trophy game. Mets fans are shocked when Yankee management won't let them bring their banners and noisemakers into the Stadium.

1967

A Houston, Texas, court finds ex-heavyweight champion Muhammad Ali guilty of draft evasion, rejecting his claim of religious exemption. However, the conviction is later overturned (1971), after Ali resumed his boxing career in 1970.

1980

Bill Svoboda, 51, linebacker for the Football Giants from 1954-59, dies in Homer, Louisiana.

1991

Frank Umont, a tackle for the Football Giants from 1943-47 and an American League umpire from 1954-73, dies in Fort Lauderdale, Florida, at age 72.

MUHAMMAD ALI

1993

Matching a record set on the same course by Jack Nicklaus in 1980, Lee Janzen shoots an eight-under 272 to win the 93rd U.S. Open, the record seventh to be played at the Baltusrol GC. The leader for the last three rounds, Janzen needs a great chip for a birdie 2 on 16 to finally shake runner-up Payne Stewart (274). Janzen earns $290,000.

1873

A National Rifle Range is opened by the NRA on a tract of land known as Creedmoor, about 12 miles east of Hunter's Point, Long Island. On opening day, the top sharpshooter is R.B. Lockwood of New York's 22d Regiment, who hits 30 of his 40 targets. Thousands attend the opening ceremonies, crowding trains on the Central Railroad of Long Island throughout the day.

1907

William A. Shea is born in New York. A politically savvy lawyer and sports fan, Shea owned a minor league football club, the Long Island Indians, and from 1958-61 was chairman of the city committee to return National League baseball to New York. His efforts were acknowledged when the ballpark built by the city to accommodate the Mets, the indirect offspring of his work, was named Shea Stadium.

1916

George (Rube) Foster of the Red Sox no-hits the Yankees, 2-0, at Fenway Park in Boston, allowing only three walks.

1916

Herbert William O'Connor is born in Montreal, Quebec. In his first year as a Ranger after being acquired from Montreal, Buddy O'Connor won the Hart Trophy as NHL MVP and the Lady Byng Trophy for effective gentlemanly play. But a car accident prevented him from reaching his full potential as a Ranger (see Oct. 8).

1932

Jack Sharkey gains a 15-round decision over Germany's Max Schmeling to win the world heavyweight championship at the Madison Square Garden Bowl in Long Island City. The crowd of 61,863 pays $432,365 to watch Sharkey avenge a controversial loss to Schmeling in a 1930 title fight. Schmeling's manager, Joe Jacobs, is not impressed with the verdict. "We wuz robbed," he famously says.

1932

Major W. Taylor dies at age 53 in Chicago, Illinois. Taylor, America's first great black athlete besides racehorse jockeys, was cycling champion in 1899. Later, managed by William Brady, he was a star attraction at the Manhattan Beach Track in Brooklyn.

1956

Robert Gardner dies at age 66. A Yale graduate, Gardner was the U.S. national amateur golf champion in 1916 and 1922, pole vault champion at the IC4A meet in 1912 (at 13'1", the first man ever to clear 13 feet) and the racquets national doubles champion (with Howard Linn) in 1926, making him perhaps the only man ever to win championships in three different sports.

1964

In the opener of a Father's Day doubleheader at Shea Stadium, Philadelphia's Jim Bunning hurls the National League's first perfect game since 1880, blanking the Mets, 6-0. John Stephenson fans for the final out.

1989

Lee Q. Calhoun, an Olympic hurdler and Yale track coach from 1976-80, dies in Erie, Pennsylvania, at age 56.

1993

Alan J. Gould, sports editor of *The Associated Press* from 1925-38 and the man who in 1936 started the *AP* weekly college football poll, dies in Vero Beach, Florida, at age 95.

1891

Tom Lovett hurls Brooklyn's first National League no-hitter, 4-0, over the Giants at Washington Park.

1891

Running on the Old Futurity Course at Sheepshead Bay, Kingston, a seven-year-old stallion, sets a track record with a 1:08 clocking on the oval that is 170 yards less than three-quarters of a mile. Over the final 18 years of the track's use, the record is never bested.

1915

Cornelius Warmerdam is born in Long Beach, California. The greatest pole-vaulter of his era, Warmerdam in 1940 became the first athlete ever to vault 15 feet and was the American champion in the event seven times (1937-38, 1940-44).

MAX SCHMELING

1927

Dr. Walter B. Peet, coach of Columbia's 1895 IRA heavyweight championship crew, dies at age 66 in Hammondton, N.J. Peet was the stroke oar on the Lions' 1881 crew and was generally credited with developing the Hudson River site at Poughkeepsie, New York, where the IRA championships were rowed for decades.

1935

Newark AC wins the New Jersey State AAU track and field team title for the *sixth straight* year with 71 $^5/_6$ points at Rutherford (N.J.) Field. The Shore AC is second. Jack Muller of the Paterson Call AA sets a meet record (52.0 seconds) in the 400 meters and Dave Andelman of the Newark AC wins his sixth straight shot put title (48' 5 $^1/_2$").

1938

In a bout rife with international political overtones, heavyweight champ Joe Louis KOs Germany's Max Schmeling at 2:04 of the first round before 70,043 at Yankee Stadium, avenging his only professional loss to date (see June 19).

1968

John Beckman, an Original Celtics star of the 1920s, dies in Miami Beach, Florida, at age 72.

1977

John A. Ziegler, Jr., is elected by the Board of Governors as NHL president. He takes office in September, succeeding the retiring Clarence Campbell, who had served since 1946.

1979

Football Giants defensive lineman Troy Archer (1976-78) dies in a car crash at age 24.

1980

Claudell Washington becomes the third Met to hit three homers in a game as he connects thrice against the Dodgers in a 9-6 Mets win at Los Angeles.

1994

Hakeem Olajuwon scores 25 points as the Houston Rockets beat the Knicks, 90-84, at Houston to win the NBA final in seven games and take their first league title. New York led the series, 3-2, but on June 19, the Rockets won at Houston, 86-84, to force a seventh game when Olajuwon deflected John Starks' three-point attempt at the buzzer.

1900

John Ross Roach, who amassed 30 shutouts and a 2.16 gaa in four seasons as Rangers goalie (1928-32), is born in Fort Perry, Ontario.

1930

Walter Dukes, the Seton Hall center who later became the Knicks' No. 1 choice in the 1953 draft and their first seven-footer, is born in Youngstown, Ohio.

1934

Wiley Post and Harold Gatty take off from New York on the initial leg of the first around-the-world flight in a single-engine plane.

1934

Ed Thorp dies in Port Chester, N.Y., at age 48. Thorp, an Eastern football referee, officiated the 1934 Rose Bowl in which Columbia beat Stanford. From 1919-23, he was NYU basketball coach and led the Violets to a 42-13 record in that time and the 1920 national AAU championship in Atlanta, where they defeated Rutgers. He was one of six brothers, one of whom, Tom, was an All-American at Columbia (see July 6).

1951

Ralph Kiner's single in the first inning is the only Pirates hit allowed by Don Newcombe in the Dodgers' 13-1 victory at Pittsburgh.

1954

William Lowell dies in East Orange, N.J., at age 91. Dr. Lowell, a dentist and former tennis player, took up golf at age 60 and in 1923 invented the wood tee. He then paid pros Walter Hagen and Joey Kirkwood to use them, and they became popular.

1977

Fred J. Corcoran dies in White Plains, N.Y., at age 72. A golf promoter and sportswriter, Corcoran, who managed Ben Hogan, among others, was tournament manager of the PGA (1937-48), founder the LPGA and tournament director of the Westchester Classic (1967-76).

1988

For the fifth (and as it turns out, final) time, Billy Martin is replaced as Yankees manager for the second straight time by Lou Piniella. The Bombers are 40-28 at the time but slumping. With Piniella, the Yankees finish 85-76, 3 $1/_2$ games out of first.

1994

P.J. Carlesimo resigns after 12 years as Seton Hall basketball coach to become head coach of the NBA Portland Trail Blazers, who fire him after the 1996-97 season having compiled a 137-109 record in three seasons. Carlesimo then becomes coach of the Golden State Warriors.

1994

Marvelous Marv Throneberry, onetime Yankee first baseman who became the symbol of the Amazin' Mets of 1962, probably the worst major league team of the 20th century, dies in Fisherville, Tennessee, at age 60.

# June 24

1895

Columbia wins the eight-oar shell varsity title at the IRA regatta, covering the four miles down the Hudson River in 21:25.0 at Poughkeepsie, N.Y. Cornell is second and Penn third. The Lions will not win the biggest prize in U.S. rowing for another 32 years.

1905

Guy Vaughn, driving a 40-horsepower Decauville at Yonkers' Empire City racetrack, sets a world record for 1,000 miles in a car. The 18-year-old is clocked in 23:33.20 for the distance, breaking the mark set by C.G. Wridgway at Brighton Beach the year before. For the full 24 hours, Vaughn logs 1,015 $^5/_8$ miles and finishes before 1,000 spectators. Wridgway serves as one of the official timers.

1913

Willie Klein, longtime sports editor of the Newark *Star-Ledger*, is born in Newark, N.J. Klein's two sons, Moss and Dave, became *Star-Ledger* sportswriters.

1916

Future heavyweight champion Jack Dempsey makes his New York debut with a consensus win in a 10-round no-decision bout with Andre Anderson at the Fairmont AC.

1929

For the second time in three years, Columbia wins the IRA regatta eight-oar heavyweight championship in the Hudson River at Poughkeepsie, N.Y., in 22:58. The University of Washington is second and Pennsylvania third.

1953

George Herbert Walker, Wall Street investment banker and president of the USGA, dies in New York at 79. The man for whom the 41st president, George H.W. Bush, is named, Walker donated the Walker Cup for international team amateur golf matches and in 1925 formed the underwriting syndicate to build Garden No. 3.

1955

Hy Turkin, sportswriter for the *Daily News*, an early advocate of Little League baseball and compiler of (with Tommy Thompson) of the first baseball encyclopedia ever published (*Encyclopedia of Baseball*, 1951), dies in New York at age 40.

1961

Returning to New York for the first time in 16 years, the AAU Nationals get off to a flying start as Frank Budd of Villanova sets a world record (9.2 seconds) in the 100-yard dash before 9,400 at Downing Stadium on the first day of the championships.

1962

Jack Reed's two-run homer in the 22d inning gives the Yankees the win in their longest game ever, a 9-7 victory at Detroit.

1978

Nathan Agar dies in New York at age 90. In 1905, Agar organized the first soccer club in the U.S., the Critchleys of Coney Island.

1995

Completing a stunning four-game sweep of the final, New Jersey wins the Stanley Cup with a 5-2 victory over the Detroit Red Wings at the Meadowlands Arena. Neal Broten breaks a 2-2 tie at 7:56 of the second period and the Devils' defense limits Detroit to only one shot on goal in the third period. Devils right wing Claude Lemieux is named the Conn Smythe Trophy winner as the playoffs' MVP.

1868

In their first baseball meeting, Yale beats Princeton 30-23, at New Haven, Connecticut.

1885

George Pinckney becomes Brooklyn's second hitter to get six hits in a game as he raps six singles in a 21-14 win over the Philadelphia Athletics in an AA game at Washington Park.

1906

On opening night for the musical "Mam'zelle Champagne," Pittsburgh millionaire Harry K. Thaw shoots and kills Stanford White, architect of Madison Square Garden No. 2, in the Roof Garden Theatre of the building. Thaw, who was eventually judged insane, is enraged over a liaison between White and Thaw's wife, showgirl Evelyn Nesbit, before their marriage.

GENE SARAZEN

1909

With a record low 290, George Sargent wins the U.S. Open by four strokes at the Englewood (N.J.) GC. Sargent shoots a 72-71-143 on the last day to pass runner-up Tom McNamara of Boston, whose second-day rounds are 75-77-152. McNamara shot 73-69-142 on the first day, the 69 being the first Open round ever to break 70.

1932

British Open champ Gene Sarazen, playing out of Lakeview in Great Neck, L.I., wins the U.S. Open with a blistering last-round 66 at the Fresh Meadows CC in Flushing, Queens. Sarazen's 72-hole 286 is three strokes better than Bobby Cruickshank and T. Philip Perkins.

1935

In his New York debut, Joe Louis KOs former heavyweight champ Primo Carnera in the sixth round before an integrated crowd of 57,000 at Yankee Stadium. The gate of $340,000 and demeanor of the crowd (estimated to be 25% black) pleases just about everyone concerned.

1950

Pittsburgh's Ralph Kiner hits for the cycle, homering twice and his eight RBI help the Bucs beat the Dodgers, 16-11, disappointing the Sunday crowd of 20,196 at Ebbets Field.

1961

Before 19,200, Frank Budd's 21-race winning streak is broken on the second day of the AAU Nationals at Downing Stadium. Paul Drayton, Budd's Villanova teammate, wins the 220 (21.0). Dyrol Burleson takes a tight three-way mile (4:04.9) with Jim Beatty second, Jim Grelle third.

1972

Nat Fleischer dies at age 84 in New York. A CCNY graduate and onetime New York City public school teacher, Fleischer was a sportswriter for various papers from 1912-27. In 1922, he founded *Ring Magazine* with three partners (all of whom were bought out by 1929), and in 1942 the *Ring Record Book & Encyclopedia*, which was discontinued in 1987. During his lifetime he was considered the world's leading authority on boxing and wrestling.

1991

Irving Cohen, 87, last promoter at St. Nicholas Arena (1961-62), promoter at Sunnyside Gardens (1962-65) and a manager of middleweight champ Rocky Graziano, dies in Scottsdale, Arizona.

June 26

1884
Former bare-knuckle heavyweight champ Jake Kilrain draws a crowd of 4,500 to the Garden for his four-round victory over Mike Cleary.

1897
R.A. Miller of the Greenwich (Connecticut) Wheelmen is the surprise winner of the Greater New York Amateur Bike Racing championship before 5,000 at Brooklyn's Manhattan Beach. Miller wins his mile heat in 2:27.4 and the final in 2:19.6 with O.B. Babcock second both times.

1900
Burly Gus Ruhlin of Akron, Ohio surprises the oddsmakers and "Sailor Tom" Sharkey with a kayo in their heavyweight bout at Coney Island's Seaside Sporting Club. Ruhlin decks Sharkey three times in the 15th of the scheduled 25-rounder and the Sailor is counted out at 2:55.

1906
Noted politician and former fighter Jim Dunne dies in Elizabeth, N.J., at 63 (see May 13).

1920
Japan's Ichita Kumagae defeats Howard Voshell, 6-0, 6-1, 6-3, in 40 minutes to win the Metropolitan Tennis Championship at the New York Tennis Club. Kumagae also won the championship, then one of the most prestigious amateur events, in 1916.

1922
Lightweight champion Benny Leonard fails to win the welterweight crown, losing to Jack Britton on a foul in the 13th round before 18,851 at the New York Velodrome.

1925
Sam Crane, who parlayed a seven-year major-league shortstop career into a three-decade career as a New York sportswriter, dies in New York at age 71.

1966
In the first sub-4:00-mile run outdoors in New York, Kansas' Jim Ryun (running for the Jayhawk Track Club) turns in a blistering 52.6 final quarter to finish in 3:58.6 in the AAU Nationals at Downing Stadium, Randalls Island. Dyrol Burleson of Eugene, Oregon, is second in 4:00.0. Ryun, helped by a slow early pace, finally took the lead because "nobody wanted it."

1987
Stan Lomax, a sportswriter and later sportscaster on WOR radio from 1934-77, dies in Ossining, N.Y., at age 88.

1993
Roy Campanella, Brooklyn Dodgers catcher from 1948-57 who was National League MVP three times (1951, 1953, 1955) and whose career was cut short by a car accident that left him paralyzed from the neck down (see Jan. 28), dies in Woodland Hills, California, at age 71.

LON KELLER

1995
Lon Keller, the sports artist who designed hundreds of sports magazines and program covers from the 1930s into the 1960s, and who created the logos of the Yankees (1946) and Mets (1961), dies in DeLand, Florida, at age 87.

1860

Patrick Thomas Powers, president of baseball's International League and the Newark (N.J.) Peps of the outlaw Federal League in 1915, is born in Trenton, N.J.

1903

Willie Anderson wins the second of his four U.S. Open championships with a two-stroke victory over David Brown in a playoff at the Baltusrol Golf Club. Playing out of Apawamis, Anderson shoots 82 in the playoff after he and Brown tie at 307 for 72 holes.

1913

World billiards champion Willie Mosconi is born in Philadelphia, Pennsylvania.

1926

James Donald Raleigh is born in Kenora, Ontario. Don (Bones) Raleigh, who came to the Rangers as a 17-year-old during World War II, was a slight center who scored 101 goals and added 219 assists in a 535-game, 10-season career, all with New York.

CHARLES OAKLEY

1928

Preparing for the Olympics at Amsterdam, the Netherlands, next month, AAU national freestyle champion Martha Norelius sets a world record of 1:12.75 for 110 yards at Rockaway's Atlantic Beach pool. Norelius, the best freestyler yet produced by the WSANY, takes gold in the 400-meter freestyle and 400-meter relay, both in Olympic record time, at the Games.

1939

Nearly two decades after their 26-inning tie (see May 1), the Brooklyn Dodgers and Boston Bees have at it again, struggling to a 2-2 deadlock in 23 innings at Boston's National League Field.

1949

Yankees beat the Giants, 5-3, in the Mayor's Trophy game at the Stadium, but the big news is the return of Joe DiMaggio. The Bombers' centerfielder, who has missed the entire season due to treatment for a painful bone spur in his right heel, is hitless in four at-bats but is cleared to make his season debut the next night in Boston.

1982

Bob Gilder shoots a record 261, breaking a 70 in each of his four rounds, to win the Westchester Classic at the Westchester CC. He shoots a final-round 69 after a 64-63-65 the first three days. One of the highlights is a double-eagle 2 on the 509-yard 18th hole on the third day when he sinks a 3-wood.

1988

Knicks trade center Bill Cartwright to the Chicago Bulls for forward Charles Oakley. The teams also exchange 1988 first- and third-round draft choices.

1992

Sandy Amoros dies in Miami at age 62. Amoros, a part-time outfielder with the Dodgers, played a critical role as Brooklyn won the 1955 World Series (see Oct. 4).

June 28

1878

Harvard and Yale, having met 14 times in the prior 25 years on four different courses, settle on New London, Connecticut, as the site of their now-annual rowing race. Harvard wins, covering the four-mile course in 20:44.75 to Yale's 21:29, and now has won 10 of 14 but Yale, starting in 1880, will win 18 of 23 (see July 21).

1879

Brighton Beach Race Course, the first major thoroughbred track in the City of Brooklyn, is opened by the Brighton Beach Racing Association. On June 19, 1880, the Coney Island Jockey Club opens the most famous of the city's three tracks, Sheepshead Bay, and in 1886, Gravesend joins the two earlier tracks (see Aug. 26).

1907

In an indication that the catcher's future greatness lies in the front office, Washington steals 12 bases off Branch Rickey in the Senators' 16-5 win over the Highlanders at Hilltop Park.

1919

Arthur Lucien Walker, Jr., son of a prominent professor of metallurgy, becomes the first Columbia golfer to win the Intercollegiate championship by beating Princeton's J. Simpson Dean, 4 and 2, at the Merion (Pa.) CC. Walker, later IGAA president, rallies after being three holes down after the 18-hole morning round, and finishes strongly with wins on three straight holes to close out the match. Walker was also the medalist with a 320 for four rounds in the team competition won by Princeton two days earlier. Columbia is 4th in the team event.

1929

Tommy Aycock, a Yale sophomore, wins the championship of the Intercollegiate Golf Association at the Hollywood CC in Deal, N.J. Aycock defeats another Yalie, Marshall Forest, in the final, 5 and 4. He is the 13th Yale winner but the first since 1924. Princeton wins the team title in the event, which isn't taken over by the NCAA until 1939.

1941

Dodgers pitcher Freddie Fitzsimmons and Boston coach Johnny Cooney umpire the first inning at Braves Field when the umpires (Lee Ballanfant, Al Barlick and Babe Pinelli) arrive late. It turns out that the umpires' boat from New York was delayed by fog.

1959

Jean Balukas, the greatest women's billiards player of her time, is born in Brooklyn. Balukas finished fifth in her first U.S. Open straight pool tournament at age nine, won her first title in 1972 and every year thereafter until the competition was discontinued after 1978. She also took six World Open championships. Lack of competition virtually forced her to stop playing.

1964

Tom O'Hara edges archrival Dyrol Burleson and sets an American record of 3:38.1 in winning the 1500-meter run as 22,000 at Rutgers Stadium watch the finals of the 76th AAU championships in New Brunswick, N.J. Bob Hayes defends his 100-meter dash title (10.3 seconds) and Ralph Boston also stars with his fourth straight to win the broad jump (26' 7 $\frac{1}{2}$").

1966

Terry Underwood, star running back for Wagner College, is born in Perth Amboy, N.J. In four seasons Underwood rushed for 5,010 yards in regular season play, setting a Division III record with an average of 201.0 yards per game in 1988.

1993

Jacques Lemaire is hired as head coach of the Devils. Under Lemaire, a former Canadiens star center and coach, New Jersey wins the Stanley Cup in 1995.

1876

Joe Start of the Mutuals hits into the major leagues' first triple play during an 8-0 loss at St. Louis. Shortstop Dickey Pearce (a former teammate of Start's with the Brooklyn Atlantics) gets the first out, goes to first baseman Herman Dehlman for the second and then third baseman Joe Batten gets out number three.

1894

Frank Hunter, a two-time winner of the U.S. Indoor singles tennis championship at the 7th Regiment Armory (1922, 1930), twice runner-up at the Nationals in Forest Hills (1928-29) and one of the early tennis pros (1931), is born in New York.

1916

Despite giving away over 35 pounds, Jack Dillon of Indianapolis scores a convincing 10-round win over heavyweight Frank Moran in the first major ballpark fight in America at Brooklyn's Washington Park. Dillon weighs 169 to Moran's 204 $\frac{1}{2}$ but takes the $40,000 purse anyway. The novelty of outdoor boxing draws many socially prominent fans to the ringside portion of the 18,000 on hand. The bulk of serious boxing fans, however, are in the $5 grandstand or $2 bleacher seats.

1923

Jacques Fournier gets six hits, including a homer and two doubles, as the Dodgers belt the Phillies, 14-5, at Philadelphia's Baker Bowl. Brooklyn racks up 25 hits.

1927

Columbia captures the IRA regatta eight-oar heavyweight championship for the first time since 1895 with a clocking of 20:57, with Washington second and California third.

1928

At the Apawamis Club in Rye, N.Y., Maurice McCarthy, Jr., of Georgetown wins the Intercollegiate Golf Championship individual title, beating John Roberts of Yale, 2 and 1. Princeton wins the team title with a four-man total of 608 in the three-day event.

1950

Yankees recall left-hander Ed (Whitey) Ford from Kansas City of the minor league AA and Ford wins his first nine decisions to help the Bombers win their second straight pennant. He finally loses, 8-7, to the Philadelphia A's in relief on Sept. 27.

1974

Charles Loftus, Yale's director of sports information from 1943-68, dies in New Haven, Connecticut, at age 55.

1982

In a swap of guards, the Nets send Ray Williams to the Kansas City-Omaha Kings for Phil Ford.

1993

Barney Stein, *New York Post* photographer from 1937-73 and official photographer of the Brooklyn Dodgers, dies in Deerfield Beach, Florida, at age 84.

1997

After opening the league's first season with three road wins, the New York Liberty takes its home opener, 65-57, over the Phoenix (Arizona) Mercury in a WNBA game at the Garden, as Vickie Johnson scores 20 points before 17,780, the largest crowd yet for a women's pro basketball game in the U.S. The Liberty wins its first seven games before losing July 7 at Phoenix.

June 30

1899
Bicyclist Charles Murphy, drafting a Long Island Rail Road train near Hempstead, N.Y., is clocked at 57 $^4/_5$ seconds for a mile. "Mile-A-Minute" Murphy's record stood until 1941.

1908
Boston's Cy Young no-hits the Highlanders (later the Yankees), 8-0, at Hilltop Park.

1925
Walter Budko, Jr., is born in Brooklyn. Walt Budko, a star forward for Columbia, averaged 14.2 ppg for the Lions from 1942-44 and 1946-48 and later played in the NBA.

1927
Shirley June Fry, Wimbledon and U.S. nationals champion at Forest Hills in 1956 when she was the world's No.1-ranked player, is born in Akron, Ohio.

1929
Bobby Jones, the last amateur to win golf's U.S. Open, does so for the third time with a 23-stroke win over pro Al Espinosa in a 36-hole playoff on the west course of the Winged Foot GC in Mamaroneck, N.Y. Jones made a 12-foot putt the day before to salvage a tie at 294 and then shoots 72-69-141, three under par, in the playoff. Espinosa gets $1,000 as the top pro finisher. Jones wins his fourth Open the following year and then retires at age 28.

BOB FISHEL

1934
Dan Topping buys the Brooklyn Football Dodgers from Chris Cagle and Shipwreck Kelly (see July 9).

1949
Playing only his third game of the season, Joe DiMaggio hits a three-run homer off Mel Parnell in the seventh inning to lift the Yankees to a 6-3 win over the Red Sox at Boston. In the Bombers' three-game sweep of the Sox, DiMaggio hits .455 with four homers and nine RBI. He missed the first 65 games of the season due to a bone spur on his right heel but finishes with 67 RBI in 76 games and a .346 average as the Yankees win the pennant by one game, edging Boston.

1956
Billy Haughton drives Belle Acton to victory in the inaugural Messenger Stakes at Roosevelt Raceway.

1962
Sandy Koufax of the Dodgers no-hits the Mets, 5-0, in Los Angeles, the first of the southpaw's four career no-hitters.

1966
Michael G. Tyson, world heavyweight champion from 1986-90, is born in Brooklyn.

1988
Bob Fishel, Yankees public relations director from 1954-74 who joined the American League in 1974, ascending to executive vice president in 1983, dies in New York at age 74.

1854

On the sixth and final day of the most successful racing meeting ever held in the Northeast, over 20,000 turn out to see Highlander win the featured club purse at the new National Course between Flushing and Newtown, Long Island (now Queens). The five-year-old chestnut horse wins two straight four-mile heats from the mare, DiClapperton, in 7:57 and 7:54.5.

1857

Roger Connor, Giants slugging star of the 1880s, is born in Waterbury, Connecticut. Star of the 1888 and 1889 world champions, Connor, the most consistent home run threat of the dead-ball era of 19th-century baseball, scored over 100 runs in a season eight times.

1882

Lon Myers of the Manhattan AC sets a U.S. record (1:11.4) in the 600-yard run in the American AC Games at the Polo Grounds. S.A. Stafford of the host club also sets a record (27.4 seconds) in the 220-yard hurdles.

1900

William B. Curtis, a founder of the NYAC in 1868 and a national champion in the hammer throw (1876, 1878, 1880), and 56-pound weight (1878), dies in a blizzard while climbing Mount Washington in New Hampshire.

1911

In the first appearance of a Japanese baseball team in New York, Waseda University scores seven runs in the 10th to beat a Manhattan team, 10-4, at the Lenox Oval. The home team is mainly college players augmented by a few semi-pros.

1912

Peter Drobach of Boston is the surprise winner of the five-mile national championship bike race at the Newark Velodrome in 10:23.4. The real surprise is that Frank Kramer finishes fourth and Alf Goullet, who was expected to battle Kramer for the title, is fifth.

1920

Tex Rickard and partner Frank C. Armstrong take over the lease on Garden No. 2 at 26th Street and Madison Avenue. In six months, Rickard is the first manager to make money consistently with the building, mainly due to his 25 boxing dates over that period starting with a September 18 card featuring Johnny Dundee against Joe Welling. By March, Rickard had drawn 910,402 with boxing (including two charity shows and five amateur tournament dates), two six-day bike races, the National Horse Show (over 60,000) and the Westminster Kennel Club dog show (40,000).

1941

Rodrigue Gabriel Gilbert is born in Montreal, Quebec. Rod Gilbert played more seasons (18), and scored more goals (406) and assists (615) than any other Ranger.

1981

Dan Daniel, 91, dies in Pompano Beach, Florida. A Columbia graduate born Daniel Margovitz, he was a baseball writer for the *Herald, Press, Evening Mail, Telegram* and *World-Telegram* for over 50 years, covering primarily the Yankees, and contributor to *Ring Magazine*.

1987

New York gets the world's first all-sports radio station when WHN (1050 AM) is converted to WFAN. At 3:00 p.m., Suzyn Waldman reads the first "Sports Update" and explains the station's format, which includes news, call-in talk shows and live event broadcasts. In 1988, WFAN displaces WNBC at 660 on the AM dial (WEVD takes over 1050) and becomes the flagship station for the Knicks and Rangers, as well as the Mets.

July 2

1872

In the most anticipated horse race of the season in the East, five-year-old Longfellow convincingly beats four-year-old Henry Bassett in a 2 $\frac{1}{2}$-mile race to win the Monmouth Cup. Longfellow is clocked in 4:34 to win the $1,500-added run by almost 200 yards as 25,000 watch.

1921

Boxing's first million-dollar gate is produced at Boyle's 30 Acres in Jersey City, N.J. Tex Rickard's promotion of heavyweight champion Jack Dempsey's title defense against France's Georges Carpentier ends with a fourth-round kayo by Dempsey. The crowd of 80,183 generates a gross gate of $1,789,238.

1925

Harry Greb defends his middleweight championship with a 15-round decision over Mickey Walker before 40,000 at the Polo Grounds.

1933

In one of the great pitching exhibitions in baseball history, Giants lefthander Carl Hubbell throws an 18-inning six-hitter to beat St. Louis, 1-0, in the opening game of a Polo Grounds doubleheader. Hughie Critz drives in the only run with a single. Hubbell strikes out 12 and walks none. In the nightcap, Johnny Vergez homers and Roy Parmalee tosses a four-hitter for another 1-0 win to complete the sweep before over 45,000.

1935

Hank O'Day dies in Chicago, Illinois, at 72. O'Day, a one-time major-league pitcher, began umpiring in 1888 and worked the first modern World Series (with Tom Connolly of the American League) in 1903. He is most famous for making the out call caused by "Merkle's Boner" (see Sept. 23).

1936

WPA Administrator Harry Hopkins calls it "the finest in the world" as the Astoria Pool is dedicated in Queens. Mayor Fiorello LaGuardia throws the switch formally turning on the lights after praising Parks Commissioner Robert Moses, who supervised the construction. Several national swimming championships are held there and the women's final Olympic trials begin here nine days after the formal opening.

1940

Former heavyweight champ Max Baer flashes enough old form to beat "Two-Ton" Tony Galento, who fails to answer the bell for the eighth round. The bout draws 22,711 to Jersey City's Roosevelt Stadium.

1948

Joe Jeannette dies at age 78 in Weehawken, N.J. Jeannette was the first black man licensed as a boxing referee in New York State (see Feb. 24) after a distinguished ring career in which he fought 154 times as a heavyweight.

1952

Lester R. Goodman, general manager of the Elias Baseball Bureau who was hired by founder Al Munro Elias in 1917, dies at age 54 in New York.

1960

Eugene Devlan dies in Los Angeles, at age 70. As Gene Fowler, Devlan became a prominent newspaperman, sportswriter and author who not only wrote for several New York newspapers but authored a number of books celebrating the so-called "Golden Age of Sports" in New York in the 1920s.

1870

As the sport steadily moves toward sanctioning professional play, the Knickerbockers, baseball's first organized club, withdraw in protest from the National Association of Base Ball Players, which they had helped found in 1858 (see Mar. 10).

1921

J. Simpson Dean of Princeton defeats defending champion Jess Sweetser of Yale, 3 and 2, to win the Intercollegiate Golf Association championship at the Greenwich (Connecticut) Country Club. Dartmouth, for the only time, wins the team title.

1922

At Shibe Park in Philadelphia, the Yankees' Bob Meusel hits for his second career cycle in a 12-1 rout of the A's.

1936

German-born Bob Rodenkirschen, a schoolboy from Jersey City's Dickinson High School, wins the junior 200-meter run in the National AAU championship at Princeton's Palmer Stadium with a record 21.2-second time. That evening, Nazi foreign minister Franz Von Papen pressures Rodenkirschen to join the German Olympic team for Berlin Games

PANCHO GONZALEZ

since his father hasn't completed his U.S. citizenship papers. But the boy refuses and runs for neither country.

1970

On the final day of the five-day Grand Circuit meeting at Historic Track in Goshen, N.Y., where harness racing has been conducted since 1838, Most Happy Fella sets a mile record of 1:58.4 for two trips around the half-mile in winning the first heat of the Orange County Cup before 3,517 fans. Pari-mutuel racing is discontinued at Historic after the 1978 meeting.

1994

Lew Hoad dies in Fuengirola, Spain, at age 59. In 1956, Hoad's bid to win tennis' Grand Slam at the U.S. Nationals at Forest Hills was thwarted in the final by fellow Australian Ken Rosewall.

1995

Pancho Gonzalez dies in Las Vegas, Nevada, at age 67. Considered by some the best tennis player of all time, the fiery Gonzalez, who spent his best years relegated to the self-imposed obscurity of the pro tour (where the money was better) before the dawn of open tennis in 1968, won the U.S. National singles title at Forest Hills in 1948 and 1949 before turning pro. His last wife, Rita, is tennis star Andre Agassi's sister.

1995

Charley Eckman, long-time college basketball and NBA referee, dies in Glen Burnie, Maryland, at age 73.

1996

Alex Ochoa of the Mets hits for the cycle at Philadelphia in only his 22d major league game (third fastest career cycle in history), collects a club-record-tying five hits, two of them doubles, and drives in three runs as the Mets down the Phillies, 10-6.

1826

Second U.S. President John Adams, at age 91, and the third president, Thomas Jefferson, at age 83, die, on the 50th anniversary of the signing of the Declaration of Independence, which Adams inspired and Jefferson drafted. (This has nothing to do with sports but is probably the most remarkable fact in American history - Ed.)

1877

George McNichol wins the 100-yard dash (10.25) and Harry Buermeyer takes the shot put (34' 11") in the Scottish-American AA Games at Manhattan's Washington Park, 69th Street and the East River, before 3,000.

1882

John L. Sullivan, soon to be heavyweight champ, knocks out Jimmy Elliot in the third round at Brooklyn's Washington Park. Although Brooklyn is still independent, it is Sullivan's second appearance in what will become New York when the cities are consolidated in 1898.

1883

Tim Keefe of the Mets pitches two complete games, allowing only three hits in winning an AA doubleheader, 9-1 and 3-0, at Columbus, Ohio.

1908

Hooks Wiltse gets a no-hitter with a 1-0 victory over Philadelphia in 10 innings for the Giants in the first game of a doubleheader at the Polo Grounds. It is the National League's first extra-inning no-hitter.

1939

Between games of a doubleheader with Washington, the Yankees retire Lou Gehrig's No. 4, the first uniform number retired in baseball history. Despite his illness, which would take his life in fewer than two years (see June 2), Gehrig tells the crowd of 61,808 that he considers himself "the luckiest man on the face of the earth."

1950

Barney Doyle, 56, an unemployed ferry worker from Weehawken, N.J., is killed in the leftfield upper deck in the Polo Grounds before a Giants-Dodgers doubleheader by a rifle bullet. Doyle took the son of a friend to see the games and is hit by a shot fired from a nearby building.

1970

Harold Stirling (Mike) Vanderbilt dies at age 85 in Newport, Rhode Island. Vanderbilt, a director of the New York Central Railroad from 1913-54, skippered three successful America's Cup defenses (1930, 1934, 1937). He also developed contract bridge in the mid-1920s.

1972

George Schuster, who drove a Thomas Flyer around the world to win the famous New York-to-Paris auto race of 1908 (see Feb. 12), dies at age 99 in Springville, N.Y.

1979

Mendy Rudolph, who refereed 2,113 NBA games over 18 seasons (1957-75), dies in New York at age 52.

1983

Southpaw Dave Righetti no-hits the Red Sox, 4-0, at the Stadium, fanning future Yankee (and 1983 batting champ) Wade Boggs for the final out. It is the first Yankee no-hitter since Don Larsen's perfect game in 1956 (see Oct. 8), the first by a Yankee lefty since George Mogridge in 1917 and the first ever by a Yankee southpaw at the Stadium.

1878

America wins its first event at London's Royal Henley Regatta as Columbia's four-oared shell rows to victory over Hertford College of England to take the Visitors' Challenge Cup.

1904

After winning 18 straight, the Giants drop a 6-5 10-inning decision to the Philadelphia Phillies.

1908

In the longest scoreless game up to that time in the International League, Jersey City and Newark go 19 innings at Newark, with Skeeters starter Ed Lafitte yielding only three hits and Indians starter King Brockett six as both go the distance.

1929

Martha Norelius, star of the WSANY team, announces that she is turning pro and giving up hope of getting her AAU suspension lifted. The two-time gold medal Olympian (1924, 1928) is stripped of her three individual and two relay wins in the nationals at Chicago (see Mar. 2), and the WSANY loses its team championship for the first time since the competition began in 1921.

1935

Al Cuccinello homers for the Giants and his brother, Tony, does the same for the Dodgers but Tony's Dodgers win, 14-4, at the Polo Grounds. It is the first time brothers ever homer for opposing teams in the same major league game.

LOU GEHRIG

1937

Germany's Bernd Rosemeyer, the pre-race favorite, wins the 300-mile Vanderbilt Cup auto race at Roosevelt Raceway in an Auto-Union that averages 82.564 mph. He covers the distance in just over three hours, 38 minutes, with Britain's John A.B. Seaman second and American Rex Mays third. Unfortunately, it is the last Vanderbilt Cup, revived in 1936, and the last win for Rosemeyer, who is killed January 28, 1938, in a road race near Berlin.

1989

Nesuhi Ertegun, recording executive with Atlantic Records who, with his brother Ahmet, founded the New York Cosmos of the North American Soccer League in 1971, dies in New York at age 71. The brothers Ertegun sold the team in 1983.

1990

David Schriner dies in Montreal, Quebec, at age 78. A native of Calgary, Alberta, Sweeney Schriner was the NHL Rookie of the Year in 1934-35 and the league's leading scorer in 1935-36 and 1936-37 as a left wing on the Americans.

1995

Samuel Deitchman, co-captain (with Red Holzman) of the 1941-42 CCNY basketball team that went 16-3, dies in New York at age 73.

1922

Frank L. Kramer equals the world bike sprint record of 15.4 seconds for one-six-teenth of a mile at the Newark (N.J.) Velodrome and, at age 41, retires from competition. In more than two decades as a champion racer, Kramer was the highest-paid athlete in the world and the most famous name in American sports. He won the League of American Wheelmen amateur title in 1898 (at age 17) and became the U.S. pro sprint champion in 1901, holding the title at one point for 16 straight years.

1940

Frederick Maxfield Hoyt, a *Titanic* survivor who became a successful yacht de-signer and sailor, dies at age 66 in New Rochelle, N.Y. Hoyt sailed with the *Atlantic* from the U.S. to Spain when she won the Kaiser's Cup before World War I.

1942

Originally scheduled for cozy Ebbets Field, the All-Star Game is played at the more spacious Polo Grounds as a benefit for war charities and the AL wins, 3-1. But the crowd is held to 34,178 by afternoon showers that precede the 6:00 p.m. planned start. Lou Boudreau and Rudy York hit first-inning homers for the winners.

PAT RILEY

1942

Tom Thorp dies in Cambridge, Massachusetts, at age 60. A Columbia football All-American in 1904, Thorp was head coach at Fordham from 1912-13 (7-7-2) and NYU from 1922-24 (14-9-2), as well as a sportswriter for the *Evening Journal* from 1906-36 and one-time general manager of the Empire City Race Track in Yonkers, N.Y.

1948

Douglas Bradford Park is born in Toronto, Ontario. Brad Park was generally considered the second-best defenseman in the NHL during the early 1970s. Rangers captain at the time of his shocking trade to Boston (see Nov. 7), he set the club mark for most goals by a defenseman (25) in 1973-74 when he became the first backliner in team history to lead the team in points (82).

1962

Rod Kanehl hits the Mets' first grand slam ever, connecting off lefty Bobby Shantz in the eighth inning of the Mets' 10-3 win over St. Louis in a night game at the Polo Grounds.

1970

Tommie Agee hits for the cycle for the Mets in a 10-3 rout of St. Louis at Shea Stadium.

1975

A much-anticipated match race nationally televised and attended by 50,764 at Belmont Park ends in tragedy as unbeaten three-year-old filly Ruffian fractures both sesamoids in her right foreleg in the first quarter of the 10-fur-long match race against Kentucky Derby winner Foolish Pleasure. The three-year old colt wins the $225,000 purse but the unfortunate filly is put down the next morning despite extensive efforts to save her, including emergency surgery. Ruffian had won all 10 of her races before her demise, including New York's Triple Crown for fillies earlier in 1975.

1995

Knicks hire Don Nelson as head coach, succeeding Pat Riley, who resigned by fax earlier in the summer to accept the job as president, general manager and coach of the Miami Heat. Subsequent events prove that Nelson and the Knicks players are unsuited for each other and he is fired before completing a full season (see Mar. 8).

1877

By winning the first innings, 129-81, and the second innings, 132-46, the St. George Cricket Club routs the University of Pennsylvania on the St. George Grounds at Hoboken, N.J. J.B. Whetham makes 45 runs in his first inning against E. Walter Clark's bowling and 37 against C.M. Clark in his second inning.

1900

Walter J. Travis wins the first of his three U.S. Amateur golf titles with a victory over Findlay S. Douglas, 2-up, in the final at the Garden City (L.I.) Golf Club.

1909

William Jennings Bryan Herman is born in New Albany, Indiana. Billy Herman was the second baseman on the 1941 pennant-winning Brooklyn Dodgers.

1962

Fencers Club of New York wins the three-weapon team final in the National Fencing Championships at the Park Sheraton Hotel but the NYAC wins the overall team title with 48 points in the eight-day event. Al Axelrod wins the foil and Jimmy Adams the epee as Fencers Club defeats Salle Csiszar of Philadelphia, Pennsylvania, the defending champion, in the three-weapon event, 2-1. Fencers Club finishes with 31 points for second place overall. NYAC's team title is its third straight.

JOHN CALLISON

1964

Johnny Callison's three-run, ninth-inning homer boosts the National League to a 7-4 victory in the only All-Star Game ever played at Shea Stadium.
Boston's Dick Radatz is on the mound protecting a 4-3 American League lead in the ninth when Orlando Cepeda's RBI single ties the game and, after two outs and a walk, Callison's shot into the rightfield stands sends the 50,844 fans home. The win enables the NL to tie the series, 17-17.

1976

Bill Swiacki, an All-America end at Columbia in 1947 whose two circus catches helped end Army's 32-game unbeaten streak (see Oct. 25), dies in Sturbridge, Massachusetts, at age 53. Swiacki also played for the Football Giants from 1948-50.

1982

New York Gov. Hugh Carey signs legislation that produces $50 million in tax breaks for Madison Square Garden over the next 10 years and also enables Con Edison to make concessions on the Garden's electric rates by tapping into the state's hydroelectric grid. The Garden claims annual losses of some $9 million.

1982

In a swap of power forwards, the Knicks send Maurice Lucas to the Phoenix Suns for Len (Truck) Robinson.

1992

Clint Frank dies in Chicago, at age 76. Frank was a Yale halfback from 1935-37, an All-American in 1936-37, and Heisman and Maxwell Trophy winner in 1937. The 1937 Bulldogs squad of which he was captain went 6-1-1 and finished 12th in *The Associated Press* national rankings.

1877

With 4,000 on hand at the end, Daniel O'Leary falls 48 $\frac{1}{2}$ miles short in his bid to walk 520 miles in six days at the American Institute Fair Building. At 30 seconds past 12:04 a.m., O'Leary has completed 471 $\frac{1}{2}$ miles since 12:05 a.m. the prior Monday.

1889

After traipsing around to Jersey City's Oakland Park and Staten Island's St. George Grounds for "home" games after their former home was demolished, the Giants win their first game at 157th Street and Eighth Avenue, beating Pittsburgh, 7-5, as Cannonball Crane oupitches Pud Galvin with 8,324 fans trying out the new grandstands (see Mar. 30).

1907

Chicago Cubs first baseman Frank Chance nearly triggers a riot at Washington Park when Dodgers fans throw bottles on the field and he throws them back, one striking a small boy. Quick response by 12 cops from the Bergen Street station averts a serious problem as they escort Chance to the clubhouse. He is then driven to his Manhattan hotel by Brooklyn club owner Charley Ebbets, who wheels past some angry fans.

1914

James Francis Elliott is born in Philadelphia, Pennsylvania. Jumbo Elliott was the Villanova track coach from 1935-81 when the Wildcats dominated collegiate indoor track-and-field events.

1923

Harrison Dillard, four-time Olympic gold medalist in 1948 (1) and 1952 (3), and winner of the 1955 Sullivan Award as the nation's top amateur athlete, is born in Cleveland, Ohio.

1929

Tommy Gorman resigns as general manager and coach of the Americans in order to expand his thoroughbred racing work when he is appointed general manager of Mexico's Agua Caliente racetrack.

1950

Greentree Stables' One Hitter, with Ted Atkinson up, wins the Questionable Stakes by a nose in a track-record 1:42.4 at Jamaica. One Hitter nips Brookmeade Stables' Greek Ship at the wire in the mile-and-a-sixteenth test and pays $17.60 to win.

1969

Robert (Red) Rolfe dies in Laconia, New Hampshire, at age 60. Rolfe played third base for the Yankees in 1931 and from 1934-42, and in 1939 set a major league record for most consecutive games scoring at least one run (18).

1987

Al Bianchi is named Knicks general manager, succeeding Scotty Stirling.

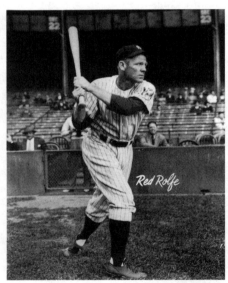

RED ROLFE

1988

Ray Barbuti, winner of two gold medals at the 1928 Olympic Games (in the 400 meters and 4x400-meter relay) and a leading Eastern football game official, dies at age 83. Barbuti called a touchdown the circus catch by Columbia's Bill Swiacki that reduced Army's lead to 20-14 in the game that ended the Cadets' 32-game unbeaten streak (see Oct. 25).

1886

Thomas Gorman, the first Americans coach in 1925-26 (12-20-4), coach again in 1928-29 (19-13-12) and later coach of the Stanley Cup champion Chicago Blackhawks of 1934 and Montreal Maroons of 1935, is born in Ottawa, Ontario.

1910

Thomas Linton Anderson is born in Edinburgh, Scotland. A left wing, Tommy Anderson played seven years with the Americans, scoring 57 goals and 125 assists. In the club's last year in the NHL, 1941-42, when it was called the Brooklyn Americans even though it still played its home games in Manhattan's Madison Square Garden, Anderson won the Hart Trophy as the league's MVP, posting 12 goals and 29 assists while playing all 48 games for the cellar-dwellers, who finished seventh.

1933

Big Bill Dwyer, sole owner of the Brooklyn Football Dodgers, having bought out former partner John Depler (see July 12), sells the club to Chris Cagle and Shipwreck Kelly.

1937

Joe DiMaggio hits for the cycle for the first time in his career. He belts two homers and drives in seven runs as the Yankees beat the Washington Senators at the Stadium, 16-2.

1962

Harry Elwood McCormick, who apparently scored the winning run on Al Bridwell's single in the "Merkle's Boner" Game of 1908 (see Sept. 23), which indirectly led to the suicide of Harry Pulliam (see July 29), dies in Lewisburg, Pennsylvania, at age 81. Moose McCormick was later head baseball coach at Army from 1926-37.

AL FRAZIN

1969

With a one-out single in the ninth, the Cubs' Jimmy Qualls breaks up Tom Seaver's perfect-game bid at Shea Stadium. The second-place Mets top front-running Chicago, 4-0, before 50,709.

1973

Dwight Filley Davis, Jr., dies at age 66 in Southampton, N.Y. Pete Davis, son of the donor of tennis' Davis Cup, was one of the original backers of a New York team in the proposed Continental League in the late 1950s and later a Mets vice president.

1988

Colonel Alfred Bender Frazin dies in Satellite Beach, Florida. Al Frazin was the chief public address announcer at Madison Square Garden from 1925-42 and then entered the U.S. Army, rising to lieutenant colonel by his retirement in 1965.

1994

Devils retain captain and defenseman Scott Stevens by matching the free-agent offer sheet Stevens signed with the St. Louis Blues July 4.

July 10

1876

Mutuals score once in the 16th inning and beat the Colonels, 6-5, at Louisville, Kentucky, in a National League game that began Saturday, two days earlier, and was called by darkness after 15 innings as a 5-5 tie to be resumed on Monday.

1922

Giacobe LaMotta is born in The Bronx. Jake LaMotta, "the Bronx Bull," was middleweight champion from 1949-51, and subject of the movie "Raging Bull."

1926

Edward Butler is awarded an NFL franchise for Brooklyn but the Lions are losers both at the field and at the box office in the war with the first AFL (which also has a team in Brooklyn) and fold at the end of their first season.

1934

With a performance that ensures the permanence of the All-Star Game as a fixture of the baseball schedule, Giants lefty and National League starter Carl Hubbell fans in succession over the first and second innings Babe Ruth, Lou Gehrig, Jimmy Foxx, Al Simmons and Joe Cronin. After a Bill Dickey single, he then fans opposing starter Lefty Gomez. But the American League wins, 9-7, at the Polo Grounds, with Brooklyn's Van Lingle Mungo taking the loss.

1945

Bill Farnsworth, sports editor of the New York *Evening Journal* (1925-37) and later an executive with Mike Jacobs' 20th Century Sporting Club, dies in New York at age 60. Wilton Simpson Farnsworth, who once negotiated with Babe Ruth as a favor to Yankee owner Jake Ruppert to solve a contract dispute, had suffered a stroke November 17, 1944, ringside at the Garden.

1946

Freddie Archer gains a 10-round decision over Jorge Morelia at Newark's Meadowbrook Bowl. The fight was halted the night before by rain after two rounds in the open-air arena and resumes in round three.

1950

Giants claim Jim Hearn on waivers from the St. Louis Cardinals. Hearn is 17-9 for the Giants in 1951 and wins the third game of that year's World Series.

1977

George Morton Levy, founder of the Roosevelt Raceway harness track in 1940 and father of the modern-day harness racing industry, dies in Mineola, N.Y., at age 89.

1979

Sam Taub dies in New York at age 92. An aide to Bat Masterson when the legendary Dodge City gunslinger was sports editor of *The Morning Telegraph*, Taub broadcast over 7,000 boxing matches, including the first bouts ever seen on television, in 1938 (from Ridgewood Grove, St. Nicholas Arena and Jamaica Arena), and the first major televised bout, in 1939 (see June 1). "The Voice of Adam Hats," Taub was so identified with that sponsor that Gillette, new underwriter of boxing programs, chose a new voice for its broadcasts—Don Dunphy.

1995

August Belmont, IV, dies in Easton, Maryland, at age 86. Belmont was a director of the American Kennel Club and its chairman from 1977-79, as well as chairman of the Jockey Club from 1982-83.

1924

Ray Lumpp, star guard at NYU, member of the 1948 U.S. Olympic gold medal basketball team, a Knick for parts of five seasons (1948-49 to 1952-53), long-time athletic director of the New York Athletic Club and frequent indoor track and field meet director, is born in Brooklyn.

1926

Tony Lavelli, an All-America basketball player at Yale who upon his graduation was the all-time leading scorer in major college basketball history with 1,964 points (20.2 ppg), is born in Somerville, Massachusetts. Lavelli, who also played 30 games for the Knicks in 1950-51, was known for playing the accordion at halftime of college and pro games.

1936

On a scalding hot Saturday when the temperature unofficially hits 108 degrees, President Franklin D. Roosevelt officially opens the Triborough Bridge while in the Triborough Stadium on Randalls Island under the new span, the U.S. Olympic team begins two days of final trials. Jesse Owens wins the 100-meter dash in 10.4 with Ralph Metcalfe second. Owens also wins the broad jump with a leap of 25' 10 $^3/_4$".

1939

Before 62,892, Joe DiMaggio's homer helps the American League to a 3-1 All-Star Game win over the National League in the first such game played at Yankee Stadium. The game is broadcast by all three radio networks: NBC (WJZ-760 AM in New York), CBS (WABC-860), and Mutual Broadcasting System (WOR-710). It is also the first All-Star game telecast, being shown on a few sets in New York by NBC's experimental station (W2XBS). Box seats are $2.20 and reserved grandstand $1.65, producing the gross gate of $75,701.

JESSE OWENS

1953

Oliver Samuel Campbell, a Brooklyn native who for exactly a century was the youngest man ever to win the U.S. national singles tennis championship, dies in Campbellton, Canada, at 82. Campbell won three in a row (1890-92), the first at age 19 as a Columbia undergraduate.

1953

Rookie righty Alan Worthington, a mid-season callup, becomes the first modern National League pitcher to break in with two shutouts as the Giants beat the Dodgers, 6-0, at Ebbets Field for their eighth straight win. Worthington allows only four hits as Brooklyn is shut out for the first time this season.

1954

Don Mueller, getting his first homer of the season, hits for cycle and helps the Giants win the opening game of a doubleheader from Pittsburgh, 13-7, at the Polo Grounds. Mueller drives in four runs in the opener but the Pirates come back to win the second game, 5-1.

1996

Riddick Bowe wins his heavyweight bout over Poland's Andrew Golota at the Garden on a foul with 27 seconds left in the seventh round. Brawls break out in the ring and among the 11,252 on hand after the decision but no serious injuries are reported.

1892

Alexander Cartwright, the surveyor whose innovations in 1845 created a form of a game recognizable as, and to-day called, baseball, dies in Honolulu, Hawaii Territory, at age 72.

1908

Paul Scott Runyon, winner of over 50 tournaments as a pro golfer, including six Westchester Opens and three Metropolitan PGAs, is born in Hot Springs, Arkansas.

1915

Guido Cribari, for over 50 years golf writer and sports editor of group of newspapers known then as the "Macy chain" (after its founder Valentine Macy) and now as the Gannett Suburban Newspapers, is born in Mount Vernon, N.Y.

1923

Argentine Luis Angel Firpo, "the Wild Bull of the Pampas," knocks out former heavyweight champ Jess Willard in the eighth round before 80,000 at Boyle's 30 Acres in Jersey City, N.J.

1930

Bill Dwyer and John Depler buy the Dayton (Ohio) Triangles of the NFL from Carl Storck and transfer the franchise to Brooklyn as the Football Dodgers playing in Ebbets Field. Brooklyn remains in the league until the end of the 1944 season.

1936

Eleanor Holm Jarrett in the 100-meter backstroke and Dorothy Poynton Hill in the high dive lead the winners in the final trials for the U.S. Olympic women's swimming squad at the new Astoria Pool. However, Mrs. Jarrett (wife of a popular band leader, and a 1932 gold medalist) doesn't swim in Berlin when she is suspended by U.S. Olympic chief Avery Brundage for "unbecoming conduct" on the trans-Atlantic ship voyage to Europe.

1949

Winning for the fourth straight year, the American League captures the only All-Star Game ever played at Ebbets Field. Virgil Trucks gets the win in the 11-7 game watched by a capacity 32,577. Brooklyn's Don Newcombe is the loser. Ebbets Field is the last active major-league ballpark to host an All-Star Game.

1951

Yankees righty Allie Reynolds pitches his first career no-hitter on the night the regular season resumes after the All-Star break, beating the Indians, 1-0, at Cleveland. Gene Woodling's 7th-inning homer off Bob Feller produces the game's only run. Feller had pitched his third career no-hitter 11 days earlier against the Detroit Tigers (see Sept. 28).

1975

Peter Robert Galiardy, who under the name Bobby Gleason was a boxing manager and owner of Gleason's Gym, dies at age 83 in New York. Gleason's was located at 149th Street and Westchester Avenue in The Bronx from 1937-74 before moving to 252 West 30th Street in Manhattan.

1991

Precious Bunny, driven by Jack Moiseyev, breaks Nihilator's record (see July 19) by winning the $1 million one-mile Meadowlands Pace in a scorching 1:49.8.

1996

Michael Francis announces his resignation as chairman of the NJSEA. Vice Chairman Ray Bateman succeeds him. Francis is under investigation for possible conflict of interest involving his maintenance company. Bateman's term is to run until February 1998.

1926

Jacques Fournier becomes the first Dodger to homer three times in a game, knocking in five runs, but the Cardinals beat Brooklyn, 12-10, at St. Louis.

1934

Babe Ruth hits his 14th homer of the year and the 700th of his career off Tommy Bridges in the second inning with a man on at Detroit's Navin Field. The Yankees win, 4-2, and Ruth pays a boy $20 for the home run ball hit over the rightfield fence.

1937

Cal Ramsey is born in Selma, Alabama. Ramsey, an NYU star who averaged 20.2 ppg in 63 games over three seasons (1956-59) for the Violets, played seven games for the Knicks in 1959-60. He later served as a commentator on Knicks telecasts for 10 seasons (1972-82) and became the team's Director of Community Relations.

1954

Henry Grantland Rice dies in New York at age 73. Grantland Rice from 1909-50 was a sportswriter for the *Evening Mail*, *Herald*, and *Herald Tribune* and appeared in *The Sun* as a syndicated columnist. He immortalized the "Four Horsemen," and they he, in 1924 (see Oct. 18).

ALEX WOJCIECHOWICZ

1960

In the second All-Star Game of the year, the NL blanks the AL, 6-0, before only 38,362 at Yankee Stadium. AL starter Whitey Ford takes the loss.

1969

Whitey Bimstein, cornerman and trainer (for many years with Ray Arcel) who handled champions including Jim Braddock, Primo Carnera, Rocky Graziano and Barney Ross, dies in New York at 82.

1977

When a power failure hits New York, several events are postponed after being interrupted in progress. At Shea Stadium, the Mets' Lenny Randle and 14,626 customers are literally left in the dark with a Ray Burris pitch speeding toward the plate. "I just hit the dirt," says Randle. The game is suspended and resumed September 16, with the Cubs winning, 5-2. At the Felt Forum, a World Tennis Team match halts. It resumes three days later and the Apples beat the Golden Gaters, 29-18.

1987

In his first major move as Knicks general manager (see July 8), Al Bianchi hires Providence head coach Rick Pitino as the new Knicks coach.

1992

Alex Wojciechowicz dies in South River, N.J. The center and linebacker for Fordham's second version of the "Seven Blocks of Granite" in the mid-1930s, "Wojie" was an All-American in 1936 and 1937 and fourth in the Heisman Trophy balloting in 1937.

1994

Roberto Baggio scores twice in the first half and Italy hangs on to beat Bulgaria, 2-1, as 77,094 watch the World Cup semifinal on a Wednesday afternoon at Giants Stadium.

1852

James Dwight, "the Father of American Tennis," is born in Paris, France. Dwight may or may not have introduced the game to the U.S. in 1874, but he certainly helped organize the United States National Lawn Tennis Association in 1881 and served 21 years over two terms as its president (1882-84, 1894-1911), still the longest tenure in the association's history. He also won five U.S. national doubles titles (1882-84, 1886-87).

1906

Eben M. Byers wins the U.S. Amateur golf championship by defeating George S. Lyon, 2-up, in the final match at the Englewood (N.J.) Golf Club.

1912

Rube Marquard loses both ends of a doubleheader in St. Louis, the first in relief as the Cardinals beat the Giants, 3-2, and the second as a starter, 4-2.

1916

Claude Harmon is born in Savannah, Georgia. The long-time golf pro at the Winged Foot GC, Harmon, winner of the 1946 and 1947 Westchester Open, the 1946 Metropolitan PGA and the 1948 Masters, was teaching pro for four presidents.

1923

Amateur Bobby Jones wins the first of his four U.S. Open golf titles in a playoff with a 76 for a two-stroke victory over pro Bobby Cruickshank at the Inwood (L.I.) Country Club. The pair tied at 296 for 72 holes.

1925

Popular Bobby Walthour, Jr., temporarily takes the lead in the American Bicycle Championship by winning the 13th of the 24 races, a third-of-a-mile sprint, at the New York Velodrome. Walthour beats defending champion Arthur Spencer and former titleholder Willie Spencer (no relation) in 37.2 seconds to give him 25 points for the season.

1925

Pancho Villa, reigning flyweight champion, dies of a jaw infection in San Francisco. Villa had won the title in 1923 when he stopped Jimmy Wilde in the seventh round at the Polo Grounds. He had lost to welterweight Jimmy McLarnin on July 4 in Oakland, California, when he suffered the infection, and became one of the rare boxers to die while a world champion.

1986

Former Rangers captain and incumbent television colorman Phil Esposito is named Rangers general manager, succeeding Craig Patrick, whose grandfather Lester and uncle Muzz had held the job earlier in the franchise's history.

1993

Robert A. Hall dies at age 86 in North Palm Beach, Florida. Hall, Yale's athletic director from 1950-54, built the largest known collection of football game films and was a member of the NCAA television committee that introduced the first national plan for the 1951 season.

1996

Knicks acquire forward Larry Johnson from the Charlotte Hornets for forwards Anthony Mason and Brad Lohaus. Knicks also sign free agent guards Chris Childs (late of the Nets) and Allan Houston (Detroit) while renouncing the rights to seven players, including guard Derek Harper.

July 15

1895
Leon A. Miller is born in Cherokee, North Carolina. "Chief" Miller was CCNY lacrosse coach from 1932-60 and head football coach from 1942-44.

1901
Christy Mathewson no-hits the Cardinals in a 2-0 Giants victory at St. Louis.

1933
Oxford student Jack Lovelock of New Zealand sets a world record for the mile at Palmer Stadium in Princeton, N.J. Clocked in 4:07.6, Lovelock is chased all the way by Princeton's Bill Bonthron, who finishes second by seven yards, but whose time of 4:08.7 is the fastest ever by an American. Both men break the world standard of 4:09.2 established by France's Jules Ladoumegue in 1931, who had eclipsed the mark of 4:10.4 posted in 1923 by Paavo Nurmi of Finland.

1947
Leonard Brumby dies at age 57 in Hicksville, N.Y. Brumby, a breeder of champion terriers, founded the Professional Dog Handlers' Association in 1927.

1951
Happy Chandler resigns as baseball commissioner under pressure from unhappy owners.

1968
Owner Arthur Brown announces that the ABA New Jersey Americans are moving to Long Island (where they will become the New York Nets).

1972
Speedy Crown beats Canada's Fresh Yankee to the wire and becomes the first American horse since Speedy Scot in 1964 to win the International Trot at Roosevelt Raceway.

1976
Paul Gallico, famed author and *Daily News* sports editor (1924-37), dies in Monaco at 78.

1986
Harness driver and trainer Billy Haughton dies in Valhalla, N.Y., at age 62. Haughton won four Hambletonians, five Little Brown Jugs and seven Messenger Stakes. He dies after being injured in a racing accident July 5.

1988
Claiming losses of $7.4 million over the previous four years, owners of Roosevelt Raceway announce that it is closing for good. The announcement cancels a meeting scheduled to begin August 4, causes layoffs for some 900 employees and ends a harness racing history that began in 1940 when the track was the first in the nation to run trotting races under lights (see Sept. 2).

1994
One month and one day after leading the club to their first Stanley Cup in 54 years, coach Mike Keenan, using the pretext of a day-late bonus payment, declares the Rangers in breach of their contract, rendering it void and Keenan a free agent able to sign with any team. Two days later, Keenan, after failing to come to terms with the Detroit Red Wings, agrees to be general manager and coach of the St. Louis Blues (see July 24).

1863

John B. Foster, a sportswriter for the *New York Telegram*, secretary of the Giants, and editor of Spalding's *Official Baseball Guide*, is born.

1871

Parke Hill Davis, a Princeton football tackle and college football historian, is born in Jamestown, N.Y.

1902

In the evening, Andrew Freedman, owner of the Giants, hires John McGraw to succeed Horace Fogel as the manager of the forlorn New York National League club. Freedman had averaged almost a manager a year during his ownership, but Freedman is gone after the 1902 season, while McGraw remains until June 1932.

1921

Arthur Albert Irwin, a journeyman infielder in the NL, AA, and Players League in the 1880s and 1890s and manager who led the Giants in 1896, and an NL umpire in 1881 and 1902, dies aboard an ocean liner in the mid-Atlantic at age 63.

1926

Jack Delaney wins the light heavyweight championship with a 15-round decision over Paul Berlenbach before an overflow 49,186 at Ebbets Field. The gross of $461,789 sets a record for non-heavyweight fights that lasts 25 years (see July 24 and Sept. 12).

1942

Margaret Smith is born in Albury, New South Wales, Australia. The winner of more major singles championships (24) than any other player in tennis history, Margaret Smith (who married Barry Court in 1967) won the U.S. Nationals at Forest Hills five times. With her triumph in 1970, she completed the second women's Grand Slam.

1948

In one of the most startling and sensational off-field events in baseball history, Leo Durocher, Dodgers skipper since 1939, quits Brooklyn and signs to manage the archrival Giants. He replaces the popular Mel Ott at the Polo Grounds while Burt Shotton, once again, succeeds him in the Dodgers' dugout.

1965

Claude Lemieux, an agitating right wing who led the NHL with 13 goals in the 1995 playoffs as the Devils won the Stanley Cup, is born in Buckingham, Quebec.

1965

Charles Smith is born in Bridgeport, Connecticut. A 6'10" forward, Smith averaged 11.3 ppg in 241 games over four seasons (1992-96) with the Knicks before his trade February 8, 1996.

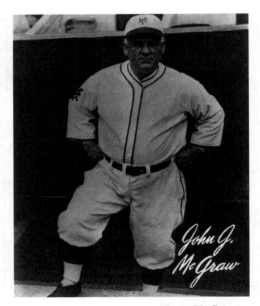

JOHN MCGRAW

1979

Basketball team owner Bobby Douglas dies in New York at age 96. Douglas owned the New York Renaissance (the Rens) in the 1930s and 1940s.

1896

Wilfred Thomas Green is born in Sudbury, Ontario. Hall of Famer Shorty Green, with his brother, Redvers (Red), was an original American in 1925-26.

1896

In the second U.S. Amateur golf championship, H.J. Whigham tops the field of 58 entries with a final-match win over J.G. Thorp, 8 and 7, at the Shinnecock Hills GC in Southampton, L.I.

1904

With pitcher-manager Clark Griffith throwing a three-hitter, the Highlanders beat Detroit, 3-1, at Newark's Weidenmayer Park, where they play this Sunday game to get around the ban on Sunday games in New York. But despite the turnout of 6,700, the club decides to discontinue the practice because of the inadequacies of the minor league park and pressure put on the American League by local clergy.

1914

In the longest game yet played in the National League, the Giants beat the Pirates, 3-1, in 21 innings at Pittsburgh's Forbes Field on Larry Doyle's two-run homer. Rube Marquard gives up 15 hits in 21 innings and gets the win while the Bucs' Babe Adams also goes the route without issuing a walk and allowing 12 safeties.

1941

Joe DiMaggio's 56-game hitting streak finally ends under the lights of Cleveland's Municipal Stadium. Indians third baseman Ken Keltner twice robs DiMaggio of potential hits with great plays. The Yankee centerfielder hits in the next 16 straight to give him safeties in 72 of 73 games en route to his second MVP award. The Yankees beat Cleveland, 4-3, improving their 41-13-2 record during the streak.

1942

Nick Werkman is born in Trenton, N.J. "Nick the Quick" averaged 32.0 ppg in 71 games at Seton Hall, leading the nation in scoring in his junior year (1962-63) despite having the lowest scoring average (29.5) in his three Pirates seasons.

1944

Soccer great Carlos Alberto, who spent his later playing years defending for the Cosmos, is born in Rio de Janeiro, Brazil.

1974

In the only home opener for the Stars of the embryonic WFL, the Birmingham (Alabama) Bulls score a 32-29 victory on this Wednesday night at Downing Stadium. By mid-season, the Stars shift to Charlotte, North Carolina, and by the end of the 1975 season, the WFL folds.

1975

Dick Conlon, manager of the Stork Club from 1950-57 and Gallagher's Steak House from 1965-75 (both athlete hangouts), dies in New York at age 60.

1977

Billy Gonsalves dies in Kearny, N.J., at age 68. Probably the greatest soccer player ever born in America, Gonsalves, an inside forward on U.S. World Cup soccer teams in 1930 and 1934, was a star on the Brooklyn Hispano national champions in 1933 and 1934 and numerous soccer clubs in the New York area.

1989

Neil Smith is named Rangers general manager after a lengthy search necessitated by Phil Esposito's firing (see May 24) and rejections of the job offer by other candidates, including former Canadiens coach Scotty Bowman.

1890

Brooklyn third baseman Jumbo Davis hits for the cycle but his AA club loses, 7-6, at Louisville.

1896

Scottish pro James Foulis, playing out of the Chicago Golf Club, wins the U.S. Open with a 74 for a 36-hole 152 at the Shinnecock Hills Golf Club in Southampton, N.Y. Horace Rawlins is second at 155.

1912

Wyatt Lee pitches a no-hitter for Newark in a 4-0 International League victory over Providence (but finishes the season with a 16-19 record).

1929

Richard T. Button is born in Englewood, N.J. Dick Button, the best male figure skater ever born in America, won gold medals at the 1948 and 1952 Winter Olympic Games, seven consecutive U.S. national championships (1946-52) and five straight world championships (1948-52). He later became a well-known television analyst covering the sport at national and international competitions.

BRYAN TROTTIER

1956

Bryan John Trottier is born in Val-Marie, Saskatchewan. The greatest center in Islanders history, Bryan Trottier won the Hart Trophy as NHL MVP in 1978-79, the Calder Trophy as Rookie of the Year in 1975-76 and the Conn Smythe Trophy as playoff MVP in 1980 when the Islanders won the first of their four straight Stanley Cups.

1967

Harold Lebair, treasurer of the United States Lawn Tennis Association from 1958-67 and long-time tennis umpire and linesman, dies at age 77 in Fairlee, Vermont.

1975

Eddie Brannick dies in West Palm Beach, Florida, at age 82. An employee of the Giants from 1905-57, Brannick at various times was the club's secretary, traveling secretary and agent renting out the Polo Grounds for non-baseball attractions.

1980

In the first $1 million event in U.S. horse racing, Niatross breezes home in a record 1:53.1 to win the one-mile Meadowlands Pace before a track-record 42,612 fans.

1986

Jacob (Buddy) Baer, brother of heavyweight champion Max, dies at age 71 in Martinez, California. Baer lost only seven of 55 professional bouts (including two to heavyweight champ Joe Louis in 1941 and 1942). In later years he appeared as a featured character actor in 17 movies.

1987

Don Mattingly hits a solo homer off Jose Guzman in the fourth inning of the Yankees' 7-2 loss at Texas to give him home runs in eight straight games. Mattingly ties the major-league record set by Pittsburgh's Dale Long (who later played for the Bombers (1960, 1962-63)) in 1956. Mattingly has 10 homers in his streak.

1858

William Trotter Porter, 48, dies in his home on Bleecker Street in Manhattan (see Jan. 3).

1871

During the 10th annual reunion of the National Pedestrian Congress, several competitons are held at the American Institute Fair Building. In the afternoon, Thomas Brown wins the four-mile walking match with William Young second and Homer Lane wins the wrestling competition by defeating Matt Grace and Peter Doyle. In the evening, J.W. McClellan takes the five-mile velocipede race with William E. Harding second.

1918

Secretary of War Newton Baker issues a "work-or-fight" order declaring baseball nonessential to the U.S. war effort. Baker later modifies the order to exempt professional baseball from automatic drafts of its players until September 1. As a direct result of this order, the baseball season ends Sept. 2 and the World Series is scheduled to start Sept. 4 (although rain delays the actual start one day).

1932

Roosevelt Grier is born in Cuthbert, Georgia. Rosey Grier, a gentle giant at 6'5" and 290 pounds, was a defensive tackle for the Giants from 1955-56 and 1958-62, spending the 1957 season in military service. He was named All-Pro in 1956.

1940

Yankees catcher Buddy Rosar hits for the cycle against Cleveland at the Stadium, scoring four runs and driving in three to lead the Bombers to a 15-6 rout of the Indians.

1946

Ilie Nastase, the gifted but vulgar tennis star of the early 1970s and the U.S. Open men's singles champion in 1972, is born in Bucharest, Rumania.

1977

In the first All-Star Game played in the renovated Yankee Stadium, the NL scores four first-inning runs and holds on for a 7-5 win over the AL before 56,683.

DON MATTINGLY

1985

Nihilator, a son sired by Niatross, breaks his sire's race record with a 1:50.3 clocking to win the one-mile Meadowlands Pace (see July 18).

1989

Claude Harmon, golf pro to four presidents (Eisenhower, Kennedy, Nixon and Ford) and at the Winged Foot GC in Mamaroneck, N.Y., dies at age 73 in Houston, Texas.

1994

Ray Flaherty dies in Coeur d'Alene, Idaho, at age 89. Flaherty, an end with the NFL Football Yankees from 1927-28 and the Giants from 1928-29 and 1931-35, coached the AAFC Yankees from 1946-48 (22-8-2), leading them to the league title games in 1946 and 1947, both losses to the Cleveland Browns. He also won NFL championships as head coach of the Washington Redskins (1937, 1942).

1858

In an embryonic "World Series" matching All-Star teams from the cities of New York and Brooklyn for the base-ball championship of America, New York wins the first game of the best-of-three set, 22-18, at the Fashion Race Course in what is now Corona, Queens. The crowd of 1,500 causes sizeable traffic jams on the country roads with their carriages, and the 50-cent admission fee is a baseball first. Brooklyn wins the next game, 29-8, but New York captures the championship with a 29-18 victory in the rubber match.

1876

In a widely-followed sloop yacht race on Long Island Sound, *Pluck & Luck* easily beats *Mary Emma* in three hours, seven minutes over a course five miles windward from New Rochelle, N.Y., and return twice around. Edward Spahn and Vice Commodore Jacob Schmidt of the Williamsburg Yacht Club collect a $500 wager from the Iselin brothers of the Seawanhaka Yacht Club, owners of the *Mary Emma*.

1906

Brooklyn's Malcolm Eason hurls a 2-0 no-hitter against the Cardinals at St. Louis.

1927

Famed public relations executive Joey Goldstein is born in Conway, South Carolina. Goldstein worked at Roosevelt Raceway and later did publicity for the New York City Marathon, the Manufacturers Hanover (later Chemical, later Chase) Corporate Challenge, the Millrose Games, the NIT, and numerous other sports events.

1929

"Wild Bill" Mehlhorn turns in a final-round 68 to win the Metropolitan Open by three strokes over Wiffy Cox of Dyker Beach at the Lido CC in Long Beach, N.Y. Tommy Armour does not defend his crown and Mehlhorn of Fenimore shoots 288.

1933

Nelson Doubleday, Jr., is born in New York. Doubleday, distantly related to Abner Doubleday (see Jan. 26), became chairman of the board when the syndicate of which he was a principal bought the Mets in 1980.

1949

Ian Wilkie, backup goalie for the WHA Raiders in 1972-73, is born in Edmonton. "We Want Wilkie!" those few hardy partisans at the Garden would chant, echoing the galleries at the 1940 Republican Convention that nominated Wendell Willkie for president. Alas, they didn't get Wilkie much—he played five games (1-3, 6.40 gaa).

1963

For the second time in three years, Su Mac Lad wins the Roosevelt International as the fifth renewal draws 40,153 to Roosevelt Raceway.

1965

Formal groundbreaking ceremonies are held for the new Belmont Park (see Oct. 27).

1965

Mel Stottlemyre hits an inside-the-park grand slam off Bill Monbouquette and also gets the win as the Yankees defeat Boston, 6-3, at the Stadium.

1988

John W. Galbreath, principal owner of the Pittsburgh Pirates (1946-85) and owner of the Darby Dan Farm from 1935-88, which produced Little Current, winner of the 1974 Preakness and Belmont Stakes, dies at Darby Dan Farm near Columbus, Ohio. Galbreath was chairman of the Greater New York Association (later NYRA) when the new Aqueduct and Belmont Park plants were built.

July 21

1855

Inaugurating the more-or-less regular annual regatta, Harvard defeats Yale at Springfield, Massachusetts, over a three-mile rowing course. Harvard won the first meeting in 1852 on Lake Winnepesaukee, New Hampshire. From 1859 on, the crews row virtually every year. The regatta changes locations several times, settling in New London, Conn., in 1878 (see June 28).

1889

Worcester beats Jersey City, 9-2, before 2,500 hushed fans at Jersey City. But police learn of the Eastern League game and, despite the quiet, arrest the 18 players. Each is fined $2 by Justice of the Peace Moore and warned that police would prevent further Sabbath violations, but the ensuing uproar among sports fans leads to an eventual relaxation of the Sunday Blue Laws (see Sept. 11).

1890

Roger Connor leads the New York Players League club to a 7-5 win at Buffalo as he hits for the cycle and scores twice.

1898

Max Kase is born in Brooklyn. Kase, sports editor of the *Journal-American* from 1939-65, won a Pulitzer citation in 1952 for his work in uncovering the 1951 college basketball scandals.

1935

Gerald Arthur Paulson is born in New York. Gerry Paulson, a guard, averaged 16.7 ppg in 69 games over three seasons (1954-57) for Manhattan College and was voted MVP of the 1956 ECAC Holiday Festival at the Garden.

1943

Charlie Paddock, the "world's fastest human" in the 1920s and a captain in the U.S. Marines, dies at age 42 near Sitka, Alaska, in the crash of a Navy plane.

1947

Will Gibson, boxing manager and promoter who owned the first New York Football Giants club (0-2 in 1921), which failed, and was a partner (with Tim Mara) of the second one (beginning in 1925), which succeeded, dies in New York at age 71.

1965

Mets righthander Al Jackson loses his no-hitter with one out in the eighth inning when Willie Stargell singles, but beats the Pirates, 1-0, at Pittsburgh on a two-hitter.

1979

Eddie Price, a running back for the Football Giants from 1950-55 and the NFL's leading rusher in 1951, dies in New Orleans, Louisiana, at age 53.

1983

Arthur M. Wirtz, owner of Chicago Stadium and the NHL Chicago Blackhawks, and a partner in the International Boxing Club syndicate that controlled boxing in the 1940s and 1950s until broken up under the anti-trust laws by the Supreme Court, dies at age 82.

1996

Free agent Wayne Gretzky, leading goal-, assist- and point-scorer in NHL history, signs a two-year contract with the Rangers, reuniting "The Great One" with former Edmonton teammate and current Rangers captain Mark Messier.

1896

Brooklyn's Brighton Beach race track opens its summer meeting with a new 3,000-seat grandstand, replacing one that burned in December 1895. Supported by steel columns on granite blocks which, in turn were supported by pilings driven into the beach sand, the roof spans 122 feet in length and 250 in width.

1916

Marcel Cerdan, middleweight champ from 1948 (when he took the title from Tony Zale at Jersey City, N.J.) to 1949 (when he lost it to Jake LaMotta), is born in Sidi Bel Abbes, Algeria.

1918

Retired Giants centerfielder Mike Donlin and St. Louis trainer Bill Bierhalter, a former minor-league ump, umpire a 15-inning 4-4 tie between the Yankees and Browns at the Polo Grounds when regular AL umps mysteriously fail to appear.

1941

Ronald Turcotte is born in Grand Falls, New Brunswick, Canada. Turcotte rode 3,032 winners in an 18-year career cut short by a July 13, 1978, injury that left him paralyzed. His most famous winners were Riva Ridge, who took the Kentucky Derby and Belmont Stakes in 1972, and Secretariat, Triple Crown winner in 1973.

1944

Albert Walter Lyle is born in DuBois, Pennsylvania. Sparky Lyle, the first American League reliever to win the Cy Young Award (in 1977), saved 141 games over seven seasons (1972-78) with the Yankees, including a league-leading 35 in 1972 and 23 in 1976.

1961

Johnny Blanchard's second pinch homer in two days helps the Yankees to an 11-9 win over the Red Sox at Fenway Park. The day before, Blanchard had a pinch grand slam off Mike Fornieles to give the Yanks an 11-8 victory over Boston (see July 26).

1970

Sergei Zubov, who in 1993-94 led the Stanley Cup champion Rangers in regular-season scoring with 89 points (77 assists), is born in Moscow, U.S.S.R.

1979

Anthony Galento, a true heavyweight contender whose girth earned him the nickname "Two-Ton," dies in Livingston, N.J., at age 69. Galento, who lost to Joe Louis in a title bout at Yankee Stadium in 1939, is famous for the quote, "I'll moider da bum."

1989

Bob Mullens, a Fordham basketball star and member of the original Knicks in 1946-47, dies in Staten Island at age 66.

1995

Luc Ouellette drives a record nine winners in a 12-race harness program at Yonkers Raceway, winning races 1, 2, 3, 4, 7, 9, 10, 11 and 12. Ouellette is a nephew of Michael LaChance, one of several drivers to drive eight winners in a single program.

RON TURCOTTE

1874

Famed horse trainer James (Sunny Jim) Fitzsimmons is born in Brooklyn.

1918

Harold Reese is born in Ekron, Kentucky. Pee Wee Reese is the Hall of Fame Dodgers shortstop of the 1940s and 1950s who helped Brooklyn to seven World Series. He scored at least 94 runs eight straight seasons (1948-55), including a league-leading 132 in 1949.

1932

William D. Gilmour is born in Lucan, Ontario. Harness driver Buddy Gilmour has won over 5,000 races in a career that began in 1952.

1943

Murray Lewin, a former boxer and past president of the New York Boxing Writers' Association, and sportswriter for the *Daily Mirror* from 1924-43, dies at age 44.

1944

Giants manager Mel Ott orders Chicago Cubs slugger Bill (Swish) Nicholson walked intentionally with the bases loaded in the eighth inning of a game eventually won, 12-10, by New York at the Polo Grounds. Nicholson had hit four homers in two days against the Giants.

1955

Bob Cerv (off Alex Kellner) and Elston Howard (off Tom Gorman) both hit pinch homers in the ninth, but the Yankees lose to the Athletics anyway, 8-7, in 11 innings at Kansas City.

1955

With one out in the ninth, pinch-hitter Chuck Harmon plops a single into shallow left, breaking up Jim Hearn's no-hitter and the hearts of 4,273 fans at the Polo Grounds as the Giants beat the Reds, 2-0. Hearn finishes with a one-hitter and Sid Gordon drives in both runs with sacrifice flies in the first and third innings.

1957

Mickey Mantle hits for the cycle in the Yankees' 10-6 win over the White Sox at the Stadium.

EMLEN TUNNELL

1968

Donald C. Lillis dies at age 66 in Westerly, Rhode Island. A member of the five-man group that bought the bankrupt Titans in 1963 (see Mar. 28) and renamed the team the Jets, Lillis became club president when the other four partners bought out Sonny Werblin's interest May 21, 1968. Lillis was also a director of the Monmouth Park Jockey Club.

1975

Emlen Tunnell, defensive back from 1948-58 with the Football Giants, dies in Pleasantville, N.Y., at age 50.

1886

Adonis Terry no-hits St. Louis, 1-0, at Washington Park for Brooklyn's second AA no-hitter and the first of his career.

1923

In the first title bout at Yankee Stadium, Benny Leonard defends his light-weight crown with a 15-round decision over Lew Tendler before 58,519, who pay $452,648 to see the glamour matchup. Both figures are records for a non-heavyweight title bout (see July 16).

1924

Harry J. Boykoff is born in Brooklyn. High-scoring Heshie Boykoff, center for St. John's, played on the 1942 NIT championship team and was an All-America choice in 1942-43.

1931

Babe Herman hits for the cycle for the second time this season and Lefty O'Doul is 5-for-5 as the Dodgers bang out 21 hits but lose, 8-7, to the Pirates at Pittsburgh's Forbes Field. Brooklyn leaves 13 men on base and hits into five double plays.

1963

Jockey Julieanne Krone, who rode Belmont Stakes winner Colonial Affair in 1993, is born in Benton Harbor, Michigan.

MIKE KEENAN

1978

At a teary-eyed Kansas City press conference, Billy Martin "resigns" as Yankees manager with the team 52-42, 10 behind first-place Boston. The day before, Martin said that Reggie Jackson, just off a five-game suspension for insubordination (he bunted three times when ordered three times to swing away), and club owner George Steinbrenner, deserved one another, on the theory that "One's a born liar, the other's convicted," referring to Steinbrenner's criminal guilty plea (see Nov. 27). Bob Lemon is named manager the next day (but see July 29).

1983

In the "pine tar" game, George Brett hits a two-out, two-run, ninth-inning homer off Goose Gossage at the Stadium to give Kansas City an apparent 5-4 lead over the Yankees. Umpires nullify the homer because Brett has pine tar on his bat beyond the 18 inches allowable, and call him out for using an illegal bat, giving New York a 4-3 win (but see Aug. 18).

1984

Rangers right wing Bryan Hextall, Sr., the NHL scoring leader in 1941-42, dies at age 70 in Portage La Prairie, Manitoba. His sons Bryan, Jr., and Dennis both briefly played for the Blueshirts, but Dennis' son, goalie Ron, played for the Islanders.

1994

As part of the settlement resolving Mike Keenan's contract dispute with the Rangers, New York acquires center Petr Nedved from the St. Louis Blues for forward Esa Tikkanen and defenseman Doug Lidster (see July 15).

1907

Six-day bike racing great Alf Letourner is born in Amiens, France.

1912

Leadoff man Bert Daniels of the Highlanders (later the Yankees) becomes the first player in franchise history to hit for the cycle, doing so against the White Sox at Hilltop Park, but Chicago wins, 6-4, in 10 innings.

1921

Pete Herman regains his bantamweight world title with a 15-round decision over Joe Lynch at Ebbets Field. The crowd of 30,000 pays $103,315 gross. The success of this fight, the first in a ballpark owned and actively used by a major league team, paves the way for a half-century of premier boxing bouts in big league ballparks.

1926

Carroll Walter Lockman is born in Lowell, North Carolina. Whitey Lockman was a member of the Giants' "Miracle of Coogan's Bluff"' team of 1951.

1927

Harness racing great Stanley Dancer is born in Edinburg, N.J. Four-time leading driver in the 1960s, Dancer steered four Hambletonian winners.

1950

Harold Hathaway Weekes, 70, Columbia halfback and third team All-American in 1899, second team All-American in 1900 and first team All-American in 1901, dies in New York.

1961

Roger Maris hits four homers in a twi-night doubleheader at Yankee Stadium against the Chicago White Sox. Maris belts two in the opener (including a two-run shot) as the Yanks win, 5-1, and two more (one a three-run homer) in the nightcap, a 12-0 win.

1965

Casey Stengel fractures his hip in a fall after the Old-Timers' Dinner at Toots Shor's and Wes Westrum is named interim Mets manager. When Stengel formally retires August 30, Westrum becomes the manager.

1971

Arnold Palmer, who took the lead on the first day with a 64, shoots 69 on the last day to finish at 270 to win the Westchester Classic at the Westchester CC. Palmer is five strokes better than Gibby Gilbert and Hale Irwin, who tie for second. Palmer had won the Thunderbird Classic on the same course in 1963.

1991

Right wing Brendan Shanahan, New Jersey's No. 1 draft choice (second overall) in 1987 and a 29-goal scorer in 1990-91, signs as a free agent with St. Louis. As compensation for their loss, the Devils are awarded by an arbitrator Blues defenseman Scott Stevens on Sept. 3, 1991.

STANLEY DANCER

July 26

1892

Alva Rosenberg is born in Brooklyn. Rosenberg was the best known dog show judge of his era from 1910 until his death in 1973, judging at over 1,000 shows.

1923

James Hoyt Wilhelm is born in Huntersville, North Carolina. The first relief pitcher ever elected to the Baseball Hall of Fame, knuckleballer Hoyt Wilhelm began his 21-season career at age 28 with the Giants in 1952, for whom he pitched five seasons.

1928

Bob Meusel of the Yankees hits for the cycle against the Tigers in Detroit. It is the third time Meusel has hit for the cycle, a major league record (equaled by Babe Herman in 1933) and setting a franchise mark that still stands. The Yankees win, 12-1, in the first game of a twinbill by scoring 11 runs in the 12th.

1950

Brooklyn's Jimmy Russell becomes the first Dodger to switch-hit homers in a game, helping the Bums to a 7-5 win over St. Louis at Ebbets Field. Russell hits a two-run shot off lefty Harry (the Cat) Brecheen in the first inning and tags righty George Munger for a solo drive in the fifth.

1952

In the fifth annual U.S. Junior Amateur golf championship, Don Bisplinghoff, a 17-year-old Orlando, Florida, high school student, eliminates defending champion Tommy Jacobs, 3 and 2, and then wins the title with a victory over Eddie Myerson, 2-up, in the final at the Yale Golf Course in New Haven, Connecticut.

1961

Johnny Blanchard homers in his first two at-bats to give him four homers in four plate appearances as the Yankees beat Chicago, 5-2, at the Stadium. Blanchard had hit two pinch homers earlier in the week against the Red Sox in Boston (see July 22).

1975

Gus Campise dies at age 58 in Manhasset, N.Y. Campise was an umpire and linesman at the U.S. Open tennis championships at Forest Hills and founder of the Mecca Tennis Club, a "watchdog" group for over 500 New York City municipal tennis courts.

1976

Ted Kiendl dies in Bronxville, N.Y., at age 86. Kiendl, a star basketball player at Columbia from 1909-11, during which time the Lions won 40 of 43 games and the mythical national championship in 1910, became a famed negligence defense attorney.

1993

Gen. Matthew Bunker Ridgway dies in Fox Chapel, Pennsylvania, at age 98. General Ridgway was a soccer player and football manager for Army who succeeded General Douglas MacArthur as commander of all forces during the Korean War.

1996

Buck Williams, a sturdy Nets forward for eight years (1981-89) before his trade to Portland June 24, 1989, signs a free agent contract with the Knicks.

July 27

1883

It's a 9-0 forfeit victory for the Mets over the Athletics when Philadelphia fails to appear for a scheduled AA game at the Polo Grounds, leaving about 2,400 fans with mixed feelings and a refund.

1918

Emerging heavyweight Jack Dempsey makes a powerful impression by knocking out rugged Fred Fulton in 18.6 seconds of the first round at the Federal League ballpark in Harrison, N.J. The audience of over 10,000 is barely in its seats before Fulton hits the deck.

1920

The longest series yet held for the America's Cup (and the first challenge since 1903) ends with the New York Yacht Club's *Resolute* defeating Sir Thomas Lipton's *Shamrock IV* by 19 minutes, 45 seconds. *Resolute*, skippered by Charles Francis Adams, won three of the seven races off Sandy Hook with *Shamrock IV* winning two and two others called because of light wind that prevents finishes within the allotted time. This is the last challenge raced in New York waters, as races move to Newport, Rhode Island, in 1930.

1927

After one season, the Brooklyn club (called the Lions) withdraws from the NFL and the league transfers the franchise to Charles (Cash and Carry) Pyle, owner of the AFL New York Yankees, who played in the first AFL in 1926. The Yankees, featuring famed running back Red Grange, play in the NFL in 1927-28 (see 1929 below).

1928

Under the aegis of Douglas C. Hertz's newly-formed American Greyhound Racing Association, dog racing comes to New York on a regular basis as a 10-race night program at Dongan Hills, Staten Island. Long Wanted, owned by stage star Billie Burke, wife of showman Florenz Ziegfeld, wins the first race. A light but steady rain holds the crowd to about 2,000, mostly celebrities gathered in the grandstand built on the old Richmond County Fair Grounds.

1929

C.C. Pyle surrenders the NFL franchise he operated for two years as the New York Football Yankees at Yankee Stadium. The franchise is awarded to the Stapleton Athletic Club of Staten Island, ostensibly for Brooklyn, but the Stapes play instead at Thompson Field in Stapleton until leaving the NFL after the 1932 season.

1941

Howard H. Jones, coach of the perfect 1909 Yale football team, dies in Toluca Lake, N.Y., at age 55. Brother of Tad, later Bulldogs coach, Howard Jones was the first paid full-time coach when he led Yale to a 5-2-3 mark in 1913, his only other season as coach. He later coached Iowa, Duke and Southern California (the latter from 1925-40).

1959

At a press conference in the Hotel Biltmore, founding of the Continental League of Professional Baseball Clubs is announced as an embryonic third major league with New York, Houston, Toronto, Denver and Minneapolis-St. Paul as charter members. On August 8, the group names 77-year-old veteran executive Branch Rickey as its president. Atlanta, Georgia, on Dec. 8, Dallas-Fort Worth, on Dec. 22, and Buffalo, in Jan. 1960, are added to round out the eight-team circuit.

1969

Betsy Rawls finishes with a 72-hole 293 to win the LPGA championship at the Concord in Kiamesha Lake, N.Y. Carol Mann and Susie Berning tie for second in the first LPGA championship played in the East.

1921

Bob MacDonald of Chicago ends Walter Hagen's three-year run as Metropolitan Open champion with a final-day 148 for a 72-hole 294 at Siwanoy CC. Pat O'Hara is second at 298, the only other golfer to break 300.

1930

John R. DeWitt dies in New York at age 48. DeWitt was a Princeton guard and field goal kicker who made the All-America teams in 1902 and 1903.

1943

William Warren Bradley is born in Crystal City, Missouri. Bill Bradley would become a Princeton basketball All-American, a Rhodes Scholar, a star with the Knicks (1967-77) and a three-term United States Senator from New Jersey.

1943

Allen Edward Atkinson is born in Philadelphia, Pennsylvania. Al Atkinson was a Jets linebacker from 1965-74.

1954

Becoming the last New York Giant ever to turn the trick, Dusty Rhodes hits three homers as the Giants club St. Louis, 10-0, at the Polo Grounds. Rhodes homers in the second, sixth and seventh innings. His middle homer follows Willie Mays 36th of the season, putting Mays 11 games ahead of Babe Ruth's 1927 pace when Ruth hit 60.

1988

Frank Zamboni, inventor of the indoor ice resurfacing machine that bears his name and revolutionized the ice care business, dies in Paramount, California, at age 87.

BILL BRADLEY

1989

Board of Regents of the University of the State of New York grants a charter to the New York Sports Museum & Hall of Fame. Initial trustees are Richard Lally, Michael J. Burns, A. Joshua Ehrlich and the authors.

1991

Ray Felix, whose college career at LIU was shortened when the Blackbirds dropped basketball in the wake of the 1951 point-shaving scandals, and who later averaged 12.0 ppg in 376 games over six seasons (1954-60) with the Knicks, dies in New York.

1995

Priming for their playoff push, the Yankees acquire veteran righty and former Met David Cone from the Kansas City Royals for three minor-league pitchers. Cone goes 9-2 to help the Yankees win the first wild-card berth in AL history by one game.

1997

Mark Messier, the 36-year-old captain and symbol of the Rangers since his acquisition from the Edmonton Oilers in October 1991, and the man who in 1994 helped deliver the Blueshirts' first Stanley Cup since 1940, signs as a free agent with the Vancouver Canucks.

1873

It's opening day for the trotting season at Deerfoot Park in what is now Brooklyn, and Lady Pfifer wins the only event completed, accumulating the best finishes in the five one-mile heats, coming in first, first, third, third and second. The day's next event is postponed due to threatening weather after Jack Draper wins the first heat.

1876

Sixteen organizations, including Yale, Harvard, and City College, gather for the first USA Amateur Championships Meet at the Mott Haven Grounds in what is now The Bronx. Amateur clubs from Boston to Philadelphia are represented. David Woods of Ontario, Canada, wins the mile (4:43), Thomas A. McEwen of the Scottish-American Athletic Club the quarter-mile in (0:53) and Frederick Wessel of Newark, N.J., the two-mile walk (15:17.0). The New York AC, which organizes the meet, wins the team title with 33 points.

1909

National League president Harry Pulliam dies the morning after shooting himself in the head in his room at the New York Athletic Club, his suicide apparently brought on by the continuing pressure of John McGraw and the Giants over the disputed 1908 National League pennant race (see Sept. 23).

1922

Sidney Hertzberg is born in Brooklyn. Sonny Hertberg became a standout guard at CCNY and was an original Knick in 1946-47.

1943

Created by wartime travel restrictions, a consolidated harness racing meeting begins at the Empire City racetrack in Yonkers. The meeting represents racing from Roosevelt Raceway, Saratoga Harness, Hamburg and Goshen's two tracks.

1957

Betsy Rawls takes the third of her four USGA Women's Open titles after Mrs. Jackie Pung is disqualified for a scorecard error. Miss Rawls thus wins the $1,800 first-place money with her 72-hole 299 over the East Course at the Winged Foot GC in Mamaroneck, N.Y. Veteran pro Patty Berg is second at 305 (and wins $1,200) while Betty Hicks and Louise Suggs tie for third, each earning $810.

1957

In his first title defense as heavyweight champion, Floyd Patterson stops Tommy (Hurricane) Jackson in the 10th round at the Polo Grounds.

1960

Mrs. C.T. Stout dies in New York at age 76. As Genevieve Hecker, she won the women's Metroplitan golf championship in 1900 and 1901 and the USGA women's amateur titles in 1901 and 1902. As Mrs. Stout, she won the Met again in 1905 and 1906.

1978

At Old-Timers' Day at Yankee Stadium, public-address announcer Bob Sheppard startles and delights the crowd by introducing the Yankees' manager in 1980, Billy Martin, who had resigned under pressure five days earlier.

1986

A U.S. District Court jury in Manhattan finds the NFL liable to the rival USFL for violations of federal antitrust laws. For damages, the jury awards the USFL one dollar of the $1.7 billion sought by the rival league (an award tripled to $3 by law).

1844

A group of influential New Yorkers, meeting aboard *Gimcrack*, John Cox Stevens' yacht, forms the New York Yacht Club, which, in 1851, successfully challenges for what becomes known as the America's Cup and establishes U.S. supremacy in international yacht racing.

1883

In their first match against local competition, the New York Lacrosse Club beats the Independent L.C., 3-0, at Brooklyn's Washington Park as 500 spectators watch. It is the first match for the Independent Club, recently organized by Canadian residents in New York. The match is refereed by Erastus Wyman, president of the National Lacrosse Association, who later becomes owner of the baseball Mets when the club moves to Staten Island after the 1885 season.

1889

Charles Dillon Stengel is born in Kansas City, Mo. The most famous baseball personality of the 1950s and '60s, Casey Stengel played for Brooklyn in the 1910s and Giants in the 1920s, and managed the Dodgers in the 1930s, the Yankees from 1949-60 and the infant Mets in the 1960s. His 10 pennants in 12 years with the Yankees and five world championships in a row (1949-53) are major league records. His 120 losses with the 1962 Mets are a 20th-century record.

CASEY STENGEL

1941

Mickey Welch, winner of over 300 games, mostly with the Giants (1883-92), dies in Nashua, New Hampshire, at age 82.

1969

Dennis Menke (off Cal Koonce) and Jimmy Wynn (off Ron Taylor) both hit grand slams in the ninth inning as Houston rallies for an 11-5 win over the Mets at Shea Stadium. It's the first time in National League history a team has hit two grand slams in one inning.

1991

Free agent forward Anthony Mason, a former Net, signs with the Knicks.

1993

Frank Leo Howley, left end and placekicker for NYU, where he was known as the "Golden Toe," dies in Warrenton, Virginia, at age 90. Howley returned to his alma mater after an Army career, during which he was military governor of Berlin from 1945-49, to serve as vice chancellor of the university from 1950-69.

1997

Heat racing, the essence of trotting for more than a century, moves closer to oblivion with the announcement that the Hambletonian, the sport's premier event, will be decided by a single one-mile dash when it is run August 9 at the Meadowlands. Since its inception in 1926, the Hambo was based on a horse winning two heats in the same afternoon. Depending on the size of the field, as many as five races could be needed to determine a winner. Instead, qualifying races will now be run to produce a 10-horse field for the $1 million Hambo and its filly counterpart, the Hambletonian Oaks.

1886

Heavyweight contender Jake Kilrain stops Jack Ashton at 1:16 of the eighth round in a bout fought with soft gloves at Ridgewood Park in Brooklyn. Under the Marquis of Queensberry rules, referee Patrick Johnson halts the action to prevent injury despite the protests of Ashton's manager.

1890

Raveloe, a three-year-old colt, wins the Newark Stakes at Monmouth Park and sets a U.S. record for the mile with a 1:39.25 clocking.

1890

George Lee Schuyler, last survivor of the founders of the New York Yacht Club, dies aboard his yacht, *Electra*, anchored off New London, Connecticut, at age 79. Schuyler was also a donor of the America's Cup and his daughter, Louisa Lee (who dies in 1926), is the founder of America's first school of nursing.

1891

Amos Rusie hurls a 6-0 no-hitter for the Giants over Brooklyn at the Polo Grounds, avenging Tom Lovett's no-hitter against New York in Brooklyn June 22.

1909

George H. Robertson and Al Poole drive their Simplex to victory in the opening 24-hour auto race at the Brighton Beach Motordrome. The Robertson team logs 1,091 miles to finish exactly 50 miles in front of a Rainier driven by Louis Disbrow and Ray Lund as five of the nine starters complete the grind.

1927

Australian native Walter J. Travis dies in Denver, Colorado, at age 65. Coming to America as a youngster, Travis took up golf at age 30 and became a leading amateur player. He won the Metropolitan Amateur four times (1900, 1902, 1909 and 1915) and the U.S. Amateur thrice (1900-01 and 1903).

1948

George Townsend Adee, Yale football quarterback from 1892-94, an All-America selection in 1894 and president of the United States National Lawn Tennis Association from 1916-20, dies in New York at age 74.

1951

Evonne Fay Goolagong, a finalist four years in a row at the U.S. Open at Forest Hills but never a champion (1973-76), is born in Griffith, New South Wales, Australia.

1954

Using a bat borrowed from reserve catcher Charlie White, Joe Adcock slams four homers and a double for 18 total bases and seven RBI at Ebbets Field as Milwaukee wins, 17-8, thumping four Dodgers pitchers. Eddie Mathews also homers twice for the Braves.

1956

David Wilfred Maloney is born in Kitchener, Ontario. Called up by the Rangers at age 18 during 1974-75, defenseman Dave Maloney became the youngest captain in team history on Oct. 11, 1978, at age 22.

August 1

1906
Brooklyn's Harry McIntyre hurls an 11-inning no-hitter against Pittsburgh at Washington Park but loses, 1-0, in the 13th.

1925
Tim Mara and Billy Gibson are granted an NFL franchise for New York at a fee of $2,500. Shortly, the team makes arrangements to play at the Polo Grounds and soon becomes known as the New York Football Giants.

1926
Vinny Richards defeats Bill Tilden, 6-3, 6-4, 4-6, 6-2, in the final of the Metropolitan Grass Court Championships at the Crescent Athletic Club in Brooklyn.

1937
For the second time in his career, the Yankees' Lou Gehrig hits for the cycle, this time against the St. Louis Browns at Yankee Stadium, leading the Bombers to a 14-5 win.

1940
Joan Joyce, one of the greatest female athletes in U.S. history, is born in Waterbury, Connecticut. A pitcher-first baseman for the Raybestos Brakettes softball team that went 509-33, she pitched 105 no-hitters from 1954-73 and hit .327 as her team won 11 national championships and was named an All-American 18 straight years. She was also a three-time AAU basketball All-American, volleyball player and bowler, and LPGA tour golf pro from 1975-85.

1946
Michael Emrick is born in Marion, Indiana. A Ph.D. holder in film, Doc Emrick was the television voice of the New Jersey Devils from 1983-86, and after a stint with the Rangers and Philadelphia Flyers, returned in 1993. He has also broadcast Stanley Cup, NHL All-Star and Olympic hockey, and NFL football, for network television.

1954
Milwaukee's Joe Adcock, who hit four homers the day before (see July 31), gets beaned in his second at-bat in the fourth inning by Dodgers reliever Johnny Podres. Adcock is carried off the field as the teams come close to a brawl, but cooler heads prevail and the Braves go on to a 14-6 win at Ebbets Field.

1959
French-bred Jamin wins the first Roosevelt International before 45,723 at Roosevelt Raceway.

1959
Jamaica Race Course on Baisley Boulevard in Queens closes. It becomes the site of Rochdale Village.

1973
Nets trade George Carter, the rights to Kermit Washington and cash to the Virginia Squires for Julius Erving and Willie Sojourner.

1986
Alvin R. Grant, Holiday on Ice executive who became a vice president at Madison Square Garden when the Garden acquired the show from Morris Chalfen, dies in Palm City, Florida, at age 65.

1989
Kevin McReynolds of the Mets hits for the cycle and drives in six runs in an 11-0 Mets win at St. Louis.

1892

John Francis Kieran is born in New York. The first "Sports of The Times" columnist for *The New York Times* in 1927, and the first byline writer on the paper's sports pages, Kieran was also a panelist on the radio show "Information Please" and later editor of the *Information Please Almanac*, published by Dan Golenpaul, the radio show's producer.

1902

Charles W. Caldwell, Jr., is born in Bristol, Virginia-Tennessee. As batting practice pitcher for the Yankees, Charlie Caldwell beaned incumbent first baseman Wally Pipp, helping to pave Lou Gehrig's way into the lineup. As Princeton football coach, Caldwell led the Tigers to consecutive perfect seasons in 1950 and 1951 and a 24-game winning streak.

1914

Oscar Fraley, *United Press International* "Sports Parade" columnist for over two decades and author of the best-seller *The Untouchables* with FBI agent Elliot Ness, is born in Philadelphia, Pennsylvania.

1923

Isiah Williams is born in Brunswick, Georgia. Ike Williams was world lightweight champion from 1947-51.

1932

Oilman Lamar Hunt, a founder of the American Football League in 1959 and World Championship Tennis (WCT), a circuit that lasted from 1967-90 and helped precipitate the open tennis era, is born in Eldorado, Arkansas.

1938

David Alexander Balon, left wing on the Rangers' original "Bulldog Line" (Walt Tkaczuk at center and Billy Fairbairn at right wing) in the early 1970s, is born in Wakaw, Saskatchewan.

1979

Yankees catcher and captain Thurman Munson dies in a plane crash outside Canton, Ohio, at age 32. Munson, American League Rookie of the Year in 1970 and MVP in 1976, had a lifetime .292 average and helped the Yankees to three straight AL pennants and consecutive World Series titles in 1977 and 1978.

1980

Walter Merrill Hall, president of the USLTA from 1934-37, dies at age 92 in New Rochelle, N.Y.

1985

Bobby Meacham and Dale Berra are tagged out almost simultaneously at home plate by Chicago catcher Carlton Fisk in the seventh inning at Yankee Stadium. The sequence proves costly for the Yankees as the White Sox beat New York, 5-4, in 11 innings.

THURMAN MUNSON

1988

Dr. Henry Chase, a Manhattan dentist who was secretary of the NHSA and trustee of the National Horse Show Foundation, dies in New York at age 64.

August 3

1890
Toledo beats Brooklyn, 9-3, at Ridgewood Park in what turns out to be the last AA game in Brooklyn. The team leaves that night for a road trip to Columbus, Toledo and Syracuse, but folds before returning home (see Aug. 25).

1895
Harry Tyler sweeps the honors on the final day of the cycling meeting at Manhattan Beach, winning the quarter mile sprint and the international mile. Tyler wins the quarter in 39.6 seconds with A.W. Porter second and Peter Berlo third. He takes the mile in 2:25.8 with Porter again second and W.L. Sanger third.

1948
Tommy Ryan (whose given name was Joseph Youngs), welterweight (1894-96) and middleweight (1898-1907) champion, dies in Los Angeles at age 78.

1949
Basketball Association of America and National Basketball League merge to form the National Basketball Association. The BAA's Maurice Podoloff is named commissioner of the new league with NBL executives Ike Duffy and Leo Ferriss on the executive committee. The NBA has 17 teams in three divisions for the 1949-50 season.

1957
Nels Stewart, another Hockey Hall of Famer who played his declining years with the Americans (1936-40), dies at age 54. Stewart scored the last 62 goals of his career with the Amerks. On his retirement, his 324 goals were the most in league history.

1975
Jack Molinas is shot in the head in his backyard and dies in Hollywood Hills, California, at age 43. Molinas, a high-scoring (17.6 ppg), sturdy rebounder for Columbia from 1950-53, was barred for life from the NBA for betting on games as a member of the Fort Wayne Pistons. He was later implicated as the fixer behind the 1961 college basketball point-shaving scandals.

1982
Irving T. Marsh, assistant sports editor of the *Herald Tribune* in the 1950s, two-time Columbia sports information director and publicity director for the ECAC, dies in Connecticut at age 75.

1982
After the Yankees drop a Stadium doubleheader to the Chicago White Sox, Gene Michael is fired as manager for the second time in less than a year. Clyde King takes over.

1983
Nihilator wins at the Meadowlands with a mile clocking of 1:49.3, a world pacing record that will stand for nearly 11 years.

1990
Thomas Macioce, Columbia basketball captain in 1938-39 and president and chief executive officer of Allied Stores (owner of, among others, Brooks Brothers and Ann Taylor) from 1970-87, dies in New York at age 71.

1996
By winning the first and third heats, Continentalvictory becomes only the second filly in 30 years (and 13th overall since 1926) to win the Hambletonian. Her first heat clocking of 1:52.2 over the Meadowlands track is also the fastest ever in the Hambo.

1909

Glenn Cunningham, world record miler and Sullivan Award winner in 1933 as the nation's top amateur athlete, is born in Elkhart, Kansas.

1914

Neil McNeil Colville is born in Edmonton, Alberta. A center who played his entire 12-year career with the Rangers and later coached them for 93 games (1950-51), Neil Colville, the Ranger captain for over three years (1945 to December 21, 1948), helped New York win the Stanley Cup in 1940 and was elected to the Hockey Hall of Fame in 1967.

1930

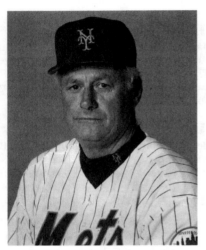

In the small hours of a Monday morning, a fire started in a nearby vacant lot destroys the 20,000-seat New York Velodrome at 225th Street and Broadway. Also lost in the blaze are 160 competition bicycles used during the three-nights-a-week racing season. A boxing card scheduled for the next night is canceled. After the $150,000 blaze is put out, co-owners Ingils M. Uppercu and John Ringling promise to rebuild but never do.

1934

Dallas Green, who managed the Yankees for less than one season (1989) and the Mets for parts of four (1993-96), is born in Newport, Delaware.

DALLAS GREEN

1942

Cleon Joseph Jones is born in Plateau, Alabama. A streaky, smooth-hitting leftfielder, Cleon Jones, one of the few players to bat righty and throw lefty, hit .340 for the 1969 world champion Mets, a club record.

1944

Beau Jack beats Bob Montgomery in a 10-round lightweight bout at the Garden, which tops a card conducted to sell U.S. War Bonds. The crowd buys $35,864,900 in bonds to watch.

1949

John Riggins, bruising Jets running back from 1971-75 who galloped to fame and fortune behind the Washington Redskins lines of the 1980s (the "Hogs"), is born in Seneca, Kansas.

1982

Joel Youngblood drives in the go-ahead run for the Mets in a 7-4 win at Chicago and then is traded to Montreal. Flying out immediately after the game, Youngblood joins the Expos in Philadelphia in time to play rightfield in the fourth inning. He gets a hit and becomes the only player in major league history to get hits for two different teams in two cities on the same day.

1984

With 37,628, the largest Meadowlands harness crowd of the year, on hand, Historic Freight, driven by Ben Webster, outlasts a 26-horse field to win the Hambletonian.

1994

Dick Bartell, Giants shortstop in the 1930s known as "Rowdy Richard" for his combative demeanor, dies in Alameda, California, at age 86.

1763

Tom Richmond, a black man who became the first famous American prize fighter in England, is born on Staten Island. During the British occupation of New York City during the Revolutionary War, Richmond became a favorite of General Earl Percy, who took him to England in 1777. Although he lost to champion Tom Cribb in 1805, Richmond was known as "the Black Terror" among the British sporting public for his impressive ring record before his death in 1829 at age 66.

1867

Jacob Ruppert is born in New York. Ruppert, a colonel in the New York National Guard, owner of Ruppert's Knickerbocker Brewery on Second Avenue and 91st Street and legislator, acquired the Yankees with Col. Tillinghast L'Hommedieu Huston in 1915 (see Jan. 11), bought out Huston's share in 1922 and owned the club to his death in 1939. Under his ownership, the Yankees laid the groundwork for the baseball dynasty that lasted over four decades.

1935

John William McCartan is born in St. Paul, Minnesota. Jack McCartan, star goalie of the 1960 U.S. Olympic gold medal hockey team, received a hero's welcome when he joined the Rangers in 1960 and showed promise with a 2-1-1 record and 1.75 gaa. But the next year he went 1-6-1 with a 4.91 gaa and never played again in the NHL.

1937

William (Bunk) MacBeth dies at age 52 in Saratoga Springs, N.Y. MacBeth, onetime sports editor of the *Montreal Herald*, was a founder of the Baseball Writers Association of America when he joined the staff of the *New York American* in 1908. Born in Ingersoll, Ontario, MacBeth was a leading advocate of hockey and helped bring the NHL to New York. After four years with the morning *Sun*, he joined the *New York Tribune* on August 16, 1916, and continued with the *Herald Tribune* when the two papers merged in 1924.

1937

Herbert Paul Brooks is born in St. Paul, Minnesota. Herb Brooks, coach of the U.S. Olympic gold medal hockey team in 1980, coached the Rangers for four seasons (131-113-41 from 1981-85), instituting a swirling attack with small, mobile players derided by critics as "Smurfs." He also coached the Devils for the 1992-93 season.

1946

Bruce Noel Coslet, Jets coach from 1990-93, is born in Oakdale, California.

1948

Cyril Walker, U.S. Open golf champion in 1924 who played out of the Englewood (N.J.) GC, dies in Hackensack, N.J., at age 56.

1962

Patrick Aloysius Ewing, the Knicks' all-time leader in games, minutes played, points and rebounds, among other categories, is born in Kingston, Jamaica.

1978

For the 16th time in 20 matches, the U.S. wins the Curtis Cup over Britain and Ireland in a match closer than the 12-6 score indicates. Leading 5-4 after the first day, U.S. women win seven of nine matches on the final day at the Apawamis Club in Rye, N.Y. Beth Daniel wins two singles and plays on a victorious foursome for the U.S.

1991

Richard Evans' resignation as president caps several months of executive turmoil at Madison Square Garden (see Mar. 1).

1906

Helen Hockenjos, a school teacher who played out of the Baltusrol GC in Springfield, N.J., and was the New Jersey amateur golf champion in 1936 and 1939, is born in Paterson, N.J.

1908

Helen Hull Jacobs, a four-time U.S. national singles tennis champion (1932-35) whose outstanding career was nevertheless overshadowed by her more accomplished contemporary, Helen Wills Moody, is born in Globe, Arizona.

1919

Pauline May Betz, winner of four U.S. national singles tennis titles (1942-44, 1946), and the world's No. 1-ranked player in 1946, is born in Dayton, Ohio.

1922

Douglas Ford is born in West Haven, Connecticut. Ford won the Metropolitan PGA championship four times (1957, 1959, 1960, 1963) and the Westchester Open in 1961, and his major victories include the PGA championship (1955), the Masters (1957) and the Canadian Open (1963).

1938

Len Grant, a tackle at NYU (1927-29) and captain of the 1929 Violets team, is killed by a bolt of lightning on the Norfolk Golf Club course near Dedham, Massachusetts, at age 33.

1946

Tony Lazzeri dies in San Francisco at age 42. Second baseman for the "Murderers' Row" Yankees of the 1920s, Lazzeri drove in 100 or more runs seven times during his 12 seasons (1926-37) with the Bombers.

1947

Hoot Mon, driven by Sep Palin, wins the second heat of the 22d Hambletonian in 2:00 flat, the fastest time ever for the race, at Good Time Park in Goshen, N.Y. Second in Heat No. 1, Hoot Mon has to go a third time, but beats Rodney handily in 2:02.25 to take the Hambo.

1968

Phil Iselin assumes presidency of the Jets following the death of Don Lillis (see July 23). Iselin will remain president until his death in 1976 (see Dec. 28).

1980

As the Woodrow Wilson becomes the first $2 million race in harness history, Del Insko drives Land Grant to a surprising victory in 1:56.8 at the Meadowlands. Land Grant pays a stakes-record $141.80 to win the two-year-old colt pace that is valued at $2,011,000 (the purse hits a record $2,161,000 in 1984).

HELEN HULL JACOBS

1994

Frank P. Kringle dies at age 91 in Springfield, Massachusetts. Kringle was the pro at the Sunnyfield CC in Linden, N.J., for three decades until 1947. During his years in New Jersey, he won the State Open in 1945, finishing two strokes ahead of touring pro Tommy Harmon.

August 7

1875

Henry Phillip Burchell, sports editor of *The New York Times* from 1902-15, is born in New York. Burchell, who was forced out at *The Times* in favor of Bernard Thompson on December 13, 1915, later became the first secretary of the New York State Athletic Commission (1921-23), but was also forced out of that job and committed suicide Jan. 17, 1924.

1906

Angered by repeated run-ins with the arbiter, Giants manager John McGraw bars umpire Jimmy Johnstone from the Polo Grounds. Johnstone retaliates by forfeiting the game to the Chicago Cubs while standing outside the ballpark.

1933

Edwin Firmani, who coached the Cosmos to North American Soccer League championships in 1977 and 1978 and had an overall 49-22 record in parts of four seasons with the Cosmos, is born in Capetown, South Africa. Firmani also coached the Tampa Bay Rowdies to the 1975 NASL title.

1937

Eddie Gerard dies at age 47 in Ottawa, Ontario. Gerard coached the Americans (1929-31) and the Montreal Maroons (Stanley Cup champs in 1926) after a brilliant career with the Ottawa Senators (1913-23). It was Gerard's stubbornness as Maroons coach that forced Rangers coach Lester Patrick to play goal in the second game of the 1928 Stanley Cup final (see Apr. 7).

1938

A.A. McLellan, bowling for Staten Island against the Crescent Athletic Club, secures all 10 wickets in an innings for only 33 runs, a record in the New York & Metropolitan District Cricket Association, at Huntington, N.Y.

1956

A.L. Walker, Jr., the only golfer from a New York City college (Columbia) ever to win the U.S. intercollegiate golf championship (1919), dies in New York at age 58.

1963

Jim Hickman becomes the first Met ever to hit for the cycle, accomplishing the feat against the Cardinals at the Polo Grounds, and the Mets beat St. Louis, 7-3, before 9,977.

1966

Dick Christy, a running back and kick returner with the Titans (1961-62) and Jets (1963), dies in an auto crash at age 30 in North Carolina.

1966

Ed (Strangler) Lewis, intermittant world heavyweight wrestling champion from 1920-32, dies at age 76 in Muskogee, Oklahoma.

JOE NAMATH

1971

In the exhibition opener, against Detroit at Tampa, Florida, the Jets lose quarterback Joe Namath for the second straight season, as he injures his knee attempting a tackle on a fumble runback. Jets lose, 28-24, and Namath misses the first 10 games of the regular season.

1868

New York Athletic Club is founded by 14 men meeting in the rear parlor of John C. Babcock's home at 200 Sixth Avenue, New York.

1870

In the first international challenge for the America's Cup, the U.S. yacht *Magic* defends with a 39-minute, 12-second win over England's *Cambria* in New York Harbor.

1889

Billy O'Brien raps three doubles and three singles to help Brooklyn to a 12-11 AA win at Columbus, Ohio.

1902

U.S. wins the second competition for the tennis international team trophy now known as the Davis Cup, defeating Britain, 3-2, at Brooklyn's Crescent Athletic Club courts.

1934

Wilbert Robinson, manager *extraordinaire* of the Brooklyn Superbas (sometimes unofficially known as the Robins in his honor), who were later known as the Dodgers, dies in Atlanta, Georgia, at age 71. Robinson managed the Brooklyn club longer than anyone else (1914-31), and captured NL pennants in 1916 and 1920.

1936

Big Frank Howard, Mets manager in 1983 after George Bamberger's resignation and Yankees coach in the late 1980s and early 1990s, is born in Columbus, Ohio. Howard, also an intimidating basketball player, set the Garden collegiate record for most rebounds in a game at the 1956 ECAC Holiday Festival (32).

1947

Bill Richardson, 62, dies in Cornwall, N.Y. Richardson was the first golf writer (1922) for *The New York Times* and succeeded Grantland Rice as editor of the annual golf guide.

1956

"Moving the Hambletonian from Goshen would be like moving the Kentucky Derby from Churchill Downs," Bill Cane, promoter of trotting's most famous event, said, but Cane died in the spring (see Mar. 27) and this is the end of the Hambos run at his Good Time Park in Goshen, N.Y. The Intruder, driven by 29-year-old Ned Bower, wins Heats Nos. 2 and 3 to capture the farewell Hambo as the race moves to the DuQuoin (Ill.) Fair Grounds in 1957.

1972

Yankees sign a 30-year lease to play at Yankee Stadium, expiring in 2002, as the city agrees to remodel the ballpark beginning after the 1973 season. During the two-year facelift (1974-75), the Yankees will play at Shea Stadium, home of the Mets.

1981

After 24 years at DuQuoin, Illinois, harness racing's most famous race, the Hambletonian, has its first running at the Meadowlands. Shiaway St. Pat wins the 56th running, taking the three-horse third heat to become only the third gelding ever to win the Hambo as 20,677 attend.

1983

Harvey Johnson, defensive back and placekicker for the AAFC Yankees (1946-49) and the NFL Yanks (1951), dies at age 64 in Bridgeton, N.J. Johnson scored 213 points for the Yankees, the sixth-highest total in the four-year history of the AAFC.

1890

C.M. Carbonell of the Manhattan Athletic Club wins the 75-yard dash at the St. George AC games but not until 17 preliminary heats, four semifinal heats and a re-run final are held on the American AC grounds at 135th Street and Railroad Avenue. Carbonell wins the second final in 8.2 seconds after the contestants disagree with the judging of the first and ask for another (even though Carbonell is judged the winner the first time, too).

1901

Frank L. Kramer wins the half-mile Grand Circuit bike race that headlines a National Cycling Association program at the Garden. Kramer is clocked in 1:09.4 in the final with Tom Cooper second, but sets a record for the distance with a blistering 58 seconds flat in a qualifying heat.

1902

Frederick Spencer, champion six-day bike racer of the 1920s and 1930s, is born in Westfield, N.J. At the New York Velodrome August 9, 1929, Spencer set world speed records for 10, 15, 20 and 25 miles and later set a half-mile sprint record at the Newark Velodrome (52.6 seconds)

1966

Wall Street broker Peter Elser and R.K.O. General, represented by executive John Pinto, form the New York Generals and apply to join the new National Professional Soccer League (see Aug. 26).

1970

Cap McEwan, Army football coach from 1923-25 (18-5-3) and head coach of the Brooklyn Football Dodgers from 1933-34 (9-11-1), dies in New York at age 77.

1976

New York Sets' World Team Tennis match against the Boston Lobsters at Nassau Coliseum is canceled by Hurricane Belle, though the two teams do play the next night in Boston.

1979

Walter F. O'Malley, who in 1957 took the Dodgers out of Brooklyn after negotiations with the city for the construction of a new ballpark to replace the dilapidated and soon-to-be-condemned Ebbets Field collapsed, dies in Rochester, Minnesota, at age 75.

1994

Buff Donelli dies in Fort Lauderdale, Florida, at age 87. Aldo T. Donelli, an international soccer star in the 1930s and all-around athlete who coached Duquesne and the Pittsburgh Steelers simultaneously briefly in 1941, was Columbia head football coach from 1957-67 and led the Lions to their only Ivy League title (shared) in 1961.

BUFF DONELLI

1997

For the first time, the Hambletonian is run as a single one-mile dash and Malabar Man, with Malvern Burroughs in the bike, comes home first in 1:55 to take the winner's share of the $1.2 million purse at the Meadowlands. Eliminations were held a week earlier to cut the field to 10 horses as the heat-racing system is dropped after 71 years (see July 30).

1887

Dave Orr of the AA Mets gets his second career cycle but it comes in a losing effort, 6-5, at Baltimore.

1905

Melville Sidney Keeling is born in Owen Sound, Ontario. A left wing, Butch Keeling assisted on Bill Cook's power-play overtime goal that gave the Rangers the 1933 Stanley Cup. In 455 games over 10 seasons with the Blueshirts, he tallied 136 goals and 55 assists.

1920

William Holzman is born in Brooklyn. A CCNY graduate, Red Holzman led the Knicks to 613 regular season victories during two terms as head coach and their only two NBA titles (1970, 1973).

1962

Ted Husing dies in Pasadena, California, at age 60. For two decades, Husing was the leading sportscaster for the CBS radio network, doing numerous major events every year, including play-by-play of Forest Hills tennis championships.

1966

Chuck Dressen, a Yankees coach who later managed the Dodgers, dies in Detroit, Michigan, at age 67. In his first year as manager, 1951, Brooklyn squandered a $13\frac{1}{2}$-game lead and lost a playoff to the Giants in the bottom of the ninth of the deciding game. In 1952, the Yankees rallied from a 3-2 World Series deficit, winning the last two games at Ebbets Field. In 1953, the Yankees won the Series in six games. In 1954, Dressen was gone.

JOE LAPCHICK

1970

Joe Lapchick, Original Celtics star, two-time St. John's coach and second coach of the Knicks, dies in New York at age 70.

1976

Giorgio Chinaglia scores five goals in the final game of the NASL regular season as the Cosmos pound the Miami Toros, 8-2, before 18,103 at Yankee Stadium. Pele scores twice the first half and Chinaglia once and the Italian striker boots in four more in the game's last 16:37. After drawing 218,719 in their 12 home games, the Cosmos move to Giants Stadium in East Rutherford, N.J., the following season.

1981

In the first regular-season baseball game in the majors since a strike began on June 12, the Mets beat the Cubs, 7-5, in 13 innings at Chicago's Wrigley Field.

1994

Bob Towers dies at age 83 in New York. Owner of an advertising agency that handled numerous sports accounts, including Generals and Cosmos soccer, and U.S. Open and Nabisco Masters tennis, Towers was also director of recreation for the Concord and Nevele hotels in Sullivan County, N.Y., where he promoted national amateur championship tennis tournaments.

 **August 11**

1916

Herbert Warren Wind, one of America's most elegant writers on golf and tennis, is born in Brockton, Massachusetts. Wind spent eight years as part of the original staff of *Sports Illustrated* (1954-62) in between two stints with the *New Yorker* magazine, where he started in 1949.

1920

Claude Earl Rayner is born in Sutherland, Saskatchewan. A Hockey Hall of Famer, Chuck Rayner was the last regular Americans goalie in 1941-42. After World War II, "Bonnie Prince Charlie" joined the Rangers and went 123-181-72 for a series of generally bad teams. In 1949-50, however, Rayner won the Hart Trophy as NHL MVP and carried the Blueshirts all the way to the seventh game of the Stanley Cup final.

1941

Lawrence J. Klecatsky is born in St. Paul, Minnesota. Larry Kletcasky, member of the New York Athletic Club, has won more U.S. and Canadian rowing championships than anyone else in the history of the sport.

1943

Volo Song is the fourth horse driven by Ben White to win the Hambletonian, taking Heat Nos. 2 and 3 after breaking and finishing third in the opener. This Hambo is run at the Empire City Racetrack in Yonkers, N.Y., instead of Goshen, N.Y., its home since 1930, due to wartime travel restrictions (see July 29).

1951

CBS presents the first colorcast of a baseball game, airing the Boston Braves' 8-1 loss to the Dodgers in the first game of an Ebbets Field doubleheader. Boston wins the nightcap, 8-4. CBS also airs colorcasts from Brooklyn on Aug. 25 (against the Chicago Cubs) and Sept, 8 (Giants).

1963

Josef Masopust's second-half goal gives Dukla Prague a 1-1 tie before 15,231 at Randalls Island, enabling the Czechoslovak team to take the ISL American Challenge Cup for the third straight year with a 2-1 total-goals win in the two-game series.

1965

Poland's Polonia Bytom ends Dukla Prague's grip on the ISL American Challenge Cup after a 1-1 tie at Randalls Island gives Polonia a 3-1 win in the two-game, total-goals series. Dukla had held the Cup since 1961 but the game proves to be the last for the ISL, which disbands during the winter of 1965-66 following litigation over date exclusivity for international games.

1970

Nets acquire former St. John's center Billy Paultz from the Virginia Squires for a draft pick and cash. Paultz three times led the Nets in rebounding.

1992

Bob Harding, a racing writer for the *Newark Star-Ledger* from 1965-90, dies in Baldwin, Maryland, at age 60. Harding was also a publicist for the International Soccer League.

1994

Both New York teams go extra innings on the final day before the longest labor stoppage in baseball history begins. The Yankees drop a day game to Toronto, 8-7, in 13 at Yankee Stadium, and the Mets go 15 that night before losing, 2-1, at Philadelphia. The strike, baseball's eighth in 23 seasons, begins the next day and prevents the World Series from being played for the first time since 1904.

1846

Richard Kyle Fox is born in Belfast, Ireland. Dick Fox came to the U.S. in 1874 and within three years became publisher of the *Police Gazette*, turning the one-time scandal sheet into the leading sports weekly in the nation. Under Fox, the *Gazette* provided prizes, trophies and awards for athletic events including a diamond-studded belt for the world heavyweight boxing champion that cost over $4,000 when made.

1902

Famed ring announcer Johnny Addie, who worked at the Garden from 1948-71, is born in New York.

1913

Bunny Hearn goes the distance for the Skeeters as Toronto battles to a 20-inning scoreless International League tie at Jersey City.

1939

Morris (Babe) Bower wins the first national midget auto championship before over 55,000 at Roosevelt Raceway. Of the 29 starters in the 150-mile race, only seven finish, with Joe Garson second. Bower is clocked in 3:02:43.1 for the 300 laps around the half-mile oval.

1947

Samuel Rosen is born in Ulm, West Germany. As a child, Rosen moved to Brooklyn and became CCNY baseball captain before starting a career in broadcast journalism. He became a play-by-play voice of the Rangers in 1984.

SAM ROSEN

1950

Beating the Rough Riders, 27-6, in an exhibition game at Ottawa, Ontario, the Football Giants become the first NFL team to play an international game.

1953

A total purse of $117,117.98 lures a record field of 23 trotters to the Hambletonian at Good Time Park in Goshen, N.Y. A filly, Helicopter (sired by Hoot Mon, the 1947 Hambo winner), finishes 17th in the first heat but then takes the next two to capture the $53,126.59 winner's share of the largest purse ever at Goshen.

1964

For the 10th time in his career, Mickey Mantle switch-hits homers in a game as the Yankees beat Chicago, 7-3, at the Stadium. Though Mantle plays four more seasons, he does not accomplish this feat again, but the 10 switch-hitting homer games remains a big-league record.

1966

Mike McTigue, world light heavyweight champion (1923-25), dies in New York at 73.

1980

Howard M. Tuckner, sportswriter for *The New York Times* who left the paper to become a television reporter broadcasting from Vietnam during the height of the U.S. involvement there, dies in New York at age 48.

August 13

1893

"Bullet Joe" Simpson, a Hall of Fame defenseman who played his entire six-year career in the NHL with the Americans (1925-31) and coached the Amerks from 1932-35, is born in Selkirk, Manitoba.

1913

Ward Cuff, a Marquette running back who became a star with the Football Giants (1937-45), is born in Redwood Falls, Minnesota. Cuff was the team's scoring leader his first six seasons and scored 319 career points.

1918

Dr. Luther Halsey Gulick dies in South Casco, Maine, at age 52. Dr. Gulick was a co-founder of the New York City PSAL in 1903 and, in 1891, urged Dr. James Naismith to invent a winter indoor game to engage the attention of students at the Springfield YMCA college. So Naismith invented basketball.

1939

Breaking an eight-game losing streak, the Athletics beat the Yankees, 12-9, in the opening game of a double-header at Philadelphia's Shibe Park as 34,570 watch. But the Bombers bounce back with a vengeance as Red Ruffing throws a three-hitter in the nightcap, getting four hits himself and both Joe DiMaggio and Babe Dahlgren homer twice in a 21-0 rout. The game is the largest shutout margin ever for the Yanks and it goes only eight innings due to darkness.

1972

Jack Nicklaus withstands Jim Colbert's final-day 65 to win the Westchester Classic by three strokes at the Westchester CC. Nicklaus shoots 68 himself to finish at 270 and collect the $50,000 winner's prize. He had won the predecessor Thunderbird Classic here in its final year (1965), and the Westchester in 1967.

1972

George M. Weiss, whose shrewd baseball eye helped establish, and then perpetuate, the Yankee dynasty, dies in Greenwich, Connecticut, at age 78. Weiss was the Yankees farm director from 1932-47 and general manager from 1947-60. In 1961, he joined the nascent New York Mets as president and helped lay the foundation for their 1969 world championship.

1973

Geraldine Rockefeller Dodge, owner of Giralda Farms in New Jersey on which she held the Morris and Essex Dog Show (at one time one of the largest dog shows in the world), dies in Madison, N.J., at age 91. Mrs. Dodge also twice showed Best-in-Show dogs at the Westminster Kennel Club Dog Show at the Garden (1932 and 1939) and in 1933 became the first woman ever to select the Best-in-Show at Westminster.

1985

Pete Sheehy, clubhouse attendant for whom the Yankees clubhouse is now named, dies in New York. Sheehy began working in the Yankees' room in 1927.

1993

Clint Miller, a member of the Titans' "chain gang" on the sidelines at the Polo Grounds and clock operator for the franchise, dies of a heart attack in the press box during a Jets exhibition game at Giants Stadium at age 60.

1995

Mickey Mantle dies in Dallas, Texas, at age 63. A three-time AL MVP and winner of the Triple Crown in 1956, Mantle despite injuries played more games (2,401) for the Yankees than anyone else.

1886

William Meharg scores the first goal at 27 minutes and J.F. McClain cracks the packed Brooklyn defense for a late goal as the New York Lacrosse Club defends its U.S. championship with a 2-0 victory at St. George, Staten Island.

1888

After winning 19 straight decisions, the Giants' Tim Keefe is beaten, 4-2, by the Chicago Cubs at the Polo Grounds, to the disappointment of the 10,240 on hand.

1916

Wellington T. Mara, son of the co-founder of the Football Giants who became 50% owner on his father's death in 1959 and president of the club in 1965 after the death of his older brother Jack, is born in New York. A Fordham classmate of Vince Lombardi, Mara has seen the franchise grow up from its birth in 1925, when he was a nine-year-old waterboy.

1917

Marty Glickman, a noted college athlete who became nearly legendary as a sportscaster of football, basketball and other sports, is born in The Bronx. Many announcers model their style after Glickman's.

MARTY GLICKMAN

1931

Calumet Butler wins the $48,079.39 Hambletonian at Good Time Park in Goshen, N.Y. The winner is bred by Calumet Farms, later one of the most famed of all thoroughbred farms (with Triple Crown winners Whirlaway (1941) and Citation (1948)).

1942

Turning seven double plays, the Yankees display both defense and offense in an 11-2 win over the A's in a night game at Philadelphia. The Yanks have double plays in every inning except the second and fourth, with catcher Bill Dickey and shortstop Phil Rizzuto each starting two.

1959

At the organizational meeting of the American Football League in Chicago, noted broadcaster Harry Wismer is revealed as the owner of the New York franchise. Other cities admitted are Dallas, Houston, Los Angeles, Denver and Minneapolis-St. Paul. The league actually adopts the name American Football League at its next meeting (in Dallas, Aug. 22).

1963

Beatrix Hoyt, the leading women's golfer of the late 1890s who played out of Shinnecock Hills on Long Island, dies in Thomasville, Georgia, at age 83. A native of Westchester who was the U.S. women's amateur champion from 1896-98, Hoyt was a granddaughter of Salmon P. Chase, Secretary of the Treasury under President Lincoln.

1977

Before the largest crowd in U.S. soccer history (77,691), the Cosmos crush the Fort Lauderdale (Florida) Strikers, 8-3, in an NASL second-round playoff game at Giants Stadium.

August 15

1895

George Davis has six hits, including a double and a triple, but the Giants are routed by the Quakers, 23-9, at Philadelphia.

1925

Joseph J. Fogarty dies of pneumonia in Williamsport, Pennsylvania. Considered one of the great forwards in the formative days of pro basketball at the turn of the century, Fogarty was Yale's head basketball coach for three seasons, leading the Elis to a 16-3 record and the EIBL championship in his first season (1922-23).

1926

In the classic exhibition of "Daffy Dodgers" baserunning, Babe Herman doubles into a double play while driving in the go-ahead run in a 4-1 Brooklyn win at Ebbets Field. Herman doubles with the bases loaded in the seventh. Hank DeBerry scores the tie-breaker but slow-running Dazzy Vance goes back to third, where Chick Fewster has advanced from first, and Herman shortly arrives after seeing the throw go home. Fewster and Herman are out.

1934

In the only four-heat Hambletonian ever run at Good Time Park in Goshen, N.Y., Lord Jim, driven by Dr. Hugh Paschall, wins the second and fourth heats to take first-place money.

1936

Perrin Walker of Georgia Tech wins the 100-yard dash in 9.8 seconds and Ernest Federoff of the Millrose AA takes a slow mile run in 4:24.6 on the opening day of the World Labor Athletic Carnival at Randalls Island Stadium. Only 5,000 show up to watch the first of two days of competition for name athletes who failed to make the Olympic squads. Among the major disappointments is Eulace Peacock, expected to be a sprint contender, who withdraws after an injury in the 100-yard dash semifinals.

1948

Mrs. Babe Didrikson Zaharias easily wins the U.S. Women's Open golf title and its $1,200 first-prize with a 72-hole 300 at the Atlantic City Country Club in Northfield, N.J. One of the 11 pros in the field, Mrs. Zaharias finishes eight strokes ahead of Betty Hicks and 12 in front of Betty Jameson. U.S. Intercollegiate champ Grace Lenczyk of Newington, Connecticut, is the low amateur at 313. This is the second of three Opens conducted by the original Women's PGA, which hands the event over to the Ladies PGA in 1949. It is taken over by the United States Golf Association in 1955.

1982

Bill Roeder, sportswriter for the *World-Telegram* from 1944-60 when he joined *Newsweek*, dies in Sharon, Connecticut, at age 60. Roeder covered the Brooklyn Dodgers until their move to Los Angeles in 1957.

1989

Roger Neilson is hired as Rangers coach, less than one month before training camp begins and less than one month after Neil Smith is named general manager (see July 17).

1997

First Union Corporation sells $25 million in private-placement bonds for the Football Giants, the first such financial deal in the history of professional sports. The funds raised enable the NFL team to pay contracts and off-season expenses at more favorable interest rates than are available for short-term loans.

1870

Before an astonished crowd at Brooklyn's Capitoline Grounds, young Fred Goldsmith proves a curveball is not an optical illusion. He pitches a baseball to the right of one pole, the left of a second and the right of a third, debunking popular theories that a ball in flight could not be caused to curve.

1920

Yankees submarining righthander Carl Mays hits Cleveland shortstop Ray Chapman, leading off the fifth inning, in the head with a 1-1 fastball. The Indians win, 4-3, at the Polo Grounds, with Harry Lunte finishing the game at short, but Chapman dies the next morning from his injuries, the only on-field fatality in major league history.

1921

In the first action of its type since its formation, the New York State Athletic Commission revokes the boxing license of the Dyckman Oval for failure to pay $2,500 of the $5,000 due to St. Paul (Minnesota) middleweight Mike Gibbons. The Commission also suspends the license of the Boxing Drome AA in The Bronx for what Commission Secretary Harry Burchell calls "financial mismanagement." Chairman William Muldoon says he is considering banning guarantees to have boxers earn a fixed percentage of the gate, to prevent promoters from guaranteeing bigger purses than they can pay. But he ultimately decides against the idea.

1930

Frank Gifford, the Football Giants career-scoring leader upon his retirement in 1964, is born in Bakersfield, California. Gifford, who starred at USC, joined the Giants in 1952. Later, he became a color commentator on ABC's "Monday Night Football" from 1971-97.

1942

Devereaux Milburn dies in Westbury, N.Y., at age 60. One of the greatest polo players produced in America, Milburn was rated at 10 goals for 12 straight years (1917-28) and played for the Meadow Brook team that won the National Open in 1916, 1919, 1920 and 1923.

1948

Babe Ruth dies in New York at 53. Considered by many the greatest player in baseball history, Ruth played 15 of his 22 big-league seasons with the Yankees (1920-34), during which time he hit 659 homers in leading the Yankees to seven pennants and four world championships and establishing the franchise as the most famous and successful in American sports history.

1961

Harry Balogh dies in New York at age 70. Balogh, the "Voice of Armories," succeeded the fabled Joe Humphreys in 1933 and was the leading ring announcer at the Garden until his retirement in 1957. He was the first announcer to work regularly in a tuxedo and learned sufficient Spanish to introduce Hispanic boxers in their language.

MAYOR WILLIAM O'DWYER AND BABE RUTH

1987

Julius Helfand, 84, New York State Athletic Commission chairman (1955-60), dies in West Palm Beach, Florida.

August 17

1901

A rarity in American cricket occurs when both S.B. Standfast and Andrew Brown bat a century as the Brooklyn Cricket Club crushes the Montclair Athletic Club at Brooklyn's Prospect Park. When the stumps are drawn, Brooklyn wins by 210 runs and eight wickets as Standfast has 116 runs and Brown 110, both not out.

1914

Albert Henry Soar is born in Alton, Rhode Island. Hank Soar, a Football Giants fullback (1937-44, 1946), was an American League umpire from 1950-71 before retiring to become AL supervisor of umpires.

1933

Kenny Sears is born in Watsonville, California. Sears, a Knicks first-round choice in the 1955 NBA draft, played seven seasons for the Knicks (1955-62) and led the team in scoring two straight seasons (18.6 ppg in 1957-58 and 21.0 in 1958-59).

1933

Thomas W. Courtney is born in Newark, N.J. As a Fordham student, Courtney was the IC4A 1,000-meter champion in 1954 and won two gold medals at the Olympic Games in 1956.

1938

Henry Armstrong becomes the only boxing champion ever to wear three crowns simultaneously with a split decision over Lou Ambers for the lightweight title at the Garden. Armstrong knocks Ambers down in both the fifth and sixth rounds of the 15-round bout. Despite the knockdowns, many of the 19,216 on hand roundly boo the verdict of referee Billy Cavanaugh and judge George Lecron. Judge Marty Monroe gives the decision to Ambers. Armstrong had won the featherweight title from Petey Sarron in 1937 and the welterweight diadem from Barney Ross earlier in the year.

1969

In a game that finally establishes football bragging rights in New York, the Super Bowl champion Jets clobber the Football Giants, 37-14, in an exhibition game at the Yale Bowl in New Haven, Connecticut, in the teams' first-ever meeting.

1981

Bill Jennings dies in Byram, Connecticut, at age 60. A New York attorney, Jennings founded the Westchester Classic golf tournament in 1967 and was president of the Rangers from 1962-81. He was the driving force behind the daring 1967 NHL expansion from six to 12 teams.

1986

John Kelly dies in Lighthouse Point, Florida, at age 76. Shipwreck Kelly was a colorful football back for the Football Giants and Football Dodgers (of which he was part owner for a time with Dan Topping) during the 1930s.

1992

A consortium of four Long Island businessmen (Robert Rosenthal, Stephen Walsh, Ralph Palleschi and Paul Greenwood) acquire managing control of the Islanders from team owner John Pickett and name assistant general manager Don Maloney as the new general manager, replacing Bill Torrey, heretofore the only general manager in club history.

1997

Davis Love, III, turns in a final-round 66, his third 66 of the four days, and wins the PGA championship with a 72-hole 269 at the Winged Foot Golf Club in Mamaroneck, N.Y. Love, who was tied for the lead after the first and third rounds, finishes five strokes ahead of Justin Leonard and takes the $470,000 top prize in the $2.4 million event.

1890

Maurice Podoloff, first commissioner of the NBA, is born in Elizabethgrad, Russia.

1925

Rough seas and high winds thwart New Yorker Gertrude Ederle's attempt to become the first woman to swim the English Channel, as she is pulled from the water nearly two-thirds of the way from France to England (on her second attempt, she succeeds, covering 31 miles in a record 14 hours, 31 minutes) (see June 15).

1940

Walter Percy Chrysler, who in 1924 brought out the first Chrysler car and in 1933 joined the Board of Directors of Madison Square Garden during the reorganization engineered by Floyd Odlum, dies in Great Neck, N.Y., at age 65.

1941

Matt Snell is born in Garfield, Georgia. A bruising fullback, Snell scored the Jets' only touchdown in their Super Bowl win over the Baltimore Colts in 1969.

1952

Deborah Elizabeth Meyer is born in Haddonfield, N.J. Debbie Meyer, a swimmer, at one time held six world records and won the Sullivan Award as the nation's top amateur athlete in 1969.

1968

Julius Boros squeezes home one stroke ahead three other golfers to win the Westchester Classic at the Westchester CC. Boros' final-round 68 for a 72-hole 272 gives him the win over defending champ Jack Nicklaus (who shoots a closing 66), Dan Sykes and Bob Murphy.

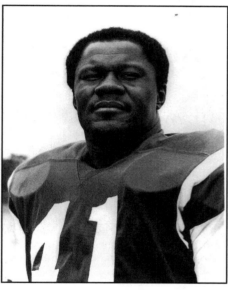

MATT SNELL

1983

In the completion of the "pine tar" game (see July 24), Kansas City reliever Dan Quisenberry retires the Yankees in order in the bottom of the ninth to seal the Royals' 5-4 victory. In protest of American League president Lee MacPhail's upholding of the Royals' protest, Yankees manager Billy Martin puts pitcher Ron Guidry in centerfield for the final out of the visiting half of the ninth and lefthanded outfielder-first baseman Don Mattingly at second. On resumption of play, New York reliever George Frazier appeals Brett's homer, but the umpires produce an affidavit from members of the crew who had worked the game in July that Brett touched all the bases.

1989

Dallas Green is fired as Yankees manager and is replaced by former Bombers hero shortstop Bucky Dent. But Dent goes 36-53 over the next 89 games and is replaced June 6, 1990, by Stump Merrill.

1994

Michael J. Kochel, the left guard on the second incarnation of Fordham's "Seven Blocks of Granite" in 1937, dies in Bellevue, Nebraska, at age 78.

1893

Harry C. Wheeler, a pro from Orange, N.J., wins the five-mile handicap race (13:11.8) and one-mile open (2:31.2) at the National Cycling Association meet staged at Manhattan Field.

1917

Managers John McGraw of the Giants and Christy Mathewson of the Reds are designated to be, and are, arrested at the Polo Grounds because the Giants play Cincinnati in violation of New York Sunday Blue Laws. Accommodating police arrange for the arrests to be processed at the ballpark so as not to interfere with the playing of the game. The ceremonial arrests of the high-profile McGraw and Mathewson are part of a continuing battle between sports fans and promoters on the one hand and religious groups on the other regarding the playing of sports events on Sundays. Cincinnati wins the game, attended by over 34,000 fans, 5-0, in a benefit for the famed 69th Regiment, which ships out for France the next day.

1931

William Lee Shoemaker is born in Fabens, Texas. Willie Shoemaker won a record 8,832 races as a thoroughbred jockey, including five Belmont Stakes, five Woodward Stakes and four Jockey Club Gold Cups.

1934

Richard Raskind is born in New York. A Yale graduate, Raskind in 1960 lost in the first round of the U.S. national singles tennis championship at Forest Hills to eventual champion Neale Fraser. In 1977, two years after a sex-change operation and shortly after a highly-publicized court battle over eligibility, Renee Richards lost her first-round singles match to 1968 U.S. Open women's champion Virginia Wade. She did reach the women's doubles final that year.

1939

Gar Wood, Jr., sweeps both Amateur Class A races before a storm halts racing in the National Sweepstakes motorboat regatta on the Shrewsbury River near Red Bank, N.J. Eastern pro class A laurels go to defending champion Fred Jacoby, Jr., of North Bergen, N.J., and the Eastern amateur class A winner is Frank Desmond of Short Hills, N.J.

1969

Lou Stillman dies in Santa Barbara, California, at age 82. Stillman, whose real name was Louis Ingber, was owner of the Stillman's Gym. Once called "an open sesame to low society" by Damon Runyon, the gym, where many famous fighters trained, was located at 919 8th Avenue, although it also operated at other locations. Ingber was business partner of Marshall Stillman and they operated a gym on 125th Street in Harlem. When the gym moved downtown, Ingber took a new partner but kept the name "Stillman's" for the gym, and many customers called him "Mr. Stillman," so he changed his name.

1975

Frank Shields, a top tennis player of the 1920s and 1930s, whose granddaughter, actress Brooke Shields, married tennis star Andre Agassi, dies at age 64 in New York.

1982

Fritz Crisler, owner of the best winning percentage of any coach in Princeton football history (35-9-5, .765, from 1932-37) and the father of two-platoon football, dies in Ann Arbor, Michigan, at age 83. His teams of 1933 and 1935 were 9-0 and in 1933 the school rejected the Rose Bowl invitation ultimately accepted by Columbia. He left the Tigers to become head coach at Michigan, where he coached the perennial national power Wolverines for 10 seasons (1938-47).

1889

Morris Park opens as New York's major racetrack (succeeding Jerome Park) on a tract now part of the Lehman College campus and part of the Jerome Park Reservoir.

1914

Racing against time, Peter Billiken sets a world record for a trotter pulling a high-wheel sulky on a half-mile track, clocking 2:14.25 for a mile at Goshen, N.Y.

1920

At the Jordan and Hupmobile auto showroom in Canton, Ohio, representatives of four Ohio-based pro football teams (Akron Pros, Canton Bulldogs, Cleveland Indians and Dayton Triangles) from the American Professional Football Conference, precursor to the NFL.

1938

Lou Gehrig hits a first-inning grand slam off Lee Ross as the Yankees coast to an 11-3 victory over the Athletics at Philadelphia. Gehrig, who also has a two-run double in the fourth, now has 24 homers for the season and 23 grand slams for his career. But this is the last of his career-record grand slams.

1945

Dodgers shortstop Tommy Brown becomes the youngest player to homer in the big leagues with a seventh-inning solo shot off Pittsburgh's Preacher Roe into the upper leftfield stands at Ebbets Field. Brown is 17 years, eight months and 14 days old. Radio announcer Red Barber, who always rolls a carton of Old Gold cigarettes down the screen for Dodgers home run hitters, decides Brown is too young to smoke and adds the carton to a donation going to a Veterans' Administration hospital. Brown's homer is Brooklyn's only run as they make seven errors (one by Brown) and disappoint a crowd of 7,368 (including 1,046 servicemen) in an 11-1 loss to the Pirates.

1949

Led by Frank Stranahan and Skee Riegel, the U.S. wins the Walker Cup with a 10-2 edge over Great Britain in the international amateur team golf matches at the Winged Foot GC in Mamaroneck, N.Y.

1960

Hairos II of Holland wins the second running of the Roosevelt International. The race, at Roosevelt Raceway, draws 54,861, largest crowd in the history of harness racing.

1968

Earl Sande, the jockey who rode Gallant Fox to the 1930 Triple Crown and won four other Belmont Stakes, dies in Jacksonville, Oregon, at age 69.

1985

Dwight Gooden fans 16 Giants in a 3-0 win over San Francisco at Shea Stadium to become the first pitcher to strike out 200 or more in each of his first two seasons. In 1986, Gooden makes it three straight with an even 200 after 276 in 1984 and 268 in 1985.

EARLE SANDE ON GALLANT FOX

233

1897

Righhanded fireballer Amos Rusie throws a five-hitter but loses his catcher in the third inning of the Giants' 7-1 victory over the Louisville Colonels at the Polo Grounds. A foul ball hits catcher Jack Warner's mask, breaking it and the prongs cause a deep cut over his left eye.

1904

Tom Greenwade, the Yankees scout who signed Mickey Mantle, is born in Willard, Missouri.

1909

Scoring the game's only run without the benefit of a hit in the first inning, the Giants defeat Cincinnati, 1-0, at the Polo Grounds behind the five-hit pitching of Christy Mathewson. Larry Doyle walks in the first, goes to third on a grounder to the mound and beats third baseman Miller Huggins' throw home on another grounder.

1915

Harold Vollmer of the New York Athletic Club swims to wins in both the 100-yard (1:05.4) and 200-yard (2:26.6) races at the Rye Beach Club meet on Long Island Sound. Helen Walsh of the host club wins the girls' 100-yard swim in 1:48.2

1928

Seabury Lawrence, a sportswriter who covered the first Rangers home game for *The New York Times* in 1926, dies in New York at age 47.

1937

Howard (Poke) Freeman, sports cartoonist for the *Newark Evening News* from 1912 until his death, dies in Avon, N.J., at age 59.

1937

Joe Morrison, Football Giants running back from 1959-72, is born in Lima, Ohio.

1965

Joe Namath, starting in the second half in relief of fellow rookie John Huarte, shows enough skill and poise to win the Jets' starting quarterback job after a 30-14 exhibition loss to Buffalo at New Brunswick, N.J. Buffalo takes a 27-0 halftime lead, in part, by converting two Huarte interceptions into touchdowns.

PELE

1965

Jack Fisher becomes the winningest righthander in Mets history after his 6-2 win over the Cardinals at Shea Stadium. Fisher is now 18-33 in his Mets career. He also stops a Mets four-game losing streak, nine-game home losing skid and 10-game schneid against St. Louis.

1966

Pele, judged by many to be soccer's greatest player, makes his U.S. debut in a match against Benfica of Portugal and its star, Eusebio. Pele's Santos club of Brazil wins, 4-0, in a match that draws an overflow 28,000 to Randalls Island, hundreds of whom sit on the running track around the field (see Sept. 5).

1851

By winning a race against 14 British yachts around the Isle of Wight off the English coast, *America*, sponsored by several members of the New York Yacht Club (see July 30) and the only U.S. yacht entered, wins a Cup that will come to be known as "the America's Cup," destined to become the greatest prize in international yachting. *America* completes the course in 10:37, 18 minutes ahead of the field. England's *Aurora* is second. J.C. Stevens, Edwin A. Stevens, Hamilton Wilkes, J. Beekman Finley and George L. Schuyler present the Cup for perpetual international competition in 1857, but the first challenge isn't accepted until 1870.

1880

William Winston Roper is born in Philadelphia, Pennsylvania. Bill Roper was an end at Princeton from 1899-1901 and served three terms as Tigers head coach (1906-08, 1910-11, 1919-30). His 1922 squad finished 8-0 and was dubbed the "Team of Destiny."

1892

Monte Ward raps two doubles, a triple and a home run as the Giants wallop the Pirates, 17-1, at Pittsburgh.

1926

Levi A. Jackson, Yale football's first black player, and, team captain in 1949, is born in New Haven, Connecticut.

1941

Duane Charles Parcells is born in Englewood, N.J. Bill Parcells led the Football Giants to Super Bowl triumphs in 1987 and 1991. In 1997, he became the first man ever to serve as head coach of both the Giants and Jets.

1944

Frank J. Hill, Rutgers head basketball coach for 28 seasons (1915-43), dies in Newark, N.J., at age 64. Hill was 223-162 for a .579 winning percentage.

1963

Johnny Blanchard becomes the first Yankee in 15 years to hit two grand slams in a season with a four-run shot against the Indians at the Stadium, but Cleveland wins anyway, 7-4. Blanchard had a grand slam at Boston in a 10-2 victory August 15. Tommy Henrich had two in 1948, and Blanchard is the sixth Yankee to hit two or more grand slams in a season.

1964

Mats Arne Olaf Wilander, winner of the 1988 U.S. Open singles tennis title, his third major championship of the year, is born in Vaxjo, Sweden.

1980

Clive Rush, Weeb Ewbank's chief assistant coach of the Super Bowl Jets and later head coach of the Patriots, dies in London, Ohio, at age 49.

CHRISTY MATHEWSON

1876

William O. Hickok is born in Harrisburg, Pennsylvania. This "Wild Bill" was a two-time All-America football guard at Yale (1893-94).

1919

Charles Pores is an upset winner in the five-mile run during the Metropolitan AAU meet at Jersey City's Pershing Field. The Millrose AA runner is one of only two finishers in the event as the new track, being used for its first major meet, causes such stars as Max Bohland and Hannes Kolehmainen to drop out with injuries. Fred W. Kelly, now competing for the New York Athletic Club, wins both hurdles (the 120-yard in 16.2 seconds and the 220 in 28.4).

1926

Molla Bjurstedt Mallory rallies from a 4-0 third-set deficit and saves a match point to top Britain's Elizabeth Ryan, 4-6, 6-4, 9-7, in the U.S. national women's singles final at Forest Hills. It is Mrs. Mallory's eighth (and final) U.S. singles title, a record.

1949

Giants sell first baseman Johnny Mize to the Yankees for a reported $40,000.

1958

Anne Quast defeats Joanne Goodwin, 3 and 2, in the 36-hole final match to win the U.S. Women's Amateur golf championship at the Wee Burn Club in Darien, Connecticut.

HERB SCHARFMAN

1961

Beals C. Wright, U.S. national singles tennis champion in 1905, dies in Alton, Illinois, at age 81.

1962

Glenn Healy is born in Pickering, Ontario. Healy, who backstopped the Islanders to their surprising Stanley Cup semifinal run in 1993, passed from the Isles to Anaheim to Tampa Bay to the Rangers in a series of expansion draft-related transactions June 24-25, 1993, and was the backup goalie for the Rangers' 1994 Stanley Cup champions.

1975

Peter Elser, one of the founders of the New York Generals of the NASL, dies at age 55 in Tuxedo Park, N.Y.

1982

Raymond (Ducky) Pond dies in Torrington, Connecticut, at age 82. Ducky Pond was Yale's football coach from 1934-40, compiling a record of 30-25-2, and coached successive Heisman Trophy winners Larry Kelley in 1936 and Clint Frank in 1937.

August 24

1852

James Henry O'Rourke is born in Bridgeport, Connecticut. Orator O'Rourke hit over .300 in a 23-season major league career that started in 1872. A member of the Giants world championship teams of 1888 and 1889, he played a variety of positions, though he was primarily an outfielder during his eight seasons with the Giants (see Sept. 22).

1909

With Governor Charles Evans Hughes leading an anti-betting mania that shut most of the state's tracks, the Orange County Driving Park's opening of a week-long nonbetting meeting draws over 10,000 to the little Goshen, N.Y., track as Quinsetta, a trotting mare owned by E.S. Harriman, wins the day's major event by taking the last two of the three heats.

1911

Herb Scharfman, photographer for the International News Service from 1932-58 and *Sports Illustrated* from 1958-80, is born in Chicago. Scharfman was also a perennial at the Brooklyn Dodgers training camp.

1912

Barney Nagler, a longtime sportswriter who started with the *Bronx Home News* in 1937 and later wrote the column "On Second Thought" for *The Morning Telegraph* (which became the *Daily Racing Form* in 1972) starting in 1950, is born in Brooklyn.

1919

In the first-ever International Small Bore Rifle competition staged, U.S. defeats Britain, 7,617-7,523, at Caldwell, N.J. Captain G.C. Wotkyns of Army Ordinance leads the mostly-military U.S. team with 391 points out of a possible 800 but 17-year-old A.M. Morgan scores 388 and Mrs. E.C. Crossman, the first woman ever to shoot in an international competition, gets 377.

1935

Hank Leiber homers twice during the eight-run second inning as the Giants pound Tex Carleton and the Cubs, 9-4, at the Polo Grounds. Leiber leads off the inning with a homer, then hits a two-run shot off the front of the left field roof. Mel Ott also has a three-run homer during the inning that excites the 17,923 fans.

1963

Hooley Smith, another hockey great spending the last years of his career with the Americans, dies at age 60. Smith, a former forward and center, played defense most of his four seasons (1937-41) with the Amerks.

1975

In the nightcap of a doubleheader, Ed Halicki no-hits the Mets, 6-0, at San Francisco.

1980

Jean Balukas of Brooklyn successfully defends her women's world open pocket billiards championship with a 100-75 win over Billie Billing at the Hotel Roosevelt in Manhattan. Miss Balukas has now lost only two matches to women in the last eight years. Nick Varner of Owensboro, Kentucky, upsets Mike Sigel of Baltimore, 150-13, to win the men's title.

1991

Abel Kiviat, one of the world's great runners in the first two decades of the century, dies in Lakehurst, N.J., at age 99. A New York native and runner for the Irish-American AC, Kiviat in 1912 broke the world record in the 1,500 meters three times in 13 days. He was later a longtime press steward at New York track meets at Madison Square Garden.

August 25

1888

In a 7-0 win at Philadelphia, Mike Tiernan becomes the first Giant to hit for the cycle. After a first-inning single, he hits a solo homer in the third, triples in two runs in the fifth and doubles in another in the seventh.

1890

One of three big league clubs in Brooklyn throws in the towel as the AA team loses at Syracuse, 5-4, and announces it is disbanding. Manager Jim Kennedy blames the AA owners, who he says are scheming to merge with the Players League, but the team is 27-72, has lost 18 of its last 20 games and attendance at remote Ridgewood Park is sparse at best. Most of the players are shifted to Baltimore by AA executives to play out the last 34 games of the schedule under new manager Billy Barnie.

1927

Althea Gibson, the first black to win a major singles title, and a two-time champ at Wimbledon and the U.S. nationals at Forest Hills (1957-58), is born in Silver, South Carolina.

1931

John Patrick Rohan is born in Floral Park, N.Y. Considered one of the best basketball minds in the country, Jack Rohan was Columbia's head coach from 1961-74 and 1990-95, compiling a 217-248 (.470) record in 18 seasons. His Lions won the 1967 ECAC Holiday Festival and the 1968 Ivy League title. That year, they finished 23-5, ranked sixth in the nation.

1939

Babe Siebert, a Rangers defenseman from 1932-34 who had been named earlier in the summer head coach of the Montreal Canadiens, drowns accidently at age 35 in St. Joseph, Ontario.

1942

Ralph Robert Baker, Jets linebacker from 1964-74, is born in Lewistown, Pennsylvania.

1952

Virgil Trucks of the Tigers hurls his second no-hitter of the year and beats the Yankees, 1-0, at Yankee Stadium. Controversy surrounds the feat as Phil Rizzuto's third-inning grounder to shortstop Johnny Pesky is ruled an error, then changed to a hit, then back to an error in the seventh by official scorer John Drebinger.

1958

After covering the Yankees' doubleheader against Detroit at the Stadium the day before, Ben Epstein dies of a heart attack in his Manhattan home. The 51-year-old *Daily Mirror* writer is honored annually by the Ben Epstein "Good Guy Award" presented by the New York chapter of the BBWAA.

1973

Delmonica Hanover is the second straight U.S. winner of the International Trot, edging Spartan Hanover at Roosevelt Raceway. Driven by John Chapman, the longshot pays $22.20 to win and covers the $1^1/_4$ miles in 2:34.2, the fastest time since 1966, in the 15th renewal of the event.

1984

Waite Hoyt dies in Cincinnati, Ohio, at age 84. A Brooklyn native who initially signed with the Giants at age 15, Hoyt won 157 games in 10 seasons with the Yankees, including a league-leading 22 in 1927 for "Murderers Row." In the 1921 World Series against the Giants, "the Schoolboy" won two of three decisions, all complete games, allowing no earned runs in 27 innings. He lost the finale, 1-0, on an unearned run.

1992

Jim Rathschmidt, 78, the Yale crew coach from 1951-70, dies in Boynton Beach, Florida.

1886

Gravesend Park, Brooklyn's third major racetrack, is opened by the Brooklyn Jockey Club. The three tracks are all within sight of each other on the Atlantic Ocean beach.

1899

Charles Mock starts a 24-hour cycle ride on the Century Road Racing Club course from Valley Stream, L.I., and back via Lynbrook, Freeport, and Hempstead. By the following morning, Mock sets a 24-hour record of 386 miles as well as a 12-hour record of 211 miles and time records for the fastest 200, 300 and 400 miles peddled.

1925

Former Yale football captain Ted Coy, now a New York stockbroker, quietly marries Broadway star Jeanne Eagels in Stamford, Connecticut, but a tabloid frenzy breaks out when news of the nuptials seeps back to New York. Miss Eagels obtains a divorce in Chicago on July 14, 1928, ending the storybook marriage of the decade (see May 24 and Sept. 8).

1929

Colonel Abraham G. Mills, 85, third National League president (1883-84) and onetime president of the NYAC, dies in Falmouth, Massachusetts. Mills wrote the National Agreement that binds baseball leagues together in the structure known as Organized Baseball. The Mills Commission, formed in 1908 after the death of Henry Chadwick, published a report wrongly concluding that baseball was created by Abner Doubleday in Cooperstown, N.Y., in 1839. In 1921, Mills proposed the creation of the American Olympic Committee.

1933

Helen Hull Jacobs defeats Helen Wills Moody, 8-6, 3-6, 3-0 ret., in the U.S. national women's singles final at Forest Hills. Mrs. Moody's mysterious retirement ends her 45-match winning streak at the nationals, the longest in tournament history.

1939

In the first regular-season major league baseball game ever televised, Bill Stern calls the action in the opener of a doubleheader from Ebbets Field over W2XBS. Bucky Walters throws a two-hitter as the Cincinnati Reds beat the Dodgers, 5-2, as 33,535 see catcher Babe Phelps make two errors in the Reds' five-run eighth inning. Brooklyn wins the nightcap, 6-1 (without television) as Hugh Casey throws an eight-hitter.

1939

Betty Jameson scores a 3 and 2 win over Dorothy Kirby in the 36-hole final match to capture the U.S. Women's Amateur golf title at the Wee Burn Club in Darien, Connecticut.

1966

National Professional Soccer League is formed in St. Louis and the Generals are admitted as the New York franchise. The NPSL, an "outlaw" league, is not recognized by FIFA, soccer's international governing body, which has sanctioned the rival United Soccer Association.

1967

Sandro Mazzola's goal eight minutes into the second half gives Internazionale of Milan a 1-0 victory over Santos of Brazil before 37,063 at Yankee Stadium and avenges an exhibition loss the year before to the Pele-led Santos (see Sept. 5).

1993

Carmine Cincotta, longtime sports producer for the three New York television network affiliates (WABC-TV, WCBS-TV, WNBC-TV), dies in New York at age 41.

1920

Bill Tilden takes his first of six straight U.S. national singles titles with a five-set win over defending champ Bill Johnston in the final at the West Side Tennis Club in Forest Hills, avenging his defeat in the final in 1919, the first of five final-round wins for "Big Bill" over "Little Bill" at the nationals. The match has a referee's overrule on a critical point, a rain delay and a crash on the grounds of a military plane that kills two fliers and barely misses the crowded stands.

1920

Monty Waterbury, one of America's greatest polo players and only the sixth ever to be rated at 10 goals, dies in Rumson, N.J., at age 42.

1930

Favorite Hanover Bertha, driven by Tom Berry, wins the fifth Hambletonian, taking the last two of three heats after finishing fifth. This Hambo is the first run at Good Time Park, a triangular-shaped mile track in Goshen, N.Y., where 25 of the next 26 renewals will be run. Promoted by Bill Cane, the Hambletonian becomes the biggest event in harness racing during its long stay in the Orange County community.

1938

Missing a perfect game by the margin of two fourth-inning walks, the Yankees' Monte Pearson no-hits the Indians, 13-0, before 4,959 at Yankee Stadium.

1966

In an attempt to bring minor league football to New York, the Brooklyn Dodgers open their season before some 8,000 fans at Randalls Island Stadium. The team, a member of the Continental Football League, has Jackie Robinson as its general manager and Andy Robustelli as head coach but opening night produces a 49-7 loss to the Orlando (Florida) Panthers as Glynn Griffing throws a pair of second-half touchdown passes.

1975

In the first night match ever played at the U.S. Open, Onny Parun defeats Stan Smith, 6-4, 6-2, before 4,949 at the West Side Tennis Club in Forest Hills.

1976

With five runs in the 15th inning, the Yankees beat the California Angels, 5-0, at Anaheim, and equal the club record for the longest shutout. Grant Jackson gets the win in relief as the Bombers match the record set in 1915. Oddly, the Yankees had gone 19 innings in their previous game two days earlier before beating Minnesota at the Stadium.

1978

Dennis Tueart scores two and Giorgio Chinaglia one as the Cosmos beat Tampa Bay, 3-1, before 74,901, for their second straight NASL title, as the Soccer Bowl comes to Giants Stadium.

BILL TILDEN

1991

Down two sets to none, 0-3 in the third set and 0-40 in the fourth game of that set, Jimmy Connors takes game, set and match from Patrick McEnroe, 4-6, 6-7, 6-4, 6-2, 6-4, in a first-round match at the National Tennis Center in Flushing Meadow, N.Y., that ends after 1:30 a.m.

1884

Mickey Welch fans the first nine hitters as the Giants roll to a 10-2 win over Cleveland at the Polo Grounds. Welch finishes with a six-hitter and 13 strikeouts and issues no walks.

1922

Opening round play inaugurates competition for American golf's oldest international team trophy, the Walker Cup, at the National Links in Southampton, N.Y. The next day, the U.S. completes an 8-4 victory over Britain.

1932

Andy Bathgate is born in Winnipeg, Manitoba. A right wing, Bathgate became the Rangers' best player and captain during the late 1950s and early 1960s, winning the Hart Trophy as league MVP in 1958-59 and tying for the NHL scoring lead in 1961-62.

1939

Charley Miller of Linden, N.J., wins the 40-lap Eastern States Midget Auto Championship in 10:06.8 at Thompson Stadium (former home of the NFL Stapletons) on Staten Island. Chet Gibbons is second and Johnny Swier third.

1951

Howie Pollet throws a six-hitter and the Pirates score twice in the eighth for a 2-0 win at the Polo Grounds, ending the Giants' 16-game winning streak that began Aug. 12 with a 3-2 win over the Phillies. The second-place Giants, like most of the 8,803 fans, nurture little hope of catching league-leading Brooklyn since they still trail by six games, seven in the loss column.

1955

In an exhibition game at Portland, Oregon, the Los Angeles Rams beat the Football Giants, 23-17, in overtime, the first time the NFL sudden-death overtime rule is used in a game involving two NFL teams.

1960

Hitting back-to-back homers twice in the second game of a doubleheader at the Stadium, the Yankees salvage a split with Detroit. Dale Long and John Blanchard, and then Mickey Mantle and Yogi Berra, hit successive homers in the 8-5 win. The Tigers won the opener, 6-2.

1977

Steve Hunt scores the first goal and assists on Giorgio Chinaglia's winner as the Cosmos capture their second NASL title with a 2-1 win over the Seattle Sounders before 35,548 in Portland, Oregon, in Soccer Bowl '77.

1978

A consortium headed by New Jersey businessmen Joe Taub and Alan Cohen buy the New Jersey Nets from Roy L.M. Boe.

1990

Stefan Edberg becomes the first No. 1-seeded men's player to lose in his first-round U.S. Open match since John Newcombe in 1971, falling to Alexander Volkov of the U.S.S.R. in straight sets. But the next year, Edberg wins the men's singles title, the first man to win the Nationals the year after losing in the first round since Mal Anderson in 1957.

1994

A partnership of ITT and Cablevision announce that they have agreed to buy Madison Square Garden and its components from Viacom for $1.075 billion. When the sale is completed March 10, 1995, the actual price is $1.010 billion.

August 29

1922
A U.S. team that includes Francis Ouimet, Chick Evans, Bobby Jones and Jess Sweetser, defeats a British team, 8-4, in the Walker Cup match at the National Golf Links of America in Southampton, L.I.

1925
Yankees manager Miller Huggins suspends Babe Ruth from the team for "off-field conduct" before a 4-1 win over the Browns at St. Louis.

1933
Major Frank Cavanaugh dies in Worcester, Massachusetts, at age 57. A major in the U.S. Army in World War I, Cavanaugh was Fordham football coach from 1927-32, posting a 34-14-4 (.694) record, including 27-4-4 the last four seasons. The 1929 squad went unbeaten (7-0-2) and its line earned the nickname, "The Seven Blocks of Granite." Cavanaugh also coached at Cincinnati, Dartmouth, Holy Cross and Boston College.

1948
Jackie Robinson hits for the cycle as the Dodgers beat the Cardinals, 12-7, in the opening game of a double-header at St. Louis. Brooklyn also wins the second game, 6-4, in 10 innings.

1951
Roger Donoghue KOs Georgie Flores in the eighth round of a middleweight semifinal bout on the Billy Graham-Kid Gavilan card at the Garden. Flores, who had lost to Donoghue two weeks before, doesn't regain consciousness and is rushed to St. Clare's Hospital, but he dies four days later.

1968
After being amateur-only since their inception, the U.S. tennis championships go Open, welcoming professional players for the first time. Defending women's champ Billie Jean King plays the first match on the Stadium Court at the West Side Tennis Club in Forest Hills, defeating Long Island dentist and alternate player Dr. Vija Vuskains, 6-1, 6-0. Pro and 10th seed Andres Gimeno is beaten by amateur Ray Moore in the biggest opening-day upset.

1972
In the first game of a Yankee Stadium doubleheader, New York's Bobby Murcer hits for the cycle against Texas and the Yankees win, 7-6, in 11 innings.

1974
Stanton Griffis dies at age 87 in New York. Griffis, a noted diplomat, was a member of the group led by Floyd Odlum that reorganized Madison Square Garden in the mid-1930s and returned it to profitability. Griffis was on the Garden's board from 1933-55 and served a term as chairman.

1974
Isador Bieber, a horse trainer and longtime partner of Hirsch Jacobs from 1928-70, dies in Hollywood, Florida, at age 87. Nicknamed "Colonel" by Damon Runyon, Bieber, with Jacobs, saddled 3,569 winners and earned over $12 million in purses.

1978
In the first U.S. Open match ever at the National Tennis Center in Flushing Meadow, Bjorn Borg whips Bob Hewitt, 6-0, 6-2, on opening night. The first full schedule of matches is played the following day.

1983
With eventual Heisman Trophy winner Mike Rozier as the feature back, Nebraska crushes Penn State, 44-6, in the first Kickoff Classic at Giants Stadium.

1864

Despite the distraction of the Civil War, trotting racing continues at Union Course with Bay Mare defeating Lady Bayard in two straight one-mile heats to win the $400 purse, clocking 2:45.25 and 2:48.25.

1900

In the last major match before the expiration of the Horton Law the next night, Jim Corbett knocks out Kid McCoy at 2:03 of the fifth round before 11,000 at the Garden. Corbett collects about $22,400 for his night's work and McCoy a bit over $9,000. The four-year-old Horton Law is New York's first experiment with fully-legalized boxing.

1906

Highlanders lefty Slow Joe Doyle becomes the first AL rookie to break into the majors with two shutouts as he throws a 5-0 two-hitter at the Senators in the first game of a doubleheader sweep at Hilltop Park. New York wins the second game, 9-8, in 10 innings, as Hal Chase raps three triples and a double. Doyle threw a six-hitter in winning his AL debut, 2-0, over Cleveland at Hilltop August 25.

1917

William Gates in born in Decatur, Alabama. One of the great basketball stars of his time, Pop Gates played with the all-black New York Rens from 1938-41 and in 1944, 1946 and 1948-49. He also played for the Long Island Grumman Flyers from 1941-43 and the Hellcats in 1945.

1925

NYU undergrad Ethel McGary, the newest star of the WSANY, sets two world records during an AAU meet at the Hotel Wentworth pool in Portsmouth, New Hampshire. Miss McGary sets a mile freestyle mark (25:35.6), beating WSA teammate Virginia Whitneck and also breaks her own 440-yard breaststroke record with a time of 7:20.8.

1939

Football Giants, defending NFL champions, beat the College All-Stars, 9-0, in a preseason game before 81,456 at Chicago.

1959

Bowling great George Young dies at age 49 in Detroit, Michigan.

1967

With a third-round 65, Jack Nicklaus wins the first Westchester Classic by one stroke over Dan Sykes at the Westchester Country Club. The tournament was halted for three days by rain after the opening round. Nicklaus finishes at 272 to Sykes' 273, with Roberto DiVicenzo at 274, Gary Player at 275, Arnold Palmer at 276 and Doug Sanders at 277. The tournament is the successor to the Thunderbird Classic, which was discontinued after 1965, and is played on the same course at the club.

1973

Yancey (Yank) Durham, manager of boxing champs including light heavyweight Bob Foster and heavyweight Joe Frazier, dies in Philadelphia, Pennsylvania, at age 53.

1979

Third-seeded John McEnroe beats Romania's Ilie Nastase, 6-4, 4-6, 6-3, 6-2, in a wild night match at the U.S. Open in Flushing Meadow, during which Nastase is defaulted by umpire Frank Hammond, only to be reinstated after the crowd starts a near riot. Following an 18-minute delay, tournament referee Mike Blanchard takes the chair from Hammond and finishes the match as umpire.

August 31

1895

J.F. Starbuck of Philadelphia, Pennsylvania, defeats Peter Berlo of Boston by half-a-wheel to win the five-mile handicap cycle race at Manhattan Beach in Brooklyn. Berlo had a 275-yard handicap advantage.

1903

Giants righty Joe McGinnity pitches and wins both ends of a double-header for the third time this season, earning him the nickname "Iron Man." McGinnity beats the Phillies, 4-1, on a five-hitter, and 9-2 on a six-hitter. At bat, McGinnity gets four hits himself (three in the second game). The games combined take 3:03 playing time, pleasing the Polo Grounds crowd of 3,496.

1915

After being delayed one day by rain, the first U.S. national tennis championships to be played in New York begin at the West Side Tennis Club in Forest Hills, Queens. Ward Dawson and Bernard C. Law are among the first-round winners on the main courts as over 5,000 attend the opening-day matches.

1940

William Vincent Campbell is born in Homestead, Pennsylvania. A diminutive guard and linebacker, Bill Campbell was captain of the Columbia Ivy League football champions of 1961 and the Lions' head coach for six seasons (1974-79, 12-41-1).

1950

Gil Hodges becomes the fourth NL player to hit four homers in a game (off, in order, Warren Spahn, Normie Roy, Bob Hall and Johnny Antonelli) to lead the Dodgers to a 19-3 rout of the Boston Braves at Ebbets Field. Hodges also singles to finish with 17 total bases, matching an NL record set by Bobby Lowe in 1894 and tied by Ed Delahanty in 1896, and has nine RBI.

BILL CAMPBELL

1987

Richard Leonard Young dies in New York at age 69. Dick Young joined the *Daily News* in 1943 and became the most famous sportswriter of his time, spending almost 40 years there before joining the rival *New York Post* in 1982.

1989

Famed bowler Lou Campi dies in Dumont, N.J., at age 84. In 1948, Campi won 13 consecutive matches as part of a live weekly televised bowling series broadcast from the Bowlmor Lanes on 14th Street in Manhattan.

1990

Nat (Sweetwater) Clifton, the first black man ever to play for the Knicks (Nov. 4, 1950, at the Tri-Cities Blackhawks in Moline, Ill.), dies in Chicago at age 65.

1997

In the first game of the season and Bill Parcells' debut as their head coach, the Jets strafe the Seahawks, 41-3, at Seattle, posting the largest road-game margin of victory in the franchise's 38-season history.

1880

A tennis tournament of national interest is held for the first time in America at the Staten Island Cricket and Baseball Club. A squabble over the weight and size of the balls used in this tournament leads to a call for a national organization to regulate the sport (see May 21).

1890

On a day when nine major league games are played in New York and Brooklyn, the NL Bridegrooms win three times over Pittsburgh at Washington Park. In the morning, Brooklyn has a 10-0 lead in the ninth and wins, 10-9. Then, the 'Grooms sweep in the afternoon, 3-2 and 8-4. Tony Carruthers wins twice (in the morning and the second game of the p.m. twinbill watched by 7,194). On the same day, the Giants sweep Cleveland at the Polo Grounds, 4-0 and 5-1, and, in the Players League, at Manhattan Field adjacent to the Polo Grounds, New York wins two from Buffalo, 7-5 and 19-7, while Brooklyn splits with Chicago, losing 13-1 and winning 7-6, at Eastern Park.

1947

Jack Lohrke's leadoff eighth-inning homer off Red Barrett gives the Giants and Larry Jansen a 2-1 victory over the Boston Braves in the opening game of a Labor Day doubleheader at the Polo Grounds. The 43,106 fans see history as Lohrke's homer is the Giants' 183d of the season, surpassing the record of 182 set by the 1936 Yankees. The Giants win the nightcap, 12-2, and finish the season with 221 homers, but struggle to finish fourth.

1947

Ted Schroeder outlasts Australia's Dinny Pails, 6-3, 8-6, 4-6, 9-11, 10-8, to clinch the Davis Cup for the United States at the West Side Tennis Club. The capacity crowd of 11,500 sits through a three-hour, five-minute match of 71 games, the longest in Cup history up to that time. Jack Kramer later defeats John Bromwich, 6-3, 6-2, 6-2, in the second reverse singles and gives the U.S. a 4-1 win in the Cup challenge round.

1951

Don Mueller hits three homers and drives in five runs as the Giants beat Brooklyn, 5-1, in the opener of a two-game set at the Polo Grounds. Mueller ties the major league record for homers in two successive games by hitting a pair the next night, again driving in five, as the Giants win again, 11-2, to pull within five games of first-place Brooklyn.

1955

En route to the first trotting Triple Crown in U.S. history, Hambletonian winner Scott Frost, driven by Joe O'Brien, wins the inaugural Yonkers Futurity over a mile-and-a-sixteenth at Yonkers Raceway. The three-year-old bay colt is clocked in 2:12 as 21,033 watch. Scott Frost, also the winner of the Kentucky Futurity to complete the Triple Crown, earns $36,550.80 in the $73,840 Yonkers Futurity (later, the Yonkers Trot), the richest night harness race run yet.

1976

On opening night of the new Meadowlands race track in East Rutherford, N.J., 42,133 fans are on hand for an 11-race harness program. Quick Baron, driven by Ray Remmen, wins the first race.

1980

Arthur Donovan dies at age 89 in The Bronx. Donovan refereed 150 boxing title bouts before retiring as a ref in 1948. He was also boxing instructor at the New York Athletic Club from 1915-65, succeeding his father at 3:00 p.m. September 1, 1915, and retiring at 3:00 p.m. September 1, 1965.

1989

Bart Giamatti, president of Yale University from 1978-86 and of the National League from 1987-89, and commissioner of baseball from April 1, 1989, dies in Martha's Vineyard, Massachusetts, at age 51.

1915

Peter A. Carlesimo, Fordham athletic director from 1968-78 and executive director of the MIBA, which runs the NIT, from 1979-88, is born in Newark, N.J.

1933

Edward J. Conlin is born in Brooklyn. Ed Conlin, a forward who averaged 18.1 ppg in four seasons with Fordham (1951-55), was the Rams head coach for two seasons (1968-70), posting a 27-24 record.

1940

Headed by lawyer George Morton Levy, the Old Country Trotting Association opens its first night harness racing meeting at Roosevelt Raceway. Martha Lee, John Hanafin driving, wins the first race and a crowd of 4,584 generates a handle of $40,742.

1944

Dixie Walker tees off on the Giants, driving in four runs and hitting for the cycle in an 8-4 Dodgers victory, to the delight of 9,623 Ebbets Field faithful.

1949

Famed bike racer Bobby Walthour, Sr., dies in Boston, Mass., at age 71.

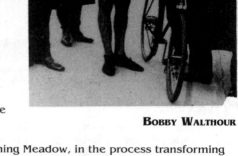

BOBBY WALTHOUR

1952

James Scott Connors is born in East St. Louis, Ill. The winner of more singles titles (109) than any other man in tennis history, volatile Jimmy Connors won the U.S. Open five times, on grass (1974) and clay (1976) at Forest Hills and on hardcourt (1978, 1982-83) at Flushing Meadow, in the process transforming from a *bete noire* to a fan favorite.

1970

For the first time at a major tennis tournament, the tie-break system is used, as the U.S. Open institutes a nine-point "sudden death" system (first to five points wins the game and set). Later, a 12-point "lingering death" format is instituted, with the first player to seven points winning the set, but requiring a two-point lead.

1971

Chris Evert and Jimmy Connors both win their first U.S. Open matches, Evert beating Edda Buding, 6-1, 6-0, and Connors, on his 19th birthday, topping Alex Olmedo, 2-6, 5-7, 6-4, 7-5, 7-5. Evert and Connors would go on to set U.S. Nationals singles records in match victories, Evert with 101 and Connors with 98.

1980

For the third time in four years (and fourth overall), the Cosmos are NASL champs, beating Fort Lauderdale, 3-0, at Washington, D.C. in Soccer Bowl '80. Julio Cesar Romero scores the first goal and Giorgio Chinaglia gets the next two before 50,768 at D.C. Stadium.

1991

On his 39th birthday, Jimmy Connors rides a raucous Labor Day crowd to a 3-6, 7-6, 1-6, 6-3, 7-6 round-of-16 U.S. Open win over Aaron Krickstein at the National Tennis Center. Connors, a wild-card entry after spending much of the year recovering from wrist surgery, advances to the semifinals.

1890

Columbia College's Oliver S. Campbell becomes only the third man to be U.S. national singles tennis champion, defeating defender Henry W. Slocum, Jr., 6-2, 4-6, 6-3, 6-1, at The Casino in Newport, Rhode Island.

1908

Hal Chase, fancy-fielding first baseman of the last-place Highlanders, jumps the club to play in the outlaw California League after a 5-2 loss to Philadelphia at Hilltop Park. Club president Frank Farrell says he is "surprised" since Chase had signed a three-year contract before the 1907 season and calls his action an "unmanly act." Chase, a notorious gambler, not only returns to the club in 1909 but becomes manager in 1910. In 1913, Chase is traded to the Chicago White Sox, then jumps to the Federal League in 1914, plays three years with the Cincinnati Reds, and finishes his career in 1919 with the Giants.

1919

Harness racer Budd Doble, who drove Dexter to 34 wins in 35 races in 1866 and also rode such famous horses as Goldsmith Maid and Nancy Hanks, dies in Philadelphia, Pennsylvania, at age 76.

1936

With John Goodman and U.S. Amateur champ John Fischer leading the way, the U.S. scores the first shutout of Great Britain, 9-0, in the Walker Cup matches at the Pine Valley GC in Clementon, N.J.

1945

Sgt. Frank Parker, on military leave, defeats Billy Talbert at Forest Hills to repeat as men's U.S. national singles tennis champion. Talbert, nursing a leg injury, wears long pants to conceal his condition and is the last man to play in the U.S. national singles final in trousers. Ironically, the day before, the Japanese formally surrendered, ending World War II.

1965

Jim Hickman's three homers help the Mets win, 6-3, at St. Louis. Hickman becomes the first Met to hit three homers in a game and also singles to finish with a club-record 13 total bases.

1978

Lee Mazzilli, in his first career two-homer game, hits home runs from both sides of the plate to help the Mets beat the Dodgers, 5-3, at Los Angeles. Mazzilli also singles twice.

1989

Chris Evert earns the last of her 101 career U.S. Open victories with a 6-0, 6-2 pasting of the highly-touted 15-year-old Monica Seles. Two days later, Zina Garrison ends Evert's Open career in the quarterfinals, 7-6, 6-2.

1989

Augie Lio, a former NFL player who was a sportswriter and sports editor for the *Passaic Herald-News* from 1947-84, dies in Clifton, N.J., at age 71.

1991

Rangers sign Edmonton free agent center Adam Graves. As compensation, they send Troy Mallette (and not Steven Rice, as the Oilers had requested) to Edmonton.

1995

Tony Fernandez of the Yankees hits for the cycle against the A's at the Stadium, but Oakland beats New York in 10 innings, 10-9.

September 4

1898

William Henry Cammeyer dies in New York at age 77. Cammeyer introduced the enclosed ballpark to baseball, opening the Union Grounds in Brooklyn on May 15, 1862, after converting a former skating rink at Lee and Rutledge Streets into a baseball ground. He provided the park to the leading clubs in the City of Brooklyn, then charged admission (initially 10 cents) to the general public to recoup his costs.

1899

Planned as a replacement for the now-closed Fleetwood in The Bronx, William H. Clark and James Butler open the Empire City Trotting Club, a harness track in Yonkers, N.Y., and over 12,000 fans are on hand for the first day's racing. But Clark dies after the inaugural season and the track remains largely unused until 1907, when Butler converts it to thoroughbred racing.

1904

Sabin W. Carr is born in Dubuque, Iowa. A Yale graduate, Carr won the 1928 Olympic gold medal in the pole vault and was three-time IC4A outdoor champion (1926-28). He was the first vaulter to clear 14 feet (14'1"), at the AAU indoor championships in 1928.

1918

William Franklin Talbert is born in Cincinnati, Ohio. Billy Talbert was a two-time U.S. national singles tennis finalist (1944-45), a respected author of tennis books and tournament director of the U.S. Open at Forest Hills from 1969-73.

1923

Sad Sam Jones becomes the first Yankee to pitch a winning shutout no-hitter, beating the Athletics, 2-0, at Philadelphia. Jones walks one and strikes out none.

1941

With a 6-3 win over the Red Sox at Boston, the Yankees clinch the American League pennant, the earliest pennant clinching date for a full season in league history. Skipper Joe McCarthy is back in New York recuperating from an illness and coach Art Fletcher manages the clincher.

1983

Buddy Young, an All-America halfback who starred for the AAFC Yankees from 1947-49 and the NFL Yanks in 1950-51, and became the first black executive for the NFL office when he was named director of player relations in 1964, dies near Dallas, Texas, at age 57.

1986

Sid Tanenbaum dies at age 60 in Far Rockaway, N.Y. A star guard with NYU from 1944-47 and winner of the Haggerty Award in 1946 and 1947 as the New York metropolitan area's best collegiate player, Tanenbaum played parts of two seasons with the Knicks.

1993

Lefty Jim Abbott, who has no right hand due to a birth defect, throws a no-hitter for the Yankees, beating Cleveland, 4-0, at Yankee Stadium.

1995

In a Giants Stadium ceremony on a Monday night, Phil Simms' #11 is the ninth Giants jersey retired, joining Ray Flaherty (1), Al Blozis (32), Ken Strong (50), Charley Conerly (42), Mel Hein (7), Y.A. Tittle (14), Joe Morrison (40) and Lawrence Taylor (56). In the game, Dallas crushes the Giants, 35-0.

1903

For the second time, Highlanders president Joseph W. Gordon challenges the Giants to a postseason series between the two teams. Giants president John T. Brush dismissed the first challenge, saying, "We do not know who these people are." Gordon retorts, "You may name any reasonable conditions and I will accept them. I wish to show the public the difference between baseball and ping-pong. When you (Brush) were keeping a small clothing store in Muncie, Indiana, I was a director of the New York baseball club (the Giants)." But Brush declines again.

1903

Winning the last of his three U.S. Amateur golf championships, Walter J. Travis triumphs, 2-up, over former champ Findlay S. Douglas at the Garden City (L.I.) GC.

1908

Brooklyn's Nap Rucker pitches a 6-0 no-hitter against Boston in the second game of a doubleheader at Washington Park.

1958

Donald Michael Maloney is born in Lindsay, Ontario. The younger brother of Rangers captain Dave, Don Maloney scored 195 goals and 307 assists in 653 games as a Ranger. He later played for and served as general manager of the Islanders before returning to the Rangers as assistant general manager in 1997.

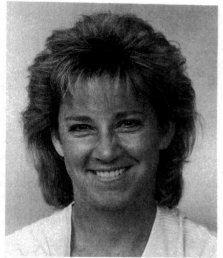

CHRIS EVERT

1966

Before a Labor Day crowd of 41,598 at Yankee Stadium, Pele and his Santos club of Brazil defeat Internazionale Milan, 4-1, with surprising ease. The gross gate is the largest in U.S. soccer history to date.

1975

After losing a women's singles semifinal match to eventual champion Chris Evert at the U.S. Open in Forest Hills, 18-year-old Martina Navratilova defects from her native Czechoslovakia, asking for political asylum in the U.S.

1978

1977 Triple Crown winner Seattle Slew is the odds-on favorite but Dr. Patches scores a major upset to win the Paterson Stakes at the Meadowlands.

1990

On his way to his first U.S. Open title, 19-year-old Pete Sampras, the No. 12 seed, thwarts Ivan Lendl's bid to reach a record-setting ninth straight final, beating the third seed, 6-4, 7-6, 3-6, 4-6, 6-2, in a quarterfinal match.

1996

In a U.S. Open quarterfinal match at humid Flushing Meadow, defending champion Pete Sampras, having already vomited twice in the fifth-set tiebreak against Alex Corretja, saves a match point at 6-7, hits a second serve ace for an 8-7 lead and wins the match when Corretja double-faults. Sampras goes on to win his fourth Open.

1899

Three of the leading harness horses in the East go head-to-head at the new Empire City Trotting Club on only its third day of racing (see Sept. 4). Joe Patchen beats Star Pointer with John R. Gentry third.

1912

Jeff Tesreau fires a no-hitter in a 3-0 victory for the Giants in the opening game of a doubleheader at Philadelphia.

1913

Jerome Travers again wins the U.S. Amateur Golf Championship, defeating John Anderson, 5 and 4, in the final match at the Garden City (L.I.) GC.

1924

Concluding a triumphant first tour in major Eastern events, the "world's fastest human," Charlie Paddock, ties world records in the 100-yard dash and the 220 on the same day. The California runner nips Loren Murchison in both events at the National AAU championships staged by the Newark AC at Colgate Field in West Orange, N.J. Paddock is clocked in 9.6 seconds for the 100 and 20.8 in the 220. With 44 points, the Illinois AC wins the team title with the NYAC second (36 points).

1951

Bowling great Joe Falcaro dies at age 55 in Cedarhurst, N.Y. Falcaro, based in Brooklyn, won the BPAA title four times in a row (1929-32) but failed to defend in 1933 when he was shot by a friend's husband. He later operated a bowling alley on West 181st Street in Manhattan.

CARL FURILLO

1953

After being hit by a Reuben Gomez pitch at the Polo Grounds, the Dodgers' Carl Furillo leaves first base and challenges Giants manager Leo Durocher. In the brawl that follows, Furillo breaks the fifth metacarpal bone (his pinky) in his left hand. He is out until the World Series but the injury proves a blessing as his average is frozen at .344. St. Louis' Red Schoendienst tries valiantly to catch Furillo, who wins the National League batting title with the Cardinal finishing at .342.

1975

Spain's Manuel Orantes saves five match points and rallies from a 5-0 fourth-set deficit to beat Guillermo Vilas of Argentina, 4-6, 1-6, 6-2, 7-5, 6-4, at Forest Hills in the second men's singles semifinal match at the U.S. Open, which ends late Saturday night. The next day, Orantes upsets No. 1 seed and defending champ Jimmy Connors in straight sets to take the title.

1981

Bob Lemon becomes Yankees manager for the second time, replacing Gene Michael.

1994

Fred Wilt dies at age 73 in Anderson, Indiana. A distance runner who staged legendary duels with Don Gerhmann in the mile, Wilt won the Columbian Mile in the Knights of Columbus Games in 1951 and 1952 at the Garden. A special agent for the FBI while he ran for the New York Athletic Club from 1949-54, Wilt won the Sullivan Award as the nation's top amateur athlete in 1950.

September 7

1889

Prompted by owner Chris Von der Ahe, who evidently (and correctly) believes that AA Brooklyn owner Charlie Byrne is planning to jump to the National League, the St. Louis Browns create a bizarre forfeit at Brooklyn's Washington Park. Manager and first baseman Charlie Comiskey, who argues every umpire's call for innings, pulls his team off the field with a 4-2 lead in the last of the ninth. Von der Ahe places candles along the foul line to support the manager's claim that it is too dark to continue. But fans among the 15,000 on hand put the candles out with beer and soda sprays. Umpire Fred Goldsmith waits five minutes after the Browns leave the field with two Brooklyn runners on base and then awards a 9-0 forfeit to the home team.

1903

Frank Kramer wins the national professional motorcycling title at Manhattan Beach, Brooklyn. Kramer beats Ivor Lawson by a half-length in the two-mile race. Mrs. Eva M. Rogers of Schenectady, N.Y., also makes history in the one-lap motorcycle skills competition. Mrs. Rogers is the first woman ever to compete for motorcycle honors in the U.S. but doesn't finish in the money.

1918

Carol Cudone is born in Oxford, Alabama. A top women's golfer, Mrs. Cudone won the women's Metropolitan Open five times from 1955-65 and the New Jersey Golf Association stroke play title 11 times in 16 years.

1928

Al McGuire, a St. John's product who played three seasons (1951-54) for the Knicks as a backup guard alongside his brother Dick, who later won an NIT (in 1970) and NCAA (1977) title as Marquette coach, and became even more famous as a television commentator, is born in New York. His son Allie played two games for the Knicks in the 1973-74 season.

1942

Ted Schroeder beats Frank Parker in five sets to win his only U.S. national men's singles championship. Owing to war-time travel restrictions, all five major championships (men's and women's singles and doubles, and mixed doubles) are held at a single site (Forest Hills) for the first time ever. This condition prevails through 1945, and then not again until 1969.

1947

After watching the Jersey City Giants beat the Baltimore Orioles, 6-3, most of the 18,332 fans remain patiently seated at Roosevelt Stadium listening to a radio broadcast of the Toronto-Montreal game. When Toronto rallies for a 6-5 win, eliminating the Royals, fans celebrate Jersey City's clinching of the International League pennant as the Giants complete an improbable last-to-first season after finishing in the International League cellar the year before. But the L'il Giants are eliminated in the first round of the playoffs by the Buffalo Bisons.

1953

Maureen Connolly completes the first women's Grand Slam, defeating Doris Hart, 6-2, 6-4, at Forest Hills, to take her third straight U.S. national women's singles championship.

1964

For the second game in a row, Tony Kubek leads off a game with a home run, this time starting the Yankees off to what proves to be a 5-4 victory in 11 innings against the Twins in Minnesota. Kubek also homered to open the Bombers' 3-2 win over the A's in Kansas City the day before.

1985

Frank (Bruiser) Kinard, a four-time all-NFL tackle with the Brooklyn Dodgers from 1938-44 who played for the AAFC Yankees in 1946-47, dies in Jackson, Mississippi, at age 70.

September 8

1935

Ted Coy, considered by both Parke Davis and Walter Camp the best fullback in college football's first half-century, dies in a New York Hospital of pneumonia at age 47. Coy, survived by his third wife (see May 24 and Aug. 26), was captain of the 1909 Yale team that included future Madison Square Garden president John Reed Kilpatrick.

1953

With a 10-2 victory over the second-place Braves in Milwaukee, their 12th win in 13 games, the Dodgers clinch the National League pennant on the earliest date in league history for a 154-game schedule. Karl Spooner's 5 $\frac{1}{3}$ innings of no-hit relief help boost Brooklyn's lead to 17 games over Milwaukee.

1957

In their last meeting as New York interborough rivals, the Giants beat the Dodgers, 3-2, at the Polo Grounds. A crowd of 22,376 watches as Hank Sauer's 25th homer, a two-run shot in the fourth inning off Don Drysdale, gives the Giants the lead for good. Curt Barclay gets the win with relief help from Marv Grissom.

1957

Althea Gibson defeats Louise Brough, 6-3, 6-2, at Forest Hills, to win the U.S. national women's singles title, becoming the first black, man or woman, to take the U.S. singles crown.

1968

Virginia Wade takes the first U.S. Open women's singles title, beating top-seeded Billie Jean King, 6-4, 6-4, at Forest Hills.

1969

Rod Laver completes his second, and history's fourth, tennis Grand Slam, beating fellow Aussie Tony Roche, 7-9, 6-3, 6-3, 6-2, on the soggy grass at Forest Hills. Laver's win, during which switches from sneakers to spikes after being broken when serving for the first set at 5-4, is seen by only 3,708 on this Monday. Rain delays the final by 95 minutes while a helicopter flies over Stadium Court to dry the surface. The next day, a throng of 135 see Ken Rosewall and Fred Stolle take the men's doubles final over Charlie Pasarell and Dennis Ralston.

1974

In the final U.S. national championships played on grass courts, 22-year-old Jimmy Connors completes one of the great single years in tennis history, crushing 39-year-old Ken Rosewall, 6-1, 6-0, 6-1, at Forest Hills, in the most lopsided men's singles final in the history of the U.S. Nationals. The next year, the championships are played on clay at Forest Hills before switching to hard court surfaces with the move to Flushing Meadow for the 1978 competition.

1993

Lillian Jenkins, director of public relations at Madison Square Garden during the 1960s, dies in New York.

1996

With 11:04 remaining the fourth quarter, the Indianapolis Colts' 21-7 win in the Jets' home opener at Giants Stadium is held up for 32 minutes by rain and lightning. The stoppage is the first in-game weather delay on record for an NFL regular-season game.

1996

In the last U.S. national singles championships played in Louis Armstrong Stadium at the National Tennis Center in Flushing Meadow, Pete Sampras routs Michael Chang, 6-1, 6-4, 7-6, for his fourth Open title, shortly after Steffi Graf beats Monica Seles in the women's final for the second straight year. In 1997, the new main stadium at the National Tennis Center is Arthur Ashe Stadium.

September 9

1895

Led by Thomas Curtain and Joseph Thum, 25 bowling proprietors form the American Bowling Congress in a meeting at Beethoven Hall in New York. The ABC promotes standard 10-pin rules and revives the sport.

1902

John T. Brush, one-time owner of the defunct Indianapolis, NL franchise, buys the Giants from Andrew Freedman, who has owned the club since January 24, 1895.

1916

Before the largest crowd ever yet to see a track meet in the United States, the AAU Nationals are run at Newark's Weequahic Park. Some 30,000 pack in to see New York's Irish-American AC score 35 points to the NYAC's 30 for the team title. George Bronder of the I-AAC sets an American record of 190' 6" in the javelin and Ican Meyers of the Illinois AC wins the mile in 4:22.

1948

Rex Barney survives a rainy night and wildness to pitch a 2-0 no-hit victory for Brooklyn against the Giants at the Polo Grounds.

1962

Rod Laver completes the second Grand Slam in men's tennis history, defeating fellow Australian Roy Emerson, 6-2, 6-4, 5-7, 6-4, to win the U.S. national singles final at Forest Hills.

1968

Arthur Ashe takes the first U.S. Open men's singles title, defeating the Netherlands' Tom Okker, 14-12, 5-7, 6-3, 3-6, 6-3, in the final at the West Side Tennis Club in Forest Hills. Ashe, who had won the U.S. Amateur championship at the Longwood Cricket Club in Boston earlier in the summer, is the first black man to win a major tennis championship and becomes the first (and to date last) amateur to win the Open. Okker cashes the $14,000 first-prize check anyway.

1979

Tracy Austin, at age 16 years, eight months, 28 days, becomes the youngest titlist in the history of the U.S. national singles, defeating Chris Evert Lloyd in the final, 6-4, 6-3. Mrs. Lloyd's loss ends at 31 her U.S. Open match winning streak. She had not been beaten since the 1974 semifinals by Evonne Goolagong on the grass at Forest Hills. Her streak is the second longest in the history of the women's U.S. Nationals (to Helen Wills Moody, 45, from 1927-33).

TRACY AUSTIN

1990

Pete Sampras, 19, becomes the youngest men's singles champion in the history of the U.S. Nationals, beating Andre Agassi in the U.S. Open final at Flushing Meadow, 6-4, 6-3, 6-2.

1995

Steffi Graf, playing despite injury and the imprisonment of her father in Germany on tax evasion charges, wins her fourth U.S. Open title, beating Monica Seles, 7-6, 0-6, 6-3, at Flushing Meadow. Seles returned to tennis in August after a 28-month absence caused when she was stabbed in the back in Hamburg and played her first Open since winning titles in 1991-92.

1995

Bill Esposito, an internationally-recognized authority on jazz music who was St. John's sports information director from 1961-84, dies in East Patchogue, N.Y., on his 67th birthday.

1890

Veteran John Clarkson pitches Boston to an 8-5 win as the Giants play their final game at the 157th Street Polo Grounds. After the end of the "Brotherhood War" this season, the NL Giants move into the immediately adjacent (and structurally superior) Brotherhood Park, which then becomes the Polo Grounds site occupied by the club until 1957 (and used by the Yankees from 1913-22 and Mets from 1962-63).

1916

In a Sunday exhibition game, the Giants beat the Yankees, 4-2, at the Polo Grounds before 20,000. The teams avoid the strict anti-sports Sunday laws by staging a concert of "religious and patriotic" songs before the game featuring popular singers Anna Fitziu and Hugh Allen with the Nahan Franko orchestra. The event is staged as a charity benefit for the *New York American* Fund for Needy Families. Still, the event shows that many New Yorkers crave sports and entertainment on Sunday, further eroding the law prohibiting such activities.

1933

Great Britain's Fred Perry thwarts Jack Crawford's bid to win the Grand Slam of tennis, beating the Australian, 6-3, 11-13, 4-6, 6-0, 6-1, in the U.S. national men's singles final at Forest Hills. The next Britain-Australian men's singles final at the U.S. Nationals takes place in 1997, with Aussie Patrick Rafter downing Canadian native, but British citizen, Greg Rusedski.

1954

Giants catcher Ray Katt sets an unwanted major league record by being charged with four passed balls in the eighth inning of the Cincinnati Reds' 8-1 win at the Polo Grounds. With knuckleballer Hoyt Wilhelm on in relief, Katt's passed balls allow two runs to score.

1961

A chapter in New Jersey sports history is closed as Jersey City defeats Richmond, 2-0, in an International League game at Roosevelt Stadium. It is the last Triple-A game played in New Jersey as the Jerseys finish seventh (70-82), missing the playoffs, and the franchise moves to Atlanta, Georgia, for the 1962 season. Lower minor classification leagues have teams in Jersey City as late as 1978 but the IL history that began in 1887 is over.

1969

Moving into first place for the first time in their eight-season history, the Mets sweep a twi-night doubleheader from Montreal at Shea Stadium, 3-2 in 12 innings and 7-1. A crowd of 23,512 watches as the Mets take a one-game lead over Chicago in the NL East and extend their winning streak to six games.

1978

Completing a four-game sweep that is instantly dubbed the "Boston Massacre," the Yankees beat the reeling Red Sox, 7-4, to move into a first-place tie with Boston in the AL East race and cap a comeback from a deficit as wide as 14 games as late as July 19. In the four games, New York beats Boston 15-3, 13-2, 7-0 and 7-4.

1987

Lou Lamoriello is named general manager of the New Jersey Devils, replacing Max McNab.

1988

Steffi Graf of West Germany completes the third Grand Slam in the history of women's tennis, taking her first U.S. Open title with a 6-3, 3-6, 6-1 final-round win over Argentina's Gabriela Sabatini at Flushing Meadow. Within a month, Graf would also win the gold medal at the Olympic Games in Seoul, South Korea. Graf reached the final a day earlier when food poisoning prevented Chris Evert from playing their scheduled semifinal match.

September 11

1898

In the first Sunday "home" game by a New York NL team, the Giants beat the Washington Senators, 8-2, at Weehawken, N.J. A crowd of 4,000 journeys across the Hudson River to see the game at the West New York Club Grounds. Prohibited by law from playing on Sunday in their own park, the Polo Grounds, the Giants try this method. The following Sunday, the Giants are the visitors as Brooklyn hosts a game rained out at Washington Park and moved to Weehawken. The Giants win, 7-3, before an even bigger crowd (more than 5,000) (see Aug. 19).

1915

Packey McFarland and Mike Gibbons battle to a 10-round no-decision before over 30,000 at the Brighton Beach Motordrome in Brooklyn. The outdoor promotion, staged by the Ocean Athletic Club and promoter William C. Marshall, is eagerly anticipated by boxing fans. Though the fight does not live up to its billing, sportswriters generally give Gibbons the edge.

1920

Charles (Chick) Evans becomes the U.S. Amateur golf champion with a 7 and 6 win over famed former U.S. Open winner Francis Ouimet at the Engineers' Country Club in Roslyn, L.I.

1924

Heavyweights Harry Wills and Argentina's Luis Angel Firpo fight a 12-round no-decision before 70,000 in Jersey City, N.J. The gross gate of $509,135 is the second-largest ever at Boyle's 30 Acres, the outdoor arena that was the site of boxing's first million-dollar-plus gate (see July 2).

1946

Cincinnati and the Dodgers play the longest scoreless tie in major-league history, a 19-inning duel at Ebbets Field. The Reds get 10 hits and Brooklyn eight in the four-hour, 40-minute marathon in front of 14,538 before the game is halted by darkness. Starter Johnny Vander Meer goes 15 for the Reds and Hal Gregg the first 10 for the Dodgers.

1960

AFL New York Titans open their first season with a 27-3 victory over the Buffalo Bills before 10,200 at the Polo Grounds.

1977

Guillermo Vilas wins the last U.S. national championship tennis match ever played at the West Side Tennis Club, defeating defending champion Jimmy Connors, 2-6, 6-3, 7-6, 6-0, on the clay at Forest Hills in the men's singles final. The next year, the United States Tennis Association abandons West Side, where U.S. championships had been held since 1915, for the city-owned National Tennis Center in Flushing Meadow.

1994

Unseeded Andre Agassi beats his fifth seeded opponent of the tournament, fourth-seed Michael Stich of Germany, 6-1, 7-6, 7-5, at Flushing Meadow, to win the U.S. Open men's singles title to become the first unseeded player, man or woman, to win a U.S. national singles title in the Open era (which began in 1968).

1997

John Olerud completes his cycle with a three-run eighth inning triple and lifts the Mets to a 9-5 victory over Montreal at Shea Stadium. Olerud has five RBI with his 4-for-4 game.

September 12

1890

John Montgomery Ward gets three hits as his Brooklyn Players League club beats first-place Boston, 8-7, in the last PL game at Eastern Park, shortened by rain after seven innings and seen by 700.

1899

Terry McGovern kayoes Pedlar Palmer in the first round to win the world bantamweight championship at Tuckahoe, N.Y. The outdoor bout had been postponed the day before by rain.

1908

Frank Kramer of East Orange, N.J., shows why he is considered bike racing's best sprinter with narrow wins over Australian champion A.J. Clarke in the National Cycling Association final at the Garden. Kramer comes home in 1:03 in the half-mile and finishes a half-wheel ahead of Clarke in the mile race, the highlight of the NCA championship program that also includes amateur events.

1928

Ernest Maurice Vandeweghe, Jr., is born. Vandeweghe averaged 9.5 ppg over six seasons (1949-54, 1955-56) with the Knicks. His son, Ernest III (better known as Kiki), also played for the Knicks.

KIKI VANDEWEGHE

1942

Max Lanier pitches a five-hitter and Whitey Kurowski hits a two-run homer off Max Macon as the Cardinals beat the Dodgers, 2-1, at Ebbets Field. The St. Louis win creates a first-place tie in the National League, wiping out Brooklyn's lead, which was 10 $\frac{1}{2}$ games on August 5. The next day, the Dodgers lose a doubleheader to Cincinnati and the Cardinals go into first place to stay.

1951

Sugar Ray Robinson regains his world middleweight championship with a 10th-round knockout of England's Randy Turpin before 61,370 to the Polo Grounds. The live gate of $767,626.17 and the total gross of $992,630 (including theatre, television and film rights) are the largest ever for a non-heavyweight championship fight.

1952

In his first professional fight, Floyd Patterson, the future heavyweight champion, records a second-round knock-out of Eddie Godbold at St. Nicholas Arena.

1964

In their first home game at Shea Stadium, the Jets beat Denver, 30-6, before a franchise-record crowd of 45,665 on a Saturday night. The old mark was 25,136 on October 15, 1961, when the Titans lost to San Diego, 25-10.

1977

Owner Roy Boe announces that the Nets are moving to New Jersey and will play at the Rutgers Athletic Center in Piscataway, N.J., until the completion of the new arena planned for the Meadowlands sports complex.

1984

Cosmos lose, 1-0, to the Sting, in Chicago, in their last NASL game ever.

1924

Once again led by Bobby Jones, Chick Evans, Francis Ouimet and Jess Sweetser, the U.S. finishes a 9-3 Walker Cup victory over Great Britain at the Garden City Golf Club.

1925

Dazzy Vance becomes the eighth Dodgers pitcher to throw a no-hitter, fanning nine and walking one to beat the Phils, 10-1, in the opener of a twinbill at Ebbets Field.

1926

Emile Francis, a one-time Rangers backup goalie (1948-52) who during his 12 years (1964-76) as general manager rebuilt a franchise moribund since World War II into a perennial contender, who coached the Blueshirts in more games (654) and to more wins (342) than anyone else, and who helped found the Metropolitan Junior Hockey League, is born in North Battleford, Saskatchewan.

1930

Tommy Armour defeats Gene Sarazen, 1-up, in a thrilling match for the PGA championship at the Fresh Meadows CC in Flushing.

1941

A six-man syndicate headed by William D. Cox announces that it has purchased the AFL team based in Yankee Stadium from Douglas G. Hertz, who was forced out by the league for failure to meet financial obligations. Cox also announces the team will be known as the Americans and Jack McBride, fired by Hertz, will remain as coach.

1949

Patty Berg is elected first president and the formation of the Ladies Professional Golf Association is announced in New York. Fred Corcoran, a former PGA executive, is the tour director and New York attorney Lee V. Eastman is legal counsel for the group, which initially includes, besides Berg, six top women pros including Babe Didrikson Zaharias, Betty Jameson and Helen Hicks. The announcement is the start of a battle with the three-year-old Women's PGA to take control of women's pro golf events.

1949

Jim Cleamons, the Cleveland guard whom the Knicks signed as a free agent in October 1977 and as compensation sent Walt Frazier to the Cavaliers, is born in Lincolnton, North Carolina.

1970

New York City fireman Gary Muhrcke, running for the Millrose AA, wins the first New York City Marathon organized by the New York Road Runners Club. Muhrcke is first out of the field of 126 who start the 26-mile, 385-yard run through Central Park this Sunday. The only woman starter, Nina Kuscsik, does 14.2 miles before dropping out but comes back to win the event twice (1972-73).

1970

For the second straight year, tennis sees an Australian complete the Grand Slam with a U.S. Open triumph at Forest Hills. Margaret Smith Court beats Rosemary Casals, 6-2, 2-6, 6-1, to take the women's singles final. Court also wins the women's doubles title (with Judy Dalton) and the mixed doubles crown (with Marty Riessen).

1981

For the first time since Bill Tilden took six U.S. national singles titles from 1920-25, a man wins a third straight. John McEnroe beats Bjorn Borg in the U.S. Open final at Flushing Meadow in four sets, just as he had at Wimbledon two months earlier. It is Borg's last appearance at a major championship.

September 14

1915

Yale wins the Intercollegiate golf championship for the 10th time in 11 years and the 13th time since 1897 at the Greenwich (Connecticut) CC. Princeton had broken Yale's nine-year winning streak the year before but the Elis recover the crown with a vengeance. Francis R. Blossom wins the individual title, 11 and 9, over Princeton's Grant A. Peacock, ending the 36-hole match on just the ninth hole of the afternoon round.

1929

Bill Tilden, 36, completes his dramatic run to the U.S. national men's singles title by beating Frank Hunter, 3-6, 6-3, 4-6, 6-2, 6-4 in the final at Forest Hills. It is his seventh (and last) U.S. singles title, tying the record set by Richard Sears (1881-87) and equaled by Bill Larned (1901-02, 1907-11).

1930

Losing to the Spartans, 13-6, at Portsmouth, Ohio, the Newark Tornadoes begin their only season in the NFL.

1940

Richard D. Chapman decisively defeats W.B. McCullough, Jr., 11 and 9, to win the U.S. Amateur golf championship at the Winged Foot GC in Mamaroneck, N.Y.

1946

In their first AAFC home opener, the Football Yankees defeat the Buffalo Bisons, 21-10, at Yankee Stadium. Coach Ray Flaherty's club had opened the season at San Francisco with a 21-7 win over the 49ers.

HORACE DAVENPORT

1946

In the first U.S. Amateur golf championship since 1941, Stanley E. (Ted) Bishop wins the title with a 1-up victory over Smiley L. Quick on the first extra hole at the Baltusrol GC. Like many other sports events, the U.S. Amateur was suspended during World War II.

1959

New Aqueduct racetrack opens after a reconstruction costing $34.5 million.

1972

Arthur (Bull) Hancock, owner of Claiborne Farm, breeder of such horses as Kelso, Nashua, Round Table and Bold Ruler, dies at age 62. Hancock is considered by some the greatest thoroughbred breeder in U.S. racing history.

1974

Graig Nettles and brother Jim both homer at Detroit, Graig off Mickey Lolich in the first inning and Jim off Pat Dobson in the second, as Graig's Yankees beat Jim's Tigers, 10-7.

1994

With major league baseball players on strike since August 12, club owners vote to cancel the remainder of the regular season, the playoffs and the World Series. It is the first time the Series will not be played since 1904.

1894

Domino, winner of 19 of his 25 career races, runs a dead heat with Henry of Navarre II in a match race at Brooklyn's Gravesend. Both horses cover the mile-and-an-eighth in 1:55.5 and divide the $5,000 purse.

1900

Ernest Roeber regains his world Greco-Roman wrestling championship by defeating Denmark's Beck Olsen before 14,000 in Copenhagen. Olsen had wrestled the crown away from Roeber earlier in the year.

1915

Hans Ohrt, the reigning national and world amateur champion, is clocked in 1:53.4 for a mile in a bike race at the Newark Velodrome, the fastest ever in track competition for an amateur. It is not recognized as a record because Ohrt, starting from scratch, does not win the race, finishing third in the handicap event, unable to make up the distance allowed his competitors at the start.

1921

Babe Ruth sets a record for homers in a season, hitting his 55th off St. Louis lefthander Bill Bayne in the opening game of a doubleheader at the Polo Grounds, a 10-6 Yankee win.

1950

For a record sixth time in his career, Johnny Mize slams three homers in a game (driving in six runs), but the Tigers hold off the Yankees, 9-7, at Detroit's Briggs Stadium.

1958

George (Snuffy) Stirnweiss, Yankees infielder (1943-50) and 1945 American League batting champ, dies at age 39 in Newark, N.J., when the Central Railroad of New Jersey commuter train on which he is riding drives onto an open lift bridge and plunges into Newark Bay.

1978

Playing its first varsity football game in 47 years, St. John's is beaten by Kean College, 20-7, in a night game in Union, N.J. The Redmen had dropped football after the 1931 season because of financial constraints (see Apr. 29) and revive it at the Division III level after several successful seasons of club-status teams.

1983

Tennis official Dick Wertheim, 61, dies in New York. Wertheim, seated as center linesman during the boys' singles final at the U.S. Open Sept. 10, had been hit by a shot from Stefan Edberg, fell backward and struck his head on the hard court surface.

1991

Andre Baruch dies in Beverly Hills, California, at age 83. Baruch was a radio and television announcer for the Brooklyn Dodgers from 1954-57. He also also an announcer on such famous radio programs as "The Shadow," "Your Hit Parade" and "Kate Smith."

1991

Horace Davenport, star rower on the Columbia 1927 and 1929 IRA champions, dies in Manchester-by-the-Sea, Massachusetts, at age 84.

1993

Ethan Allen, a Giants outfielder who coached Yale for 23 seasons (1946-68), dies in Brookings, Oregon, at age 89. Allen's 1947 and 1948 squads played in (and lost) the College World Series, when the regular first baseman was future president George Bush.

September 16

1897

Louis Phal, who as Battling Siki became world light heavyweight champion from 1922-23, is born in St. Louis, Senegal, at the time part of French West Africa.

1911

Harold L. Hilton goes 37 holes to defeat Fred Herreshoff, 1-up, for the U.S. Amateur golf championship at the Apawamis Club in Rye, N.Y. The extra hole is needed to break a tie after the regulation 36 holes in the championship match.

1914

James E. Sullivan dies in New York at age 51. Sullivan was a founder of the AAU and founded the American Sports Publishing Company in 1893, publishers of the famous Spalding annual guides in most major sports. The Sullivan Award is given annually in his honor to the nation's premier amateur athlete.

1919

James Lansing, All-America end at Fordham in 1941, and Rams coach who led the program out of club status and into Div. III in 1970, is born in Mount Vernon, N.Y.

1920

Billy Southworth's first-inning single is the only hit allowed by Art Nehf and no Pirate advances beyond first base (Nehf walks one) as the Giants salvage a split of a doubleheader with a 4-0 win over Pittsburgh at the Polo Grounds.

1924

St. Louis slugger Sunny Jim Bottomley sets a major league record with 12 RBI as the Cardinals clout the Dodgers, 17-3, at Ebbets Field. Bottomley has six hits, including a grand slam in the fourth, a two-run homer (in the sixth) and an RBI double.

1938

James Larry Grantham is born in Crystal Springs, Mississippi. Larry Grantham, a linebacker, was the only Titan selected in the first AFL draft who played for the 1969 Super Bowl Jets.

WILLIE MOSCONI

1942

Dennis Conner is born. Conner successfully defended the America's Cup for the New York Yacht Club with *Freedom* in 1980 but became the first U.S. skipper to lose the Cup, with *Liberty* in 1983. Conner, then sailing for the San Diego Yacht Club, regained the Cup for the U.S. with *Stars & Stripes* in 1987.

1948

Rosemary Casals, four-time U.S. nationals doubles champion and a strong promoter of women's tennis at the dawn of the Open era that began in 1968, is born in San Francisco.

1969

Charles Johnston, who managed boxers Sandy Saddler and Archie Moore and was a wrestling promoter at Madison Square Garden, dies in New York at age 74.

1993

Billiards champion Willie Mosconi dies in Haddon Heights, N.J., at age 80.

September 17

1898

Findlay S. Douglas, later a president of the USGA, wins the U.S. Amateur golf championship, 5 and 3, over Walter B. Smith. Douglas and Smith are the survivors from 120 entrants at the Morris County GC in Morristown, N.J.

1910

Clifford Earl Montgomery is born in Natrona Heights, Pennsylvania. Cliff Montgomery was quarterback and captain of the 1933 Columbia football team that won the 1934 Rose Bowl (see Jan. 1). The next year he played for the Brooklyn Football Dodgers and in later years was an Eastern college football official.

1920

George Burns hits for the cycle and collects an extra double in the Giants' 10-inning, 4-3 win over Pittsburgh at the Polo Grounds. He finishes 5-for-5.

1930

In their NFL home opener, the Newark Tornadoes lose to the Football Giants, 32-0.

1934

Maureen Catherine Connolly is born in San Diego, California. Winner of the Grand Slam in 1953 and three U.S. national singles tennis titles at Forest Hills (1951-53), "Little Mo" (as powerful in her own way as "Big Mo," the Battleship Missouri), had her career cut short when hit by a truck while riding a horse in 1954 and died of cancer at age 34.

1945

Phil Jackson is born in Deer Lodge, Montana. A slender 6'8" forward who appeared to be all knees and elbows, Jackson, the Knicks' second choice (after Walt Frazier) in the 1967 NBA draft, was a reserve on the 1972-73 titlists (though a member of the 1969-70 club, he missed the entire season after spinal fusion surgery). After 10 seasons with the Knicks, he played his last two years (1978-80) with the Nets. He later coached Michael Jordan and the Chicago Bulls to six NBA titles in eight seasons.

1946

In the opening game of the Negro World Series, the Kansas City Monarchs of the Negro American League defeat the Newark Eagles of the Negro National League, 2-1, before 19,423 at the Polo Grounds. Satchel Paige gets the win in relief with eight strikeouts (and four hits allowed) in the final four innings. Newark loses third baseman Clarence Israel, who dislocates a kneecap diving into the box seats to catch a foul in the third inning (see Sept. 29).

1961

For the first time in the franchise's 36-year history, the Football Giants open at home, losing to the St. Louis Cardinals, 21-10, at Yankee Stadium.

1984

Mets rookie Dwight Gooden fans 16 but loses, 2-1, at Philadelphia. His strikeouts give him 32 in two straight starts, tying a major league record. On Sept. 12, he whiffed 16 Pirates.

1986

With a 4-2 win over the Cubs at Shea Stadium, the Mets, with 17 games left in the regular season, clinch the National League East title. They finish with a 108-54 record, the best in club history.

September 18

1886

Godfrey M. Brinley wins the singles title with a 6-0, 6-2, 6-3 victory over J.F. Bacon at the Orange (N.J.) Lawn Tennis Club tennis tournament. National champion Richard Sears and partner James Dwight, immediate past president of the USNLTA, win the doubles, 6-1, 6-2, 6-1, over Bacon and J.M. Thomas.

1886

Malcolm W. Ford of the New York Athletic Club begins his dominance of America's decathlon national championship, winning the N4A event at the Mott Haven Grounds. Ford wins five events outright, ties for first in the pole vault (9'3") and is second in the 56-pound weight throw. He doesn't bother running the mile but still has 45 points to the 26-point totals of runners-up Alexander A. Jordan (Manhattan AC) and teammate J.P. Thornton (see June 10).

1890

On the final day of the only Players League season, Brooklyn holds off a three-run, ninth-inning rally to beat New York, 8-7, before 3,642 at Brotherhood Park (home to the National League Giants beginning in 1891). Brooklyn (72-50) finishes second in the Players League race, while New York (68-51) is third.

1903

Frederick Joseph Cook is born in Kingston, Ont. Bun Cook, an original Ranger for 10 years, played left wing on the team's top line with he and his brother Bill on the right flanking Frank Boucher as the Rangers won the Stanley Cup in 1928 and 1933.

1911

Larry Doyle steals home in the three-run first and again in the four-run second as the Giants whip the Pirates, 7-2, at Pittsburgh's Forbes Field. The second steal of home comes when the plate is left uncovered after a wild pitch with the bases loaded scores two runs.

1912

Sarah Hammond Palfrey is born in Sharon, Massachusetts. Sarah Palfrey (who later added last names Fabyan, Cooke and Danzig) twice won the U.S. national singles title at Forest Hills (1941, '45), and the doubles crown nine times. She also handled broadcast duties during the Knicks' first radiocast, teaming with Marty Glickman in St. Louis on WHN November 7, 1946, as the Knicks beat the Bombers, 68-63, in their third game.

1918

Henry Wittenberg is born in New York. Wittenberg won AAU national wrestling titles seven times from 1940-52, twice as a middleweight and five times as a light heavyweight and a gold medal in 1948 and silver medal in 1952 at the Olympics. He also coached wrestling at CCNY from 1968-78.

1926

In one of the major golf upsets of the 1920s, George von Elm defeats Bobby Jones, the two-time defender, 8 and 7, for the U.S. Amateur title at the Baltusrol GC. Jones won four of the five Amateurs from 1924-28, his only loss coming in this match.

1963

In the final major league baseball game ever played at the Polo Grounds, the Mets lose a Wednesday afternoon game to the Philadelphia Phillies, 5-1.

1982

For the fifth (and final) time, the Cosmos capture the NASL championship, winning Soccer Bowl '82, 1-0, over Seattle at San Diego. Just 22,634 are on hand as Giorgio Chinaglia gets the game's only goal.

1896

The first marathon ever in America is won by John J. McDermott of the Pastime AC. It is run at 25 miles from the Armory (South and Main Streets) in Stamford, Connecticut, and finishes at the Columbia Oval in Williamsbridge (now The Bronx) as part of the annual outdoor games of the Knickerbocker AC. Johnny McDermott leads a field of 30 with a clocking of 3:25.55. Hamilton Gray of the St. George AC finishes second by two minutes. Eugene Estoppey, Jr., of the Mount Vernon CC is third, 11 minutes behind the leader, and the Knickerbockers' E.H. Baynes fourth. In other events, Dick Sheldon of Yale sets a discus record with a toss of 111'8" and Thomas Burke of the Boston AA wins the 440 in 1:11. Even though the standard marathon distance is increased to 26 miles, 385 yards in 1908, the KAC continues to run at 25 miles until the race is discontinued in 1932.

1908

Jerome Travers wins the first of his four U.S. Amateur golf titles, defeating Max H. Behr, 8 and 7, at the Garden City GC.

1914

Mrs. Katharine Harley Jackson wins the U.S. Women's Amateur golf championship, defeating Elaine Rosenthal, 1-up, at the Nassau CC in Glen Cove, L.I.

1914

Brooklyn's Ed Lafitte pitches the first Federal League no-hitter as the Tip Tops beat Kansas City, 6-2, in the opening game of a doubleheader at Washington Park. Lafitte walks eight, hits a batter and strikes out only one. The Brookfeds also win the second game, 12-6.

1922

William Papaleo is born in Middletown, Connecticut. As Willie Pep, he was two-time featherweight champion (1942-48, 1949-50) who won 230 of 242 career bouts.

1925

Bill Tilden captures his sixth straight U.S. national men's singles tennis title, beating Little Bill Johnston in the final for the fourth straight year, 4-6, 11-9, 6-3, 4-6, 6-3. On August 25, 19-year-old Helen Wills won her third straight women's singles crown, beating Kitty McKane of Great Britain, 3-6, 6-0, 6-2. From 1924-34, the men's and women's singles competitions (which before had been held at different sites) are staged at Forest Hills, but never concurrently.

1925

Helen Filkey of Chicago, generally considered America's best female athlete, wins the 60-yard hurdles in nine seconds flat despite a one-yard penalty for a false start, in the highlight of New York's first women's track meet, sponsored by the *Evening Graphic*, at City College's Lewisohn Stadium. Miss Filkey narrowly beats Hazel Kirk of Newark's Prudential AA at the finish. The Paterson (N.J.) Recreation Centre wins the team trophy with 25 points to 20 for Prudential. Over 200 young women compete.

1936

At the Garden City GC, John W. Fischer survives a field of 208 starters and a 37th hole in the championship match to win the U.S. Amateur, defeating Jack McLean, 1-up, in the final.

1936

Al Oerter, a New York Athletic Club member who won four Olympic gold medals in the shotput (1956-68), is born in New York.

1913

Newark wins the International League pennant for the first time with a 2-1 victory over Jersey City in the opening game of a doubleheader at Weidenmeyer Park. The Indians win their final five games, closing with a 5-4 triumph at Jersey City the next day.

1919

Jim Barnes waits three years but successfully defends his PGA championship, turning back Fred McLeod, 5 and 4, at the Engineers Country Club in Roslyn, L.I. Barnes won the inaugural tournament in 1916 but no competition was held the next two years because of World War I. Barnes had won three major pro events this season (the Southern, the Western and the North-South) before his 32-hole win in the PGA final.

1940

Andrew Ponzi closes out his pocket billards match with Onofrio Lauri at Julian's 14th Street Academy, 125-65. Ponzi has a high run of 57 to Lauri's 47 and wins the five-inning match, 520-468.

1951

Ford C. Frick is elected commissioner of baseball, succeeding A.B. (Happy) Chandler, after owners refuse to renew Chandler's contract.

1958

Orioles knuckleballer Hoyt Wilhelm no-hits the Yankees, 1-0, at Memorial Stadium in Baltimore.

BOB GUTKOWSKI

1969

Pittsburgh's Bob Moose temporarily derails the Mets' express to the NL Eastern Division title, no-hitting New York, 4-0, at Shea Stadium.

1973

Nets trade John Baum and Jim Ard to the Memphis Tams for forward Larry Kenon.

1982

In the last game played before what would become a 57-day NFL players' strike, the Green Bay Packers beat the Football Giants, 27-19, on a Monday night at Giants Stadium, dropping the Giants to 0-2.

1991

Devils trade captain Kirk Muller and goalie Roland Melanson to the Canadiens for right wings Stephane Richer and Tom Chorske.

1994

Bob Gutkowski is dismissed as president of the Garden by the new owners (ITT/Cablevision) and Knicks president Dave Checketts is appointed interim president.

September 21

1895

In the first international amateur track and field meet ever, the New York Athletic Club faces the London AC before 10,000 at Manhattan Field, 155th Street and 8th Avenue. The NYAC wins all 11 events with Bernie Wefers setting a world record in the 220-yard run (21.6 seconds) and equaling the world mark in the 100 (9.8 seconds). Charles Kilpatrick wins the 880 in record time (1:53.4) and Mike Sweeney sets a high jump record (6'5 $^5/_8$"). Tommy Conneff of the Manhattan AC becomes the first American to set the world record in the mile (4:18.2), beating fellow American George Orton (4:27.6) and Englishman William Lutyens. Later the same day, Conneff wins the three-mile and is then carried off the field exhausted.

1906

Bertrand Freishon, a 16-year-old apprentice jockey, is killed in a three-horse collision during the fifth race at Brooklyn's Gravesend track. Freishon's mount, Joe Levy, is bumped by Sonoma Belle, George Burns up, and both horses go down, throwing their riders. Louie H., ridden by Charlie Basquite, then goes down trying to leap over the fallen horses. Burns and Basquite are hospitalized but recover. Freishon is New York's second racing fatality of the season.

1930

In their first NFL game ever, the Brooklyn Football Dodgers play a scoreless tie with the Bears at Chicago's Wrigley Field.

1948

France's Marcel Cerdan wins the middleweight championship with a TKO of Tony Zale, who fails to answer the bell for the 12th round at Jersey City's Roosevelt Stadium, as 19,272 pay a gross gate of $242,840 for the Tournament of Champions promotion. The next day, 70-year-old Hudson County Police Chief Patrick Dolan, who worked 20 hours on the day of the fight to supervise traffic and crowd control, dies of a stroke in front of Kearny, N.J., police headquarters.

1970

In the first regular-season Monday Night Football game televised on ABC, the Jets lose to the Browns, 31-21, in the season opener at Cleveland.

1980

Richard Todd completes an NFL-record 42 passes (for 447 yards and three touchdowns), but the Jets, playing catch-up all day, lose, 37-27, to San Francisco at Shea Stadium.

1987

Arbitrator Thomas J. Roberts announces that he has sustained the grievance filed on behalf of 62 major league players who became free agents after the 1985 baseball season. Roberts rules that team owners conspired to restrict player movement in violation of the 1976 Basic Agreement between owners and players.

1989

Tony Sparando dies in Rego Park, N.Y., at age 83. Sparando, despite severely impaired vision, was a bowling standout for over 20 years who won the American Bowling Congress championship in 1954, the New York State All-Events, the Peterson Classic and the Landgraf Classic.

1995

Tony Cuccinello, an infielder with the major-league Brooklyn Dodgers (1932-35) and Giants (1940), and the semi-pro Bushwicks (1946-47), dies in Tampa, Florida, at age 87.

September 22

1901
Frank Kramer wins the 25-mile feature race at the Newark (N.J.) Velodrome in Vallsburg, N.J., with Floyd McFarland second. Kramer is timed in 58:35.4 for the distance before 5,000 fans.

1904
By winning their 100th game with 15 to play, the Giants clinch the pennant, beating Cincinnati, 7-5, in the first game of a Polo Grounds doubleheader. Former Giant Jim O'Rourke, now a 52-year-old lawyer in Bridgeport, Connecticut, catches Joe McGinnity in the clincher and is 1-for-4 at the plate. Cincinnati takes the nightcap, 7-3, while O'Rourke watches from the stands.

1920
Bob Lemon, the great Cleveland Indians righthander who managed the Yankees to the 1978 World Series title, is born in San Bernardino, California.

1961
To celebrate the 75th International Race, the six-day bikes return to the Garden for the first time since 1939, but the event becomes a fiasco when the prefabricated track doesn't fit and the start of the race is pushed back to 2:00 a.m. September 23.

1967
One-time world wrestling champion Stanislaus Zbyszko, 87, dies in St. Joseph, Missouri.

1982
Dusty DeStefano dies of a heart attack at Yankee Stadium in The Bronx at age 64. DeStefano was St. John's basketball coach between the Frank McGuire and second Joe Lapchick regimes (1952-56), compiling a 49-38 record over four seasons.

1987
Two games into the season, the NFLPA strikes the NFL, causing the games of the weekend of September 26-27 to be canceled. But club owners respond by forming "replacement teams" of free agents and non-striking veterans to play the schedule starting October 4 (see Oct. 15). In the last game before the strike, the Jets whip the New England Patriots, 43-24, on Monday night, September 21, at Giants Stadium.

1988
Abe Greene, sports editor of the *Paterson Evening News*, New Jersey State Athletic Commissioner, and president (in 1943) and commissioner (in 1948) of the National Boxing Association, dies in Paterson, N.J., at age 89.

1990
In the 10th annual Fifth Avenue Mile, PattiSue Plumer sets a women's record, breezing home in 4:16.68, surpassing the mark set by Maricia Puica (4:19.48) in 1984. Peter Elliott wins the men's elite division (3:52.95) for the second straight year and the third in the last four.

1994
Irving Mitchell Felt, chairman and chief executive officer of Madison Square Garden when the Garden moved in 1968 from its location at 49th Street and Eighth Avenue to 33rd Street and Seventh Avenue, dies at age 84.

September 23

1903

Prince Alert, a 12-year-old bay gelding driven by Jack Curry, sets a record of 1:57 for the mile, running against time at the Empire City track in Yonkers, N.Y.

1908

Famous as "Merkle's Boner," Fred Merkle's failure to touch second after Al Bridwell's single, which apparently scores the winning run in the bottom of the ninth against Chicago at the Polo Grounds, results in umpire Hank O'Day calling Merkle out when Cubs second baseman Johnny Evers steps on second with a ball. National League president Harry Pulliam rules the game a 1-1 tie and eventually a rematch is played (see Oct. 8). On July 29, 1909, Pulliam commits suicide, in part due to the controversy over his ruling.

1915

William (Brickyard) Kennedy dies in Bellaire, Ohio, at age 46. Kennedy was 174-150 in 10 years (1892-1901) with Brooklyn, including 22-8 in 1899 and 20-10 in 1900.

1916

At Travers Island, Fred W. Kelly of the Los Angeles AC wins the national AAU pentathlon championship, run in conjunction with the annual outdoor games of the New York Athletic Club.

1937

A crowd of 32,600 turns out to see boxing's "Carnival of Champions" at the Polo Grounds. In the world bantamweight title bout, Harry Jeffra decisions Sixto Escobar in 15 rounds. Lou Ambers retains his lightweight crown in 15 rounds over Pedro Montanez and Barney Ross defends his welterweight diadem, also in 15, outpointing Ceferino Garcia. Freddie Apostoli KOs Marcel Thil at 44 seconds of the 10th in what should have been a middleweight title bout, but the New York State Athletic Commission withholds recognition of this bout as a championship. Mike Jacobs' successful promotion (the gate is $232,643.35) enables him to move his 20th Century Sporting Club promotion organization into Madison Square Garden a month later.

1939

Cookie Lavagetto becomes the last Brooklyn Dodger to get six hits in a game in a 22-4 rout of the Phillies in the first game of a doubleheader at Shibe Park. Lavagetto has a double, triple and four singles but is the only Dodger without an RBI in the 27-hit assault. He is walked by Ike Pearson in the ninth, losing his shot at a record seven straight hits.

1939

Resuming football after an eight-year hiatus, LIU trounces Brooklyn College, 26-0, before 9,480 in a night game at Ebbets Field. Bob Trocolar throws a 29-yard pass to Dolly King for a first-quarter touchdown and runs for another in the fourth quarter.

1948

Edward Bayard Moss, a former sports editor of *The Sun*, who founded *The Associated Press* sports department in 1913, dies in Niantic, Massachusetts, at age 74. The Brooklyn-born Moss started his newspaper career in Syracuse, N.Y., joined *The Sun* in 1900, served as general sports editor of the *AP* from 1913 to 1923 and then became the first executive secretary of the U.S. Lawn Tennis Association until ill health forced his retirement in 1942.

1973

In their final game at Yankee Stadium, the Football Giants rally to tie the Philadelphia Eagles, 23-23. The Giants had moved to the Stadium for the 1956 season after 31 years in the Polo Grounds but are forced out by renovations to the Stadium and play their five remaining home games that year at the Yale Bowl.

1921

James Kenneth McManus is born in Philadelphia, Pennsylvania. As Jim McKay, he became the first television sportscaster ever to an Emmy (1968) and the first to win two (1973). He was with CBS from 1960-71 and ABC from 1971, and worked major events including the Olympics, Triple Crown horse races and "Wide World of Sports," ABC's sports anthology show.

1927

Mrs. Miriam Burns Horn wins the U.S. Women's Amateur golf title with a 5 and 4 victory over 20-year-old Maureen Orcutt at the Cherry Valley Club in Garden City, N.Y.

1938

After six days of rain that force the U.S. men's singles final to its latest date ever, Don Budge defeats Gene Mako, 6-3, 6-8, 6-2, 6-1, to complete the first Grand Slam in tennis history. In the women's final, Alice Marble tops Australia's Nancye Wynne, 6-0, 6-3, in 22 minutes.

1948

Long-time boxing manager Bill McCartney dies in New York at age 76.

1950

Thomas Angelo Lombardo, a football player at Army (1942-44) and Cadets assistant coach in 1947, dies in Korea at age 27.

1957

On a Tuesday, a crowd of 6,702 shows up for a night game at Ebbets Field that proves to be the last major league baseball game ever played in Brooklyn. The Dodgers beat the Pirates, 2-0, behind Danny McDevitt. Gil Hodges is the last Dodger to bat and he strikes out (swinging) in the home eighth. Organist Gladys Goodding, an Ebbets Field fixture since 1939, plays "Auld Lang Syne" at the finish.

DON BUDGE

1969

Behind the shutout pitching of Gary Gentry, who throws a six-hitter, and homers by Donn Clendenon and Ed Charles, the Mets clinch the National League East title in their last home game of the season with a 6-0 victory over St. Louis before 54,928 at Shea Stadium. The season's home attendance for 70 dates is a club-record 2,175,373.

1972

Joe Namath completes 15 of 28 for club-records 496 yards and six touchdowns as the Jets beat the Colts, 44-34, at Baltimore. Rich Caster had three touchdown catches.

1980

Franz Beckenbauer's farewell game draws 71,413 to Giants Stadium but the Cosmos lose, 3-2, to the NASL All-Stars.

1866

Jerome Park, perhaps the most sociologically significant racetrack ever built in America, is opened by the American Jockey Club in what is now The Bronx. Led by socially-prominent Leonard W. Jerome (a part-owner of *The New York Times*), builders of the new track include the elite of New York life, making thoroughbred racing not just respectable but desirable for the "400." R.A. Alexander's colt Bayswater wins the first race, a 1 $^1/_4$-mile run for three-year olds, in 2:17 flat.

1901

A combined Harvard-Yale team wins six of nine events against an Oxford-Cambridge combination before 6,500 at Berkeley Oval atop Morris Heights. Yale's Jim Spraker takes the high jump and broad jump while Rev. H.W. Workman, a Cambridge grad student, takes the half-mile and two-mile runs.

1926

Walter Hagen wins another PGA championship with a 5 and 3 victory over Leo Diegel at the Salisbury Golf Club in Salisbury Plains (now Westbury), L.I.

1927

Carl Braun is born in Brooklyn. Braun, a forward, averaged 14.1 ppg in 740 games over 12 seasons for the Knicks (1947-61, missing two seasons—1950-52—due to military service). He led the team in scoring seven times and served as player-coach for the final 48 games (19-29) of 1959-60 and all of 1960-61 (21-58).

1929

Yankees manager Miller Huggins dies in New York at age 50 with 13 games left in the season and the Bombers in second place in the American League. Huggins, manager since 1918, led the Bombers to their first six pennants (1921-23, 26-28) and three World Series (1923, 1927, 1928).

1933

Ring W. Lardner, a sportswriter who authored the baseball book *You Know Me, Al*, articles for the *Saturday Evening Post*, sketches and lyrics for the Ziegfeld Follies, and (with George Kaufman) the hit play *June Moon*, dies in East Hampton, N.Y., at age 48.

1956

Sal Maglie, long-time archenemy when hurling for the Giants, becomes the last Brooklyn Dodger to pitch a no-hitter, beating Philadelphia, 5-0, at Ebbets Field.

1973

"Willie Mays, it's time to say good-bye to America," the great star tells a crowd of 56,603 at Shea Stadium. Mays, a long-time New York fan favorite finishing out his career with the Mets, had announced his retirement five days earlier. The Mets, involved in a weird pennant race, beat the Montreal Expos, 2-1, behind lefthander Jerry Koosman to keep their precarious hold on first place in the National League East.

1975

Bob Considine dies in New York at age 68. A famed sportswriter who worked for the *New York American*, *Daily Mirror*, *Journal-American*, International News Service and *World Journal Tribune*, Considine authored biographies of Jack Dempsey, Babe Ruth and Toots Shor. At his death, his column was syndicated to 105 newspapers.

1977

Presaging their move in 1984 to the Meadowlands, the Jets open their home regular season schedule at Giants Stadium, and 43,439 see them lose to the Baltimore Colts, 20-12.

September 26

1925

At a special Board of Governors meeting in New York, a deal is finally approved to bring the NHL to the "new" Garden (No. 3). The New York Hockey Club is allowed to buy the players suspended from the Hamilton (Ontario) club after having broken off efforts to buy the club itself September 15. The new club will be known as the Americans (see Dec. 2 and Dec. 15).

1926

It takes only 2:07 for the Yankees to complete a doubleheader at St. Louis with the sluggish first game taking a boring 1:12 before the nightcap is completed in 55 minutes. The Browns take both games, 6-1 and 6-2, from the pennant-winning Bombers.

1936

Inaugurating the new Municipal Stadium on Randalls Island for football, Manhattan defeats St. Bonaventure, 32-7, as Vic Fusia stars with an 88-yard interception return and three touchdown passes. The Jaspers move back to their regular home at Ebbets Field for a 33-7 win over Niagara on October 2 despite drawing over 10,000 at Randalls Island.

1948

Israel's national soccer team becomes the first representative of the new nation to appear in the U.S., losing 3-1 to the American Olympic team before 25,000 at the Polo Grounds. Eddie Souza scores two goals for the U.S.

1953

William Woodward, owner of the Belair Stud breeding farm that produced horse racing Triple Crown winners Gallant Fox (1930) and Omaha (1935), dies at age 77.

1954

Karl Spooner pitches his second straight shutout and sets a big-league record with 27 strikeouts in the first two starts of his career. He downs Pittsburgh, 1-0, at Ebbets Field, fanning 12, after breaking in September 22 with a three-hitter against the Giants in which he struck out 15.

1964

Mel Stottlemyre is five-for-five and hurls a shutout as the Yankees, closing in on a fifth straight pennant, whip the Senators, 7-0, before 7,642 at Griffith Stadium in Washington.

1965

Joe Namath starts his first regular-season game as Jets quarterback and throws for 287 yards and two touchdowns at Buffalo, but the Bills beat New York, 33-21.

1980

Thoroughbred owner and breeder, and occasional steeplechase rider, A.C. Bostwick dies in Old Westbury, N.Y., at age 79.

1981

South African Sydney Maree of Villanova wins the first Fifth Avenue Mile in a startling 3:47.52, the second fastest time ever. Running downtown from 82nd Street, 13 runners in the elite men's field produce 10 sub-four-minute times with Mike Boit of Kenya (3:49.59) second, Dr. Thomas Westinghage of West Germany (3:50.48) third and Steve Cram of Great Britain (3:50.78) fourth. Leann Warren of the University of Oregon wins the women's race in 4:25.31. An estimated 150,000 line the 20-block route and produce a roaring wall of cheers for the runners. Only times made on running tracks are eligible for world recognition since running without curves can be expected to produce faster times. Yet the straight course down Fifth Avenue has some ups and downs of its own, not to mention a few grates and potholes not normally found on running tracks.

1847

Mike Donovan is born in Chicago. Generally recognized as the first middleweight boxing champion under the Marquis of Queensberry rules (1881), Donovan later became a boxing instructor at the New York Athletic Club until succeeded in 1915 by his son, Art, a famed ring referee. His grandson, Art Jr., was an All-Pro defensive tackle with the Baltimore Colts.

1894

Aqueduct Racetrack, operated by the Queens County Jockey Club, opens.

1925

Harry Stuhldreyer, quarterback in the fabled Notre Dame "Four Horsemen" backfield, makes his pro football debut, steering the Waterbury Blues to a 32-0 victory over the Knights of Columbus of Yonkers (N.Y.) at Waterbury, Connecticut.

1925

George Chapman needs a tie-breaking 50-mile race to win the National Motorpace championship for the sixth straight year. Chapman beats Vincent Madonna before 20,000 at the New York Velodrome after both finish the 24-race regular season tied with 59 points each.

MEL STOTTLEMYRE

1930

Eddie Tolan of the University of Michigan wins the 100-yard dash (10.0 seconds) and Gene Venzke of the Swedish-American AC takes the mile (4:25.0) as some 30,000 cram into Jersey City's Pershing Field for the city's Tercentenary Celebration Track Meet that also includes international relays and a 12-mile "modified marathon."

1931

New Daylight Saving Time costs the Giants' Bill Terry a batting title as the second game of a season-ending doubleheader at Ebbets Field is called by darkness, wiping out the hit he needs to win his second straight National League hitting crown. Terry is 1-for-4 in the opener that Brooklyn wins, 12-3, and 1-for-2 in the nightcap with the Giants ahead, 6-1, when play stops in the fourth. St. Louis' Chick Hafey winds up at .3489 to Terry's .3486.

1936

Opening the first season of AFL No. 2, the Football Yankees defeat the Syracuse Braves (soon to shift to Rochester), 13-6, at the new Municipal Stadium on Randalls Island. Despite the presence of Ken Strong and rookie end King Kong Klein of NYU in the lineup, the game draws only 6,500. Charlie Siegel runs for a touchdown and passes to Al Rose for another to power the Yanks offense, while Strong kicks the point after Siegel's second-quarter score.

1942

Despite gaining only one yard rushing, completing only one pass and making no first downs, the Football Giants beat the Redskins, 14-7, at Washington, in the season opener.

1963

Andy Coakley dies in New York at age 80. A big league pitcher who spent the 1911 season with the Highlanders, Coakley coached Columbia from 1914-51 (except 1919), compiling a 306-289-11 record. His prize student was Lou Gehrig.

September 28

1865

In a surprising baseball result, the Eckfords of Brooklyn beat the New York Mutuals 28-11, at Elysian Fields in Hoboken, N.J. It is later learned that three Mutuals players (Ed Duffy, William Wansley and Thomas Devyr) are involved in a conspiracy to throw the game as part of a betting coup. The plot becomes the most sensational sports scandal of its time, helping to pave the way for professional leagues with enforcement rights, although the amateur Players Association eventually reinstates all three.

1911

Birdie Cree and Hal Chase lead the way with four each as the Highlanders steal 15 bases during their 18-12 win over the St. Louis Browns at Hilltop Park. Cozy Dolan and Bert Daniels steal three bases apiece and Roy Hartzell one to complete the thievery.

1919

Playing "Beat the Clock" as well as "Beat the Phils," the Giants sweep a doubleheader at the Polo Grounds, stopping Philadelphia, 6-1 and 7-1, on the last day of the season. The first game takes only 51 minutes, a major league record that still stands.

1940

Montclair State, trailing 12-0 with fewer than six minutes to play, beats CCNY, 13-12, as Romeo DeVito throws two touchdown passes and kicks the extra point after the first score.

1946

First Flight, a two-year-old filly, turns in a blistering 1:08.6 for six furlongs to win the Matron Stakes on the Widener Course at Belmont Park. It is the fastest six furlongs by a filly since Artful's 1:08 in 1904 at Morris Park on the famed "Toboggan Slide" track.

1951

Yankees righty Allie Reynolds becomes the first American League pitcher to hurl two no-hitters in a season and clinches a tie for the pennant in an 8-0 victory over Boston in the first game of a doubleheader at the Stadium. Ted Williams is the game's final out on a foul pop to catcher Yogi Berra on the pitch after Berra dropped a similar foul for an error. In the second game, the Yanks clinch the pennant with an 11-3 win behind Vic Raschi. Oddly, both of Reynolds' no-hitters take exactly 2:12 to play and both are witnessed by slightly over 39,000 fans (39,195 at Cleveland July 12 and 39,038 in New York).

1952

After ushering the Yanks out of the league December 16, 1951, with a 27-17 road win at Yankee Stadium, the Football Giants welcome the Yanks' successor franchise, the Dallas Texans, to the NFL with a 24-6 win at Dallas. The Texans finish 1-11 in their only season before shifting to Baltimore.

1959

Vinnie Richards, one of the first tennis pros when he joined promoter C.C. Pyle's 1926-27 tour and the winner of the first U.S. professional championship (and the $1,000 first prize), which was held in New York in 1927, dies in New York at age 56.

1982

Knicks sign free agent forward Bernard King to an offer sheet. After they match the Knicks' offer, the Golden State Warriors trade King to New York October 22 for Micheal Ray Richardson and a draft choice.

1990

Larry O'Brien, NBA commissioner from 1975-84, dies in New York at 73. O'Brien, adviser to President Kennedy and postmaster general under President Johnson, served two terms as chairman of the Democratic National Committee. It was O'Brien's Watergate office that was bugged when burglars were arrested in June 1972.

September 29

1880

In the first baseball game at the original Polo Grounds, the Metropolitans defeat the Nationals of Washington, D.C., 4-2, in a game shortened to five innings by darkness. The Mets actually score four more runs in the sixth and the Nats one but the inning could not be completed and the score reverts to the last completed inning. Some 2,500 are on hand for the opener of a three-game series between the two top independent pro teams.

1923

Gene Sarazen captures his second PGA title in a classic struggle with Walter Hagen, 1-up, on the 38th hole of the final at the Pelham Country Club in Pelham, N.Y.

1929

Orange (N.J.) enters the NFL by playing a scoreless tie with the Football Giants at Orange to begin its only season in the league.

1944

In the first world championship bout ever televised, Willie Pep defends his featherweight title with a unanimous 15-round decision over Chalky Wright at the Garden. This fight is the first under a one-year deal between Mike Jacobs and the Gillette Safety Razor Co. NBC's New York outlet (WNBT) originates the telecast.

1946

Newark wins the Negro League World Series with a come-from-behind 3-2 win over the Kansas City Monarchs, thrilling a crowd of 7,200 at Ruppert Stadium. After stops in New York, Chicago and Kansas City, the Eagles take the series, four games to three. After Larry Doby and Monte Irvin walk in the sixth, John Davis' double drives in two runs to put the Eagles in front to stay. Irvin also has an RBI single earlier. It is the final series between the two Negro Leagues before Jackie Robinson joins the Brooklyn Dodgers, beginning the exodus of talented black players to the major leagues.

1954

Willie Mays' spectacular catch off Vic Wertz in the eighth inning and Dusty Rhodes' three-run pinch homer give the Giants a 5-2 win over Cleveland in the opening game of the World Series at the Polo Grounds. Mays' great play is both sensational and critical as the Indians have men on first and second with no one out when Wertz blasts his 450-foot plus drive to center, which Mays, back to the infield, basket-catches to preserve the 2-2 tie broken by Rhodes two innings later.

1957

Giants play their last game as a New York team, losing to the Pittsburgh Pirates, 9-1, before 11,606 at the Polo Grounds, their home since 1891. The Giants played in New York from 1883 until now, after which they move to San Francisco.

1962

Army defeats Syracuse, 9-2, in the final major college football game at the Polo Grounds.

1966

Bernard Feustman Gimbel dies in New York at age 81. Gimbel, president of the Gimbel's department store chain from 1927-53 and chairman of the board from 1931-66, was a director of Madison Square Garden Corp.

1987

Don Mattingly slugs his sixth grand slam of the season to back the tight pitching of Charles Hudson as the Yankees beat Boston, 6-0, at the Stadium, and 20,204 see a major league record set. Mattingly breaks the record (five) set by Ernie Banks of the Chicago Cubs in 1955 and tied by Baltimore's Jim Gentile in 1961. Mattingly finishes with a .474 average and 33 RBIs in bases-loaded situations for the season. They are the only six grand slams of Mattingly's 14-season career.

1915

Thanks to two days of rain, a premature end comes for the Federal League Tip Tops at Washington Park as they lose to Buffalo, 3-2. Friday's game with the Buffeds is rained out and rescheduled as part of a Saturday double-header October 2—but that's washed out, too.

1915

John Isaacs, a member of the New York Renaissance, a black touring pro basketball team, is born in the Panama Canal Zone.

1916

Winning their record 26th straight game, the Giants beat the Boston Braves, 4-0, behind Rube Benton's one-hitter before 38,000 at the Polo Grounds. In the second game of the doubleheader, the Braves break a 2-2 tie with a five-run seventh to end the streak with an 8-3 victory. The streak is still the longest in major-league history.

1927

Babe Ruth hits his major-league record 60th homer of the year, a two-run eighth inning shot off Washington southpaw Tom Zachary, as the Yankees beat the Senators, 4-2, at the Stadium. Ruth's homer, his 17th in September, breaks the mark of 59 he set in 1921, which broke the standard of 54 he established in 1920, which shattered the record of 29 he set in 1919. Ruth's drive down the rightfield line is fair by about six inches.

1931

In his first year as the pro at Metropolis, Paul Runyon wins the Westchester Open by shooting a final day 70-73 for a 72-hole 290. Yale's Sidney Noyes is second at 294 after a final day 74-74 costs him the lead. Paul Shindo of the Westchester CC is third at 299 and Herman Barron is fourth at 300.

1936

In the return of the "Subway Series," the Giants and Yankees meet for the fourth time, but the first since 1923, and the Giants win, 6-1, behind Carl Hubbell at the Polo Grounds, snapping the Yankees' 12-game World Series winning streak. The game is played in a steady rain.

1939

Fordham defeats Waynesburg (Pennsylvania), 34-7, at Randalls Island Stadium in the first football game ever televised. Bill Stern is at the microphone for NBC's W2XBS.

1940

Hank Borowy throws a five-hitter in the seventh game as the Newark Bears win the International League playoffs with a 3-2 win over the Baltimore Orioles at Newark's Ruppert Stadium. On October 9, the Bears beat the AA Louisville Colonels, 6-1, behind Steve Peek's six-hitter to win the Little World Series in six games.

1973

In the last game before the remodeling of Yankee Stadium, Detroit beats New York, 8-5, before 32,238. After the game, Ralph Houk, who has been in the Yankee organization continuously since 1939, manager of the 1961 and 1962 world champions and incumbent manager since 1966, resigns. He will be succeeded by Bill Virdon.

1994

NHL Commissioner Gary Bettman announces a two-week delay in the start of the 1994-95 season, in effect locking out players who are seeking a new contract. On October 11, both sides reject a suggested deal and Bettman announces on Dec. 29 that the season will be canceled if no settlement is reached by Jan. 16 (see Jan. 11).

October 1

1884

Yale Field, first permanent home for Yale football, opens and the Elis rout Wesleyan, 31-0. Eventually expanded to hold over 30,000, Yale Field was supplanted by the Yale Bowl in 1914 (see Nov. 21).

1885

When the Mets beat Cincinnati, 5-1, at the Polo Grounds, they close out the history of AA baseball in Manhattan. Under pressure from fellow National League owners, John B. Day sells the Mets to August Wiman, who moves them to Staten Island.

1910

For the second straight year, Bostonian Harry F. Grant wins the Vanderbilt Cup auto race on Long Island. Using the specially-built Motor Parkway and a combination of state roads, the race has become one of the most important in the world since its inauguration in 1904. Grant in his Alco finishes only 30 seconds in front of Joe Dawson (driving a Marmon) but the big news is again tragedy. Accidents kill two and injure more than a dozen, including drivers Louis Chevrolet and Harold Stone. Both Chevrolet's mechanic, Charles Miller, and Stone's, Milt Bacon, are killed in crashes. Other drivers and some in the crowd of over 250,000 are injured. The race is moved the following year to Savannah, Georgia, goes to Milwaukee in 1912, and then California before being discontinued in 1917.

1921

Walter Hagen wins the first of his five PGA championships with a 3 and 2 triumph over two-time winner Jim Barnes at the Inwood (L.I.) Country Club. Hagen would also win the PGA four years in a row from 1924 to 1927, making "the Haig" not only the most colorful but also the best pro of his time.

1921

Yankees beat Philadelphia, 5-3, in the opening game of a doubleheader at the Polo Grounds, behind Carl Mays to win their first American League pennant. Yankees also win the nightcap, 7-6, with Babe Ruth getting the win in relief.

1932

In the fifth inning of World Series Game 3, Babe Ruth hits his 15th (and last) Series homer at Chicago. Shrouded in controversy but generally referred to as the Babe's "called shot," it, according to many witnesses, comes after Ruth points to the centerfield bleachers before an 0-2 pitch from the Cubs' Charley Root, snapping a 4-4 tie in a 7-5 Yank win for a 3-0 Series lead. (Lou Gehrig hits the next pitch for another homer.)

1950

Dick Sisler's three-run, opposite-field homer in the 10th inning gives the Phillies a 4-1 victory over the Dodgers at Ebbets Field on the final day of the season as Philadelphia wins its first pennant since 1915. The Dodgers start the day one game out of first after 153 games and blow two chances to win in the ninth when Cal Abrams is thrown out (by plenty) at the plate and Carl Furillo pops out with the bases loaded and one out.

1961

In the last game of the season and on a 2-0 pitch from Boston pitcher Tracy Stallard in the bottom of the fourth, Roger Maris hits his 61st homer of the year, breaking Babe Ruth's 34-year-old record for most home runs in a season. Sal Durante catches the ball and wins a $5,000 prize.

1973

With a 6-4 win over the Cubs in the opener of a scheduled makeup doubleheader on the day after the regular season was supposed to end, the Mets, 82-79, clinch the National League East. The second game is canceled. Yogi Berra's club is the only NL East team over .500 after winning 21 of their last 29.

October 2

1861

In a so-called "Grand Match" for a silver baseball and the U.S. championship, Brooklyn clubs New York, 18-6, before some 15,000 fans at Hoboken's Elysian Fields.

1880

New York's first major bicycle racing competition is held, using the newly-installed track at the Polo Grounds. Six races are run at distances from one to five miles in the event sponsored by the Manhattan Polo Association, owner of the Polo Grounds. Martin Wrigley of the Brooklyn BC wins the first event—a two-mile handicap race.

1932

Winning their record 12th straight World Series game, the Yankees put the final touches on a four-game sweep of the Cubs with a 13-6 victory at Wrigley Field in Chicago.

1936

Evening the current edition of the Subway Series at a game apiece, the Yankees hammer the Giants, 18-4, at the Polo Grounds in the most lopsided World Series game ever.

1949

On the final day of the season, Tommy Henrich's leadoff eighth-inning homer gives the Yankees a 2-0 lead and propels the Bombers to a 5-3 win over the Red Sox in front of 68,055 roaring fans at the Stadium. The win gives the Yanks the American League flag by one game over Boston and first-year manager Casey Stengel the first of his 10 pennants.

1953

Fanning Mickey Mantle four times, Brooklyn's Carl Erskine sets a World Series record with 14 strikeouts in the Dodgers' 3-2 victory over the Yankees at Ebbets Field to shave the Bombers' Series lead to 2-1. Two days later, Mantle hits a grand slam that helps the visiting Yanks win Game 5, 11-7, and take a 3-2 Series lead.

1954

Completing their stunning four-game sweep of the World Series, the Giants beat the Indians, 7-4, before 78,102 at Cleveland's Municipal Stadium. After jumping out to a 7-0 lead, the Giants wrap up the Series as Johnny Antonelli finishes in relief of starter Don Liddle and Hoyt Wilhelm. The Giants become only the second National League team (Boston Braves, 1914) to earn a clean four-game sweep (no ties). The four-game attendance of 251,507 produces a record winning share of $11,147.90 for each Giant.

1960

Yankees beat Boston, 8-7, at the Stadium, to finish the season with 15 straight wins, a record. The Bombers trailed Baltimore by two games on Labor Day morning but win the pennant by eight games, clinching on September 25 thanks to the late-season streak.

1963

Dodgers lefty Sandy Koufax fans a record 15 as Los Angeles beats the Yankees, 5-2, in the opening game of the World Series at Yankee Stadium. Koufax breaks the record set 10 years to the day earlier by Carl Erskine when the Dodgers were still in Brooklyn.

1978

Bucky Dent's three-run seventh-inning homer erases a 2-0 Red Sox lead and helps the Yankees to a 5-4 victory in a one-game American League Eastern Division playoff at Fenway Park in Boston, giving the Bombers their third straight division title and capping their comeback from a 14-game deficit in the standing on July 17. Ron Guidry wins his 25th game of the year with relief help from Goose Gossage, who leaves the tying run on third and winning run on first in the bottom of the ninth by inducing clean-up hitter Carl Yastrzemski to pop up. Reggie Jackson's eighth-inning solo homer, which gives New York a 5-2 lead, provides the margin of victory.

October 3

1878

Australia wins a two-day cricket match over a New York All-Star team at the St. George Cricket Grounds in Hoboken, N.J. Australia has 98 runs (not out) in its second inning in what *The New York Times* calls "the finest exhibition of batting ever seen in this country." The New York team is held to 63 runs in its first inning and retired for 98 in its second.

1915

Ed Reulbach's three-hitter gives the Newark Peps a 3-0 win in the second game and a split of their doubleheader with Baltimore in the final Federal League game at Harrison, N.J. The Terrapins win the opener, 9-5. The FL goes out of business with the close of the 1915 season.

1931

Quarterback Bob Sheppard runs for one touchdown and passes to Tom Neary for another as St. John's routs Vermont, 38-7, before 2,000 at Woodhaven's Dexter Park.

1936

John W. Heisman, former football player and coach who was athletic director at the Downtown Athletic Club (1930-36), dies at 68 in New York. The DAC Trophy, annually awarded to the country's best college football player beginning in 1935, is renamed the Heisman Trophy.

1947

Cookie Lavagetto of the Dodgers ruins Yankees righthander Bill Bevens' bid to pitch the first World Series no-hitter with a two-out, two-run double in the ninth off the rightfield wall that gives Brooklyn a 3-2 home win over the Yankees and ties the Series at two games apiece.

1948

Johnny Mize hits a home run in the second inning (his only at-bat of the game) on the last day of the season at the Polo Grounds to tie Pittsburgh's Ralph Kiner for the National League homer title for the second straight season. Both hit 51 in 1947 and 40 in 1948. Mize was benched by manager Leo Durocher after his homer and the pennant-winning Boston Braves blast the Giants, 11-1.

1951

Bobby Thomson hits a three-run homer with one out in the bottom of the ninth inning to carry the Giants to an improbable 5-4 victory over Brooklyn before 34,320 at the Polo Grounds, giving the Giants their first National League pennant since 1937. Thomson's homer on an 0-1 pitch from reliever Ralph Branca caps a four-run rally in the final inning of the final game of a three-game playoff. The Dodgers held a 13 1/2-game lead on August 11 and appeared destined to win the pennant easily, but the Giants won 37 of their last 44 to tie. Thomson's two-run homer off Branca and Jim Hearn's five-hitter gave them a 3-1 win in the playoff opener at Ebbets Field before Brooklyn won, 10-0, behind Clem Labine at the Polo Grounds. In the third game, Don Newcombe has a 4-1 lead in the ninth, yielding only four hits. But after two singles and a pop-up, Whitey Lockman doubles to left to cut the lead to 4-2. Don Mueller breaks his ankle sliding into third. Newcombe is relieved by Branca. Clint Hartung runs for Mueller and Thomson homers into the lower deck in left field. Larry Jansen gets the win in relief of starter Sal Maglie.

1970

Fordham plays its first varsity football game in nearly 16 years and defeats St. Peter's. 14-0, at Jack Coffey Field. Coach Jim Lansing's Rams finish 5-1-2 in Division III, moving out of the club program that began in 1964 (see Nov. 7). Fordham dropped its "big-time" program after the 1954 season with heavy financial losses and all-too-numerous on-field defeats (see Dec. 17).

1990

Charlotte Boyle Clune, a freestyle swimmer who set four world and eight American records from 1917-21, dies in Scottsville, N.Y., at age 91.

October 4

1884

Righthander Sam Kimber pitches Brooklyn's first major-league no-hitter but doesn't get a win. Kimber hurls his gem in a game against AA rival Toledo at Washington Park but the game is called due to darkness in the 11th inning, ending in a scoreless tie. Kimber is the first pitcher ever to throw an extra-inning no-hitter.

1904

Sam Mertes gets six hits for the Giants in a 7-3 loss to St. Louis in the first game of a doubleheader, but the real action is in the second game, when umpire Jimmy Johnstone forfeits the game to the Cardinals (who lead 2-1) in the fourth inning after a protracted dispute with Giants manager John McGraw (see Aug. 7).

1922

In radio's first broadcast direct from the field, Graham McNamee is behind the mike for NBC at the Polo Grounds for the opening game of the World Series between the Yankees and Giants. Previous experimental sportscasts had been relayed by telephone line to a studio and then rebroadcast onto another set of lines. The Giants win, 3-2.

1934

Robert Lee Huff is born in Edna Gas, West Virginia. Sam Huff, a linebacker with the Football Giants from 1956-63, was a Pro Bowl selection four straight seasons (1958-61).

HUGH CASEY

1955

It is the blazing red headline on this afternoon's late editions of the *Journal-American* that says it best. "This is Next Year!" For the first time, Brooklyn wins the World Series as the beloved Dodgers finally beat the hated Yankees, taking the seventh game, 2-0, at Yankee Stadium and the Series, 4-3. Southpaw Johnny Podres wins his second Series game with an eight-hitter, and is rescued in the bottom of the sixth when leftfield defensive replacement Sandy Amoros corrals Yogi Berra's slicing opposite-field drive with two on and none out, turning a likely double into a rally-killing double play as Gil McDougald is doubled off first base.

1969

Scoring five runs in the eighth off Phil Niekro, the Mets, in their first postseason game, rally for a 9-5 victory in the first National League Championship Series game ever played. Tom Seaver, with relief help from Ron Taylor, gets the win before 50,270 at Atlanta-Fulton County Stadium.

1975

Joan Whitney Payson, founding owner of the National League expansion New York Mets in 1961 and partner in the Whitney family Greentree Stable with her brother, John Hay (Jock) Whitney, and other family members, dies in New York at age 82.

1986

Paul Koster passes for a school-record 443 yards as St. John's beats Fordham, 38-7, at Redmen Field.

1991

Instantly transforming themselves into serious Stanley Cup contenders, the Rangers acquire Oilers center Mark Messier, plus future considerations (see Nov. 12) from financially weaker Edmonton for center Bernie Nicholls and wingers Steven Rice and Louie DeBrusk.

October 5

1859

On the final day of a three-day match, a touring England cricket team decisively defeats a U.S. team at the St. George Cricket Club grounds in Hoboken, N.J. England wins by 64 runs and an inning in a match that draws over 25,000 in three days. On the second day, Tuesday, some 12,000 flock to the test, causing ferry companies to scramble for sufficient boats to handle the traffic over the Hudson.

1889

Tim Keefe throws a six-hitter as the Giants beat the Spiders, 5-3, at Cleveland, to clinch the National League pennant on the last day of the season as Boston loses, 5-1, at Pittsburgh.

1912

Brooklyn's wooden ballpark era ends as the Giants score in the 7th inning for a 1-0 victory over the Dodgers in the last National League game at Washington Park (see Apr. 9).

1921

Playing in their first World Series game ever, the Yankees blank the Giants, 3-0, on Carl Mays' five-hitter at the Polo Grounds. It is the first "Subway Series" game and the first played under the supervision of a commissioner of baseball.

1941

Brooklyn is about to tie the World Series at two games apiece at Ebbets Field when reliever Hugh Casey strikes out Tommy Henrich for the final out. But Dodgers catcher Mickey Owen can't hold the third strike, Henrich reaches first and the Yankees go on to score four times with two out in the ninth for a 7-4 victory. Casey becomes the first pitcher ever to lose consecutive Series games. The next day, Ernie Bonham throws a four-hitter; the Yankees take the game, 3-1, and the Series, four games to one.

1941

Lawrence David Glueck is born in Norristown, Penna. Larry Glueck took Fordham's football team from Division III to Division I-AA as coach and saw the Rams' fortunes reverse, going from 9-2 in 1988 to 2-6 in 1989.

1942

After an opening-game win in St. Louis, the Yankees suffer one of their most stunning reversals, dropping four straight to the underrated Cardinals, who finish the World Series with a 4-2 win in the fifth game at Yankee Stadium.

1953

Becoming the only team in baseball history ever to win five straight World Championships, the Yankees capture the sixth game of the World Series, 4-3, at Yankee Stadium on Billy Martin's record 12th hit of the Series, a one-out single to center in the bottom of the ninth off Brooklyn's Clem Labine.

1979

NYU and Football Giants great Ken Strong dies in New York at age 73.

1982

Playing their first game as a New Jersey team, the Devils settle for a 3-3 tie with Pittsburgh in the initial regular-season NHL game at the Meadowlands Arena. Captain Don Lever scores the first Devils goal.

1988

Terry Underwood rushes for a school-record 363 yards as Wagner defeats Hofstra, 30-24, before 6,315 at Staten Island's Fischer Memorial Field.

# October 6

1857

On the same day the American Chess Association is organized in New York at the first American Chess Congress, A.B. Meek of Alabama is elected president and Paul C. Morphy, a 20-year-old chess wizard from New Orleans, Louisiana, wins the first U.S. championship.

1906

With almost 300,000 fans crowding onto the roads, Louis Wagner of France wins the third Vanderbilt Cup race in his Darracq but Elliott Shepard's Hotchkiss racer kills a spectator on Jericho Turnpike. The death of 33-year-old Curt Gruner of Passaic, N.J., plus other injuries caused when some of the 45 entrants miss curves, forces cancellation of the 1907 race and prompts construction of special roads before road racing is resumed in 1908.

1923

Edith Cummings wins the U.S. Women's Amateur golf title, defeating Alexa Sterling, 3 and 2, in the 36-hole final at Rye's Westchester-Biltmore course (now the Westchester Country Club).

1926

Babe Ruth clubs three homers, the first ever to do so in the World Series, and the Yankees tie the Series, 2-2, with a 10-5 rout of the Cardinals at Sportsman's Park in St. Louis, Missouri.

1928

Facing a challenger other than England for the first time in the 42-year history of the series, the U.S. defeats Argentina, 2-1, in the International Polo Match at the Meadow Brook in Westbury, N.Y. The U.S. had won Sept. 29 and lost Oct. 3.

1929

With NYU great Ken Strong making his pro debut, the Staten Island Stapletons play their first NFL game, a 12-0 victory over the Dayton Triangles at Thompson Field. The Stapes, reputedly owned by bootleggers, pay lavish salaries during their four seasons. When Prohibition ends, however, the Stapes' owners' cash flow dries up and the club quits the league.

1936

Yankees score seven times in the ninth to clinch the World Series, 4-2, with a 13-5 win over the Giants at the Polo Grounds as President Franklin D. Roosevelt attends.

1940

Trying for the third time, the AFL debuts in New York, and the Columbus (Ohio) Bullies defeat the Yankees, 23-13, before 5,312 at Yankee Stadium. Three nights later, the Yankees get their first win as Bill Hutchinson scores two touchdowns in a 40-13 rout of the Cincinnati Bengals, but the Stadium crowd that night is only 4,296.

1947

Joe Page throws five innings of one-hit relief as the Yankees beat the Dodgers, 5-2, at the Stadium to take the World Series in seven games. Yankees co-owner Larry MacPhail fires general manager George Weiss and announces he is quitting. The firing doesn't stick but the retirement does as his partners, Dan Topping and Del Webb, buy MacPhail's share and reinstate Weiss.

1963

For the first time ever, the Yankees are swept in four straight games in the World Series, losing, 2-1, to Sandy Koufax and the Dodgers at Los Angeles.

1969

Nolan Ryan's seven innings of three-hit relief lifts the Mets to a 7-4 win over the Atlanta Braves at Shea Stadium, finishing New York's three-game sweep of the National League Championship Series.

1904

Righty Jack Chesbro wins his 41st game as the Highlanders beat Boston, 3-2, at Hilltop Park. Chesbro's five-hitter puts New York in first place with four games to go in the season.

1904

Columbia's Robert LeRoy wins the national intercollegiate singles tennis title with a 4-6, 6-3, 7-5, 2-6, 6-0 victory over Penn's E.B. Dewhurst at Philadelphia's Merion Country Club.

1916

John Reid, 76, the "Father of American Golf," dies in Yonkers, N.Y. Reid formed the St. Andrews Club in Yonkers on Nov. 14, 1888, served as the club's first president (1888-97) and was one of the founders of the USGA in 1894.

1925

Christy Mathewson dies in a sanitorium in Saranac Lake, N.Y., at age 45. A 373-game winner for the Giants, Mathewson inhaled poison gas while serving in World War I.

1933

Mel Ott's 10th-inning homer gives the Giants a 4-3 win over the Senators at Washington and the World Series, 4-1. Dolph Luque wins the finale in relief.
1950
Yale beats Fordham, 21-14, at the Yale Bowl, spoiling Fordham's chance at an unbeaten season. The Rams finish 8-1.

1950

Allie Reynolds, the complete-game winner two days earlier, comes out of the bullpen to strike out Stan Lopata for the final out as the Yankees complete a four-game World Series sweep of the Philadelphia Phillies with a 5-2 win at Yankee Stadium.

1951

With the Giants holding a 2-1 World Series lead, the fourth game at the Polo Grounds is rained out. The one-day respite allows the Yankees to reorganize their pitching and use their ace, Allie Reynolds, when the Series resumes. Sure enough, Reynolds wins, 6-2, tying the Series and setting up the Yankees' eventual victory (see Oct. 10).

1952

Second baseman Billy Martin's dash to the mound to snare Jackie Robinson's two-out bases-loaded pop-up in the seventh ends the last Brooklyn rally as the Yankees, in the seventh game, win their fourth straight Series, matching their record (1936-39), 4-2, at Ebbets Field.

1972

Opening their first season in the NHL, the Islanders lose, 3-2, to their fellow expansion team, the Atlanta Flames, at Nassau Coliseum on Rey Comeau's goal.

1991

In the first triple dead heat in New York racing in 47 years, Cafe Lax, Scoreboard Harry and Space Appeal all hit the wire at precisely the same second in the ninth race at Belmont Park. It is only the 19th triple dead heat in the U.S. since 1940 but it creates six triples, six exactas and three daily double payoffs (see June 10).

1995

Columbia quarterback Matt Cavanaugh runs for two touchdowns as the Lions beat Pennsylvania, 24-14, at Wien Stadium, ending the Quakers' 24-game winning streak, the longest in Division I football.

# October 8

1878

For the second time in five months, Charles A. Harrison wins a professional walking competition in New York. He does 106 miles plus three laps in a 24-hour match at Gilmore's Gardens, and wins the top prize of $200.

1894

Giants complete a four-game sweep of the pennant-winning Baltimore Orioles to win the Temple Cup, 16-3, at the Polo Grounds. The series is a matchup of the top two finishers in the National League race in the absence of a World Series (or another major league).

1904

British driver George Heath brings his 90-horsepower Panhard home 88 seconds ahead of Albert Clement in the first Vanderbilt Cup road race run over a 30-mile course from Westbury to Queens and back. Each car makes 10 trips around the loop.

1908

In the playoff of the tie game of Sept. 23, the Chicago Cubs score four runs in the third inning to defeat the Giants and Christy Mathewson, 4-2, and win the NL pennant before 35,000 at the Polo Grounds.

1922

For the second straight year, lefthander Art Nehf shackles the Yankees in the final game of the World Series as the Giants win, 5-3, at the Polo Grounds, to take the Series, 4-0 (with one tie).

1927

Generally considered the greatest team in baseball history, the "Murderers' Row" Yankees complete their four-game sweep of the Pittsburgh Pirates, 4-3, at the Stadium. On the day after the Series, Babe Ruth and Lou Gehrig play an exhibition game at a school in The Bronx.

1948

Four Rangers, including center (and 1947-48 league MVP) Buddy O'Connor, are injured when their car collides with a truck near Lacolle, Quebec. O'Connor has damaged ribs (one broken) which sideline him for most of the first half of the season.

1956

Don Larsen hurls a perfect game, the only no-hitter in World Series history and the first perfect game in the majors since 1922, and the Yankees beat Brooklyn, 2-0, at the Stadium to take a 3-2 Series lead. Mickey Mantle homers in the fourth to snap a scoreless tie.

1973

In a scene without contemporary precedent in New York, the Mets take a 2-1 lead in the NLCS with a 9-2 trouncing of Cincinnati. But the indelible memory of the game is a fifth-inning bench-clearing confrontation precipitated by a fight between Reds leftfielder Pete Rose and Mets shortstop Bud Harrelson after Rose's unsuccessful attempt to break up a double play. Fans in leftfield at Shea Stadium shower Rose with garbage when he takes his position in the bottom of the inning and the Mets ahead 9-2, prompting Reds manager Sparky Anderson to pull his club off the field. Finally, manager Yogi Berra and players Willie Mays, Rusty Staub, Cleon Jones and Tom Seaver go to left field to calm the crowd so that the game can be completed.

1985

Fabled New York Athletic Club fencing coach Giorgio Santelli dies in Teaneck, N.J., at age 87.

1988

Columbia astonishes 5,420 fans at Wien Stadium with a 16-13 come-from-behind victory over Princeton to end the Lions' 44-game losing streak.

October 9

1896

Beatrix Hoyt, a sixteen-year-old playing out of Shinnecock Hills, wins the first of her three successive national championships by taking the initial Women's Amateur sponsored by the United States Golf Association with a 2 and 1 victory over her clubmate, Mrs. Arthur Turnure, at the Morris County GC in Morristown, N.J.

1916

In the longest World Series game ever played, Del Gainor's 14th-inning double off Brooklyn's Sherry Smith drives in the winning run as the Red Sox win, 2-1, at Braves Field in Boston and take a 2-0 Series lead. Smith goes the distance as does Boston lefthander Babe Ruth, who shuts out Brooklyn for the last 13 innings.

1926

Quarterback Tubby Raskin runs for a touchdown, sets up two more with his passes and kicks two extra points as City College ends St. Lawrence's 10-game winning streak with a 20-7 victory at Lewisohn Stadium.

1928

Closing out another World Series sweep with their eighth straight Series win, the Yankees get three homers from Babe Ruth in a 7-3 victory over the Cardinals at St. Louis.

1938

Despite the presence of the immortal and gallant Dizzy Dean and former Yankees great Tony Lazzeri, the Chicago Cubs prove no match for the Bombers, who complete yet another four-game World Series sweep with an 8-3 victory at the Stadium.

1948

Jerry Edwards sprints 65 yards for a second-quarter touchdown to give Brooklyn College a 7-2 halftime lead, but NYU rallies for a 21-7 victory before 14,128 in a night game at Ebbets Field.

1949

Joe Page snuffs out a Dodgers rally and the Yankees end the World Series with a 10-6 victory over Brooklyn at Ebbets Field and a four-games-to-one Series win.

1958

Becoming only the second team to trail, 3-1, and win a seven-game World Series (after Pittsburgh in 1925), the Yankees beat the Braves, 6-2, at Milwaukee, to avenge their 1957 Series loss.

1960

Howard Glenn, linebacker with the Titans, dies at age 25 at Jeppeson Stadium in Houston, Tex., of a broken neck suffered in the game against the Oilers.

1961

With a mighty display of power hitting, the Yankees, scoring five times in the first and fourth innings, whip the Reds, 13-5, at Crosley Field in Cincinnati to close out the World Series, four games to one.

1977

With a run in the eighth and three in the ninth, the Yankees stun the Royals, 5-3, at Kansas City, to take the ALCS and their second straight pennant, three games to two. Reliever Sparky Lyle earns his second win in as many days, but the pitching hero is Mike Torrez, who hurls 5 $\frac{1}{3}$ innings of scoreless ball in relief of Ron Guidry.

1994

Fred Lebow, founder of the New York City Marathon, dies in New York at age 62. Lebow was president of the New York Road Runners Club for 20 years and began the Marathon as a run around Central Park in 1970.

# October 10

1874

Edward P. Weston fails to reach his goal of walking 500 miles in five days at Barnum's Hippodrome (later Madison Square Garden No. 1), finishing with 346 miles in spite of his 101-mile performance on the first day.

1904

Jack Chesbro's ninth-inning wild pitch sends home the winning run as Boston clinches the AL pennant on the season's final day with a 3-2 win over the Highlanders in the first game of a twinbill at Hilltop Park.

1923

In the first World Series game played in Yankee Stadium, Casey Stengel's ninth-inning inside-the-park homer, a solo "shot," lifts the visiting Giants to a 5-4 win and a 1-0 Series lead.

1924

Walter Johnson wins in relief and the winning run scores in the 12th on a bad-hop Earl McNeely hit as the Senators beat the Giants, 4-3, in Washington in the seventh game of the World Series.

1926

Grover Cleveland Alexander, complete-game winner the day before, fans the Yankees' Tony Lazzeri in relief with the bases loaded and two out in the bottom of the seventh inning of the seventh game of the World Series. St. Louis wins, 3-2, at the Stadium, to take the Series, four games to three.

1926

Brooklyn teams in the warring football leagues open their home schedules on a rainy Sunday. Matt Brennan's 30-yard fourth-quarter pass to Rex Thomas gives the NFL Lions a 6-0 win over the Hartford Blues before 3,000 at Ebbets Field, while the AFL Horsemen lose, 23-0, to Wilson's West Coast Wildcats as George Wilson scores the first touchdown before 6,000 at Commercial Field, Albany Avenue and Lincoln Road. Two "horsemen," Harry Stuhldreyer and Elmer Layden, play for Brooklyn.

1951

Hank Bauer's diving catch of Sal Yvars' liner to right with the tying run on base ends the World Series, as the Yankees beat the Giants, 4-3, in the sixth game at the Stadium (see Oct. 7).

1956

It's "Wait 'Till Last Year" for the Dodgers as the defending champs are dethroned, 9-0, by the Yankees, who take the World Series, four games to three, in the last Series game played at Ebbets Field.

1957

Former Yankees farmhand Lew Burdette tosses his third complete-game victory of the World Series (and second straight shutout) as Milwaukee beats the Yankees at the Stadium, 5-0, in the seventh game. It is the first time the world title has left New York City since 1948.

1973

Breaking a 2-2 tie with four runs in the fifth inning, the Mets win the NL pennant with a 7-2 victory over Cincinnati at Shea Stadium, taking the NLCS, 3-2. Many in the crowd of 50,323 storm onto the field after the final out and engage in an unruly, destructive "celebration," tearing up sod and causing extensive damage to the ballpark.

1976

Building a 17-0 halftime lead, the Dallas Cowboys defeat the Football Giants, 24-14, in the first event at Giants Stadium. The opening draws 76,042.

1896

Heavyweight contender Luis Angel Firpo is born in Junia Province, Buenos Aires, Argentina. In his most memorable fight, at the Polo Grounds, the "Wild Bull of the Pampas" knocked champ Jack Dempsey through the ropes and nearly out. Dempsey climbed back into the ring and knocked Firpo down seven times en route to a second round KO. Dempsey's clubbing of Firpo led to the adoption of the "neutral corner" rule that some say cost Dempsey the win in his rematch with Gene Tunney in the famous "Long Count" fight in Chicago in 1927.

1902

Lawrence (Laurie) Auchterlonie, playing out of the Chicago Golf Club, scores a comfortable six-stroke victory in the U.S. Open at the Garden City GC. Stewart Gardner and amateur Walter J. Travis tie for second at 313. The introduction of the Haskell rubber core ball helps cut scores. The total prizes for pros are $970 with Auchterlonie collecting $200.

1913

For the second time in three years, the Philadelphia A's beat the Giants in the World Series, winning, 3-1, behind Eddie Plank's two-hitter before 36,682 at the Polo Grounds to take the Series, 4-1.

1925

Beginning their inaugural season in the NFL, the Football Giants are flattened by the Steam Roller, 14-0, at the Cycledrome in Providence, R.I.

FRANK McGUIRE

1932

J.H. Dillon, a leading breeder of trotting horses, dies in New Haven, Connecticut, at age 75.

1936

Elijah West Price, who set a world's speed record on an ice boat in 1908, dies in Long Branch, N.J., at age 83. Price hit 140 m.p.h. aboard the *Clarel* over a 15-mile course on Pleasure Bay (N.J.) in 1908 and averaged 105 mph for the entire course. At the time, it was the fastest any vehicle had ever traveled on any surface anywhere in the world.

1943

Bill Dickey's two-run homer in the sixth inning accounts for all the scoring as the Yankees close out the World Series with a 2-0 fifth-game victory at St. Louis, avenging their 1942 Series loss to the Cardinals.

1946

Brooklyn, the last AAFC club to play at home in the league's first season, ties the Chicago Rockets, 21-21, at Ebbets Field.

1969

In the final meeting between Army and Notre Dame in New York City, the Irish rout the Cadets, 45-0, before 63,786 at Yankee Stadium. The series returns to the metropolitan area in 1977 at Giants Stadium (see Oct. 15).

1994

Basketball coaching legend Frank McGuire, 80, St. John's alumnus who led the Redmen to a 102-36 record in five seasons (1947-52) as head coach before going to North Carolina, where his Tar Heels in 1957 went 32-0 and won the NCAA title, dies in West Columbia, South Carolina.

October 12

1872

Nickajack sets a wagering return record of $1,178 for a $5 win bet at Jerome Park. The standard bet was $5 instead of $2 in the original "Paris-Mutuel" betting format, which is replaced by on-track bookmakers in the 1880s.

1873

Over 100,000 attend the five days of the first annual National Shooting Competition at the Creedmoor Range. On the final day, the 22d Regiment, New York National Guard, captures the 1st Division championship by 28 points over the 12th Regiment. The 22d Regiment marksmen hit 155 targets at 200 yards and 108 at 500 yards for 263 hits out of a possible 480.

1920

Stan Coveleski tosses a five-hit shutout as the Indians clinch their first World Series with a 3-0 win over the Dodgers in Cleveland. The Tribe had lost two of the first three games, all in Brooklyn, but then swept four straight at home to take the best-of-nine Series, five games to two.

1925

William Steinkraus is born in Cleveland, Ohio. Bill Steinkraus was an Olympic gold medalist in equestrian events in 1968 and president of the USET from 1972-82.

1930

In their home opener at Ebbets Field, the Brooklyn Football Dodgers blank the Newark Tornadoes, 32-0, to raise their record to 2-1-1 in their first NFL season. Having shifted from Dayton, Ohio, after being sold, the new Dodgers are 7-4-1 under coach (and co-owner) John Depler in their first year (see July 12).

1936

For the first time since 1910, the Vanderbilt Cup auto race is run on Long Island. Italy's celebrated Tazio Nuvolari wheels his Alfa-Romeo home in this closed-course revival of the famed 300-mile race run over the newly-dedicated Roosevelt Raceway on Salisbury Plan (now Westbury), L.I. Over 50,000 turn out to watch Nuvolari and 44 others spin around the dirt track at speeds approaching 100 mph. Nuvolari wins the $23,600 top money with his 65.998 mph average.

1975

Making their Shea Stadium debut, the Football Giants lose to the Dallas Cowboys, 13-7, on Roger Staubach's four-yard scoring pass to Jean Fugett in the fourth quarter. With a home-opener crowd of 60,372 watching, the Giants make Shea the first stadium ever to house four pro teams in the same season. In addition to the Mets and Jets, Shea is temporary home to the Yankees while their stadium is being renovated. The Giants spend only one season at Shea after leaving the Yale Bowl before moving to Giants Stadium in 1976.

1976

In his fourth game as a Ranger, right winger Don Murdoch sets a club record with five goals as the Blueshirts strafe the North Stars, 10-4, at Minnesota.

1991

Sophomore Al White scores five touchdowns to lead William Paterson to a 46-12 win over Upsala at East Orange, N.J. White ties a Pioneers record set in 1978 by Terry McCann, who scored five times against Jersey City State.

1996

Fordham starting strong safety Bill Tierney collapses during pregame warmups before the Rams' game with Lafayette at Jack Coffey Field in The Bronx. Tierney is pronounced dead at St. Barnabas Hospital and a subsequent autopsy reveals an irregular heartbeat caused his death. The game is canceled.

1894

L.B. Stoddard of St. Andrews defeats Charles B. MacDonald of the Chicago Golf Club, 1-up, to win the National Amateur Golf Championship at St. Andrews Golf Club in Mount Hope (now Hastings-on-Hudson), N.Y. The presence of this tournament and a similar one at Newport, R.I., a month earlier leads to the creation of the United States Golf Association to avoid duplicating championships.

1917

Famed publicist "Unswerving Irving" Rudd is born in New York. Rudd is perhaps most famous for deliberately switching the last letters of the harness racing track's billboard, allowing all to see "YONKERS RACEWYA" from the highway.

1921

A brilliant four-hitter by lefty Art Nehf makes an unearned first-inning run off Waite Hoyt stand up as the Giants defeat the Yankees, 1-0, in the eighth game to win the World Series, five games to three, their first Series triumph since 1905. The Yankees become the first team to take a 2-0 lead in games and lose the Series. All the games were played at the Polo Grounds (where the Yankees are the Giants' tenants).

1923

Notre Dame begins its annual series with Army, scoring a 13-0 victory at Ebbets Field in Brooklyn, where the game is played when the World Series forces it out of the Polo Grounds.

1929

In their first-ever meeting, the Football Giants beat the Staten Island Stapletons, 19-9, at the Polo Grounds.

1960

Bill Mazeroski leads off the bottom of the ninth with a homer off Yankees reliever Ralph Terry's first pitch of the inning to give the Pirates a wild 10-9 victory at Pittsburgh's Forbes Field and their first World Series title since 1925, four games to three.

1964

Bing Miller, a tackle at NYU and with the NFL Stapleton Stapes from 1929-31 before returning to his alma mater as athletic director, dies in The Bronx at age 60.

1974

Ed Sullivan dies in New York at age 73. Before making acts such as Elvis Presley, the Beatles and himself famous on his Sunday night variety show, Sullivan was sports editor of the *Evening Graphic* and a Broadway columnist for the *Daily News*.

1989

John F.X. Condon, the Garden basketball public address announcer from 1947-89 and president of Madison Square Garden boxing from 1979-86, dies in New York at age 75.

IRVING RUDD

1996

Yankees score six runs in the third inning on three homers and beat the Orioles, 6-4, to take the American League Championship Series, 4-1. In winning their first pennant since 1981, the Yankees defeat the Orioles for the ninth time this season (against no losses) at Baltimore.

October 14

1889

Adonis Terry's five-hitter gives Brooklyn a 6-1 win at Columbus, Ohio on the final day of the AA season, but whether manager Bill McGunnigle's Bridegrooms will win the pennant hinges on seven rain-out make-ups St. Louis intends to play to force a tie for first (see Oct. 15).

1898

Winning her third (and final) national golf title, Beatrix Hoyt defeats Maude Wetmore, 5 and 3, in the U.S. Women's Amateur final at the Ardsley Club in Ardsley-on-Hudson, N.Y.

1905

Christy Mathewson throws his third shutout in six days as the Giants clinch the World Series, 4-1, with a 2-0 victory over the Philadelphia A's before 24,187 at the Polo Grounds. All five games of the Series are shutouts.

1905

Pauline Mackay defeats Margaret Curtis, 1-up, at the Morris County Golf Club in Convent, N.J., to win the U.S. Women's Amateur golf championship. Miss Curtis later wins three national titles and with her sister, Harriot, who also won this event, donates the Curtis Cup for international competition between the women golfers of the U.S. and the British Isles.

CHRIS CHAMBLISS

1911

Margaret Curtis defeats Lillian B. Hyde, 5 and 3, to win the U.S. Women's Amateur golf championship at the Baltusrol Golf Club for the second of her three national titles.

1931

Richard Powers is born in New York. A St. John's product, Richie Powers was an NBA referee from 1956-80. He also umpired in the International League from 1961-62.

1945

Theoretically representing both Boston and Brooklyn in the NFL, the Yanks play a 13-13 tie with the visiting Football Giants at Yankee Stadium.

1965

Two days before their season opener, the Knicks trade forward Bob Boozer to the Los Angeles Lakers for guard Dick Barnett.

1969

Centerfielder Tommie Agee's two spectacular catches highlight the Mets' 5-0 victory over Baltimore at Shea Stadium as the World Series returns to a New York National League park for the first time since 1956. The Mets take a 2-1 Series lead.

1976

Chris Chambliss' leadoff homer in the bottom of the ninth lifts the Yankees to a 7-6 win over the Kansas City Royals in the fifth and deciding game of the American League Championship Series and puts the Bombers in their first World Series since 1964.

1991

Rangers right wing Mike Gartner scores the 500th goal of his NHL career but the Washington Capitals beat the Blueshirts, 5-3, at the Garden.

October 15

1887

Detroit beats St. Louis, 9-0, at the Polo Grounds, in the sixth game of the World Series. The day before, the touring championship was played at Brooklyn's Washington Park, with the Browns winning, 5-2. All told, the Series goes 14 games in 11 cities, with Detroit's National League champions winning 10.

1889

Brooklyn wins its first major-league pennant while riding the Pennsylvania Railroad. Upon arriving at Jersey City's Exchange Place terminal, the Bridegrooms learn that second-place St. Louis has lost a rainout makeup, 8-3, at Cincinnati (see Oct. 14), and is eliminated. Several hundred fans join in the celebration at the station. The Annex Ferry boat is saluted by whistles and horns while going around the Battery to Fulton Ferry, where the real celebration breaks out.

1900

Miss Marguerite Gast sets women's world records for cycling mileage, becoming the first female ever to reach 2,000 miles of continuous peddling. She has been traveling around the Century Road Club course on Long Island for 222 hours, 5 $^1/_2$ minutes, reaching her goal despite two days of rain. The 23-year-old Bavarian-born New York milliner then decides to resume peddling the triangular 25-mile course for another 1,000 miles. But police finally stop her on October 19 after she completes 2,600 miles in 12 days, seven hours, and 55 minutes, including brief stops for food, rest and medical attention.

1923

With a five-run rally in the eighth, the Yankees beat the Giants, 6-4, at the Polo Grounds, to win their first World Series, 4-2, and gain some revenge after losing the first two Subway Series to the Giants in 1921 and 1922.

1927

NYU beats Fordham, 32-0, at Yankee Stadium, the Violets' largest winning margin in the schools' football series.

1933

In their home opener, the Football Giants (3-2) demolish the new Philadelphia Eagles (in the franchise's first game), 56-0, at the Polo Grounds, the biggest victory in the team's history. The 56 points are the most ever by an NFL team (a record broken next season when the same Eagles rout the hapless Cincinnati Reds, 64-0).

1977

In the first visit of their storied rivalry to the metropolitan area since 1969, Army meets Notre Dame at Giants Stadium, and the Irish grind out a 24-0 victory over the stubborn, but outmanned, Cadets before 72,594. Subsequently, Notre Dame becomes a frequent visitor to East Rutherford, N.J., not only renewing their series with Army (1983 and 1995) but also facing Virginia (1989) and Navy (1980, 1982, 1984, 1990 and 1992).

1983

Columbia beats Yale, 21-18, at the Yale Bowl. The Lions' win is their last for 48 games until October 8, 1988. During this period, Columbia sets a Division I record with 44 straight losses (subsequently broken by Prairie View A&M).

1986

In one of the most tense National League Championship Series games ever, the Mets win the sixth game and the National League pennant with a 7-6 triumph over the Astros in 16 innings at Houston's Astrodome.

1987

A 24-day walkout by its some 1,585 players against the NFL is ended by the players' union, which the same day files an antitrust suit against the league in Minneapolis federal court. The league's replacement teams play that weekend.

October 16

1912

In the "Snodgrass Muff" game, the Boston Red Sox take the World Series with two unearned runs in the 10th, winning, 3-2, at Fenway Park. Giants centerfielder Fred Snodgrass drops Clyde Engle's routine fly to help the Sox to wipe out a 2-1 Giants lead. The Series goes eight games thanks to a 6-6 tie in Game 2 that is called because of darkness after 11 innings.

1929

Walter Michaels is born in Swoyersville, Pennsylvania. A Jets assistant coach from 1963-72 and in 1976, Walt Michaels was Jets head coach for six seasons (1977-82), leading the Jets to the playoffs his last two seasons. He also coached the USFL New Jersey Generals from 1984-85.

1940

Dave DeBusschere is born in Detroit. DeBusschere, his era's prototype big forward at a muscular 6'6", was a former two-sport pro athlete (baseball also) whose trade to the Knicks (see Dec. 19, 1968), turned New York into championship contenders. A reliable scorer and sturdy rebounder, he helped the Knicks to the 1970 and 1973 NBA titles, became New York Nets general manager after his retirement in 1973-74, and after one season took the job as ABA commissioner for that league's last season (1975-76). He later served as Knicks G.M. (1982-86).

1945

Announcement is made that William D. Cox, former owner of the Philadelphia Phillies, will operate an AAFC club known as the Brooklyn Football Dodgers at Ebbets Field when the new pro football league begins play in 1946 (see Jan. 6).

1960

Arch McDonald, briefly a radio broadcaster for the Yankees and Giants in 1939, who spent most of his career working Washington Senators games, dies at age 59 aboard a train between New York and Washington.

1962

Ralph Terry hurls a shutout and the winning run scores on a bases-loaded double-play grounder in the fifth as the Yankees win their 20th World Series in 40 seasons, defeating the Giants, 1-0, at San Francisco, to take the Series, 4-3. With runners at second and third and two out in the bottom of the ninth, Giants cleanup hitter Willie McCovey lines out to second baseman Bobby Richardson to end the game and the Series.

1969

Cleon Jones and Ron Swoboda double in the eighth to produce the winning runs as the Mets defeat the Baltimore Orioles, 5-3, to win the World Series, four games to one, at Shea Stadium. The stunning upset of the heavily-favored Birds completes an improbable rise for the Mets, who had finished ninth at 73-89 in the 10-team National League the year before, the highest finish and best record in their seven-season history.

1973

In the first night World Series game ever played in New York, the Oakland A's edge the Mets, 3-2, in 11 innings, at Shea Stadium, to take a 2-1 Series lead. New York leads 2-0 after the first but four Oakland pitchers allow no more runs.

1976

In their first World Series game in 12 years and one day, the Yankees are beaten by the Reds, 5-1, in the Series opener at Cincinnati.

1906

Willie Hoppe successfully defends his world 18.1 balkline billiards championship at the Garden's Concert Hall, finishing a 500-472 victory over Jake Schaefer, Sr.

1914

In the only meeting ever between these two storied football schools, Yale routs Notre Dame, 28-0, at Yale Field.

1926

Newark Bears open their AFL season before 6,000 at David's Stadium, but Wilson's West Coast Wildcats get the win, 7-0, on a 30-yard pass from George Wilson to Ray Flaherty in the third quarter.

1928

Robert Schnelker, an end with the Football Giants from 1954-60, is born in Galion, Ohio.

1960

Casey Stengel, after 10 pennants and seven World Championships in 12 years, is discharged as Yankees manager at age 71.

1956

Kenneth Morrow is born in Davison, Michigan. A stay-at-home defenseman, Ken Morrow went from the 1980 U.S. Olympic gold medal hockey team to the Islanders and played on their four straight Stanley Cup champions (1980-83). Of his 11 career playoff goals, three came in overtime, including the one that ended the great Islanders-Rangers first-round series of 1984 (see April 10).

1960

Expansion franchises are awarded to New York and Houston by National League owners at Chicago's Blackstone Hotel, increasing league membership from eight teams (where it had been since 1900) to ten. The new clubs begin play in 1962.

1964

Yogi Berra, after winning the pennant in his first season as a manager and guiding the Yankees to the seventh game of the World Series, is fired. Johnny Keane, skipper of the St. Louis team that won the Series, will be named to replace him.

1978

Behind the pitching of Catfish Hunter, the Yankees belt the Dodgers, 7-2, at Dodger Stadium in Los Angeles to take the World Series for the second straight year. In doing so, New York becomes the first team ever to win the Series in six games after dropping the first two.

WILLIE HOPPE

1990

Jordan Olivar, Yale football coach for 11 seasons (1952-62), dies in Inglewood, California, at age 75. A Brooklyn native, Olivar had a 61-32-6 record at Yale, including the undefeated (9-0) 1960 Ivy League champions. His Bulldogs also won the first formal league title in 1956.

October 18

1862

James Creighton, generally believed to be the first professional baseball player and certainly a dominant pitcher on the Brooklyn Excelsiors (1860-62), dies in Brooklyn at age 21.

1879

During the first annual fall meeting of the Pastime Athletic Club, held at the Manhattan AC grounds, Lon F. Myers of the MAC defeats W.F. Benham of the Harlem AC in a speedy quarter-mile, but no one is certain how quick it was, because the timekeeper neglects to take the time. P.H.G. Bissel wins the final heat the 100-yard dash (10.5) and Elliot Marshall wins the hammer throw (64'9").

1900

Brooklyn wins a postseason challenge series with a 6-1 win over the Pirates at Pittsburgh's Exposition Park. A Pittsburgh newspaper, the *Chronicle Telegraph*, offered a trophy for a series between the two top National League teams, and the pennant-winning Brooklyn club beat runner-up Pittsburgh, 3-1, in the best-of-five series, with all games in Pittsburgh.

1915

Robert B. Ward, probably the most important single financial figure in the Federal League, dies of a heart attack at age 64 in Homewood, his estate in New Rochelle, N.Y. Ward was president of the Ward Bread Co. (Tip Top bread) and the Brooklyn FL club (the Tip Tops), as well as the leading member of the FL finance committee. His demise fewer than three weeks after the end of the season convinces other FL owners to abandon their third-major-league aspirations and make their best deal with the American League and National League (see Dec. 18).

1924

Notre Dame tops Army, 13-7, at the Polo Grounds. This comes to be known as the "Four Horsemen Game" owing to sportswriter Grantland Rice's lead, which appeared the following day in the New York *Herald Tribune*: "Outlined against a blue-gray October sky, the Four Horsemen rode again. In dramatic lore they are known as Famine, Pestilence, Destruction and Death. These are only aliases. Their real names are Layden, Crowley, Miller, and Stuhldreher. They formed the crest of a South Bend cyclone before which another fighting Army team was swept over the precipice at the Polo Grounds yesterday as 55,000 spectators peered down on the bewildering panorama spread out on the green plain below."

1925

Following road games at Providence, R.I. and Frankfort (Philadelphia), the Football Giants play their first home game at the Polo Grounds. It is the back end of a weekend home-and-home with the Yellow Jackets, who beat the Giants, 5-3, Saturday in Philadelphia and 14-0 on this Sunday in New York. But the Giants, now 0-3, play their next eight games at home, win the first seven, and finish 8-4.

1977

In the sixth game of the World Series, rightfielder Reggie Jackson belts three homers, all on the first pitch, in three at-bats (his first plate appearance was a four-pitch walk) to lead the Yankees to an 8-4 victory over the Los Angeles Dodgers at Yankee Stadium and the Series title, four games to two, their first since 1962. Counting his last at-bat in the fifth game, Jackson, the Series MVP, homers on four consecutive swings, and totals five Series round-trippers, a record. Mike Torrez wins his second game of the Series with a second complete game.

1978

Nets absorb their worst beating in franchise history, losing at Houston, 139-87.

1995

Michael Rowe, executive vice president of Giants Stadium and the Meadowlands Arena, is named president and chief operating officer of the New Jersey Nets.

1872

Joseph Humphreys is born in New York. The most famous ring announcer of his time, Humphreys became the official announcer at Madison Square Garden in 1920 and resisted using microphones, even after they were installed when the new (third) Garden was opened in 1925.

1873

Columbia, Rutgers, Yale and Pennsylvania meet at the Fifth Avenue Hotel to draft a code of basic rules for intercollegiate football competition. As the pioneers of the sport, these schools are able to impose the code on most all newcomers. Harvard stands alone playing by its own rules, and eventually the two camps reconcile their differences to create uniform playing rules.

1896

Nat Holman, one of the great professional basketball players of the 1920s with the Whirlwinds and Original Celtics, who later coached CCNY during the halcyon days of Beavers basketball from the 1930s to 1951 and again in the late 1950s, is born in New York.

1897

Oliver Hazard Perry Caylor, the sportswriter who became a big-league manager, dies at age 47 in Winona, Minnesota. Caylor managed the AA Mets for 42 games in 1887 after two years at the helm in Cincinnati and then returned to sportswriting in New York.

1900

Roy Worters is born in Toronto, Ontario. A Hockey Hall of Famer, Worters won the Hart Trophy as NHL MVP in 1928-29 and the Vezina Trophy as the league's stingiest goalie in 1930-31 while minding the nets for the Americans.

1941

Augmented by the late signings of Tom Harmon and John Kimbrough, the New York Americans (see Sept. 13) open their AFL home season with a 7-7 tie against the Columbus Bullies at Yankee Stadium. Harmon of Michigan and Kimbrough of Texas A&M finished 1-2 in the 1940 Heisman Trophy vote and help lure 25,385 fans. Harmon scores the Americans' touchdown on a four-yard run 5:40 into the third quarter but leaves the team and doesn't play pro football again until 1946, when he starts a two-year career with the NFL Los Angeles Rams.

1987

Lou Piniella, having just completed his second consecutive full season as Yankees manager, the first Bombers skipper to pull that trick since Billy Martin (1976-77), replaces Woody Woodward as general manager and is succeeded as manager by—surprise!—Billy Martin, whose fifth term will last 68 games.

1991

Tim Lynch completes 50 of 69 passes for five touchdowns and an astonishing 585 yards as Hofstra beats Fordham, 50-30, at Jack Coffey Field in The Bronx. He breaks his own school-record 69 attempts two weeks later, throwing 70 times in a 30-26 win at Towson (Md.) State.

NAT HOLMAN (SECOND FROM RIGHT) AND THE ORIGINAL CELTICS.

1888

With a 6-4 victory, the Giants take a 4-1 lead in the best-of-10 World Series over the St. Louis Browns. This game, played before 9,124, proves to be the last baseball game played at the original Polo Grounds, 110th Street and Fifth Avenue (see Mar. 30). After a game in Philadelphia October 22, the Giants wrap up the Series in St. Louis (see Oct. 25).

1899

United States retains the America's Cup as New York Yacht Club defender *Columbia* completes a three-race sweep over *Shamrock*, 3:38.09 to 3:44.43, in New York Harbor.

1906

William (Buck) Ewing, who played nine seasons with the Giants (1883-89, 1891-92), primarily as a catcher, and managed them in 1900 for 64 games, dies in Cincinnati, Ohio, at age 47.

ROOSEVELT BROWN

1923

Zev, the Kentucky Derby winner, defeats Papyrus, the Epsom Derby winner, by five lengths in a match race at Belmont Park. Zev, ridden by Earle Sande, wins $80,000 and a $5,000 gold cup. The loser earns $20,000.

1923

Before 30,000 at Palmer Stadium, Notre Dame whips Princeton, 25-2.

1931

Mickey Charles Mantle, the Commerce Comet, is born in Spavinaw, Oklahoma.

1932

Roosevelt Brown, Jr., star offensive tackle for the Football Giants from 1953-65, is born in Charlottesville, Virginia. Brown was All-Pro eight times from 1956-63.

1936

Arthur August Zimmerman, the bicycle racing world champion in 1893 and one of the sport's greats, dies in Atlanta, Georgia, at age 67.

1953

Keith Hernandez is born in San Francisco. Hernandez, a smooth-fielding first baseman, was the field general of the 1986 world champion Mets. The 1979 National League co-MVP (with Pittsburgh's Willie Stargell) who led the league in hitting (.344), Hernandez three times hit over .300 with the Mets after his 1983 trade from St. Louis.

1969

Al Weill, the boxing matchmaker at Madison Square Garden who resigned to be heavyweight champion Rocky Marciano's manager, dies in Miami, Florida, at age 75. *Daily Mirror* columnist Dan Parker, referring to Weill's reputation, called him "the Vest," because, he said, "The vest gets all the gravy."

1976

Facing a cash crunch that threatens their first NBA season before it can even start, the Nets sell their best player and the former ABA's marquee attraction, Julius Erving, to the Philadelphia 76ers.

1845

In another of the continuing series of baseball games between the cities of New York and Brooklyn, New York beats Brooklyn, 24-4, in a four-inning game at Elysian Fields, Hoboken, N.J. The teams dine together at McCarty's restaurant afterwards.

1880

Lon F. Myers of the Manhattan Athletic Club sets a record of 39.5 seconds in the 350-yard run at the Elizabeth (N.J.) AC track meet.

1910

After one tie, a non-playing Sunday and a day of rain, the first New York City Series finally ends with a 6-3 Giants victory over the Highlanders at the Polo Grounds. Christy Mathewson gets his fourth win in the best-of-seven series while rookie Russ Ford is the loser. The Giants win the series, four games to two (and the tie), with a paid attendance of 103,033 for the seven games producing a gross gate of $81,462.50. Larry Doyle's three-run homer in the third inning is the decisive blow in the finale.

1956

After 31 seasons at the Polo Grounds, the Football Giants open their first season at Yankee Stadium with a 38-10 win over Pittsburgh. The Giants had played several games in the Stadium in earlier years as visitors.

1964

Francis (Happy) Felton, host of the "Knothole Gang" television show on WOR-TV (Channel 9) before Brooklyn Dodgers home games at Ebbets Field, who also hosted the postgame show, "Meet the Stars," dies in New York at age 56.

1973

Completing their rebound from a 3-2 Series deficit, the A's beat the Mets, 5-2, at Oakland to win the World Series, 4-3. Bert Campaneris and Reggie Jackson, both of whom later play for the Yankees, hit two-run homers in the third inning off Mets starter Jon Matlack, Oakland's first homers of the Series.

1973

Playing their sixth straight road game to open the season, the Jets lose, 26-14, to the Steelers in a game originally scheduled for Shea Stadium but moved to Pittsburgh because of the World Series. The Jets play only six home games (out of 14 total) this season.

1976

Knicks retire Willis Reed's No. 19 in a ceremony at the Garden, the first uniform number retired by the club. The Knicks subsequently retire Nos. 10 (Walt Frazier, 1979), 22 (Dave DeBusschere, 1981), 24 (Bill Bradley, 1984), 15 (Earl Monroe, 1986 and Dick McGuire, 1992), 12 (Dick Barnett, 1990) and 613 (Red Holzman, honoring his Knicks coaching victories, 1990).

1976

Johnny Bench drives in five runs with a pair of homers as the Cincinnati Reds beat the Yankees, 7-2, at the Stadium, and sweep the World Series in four straight games.

1987

Dr. Sidney S. Gaynor, Yankees team physician from 1948-76, dies in Columbus, Indiana, at age 82. Gaynor was on the staff at Manhattan's Lenox Hill Hospital from 1934-76.

1993

Irving Torgoff, an All-America forward at LIU in 1938-39 when the Blackbirds went 24-0 and won the NIT, dies in Fort Lauderdale, Florida, at age 76.

October 22

1845

On page two of this morning's *New York Herald*, the following item appears in column 4: "Base Ball Match - A very closely contested match of this well-known and old-fashioned game took place yesterday at Hoboken between nine Brooklyn men and nine New Yorkers. We were informed last evening that the Brooklynites were the victors." It is the first known report of baseball in a major newspaper. It is also incorrect (see Oct. 21).

1883

Opening day of the first National Horse Show at Madison Square Garden with the fire engine horse judging at 10 a.m. At 3:45 p.m., Mayor Franklin Edson delivers the formal opening remarks. The show is now the oldest indoor equestrian competition in the world (see Oct. 30).

1900

A thoroughbred racing meeting is held for the first time at Empire City in Yonkers, N.Y., but regular racing won't begin until 1907. Harness racing (briefly) returns and auto racing is tried before James Butler establishes racing for 35 years at the track.

1910

The first international aerial tournament is held for airplanes at Belmont Park, running through October 31. Claude Graham-Whitlaw wins the $5,000 Gordon Bennett Trophy Race. On October 30, John B. Moisant of the United States wins the $10,000 Statue of Liberty Race by 43 seconds. Ralph Johnstone sets an altitude record during the tournament of 9,714 feet and also wins a $5,000 prize.

1939

In the first televised NFL game, the Brooklyn Football Dodgers defeat the Philadelphia Eagles (coached by Bert Bell), 23-14, at Ebbets Field. A live audience of 13,057 far outnumber those watching over NBC's W2XBS.

1942

Allen J. Coage, AAU heavyweight judo champion six times (1965-66, 1968-70, 1975) and later a personal celebrity bodyguard, is born in New York.

1955

Yankees open a 16-game tour of Japan with a 10-2 victory over the Mainichi Orions in Tokyo. The tour also includes five games in Hawaii on the way out and stops in Okinawa, Manila and Guam on the return. The Yankees win 24 of the 25 games and tie the other, 1-1.

1966

For the third straight year, club football teams from Fordham and NYU meet, with the Violets winning, 7-0, at Jack Coffey Field. But NYU disbands its team after the season while the Rams, despite a 1-5 record, continue for three more until varsity status is restored in 1970.

1979

John Drebinger dies in Greensboro, North Carolina, at age 88. Drebinger, a *Staten Island Advance* sportswriter from 1916-24, wrote primarily baseball for *The New York Times* from 1924-64. He wrote *The Times'* World Series main lead 203 times.

1992

Red Barber, one of the most famous broadcast voices in baseball history, dies in Tallahassee, Florida, at age 84. Barber broadcast for the Dodgers (1939-53) and Yankees (1954-66), being dismissed after the 1966 season by Yankees president Mike Burke.

1863

Seton Hall beats Fordham, 20-13, in the first intercollegiate baseball game played in New Jersey.

1884

In the opening game of the first officially-sanctioned World Series, the Providence Grays, behind the two-hit pitching of Charley (Old Hoss) Radbourne, beat the Mets, 6-0, at the Polo Grounds. The next day, Radbourne outpitches the AA Mets' Tim Keefe again in a 3-1 victory for the National League champs, who complete the three-game sweep Oct. 25, 12-2. Radbourne, who was 60-12 during the regular season, pitches complete games in all three wins.

1906

Gertrude Ederle is born in New York. Perhaps the most famous woman's swimmer in American history, she was the first woman to swim the English Channel (August 6, 1926), making the crossing in record time, and was honored with a ticker-tape parade up Lower Broadway.

1915

Columbia plays its first varsity football game in 10 years and routs St. Lawrence, 57-0, at South Field on the Columbia campus.

JIM LEYRITZ

1967

New Jersey Americans play their first game, losing, 110-107 to the Pittsburgh Pipers before 3,089 at the Teaneck (N.J.) Armory. Center Dan Anderson leads all scorers with 41 points. The Americans spend one season in New Jersey before shifting to Long Island to become the New York Nets.

1976

Rutgers beats Columbia, 47-2, before 42,382 in the first college football game at Giants Stadium in East Rutherford, N.J.

1983

In one of the event's most dramatic finishes, New Zealand's Rod Dixon becomes the first non-American man to win the New York City Marathon. He makes a powerful sprint in Central Park to catch the leader, Geoff Smith, who vainly tries to stagger the final yards. Smith's punishing pace forces Dixon to run the distance in 2:08:59, only 46 seconds off the world record.

1995

Bob Watson is named Yankees general manager and, within about a year, becomes the first black general manager of a world championship team. But Watson, the 16th general manager in the George Steinbrenner era, resigns February 3, 1998, and is succeeded by his 30-year-old assistant, Brian Cashman.

1996

Trailing two games to one in the World Series and 6-0 after five innings, the Yankees rally to stun the Braves, 8-6, in 10 innings at Atlanta. After three runs in the sixth, the Bombers tie it on Jim Leyritz's three-run homer in the eighth, and win it on Wade Boggs' bases-loaded, two-out walk. With a 1-0 win the following night to take a 3-2 Series lead, the Yankees finish their road 1996 postseason with an 8-0 record.

1845

In a return match of the baseball game played three days earlier, New York defeats Brooklyn again, 37-19, this time on the grounds of the Star Club, Myrtle Avenue, Brooklyn (see Oct. 21).

1891

First six-day bike race run at the Garden is won by Irish-born Bill Martin, a Detroit resident who came to the United States at age 3. Martin logs 1,466 miles and four laps in the 142-hour event, setting a world record. The record of 1,405 miles was set by Albert Schock in Minneapolis in December 1886 but Schock, considered the world champion, finishes fourth in the first Garden event behind Charles Ashinger and England's William Lamb. A final day crowd of 8,000 packs the Garden and the receipts of over $25,000 for the six days include $8,000 prize money, of which Martin wins $3,000.

1906

In something of a racing rarity, a 100-to-1 shot, a three-year-old bay colt named Young Davis, wins the sixth race at Jamaica. One wise bettor, Eugene Woods, bets $40 on Young Davis each of three ways and collects over $5,000.

1908

George H. Robertson becomes the first American driver to win the Vanderbilt Cup auto race as the competition resumes after a year's absence. Robertson wins by 1:48.4 in his 90-horsepower Locomobile over Herbert Lytle in his Isotta. With 500 National Guard troops and squads of special Nassau County deputy sheriffs to control the crowd of over 200,000 on the 23.46-mile circuit, the race uses nine miles of the new Long Island Motor Parkway. The Parkway was privately financed expressly to be used in the race after spectator fatalities in 1906.

1914

Princeton beats Dartmouth, 16-12, in the first game at the Tigers' new Palmer Stadium. A bit over 82 years later, Dartmouth gets revenge with a 24-0 win in the final game at Palmer, Nov. 23, 1996.

1926

Red Grange draws 18,521 fans to Yankee Stadium on a gloomy Sunday but Eddie Tryon is the hero with a 76-yard run in the fourth quarter that gives the AFL Yankees a 6-0 win over Wilson's West Coast Wildcats in their home opener. In other local pro games, Rock Island and Newark play a scoreless AFL tie at David's Stadium as the teams trade 23 punts in the mud and, at Brooklyn's Commercial Field, the AFL Horsemen's game against the Philadelphia Quakers is rained out. Across the Harlem River from Yankee Stadium, the Football Giants beat the Kansas City Cowboys, 13-0, at the Polo Grounds, but only 5,000 brave the weather for the NFL game.

1972

Jackie Robinson, who broke the major league baseball color line in 1947 when he joined the Brooklyn Dodgers and went on to a Hall of Fame career, dies in Stamford, Connecticut, at age 53.

1976

Bill Rodgers starts his four-year winning streak as the New York City Marathon goes city-wide for the first time. Rodgers sets an event record of 2:10:10 to beat Frank Shorter in the first five-borough race while Miki Gorman is the first woman finisher. In an effort to minimize traffic disruption, the now-fabled First Avenue section in Manhattan is not part of the course. The runners instead use the East River Promenade and, as a result, have to run up 25 steps along the FDR Drive.

1988

Henry Armstrong, who in 1938 became the first boxer to hold three world titles (featherweight, welterweight, lightweight) simultaneously, dies in Los Angeles, California, at age 75.

October 25

1888

With Buck Ewing and Mike Tiernan hitting homers, the Giants wrap up their first World Series title with an 11-3 victory over the AA Browns at St. Louis in the eighth game of a best-of-10 series. Although the National League winners have already clinched, six games to two, the Browns want to play the last two games and beat the Giants reserves, 14-11 and 18-7.

1921

Bat Masterson dies in New York at age 67. William Barclay Masterson, famed western frontier gunslinger, former Marshall of Dodge City, Kansas, and inspiration for the character Sky Masterson in Damon Runyon's *Guys and Dolls*, worked as a boxing referee and sportswriter, became sports editor of *The Morning Telegraph* and died at his desk in the newspaper's office. He was found by his aide, Sam Taub, later a famed boxing announcer.

1946

Dr. Mal Stevens resigns as head coach of the Brooklyn Football Dodgers on the day of a home game against the Miami Seahawks after a dispute with owner Bill Cox. The Dodgers beat Miami, 30-7, under interim coach Thomas Scott and Cliff Battles is hired as head coach November 1. Battles lasts through the 1947 season.

1947

Overcoming a 20-7 halftime deficit, Columbia upsets Army, 21-20, at Baker Field, ending the Cadets' 32-game unbeaten streak. End Bill Swiacki is the star, making two acrobatic catches in the fourth quarter, one resulting in a touchdown and the other setting up Lou Kusserow's tying score. Ventan Yablonski's extra point provides the margin of victory. The Lions finish the season 7-2, ranked 20th in the nation.

1976

Claire (Mrs. Babe) Ruth dies in New York at age 76.

1981

Alberto Salazar of Eugene, Ore., wins the second of his three straight New York City Marathons and sets a world record in the process, dashing home in 2:08:13 in the first nationally-televised marathon (ABC). Salazar's record is a New York standard until Jumal Kangaa of Tanzania is clocked in 2:08:01 in 1989. Alison Roe of New Zealand breaks the city's women's record with her 2:25:27 finish (surpassed by Australia's Lisa Ondieki in 1992). The twin record performances on national television ignite the American running mania and confirm running as, once again, a major sport.

1982

Winston Frederick Churchill Guest, a Yale graduate, international polo star, father of a famous debutante and relation of Winston Churchill, dies in Mineola, N.Y., at age 76.

1986

Twice a strike from elimination, the Mets tie the World Series three games all with a 6-5 10-inning win over Boston at Shea Stadium. After the first two men in the home half of the tenth are retired, the Mets, trailing 5-3, get three runs after three singles score a run, Bob Stanley's wild pitch with Mookie Wilson up ties it, and Wilson's roller to first slides under Bill Buckner's glove as Ray Knight scores the winning run from second.

1986

Emerging from a disastrous fire, Freehold (N.J.) Raceway hosts the Breeder's Crown three-year-old Filly Trot with a new grandstand. JEFS Spice, driven by Bill O'Donnell, wins in 1:59 for O'Donnell's third straight victory in the annual event.

1991

Anthony Russo runs for five touchdowns as St. John's defeats C.W. Post, 54-14, at Redmen Field to win the Liberty Conference championship for the second time in three seasons.

October 26

1911

In the latest ending of a World Series until 1981, the Athletics beat the Giants, 13-2, at Philadelphia, to close out the Series, 4-2. Chief Bender holds the Giants to four hits in the finale after four days of rain and Sunday Blue Laws extend the six games over 13 days.

1923

In its first season of football, St. John's scores a major upset by beating Fordham, 13-0, at the Polo Grounds. Coach Ray Lynch's team ends the season 5-0-1 as only a season-ending 6-6 tie with Providence mars an otherwise perfect inaugural campaign.

1930

Harry Payne Whitney, one of America's finest international polo stars, dies in New York at age 58.

1950

Walter F. O'Malley and Mrs. John L. Smith exercise their options on Branch Rickey's 25% interest in the Brooklyn Dodgers, purchasing the share for $1.025 million, and announce that Rickey's contract as president and general manager (which expires October 28) will not be renewed. O'Malley becomes president of the Dodgers and Rickey moves to the Pittsburgh Pirates as executive vice president and general manager.

1956

Knicks trade Walter Dukes and the draft rights to Burdette Haldorson to Minneapolis for guard Slater Martin and forward Jerry Bird. Martin and Bird, combined, play 24 games for the Knicks.

1968

Rum Customer, driven by Billy Haughton, wins the $189,018.15 Messenger Stakes, the richest harness race ever run, at Roosevelt Raceway.

1981

Free agent guard Ray Williams signs an offer sheet with the Nets. To induce the Knicks not to match the offer, the Nets send power forward Maurice Lucas to New York.

1983

Mike Michalske, a guard for the Football Yankees of the AFL (1926) and NFL (1927-28), dies at age 80.

1984

Howard Samuels dies in New York at age 64. A loser to future governor Hugh Carey in the 1974 New York Democratic gubernatorial primary, "Howie the Horse" was the first president of New York City Off-Track Betting (1971) and later president of the dying North American Soccer League (1982).

1996

Making three runs in the third stand up, the Yankees beat Atlanta, 3-2, at Yankee Stadium to take the World Series, 4-2, becoming the first team in baseball history to win the Series in six games after dropping the first two at home. Joe Girardi's RBI triple keys the inning and Jimmy Key, pitching his last game as a Yankee, gets the win. MVP John Wetteland gets his fourth save of Series despite allowing a run in the ninth.

1922

Ralph McPherran Kiner is born in Santa Rita, New Mexico. National League leader (either outright or tied) in homers a record seven straight seasons (1946-52), Ralph Kiner became a broadcaster with the original Mets in 1962 and stayed with them for over 35 years.

1923

West Virginia and Penn State battle to an exciting 13-13 tie that draws 50,000 to Yankee Stadium. The year before, the Nittany Lions inaugurated their long-running series with Syracuse at the Polo Grounds with a scoreless tie.

1924

Columbia football coach Percy D. Haughton dies of angina pectoris at age 48 in New York after a practice. Haughton, who earned his greatest fame at Harvard, where he restored the Crimson as a major national power, came to Columbia to do the same, but died midway through his second season with the Lions 4-1. His final words were, "Tell the squad I'm proud of them."

1955

Clark Griffith, the first manager of the Highlanders in 1903 (who became the Yankees), and later owner of the original American League Washington Senators, dies in Washington, D.C., at age 85.

1962

Beau Purple beats Kelso in the Man O' War Stakes on the final day before Belmont Park closes for a renovation project that will take almost six years as the old stands are demolished. Most thoroughbred racing is conducted at Aqueduct, including the Belmont Stakes, before Belmont reopens in 1968.

1973

Islanders beat the Rangers, 3-2, at Nassau Coliseum, their first win ever over their cross-county rivals after six losses the year before. Denis Potvin scores his first career goal.

1975

Georges Carpentier, a French native and the only boxer known to have fought professionally in every existing weight class, dies in Paris, France, at age 81. His most famous bout was a loss to heavyweight champ Jack Dempsey in 1921 (see July 2).

1986

After a one-day postponement caused by rain, the Mets win the World Series for the second time in their 25-season history with an 8-5 victory over the Red Sox in the seventh game to take the Series, four games to three. Ray Knight and Darryl Strawberry homer as the Mets wipe out a 3-0 Boston lead with three in the sixth and seventh, and two more in the eighth after Boston's pair in the top half cut the lead to 6-5. Roger McDowell gets the win and Jesse Orosco the save, but the unsung pitching star is Sid Fernandez, whose three innings of scoreless relief hold Boston while the Mets catch up.

DENIS POTVIN

1996

Jets beat the Cardinals, 31-21, at Arizona, snapping a club-record 12-game losing streak. But the Jets lose their last seven games to finish 1-15, the worst mark in team history.

1890

With public interest drained by the war among three baseball leagues, the World Series fizzles to an anti-climax at Brooklyn's Eastern Park. Louisville's Red Ehret outpitches Tom Lovett to give the AA Colonels a 6-2 victory over Brooklyn that ties the series 3-3-1. But when only 300 fans show up, the balance of the series is canceled. Brooklyn won the National League pennant in its first year in the league but begins a World Series frustration that would last 65 years.

1899

Harold Weekes sprints 70 yards for the game's only touchdown as Columbia shocks Yale, 5-0, at Manhattan Field. It is the first time in its 28-season football history that Yale has ever been shut out by a team other than Harvard, Princeton or Pennsylvania.

1922

Surging back from an 18-7 deficit in the fourth quarter, Princeton stops the University of Chicago, 21-18, at Chicago. The Tigers also need a great goal-line stand in the last minute to save the victory. Radio history is made, too, when Gus Falzer calls the action on Newark's WOR in the first football broadcast ever.

1925

Rev. Dr. William J. Leggett, captain of the Rutgers team that won the first intercollegiate football game ever played (see Nov. 6), dies at age 77 in Nyack, N.Y.

HAROLD WEEKES

1926

Bowie Kent Kuhn, baseball commissioner from 1969-84, is born in Tacona Park, Maryland. Kuhn presided over some of the most revolutionary times in baseball history, including splitting the leagues into divisions (1969), the first players' strike (1972), the death of the reserve clause (1975), night World Series games (1971), the designated hitter (1973) and the first billion-dollar television contract.

1932

Nine local teams meeting at the Jamaica Arena in Queens form the Metropolitan Amateur Hockey League and elect Julius Weibel of the Van Cortlandt Bronks the first president. George B. Smith, Jr., of the Morristown (N.J.) Millionaires is named vice president, Harold Heinze (New York Stock Exchange Brokers) first secretary and Reggie Proud (Bayside Bears) treasurer.

1979

Dick Howser is named Yankees manager, replacing Billy Martin, whose second term ends after he punches out a marshmallow salesman in a Minneapolis hotel.

1981

Los Angeles, after dropping the first two games of the World Series, takes the Series, four games to two, beating the Yankees at the Stadium, 9-2, their fourth comeback win in a row. New York reliever George Frazier ties a dubious record with his third Series loss. The mark was set by crooked "Black Sox" pitcher Lefty Williams in the 1919 Series.

1993

Bob Seeds, 86, outfielder for the Yankees (1936), Giants (1938-40) and 1937 International League Newark Bears (considered by many the greatest minor-league team ever), dies in Erick, Oklahoma.

1889

Rallying from a three-games-to-one deficit, the Giants win their second straight World Series with a 3-2 ninth-game victory over Brooklyn at the Polo Grounds. The Giants lost three of the first four to the A.A. champs but then win five straight in the best-of-10 series.

1920

Ed Barrow, former manager of the Boston Red Sox, is named Yankees general manager, beginning his 24-year tenure during which he will establish the Yankees as baseball's dominant team.

1937

Amateur Hockey Association of the United States (AHAUS) is formed in New York and New York's Tommy Lockhart is elected its first president. John B. Sollenberger of Hershey, Pennsylvania, is elected vice president and Philip E.M. Thompson of Atlantic City, N.J., secretary-treasurer of the organization that still controls amateur hockey in the United States.

1953

Denis Charles Potvin is born in Ottawa, Ontario. Captain of all four Islanders Stanley Cup champions (1980-83), Denis Potvin, best defenseman in club history, won the Norris Trophy as the NHL's best backliner three times and was runnerup twice. He finished his career with 310 goals and 742 assists for 1,052 points, all NHL records for defensemen when he retired.

1956

Frederick M. Linder, president of the Jacob Ruppert Brewery and treasurer of the Yankees, dies in New York.

1965

William Boyd McKechnie dies in Bradenton, Florida, at age 79. Bill McKechnie cut his managerial teeth with the Newark Peps of the Federal League in 1915, succeeding Bill Phillips and managing the last 99 games of the season (54-45). McKechnie later managed 24 years in the National League, winning pennants at Pittsburgh (1925), St. Louis (1928) and Cincinnati (1939-40). He also briefly played third base for both the Yankees and Giants.

BUCK SHOWALTER

1966

For the second straight year, there is a pacing Triple Crown winner as Romeo Hanover wins the Messenger Stakes at Roosevelt Raceway.

1991

Buck Showalter is named Yankees manager, succeeding Stump Merrill. Showalter lasts four seasons, the longest tenure since Ralph Houk (1966-73), and after guiding the Bombers to a 76-86 record in 1992, leads them to second-, first- and second-place finishes.

1992

Homer Zink, a Rutgers oarsman who later starred as a single sculler for the Nereiod Boat Club (Belleville, N.J.) and as an independent, dies in West Trenton, N.J., at age 73.

1992

Tom Cahill, a three-sport athlete at Army from 1940-42 who coached the Cadets football team from 1966-73 (40-39-2), dies at age 73 in Schenectady, N.Y.

1871

Forced to play a "home" game at Brooklyn's Union Grounds, the Chicago White Stockings lose, 4-1, to the Athletics, giving Philadelphia the NA championship on the final day of professional baseball's first pennant race. The great Chicago fire earlier in the month destroyed the White Stockings' ballpark.

1898

William Harold Terry is born in Atlanta, Georgia. "Memphis Bill" Terry, a Giants first baseman, was the last National Leaguer to hit .400 (.401 in 1930) and, after succeeding John McGraw in 1932, managed the Giants to three pennants (1933, 1936, 1937).

1944

Graeme Hammond, president of the American Olympic Association (predecessor of U.S. Olympic Committee) and the New York Athletic Club, dies at age 86.

1954

In their first game playing with a 24-second clock, the Knicks down the Minneapolis Lakers, 94-83, at the Garden.

MIKE RICHTER

1956

Ebbets Field is sold to real estate developer Marvin Kratter, with the Dodgers holding a lease through the 1959 season. Kratter plans a housing project for the site.

1973

Righthander Tom Seaver wins the second of his three Cy Young Awards as the NL's best pitcher. The Mets star was 19-10 and is the first non-20-game winner chosen for the award by the BBWAA. Seaver won the award in 1969 and would win again in 1975.

1981

New Jersey Nets play their first game at the Meadowlands Arena in East Rutherford, N.J., but lose to the Knicks, 103-99.

1981

Daniel J. Lynch, a guard with St. Francis from 1935-38 who served as Terriers head coach from 1948-69 (282-237) and athletic director from 1956-75, dies in New York at age 65.

1989

Leonard Cohen, sportswriter at the *Evening World* from 1924-26 who was both a sports editor and columnist with the *Post* from 1926-74, dies in Lauderdale Lakes, Florida, at age 87.

1996

After seven years at New Jersey's Meadowlands Arena, the 113-year-old National Horse Show returns to Madison Square Garden for a four-day run entitled "Homecoming 1996" (see Oct. 22).

1996

Devils set a club record with 54 shots, but Rangers goalie Mike Richter stops 53, and the Blueshirts shoot 6-for-23 to beat New Jersey at the Meadowlands, 6-1.

1905

Organized as the local affiliate of the AAU, the Metropolitan AAU is formed in a meeting at the St. Bartholomew's Club. When permanent officers are elected November 16 at the Pastime Athletic Club, P.F. Walsh of the NYAC is elected president.

1911

Wilfred Kennedy McDonald is born in Fergus, Ontario. Bucko McDonald played defense on the terrible Rangers teams of 1943-44 and 1944-45 before being elected to the Canadian Parliament.

1916

Nicholas E. Young dies in Washington, D.C., at age 76. Young, secretary of the player-run National Association of Professional Ballplayers from 1871-75 and secretary and treasurer of the National League from its inception in 1876 to 1902, was also league president simultaneously from 1885-1902.

1941

Making its seventh (and final) football appearance in New York City, Penn State routs NYU, 42-0, before 10,690 at the Polo Grounds.

1959

In their first football meeting ever, Army and the Air Force Academy play to a 13-13 tie before over 70,000 at Yankee Stadium.

1964

Maine Maritime scores a 42-0 victory over visiting Fordham in a game that marks the debut of the Rams' club football team and the return of the sport to the Rose Hill school after a 10-year hiatus (see Dec. 17). Senior David Langdon acts as the student coach of the team.

1975

Rangers goalie Eddie Giacomin is claimed on waivers by the Detroit Red Wings (see Nov. 2).

1992

Hugh (Bones) Taylor, Titans assistant coach from 1960-62, dies in Wynne, Arkansas, at age 69.

1993

In a neutral-site game as part of the NHL's effort to introduce hockey to new markets, the Rangers beat the Devils at Halifax, Nova Scotia, 4-1. The plan, introduced the year before, is dropped after this season.

1993

In their first regular-season meeting in five years, the "visiting" 2-4 Jets beat the "home" 5-1 Football Giants, 10-6, before 71,659 at Giants Stadium, igniting a five-game Jets winning streak. Despite earning local bragging rights, the Jets lose their last three games to wind up 8-8, missing the playoffs, while the Giants make it, finishing 11-5.

EDDIE GIACOMIN

November 1

1913

Notre Dame meets Army for the first time and defeats the Cadets, 35-13, in a major upset on the plains of West Point as Gus Dorais completes 14 of 17 passes for 243 yards, including a 40-yard scoring toss to Knute Rockne. The matchup is made after Army's scheduled game with Yale is canceled in a dispute over player eligibility.

1922

Mickey Walker wins the welterweight championship with a 15-round decision over Jack Britton at the Garden.

1928

Yale football reports gross revenue in excess of $1 million for the first time, announcing that the 1927 season produced $1,033,211.98, with a net profit of $543,084.76.

1944

Branch Rickey, president of the Brooklyn Dodgers, announces that he has purchased 25% of the club, along with Walter F. O'Malley and Andrew J. Schmitz.

1946

In their first game, the Knicks beat the Huskies, 68-66, at Toronto's Maple Leaf Gardens.

1947

Man O'War, the greatest racing thoroughbred of his generation, dies at age 30 a few miles from Lexington, Kentucky. Man O'War won 20 of his 21 career starts, including a match race against Sir Barton, the first Triple Crown winner (1919). His only career loss was to Upset in Saratoga, N.Y. Of his 21 races, 20 were run on New York tracks.

1957

On the day before his Princeton football team is to meet Brown at Providence, R.I., head coach Charlie Caldwell dies in Princeton, N.J., at age 56. (The Tigers win the next day, 7-0, under acting coach Dick Colman, who had taken over for the ailing Caldwell at the start of the season.)

1967

Dear Brutus, ridden by Russell Stewart, sets a Garden record with a jump of 7'3" to win the $1,250 Puissance Stake at the last National Horse Show to be staged at Garden No. 3. The crowd of over 7,000 responds with a rare standing ovation. The next night, Bold Minstrel, ridden by U.S. Olympian Bill Steinkraus, matches the record.

1967

Willis Reed scores 53 points, the highest road game total in club history, as the Knicks beat the Lakers, 129-113, at the Los Angeles Sports Arena.

1971

After two days of meetings in New York, the World Hockey Association is organized as a second major league with franchises in St. Paul, Chicago, Dayton, Edmonton, Los Angeles, Winnipeg, Calgary, San Francisco and Miami, as well as New York. Ontario and New England join November 21, San Francisco is shifted to Quebec City Feb. 11, 1972, Dayton switches to Houston in March 1972 and Cleveland and Philadelphia join in June 1972. Play starts with 12 teams on Oct. 11, 1972.

1974

Junie McMahon dies in Hackensack, N.J., at age 62. McMahon, who bowled in the first nationally-televised match in 1959, was the BWAA Bowler of the Year in 1950.

1893

Pascal, a black gelding driven by J.P. Gibbs, sets a world speed trotting record for 10 miles during the Driving Club of New York meeting at Fleetwood Park (now The Bronx), clocking 26:15 for the distance. The feat is performed before 12,000 fans, who also see the trotter Directum score a surprising win over the pacer Mascot in three straight one-mile heats.

1906

Paul Ivan Thompson, an original Ranger in 1926 as a left wing, is born in Calgary, Alberta.

1916

Alexander Sebastian Campanis is born in Cos, Greece. Captain of the 1940 NYU baseball team, Al Campanis, as a Brooklyn scout in 1955, signed lefthander Sandy Koufax to a Dodgers contract. He gradually moved up in the Dodgers organization until some ill-advised remarks on the nationally-televised "Nightline" show with Ted Koppel regarding the supposed lack of baseball "necessities" among blacks seeking management positions led to his swift termination.

1923

In the eighth meeting between the schools' football teams and the first at Yankee Stadium, NYU defeats Fordham, 20-0, for the Violets' first victory in the series.

1934

Kenneth Robert Rosewall is born in Sydney, Australia. Durable Ken Rosewall won the U.S. national tennis title at Forest Hills in 1956 as an amateur and the 1970 Open as a pro. The 14-year gap between championships is by far the largest in the tournament's history.

1964

For $11,200,000, Dan Topping and Del Webb sell 80% of the Yankees, coming off their fifth straight pennant and 14th in 16 years, to CBS. The network has bought a pig in a poke. Over the next three years, the Yankees finish sixth (out of 10), 10th and ninth.

1965

Knicks trade forward Jim (Bad News) Barnes, the No. 1 overall pick in the 1964 draft, to Baltimore with forward Johnny Green, guard John Egan, and cash for center Walt Bellamy.

1975

Two days after being claimed on waivers by Detroit, Eddie Giacomin returns to Madison Square Garden as a Red Wing. The fans root for the visitors, who do not disappoint, jumping out to a 4-0 lead and winning, 6-4, with Giacomin making 42 saves.

1979

Feeling they need a dominant defenseman to complete a team that lost that spring's Stanley Cup final, the Rangers acquire 22-year-old 6'3" backliner Barry (Bubba) Beck from the Colorado Rockies for left wing Pat Hickey, right wing Lucien DeBlois, defensemen Mike McEwen and Dean Turner and future considerations. Beck by himself never does compensate for the loss of three important starters (Hickey, DeBlois and McEwen) and the Rangers never reach the final in his seven seasons in New York.

1988

Nets trade Tony Brown, Frank Johnson, Tim McCormick and Lorenzo Romar to Houston for Rockets center Joe Barry Carroll and Lester Conner.

November 3

1877

"Roughest game ever seen in America" is the *Herald* headline after Princeton defeats Harvard in the first meeting ever between the schools in football. A heavy Friday rain makes the St. George Cricket Grounds in Hoboken, N.J., soggy for the game and perhaps also accounts for the small crowd (500).

1892

Robert Lindley Murray is born in San Francisco, California. Murray won both "Patriotic" national men's singles tennis tournaments held at Forest Hills during World War I to raise money for the Red Cross (1917-18).

1900

Madison Square Garden is the site for the first National Automobile Show, where 40 manufacturers exhibit over 300 different vehicles. The seven-day event draws more than 48,000 to see the greatest display of the new "horseless carriage" ever yet presented.

1911

John Joseph Keane is born in St. Louis, Missouri. After managing St. Louis to the 1964 World Series over the Yankees, Keane left the Cardinals to replace Yogi Berra as the Bombers' skipper just in time to preside over the disintegration of the Yankee dynasty.

IRVING MITCHELL FELT

1936

Roy Stanley Emerson is born in Black Butt, Queensland, Australia. Roy Emerson has won more major singles titles (12) than any other man in tennis history, including the U.S. nationals at Forest Hills twice (1961, 1964).

1960

Adm. John J. Bergen, chairman of Graham-Paige Corporation, owner of Madison Square Garden, and Irving Mitchell Felt, president of the investment house, announce plans for a new Garden, the fourth. Several sites are under consideration, but the site ultimately becomes the existing Pennsylvania Station at 33rd Street and 7th Avenue. Demolition of Penn Station to make way for the new Garden begins in 1962. Construction starts in 1965 and the new facility opens in segments beginning in the fall of 1967, though the main arena does not open until February 11, 1968. Outcry over the destruction of Penn Station leads to the enactment of New York's landmark Landmarks Preservation Law, the first of its kind in the country. That law is invoked in the mid-1970s to prevent the destruction of Grand Central Terminal (built in 1913 to rival Penn Station's grandeur), successor to Grand Central Depot, built in 1871 when the New York and Harlem Railroad vacated its terminal at 26th Street and Madison Avenue, later site of the first Garden.

1964

Clarence C. Pell, 12-time U.S. racquets champion in singles from 1915-33 and nine-time doubles champion with Stanley G. Mortimer, dies in Westbury, N.Y., at age 79.

1992

Nicholas J. Miranda, a major organizer of the semi-pro Queens Baseball Alliance, dies in Millbrook, N.Y., at age 84.

1888

John J. O'Brien is born in Brooklyn. A St. John's product and basketball referee for 20 years, O'Brien helped organize the Interstate League in 1914 and was its president from 1915-17. He headed the Metropolitan Basketball League from 1922-28 and was president of the first American Basketball League from 1928-54.

1889

Celebrated billiards player Harvey McKenna dies in New York.

1890

Princeton's Phil King runs for 11 touchdowns as the Tigers roll to an 85-0 victory over Columbia, the Lions' second-worst football loss ever (93-0, Yale, 1883).

1929

Donald J. Tierney, a member of the New York Athletic Club and the U.S. Olympic bronze medal water polo team of 1948, is born in Brooklyn.

1929

Raymond Wietecha, Football Giants center from 1953-62, is born in East Chicago, Indiana.

1939

Emmette Bryant, a backup guard for four seasons (1964-68) for the Knicks, averaging 5.9 ppg, is born in Chicago.

1942

Arthur James Roberts is born in Holyoke, Massachusetts. Archie Roberts was a star quarterback at Columbia from 1962-64 who later played for the NFL Cleveland Browns and AFL Miami Dolphins.

1962

Blanche (Mrs. John) McGraw dies at age 81 in New York.

1985

Cus D'Amato, who trained heavyweight champion Floyd Patterson and was guiding 19-year-old Mike Tyson at the time of his death, dies in New York at age 77.

1996

Yankees shortstop Derek Jeter is chosen unanimously as the American League Rookie of the Year, sweeping all 28 first-place votes in the BBWAA national poll.

DEREK JETER

November 5

1869

Cincinnati's Red Stockings, baseball's first openly-pro team, ends its initial season with a 17-8 victory over the Mutuals at Union Grounds in Brooklyn. Cincinnati finishes the season with a 57-0-1 record.

1884

Wyllys Terry runs 115 yards for a touchdown to highlight Yale's 46-0 victory over Wesleyan at New Haven.

1900

Harvey J. Harman, Rutgers head football coach from 1938-41 and 1946-55, is born. Harman, who later served as executive director of the National Football Foundation and Hall of Fame, posted a 74-44-2 record with the Chanticleers.

1935

Frank L. Lambrecht dies at age 72 in White Plains, N.Y. Lambrecht was a star with the Manhattan Athletic Club, winning the national amateur championship in the shotput four times and the hammer throw thrice. He won both titles three straight years (1883-85).

1938

Rutgers breaks a 33-game losing streak against Princeton, dating back to the second college football game ever played, in 1869 (see Nov. 6), with a 20-18 victory in the dedication game for the new Rutgers Stadium in New Brunswick, N.J.

1953

Walter Koppisch dies at age 52 in New York. Koppisch, a halfback who was the only three-time captain in Columbia football history (1922-24), was also the Lions' track captain in 1924 and won the Buermeyer 500 at the NYAC Games, among other major sprint events. He later played for the Football Giants in 1926.

1962

Steven Dwayne Burtt is born in New York. A guard at Iona, Steve Burtt averaged 20.9 ppg in four seasons (1980-84) while leading the Gaels to a 84-40 record. Upon his graduation, he was the school's career scoring leader.

1966

Roscoe E. McGowen, baseball writer for *The New York Times* from 1929-59 who mainly covered the Brooklyn Dodgers, dies in North Woodstock, Connecticut, at age 80. His son Deane was also a long-time sportswriter for *The Times*.

1974

Marge Mason, the winner of 14 New Jersey women's golf championships and the 1960 women's Metropolitan Open, dies in Teaneck, N.J., at age 56.

1991

David Novick, a Rand Corporation economist who was noted for his studies of the horse-racing industry, dies in Bethlehem, Pennsylvania, at age 85.

1992

Rod Scurry, a lefthanded reliever who pitched briefly (and ineffectively) for the 1986 Yankees, dies in Reno, Nevada, at age 36.

1869

Rutgers beats Princeton, 6-4, in the first intercollegiate football game ever played. Captains William Leggett of Rutgers and William Gummere of Princeton organize the teams for the game at New Brunswick, N.J., and a return match at Princeton, N.J., which the Tigers win, 8-0, Nov. 15.

1915

Howard Cann sprints 55 yards for a touchdown in the fourth quarter and then kicks the conversion to give NYU a 7-0 victory over Stevens Tech at Ohio Field.

1922

Morgan G. Bulkeley, first president of baseball's National League, dies in Hartford, Connecticut, at age 84. A Civil War veteran, Bulkeley was president of the Aetna Insurance Co. from 1879 to his death, mayor of Hartford (1880-88), governor of Connecticut (1889-93) and U.S. Senator (1905-11). Bulkeley, league president in 1876, was president of the Hartford club in the NL (1876-77) and head of Hartford's Charter Oak Driving Park trotting track when it was the premier trotting facility in New England.

1922

John Joseph (Buddy) Kerr, the Giants' regular shortstop for six seasons (1944-49), is born in Astoria.

HOWARD CANN

1928

New York gambler Arnold Rothstein, who was suspected (but never convicted) of bankrolling the 1919 Black Sox scheme to throw the World Series, dies at Manhattan's Polyclinic Hospital of a gunshot wound. Rothstein was shot two days earlier during a Sunday night meeting over gambling debts at the Park Central Hotel by an assailant he refused to identify. On this day, the Football Giants beat Pottsville (Pennsylvania), 13-7, before 20,000 at the Polo Grounds, West Virginia blanks Fordham, 18-0, before 30,000 at Yankee Stadium, Manual Training defeats Erasmus Hall before 25,000 at Ebbets Field, and Herbert C. Hoover is elected president of the United States.

1949

New York Bulldogs beat the Football Giants, 31-24, at the Polo Grounds, for the only win of their 1-10-1 season, their only one (by that name) in team history.

1971

Linebacker Paul Kaliades' wobbling 34-yard field goal with 48 seconds left lifts Columbia (4-3) to a 31-29 upset of Dartmouth before 18,319 at Baker Field. Kaliades' kick enables the Lions to snap the Indians' 15-game winning streak. It is also Columbia's seventh straight game decided by three points or less, an NCAA record.

1988

Norway's Grete Waitz wins the women's championship in the New York City Marathon for the ninth time in 11 years in 2:28:07. Italy's Laura Fogli is second while Steve Jones of Great Britain wins the men's title in 2:08:20. Jones misses the event record by seven seconds with Italy's Salvatore Bettiol second. Both winners earn a Mercedes and $26,385. Waitz also won 1978-80 and 1982-86, setting world records in 1978, 1979 and 1980.

1994

Mexico's German Silva wins the New York City Marathon despite taking a wrong turn in Manhattan less than a mile from the finish. Silva overtakes countryman Benjamin Paredes by two seconds, the smallest winning margin ever, in 2:11:21. Tegla Loroupe of Kenya becomes the first African black woman to win a major marathon with a clocking of 2:27:37. Tragedy strikes at the finish as two seemingly-healthy finishers, France's Bernard Rollin (age 50) and Swiss-born Pierre Marquet (age 27) die of heart attacks.

1877

Manhattan Athletic Club is formed by George W. Thomas, William S. Ridabock, Jr., Robert B. Culbert and George W. Carr, becoming the fifth major athletic club in the city, joining the New York AC, the Scottish-American AC , the Harlem AC and the American AC. Carr is chosen president when the club is incorporated April 1, 1878.

1936

Chick Meehan's Manhattan Jaspers score one of the their most significant football victories, upsetting Kentucky, 13-7, at Ebbets Field.

1938

Jerry D. Gibbs is born in Grenada, Mississippi. Jake Gibbs, a quarterback at the University of Mississippi who finished third in the Heisman Trophy balloting in 1960, was a Yankees catcher from 1962-71 when he was replaced by Thurman Munson.

1964

Fordham defeats NYU, 20-14, in a club football game at Fordham that marks the start of a three-year resumption of the storied Violets-Rams rivalry (see Oct. 22).

GENE TUNNEY

1967

Sammy Mandell, world lightweight champion from 1926-30, dies in Oak Park, Illinois, at age 63.

1970

Most Happy Fella wins the Triple Crown of pacing, the fifth in harness history, with a victory in the Messenger Stakes at Roosevelt Raceway.

1975

In the most celebrated trade to that time in NHL history, the Rangers send defenseman Brad Park, center Jean Ratelle and defenseman Joe Zanussi to Boston for center Phil Esposito and defenseman Carol Vadnais.

1977

Nets trade Al Skinner and two draft choices for guard Kevin Porter, forward Howard Porter and cash.

1978

Gene Tunney dies in Greenwich, Connecticut, at age 80. Born James Joseph Tunney in New York, Tunney was world heavyweight champ from 1926-28, dethroning Jack Dempsey and winning the rematch in the famous "Long Count" bout in Chicago in 1927. He retired undefeated as a heavyweight.

1994

Archie San Romani, a leading miler of the 1930s, dies in Auberry, California, at age 82.

1996

Yankees manager Joe Torre and Johnny Oates of Texas share American League Manager of the Year honors in the first tie ever in the BBWAA national voting in that category.

1909

After financially rescuing the National Horse Show by buying control of it in February, Alfred G. Vanderbilt presents his first opening night as NHSA president at the Garden. A British contingent headed by Maj. the Hon. J.G. Beresford, D.S.O., 7th Hussars, Aldershot, makes the show international for the first time and the 1,500 entries are the most ever. Vanderbilt succeeds Cornelius Fellowes, NHSA president since its founding in 1883, when financial instability, caused by a disastrous 1908 show, threatens its continuance.

1921

Making their first New York City appearance, the Notre Dame Ramblers beat Rutgers, 48-0, before an Election Day crowd of 12,000 at the Polo Grounds. Only three days earlier, Notre Dame defeated Army, 28-0, at West Point. The nickname "Fighting Irish" isn't adopted by Notre Dame until 1927. (In the election, Mayor John F. Hylan is reelected to a second term.)

1924

John William Bower is born in Prince Albert, Saskatchewan. Bower as a Rangers rookie goalie in 1953-54 played every minute of all 70 games. Over the next three seasons, he played only seven more for the Blueshirts. Drafted by Toronto June 3, 1958, he helped the Maple Leafs to three straight Stanley Cups (1962-64).

1934

Former New York sportswriter and broadcaster Ford C. Frick is elected president of the National League.

1938

Thomas Sanders is born in New York. Satch Sanders, a 6'6" forward, averaged 16.8 ppg over three seasons at NYU. During those years, the Violets posted a 47-24 record, including 22-5 in 1959-60, when they went to the NCAA Final Four with Sanders as captain.

1951

Yankees catcher Yogi Berra is voted the first of his three American League MVP awards by the BBWAA (Berra is also the MVP in 1954 and 1955.)

1962

AFL assumes control of the New York Titans for the balance of the season after club owner Harry Wismer fails to meet payroll (see Mar. 28).

1964

Before 60,300 at Shea Stadium, the first home sellout in franchise history, the Jets lose to Buffalo, 20-7.

1971

Long Island and Atlanta are granted expansion franchises by the NHL. A syndicate headed by Roy L.M. Boe, owner of the ABA New York Nets, gets the Long Island franchise and, surprisingly, names the new club the New York Islanders. The Atlanta team is nicknamed the Flames and moves to Calgary, Alberta, in 1980.

1972

Potsy Clark, head coach of the NFL Brooklyn Dodgers from 1937-39 (11-17-5), dies in La Jolla, California. Clark also coached the Detroit Lions to the 1935 NFL title.

1977

Stanley Raymond Harris dies on his 81st birthday in Bethesda, Maryland. Bucky Harris was the Boy Wonder player-manager who led the Washington Senators to their first (and only) World Series title in 1924. In 1947, he guided the Yankees to the championship in the first of his two seasons as Bombers skipper.

1853

Stanford White, one of the most creative architects of his time and a partner in the famed firm of McKim, Mead and White, is born in New York. Among his other creations, White designed the second Madison Square Garden, in whose roof garden he was shot in one of the most celebrated crimes of all time (see June 25).

1895

With 13 starters playing 18 holes at the Meadow Brook Club in Hempstead, L.I., the first recognized national Women's Amateur golf championship is played, with Mrs. C.S. Brown of Shinnecock Hills taking top honors with a 132 and Miss N.C. Sargent of Essex County in second at 134. Although this event predates the formation of the United States Golf Association national championship program, it is later accepted as the first Women's Amateur.

1909

Mary Cherbonnier of Baltimore, Maryland, a 16-year-old, causes a stir by riding four hunters and jumpers astride at the second night of the National Horse Show at the Garden. Previously, all women rode sidesaddle. William H. Moore (who, with A.G. Vanderbilt, helped save the NHSA), collects six more blue ribbons on the second day in the harness classes. Judge Moore ordinarily drives his own horses but he wins a blue with Lady Seaton driven by Eleanora Sears of Boston, a noted tennis player and all-around athlete. Judge Moore's horses eventually rake in 25 firsts during the week.

1944

Frank J. Marshall, 67, considered the dean of U.S. chess masters, dies in Jersey City, N.J. The Marshall Chess Club in Manhattan became a breeding ground for chess growth in the U.S.

1946

Ranked as the top two teams in college football, Army (No. 1) and Notre Dame (No. 2) play a thrilling scoreless tie at Yankee Stadium that leaves most of the 74,121 on hand limp at the end. It is the last of the annual games in the fabled series, which renews only sporadically (starting in 1958) and returns to New York City only twice (1965, 1969).

1948

Col. Humberto Mariles leads the Mexican Army team to the International Jumping championship in the National Horse Show at the Garden. France is second, Canada third and, for the first time since 1908, there is no U.S. squad in the International competition (the U.S. Army team was disbanded after the Olympic Games, where Mexico won the gold medal). Mariles wins four individual firsts during the National and shares four others. (Mexico wins the team title nine times in 11 years from 1946-56.)

1950

Mel (Killer) Davis, the Knicks' No. 1 draft choice (14th overall) in the 1973 NBA draft, is born in New York. Davis, a 6'7" forward who averaged 20.9 ppg for St. John's for two seasons (1970-72) and also played for the Nets in 1976-77, averaged 4.6 ppg in 156 games over four seasons (1973-74 to 1976-77) with the Knicks.

1976

Paul John Carbo dies at age 72 in Miami Beach, Florida. Frankie Carbo, often referred to as "Mr. Gray," was reputedly the major underworld figure in boxing in the 1940s and 1950s. He allegedly acted as a "shadow manager," owning a piece of dozens of champions and contenders, taking cuts of their purse shares.

1985

Rushing for five touchdowns, freshman Terry Underwood leads Wagner to a 57-6 thrashing of Ramapo at Mahwah, N.J.

November 10

1906

First indoor championships of the AAU in track and field are held. Lawson Robertson of the Irish-American Athletic Club wins the first final running event (the 150-yard run in 16.2 seconds) at the Garden, helping his club to the team title (with 89 points).

1928

Underdog Notre Dame rallies for a 12-6 win over Army before 78,188 at Yankee Stadium in the "Win One for the Gipper Game," so called because Irish coach Knute Rockne at halftime invokes the name of George Gipp, a halfback who had played for Notre Dame and died in 1920. On his deathbed, the 28-year-old Gipp supposedly told Rockne, in part, "One day, when things are looking bad and the breaks are beating the boys, tell them to just go out and win one for the Gipper."

1930

Famed dog show breeder and judge Michelle Billings is born in Chicago.

1942

In their last regular-season overtime game before discontinuance of the rule (see Nov. 21), the Rangers beat Chicago, 5-3, at the Garden, for their second win of the season (2-3-0), both coming in an extra session (also November 7 against the Canadiens, 4-3).

1956

Harry F. Sinclair, millionaire sportsman and oil magnate, dies in Pasadena, California, at age 80. Sinclair owned a noted racing stable and backed the Newark Federal League club, losing a reported $500,000 on it in 1915. He was also a principal player in the "Teapot Dome" scandal of the 1920s, being acquitted of complicity in the fraud but serving a jail sentence for contempt of Congress and contempt of court for refusing to testify against Secretary of the Interior Albert Fall (who was convicted anyway).

1971

Knicks send guard Mike Riordan, forward Dave Stallworth and cash to the Baltimore Bullets for high-scoring guard Earl Monroe.

1974

Joe Namath's five-yard pass to Emerson Boozer at 6:53 of overtime gives the Jets a 26-20 victory over the Football Giants at the Yale Bowl in the first regular-season overtime game for both teams, and the only second in NFL history. The league instituted its 15-minute overtime rule before the 1974 season.

1975

Jake Schaefer, Jr., five-time 18.2 balkline billiards champion (1921, 1925-27, 1929), dies in Cleveland, Ohio, at age 81. His father was one of the great billiards players of the 19th century.

1992

Kevin Joseph (Chuck) Connors, a Seton Hall basketball forward whose one at-bat with the Brooklyn Dodgers produced a double play, dies in Los Angeles, California, at age 71. Connors achieved substantially more fame as "The Rifleman" on television.

EARL MONROE

November 11

1868

First track and field meet held by the New York Athletic Club takes place at the partly-covered unfinished Empire Skating Rink at Third Avenue and 63rd Street in Manhattan. Owing to rain, the roof is completely covered before H.L. Magrane, Frank Johnson, W.L. Campbell, John Goldie and P.M. Broderick win two events each on the 14-event program. One of the club's founders, W.B. Curtis (who introduced spiked shoes to America), takes the 75-yard dash in 9.0 seconds.

1898

George Dixon recaptures the featherweight title on a 10th-round disqualification of Dave Sullivan when Sullivan's brother "Spike" and his other seconds enter the ring at the Lenox AC. It is the first disqualification under the Marquis of Queensberry rules to cause a championship to change hands.

1914

Richard Colman is born in New York. Dick Colman was Princeton head football coach from 1957-68, posting a 75-33 record and leading the 1964 team to a perfect record (9-0) and a No. 13 ranking in the year-end *UPI* poll. He was also the Tigers' lacrosse coach from 1946-49 (30-15).

1915

Loula Long wins the Waldorf-Astoria Cup for hackneys driven to a single harness with Realization on the next-to-last night of the National Horse Show at the Garden. Her victory is especially popular since her principal competition twice cuts off her horse, causing it to break and inducing the crowd to a rare display of vociferous rooting. This show, under new NHSA president Edward T. Stotesbury, also marks the large-scale presence of U.S. Cavalry officers as competitors, who fill the gap created by the absence of foreign riders due to World War I.

1917

Anthony Pilleteri is born in Garfield, N.J. As Tippy Larkin, he fought 153 bouts as a welterweight, including 19 main events at the Garden.

1922

Dartmouth, which annually plays major games in New York during this time, is beaten by Cornell, 23-0, as more than 40,000 flock to the Polo Grounds, the largest New York crowd ever for a football game, except for the Army-Navy game, then an annual fixture at the Polo Grounds.

1944

Having ended the prior season 0-17-4, the longest single-season winless streak in club history, the Rangers picked up where they left off with four losses to start 1944-45. But today, they beat Detroit, 5-3, at the Garden, their first win since Jan. 22, 1944, a 5-1 victory at Toronto.

1946

Knicks play their first game at the Garden, losing, 78-68, to the Chicago Stags in overtime.

1950

With tailback Dick Kazmaier showing the way, unbeaten Princeton roars off to a 28-0 lead and buries Harvard, 63-26, at Palmer Stadium, extending the Tigers' winning streak to 11 games. Kazmaier runs 65 and 13 yards for two touchdowns and throws for two more (15 yards to Ed Reed and 50 yards to wingback Bill Kleinsasser).

1978

Benny Borgmann, a high-scoring guard with the Original Celtics and other pro teams, dies in Pompton Plains, N.J., at age 79. Borgmann played over 2,500 pro games with various teams in several leagues from 1918-40.

1853

Conqueror, an aged trotter, sets a world record by covering 100 miles in eight hours, 55 minutes, 53 seconds at Centerville, L.I.

1870

Columbia becomes the third college in America to play football, losing to Rutgers, six goals to three, in a 20-men-a-side match in New Brunswick, N.J. Major schools reduce the size of teams to 15 in 1877 and 11 in 1880.

1931

Yankees owner Jacob Ruppert buys the Newark (N.J.) International League club from newspaper publisher Paul Block for $350,000, setting the foundation for the Yankees farm system that creates a 30-year baseball dynasty. Block acquired the Bears for $360,000 at a bankruptcy receiver's sale after the 1927 season and claims to have spent another $250,000 in four seasons (the 1931 team finished second). Ruppert changes the name of the ballpark to Ruppert Stadium (see May 15) and begins stocking it with talent such as righthander Don Brennan and outfielders Dixie Walker and Bubbles Hargreaves.

1942

Joseph F. Hagen dies in New York at age 64. As "Philadelphia Jack" O'Brien, Hagen held the light heavyweight title from 1905 to his retirement in 1912. In 1911, he lost to heavyweight Sam Langford in New York by a fifth-round knockout in a rare (at that time) bout between a black fighter and a white one.

JOHN SCHMITT

1942

John Charles Schmitt is born in Brooklyn. A Hofstra graduate, Schmitt was the Jets center from 1964-73.

1974

Weeb Ewbank announces he will retire as Jets vice president and general manager at season's end. Jets win their next five to finish the season with a 7-7 record and a six-game winning streak.

1983

Columbia loses to Cornell, 31-6, at Ithaca, N.Y., starting its then-record 44-game football losing streak. A week earlier, a late Dartmouth field goal lifted the Big Green into a 17-17 tie with the Lions at Giants Stadium in East Rutherford, N.J., for what would prove to be the Lions' last non-loss in almost five years.

1983

Mickey Kwiatkowski's Flying Dutchmen beat Coast Guard, 31-10, at Hofstra Stadium to finish a 10-0 season, but a week later, Union eliminates Hofstra from the Division III playoffs, 51-19.

1991

To complete the trade that brought Mark Messier to New York (see Oct. 4), the Rangers send defenseman David Shaw to Edmonton for defenseman Jeff Beukeboom.

1993

Yankees catching great Bill Dickey dies in Little Rock, Arkansas, at age 86.

November 13

1875

Harvard defeats Yale, four goals to zero, at New Haven, Connecticut, in a football game played under the so-called "concessionary rules" (see Oct. 19). It is the first time these rivals meet in football.

1905

England's Prince Louis of Battenburg proves to be the big draw as 10,000 jam the Garden for opening night of the National Horse Show. The arena is festooned with Union Jacks for the Prince's 45-minute appearance and the band plays "God Save the King" when he enters. Miss Alice Roosevelt, daughter of the president, is the star social attraction for the afternoon session but only 4,000 show up and most of them actually watch the horses.

1909

Alfred G. Vanderbilt wins the race for the four-in-hand coaches on the last day of the National Horse Show, capping his first year as NHSA president with a personal blue ribbon. Vanderbilt drives his team and coach from 177th Street and Fort Washington Avenue in Manhattan to the Garden at 26th Street and Madison Avenue in 38 minutes, cutting three minutes off the record set in 1906. Vanderbilt's victory comes on a day largely devoted to children showing ponies (moving the *New York Herald* to call the day "the Lilliputian Horse Show").

1913

Pocket billiards great Irving Crane is born in Livonia, New Hampshire. Crane, the first player ever to run 300 balls without a miss (in 1939), won six world championships over a 30-year span (1942-72).

1940

On the strength of clean final rounds by Captains Marshall Frame, Frank Henry and Franklin Wing, the U.S. Army wins the International Jumping Championship on the closing night of the National Horse Show at the Garden. Mexico (with 16 faults) is second, Cuba (36 1/2) third and Chile (40) fourth. In the morning, famous Chilean team horse Chilena was killed while schooling. Chilena, a mare popular with NHS audiences, had competed in New York six times since 1934 and is buried with military honors the next day at Staten Island's Fort Wadsworth.

1943

At rain-swept Baker Field, Navy sinks Columbia, 61-0, in a game neither coach attends, the Lions' Lou Little owing to illness and the Midshipmen's Capt. John Welchel to scout upcoming opponent Army. After taking a 54-0 lead with 12:35 left, Navy punts on first down on every possession but scores a final touchdown anyway on Dick Gay's 60-yard punt return with 10 seconds left.

1949

Providing plenty of action but not much entertainment for their fans at the Polo Grounds, the NFL New York Bulldogs are hammered by the Chicago Cardinals, 65-20.

1954

Wolfgang Westl's second-half goals lifts CCNY to a 1-0 victory at Brooklyn College and gives the Beavers the championship of the Metropolitan Intercollegiate Soccer League for the second straight year.

1954

Quarterback Tom Roberts comes off the bench in the fourth quarter, completes five of six passes and then runs one yard for the touchdown that ties the game as Holy Cross beats Fordham, 20-19, on the strength of Dale Hohl's extra point before 13,557 at the Polo Grounds.

1983

John Roosma dies at age 83. Roosma, an Army guard, is believed to be the first college basketball player to score 1,000 points, amassed over 86 games in five seasons (1921-26).

1888

John Reid, "the father of American Golf," founds the St. Andrews Golf Club in Yonkers, N.Y. Incorporated in 1894, the course subsequently relocates and is redeveloped a century later by Jack Nicklaus.

1922

Richard K. Fox, publisher of the *Police Gazette*, the leading sports weekly in the nation, dies in Red Bank, N.J., at age 76.

1929

"Iron Man" Joe McGinnity, who pitched both ends of doubleheaders five times in his career, dies in Brooklyn at age 58. McGinnity won 247 games in 10 big-league seasons (1899-1908) and hurled a modern-record 434 innings in 1903.

1942

In the 15th renewal of the series to be played in New York City, Yale tops Princeton, 13-6, in a game held at Columbia's Baker Field due to wartime travel restrictions.

1956

Yankees centerfielder and Triple Crown winner Mickey Mantle is unanimously chosen the American League MVP. (Mantle is the league MVP in 1957 and 1962 as well.)

1966

George M. Weiss, president and general manager of the Mets since October 1961, announces his retirement and Vaughn (Bing) Devine is introduced as the new general manager. Weiss was with the Yankees from 1932-60, the last 13 years as general manager, before joining the Mets.

1974

Jimmy Phelan, head coach of the NFL Yanks in their second (and last) season in New York (1951), dies in Honolulu, Hawaii, at age 81. The Yanks finished 1-9-2 and moved to Dallas, where as the Texans they were even worse (1-11).

1976

Behind Joe Danelo's four field goals, the Football Giants, in the fourth game at their new home, post their first Giants Stadium win, 12-9 over Washington, their first victory over the Redskins since 1970.

1984

Ralph Furey, Columbia athletic director from 1943-68 and first president of the ECAC in 1947, dies in Durango, Colorado, at age 81.

1986

Club chairman Nelson Doubleday and president Fred Wilpon become 50-50 partners in the Mets by forming Sterling Doubleday Enterprises, L.P. to purchase the team from Doubleday Publishing, which is being sold to a West German conglomerate.

MICKEY MANTLE

1873

Princeton beats Yale, 3-0, at New Haven, Connecticut, in the first meeting of what becomes one of college football's most storied rivalries (see Nov. 30).

1900

Joseph R. Brennan, a pro basketball player for the Brooklyn Visitations and Dodgers and coach for seven years (1941-48) at St. Francis (Brooklyn) College, is born in Brooklyn. "Poison Joe" was 90-46 with the Terriers.

1905

City Magistrate Baker deals a severe blow to the anti-boxing forces when he throws out charges against two men arrested for engaging in a prize fight at the Bleecker Athletic Club on Bleecker Street. Baker rules that the fight was legal because it was conducted by members of the club for an audience of club members. Boxing has technically been illegal since the expiration of the Horton Law in August 1900 (see May 31). Captain Hodgkins ordered the arrests after a three-round bout at the club November 13.

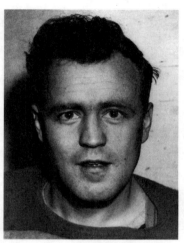

FRANK BOUCHER

1929

Albert Richard Dorow is born in Imlay City, Michigan. Al Dorow was the Titans' first regular quarterback, completing 398 of 834 passes for 5,399 yards with 45 touchdowns and 56 interceptions in the wide-open days of the early AFL (1960-61).

1939

Gregory Kenneth Larson is born in Minneapolis, Minnesota. Greg Larson was the No. 1 center for the Football Giants from 1961-73.

1960

Appearing in New York for the first time since the Lakers' move to Los Angeles from Minneapolis, Elgin Baylor sets a Garden pro scoring record with 71 points in a 123-108 win over the Knicks. Baylor's outburst surpasses the record set nine months earlier by Warriors' Wilt Chamberlain (see Feb. 21), but Chamberlain will recover the record in 1962 (see Nov. 16).

1968

Charlie Goldman, 80, former bantamweight, fight manager and trainer, dies in New York.

1972

WHA steps in to take financial control of the New York Raiders, who are unable to make their payroll, and the team continues to the end of the season (see Mar. 15).

1972

Rookie left wing Steve Vickers becomes the first player in Rangers history to score hat tricks in consecutive games, notching three goals in a 7-3 win over Philadelphia at the Garden three days after doing the same against Los Angeles in a 5-1 home Ranger win.

1973

John D. (Honey) Russell dies in Livingston, N.J., at age 71. Russell had a long playing career in the early days of pro basketball and was Seton Hall head coach from 1936-43 and 1949-60, posting a 292-129 record (.694). He was also the first coach of the Boston Celtics.

November 16

1872

Yale plays its first intercollegiate football game, defeating Columbia, 3-0, at Hamilton Park in New Haven, Connecticut, with Thomas Sherman scoring Yale's first point.

1889

NYU and Fordham meet in their first football game, with the Rams winning, 34-6, at Fordham. During the 1920s and 1930s, the "Battle of The Bronx" will become a major New York sports attraction, annually filling Yankee Stadium or the Polo Grounds.

1919

David Polansky, who three times replaced Nat Holman as CCNY head basketball coach, is born. Polansky compiled a 127-135 record in 15 seasons, replacing the lengendary Holman in 1952, 1956 and 1959, the latter time when Holman retired after an 0-4 start. Polansky himself abruptly resigned in February 1971, after an 82-80 loss to Pace, and was replaced by assistant coach and LIU alumnus Jack Kaminer.

1926

Rangers play their first NHL game ever, defeating the Stanley Cup champion Montreal Maroons, 1-0, on Bill Cook's goal on a pass from brother Bun at 18:37 of the second period. The Garden crowd of over 13,000 sees movie star Lois Moran do the ceremonial opening faceoff, Katy Schmidt conduct an ice ballet during the first intermission and referee Lou Marsh call 18 penalties. Maroons right wing Bill Phillips cuts Rangers center Frank Boucher on the neck with the butt of his stick in a third-period brawl, finishing Boucher for the night. Boucher is assessed a five-minute penalty for his part in the battle, the only fighting major of his career.

1946

Knicks play their first game at the 69th Regiment Armory, 25th Street and Lexington Avenue, and beat the Pittsburgh Ironmen, 64-62, in overtime. Of their 30 home games in 1946-47, 24 are played at the Armory.

1958

Gordon H. Ridings dies in Ardsley, N.Y., at age 51. Ridings was Columbia's head basketball coach for four seasons, winning the EIBL championship in his first two years (1946-47, 1947-48) and finishing second twice (1948-49, 1949-50) before ill health forced his retirement. The 1950-51 team he assembled also won the league title (22-0 regular season) although it was coached by Lou Rossini. Ridings had a 69-20 (.775) record in his four seasons.

1962

Wilt Chamberlain of the now-San Francisco Warriors regains the Garden pro scoring record with 73 points in the Warriors' 127-111 win over the Knicks (see Nov. 15)

1982

After 57 days, the NFL's first major work stoppage ends when NFLPA executive director Ed Garvey drops his wage-scale demands. With seven weeks of games wiped out, the NFL finishes a nine-game season and creates a 16-team "Super Bowl Tournament" (see Jan. 2 and Jan. 23).

1979

Jack Butterfield, head of player development for the Yankees from 1977-79, dies at age 50 in an auto accident on Route 17 in Paramus, N.J.

1994

Jim Poole, a Football Giants end from 1937-41 and in 1946, dies in Oxford, Mississippi, at age 79. Poole was All-Pro in 1939.

1877

Columbia journeys to Princeton, N.J., for a football match and loses, but Lions captain Charles Brower says, "if you must lose, it's a pleasure to lose to gentlemen and I am well satisfied. But in the future, we'll field a better side and the outcome will not always be as it was today." The teams, due to illness, agreed to play 14 men-a-side.

1890

Robert John Herman Kiphuth is born in Tonowanda, N.Y. Bob Kiphuth, Yale's athletic director from 1946-49, was the swimming coach from 1918-59, posting a 528-12 record. He served five times as U.S. Olympic swimming coach.

1898

A capacity crowd is on hand at the Garden when the new New York City Mounted Police detail makes its first appearance at the National Horse Show. The city police mounted unit replaces the disbanded Park Police mounted squad that represented the city prior to its consolidation Jan. 1, 1898.

1913

Wilbert Robinson is named manager of the Brooklyn Superbas, succeeding Bill Dahlen. Robinson will manage the club, which comes to be known as the Dodgers, for 18 seasons through 1931, including the pennant-winning years of 1916 and 1920.

1944

George Thomas Seaver is born in Fresno, California. Dubbed "The Franchise" when he joined the Mets, righthander Tom Seaver was the National League Rookie of the Year in 1967 and won the Cy Young Award three times (1969, 1973, 1975) with the Mets.

1956

Yale clinches no worse than a tie for the first formal Ivy League championship with a smashing 42-20 win over previously-unbeaten Princeton at Yale Bowl. The following Saturday, Jordan Olivar's Bulldogs bury Harvard, 42-14, to finish 7-0 in the league and 8-1 overall.

1968

With the Jets leading, 32-29, and 1:05 left in the fourth quarter at Oakland, NBC discontinues coverage of the game to put on the children's tale "Heidi." Irate fans complain and later learn that the Raiders scored twice in the last 42 seconds to win, 43-32. It is the last Jets loss of the season.

1979

Sixto Escobar, bantamweight champion from 1935-39, dies in Puerto Rico at age 66.

TOM SEAVER

1982

John (Cherokee) Davis, an outfielder with the Newark Eagles of the Negro Leagues from 1941-49, dies in Fort Lauderdale, Florida, at age 64.

1985

Avenging a "run-up-the-score" defeat from the year before, the Jets trounce Tampa Bay, 62-28, at Giants Stadium, setting a club record for points scored in a game.

November 18

1922

Bill Roper's Princeton Tigers complete their second undefeated season in three years with a 3-0 victory over Yale at Palmer Stadium.

1928

Gus Moore of the Brooklyn Harriers wins the National AAU senior cross-country run at Van Cortlandt Park, covering the six-mile course in 31:18. Verne Booth of the Millrose AA is second (31:48), helping the Millrose win the team title with 40 points for five finishers (second, sixth, seventh, 11th and 14th).

1945

Gothams, coached by Barney Sedran, open their American Basketball League season at St. Nicholas Arena with a 68-65 loss to the Philadelphia Sphas.

1946

Jimmy Walker, who introduced the legislation, later known as the Walker Law, that in 1920 legalized boxing in New York State, dies in New York at age 65. The dapper Walker was mayor of New York City from 1926-32.

1949

Brooklyn second baseman Jackie Robinson is chosen NL MVP by the BBWAA. Robinson led the league in batting (.342) and stolen bases (37) and had a career-high 124 RBI in leading the Dodgers to the pennant.

1961

Tom Haggerty gains 119 yards in 20 rushes as Columbia clinches at least a tie for the Ivy League title with a 37-6 whipping of Penn before 17,066 at Baker Field. The Lions finish their league season with a 6-1 record (Harvard ties for the title with its 27-0 win over Yale November 25).

1963

Gladys Goodding, organist at the Garden (1937-63) at Ebbets Field (1939-57), dies in New York at age 70.

1972

In perhaps the greatest single-game comeback in NBA history, the Knicks score the last 19 points of the game to defeat the Milwaukee Bucks, 87-86, at the Garden.

1973

Football Giants defeat St. Louis, 24-13, at the Yale Bowl. It would prove to be the Giants' only home victory during the two years they called the Bowl home (1-11).

1980

Conn Smythe dies in Toronto, Ontario, at age 85. Smythe, the Rangers' first general manager, signed most of the players who formed the core of the team that won the 1928 and 1933 Stanley Cups, but was released in a dispute with Garden management before the team ever played a game, to be replaced by Lester Patrick. Smythe went to Toronto, took over the St. Patricks, changed their name to the Maple Leafs, built Maple Leaf Gardens and developed a team that became a perennial contender.

1992

Ed Franco, one of Fordham's Seven Blocks of Granite (Version No. 2—the first was the 1929 team), dies in Bayonne, New Jersey, at age 77. A consensus All-American in 1936 and 1937, Franco was the left tackle on a line that generally had Leo Paquin at left end, Nat Pierce at left guard, Alex Wojciechowicz at center, John Druze at right guard, Al Barbartsky at right tackle and Vince Lombardi at right end.

November 19

1913

Patrick J. Ryan sets a world record in the hammer throw with a toss of 213' 9 $^1/_3$" in the Irish-American Athletic Club field events meet at Celtic Park. With only 1,500 watching on a rainy, cold day, Ryan breaks the mark of 207' 7 $^3/_4$" set by John J. Flanagan on October 24, 1910. Ryan, one of the I-AAC's stars, also wins the 35-pound weight throw event.

1938

Robert E. Turner, III, is born in Cincinnati, Ohio. Owner of several major league sports franchises, head of a communications empire and underwriter of the Goodwill Games, Ted Turner skippered *Courageous* for the New York Yacht Club in a successful America's Cup defense in 1977.

1951

Quarterback John Rauch is released by the Yanks and signed by the Philadelphia Eagles. Rauch was drafted by the Detroit Lions in 1949 but traded to New York for the rights to Doak Walker. Detroit signs Walker, the SMU All-American, who leads the NFL in scoring as a rookie in 1950 and again in 1955.

1960

Starting their second (and last) season in the National Industrial Basketball League, the Tuck Tapers surprise the Akron Goodyears, 133-119, at the 69th Regiment Armory. Charlie Curtis leads the Tapers, coached by Hank Rosenstein, with 31 points. In 1961, the Tapers join the pro American Basketball League.

1965

Bret Hanover completes a sweep of the Triple Crown of pacing, winning the $152,252 Messenger Stakes at Roosevelt Raceway.

1972

Ground is broken for the construction of what would become Giants Stadium in East Rutherford, N.J.

1973

WHA takes over management the floundering New York Golden Blades (6-12-2 and last in the Eastern Division), firing general manager Jerry DeLise and replacing coach Camille Henry with Harry Howell. The next day, the team moves from Madison Square Garden to Cherry Hill, N.J., and becomes the Jersey Knights.

1975

Three days after their sixth straight loss, a 52-19 rout at Baltimore, the Jets fire head coach Charley Winner. Offensive coordinator Ken Shipp coaches the last five games (1-4).

1983

Ed Christensen scores three first-quarter touchdowns on runs of 77, 14 and 10 yards as Wagner wins the ECAC Metro New York football championship with a 48-7 rout of St. John's at Redmen Field.

1983

Devils lose, 13-4, at Edmonton, the greatest margin of defeat in club history, as Oilers right wing Jari Kurri scores three goals in a 4:42 span of the third period, to fall to 2-18-0. After the game, Edmonton star Wayne Gretzky, embarrassed for his friend and former teammate, beleaguered New Jersey goalie Ron Low, calls the Devils a "Mickey Mouse" organization. Three days later, a shakeup begins in New Jersey (see Nov. 22).

1866

Kennesaw Mountain Landis, named after a Civil War battle site in Georgia, is born in Millville, Ohio. A federal judge, Landis was chosen as the first baseball commissioner in 1920 to restore the sport's integrity after the "Black Sox" betting scandal of 1919.

1897

For the second year running, C.F. Bates is the major winner at the National Horse Show. Bates' horses snare 20 ribbons (12 firsts), worth $2,645, as the show closes its Garden run.

1900

William Burch is born in Yonkers, N.Y. Billy Burch was NHL MVP in 1924-25 (the only American-born MVP until 1990-91) with the Hamilton Tigers, who took the league's regular season title. He then led a team players' strike before the playoffs began which resulted in the Tigers' forfeiture of their games and transfer of the franchise to New York where it became the city's first NHL team. Burch was an original Amerk, whose artistic success in the Garden (even though they finished last) led to the granting of a franchise to the Garden itself (see May 15).

1920

Returning to the ranks of major college teams, Columbia faces Pennsylvania in football for the first time since 1905 and draws over 25,000 to the Polo Grounds, but loses, 27-7. The Lions dropped football after 1905, restored it on a limited basis in 1915 and then slowly rebuilt.

1937

Harold Humphrey Hackett, a Yale graduate who teamed with Fred Alexander to form one of the most successful doubles teams in the history of men's tennis, dies in New York at age 59. Hackett and Alexander are the only men's doubles team ever to win four straight U.S. national titles (1907-10).

1956

Mark Gastineau, flamboyant defensive end for the Jets from 1979-88, is born in Ardmore, Oklahoma. Gastineau, who left the team during the 1988 season to care for his girlfriend, Brigitte Nielsen, who had cancer (she was cured), was the club career leader in sacks with 107 $\frac{1}{2}$. His "Sack Dance" infuriated opponents and led to league rules prohibiting excessive celebrations after plays.

1964

Right wing John MacLean, a clutch performer and the Devils' career leader in games played (945), goals (347), assists (354), and points (701), is born in Oshawa, Ontario. MacLean was traded to San Jose Dec. 7, 1997, and signed with the Rangers as a free agent in July 1998.

1966

Matty Begovich dies in Miami Beach, Florida, at age 56. Begovich was the center on the St. John's "Wonder Five" teams that from 1928-31 won 88 of 96 games. (The other four "Wonders" were Mac Kinsbrunner, Max Posnak, Rip Gerson and Allie Shuckman.) When the team was ruled ineligible for playing pro clubs, they turned pro and formed the New York Jewels.

1976

Rutgers completes only the second undefeated season in its 107-year football history (11-0) with a 17-9 victory over Colgate before a Thanksgiving Day crowd of 33,405 at Giants Stadium.

1982

Brown beats Columbia, 35-21, in the 323d and last game played at the Lions' Baker Field, the nation's oldest wooden major-sports stadium. Brown angers Columbia by calling two timeouts trying to score in the game's final minute—but fails.

1914

Yale Bowl, the largest stadium ever built in the U.S. up to that time, officially opens with a 36-0 Elis loss to Harvard.

1914

Alfred Goullet of Australia and his partner Alf Grenda of Tasmania set a record with 2,759 miles and two laps in the six-day bike race at the Garden. Achieved in 142 hours, the record is not broken even after the event is extended to 144 hours in 1917.

1916

Sidney Luckman, star Columbia quarterback from 1936-38 who went on to a brilliant career with the NFL Chicago Bears, is born in Brooklyn. Despite the Lions' 3-6 record his senior year, Luckman finished third in the Heisman Trophy balloting. He died July 5, 1998.

SID LUCKMAN

1934

Yankees risk $25,000 and four players to buy Joe DiMaggio, coming off knee surgery, from the San Francisco Seals of the Pacific Coast League. DiMaggio would spend one more year with the Seals before joining the Bombers in 1936.

1942

Owing to war-time travel restrictions and railroad timetables, the NHL discontinues the use of overtime in the regular season, a full 10-minute extra session. Regular-season overtime is not reinstated until the 1983-84 season, shortened to five minutes and changed to sudden death.

1948

After allowing 298 points in the previous six games (five losses), the Football Giants hammer Green Bay at Milwaukee, 49-3.

1952

Eamonn Coghlan, one-time world indoor record holder in the mile who won the Wanamaker Mile at the Millrose Games seven times (1977, 1979, 1980, 1981, 1983, 1985, 1987), is born in Dublin, Ireland.

1971

Rookie Pierre Jarry scores two of the three goals he would tally in his 34-game career as a Ranger in an eight-second span of the third period, the fastest two goals ever scored by a Ranger, and New York blitzes California, 12-1, at the Garden, the largest margin of victory in club history.

1980

After a 4-13-3 start, Fred Shero is fired as Rangers general manager and coach. Assistant general manager Craig Patrick, grandson of Lester Patrick, assumes both jobs the next day, and the team goes 7-2-1.

1980

Gene Michael is named Yankees manager, the Bombers' fourth in less than eighteen months, after Dick Howser "resigns" to pursue business opportunities.

1988

Carl Hubbell, 85, greatest lefthanded pitcher in Giants history, dies in Scottsdale, Arizona.

1898

Referee John Kelly and announcer Charlie Harvey avert a major boxing crisis at the Lenox Athletic Club when Kelly forfeits a fight to "Sailor Tom" Sharkey. Midway through the ninth round of the scheduled 20-rounder, Sharkey appears to be getting the best of former heavyweight champ Jim Corbett when Connie McVey, a former fighter and one of Corbett's cornermen, jumps into the ring. Kelly awards the win to Sharkey on a foul and orders "all bets are off." Both men are aware of the heavy wagering on the fight and successfully quiet the overflow crowd of 10,000.

1917

Four clubs, including two from Montreal, Quebec, organize the National Hockey League in Montreal. Frank Calder (who will serve until 1943) is elected president.

1936

Fred Wilpon is born in Brooklyn. Wilpon became Mets president when the syndicate of which he was a principal bought the club in 1980 (see Jan. 24).

1943

Billie Jean Moffitt is born in Long Beach, California. Sister of future major-league pitcher Randy Moffitt, Billie Jean King won six Wimbledon titles and four U.S. national singles championships (1967, 1971-72, 1974). She used her prominence as a No. 1-ranked tennis player to act as a pioneer for women and women's sports, helping to form World Team Tennis, the Women's Tennis Association, and the Women's Sports Foundation.

1959

Notre Dame quarterback George Izo is the New York Titans' first-round choice as the AFL conducts its first draft, which lasts 33 rounds. Izo never plays a game for the Titans, but a selection who does, Larry Grantham, becomes the only original club draftee to play for the 1969 Super Bowl champions.

1959

Molla Bjurstedt Mallory, 75, the Norwegian native who won more U.S. national singles tennis championships (eight) than anyone else, man or woman, dies in Stockholm, Sweden.

1977

Righty reliever Rich "Goose" Gossage signs a six-year contract with the Yankees for $2.75 million, leaving the Pittsburgh Pirates as a free agent. The fireballer earns 150 saves with New York and is on the mound when in 1978 the Yankees win the American League East playoff against Boston, the pennant against Kansas City and the World Series against Los Angeles.

1983

Following the 2-18-0 start that culminated with their "Mickey Mouse" loss at Edmonton (see Nov. 19), the Devils fire general manager and coach Billy MacMillan. Max McNab takes over as general manager and Tom McVie begins the first of his two terms as New Jersey coach.

1986

Rangers left wing Tony McKegney scores four goals and Canucks wing Petri Skriko also has four as the Rangers win in Vancouver, 8-5.

1986

Mike Lee dies in Jamaica, N.Y., at age 76. Lee, a sportswriter for the *Nassau Daily Review* from 1931-32 and the *Long Island Daily Press* from 1932-34, was sports editor of the *Long Island Press* from 1934 until the paper folded in March 1977.

1930

Dick Kazmaier is born in Maumee, Ohio. Kazmaier won the Heisman Trophy at Princeton in 1951 as he led the Tigers to a second straight 9-0 season and the No. 6 ranking in the nation.

1930

Hap Moran sets a Football Giants club record with a 91-yard run against the Packers as the Giants beat Green Bay, 13-6, at the Polo Grounds.

1935

Princeton (8-0) closes in on an undefeated season with a 26-6 victory over Dartmouth before 56,000 packed into Palmer Stadium despite a near-blizzard. A local cook plays one play as a "Twelfth Man" on the Dartmouth line in the fourth quarter before police escort him off the field.

1947

A record New York pro football crowd of 70,060 at Yankee Stadium watches as the AAFC Football Yankees forge a 28-28 tie with the Cleveland Browns.

1957

Tailback Dan Sachs scores three touchdowns (one each on a run, interception runback and punt return) and passes for another as Princeton posts a surprisingly-convincing 34-14 win over Dartmouth in a snowstorm at Palmer Stadium to win the Ivy League title.

DICK KAZMAIER

1968

Yale completes its 29th undefeated season but settles for a share of the Ivy League championship with Harvard at 6-0-1 as the Crimson's miracle rally produces 16 points in the last minute and a 29-29 tie at Harvard Stadium.

1970

In their first Monday Night Football game on ABC, the Football Giants lose, 23-20, at Philadelphia, snapping their six-game winning streak.

1979

Middleweight Wilfredo Scypion knocks out Willie Classen in the 10th round of their bout at the Garden, and Classen dies of his injuries five days later. Classen's widow later sues referee Lew Eskin, the Garden and several doctors for negligence. Classen had been knocked out in two earlier bouts in 1979 (April 6 in New York, Oct. 9 in London).

1982

Benny Friedman, an All-America quarterback at Michigan who played for the Football Giants (1929-31) and Dodgers (1932-34) before coaching at CCNY from 1934-41 (27-31-1), dies in New York at age 77, an apparent suicide.

1995

Frank Hammond dies in Staten Island at age 66. Hammond, a leading tennis umpire at the U.S. Open from 1968-80, was considered the first full-time professional tennis match umpire in the 1980s.

1871

Formation of the National Rifle Association takes place in New York for the primary purposes of conducting competition and improving the marksmanship of National Guard members (see June 21 and Oct. 12).

1897

In a substantially larger event than its first effort the year before, the Metropolitan Kennel Club opens its second dog show at the Old 13th Regiment Armory, Hanson Place and Flatbush Avenue in Brooklyn. Over 700 dogs, 130 classes and six judging rings are under the direction of manager James Mortimer. Some 40 women are among the exhibitors as the four-day event begins.

1910

Earl Cooper Robertson is born in Bingorgh, Saskatchewan. Robertson replaced Detroit starting goalie Norm Smith in the first game of the 1937 Stanley Cup final against the Rangers and led the Wings to the Cup, posting shutouts in the last two games to give Detroit a 3-2 series win. The next year, Robertson, in his first full year in the league, was the full-time Americans goalie and beat the Rangers in the playoffs, this time backstopping the Amerks to their most famous victory (see Mar. 27).

1919

Napoleon Reyes y Aguilera is born in Santiago, Cuba. Napoleon Reyes was an infielder with the Giants (1943-45, 1950) and manager of the last International League teams in Jersey City, N.J. (1960-61, 146-159).

1923

Yale football coach T.A.D. Jones utters one of sports' most famous lines, "Gentlemen, you are now going out to play football against Harvard. Never again in your whole life will you do anything so important." The psych works. The Bulldogs win, 13-0, at Cambridge, Massachusetts.

1929

Giants lose, 20-6, to Green Bay at the Polo Grounds for their only loss of the season. Packers go on to finish 12-0-1 to the Giants' 13-1-1 and are declared NFL champions.

1940

Paul Tagliabue, fourth commissioner of the NFL, is born. A lawyer, Tagliabue succeeded Pete Rozelle Nov. 5, 1989, after a process that required 12 ballots spread over almost four months in three cities (two in Chicago in July, four in Dallas in October and six in Cleveland later in October). New Orleans general manager Jim Finks was the other strongest candidate.

1963

Two days after the assassination of President John F. Kennedy, the NFL plays its full slate of games. The Giants lose, 24-17, to the St. Louis Cardinals at Yankee Stadium. AFL games are postponed.

1985

Maurice Podoloff dies in New Haven, Connecticut, at age 95. A Yale and Yale Law School alumnus, Podoloff was the first commissioner of the Basketball Association of America in 1946 and was tabbed commissioner of the new NBA when the BAA and National Basketball League merged in 1949.

1990

Malik Sealy leads St. John's to a 135-92 victory over Central Connecticut State in the opening round of the Lapchick Memorial Tournament, setting an Alumni Hall record with 43 points.

November 25

1908

In a rematch of their famous race at the London Olympics four months earlier, the now-professional Dorando Pietri of Italy and Johnny Hayes of the U.S. meet in a marathon at the Garden. Hayes had been declared the winner in London when Pietri was disqualified (he was assisted to the finish) but this night, it was Dorando's race without question (or aid). The Italian takes the lead for good in the 17th mile and is clocked in 2:44:20.4, 11 minutes faster than his time at the Olympics. This race is run at the new marathon distance of 26 miles, 385 yards established at the London Olympiad (previous marathons had been run at various distances, mostly 25 miles). Hayes is clocked in 2:45:05.2.

1914

Joseph Paul DiMaggio, the Yankee Clipper, is born in Martinez, California.

1915

Columbia concludes the only undefeated season in its football history with an 18-0 victory over Wesleyan at South Field. The Lions, coached by T. Nelson Metcalfe, finish 5-0 in their first season after abandoning football after the 1905 season.

1920

Capt. C.C. Mosley of the U.S., in a Verville with a Packard engine, wins the Pulitzer Trophy International Air Race at Mitchel Field in Mineola, L.I., by about 2 $\frac{1}{2}$ minutes. Mosley completes the four laps (33 miles) in 44:29.57. Captain H.E. Hartney (U.S.) is second in 47:00.03.

1939

Cesar Moretti of Italy and Cecil Yates of Chicago team to win the six-day bike race at the Garden, edging the Peden brothers (Torchy and Doug) by one lap. The winners log 2,079 miles and eight laps. The onset of World War II in Europe and Asia renders international competition impossible and this becomes the last annual race in the series dating to 1891.

1950

Hurricane-force winds of 80 mph (with gusts reaching 108) and driving rain mar Princeton's game with Dartmouth at Palmer Stadium. There are 19 fumbles, 13 by the visiting Indians, and the Tigers win, 13-7, to finish the season 9-0.

1961

Rutgers, scoring 25 points in the fourth quarter, completes its first undefeated season with a 32-19 victory over Ivy League co-champion Columbia at New Brunswick, N.J. Rutgers partisans in the overflow crowd of 25,500 pour into the end zones before the final seconds even elapse to tear down both sets of goalposts as the Knights finish 9-0 and extend their two-year winning streak to 12 games.

1978

Manhattan christens its new Draddy Gymnasium with a 64-53 loss to C.W. Post. It is also Brian Mahoney's first game as head coach of the Jaspers. Manhattan ends its days as the only Division I team without a home court but finishes 6-20 for the season. Mahoney is 16-62 in three years before Gordon Chiesa takes over in 1981.

1980

Lincoln Werden dies in Brooklyn at age 76. A classmate of Lou Gehrig at the High School of Commerce and Columbia, Werden joined *The New York Times* in 1928 and later became the first writer ever assigned regularly to the PGA Tour.

1997

In his first game at the Garden since signing as a free agent with Vancouver in July, former Ranger captain Mark Messier scores a breakaway goal and is voted the game's No. 1 star as the Canucks beat the Rangers, 4-2.

1912

John T. Brush dies in St. Charles, Missouri, at age 67. Owner and president of the Giants from 1903-12, Brush's refusal to play the 1904 World Series led to the adoption of the so-called "Brush Rules," which he created, that governed the playing of the Series thereafter. Brush rebuilt the Polo Grounds as a concrete stadium after a 1911 fire.

1936

NYU defeats Fordham, 7-6, at Yankee Stadium, destroying the Rams' hopes of making the trip from "Rose Hill to the Rose Bowl." Sal Somma's extra point is the difference and the Violets' Howard Dunney wins the Madow Trophy as the game's MVP in the Thanksgiving Day clash.

1941

Jeffrey Allen Torborg is born in Plainfield, N.J. Jeff Torborg, an All-America catcher at Rutgers in 1963, played 10 years in the major leagues and was later a manager, coach, and television commentator. He was a Yankees coach for 10 years (1979-88) and managed the Mets for 200 games (1992-93).

1959

In the midst of a 16-game unbeaten streak, coach Howdy Myers' Flying Dutchmen complete Hofstra's first undefeated season with a 35-0 Thanksgiving Day win over Scranton at Hofstra Field.

MARK MESSIER

1966

Susan Joy Wicks is born in Center Moriches, N.Y. A Rutgers basketball center from 1984-88 who set a school record with 2,655 points in 126 games for a 21.1 ppg average, Wicks played pro ball in Italy, Japan, Israel, Hungary and Spain before joining the WNBA Liberty in 1997.

1972

Setting a club record for most points scored in a game, the Football Giants belt the Eagles, 62-10, at Yankee Stadium.

1974

Bill Slocum, Jr., dies in Somerville, Massachusetts, at age 62. Slocum was a sportswriter and columnist for a variety of New York papers from 1935-67 (the *American, Journal-American, World-Telegram, Daily Mirror,* and *World Journal Tribune*) before being syndicated by the Hearst Headline Service from 1967-72.

1996

John Spano announces that, pending approval of the NHL Board of Governors, he has purchased control of the Islanders from John O. Pickett, the owner since 1978. After considerable negotiation, principally over the team's Cablevision telecasting contract, the board unanimously approves the sale Feb. 24, 1997. On June 30, 1997, the NHL orders Spano to suspend his involvement with the team during a dispute with Pickett over payments related to the sale. NHL commissioner Gary Bettman announces July 11 that the sale to Spano has been rescinded and ownership reverts to Pickett.

1997

Charles Jones scores a school-record 53 points to lead LIU to a 179-62 pounding of Division III Medgar Evers at the Blackbirds' court in Brooklyn. The 117-point margin of victory sets an NCAA record. Jones, the 1996-97 Division I scoring leader, makes 21 of 27 shots.

November 27

1890

Yale routs Princeton, 32-0, at Brooklyn's Eastern Park, where the teams meet because the original Polo Grounds has been demolished and the new one isn't available.

1915

Army defeats Navy, 14-0, as the annual classic returns to the Polo Grounds.

1927

In the *de facto* NFL championship game, the Football Giants beat the Chicago Bears, 13-7, at the Polo Grounds, effectively assuring themselves their first league title.

1942

Rangers trade defenseman Babe Pratt to Toronto for Hank Goldup and Red Garrett. The next season, Pratt wins the Hart Trophy as the NHL's MVP.

1943

Due to wartime travel restrictions, the Army-Navy game is played at West Point's Michie Stadium and Navy wins, 13-0.

GEORGE STEINBRENNER

1945

Frank A. Brennan dies at New York's St. Vincent's Hospital at age 61. Born in New York, Brennan became captain of the Pastime AC track team in 1908 and had served as meet director of the New York chapter of the Knights of Columbus Games track and field meet since 1936.

1947

Yankees centerfielder Joe DiMaggio is the American League MVP by a single point over Ted Williams, 202-201, in the national BBWAA poll even though the Boston slugger won the Triple Crown. (Ten years later, Williams loses the award again by a single point to a Yankee centerfielder, this time Mickey Mantle.)

1955

Closing out their 31st and final season at the Polo Grounds, the Football Giants play a 35-35 tie with the Cleveland Browns.

1966

Yielding the most points ever allowed in an NFL regular-season game, the Football Giants are shellacked, 72-41, by the Washington Redskins at D.C. Stadium.

1974

Yankees principal owner George Steinbrenner is suspended by baseball commissioner Bowie Kuhn after pleading guilty to conspiracy to make illegal contributions to president Richard Nixon's 1972 reelection campaign. Kuhn later reduces the suspension to 16 months.

1994

Jets blow a 24-6 lead in a first-place battle with Miami and lose, 28-24, at Giants Stadium, before 75,606, the largest home crowd in franchise history. The winning points come in the final minute on a "fake-spike" touchdown pass from Dan Marino to former Giant Mark Ingram, his fourth touchdown reception of the day. The loss is the Jets' first of five straight to end the season and 33 of the team's next 37 games.

1907

Johnny Hayes (see Nov. 25) of the St. Bartholomew AC, in 2:43.00.6, wins the first Yonkers (N.Y.) Marathon, sponsored by the Mercury AC.

1925

An evening of bike racing sprints draws a crowd of over 15,000 to the opening of the third Madison Square Garden. The $5.5 million edifice, built in 249 days at 49th Street and Eighth Avenue, formally opens with a hockey game (see Dec. 15). But this *de facto* opening is good enough for most of the press and public. Ross Winans wins a 1/2-mile handicap sprint in the first race. A day later, a six-day bike race becomes the first major event.

1926

Brooklyn's first NFL franchise ends its first (and only) season with a 27-0 loss to the Giants at the Polo Grounds, three days after a 17-0 loss to the Giants at Brooklyn.

1935

Frank Mautte provides the decisive run as Fordham (6-1-2) upsets NYU (7-1), 21-0, at Yankee Stadium, depriving the Violets of a chance for a postseason bowl bid.

1945

Dwight Filley Davis dies at age 66 in Washington, D.C. Davis, a former governor of the Philippines when it was a United States colony and an avid tennis player both on the Harvard varsity team and as an amateur, donated the Davis Cup for international team competition.

1953

Max Rosner, 77, owner of the Bushwicks, a semipro baseball team based in Dexter Park that produced many major-leaguers and hired some for postseason games, dies in Brooklyn.

1959

Unbeaten Pratt (15-0-2) wins the NAIA soccer championship with a 4-3 overtime victory over Elizabethtown (Pennsylvania) at Slippery Rock, Pennsylvania.

1967

Douglas G. Hertz dies in Novato, California, at age 84. The man credited with introducing dog racing to the U.S. with a track on Staten Island in 1928 and ill-fated owner of the AFL Yankees in 1940-41 (see Dec. 9), Hertz also managed heavyweight champion Jack Johnson from 1912-15 and future heavyweight titlist Jersey Joe Walcott in the 1930s.

1969

Rallying from a five-point deficit with 16 seconds remaining, the Knicks beat the Cincinnati Royals, 106-105, at Cleveland, Ohio, and set an NBA record with their 18th consecutive victory.

1979

For the first time in NHL history, a goalie scores a goal. Netminder Billy Smith is the last Islander to touch the puck before Colorado pulls their goalie on a delayed penalty, the strategy backfiring when the Rockies shoot the puck into their own net. Smith's "heroics" help little as Colorado thumps the Isles, 7-4, at Denver.

1989

Walter McLaughlin, St. John's athletic director from 1934-73, dies in Largo, Florida, at 83.

November 29

1890
Navy routs Army, 24-0, at West Point, in the first football game between the two senior service academies.

1913
For the first time, the Army-Navy football game is held in New York City. Army wins, 22-9, at the Polo Grounds, and the first program for the classic is published by Harry M. Stevens.

1925
American Soccer League leader Fall River (Massachusetts) is tied, 2-2 by the Soccer Giants before 5,000 fans at New York Oval. Fall River is 13-1-3 and the Giants only 6-5-2 when the match begins.

1933
William O'Connell McGeehan dies at age 54 in Brunswick, Georgia. Known to two generations of New York sports fans as W.O. McGeehan and to his friends as Bill, McGeehan joined the *Evening Journal* in 1914 and served as sports editor of both the *Tribune* (1915-20) and the *Herald* (1922-24), but was best known for his column, "Down the Line," in the *Herald Tribune* after the two papers merged in 1924.

1952
Fordham routs NYU, 45-0, at Randalls Island in the final varsity football game between the two longtime rivals. Fordham leads the series, 23-6, with four ties. Club teams representing the two schools will meet three times in the 1960s (see Nov. 7).

1961
Franklin J. (Cappy) Cappon, head basketball coach at Princeton from 1939-43 and 1947-61, dies of a heart attack in the shower at the university's Dillon Gym at age 61. Cappon led the Tigers to a 250-181 record and five league championships.

1965
Rufus Stanley Woodward, Jr., dies at age 70 in White Plains, N.Y. Stanley Woodward is considered by many the greatest sports editor of all time. He served two terms at the *Herald Tribune* and supervised a staff that included the likes of Red Smith, Jesse Abramson, Harold Rosenthal, Joe Palmer, Tommy Holmes (a one-armed sportswriter) and Rud Rennie.

DENNIS BYRD

1976
Free agent rightfielder Reggie Jackson, who played out his option year with the Baltimore Orioles, signs a five-year contract with the Yankees.

1981
Barclay Cooke, a Yale hockey player who was considered one of the world's best backgammon players in the 1970s, dies in Englewood, N.J., at age 69.

1992
Attempting to sack Kansas City quarterback Steve DeBerg, Jets lineman Dennis Byrd smacks teammate Scott Mersereau head-first in the chest and is partially paralyzed from the neck down. After a long rehabilitation, Byrd recovers but never plays again. Chiefs win, 23-7, at Giants Stadium.

1876

Yale beats Princeton, 2-0, at Hoboken, N.J., in the resumption of their series. The two schools, in what is the second most frequently-played series in college football, meet annually for the next 40 years. They miss 1917-18 because of World War I and 1944 during World War II.

1893

Princeton scores its first football win over Yale since 1889 with a 6-0 victory at Manhattan Field that thrills about half of the 25,294 who pay over $41,000 to watch (the schools divide $30,000 after expenses), and ends the Elis' 37-game winning streak.

1901

Clyde LeRoy Sukeforth, a catcher with the Reds (1926-31) and Brooklyn Dodgers (1932-34, 1945), is born in Washington, Maine. Sukeforth brought Jackie Robinson to be interviewed by Branch Rickey in 1945 when the Dodgers president was deciding whom he should sign to break the baseball color barrier, and was Robinson's first manager in the major leagues, piloting the club in the first two games of the 1947 season (see Apr. 9).

1930

Richard Jean Regan is born in Newark, N.J. Richie Regan played guard for Seton Hall from 1950-53, when the Pirates went 80-12, including 31-2 in 1952-53, when they won the NIT. He later served as Pirates head coach from 1960-70, posting a 112-131 mark.

1930

In their first-ever meeting, the Brooklyn Football Dodgers beat the Giants, 7-6, at the Polo Grounds. But two weeks later, the Giants beat the Dodgers, 13-0, at Ebbets Field, concluding a 13-4 season, the only one in which four New York-area teams (Newark and Staten Island being the others) operate in the NFL. Green Bay takes the league title for the second straight year, finishing 10-3-1, including a split of two games with the Giants.

1939

Rutgers blows a chance for its first unbeaten season, losing to Brown, 13-0, at Providence, Rhode Island. The Thanksgiving Day loss leaves the Chanticleers with a 7-1-1 record.

1940

Steve Filipowicz scores three touchdowns as Fordham thumps NYU, 26-0, before 35,000 at Yankee Stadium, and, immediately after the game, the Rams accept a bid to face Texas A&M in the Cotton Bowl.

1952

Football Giants absorb the worst beating in their history, losing at Pittsburgh, 63-7.

1959

World War II hero pilot Joe Foss is named first commissioner of the AFL.

1974

Iona opens its Mulcahy Center in New Rochelle, N.Y., with a 95-90 double-overtime win over Marist but the Gaels will finish 4-19. Head coach Gene Roberti is fired and replaced by Jim Valvano after the season.

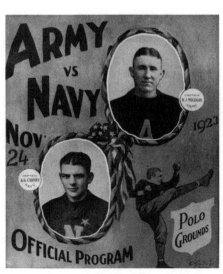

ARMY-NAVY FOOTBALL PROGRAM

December 1

1902

Morris Badgro is born in Orilla, Washington. A four-time All-NFL selection, Red Badgro was an end for the NFL Yankees (1927), Giants (1930-35) and Dodgers (1936).

1911

Walter Alston, Dodgers manager from 1954-76 who skippered the Bums when they finally brought the world championship to Brooklyn in 1955, is born in Venice, Ohio.

1912

Harry A. Lavagetto is born in Oakland, California. Dodgers infielder Cookie Lavagetto is most famous for breaking up Yankees pitcher Bill Bevens' no-hit bid with two out in the bottom of the ninth inning of the fourth game of the 1947 World Series with a two-run double that won the game for Brooklyn and tied the Series (see Oct. 3).

COOKIE LAVAGETTO

1939

Golf great Lee B. Trevino is born in Dallas, Texas.

1945

City College routs La Salle, 94-52, as Sonny Jameson scores 25 points at Wingate Gym. The score sets a Beavers record for points, eclipsing the 90 scored against Upsala in 1919.

1948

George Arthur Foster is born in Tuscaloosa, Alabama. Foster, who hit 92 homers and drove in 269 runs for the Cincinnati Reds in 1977-78, when he led the National League in both categories each season, had only 99 homers and 361 RBI for the Mets from 1982-86.

1963

Jets post the first shutout in franchise history, beating Kansas City, 17-0, before 18,824 at the Polo Grounds.

1975

Dave Koslo, Giants righthander whose pitching contributed to the 1951 "Miracle of Coogan's Bluff," dies in Nebasgam, Wisconsin, at age 55.

1986

Hubie Brown is fired 16 games into his fifth season as Knicks coach with a 4-12 record and is replaced by his assistant, Bob Hill, who completes the season (20-46). Brown was 142-202 during his four-plus seasons at the helm.

1986

NFL quarterback great Bobby Layne, who spent one season (1949) with the New York Bulldogs, who played in the Polo Grounds as part of the NFL strategy to drive the competing All-America Football Conference out of business, dies in Lubbock, Texas, at age 59.

1986

In a game made memorable by Mark Bavaro's tacklers-dragging reception in the third quarter, the Football Giants erase a 17-0 halftime deficit and beat the 49ers, 21-17, in a Monday night game at San Francisco, extending their winning streak to six games.

December 2

1905

Playing their annual football classic at Princeton, N.J., Army and Navy tie, 6-6.

1925

In the first game played by a New York team in the NHL, Charlie Langlois' goal at 3:10 of overtime gives the Americans a 2-1 victory over the Pittsburgh Yellow Jackets at Duquesne Gardens. Captain Billy Burch, assisted by Ken Randall, gives the visitors a 1-0 lead at 6:12 of the second period, accounting for the first NHL goal credited to New York. Vernon Forbes is in the nets for the winners (see Dec. 15).

1933

With sophomore Homer Spoffard scoring two touchdowns, Princeton finishes an unbeaten season by clouting Yale, 27-2, before 50,000 at the Yale Bowl. Fritz Crisler's Tigers are 9-0 and extend their winning streak to 15 before a 7-0 loss to Yale in 1934. When the Tigers decline a Rose Bowl invitation, Columbia (a 20-0 loser to Princeton) goes instead (see Jan. 1).

1941

Owner Horace Stoneham announces that Mel Ott, a player for the club since 1926, has been named playing manager of the Giants, succeeding Bill Terry, who resigned to head the farm system. Ott is only the third Giants manager since 1902.

1949

Rocky Marciano makes his New York debut with a KO of Pat Richards of Columbus, Ohio at 0:39 of the second round on the undercard of the Roland LaStarza-Cesar Brion heavyweight bout at the Garden. A crowd of 12,035 sees LaStarza run his record to 37-0 with a unanimous 10-round decision in a boring fight.

1958

Army's Pete Dawkins becomes the third Cadets back to win the Heisman Trophy as the nation's best football player in the balloting conducted by the Downtown Athletic Club.

1967

Neil Cohalan, first coach of the Knicks in 1946-47, dies in New York at age 61. A Fordham Law graduate, Cohalan, who won 11 letters at Manhattan College in football, baseball, basketball and track, coached the Jaspers to a 163-83 record from 1930-42.

1977

A major racing fraud is revealed as Dr. Mark Gerard is indicted for his role in a horse-switching scam. Cinzano, a champion four-year-old thought dead, was entered in a September 23 race at Belmont Park under the name Lebon and won as a 57-1 longshot.

1984

Playing their first game in Giants Stadium as the visiting team, the Giants beat the Jets, 20-10, before 74,975, their third straight win and the "hosts'" sixth loss in a row.

1987

With the team 2-13, Dave Wohl is fired as Nets head coach, and is replaced by assistant general manager Bob MacKinnon, serving his second stint as interim coach (as assistant coach, he replaced Kevin Loughery in Dec. 1980).

1995

Don Maloney is fired as Islanders general manager and is replaced by coach Mike Milbury.

1890

A deal is struck in which Charlie Byrne, the owner of Brooklyn's National League club, will shift his home games to Eastern Park. In exchange, the owners of the Players League club will give a 75% interest in their team to Byrne so he can fold that franchise. By moving from Washington Park (which he does not own), Byrne will provide traffic to Eastern Park on the Kings County Elevated Line, owned by the principal backers of the PL club. This deal enables all the magnates to concentrate on their primary business, with Byrne getting the baseball monopoly in Brooklyn and the elevated operators getting more customers on their lines to Eastern Park, which was built principally for that purpose.

1896

Clermont Avenue Skating Rink in Brooklyn is opened to members. It opens to the public the next day and serves as the necessary second venue that brings about the formation of the Amateur Hockey League of America.

1907

In the largest baseball trade in National League history up to this point, the Giants and Boston Braves swap eight players. Infielders Fred Tenney and Al Bridwell come to New York with catcher Tom Needham in exchange for infielders Bill Dahlen and Dan McGann, pitcher George Ferguson, outfielder George Browne and catcher Frank Bowerman.

1921

Charley Brickley's New York Giants play the second game of their only NFL season and the only one at home, losing, 17-0, to Cleveland at the Polo Grounds. Despite a drop-kicking contest at halftime between the former Harvard star and Jim Thorpe (who wins), only 3,000 fans show up, ending Brickley's career as a pro football promoter. Brickley later forms a pro basketball team also named for his favorite baseball club, but it fails, too.

1949

On "Father and Son Day," the Knicks pound the Baltimore Bullets, 85-55, in a Garden matinee, as Harry Gallatin scores 16 points and Vince Boryla adds 14, before 8,153 drawn by half-price children's tickets.

1949

That night, 18,393 drawn by the excitement of college basketball watch Ed Roman score 18 as CCNY clobbers Lafayette, 76-44, after Siena, making its Garden debut, surprises Manhattan, 48-33.

1950

Football Giants beat the Yanks, 51-7, at the Polo Grounds, in the first of the three games played between the two clubs during the Yanks' two-season existence. The Giants win both games in 1951 as well.

1969

Ray Hodge sets a Wagner record with 49 points in the Seahawks' 114-70 victory over Moravian at Sutter Gym (see Jan. 29).

1990

Knicks general manager Al Bianchi fires head coach Stu Jackson and replaces him with John MacLeod. But both Bianchi and MacLeod are gone by the end of a 39-43 regular season and three-game sweep at the hands of the Chicago Bulls in the first round of the playoffs.

1990

Clint Thomas, a Negro Leagues outfielder with the New York Lincoln Giants, Harlem Stars, Black Yankees, New York Cubans and Newark Eagles from 1928-38, dies in Charleston, West Virginia, at age 94.

1914

Southpaw Rube Marquard signs with the new Brooklyn Federal League club for a reported $1,500 bonus, but that spring reports to the Giants when they begin training at Marlin, Texas.

1915

Andrew Freedman dies in New York at age 55. Freedman, who brought John McGraw to New York in 1902, was president and owner of the Giants from 1895-1902 before selling to John T. Brush. An influential machine Democrat, he also formed the company that helped finance construction of the Interborough Rapid Transit Co., which opened the first New York City subway line in 1904.

1920

In the first significant pro football game in New York, the Buffalo All-Americans beat the Canton Bulldogs, 7-3, before 15,000 at the Polo Grounds on a Saturday afternoon. Swede Youngstrom scores the game's only touchdown when he blocks Jim Thorpe's punt and runs 15 yards into the end zone with the recovered ball. Buffalo then boards a train for a Sunday home game against Akron (a scoreless tie).

1945

Felix (Doc) Blanchard, Army's "Mr. Inside" running back, is announced as the winner of the Heisman Trophy by the Downtown Athletic Club. Blanchard is also selected as the winner of the Sullivan Award by the AAU and is the only athlete ever to win both awards.

1949

In their final AAFC game, the Football Yankees lose to the 49ers, 17-7, at Yankee Stadium in the first round of the league playoffs. When the AAFC merges with the NFL after the season, the 49ers are included in the merger but the Yankees are not since the NFL already has two teams in New York (see Jan. 23).

1956

Bernard King is born in Brooklyn. King teamed with Ernie Grunfeld at Tennessee in the 1970s to produce the "Bernie and Ernie Show" and led the Knicks in scoring in each of his first three seasons (1982-85) with the team until a knee injury March 23, 1985, ended his season and threatened his career. The only Knick to lead the league in scoring (32.9 ppg in 1984-85, a club record), he left as a free agent in 1987. King had two stints with the Nets (1977-79, 1992-93).

1967

Harry Wismer dies in New York at age 56. A famed radio sportscaster in the 1950s of Notre Dame football who owned pieces of the NFL Detroit Lions and Washington Redskins, he founded the Titans of the infant AFL in 1959, helped negotiate the league's first television contract and persuaded the wire services to treat AFL games on equal footing with those of the NFL. But the Titans went bankrupt in 1962 and Wismer was forced to sell (see Mar. 28).

1995

John Lorch, Columbia basketball star from 1924-27 who was the EIBL's leading scorer in 1926-27 (7.4 ppg), dies in Chicago.

DOC BLANCHARD

1877

Hartford, which played its home games at Brooklyn's Union Grounds, resigns from the National League during the annual meeting at Cleveland, leaving New York and Brooklyn bereft of big-league baseball starting with the 1878 season.

1925

Belgians Gerard DeBaets and Alphonse Goosens win the first international six-day bike race held in Garden No. 3 with 2,294 miles, nine laps. Police served four individuals with summonses because the race began 9 p.m. on a Sunday (Nov. 29). Protests by Sabbath-protective groups cause Captain Charles Burns of the West 49th Street Station to serve track manager Joseph Fogler, ticket taker George Bicks, ticket seller Charlie Hutchinson and Eddie Madden, a noncompeting rider. This is something of an embarrassment to former state Assemblyman Martin G. McCue, the celebrity starter of the race, but all charges are eventually dropped.

1927

Gerald Mastellone, a harness racing handicapper with the *World-Telegram* who was considered the best standardbred handicapper of his time, is born.

JIMMY CANNON

1948

In what proves to be the last major league pro football game ever in Brooklyn, the Football Dodgers lose to the Cleveland Browns, 31-21, at Ebbets Field. The AAFC game ends a pro football history in Brooklyn encompassing four teams in three leagues dating back to 1926. The Dodgers merge with the Football Yankees in the off-season.

1961

Emil E. Fuchs, a New York City Magistrate from 1915-18, Giants attorney from 1919-22 and president and owner of the Boston Braves from 1923-35, dies in Boston, Massachusetts. Fuchs brought Babe Ruth back to Boston after Ruth's Yankees career ended in 1934, but Ruth retired less than two months into the 1935 season.

1965

Rangers general manager Emile Francis fires Red Sullivan and takes the helm as Blueshirts coach for the first of his three separate terms behind the bench.

1973

Jimmy Cannon, sportswriter for over 40 years with various New York papers, most famous for his "Nobody Asked Me, But . . ." column, dies in New York at age 63.

1974

Hazel Hotchkiss Wightman, a four-time U.S. national singles tennis champion who donated a Cup for annual tennis competition between the U.S. and Great Britain, dies at age 87 in Chestnut Hill, Massachusetts. The Wightman Cup competition was discontinued after 1989.

1997

Alex (Lefty) Antonio, the only lefthanded player ever to win the New Jersey Amateur golf championship, dies at 84 in Youngstown, Ohio. Antonio had been a teaching pro in New Jersey and Ohio after his 1946 championship win.

1904

In an exhibition of teeth lifting, John Whitman (Ajax) lifts 350 pounds at the Grand Central Palace.

1906

Jim Braddock, the "Cinderella Man" who was world heavyweight champion from 1935-37 when he lost the crown to Joe Louis, is born in New York. In negotiating the terms of his fight with Louis, which he strongly suspected he might lose, Braddock got a percentage of Louis' purses for all future title defenses. After 25 defenses by his conqueror, Braddock was a wealthy man.

1907

St. John's begins its illustrious basketball history, but the new team, coached by Reverend John Chestnut, C.M., is trounced in its opener, 34-13, by NYU.

1912

Eleanor Holm, Olympic 100-meter backstroke gold medalist in 1932 who was sent home before the 1936 Berlin Games (see July 12) and later married famed showman Billy Rose, is born in Brooklyn.

1925

Andrew Robustelli is born in Stamford, Connecticut. Andy Robustelli was a defensive end for the Football Giants from 1956-64 and *de facto* Giants general manager in the mid-1970s.

1925

Before 73,000 at the Polo Grounds, the Football Giants lose, 19-7, to the Chicago Bears and the nation's most famous football player, Red Grange. The loss snaps a seven-game Giants winning streak but the crowd helps assure the stability of the New York franchise. A week later, the Giants beat the Bears in Chicago, 9-0, to finish their first season 8-4.

1933

NYU basketball star Boris Alexander Nachamkin is born in Brooklyn. Nachamkin averaged 17.1 ppg over three seasons (1951-54) for the Violets.

1945

Owner Dan Topping announces he is withdrawing his Brooklyn team from the NFL to join the new All-America Football Conference that will begin play in 1946. NFL commissioner Elmer Layden declares the Brooklyn franchise forfeit and assigns the players to the Boston Yanks. Topping eventually becomes owner of the Yankees in the AAFC playing in Yankee Stadium, having previously joined a triumvirate that had purchased both the Yankees baseball club and the Stadium (see Jan. 25).

1947

In their second season, the Knicks finally crack the 100-point barrier, routing the Providence Steamrollers, 114-85, at the Rhode Island Auditorium. Carl Braun sets a club record with 47 points for the Knicks.

1959

A 20-minute riot by marauding fans who surge onto the field and dismantle one set of goalposts with 1:53 to play delays completion of the Football Giants' 48-7 rout of Cleveland at Yankee Stadium. When the game is actually being played, the Giants roll up 526 yards total offense and clinch their third Eastern title in four years.

1961

St. John's plays its first basketball game at Alumni Hall and the Redmen defeat George Washington, 79-65.

December 7

1876

At the National League meeting in Cleveland, clubs representing the nation's largest cities—New York and Philadelphia—are expelled from the year-old pro baseball major league after one season. The clubs refused to take their final trip to the western cities since neither could win the pennant and they believed the young league was powerless to punish them. The next day, league president Morgan G. Bulkeley steps down and is replaced by Chicago club president Bill Hulbert, who had pushed for the expulsions. Bulkeley, a very prominent politician in Connecticut, is also president of the Hartford National League club and arranges to have his team play its home games in Brooklyn's Union Grounds, the home of the expelled New York Mutuals, in 1877 (see Dec. 5).

1882

New York returns to the National League as John B. Day, the owner of the independent Metropolitans, is granted the franchise vacated the day before by Troy, N.Y., as the league's annual meeting wraps up in Providence, Rhode Island. Instead of putting the Mets in the NL, Day acquires the assets of the Troy club, including players, and forms a new team, then places the Mets in the AA, giving him a team in each major league. He then takes over the Polo Grounds when the Westchester Polo Association moves to new grounds. Day will own the NL team, soon to be known as the Giants, until January 1893.

1895

Yale, coached by Dr. Henry Anderson, plays its first basketball game, defeating the Waterbury (Connecticut) YMCA, 9-4, under nine-men-a-side rules at New Haven.

1898

Ivan Wilfred Johnson is born in Winnipeg, Manitoba. Ching Johnson, an original Ranger in 1926, was a bruising defenseman who played on the team's first two Stanley Cup champions (1928, '33). After 11 seasons there, he spent his final season (1937-38) with the Americans.

1925

Max Zaslofsky, a St. John's and Knicks star who averaged 13.1 ppg in 161 games over three seasons with the Knicks, and who coached the expansion ABA New Jersey Americans in 1967-68, is born in Brooklyn.

1941

On a day which will live in infamy, the Brooklyn Football Dodgers upset the Giants, 14-7, at the Polo Grounds, ruining Tuffy Leemans Day celebrations. Broadcasts of the game are interrupted by bulletins through which millions of Americans learn of the Japanese attack on Pearl Harbor, causing U.S. entry into World War II. During the second half, numerous public address announcements at the ballpark call military personnel and reservists to their units as America begins the greatest mobilization in its history.

1974

Joe Greco's layup breaks a 76-76 tie as Vermont beats Columbia, 82-78, in the dedication game for the Lions' new Levien Gymnasium. Terry Green leads the Catamounts, coached by former Columbia player Peter Salzberg, with 27 points while Joe Stewart has 19 for the Lions. Mark Hardaway gets Columbia's first points. Levien replaces University Hall, opened in 1898 and used by Lions basketball teams since 1900.

1982

Frederick S. Buck, who with Bill Cane reestablished the Empire City Trotting Club in 1950, starting its development into Yonkers Raceway, dies in Yonkers, N.Y., at age 82. Buck was also director of Pari-Mutuel Revenue for New York State in 1940 when pari-mutuel wagering was legalized at New York tracks.

1992

Bill Shockley, Titans placekicker who scored the franchise's first points with a 15-yard field goal against Buffalo at the Polo Grounds Sept. 11, 1960, dies in New York.

1877

Yale and Princeton play a scoreless football tie at the St. George Cricket Grounds in Hoboken, N.J., with 15-a-side teams. Over 2,000 fans attend and pay a 25-cent admission.

1928

Jack Swartz sets a world record for skipping rope with 15,500 skips in 90 minutes at the New York Educational Alliance (the record is broken four years later at Pueblo, Colorado).

1932

Marcel Paille, who played from 1957-65 for the Rangers, primarily as a backup goalie (with a 33-52-21 record and a 3.42 gaa), is born in Shawingan Falls, Quebec.

1933

Johnny Green is born in Dayton, Ohio. "Jumpin' Johnny," a three-time NBA All-Star with the Knicks who led them in rebounding three straight seasons (1961-64), averaged 13.0 ppg in 465 games over six seasons (1959-65) with the team, including a high of 18.1 ppg in 1962-63.

1941

Frank (Pop) Morgenweck, a pro baketball promoter who operated teams in 14 different cities from 1901-32, including a championship squad in Paterson, N.J., dies at age 66.

1944

Edward Amos Irvine is born in Winnipeg, Manitoba. Ted Irvine played left wing for six seasons with the Rangers in the early to mid-1970s, twice scoring 20 or more goals.

1956

St. John's beats Roanoke, 89-62, to close out 24 years of college basketball at DeGray Gym, Lewis and Willoughby Streets, in Brooklyn (the Redmen played their first home game at DeGray Dec. 9, 1932). For the next five years, St. John's is, in effect, without a home court, playing 56 "home" games at several locations, including 37 at the Garden, six at the 69th Regiment Armory, nine at Martin Van Buren High School in Queens and several at other colleges.

1968

Elmore Harris, a track star of the 1940s, dies in St. Albans, N.Y., at age 46.

1977

In a four-team trade at the winter meetings in Honolulu, Hawaii, the Mets obtain first baseman Willie Montanez and outfielder Tom Grieve from Texas after the Rangers get Montanez from Atlanta. The Mets send pitchers Jon Matlack and outfielder-first baseman John Milner to Texas and Milner then moves on to Pittsburgh as part of another four-player deal.

TUFFY LEEMANS

1992

Hugh J. Devore, NYU's last football coach before the school dropped the sport, dies in Edmond, Oklahoma, at age 82. Devore, whose Violets were 4-17-2 from 1950-52, also coached the Philadelphia Eagles (1956-57) and Notre Dame twice (1945, 1963).

1899

Charlie Miller and Frank Waller pair to win the first six-day international bike race at the Garden to be raced by teams. Miller and Waller rack up 2,733 miles and four laps to win by two laps. Two-man teams (known as "Madisons") are created after the New York State legislature outlaws one-man racing in six-day events that began in the Garden in 1891. Miller won the last two of those events and Waller was the runner-up in 1898 (see Dec. 10).

1925

Nat Holman's foul shot starts a 6-0 second-half run that carries the Original Celtics to a 35-31 win over the Palace Club of Washington, D.C., in the first pro basketball game at Garden No. 3. A crowd of about 10,000 sees a rough game in which the champion Celtics make 29 free throws and only three baskets against a team sponsored by George Preston Marshall's laundry.

1934

In the "Sneakers Game," the Football Giants rally for 27 fourth-quarter points to beat the Chicago Bears at the Polo Grounds, 30-13, and win the NFL title. During the game, the Giants change from cleats to sneakers "borrowed" from the Manhattan College gym for better footing.

1940

Douglas C. Hertz, a colorful English-born sports promoter, buys the AFL Yankees from the Wall Street syndicate headed by Giles, Norris & Hay after the team flounders through its first season. Hertz, who survived the *Lusitania*'s sinking by a German torpedo in 1915, built a dog-racing track on Staten Island in 1928 and is the owner of the Pegasus Club, a year-round polo facility in Rockleigh, N.J. But, in less than a year, the league will force Hertz to sell the Yankees.

1945

Tony Kappen sets an American Basketball League record by scoring 29 points in the Gothams' 61-46 victory over the Trenton Tigers at St. Nicholas Arena.

1961

New York's first college football bowl game, the Gotham Bowl, is played at the Polo Grounds, as Baylor defeats Utah State, 24-9. A crowd of 15,123 sits in 36-degree weather to watch Baylor's right halfback Ronnie Bull earn the game MVP honors with 62 yards rushing and one touchdown on 13 carries and four receptions for 25 yards.

1967

Dave Davis becomes the first champion in the new Madison Square Garden Center by winning the Professional Bowlers Association national title. Davis beats Pete Tountas, 216-191, in the final of the 192-man event at the Garden's newly-opened Bowling Center.

1967

For the first time in their 22-year history, the Knicks have a sellout crowd at the Garden for a single game (see Dec. 27), and they beat Detroit, 124-121, before 18,499.

1988

Yankees sign a 12-year, $500-million contract with Madison Square Garden under which the Garden network will televise the majority of all Yankees games on cable television.

1990

Mike Mazurki, a Manhattan College football tackle from 1928-29 who later wrestled professionally and then had a long career (1941-65) as a movie actor, dies in Glendale, California, at age 82. Mazurki appeared in such films as "The Shanghai Gesture" (1941), "Some Like it Hot," (1959) and "Requiem for a Gunfighter" (1965).

December 10

1831

William Porter starts publication of *Spirit of the Times*, America's first major sports weekly newspaper, in Baltimore (see Jan. 3).

1898

In the final one-man six-day international bike race at the Garden, Charlie Miller wins for the second straight year and in addition to the championship gains a bride. On this Saturday at 4:30 p.m., a gun is fired telling the remaining riders to stay in place while Miller dons a clean white sweater and heads to Box 45 on the 27th Street side of the Garden. There, he is married to Genevieve Hanson of Chicago in the presence of her mother and Miller's best man, Eddie (The Cannon) Bald, the national one-mile sprint champion. Miller totals a record 2,007 miles and four laps while Frank Waller is second with 1,985 miles and two laps. Miller wins the $1,500 first prize and an additional $200 bonus for setting the world record. Waller earns $1,000 and gets to kiss the bride.

1939

In a rematch of the prior year's title game, the Packers pound the Football Giants, 27-0, at Milwaukee's State Fair Park to win their fifth NFL championship. Packers fans are particularly delighted by the first title game shutout after the New York agitation forced the game out of Green Bay's City Stadium (which Easterners consider "minor league").

1946

Damon Runyon, 62, sportswriter for the *American* covering the Giants who became most famous for writing the story that became the hit play *Guys and Dolls*, dies in New York.

1946

Big Bill Dwyer, the "King of the Bootleggers" who at one time owned the Brooklyn Football Dodgers and NHL Americans, dies in Belle Harbor, N.Y., at age 63.

1970

New York and Toronto are added as expansion franchises by the North American Soccer League. Soon to be known as the Cosmos, the New York club will become the most famous team in the history of the NASL.

1971

In maybe the most criticized of the organization's many bad trades, the Mets send righthander Nolan Ryan to California for third baseman Jim Fregosi.

1983

Jets lose to the Pittsburgh Steelers, 34-7, in their last game at Shea Stadium.

1983

Indiana University defeats Columbia, 1-0, in double overtime in the NCAA national soccer championship game in Tampa, Fla., spoiling the Lions' perfect season (18-0).

1984

In maybe the most highly praised of the organization's few good trades, the Mets acquire catcher Gary Carter from the Montreal Expos for catcher Mike Fitzgerald, third baseman Hubie Brooks, outfielder Herm Winningham and pitcher Floyd Youmans.

1988

Lawrence A. Wien, 83, a New York real estate owner who donated $6 million for the construction of a football stadium at his alma mater, Columbia, dies in Westport, Connecticut.

1925

In the opening boxing event at Garden No. 3, Paul Berlenbach defends his light heavyweight championship with a 15-round decision over Jack Delaney in the featured bout. A crowd of 16,913 pays $148,155 to initiate the new arena for fisticuffs.

1927

Football Giants conclude their first NFL championship season with a 13-0 victory over the Yankees at Yankee Stadium. On December 4, the Giants beat the Yankees, 14-0, at the Polo Grounds. In finishing 11-1-1, the Giants allow only 20 points and post 10 shutouts. The Yankees wind up 7-8-1.

1938

Football Giants beat Green Bay, 23-17, at the Polo Grounds to win their third NFL championship. The crowd of 48,120 is the largest to see any one of the first 13 NFL title contests (1933-45).

1951

William Schaeffer is born in Bellerose, N.Y. Billy Schaeffer was a star forward for St. John's from 1970-73, averaging 18.8 ppg, and a reserve for the Nets from 1973-76.

WILLIE RANDOLPH

1951

Joe DiMaggio announces his retirement. During his 13 years with the club, the Yankees centerfielder since 1936 (he missed three years for military service) hit .325 with 361 homers, won three MVP awards and led New York to 10 pennants and nine world championships.

1955

Stu Jackson, Knicks head coach from July 10, 1989 to December 3, 1990, is born in Reading, Pennsylvania. Jackson's record in just over one season was 52-45.

1959

Richie Guerin sets a club record with 57 points as the Knicks crush the Syracuse Nationals, 153-121, at the Garden.

1959

In a trade that helps prolong the Yankee dynasty for another five years, the Bombers send pitcher Don Larsen, first baseman Marv Throneberry and outfielders Hank Bauer and Norm Siebern to the Kansas City A's for rightfielder Roger Maris, shortstop Joe DeMaestri and first baseman Kent Hadley. Maris wins the American League MVP awards in 1960 and 1961.

1975

Righthander Doc Medich, who was 49-40 in the three previous seasons, is traded by the Yankees to the Pittsburgh Pirates for lefty Ken Brett, righty Dock Ellis and second baseman Willie Randolph, a mainstay of the Yankees infield for 13 seasons.

1990

Billy Myer, harness racing driver from 1931-80 who won 1,840 races and earned $6.8 million in purses during his career, dies in Harrington, Delaware, at age 74.

1896

Teddy Hale becomes the first non-U.S. resident to win a six-day bike race at the Garden and the Irish rider amasses a record 1,910 miles, eight laps, breaking the record set by Albert Schock in 1893. J.S. Rice is second with 1,882 miles and six laps as the top five finishers on the new safety two-wheelers surpass Schock's record (including Schock himself, who finishes fifth). Major Taylor, then 19, who will become the first great black rider in the sport, finishes eighth.

1896

With A.G. Fry and J.A. Fenwick scoring two goals each, the NYAC defeats the Hockey Club of New York, 4-1, at St. Nicholas Rink. A month before, both Fry and Fenwick had belonged to the HCNY.

1919

Louis Requena, longtime Yankee Stadium photographer for Spanish-language newspapers and later *United Press International* and *The Associated Press*, is born in San Juan, Puerto Rico.

1931

Army wins, 17-7, at Yankee Stadium, in the last Army-Navy game played in New York City. After this meeting the series moves to Philadelphia more or less permanently. However, games are occasionally played elsewhere, including at Giants Stadium in East Rutherford, N.J., decades later (1989, 1993, 1997).

1940

Howard J. Krongard is born in Baltimore, Maryland. An All-America lacrosse goalie in 1961 with Princeton, Cookie Krongard, who led the Tigers to three successive Ivy League titles (1959-61), is the first goalie known to have scored a goal in lacrosse. He was also a star with the New York Lacrosse Club and Long Island AC.

1962

Tracy Ann Austin, the youngest U.S. national tennis champion ever when she took the title at Flushing Meadow in 1979 at 16 years, eight months, 28 days, is born in Palos Verdes, California. Austin won another Open in 1981, but back woes curtailed her career.

1975

Mets trade rightfielder Rusty Staub and pitcher Bill Laxton to Detroit for Tigers lefty Mickey Lolich and outfielder Billy Baldwin.

1977

Frank Boucher, star center, later coach and later still general manager of the Rangers, dies in Ottawa, Ontario, at age 76. An original Ranger in 1926, Boucher won the Lady Byng Trophy for gentlemanly and effective play seven times in eight years (1928-31, 1933-35) before the trophy was permanently given to him (and replaced with another). His proposal to introduce the center red line and allow onside passing by the defense to that point was adopted for the 1943-44 season and marks the inception of the modern era of the NHL.

1987

Quarterback Greg Kovar completes 18 of 30 passes for 301 yards as Wagner wins the NCAA Division III championship with a 19-3 victory over Dayton at Phenix City, Alabama. After winning four NCAA playoff games en route to the title, coach Walt Hameline's Seahawks finish 13-1.

1988

Joe Reichler, *Associated Press* baseball writer from 1944-65, the first publicist for the baseball commissioner (1966-74) and editor of the Macmillan Baseball Encyclopedia, dies in Roslyn Heights, N.Y., at age 73.

December 13

1890

In place of the usual track and field events, the Staten Island Athletic Club presents an athletic carnival at the Garden consisting of one half of college football, a lacrosse match and a Gaelic football game. In the college game, Penn beats Rutgers, 20-12, while the SIAC tops the Manhattan AC, 2-1, in the lacrosse match, and the New York Gaelic Football Club wins, 2-1, over Portchester.

1920

Strangler Lewis takes the heavyweight wrestling championship by pinning champion Joe Stecher in 1:41:56 before over 8,000 at the 71st Regiment Armory.

1930

Having not played for two years due to a dispute over player eligibility, Army and Navy resume their football series at the behest of President Herbert Hoover and Army wins, 6-0, at Yankee Stadium.

1930

Helen Hendry of the WSANY wins the Metropolitan AAU 100-meter freestyle championship in 1:05, breaking the short-course record set by Eleanor Holm the year before. Constance Hanf, the 13-year-old prodigy, finishes second in 1:07.4.

1933

Dick Glendon, coach of the Columbia crew teams that won the IRA regattas in 1927 and 1929, dies in South Chatham, Massachusetts, of a self-inflicted gunshot wound at age 38.

DICK GLENDON

1936

Fed up with poor fan response in Boston, Redskins owner George Preston Marshall moves his team's NFL title game to New York but the Green Bay Packers win, 21-6, at the Polo Grounds before 29,545 paid. The next season, the Redskins relocate to Washington, D.C.

1953

In Steve Owen's last game as head coach, the Football Giants lose, 27-16, to Detroit at the Polo Grounds, concluding a 3-9 season. Owen finishes his 23-season career at the Giants' helm with a 153-100-17 record, eight divisional titles and two league championships.

1956

Jackie Robinson is traded by the Dodgers to the archrival Giants for southpaw Dick Littlefield and $30,000. Rather than report, Robinson retires, and the trade is canceled.

1990

Alice Marble dies in Palm Springs, California, at age 77. An athletic serve-and-volleyer, she won four U.S. national singles tennis titles at Forest Hills (1936, 1938-40) and as an American spy in Switzerland during World War II was shot in the back, curtailing her postwar pro career.

1992

Cornelius Vanderbilt Whitney dies in Saratoga, N.Y., at age 93. C.V. (Sonny) Whitney owned a stable that bred over 450 thoroughbred stakes winners, including Phalanx, the 1947 Belmont Stakes winner, and Counterpoint, the 1951 Belmont winner.

December 14

1920

Heavyweight champ Jack Dempsey, making his first and only Garden appearance, has a surprisingly-difficult title defense against Bill Brennan. Dempsey finally knocks Brennan out at 1:57 of the 12th round but the crowd of 13,000, a boxing record at Garden No. 2, gives the challenger a standing ovation for his game effort.

1930

Football Giants beat a team of former Notre Dame players coached by Knute Rockne, 22-0, before 55,000 at the Polo Grounds in a benefit game that raises $115,153 for Mayor Walker's Unemployment Fund. It is Rockne's last game as the Fighting Irish coach, as he is killed in a plane crash the following spring.

1944

Ernest Roeber dies at age 82 in Auburndale, Queens. Roeber was the successor to William Muldoon as the Greco-Roman wrestling champion of the world (see Apr. 30).

1947

Otto Graham completes 14 of 21 passes and runs for a touchdown as the Cleveland Browns top the Football Yankees, 14-3, for the AAFC title before 60,103 at Yankee Stadium.

1953

Floyd Patterson extends his record to 9-0 and vaults into national attention with a fifth-round TKO of No. 8 ranked heavyweight contender Dick Wagner of Toppenish, Washington, in a scheduled eight-rounder at Brooklyn's Eastern Parkway Arena. Patterson, although weighing only 167 pounds, is now considered a main-event heavyweight. The fight is an interesting test for the eventual heavyweight champion since he won a hotly-contested split decision over Wagner just eight months earlier.

1958

In the last game of the regular season, the Football Giants beat the Browns, 13-10, at snowy Yankee Stadium on Pat Summerall's long (hash marks are obscured) field goal, believed to be between 49 and 51 yards. The win creates a first-place tie in the Eastern Conference standing between the Browns and Giants and forces a playoff the following week (see Dec. 21).

1959

Billiards great Willie Hoppe dies in Miami, Florida, at age 72. In 1906, at age 18, Hoppe, who much later won the three-cushion championship 10 times from 1940-52, first received notice when he took the world 18.1 balkline championship in Paris, France.

1963

Buffalo beats the Jets, 19-10, before 6,526 (5,826 paid) in an AFL game that is the final major sporting event ever played at the Polo Grounds. The game was postponed from November following the assassination of President John F. Kennedy. Buffalo's Mack Yoho tackles the Jets' Galen Hall in the end zone for a safety at 6:20 of the fourth quarter, accounting for the final points. The first pro football game was played in the Polo Grounds in 1920 and major league baseball was first played there in 1890.

1980

Elston Howard, the first black to play for the Yankees (1955-67) and the American League MVP in 1963, dies in New York at age 51. A catcher, Howard later served as a Yankees coach.

1985

Roger Maris, the Yankees rightfielder who broke the most famous record in sports when he beat Babe Ruth's single-season home run mark with 61 in 1961 (see Oct. 1), dies in Houston, Texas, at age 51. Maris helped the Yanks to five straight pennants from 1960-64.

December 15

1896

In the opening game of the first hockey league season in America, the St. Nicholas Club blitzes goalie H.C. MacKenzie in a 15-0 victory over the Brooklyn Skating Club at the St. Nick's Rink. E.A. Crowninshield nets six goals, Thomas Barron gets five and captain Bill Larned four from his cover point position. The other two teams in the league—the NYAC and the Crescent AC—open their season a week later (see Dec. 22). The league (later known as the American Amateur Hockey League) lasts until 1917.

1900

Giants trade fading fireballer Amos Rusie to Cincinnati for young righthander Christy Mathewson. Mathewson is 373-188 for the Giants, Rusie 0-1 for the Reds.

1925

In the first NHL game ever in New York, the Canadiens beat the Americans, 3-1, before a black-tie audience of over 17,000 at the Garden. The Amerks' Red Green scores the game's first goal at 11:55 of the first period but goalie Vernon Forbes can't hold off Montreal. The event draws Mayor John Hylan, Mayor-elect Jimmy Walker and bands from two countries—the West Point USMA and Canada's Royal Footguards.

1925

Former world lightweight champion Battling Siki is shot to death in a street brawl in Flushing at age 28.

1935

Detroit whips the Giants, 26-7, before 15,000 at the University of Detroit Stadium to win the NFL championship.

1940

Jersey City wins the championship of the American Football Association for the second time in three years by beating the Wilmington (Del.) Clippers, 17-7, before 15,245 at Roosevelt Stadium. The Giants, a farm club of the NFL Giants, get touchdowns from Grenny Lansdell on a one-yard run and Don Lieberum on a 13-yard pass from Ed Danowski. Jersey City made the championship game with a 7-6 victory over Newark the week before.

1946

Football Giants lose the NFL title game to the Chicago Bears, 24-14, at the Polo Grounds but the real fireworks occur in the morning before the game when new NFL commissioner Bert Bell suspends Giants halfback Merle Hapes for not reporting a bribe attempt. Giants quarterback Frankie Filchock denies being offered a bribe and plays the game despite a broken nose. When it develops that both Hapes and Filchock are implicated, both are suspended for life (see Jan. 8). The attendance is an NFL championship record 58,346, not exceeded until 1955 in Los Angeles.

1962

In the second (and last) Gotham Bowl, fullback Bill (Thunder) Thornton scores two touchdowns to lead Nebraska to a 36-34 win over Miami (Fla.) in bone-chilling cold at Yankee Stadium. Quarterback George Mira is 24 of 36 passing for 321 yards and two touchdowns for the Hurricanes.

1980

Free agent outfielder Dave Winfield signs a 10-year contract with the Yankees.

1996

St. John's wins the NCAA Division I soccer championship with a 4-1 win over Florida International in Richmond, Virginia. Jesse Van Saun's goal gives the Red Storm a 2-1 halftime lead, and a crowd of 20,874 watches as Ben Hickey's goal in the 68th minute makes it 3-1.

1896

Princeton football reports a profit of $14,709.72. The bulk of the receipts come from the games against Harvard ($10,277.25) and Yale ($14,156.83).

1917

Frank Gotch, the first American to be the undisputed world professional wrestling champion, dies at age 41 on his farm near Humboldt, Iowa.

1920

Wagner plays its first home basketball game, losing, 16-10, to Upsala. Coach Erastus LaRue Ely's team opened its 1-4 season with a 57-25 loss at Staten Island Academy.

1928

In their third meeting of the season, the Football Yankees beat the Giants, 7-6, at Yankee Stadium, and win the season series, 2-1. But both teams finish below .500 (Yankees at 4-8-1, Giants at 4-7-2) and it is the Yankees' last NFL season.

1944

Randolph Field (Texas) Air Force Base Ramblers defeat the 2d Air Force (Colorado Springs, Colo.) Superbombers, 13-6, in the "Treasury Bond Bowl" at the Polo Grounds. The crowd is held to 8,356 by snow despite the lure of the Ramblers' Bill Dudley and the Superbombers' Glenn Dobbs, two famous college stars. Randolph finishes 11-0 to capture the Army Air Force football championship.

1958

Journal-American sportswriter Bill Corum dies in New York at age 63.

1973

In Weeb Ewbank's last game as Jets' head coach, Buffalo's O.J. Simpson rushes for 200 yards to give him 2,003 for the year, becoming the first running back to rush for at least 2,000 yards in a single season. The Bills clobber New York, 34-14, before 60,418 at snowy Shea Stadium. Ewbank ends his 11-year Jets coaching career with a 71-77-6 regular-season record and a 2-2 mark in the playoffs, including the 1969 Super Bowl win. Ewbank remains the only man to coach both an NFL team (Baltimore, 1958-59) and an AFL team (Jets, 1969) to world championships.

1974

Helen Hicks dies at age 63. Hicks, a two-time winner of the Metropolitan Open (1931, 1933) and the USGA women's championship in 1933, became the first woman golfer to turn pro when in 1934 she signed with Wilson Sporting Goods.

1977

Sonny Werblin holds a press conference at Manhattan's posh "21" Club to announce that he has accepted the presidency of Madison Square Garden in the wake of having created the Garden's principal rival, the Meadowlands Sports Complex, across the Hudson River in East Rutherford, N.J., six miles west.

1978

Mark Malone passes for three touchdowns to lead Arizona State to a 34-18 win over Rutgers in the inaugural Garden State Bowl postseason game at Giants Stadium. A crowd of 33,402 shows up for the first Bowl game in the New York area since 1962 (see Dec. 15), but the game is discontinued after 1982.

1983

Doug Kotar, Football Giants running back from 1974-81, dies of cancer at age 32 in Pittsburgh, Pennsylvania.

1891

Four teams join the National League as the league expands to 12 clubs coincident with the collapse of the A.A. after 10 seasons. The St. Louis Cardinals, Baltimore Orioles, Louisville Colonels, and Washington Nationals are added to the "Big League."

1897

Charles (Kid) McCoy wins the middleweight title when Australian Dan Creedon's corner throws in the towel after 15 of a scheduled 25 rounds at the Long Island City Athletic Club.

1932

NYU dedicates its partially-completed Alumni Gymnasium adjacent to Ohio Field with a 39-20 basketball victory over the University of Toronto.

1933

In the first NFL championship game, the Bears beat the Football Giants, 23-21, at Chicago's Wrigley Field, in a contest that sees six lead changes on a 32-yard pass/lateral play for a touchdown started by Bears fullback Bronco Nagurski with under a minute left.

1944

Green Bay Packers hold off a furious late rally by the Football Giants to win the NFL championship, 14-7, at the Polo Grounds, disappointing 46,016 fans. Ward Cuff scores on the first play of the fourth quarter and Ken Strong kicks the extra point to cut the Packers' 14-0 lead in half, but Green Bay withstands three later drives.

1953

Yankees owners Dan Topping and Del Webb sell Yankee Stadium to Arnold Johnson of Chicago for $6.5 million ($3.6 million cash and a $2.9 million mortgage). Johnson also acquires the Yankees' ballpark in Kansas City, Missouri, and later sells the land under Yankee Stadium to the Knights of Columbus for $2.5 million. A year later, Johnson buys the Philadelphia Athletics and transfers them to Kansas City.

1954

Fordham University Rector Lawrence McGinley, S.J., announces that the school is dropping intercollegiate football with a $200,000 deficit after a 1-7-1 season.

1954

New York teams complete a sweep of MVP honors as Willie Mays of the Giants is selected as the NL winner. Catcher Yogi Berra of the Yankees had won AL honors Dec. 9. It is the start of a three-year run in which both MVP awards are won by players on New York teams (this also occurred in 1936, 1941 and 1951).

1992

Ben Johnson, the Columbia sprinter who set an unrecognized 60-yard dash record in 1938, dies at age 78 in Harrisburg, Pennsylvania. After a brief coaching career, Johnson became an Army officer in World War II and retired as a colonel in 1968 (see Feb. 5).

1992

Howard Cann dies at age 97. An NYU football, basketball and track star, Cann led the Violets hoopsters in scoring in 1919-20, the season the team won the AAU national tournament and the same year he won the shotput competition at the IC4A championships. He served as head football coach at NYU from 1932-33 (7-7-1) and head basketball coach from 1923-58.

December 18

1896
Hockey Club of New York and the New York Athletic Club inaugurate hockey at the Ice Palace, 107th Street and Lexington Avenue, with a 1-1 tie.

1897
J.H. Rush of Princeton stuns a Garden crowd at the NJAC Games by beating Bernie Wefers twice in the same night, winning the 40-yard dash in 4.8 seconds and the 220 in 24.8.

1915
After two days of intense negotiations at the Waldorf-Astoria on 34th Street and Fifth Avenue, a peace agreement to settle the Federal League war is reached, with representatives of the American League and National League, ending the existence of the putative third major league. The agreement is formally signed Dec. 22 at Cincinnati, Ohio.

1939
Sportswriter, drama critic and political columnist Heywood Broun dies in New York at age 51. Broun, who started with the *Morning Telegraph* in 1908 and worked for the *Tribune*, *World* and *Evening Telegram*, primarily covered the Giants. He helped found the American Newspaper Guild and was its first president from 1933 to his death.

1959
Fuzzy Levane, the fourth coach in Knicks history, is fired with an 8-19 record. He is replaced by Carl Braun, who guides New York to a 19-29 mark the rest of the way.

1959
Sammy Baugh is named head coach of the New York Titans, the AFL franchise that begins play the following September. Baugh coaches the Titans for two seasons, posting consecutive 7-7 records. His .500 winning percentage is the highest of any of the franchise's coaches until Bill Parcells completes his inaugural 1997 season at 9-7.

1964
Warren Isaac scores a school-record 51 points to lead Iona to a 92-63 victory over Bates in a game played at Mount St. Michael High School in The Bronx.

1988
Ken O'Brien's five-yard touchdown pass to Al Toon with 37 seconds left in the fourth quarter lifts the host Jets to a 27-21 win over the Giants at Giants Stadium, knocking the Giants out of a playoff berth.

1989
The Jets, one game before the end of a 4-12 season, hire respected talent evaluator Dick Steinberg as general manager. Five days later, they lose at home to the Bills, 37-0.

1996
Devils allow only eight shots on goal as they beat the Canucks, 2-1, at Vancouver.

HEYWOOD BROUN

1882

Paul Krichell, the scout who signed or discovered Lou Gehrig, Whitey Ford, Tony Lazzeri, Mark Koenig and Vic Raschi for the Yankees, is born in New York. Krichell was a Yankees scout from 1920-57 and director of scouting from 1946-57.

1917

Raymond Poat is born in Chicago. Poat won his first six decisions for the Giants in 1948 and the club tore up his contract and gave him a new one. He then lost 10 of his last 15 decisions and finished the season 11-10.

1924

Douglas Norman Harvey is born in Montreal, Quebec. Doug Harvey won six Norris Trophies with the Montreal Canadiens as the NHL's best defenseman. After being sold to the Rangers and taking the Blueshirts' head coaching job as well, he won a seventh Norris in 1961-62 as he led New York to their first Stanley Cup playoff berth in four seasons.

1924

August Belmont, II, a leader in the founding of the Westchester Racing Association, which built Belmont Park, and the formation of the Jockey Club, dies in New York at age 71. Belmont, the breeder of Man O'War, also financed the building of the Interborough Rapid Transit system, New York's first subway, which opened in 1904.

AUGUST BELMONT II

1943

After beating the Redskins in consecutive weeks (14-10 at the Polo Grounds Dec. 5 and 31-7 at Washington Dec. 12) to force a playoff for the Eastern Division title, the Football Giants lose to Washington, 28-0, at the Polo Grounds.

1968

In a trade that instantly transforms them into contenders for the NBA title, the Knicks send center Walt Bellamy and guard Howie Komives to Detroit for Pistons forward Dave DeBusschere. Immediately, the Knicks improve at three positions—Walt Frazier replaces Komives at starting guard, DeBusschere succeeds Willis Reed at big forward and Reed reassumes his natural position at center with Bellamy's departure.

1980

Charles (Tarzan) Cooper, center on the New York Renaissance Five basketball team from 1929-40, dies in Philadelphia, Pennsylvania, at age 73.

1981

Football Giants beat Dallas, 13-10, in overtime, at Giants Stadium on a Joe Danelo a 35-yard field goal at 6:19 to remain alive in the NFC wild-card playoff race (see Dec. 20).

1997

Prince Naseem Hamed defends his World Boxing Organization featherweight title with a KO of Kevin Kelley at 2:27 of the fourth round before 11,954 at the Garden after being knocked down three times himself.

1997

Devils owner Dr. John McMullen announces plans to build an arena on the Hoboken (N.J.) waterfront as a new home for his NHL team.

1879

Captain A.H. Bogardus wins the $1,000 purse at his Shooting School on 8th Street at Third Avenue by smashing 5,000 glass balls in seven hours, 30$^1/_2$ minutes, standing 15 yards from the trap and loading his own gun.

1881

Wesley Branch Rickey is born in Stockdale, Ohio. Branch Rickey became perhaps the most important baseball executive of the 20th century, his most famous (but by no means only) accomplishment being breaking the color line that prevented blacks from playing major league baseball when he brought Jackie Robinson into the Brooklyn Dodgers organization.

1910

Charles William Conacher is born in Toronto, Ontario. Charlie Conacher, a Hockey Hall of Famer like linemate Busher Jackson, was another member of Toronto's Kid Line who spent the last years of his waning career (1939-41) with the Americans.

1947

In their first afternoon game at the Garden, the Knicks beat Boston, 70-58.

1961

Arch Murray, *New York Post* sportswriter from 1936-61, dies in New York at age 51.

1969

With a fourth-quarter touchdown the series after forcing New York to settle for a field goal when the Jets have first-and-goal on the Chiefs' 1-yard line, Kansas City dethrones the Super Bowl champs, 13-6, at Shea Stadium in an AFL divisional playoff game.

1972

Marty Cassio dies in Rahway, N.J., at age 68. Known as "The Bowling Tailor" owing to his occupation when not bowling, Cassio was famous for his accuracy, which he needed because a childhood injury had shrunk his hand, curled his fingers and robbed him of arm strength.

1981

With a 27-3 win over the Green Bay Packers at Shea Stadium, the Jets clinch their first playoff spot since 1969 and give the Giants their first berth since 1963.

1985

Denis Potvin's first-period assist on Mike Bossy's goal at the Garden is the 916th point of his career, one more than Bobby Orr's career record for defenseman, as the Islanders and Rangers tie, 2-2.

1990

Robert F.X. Sillerman, a broadcasting entrepreneur, acquires ownership rights to the New York area franchise in the NFL-sponsored World League of American Football. Sillerman announces that the team, opening its schedule in late March 1991, will be known as the New York-New Jersey Knights and that former Cincinnati Bengal Reggie Williams will be the general manager. The team will play its home games in Giants Stadium, but after two seasons the WLAF decides to continue in European markets only.

1996

After two disastrous seasons (3-13 followed by 1-15), Rich Kotite resigns as Jets head coach, effective after the season's final game, a 31-28 loss to Miami at Giants Stadium Dec. 22.

December 21

1924

Joseph Schaefer, Rangers off-ice official and "house goalie" during the late 1950s and early 1960s who played in two NHL games, is born in Long Island City, Queens.

1941

Winning their second straight NFL title, the Chicago Bears beat the Football Giants, 37-9, before 13,341 at Wrigley Field, with four second-half touchdowns snapping a 9-9 tie.

1944

George E. Roosevelt is reelected for his fourth one-year term as commodore of the New York Yacht Club. All officers are reelected without opposition during the course of World War II, following a tradition established during the First World War when George F. Baker, Jr. was commodore.

WILLARD MULLIN

1948

After 23 games of the club's 23d season, Frank Boucher, the Rangers' second coach, resigns (though he stays on as general manager) and is succeeded by one of his former players, Lynn Patrick. In 1939-40, Boucher, who succeeded Lynn's father and his former coach, Lester Patrick, led New York to the Stanley Cup, but compiled only a 166-243-77 record in nine-plus years at the helm. Boucher would later coach the Blueshirts for another 39 games in 1953-54 before being succeeded by another of his former players, Lynn's brother Muzz.

1954

Christine Marie Evert is born in Fort Lauderdale, Florida. A six-time U.S. Open champion (1975-78, 1980, 1982), "Chris America," the stolid queen of women's tennis and the sport's dominant player in the 1970s, taught an entire generation of youngsters to hit the two-handed backhand from the baseline.

1958

Harry Wills dies in New York at age 69. Known as the "Black Panther," Wills, a famed black heavyweight in the 1910s and 1920s, fought over 100 pro fights, but was denied the opportunity to fight for the title because of his race. His 1924 bout against Luis Firpo (see Sept. 11) is believed by many to be a payday from Jack Dempsey 's manager, Garden president Tex Rickard, for ceding his claim to challenge for the title.

1958

In an Eastern Conference playoff game for the right to play for the NFL championship, the Football Giants hold Cleveland running back Jim Brown (who ran for 1,527 yards during the season) to eight yards rushing and beat the Browns, 10-0, at Yankee Stadium.

1978

Willard Mullin dies in Corpus Christi, Texas, at age 76. Sports cartoonist with the *World-Telegram* from 1934-67, Mullin is generally considered the most literate and creative, and funniest, cartoonist in sports history.

1996

New England storms back to from a 22-0 deficit to earn a first-round bye in the AFC playoffs with a 23-22 victory over the Football Giants at Giants Stadium. It is Patriots coach Bill Parcells' first game against his former team and Dan Reeves' final game as Giants head coach.

1997

With a chance to become the first team in NFL history to make the playoffs one year after winning only one game, the Jets blow a 10-0 lead and lose at Detroit, 13-10, nevertheless finishing 9-7 in Bill Parcells' first year as head coach.

1883

Marcus L. Hurley, three-time Columbia basketball All-American (1905-07) and winner of three cycling gold medals at the Olympics in St. Louis in 1904, is born in New York.

1894

Five golf clubs meeting at the Calumet Club—Shinnecock Hills (N.Y.), St. Andrews (N.Y.), Brookline (Massachusetts), Chicago (Illinois) and Newport (Rhode Island)—form the U.S. Golf Association.

1896

Exhibiting the new-found power of its recruits from the Hockey Club of New York, the New York Athletic Club routs the Crescent AC., 20-0, at the Clermont Avenue Rink in an Amateur Hockey League game. Frank Wonham scores seven goals and A.G. Fry and J.A. Fenwick get five each.

1937

Jake Kilrain, heavyweight champion before being dethroned by John L. Sullivan in 1882, dies in Quincy, Massachusetts, at age 78. Kilrain also lost a rematch with Sullivan in 1889, the last championship fight of the bareknuckle era.

1946

Otto Graham's fourth-quarter touchdown pass to Dante Lavelli helps the Cleveland Browns defeat the Football Yankees, 14-9, at Cleveland, in the first AAFC title game.

1954

Ronald S. Greschner is born in Goodsoil, Saskatchewan. A lithe, nimble defenseman who occasionally played forward, Ron Greschner in 16 seasons scored 179 goals and 431 assists in 982 games as a Ranger, the third-most in club history.

1972

Jimmy Patton, Football Giants defensive back from 1955-66, dies in Atlanta, Georgia, at age 39, from injuries suffered in an auto accident.

1978

In the first Major Indoor Soccer League match ever, the New York Arrows defeat the Cincinnati Kids, 7-2, before 10,386 at the Nassau Coliseum.

1989

Arthur J. Brown, founding owner of the ABA New Jersey Americans in 1967, dies in Englewood, N.J., at age 78. Brown moved the team from New Jersey to Long Island in 1968 and changed its name to the Nets. He then sold the club to Roy Boe in 1969. Brown was also a harness horse owner whose Historic Freight in 1984 won the Hambletonian.

1989

Ernie Sisto dies in Grass Valley, California, at age 85. Sisto was a primarily a sports photographer for *The New York Times* from 1923-74.

1991

Jets win at Miami, 23-20, in overtime, to nose the Dolphins out of the last AFC wild-card berth. After the Dolphins score a touchdown with 44 seconds left to take a 20-17 lead, the Jets tie on a 44-yard Raul Allegre field goal as regulation expires and win on a 30-yard Allegre field goal 6:15 into the extra session.

December 23

1942

Jerome Martin Koosman is born in Appleton, Minnesota. A rookie sensation in 1968, finishing 19-12 with a 2.08 ERA for the ninth-place Mets, southpaw Jerry Koosman won 222 games in a 19-season major league career (140 with the Mets from 1967-78). A 20-game winner in 1976 and a 20-game loser in 1977, he was 3-0 in two World Series, winning the second and clinching fifth game of the 1969 Fall Classic.

1944

Director of War Mobilization and Reconversion James Byrnes announces a government ban on horse racing effective January 3, 1945 (the ban is lifted May 9, 1945, after V-E Day).

1947

William Rodgers is born in Hartford, Connecticut. Bill Rodgers won the New York City Marathon the first four years the race was run in all five boroughs of the city (1976-79).

1975

In a seminal decision, arbitrator Peter Seitz declares pitchers Andy Messersmith and Dave McNally free agents able to immediately sign with any club. Under old interpretations, players at the end of contracts could be renewed for one year by their clubs, with the renewed contracts including another renewal provision, thus binding players to their clubs, one year at a time, in perpetuity. Seitz's ruling allows players to be renewed only once, and after "playing out their options," eligible to sign anywhere. Free agents after the 1976 season as a result of this ruling include Reggie Jackson, Don Gullett, Joe Rudi, Bobby Grich and Don Baylor.

1978

Bryan Trottier scores a club-record five goals and eight points as the Islanders paste the Rangers, 9-4, at Nassau Coliseum, with a club-record seven goals in the second period. Trottier's six points that period are an NHL record.

1979

Rangers blow a 3-1 lead to the Bruins and lose, 4-3, at the Garden. After the game, players from both teams congregate near the boards and during a testy but nonphysical confrontation, fans reach over the boards and start grabbing sticks and otherwise attacking the Boston players. Thus provoked, several Bruins players vault the protective glass and storm the lower seats, with Mike Milbury, future Islanders coach and general manager, smacking one patron with the fan's own shoe.

1984

Ali Haji-Sheikh kicks three field goals as the Football Giants defeat the Rams, 16-13, in an NFC wild-card game at Anaheim Stadium.

1995

A hail of snowballs from the stands at Giants Stadium causes the Football Giants-San Diego Chargers game to be halted for three minutes in the fourth quarter under threat of forfeit. Trailing 17-10 at the time of the stoppage, the Chargers rally for a 27-17 win to clinch a playoff berth. Referee Ron Blum later says, "We were relatively close" to a forfeit. At least two dozen people are injured, three security guards hospitalized, the Chargers equipment manager knocked out on the sidelines by a snowball, 14 people arrested, 175 ejected from the Stadium and a $1,000 "bounty" placed on the head of one fan whom an *Associated Press* photographer snapped slinging a snowball.

1996

Martin Brodeur of the Devils and Dominik Hasek of the Sabres each toss shutouts at the Meadowlands as Buffalo and New Jersey skate to a scoreless tie, the first in Devils history.

1809

William Trotter Porter, founder of America's first well-known sports newspaper (see Jan. 3), is born in Newbury, Vermont.

1889

Paul Franklin Otis is born in Scituate, Massachusetts. Bill Otis, an outfielder, played four games for the Highlanders in 1912 in his only major league appearances, and died December 15, 1990, nine days shy of his 101st birthday. At his death he was the oldest living Yankee.

1929

George James Sullivan is born in Peterborough, Ontario. Red Sullivan, a Rangers center for five seasons (1956-61), coached the Blueshirts from December 28, 1962, to December 5, 1965, posting a 58-103-35 record before being fired by his successor, general manager Emile Francis.

1931

Mel Triplett is born in Girard, Ohio. Triplett was an outstanding fullback for the Football Giants who scored the first touchdown in the Giants' 47-7 win over the Chicago Bears in the 1956 NFL championship game at Yankee Stadium.

1949

It's another holiday eve double shutout as the Rangers and Canadiens play to a scoreless tie at the Montreal Forum. New York's Charlie Rayner and Montreal's Bill Durnan each get shutouts, just as they did December 31, 1945, at the Garden.

1967

Joe Namath passes for 343 yards to finish the season with 4,007 yards passing, the only quarterback in pro football history to exceed the 4,000-yard mark in a 14-game season, as the Jets beat San Diego, 42-31, to complete the first winning season (8-5-1) in club history.

1981

Nets trade Bob McAdoo to the Los Angeles Lakers for a draft choice and cash.

1984

Jack Murphy, one of the first television sports directors, who worked on Yankees telecasts for WPIX-TV for over 30 years, dies in Fort Lauderdale, Florida, at age 70.

1987

John Wesley Hanes, Sr., dies in Millbrook, N.Y., at age 95. Hanes was elected chairman of New York Racing Association in 1960 after heading the committee that recommended its formation.

JACK MURPHY

1997

In his first season with the team, Jim Fassel becomes the second Football Giants head coach in a row to be named NFL Coach of the Year, gaining 20 of the 48 votes in the nationwide poll. Predecessor Dan Reeves won the honor in 1993. Three days later, Fassel's Giants, the NFC East champions, are eliminated in a first-round playoff game when Minnesota scores 10 points in the last 1:30 for a 23-22 win at Giants Stadium.

1905

George Standing and Edward Rodgers beat world champion Peter Latham of England and David Gardiner, 4-2, in a racquets match at the Racquet & Tennis Club on West 43d Street. Standing and Rodgers win, 15-11, 9-15, 10-15, 17-14, 15-10, 15-2.

1933

Charles LeRoy McGill, sports cartoonist with the *Bergen Record* starting in 1954, is born in Englewood, N.J.

1935

Alvin Neil Jackson is born in Waco, Texas. Al Jackson was good enough to lose 20 games twice for the atrocious early Mets (8-20 in 1962 and 1965). Traded to St. Louis in 1965 and back to the Mets in 1967, he was sold to Cincinnati June 13, 1969.

1937

Bobby Bauer, assisted by Kraut Line mates Milt Schmidt and Woody Dumart, scores with 2:18 left to give Boston a 1-0 win over the Americans before 12,500 at the Garden, enabling the Bruins to maintain their four-point lead over the Rangers in the American Division.

HARRY GALLATIN

1947

In the first of what would become a traditional Christmas Day game, the Knicks beat Providence, 89-75, at the Garden. The Knicks would play 39 of the next 40 years on Christmas Day, missing only 1949, including 27 in a row at home (1961-87).

1952

Ernie Vandeweghe scores 21 points and Harry Gallatin adds 19 as the Knicks beat Boston, 97-84, before 13,825 at the Garden to maintain their hold on first place in the NBA Eastern Division.

1964

Wayne Kitchen scores at 3:45 of sudden death overtime to give the Long Island Ducks a 5-4 Eastern Hockey League win over the New York Rovers at the Norwalk (Connecticut) Crystal Ice Skating Rink. Gordy Stratton scores two goals for the Ducks, who end the Rovers' four-game winning streak.

1971

Rangers beat the North Stars, 2-1, at Minnesota, improving their Christmas Day record to 25-11-2 in 46 NHL seasons. It is the last time the Blueshirts play on that day.

1984

Bernard King scores 40 first-half points and finishes the night with a club-record 60, but the Nets rally to beat the Knicks, 120-114, at the Garden.

1989

Former Yankees second baseman and five-time manager Billy Martin dies at age 61 in a one-vehicle accident in Binghamton, N.Y.

1992

Lieutenant General Gar Davidson, Army head football coach from 1933-37 (35-11-1), dies in Oakland, California, at age 88.

1924

Glenn W. Davis, "Mr. Outside" running back to Doc Blanchard's "Mr. Inside" on the unbeaten Army teams of 1944-46, is born in Claremont, California. Davis won the Heisman Trophy in 1946.

1925

Americans beat the Pirates, 3-1, at the Garden. The teams combine for an NHL-record 141 shots on goal, 73 by the Amerks and 68 by Pittsburgh.

1928

Red Foley, longtime sportswriter for the *Daily News,* is born in New York. Foley earned distinction as a highly-rated official scorer in both major leagues.

1929

A crowd of 18,120, the largest ever to watch a hockey game in the U.S. up to that time, packs the Garden to see Boston beat the Rangers, 4-2. Fire regulations later reduce the hockey capacity of the building to 15,925.

1936

LIU ends Illinois Wesleyan's 24-game winning streak and extends its own to 43 in a row with a 41-29 victory before a capacity house of 7,000 at the Hippodrome on 6th Avenue between 43d and 44th Streets in Manhattan. In the opener of the doubleheader, City College beats Marshall, 49-33.

1942

Chris Cagle, three-time All-America halfback at Army (1927-29), dies in New York at age 37. Cagle played with the Football Giants from 1930-31 and from 1932-33 held an interest in the Brooklyn Football Dodgers.

1943

Rangers beat the Blackhawks, 7-6, at the Garden, for their fourth win in five games. They would win only two other games the rest of the year, finishing 6-39-5.

1947

New York tennis fans make headlines around the world, showing up at the Garden despite a 26-inch snowfall to watch Bobby Riggs beat Jack Kramer. Snow begins falling early this Friday morning and produces the biggest measured single-day blizzard in city history by 8:00 p.m. All traffic, including buses and streetcars, is out of commission but most of the subway system works. Many come by subway and thousands walk miles with 15,114 on hand for the match that pits Riggs, the pro champ, against the amateur titlist (Kramer) making his pro debut. Riggs wins in four sets, 6-4, 10-8, 4-6, 6-4, just as he predicted.

1974

Nets post the largest margin of victory in franchise history, pasting the Squires, 130-85, at Virginia.

1989

New Jets general manager Dick Steinberg fires head coach Joe Walton.

GLENN DAVIS

December 27

1879

Frank Hart wins the six-day American International Walking match at the Garden by completing 540 miles to earn the $3,000 first prize. Only 14 of the 65 starters complete the grueling test around the Garden track but seven exceed 500 miles walked.

1909

Frederic Remington dies in Ridgefield, Connecticut, at age 48. A Yale football player from 1879-80, Remington, the most famous artist of the American West, produced 2,800 paintings and drawings, as well as magazine illustrations, 25 statues and 13 books.

1946

John J. (Jack) Weinheimer resigns as NYU football coach. Weinheimer, an NYU grad who has been associated with the athletic department for over two decades, became head coach in June 1944 when football was resumed at the school after a two-year shutdown because of wartime manpower restrictions.

1952

DePaul surprises NIT champion LaSalle, 63-61, and Manhattan beats Cincinnati, 75-60, before 8,134 in the first games ever at the ECAC Holiday Festival on a Saturday afternoon at the Garden. That night, Miami (Ohio) stops St. John's, 68-65, and eventual tourney champ Utah State defeats NYU, 67-61. The Holiday Festival, a tournament born in the wake of the point-shaving scandals of 1951, is begun by the Garden to add dates to a schedule depleted by the loss of traditional home teams who abandoned or deemphasized the sport.

1956

Aldo (Buff) Donelli, head coach at Boston University for the previous 10 seasons, becomes Columbia's football coach, replacing the legendary Lou Little, who is retiring.

1957

For the first time in the club's 12 seasons, Madison Square Garden is sold out for a Knicks game. A record 18,255 on hand for the doubleheader see the Knicks beat Detroit, 125-120, after the *real* attraction, the Celtics-Warriors game (pitting centers Bill Russell of Boston against Wilt Chamberlain of Philadelphia) ends in a 110-106 Warriors win.

1959

For the second straight year, the Colts beat the Football Giants in the NFL title game, outscoring New York 24-7 in the fourth quarter to win, 31-16, at Baltimore.

1967

Dick McGuire, Knicks head coach, and Red Holzman, the chief scout, swap positions. Holzman becomes the winningest head coach in team history.

1981

In their first playoff game since 1969, the Jets fumble the opening kickoff, which is returned for a Buffalo touchdown. Trailing at various times 24-0 and 31-13, New York rallies but the Bills hang on, 31-27, at Shea Stadium.

1981

Returning to postseason football for the first time in 18 years, the Football Giants race to a 20-0 first-quarter lead and hold on to beat the Eagles, 27-21, at Philadelphia.

1902

In pro football's first indoor game ever, Syracuse (N.Y.) defeats the Philadelphia Nationals, 5-0, in the opening game of a five-team "World Series" of pro football at the Garden. Syracuse goes on to win the tournament.

1922

William V. Gallo is born in New York. Bill Gallo succeeded Leo O'Mealia as *Daily News* sports cartoonist in 1960.

1936

Columbia's touring basketball team defeats the Hispano Club, 35-20, for its second win in as many games in the Winter Sports Carnival tournament at Havana, Cuba. The Lions opened the tour with a 45-30 victory over the Vedado Club and on December 30 win their third straight, 52-22, over the Athletic Club of Cuba.

1937

Eugene Lytton Scott is born in New York. Gene Scott, a Yale tennis player from 1958-60 and a top U.S. amateur, founded *Tennis Week* magazine in 1974.

1949

Charlie Brickley, a Harvard football star who organized a team called "Brickley's New York Giants," dies in New York at age 58. These Giants played two games in 1921 in the American Professional Football Association, which became known as the NFL.

1958

In what is often called the "greatest game ever played," Baltimore beats the Football Giants, 23-17, in overtime at Yankee Stadium to win the NFL title before 64,185. Down 14-3 at the half, the Giants rally to take a 17-14 lead, but Steve Myhra's 20-yard field goal with seven seconds left in regulation ties it, and Alan Ameche's one-yard run at 8:15 of overtime wins it.

1962

Upholding the NFL's "blackout" policy forbidding the telecast of games within a 75-mile radius of the home team's ballpark, U.S. District Court Judge Edward Weinfeld denies an injunction that would have forced the Dec. 30 Green Bay-Football Giants NFL title game at Yankee Stadium to be televised in the New York area.

1975

In the first of the eight "Super Series" games matching two Soviet teams against eight NHL clubs, the Red Army team, the better Soviet squad, humiliates the Rangers, 7-3, at the Garden. On January 10, 1976, the Soviet Wings edge the Islanders, 2-1, at Nassau Coliseum. The Soviet teams win the overall series, 5-2-1.

1976

Phil Iselin, 74, one of five partners who in 1963 bought the Titans and turned them into the Jets, dies in New York. Iselin was club president, having succeeded Don Lillis August 6, 1968.

1985

In the first NFL playoff game ever played in New Jersey, New England defeats the Jets, 26-14, in an AFC wild-card game at Giants Stadium as Tony Franklin boots four field goals.

1986

After losing the last five games of the season to tarnish a 10-1 start, the Jets redeem themselves by shellacking Kansas City, 35-15, in a wild-card game at Giants Stadium. Backup quarterback Pat Ryan starts and throws three touchdown passes.

December 29

1927

Andy Stanfield is born in Washington, D.C. At Seton Hall, Stanfield won the IC4A indoor 60-meter dash and outdoor 100-meter dash three straight years (1949-51), and the outdoor 200-meter dash in 1949 and 1951. The Olympic gold medalist in the 200-meter dash in 1952 at Helsinki, Finland (as well as in the 4x100-meter relay), he was the AAU 100- and 200-meter dash champion in 1949 and the AAU national 200-meter champion in 1952 and 1953.

1934

Ned Irish presents his first regular college basketball doubleheader at the Garden, with Westminster (Pennsylvania) defeating St. John's in the opener, 37-33, behind 21 points by Les Bennett. In the feature game, NYU tops Notre Dame, 25-18. A crowd of 16,138 attends, encouraging Garden management to allow Irish to present more doubleheaders, and the program eventually expands to more than two dozen dates a year. Success of the Garden doubleheaders spawns not only the NIT in 1938 but its imitator, the NCAA championship, in 1939. Irish's success with intersectional matchups also spurs the development of preseason and holiday tournaments, boosting basketball into a major college sport around the country.

1956

Jumping to a 22-8 lead, Manhattan, behind Gerry Paulson's 27 points, takes the title in the ECAC Holiday Festival at the Garden before a paltry 9,715 with an 86-79 victory over Notre Dame despite 35 points and 21 rebounds by the Irish's Tom Hawkins. Angelo Lombardo adds 20 for the winners.

1963

For the third straight year, the Football Giants lose the NFL title game, this time to the Bears, 14-10, at Chicago's frigid Wrigley Field, as quarterback Y.A. Tittle throws five interceptions.

1967

Harry Fisher, a Columbia All-America forward (1905) and head basketball coach (1906-16), dies in New York at 85. Under Fisher, the Lions won 101 of 140 games and the mythical national championship in 1910. He also coached Army, Fordham and St. John's and was the editor of the *Official Basketball Guide* from 1906-15.

1968

In their first-ever postseason game, the Jets rally to beat Oakland, 27-23, before 62,627 at Shea Stadium in the AFL championship game. Joe Namath throws three touchdown passes, including a six-yarder to Don Maynard for the final points.

1984

For the second time in four seasons, the Football Giants' season ends in Candlestick Park. San Francisco once again uses New York as a stepping-stone to the Super Bowl, winning, 21-10, in an NFC divisional playoff game. Linebacker Harry Carson's 14-yard interception return accounts for the only Giants touchdown.

1985

On their home turf in the playoffs for the first time ever against the 49ers, and the first time since 1962, the Football Giants finally beat San Francisco in the playoffs, stopping the Niners, 17-3, at Giants Stadium, in an NFC wild-card game as Phil Simms tosses two touchdown passes.

1991

In their first playoff appearance in five seasons, the Jets lose, 17-10, at Houston.

1995

Held to a record low of 12 points in the second half, Princeton loses to Wisconsin-Green Bay, 55-35, in the championship game of the Green Bay (Wisconsin) Classic. Brian Earl leads the Tigers with 10 points while Jeff Nordgaard has 28 for the Fighting Phoenix.

December 30

1893

Albert Schock of Chicago recaptures the world record he lost two years earlier (see Oct. 24) by winning the third six-day bike race at the Garden with 1,600 miles plus one lap in 142 hours. Germany's Frank Waller is second (1,484 miles, eight laps) and former record holder Bill Martin of Detroit third (1,430 miles, one lap). The introduction of safety bicycles this year to replace the old high-wheelers make the races both safer and more exciting, but by 1898 the New York legislature outlaws individual six-days, so they are replaced by two-man teams (known world over as "Madisons") in 1899 (see Dec. 9).

1925

Frank Hinkey dies in Southern Pines, North Carolina, of tuberculosis at age 54. A Yale end from 1891-94, Hinkey, known as the "Disembodied Spirit" because of his knack of avoiding blockers, is one of only three men ever selected as first team All-American four times (Yale's Slim Brown and Penn's T. Truxton Hare being the others). Hinkey also coached Yale in the 1910s.

1936

Hank Luisetti scores 15 points with his one-handed shooting style as Stanford defeats LIU, 45-31, at the Garden, ending the Blackbirds' 43-game winning streak. Many in the crowd of 17,623 (then a sellout for basketball at the Garden) begin cheering for the Indians as they enjoy the Californians' up-tempo style. In the opening game, NYU (4-1) suffers its first loss of the season, a 46-40 defeat by Georgetown.

1955

Led by Bill Russell and K.C. Jones, San Francisco wins the ECAC Holiday Festival by routing UCLA, 70-53, at the Garden.

1956

In the last game of their first season in their new home, Yankee Stadium, the Football Giants rout Chicago, 47-7, before 56,836, to win their first NFL championship in 18 years. Alex Webster has two short touchdown runs and Charlie Conerly throws a pair of scoring passes.

1962

On a bitterly cold day at Yankee Stadium, Green Bay, behind three field goals by guard Jerry Kramer, beat the Football Giants, 16-7, to win the NFL title game from New York for the second straight year.

1964

In one of the most celebrated college basketball games of all time, Michigan, led by All-American Cazzie Russell, defeats Princeton, led by All-American Bill Bradley (Russell's future Knicks teammate), 80-78, in a semifinal match at the ECAC Holiday Festival at the Garden. Princeton leads, 75-63, when Bradley fouls out with five minutes left.

1967

Columbia defeats St. John's, 60-55, to win the ECAC Holiday Festival at the Garden.

1968

Lew Alcindor and UCLA capture the first ECAC Holiday Festival at Garden No. 4 with a 74-56 win over St. John's before a sellout 19,500.

1977

Jets General Manager Al Ward resigns after a third straight 3-11 season.

1994

Francis Dale (Hap) Moran, a Football Giants halfback from 1928-34, dies in New Milford, Connecticut, at age 93.

December 31

1891
Manhattan Athletic Club's water polo team defeats the Produce Exchange, 3-0, in the MAC tank on Madison Avenue as Jerome Carter scores to snap a scoreless tie.

1897
On the final night of Brooklyn's independent existence, the city's National Athletic Club dedicates its new clubhouse with a 40-round program of boxing, concluding with a 20-rounder matching Jack Fox against Tommy Butler.

1928
Toronto U. builds a 3-0 lead and hangs on for a 3-2 hockey upset over Harvard before 9,000 at the Garden.

1928
Bill Conroy scores a game-high 16 points and leads NYU to a 30-14 victory over Princeton at the 102d Engineers' Armory at 168th Street and Fort Washington Avenue, where the Violets played many home games before the opening of Alumni Gym in The Bronx.

1929
New York State Athletic Commission, which created the weight classes in 1922, votes to discontinue official recognition of the junior welterweight (maximum 140 pounds) and junior lightweight (130 pounds) championships, although competition in both classes continue for several years and then is revived periodically to suit promoters' needs for more champions.

1960
Jerry Lucas scores 32 points and Ohio State hangs on for an 84-82 victory over St. Bonaventure in the final of the ECAC Holiday Festival at the Garden. Early arrivers in the crowd of 12,897 see St. John's win third-place honors with a 73-65 win over Utah after Seton Hall beats St. Joseph's (Pennsylvania), 91-83, for fifth place.

1961
Green Bay routs the Football Giants, 37-0, before 39,029 at City Stadium in Green Bay to win the NFL title as Paul Hornung scores 19 points.

1962
Commissioner Abe Saperstein announces in Chicago that the American Basketball League, midway through its second season, is discontinuing operations immediately. Down to six teams, the would-be rival of the NBA reportedly loses several million dollars for Saperstein and other owners. The Kansas City (Missouri) Steers, with a 22-9 record and a $3\frac{1}{2}$-game lead over the Long Beach (California) Chiefs, are declared league champions for the truncated 1962-63 season. Other remaining teams are the Pittsburgh Rens, Oakland Oaks, Philadelphia Tapers (formerly based in Commack, Long Island) and Saperstein's Chicago Majors.

1974
Winning the first major bidding war of the free agency era, the Yankees announce that they have signed A's ace Catfish Hunter to an unprecedented five-year, $2.3 million contract.

1980
Bob Shawkey dies in Syracuse, N.Y., at age 90. A star righthander for the Yankees from 1915-27 (168-131) and Bombers manager in 1930 (86-68), Shawkey won the first game ever played at Yankee Stadium (see Apr. 18) and hit the Yankees' second homer there. In 1976, he threw out the ceremonial first pitch at the refurbished Stadium.

Appendix I

Abbreviations used in this book:

AA	American Association (baseball 1882-91)
AA	Athletic Association
AAFC	All-America Football Conference (1946-49)
AAU	Amateur Athletic Union of the United States
ABA	American Basketball Association (1967-76)
ABC	American Bowling Congress
ABC	American Broadcasting Company
ABL	American Basketball League (1925-54; 1961-62)
AC	Athletic Club
AFC	American Football Conference
AFL	American Football League (1926; 1936-37; 1940-41; 1960-69)
AFL	Arena Football League
AHL	American Hockey League
AIAW	Association of Intercollegiate Athletics for Women
AL	American League
ALCS	American League Championship Series
AP	Associated Press
ASL	American Soccer League
A & M	Agriculture and Military
BAA	Basketball Association of America (1946-49)
BBWAA	Baseball Writers Association of America
BC	Bicycle Club
BPAA	Bowling Proprietors' Association of America
BWAA	Bowling Writers Association of America
CBS	Columbia Broadcasting System
CC	Country Club
CCNY	City College of New York
CFA	College Football Association
CUNY	City University of New York
DAC	Downtown Athletic Club
ECAC	Eastern Collegiate Athletic Conference

EHL	Eastern Hockey League
EIBL	Eastern Intercollegiate Basketball (or Baseball) League
EL	Eastern League
EPBL	Eastern Professional Basketball League
ERA	Earned Run Average
ETA	Eastern Tennis Association
ETO	European Theater of Operations
FIFA	Federation Internationale de Football Association
FL	Federal League (1914-15)
FL of A	Fencers League of America
GAA	Goals Against Average
GC	Golf Club
GM	General Manager
HC	Hockey Club
IBC	International Boxing Club
IC4A	Intercollegiate Association of Amateur Athletes of America
IFA	Intercollegiate Fencing Association
IGAA	Intercollegiate Golf Association of America
IL	International League
ILTF	International Lawn Tennis Federation
INS	International News Service
IRA	Intercollegiate Rowing Association
ISL	International Soccer League (1960-65)
ITF	International Tennis Federation
K of C	Knights of Columbus
LAW	League of American Wheelmen
LC	Lacrosse Club
LI	Long Island
LIU	Long Island University
LPGA	Ladies Professional Golfers Association
MAAC	Metro Atlantic Athletic Conference
MAC	Manhattan Athletic Club
MIBA	Metropolitan Intercollegiate Basketball Association
MISL	Major Indoor Soccer League (1969-84)
MLS	Major League Soccer

MSG	Madison Square Garden	PGA	Professional Golfers Association
MSGN	Madison Square Garden Network	PL	Players League (1890)
MVP	Most Valuable Player	PPG	Points Per Game
NA	National Association (1871-75)	PSAL	Public School Athletic League
N4A	National Association of Amateur Athletes of America	RAC	Rutgers Athletic Center
		RBI	Run Batted In
NABF	North American Boxing Federation	RHI	Roller Hockey International
NAIA	National Association of Intercollegiate Athletics	SMU	Southern Methodist University
		TAC	The Athletics Congress
NASL	North American Soccer League (1968-85)	TC	Tennis Club
		UP	United Press
NBA	National Basketball Association	UPI	United Press International
NBA	National Boxing Association	USA	United Soccer Association (1967)
NBC	National Broadcasting Company	USET	United States Equestrian Team
NBL	National Basketball League	USFL	United States Football League (1984-85)
NCA	National Cycling Association	USGA	United States Golf Association
NCAA	National Collegiate Athletic Association	USLTA	United States Lawn Tennis Association
NFC	National Football Conference	USMA	United States Military Academy
NFL	National Football League	USNLTA	United States National Lawn Tennis Association
NHA	National Hockey Association (1910-17)		
NHL	National Hockey League	USO	United Service Organization
NHS	National Horse Show	USSF	United States Soccer Federation
NHSA	National Horse Show Association	USSFA	United States Soccer Football Association
NIT	National Invitation Tournament		
NJAC	New Jersey Athletic Club	USTA	United States Tennis Association
NJSEA	New Jersey Sports & Exposition Authority	WBA	World Boxing Association
		WBC	World Boxing Council
NL	National League	WBL	Women's Basketball League (1979-82)
NLCS	National League Championship Series	WBO	World Boxing Organization
NPSL	National Professional Soccer League (1967)	WFL	World Football League (1974-75)
		WHA	World Hockey Association (1972-79)
NRA	National Rifle Association	WKC	Westminster Kennel Club
NTC	National Tennis Center	WLAF	World League of American Football
NYAC	New York Athletic Club	WNBA	Women's National Basketball Association
NYRA	New York Racing Association	WPA	Works Progress Administration
NYSAC	New York State Athletic Commission	WSANY	Women's Swimming Association of New York
NYU	New York University		
NYYC	New York Yacht Club	WTT	World Team Tennis
OTB	Off-Track Betting	YMCA	Young Men's Christian Association
PBA	Professional Bowlers Association		

Appendix II

Numerous references are made throughout this book to military actions involving United States forces since the events affect the availability of athletes as well as domestic support for sports events. As a convenience to readers, the dates of these events and U.S. involvement are listed below.

1775-83	American Revolution (U.S. colonies vs. Britain)
1812-15	War of 1812 (U.S. vs. Britain)
1845-46	Mexican War (U.S. vs. Mexico)
1861-65	American Civil War (northern states vs. southern states)
1898	Spanish-American War
1914-18	World War I (U.S. formally enters April 6, 1917)
1939-45	World War II (U.S. formally enters Dec. 8, 1941)
1950-53	Korean War (United Nations forces vs. North Korea and China)
1961-75	Vietnam War (U.S. and South Vietnam vs. North Vietnam - U.S. withdraws Jan. 1973)

Appendix III

Throughout this book, mention is made of various venues in the New York area, often where several teams played or different events are held. Readers should bear in mind that some arenas had slightly different names at different times. A prime example is St. Nicholas Rink (opened in 1896), which was known as St. Nicholas Palace in the 1930s and then, during its last 25 years (until 1962) as St. Nicholas Arena.

Other venues moved and their names went with them. Best known among these are the Polo Grounds, Madison Square Garden, and Brooklyn's Washington Park. For convenience, their locations and dates are listed below:

Polo Grounds No. 1 - 110th St. and 5th Ave. (1880-89);
Polo Grounds No. 2 - 155th St. and 8th Ave. (1891-1963).

Madison Square Garden No. 1 - 26th St. and Madison Ave. (1879-89);
Madison Square Garden No. 2 - 26th St. and Madison Ave. (1890-1925);
Madison Square Garden No. 3 - 49th St. and 8th Ave. (1925-68);
Madison Square Garden No. 4 - 7th Ave. between 31st and 33rd Sts. (since 1968).

Washington Park No. 1 - 4th St. and 5th Ave. (1882-91);
Washington Park No. 2 - 3rd St. and 4th Ave. (1898-1912);
Washington Park No. 3 - 3rd St. and 4th Ave. (1914-20).

Index

(N.B.—Certain sports—baseball, basketball, football, boxing, and hockey—and certain geographical locations—New York City, Brooklyn, New York State, Borough of Manhattan, The Bronx, and Queens—are omitted from this index because their appearance is nearly universal.)

393

OTHER TITLES FROM SPORTS PUBLISHING INC.

The Yankee Encyclopedia: Volume 3
by Mark Gallagher

Who was the first manager of the Yankees? What year did the Yankees win their first World Series? Who pitched the shutout in Game 5 of the 1996 World Series? Who had the key hit in Game 4 of the 1996 World Series? These questions, along with hundreds more, are answered in *The Yankee Encyclopedia: Volume 3*.

1997 • 575 pp • 9 x 12 hardcover • ISBN 1-57167-114-5 • $39.95

The Yankee Encyclopedia: Volume 3 leatherbound edition
Limited edition of 250 • Includes the signatures of 11 former Yankees including:

• Hall of Famer Enos "Country" Slaughter
• Hall of Famer Jim "Catfish" Hunter
• Future Hall of Famer Dave Winfield
• Joe Pepitone
• Hank Bauer
• John Kucks
• Tommy Byrne
• Goose Gossage
• Roy White
• Bobby Murcer
• Bobby Richardson

$129.95. To order, call Sports Publishing Inc. at 1-800-327-5557.

Yogi Berra: An American Original
Edited by Bill Madden
From the archives of *The New York Daily News*

Yogi Berra: An American Original recalls the legendary life and times of one of America's most enduring personalities. Drawn from the archives of *The New York Daily News*, this book represents the most complete collection of Yogi Berra materials ever published. With over 150 classic photographs, Yogi's Hall of Fame career is captured in beautiful detail — including rarely seen pictures from his early years in Yankee pinstripes, to his World Series heroics on the great Yankee teams of the 1950s and early 1960s, through his ups and downs as manager and coach of the tradition-rich Yankees and the upstart Mets, and concluding with his life after baseball. From Bronx Bomber to Amazing Met, both on and off the field, Yogi Berra has entertained America for more than five decades.

$29.95 • 250 pp • 8½ x 11 hardcover • Available in October

Mickey Mantle: The American Dream Comes to Life—Commemorative Edition
by Mickey Mantle and Lewis Early

The companion volume to the award-winning Public Television Videography Program Special on Mantle's career with more than 180 rare photographs, headlines, articles, cartoons, and text. Mantle offers readers an intimate and insightful portrait of his life and career.

1995 • 128 pages • 182 photos • 8½ x 11 hardcover • ISBN 1-57167-071-8 • $29.95

The Perfect Yankee
by Don Larsen with Mark Shaw

By all accounts, the no-hit, perfect game pitched by New York Yankee right-hander Don Larsen in the 1956 World Series qualifies as a true miracle. No one knows why it happened, or why an unlikely baseball player like Don Larsen was chosen to perform it. In *The Perfect Yankee*, Larsen and co-author Mark Shaw describe for the first time the facts surrounding one of the most famous games in baseball history.

Autographed copies (Larsen) are available by calling Sports Publishing Inc. at 1-800-327-5557. **Bonded leatherbound edition available.** The leatherbound edition of *The Perfect Yankee* is limited to 500 and is autographed by Don Larsen and Yogi Berra.

1996 • 272 pages • 16-page photo section • 6 x 9 hardcover • ISBN 1-57167-043-2 • $22.95

Charlie Ward: Winning by His Grace
by Charlie Ward with Joe Cooney

Officially endorsed by the Fellowship of Christian Athletes

Americans have always possessed a fanatical fascination for those athletes talented and blessed enough to make it in the world of professional sports. And most of these "star" ballplayers revel in the limelight and relish playing the role of "celebrity".

In a world known more for loud "trash talk" and egotistical boasting, 27-year-old Charlie Ward stands out with his reserved, unassuming nature and lifestyle. He is a quiet man. A man at peace, maintaining a lifestyle that is based on high ethical standards, integrity and character.

1998 • 50 pp • 10 x 8 hardcover • ISBN 1-57167-242-7 • $14.95

Jets: Broadway's 30-Year Guarantee
by the Editors of *The New York Daily News*

Jets: Broadway's 30-Year Guarantee looks back on Joe Namath's guaranteed victory, which New Yorkers recently voted as the greatest moment in their city's sports history. With game stories, features and more than 100 classic photos drawn from the archives of the *New York Daily News*, this book takes fans back 30 years to relive the Jets' 1968 season and their astonishing 16-7 triumph in the 1969 Super Bowl.

1998 • 200 pages • 8½ x 11 hardcover • $29.95

The New York Rangers: Broadway's Longest-Running Hit
by Lou Friedman and John Kreiser

After 70 years of waiting, New York area hockey fans finally have a book that chronicles the history of their favorite team. In *The New York Rangers: Broadway's Longest-Running Hit*, Rangers' fans can read about the legendary feats of such stars as Brad Park, Andy Bathgate, Mark Messier, and newest star Wayne Gretzky.

Bonded leatherbound limited edition available. Autographed by Emile Francis, Brad Park, Ron Greschner, Harry Howell, and Vic Hadfield. Limited to 300. Includes Certificate of Authenticity. Available from Sports Publishing Inc. only by calling 1-800-327-5557.

1996 • 400 pages • 12-page color section • 8½ x 11 hardcover • ISBN 1-57167-041-6 • $29.95